The Light Inside

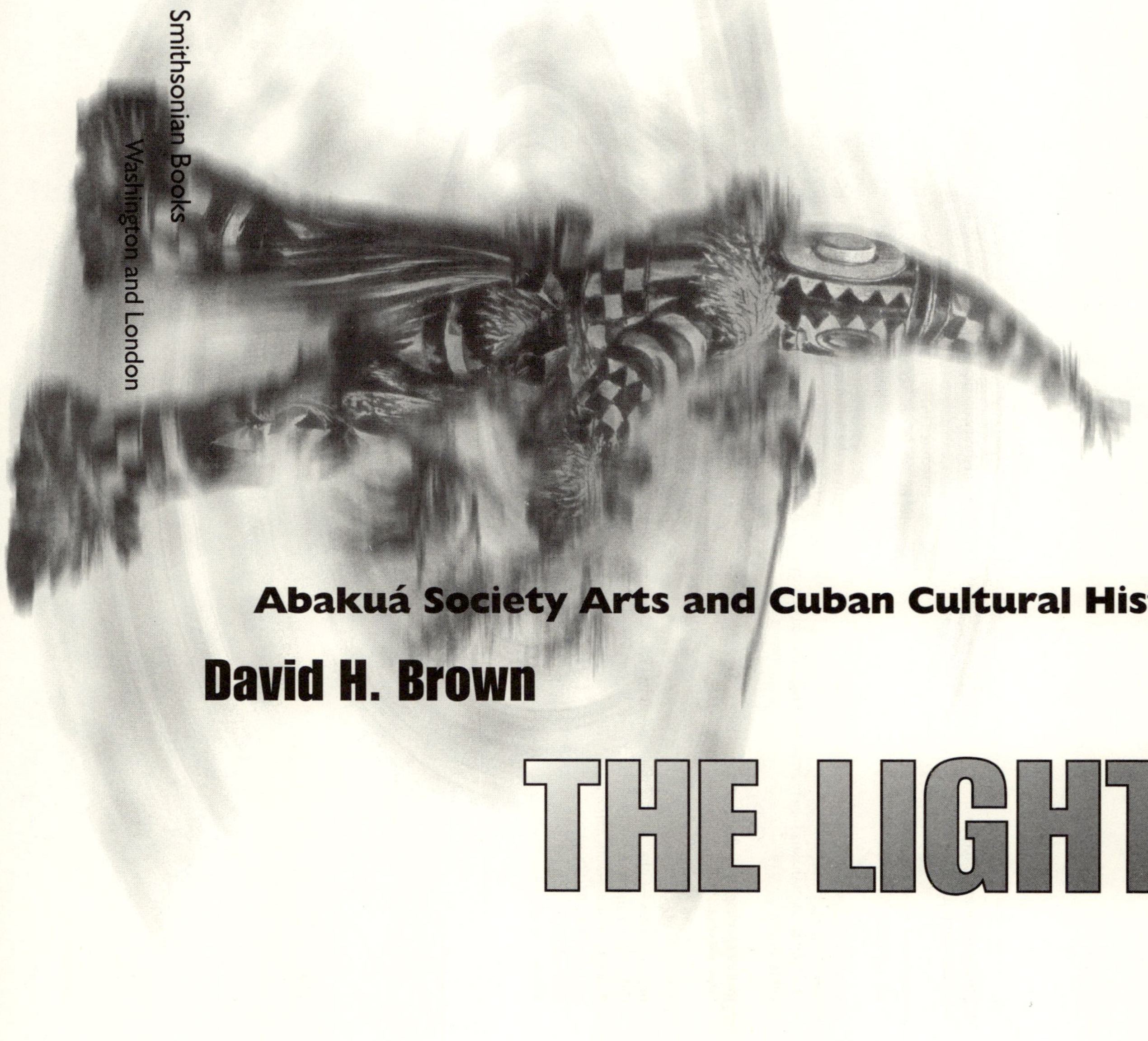

THE LIGHT INSIDE

Abakuá Society Arts and Cuban Cultural History

David H. Brown

Smithsonian Books
Washington and London

Copy editor: Gregory McNamee
Designer: Janice Wheeler

Library of Congress Cataloging-in-Publication Data
Brown, David H., Ph.D.
The light inside : Abakuá society arts and Cuban cultural history / David H. Brown.
p. cm.
Includes bibliographical references and index.
ISBN 1-58834-123-2 (alk. paper)
1. Sociedad Abakuá (Cuba). 2. Secret societies—Cuba. 3. Men—Cuba—Societies and clubs. 4. Altars—Cuba. 5. Ceremonial objects—Cuba. 6. Art, Primitive—Cuba. 7. Blacks—Cuba—Rites and ceremonies. 8. Blacks—Religious life—Cuba. 9. Blacks—Cuba—Material culture. I. Title.
HS1355.S64 C84 2003
366—dc21 2002030433

British Library Cataloguing-in-Publication Data available

Manufactured in the United States of America
10 09 08 07 06 05 04 03 5 4 3 2 1

♾ The paper used in this publication meets the minimum requirements of the American National Standard for Information Sciences—Permanence of Paper for Printed Library Materials ANSI Z39.48-1984.

For Guango

[Ñañiguismo] desires the domination of the dark of night, veiling perpetually the brilliant light of the sun.

—Enrique Fernández Carrillo (1881)

The [Abakuá] aesthetic recreates—how can I explain it to you?—the light inside, *la luz interior*. Do you understand? The interior light comes to reflect from [the exterior adornments], giving spirituality to the piece.

—Jesús Nasakó (1996)

Contents

Illustrations

Plates

Following page 30

Figures

Maps

Tables

Acknowledgments

I have received invaluable moral and material support from many people during the researching and writing of this book, for which I am extremely grateful. I would like to thank, in alphabetical order, Perico Abasonga; Pedro Alemañy; Pedro Álvarez; Pedro Emilio Álvarez Martín; Andrew Apter; Herman Bennett; Judith Bettelheim; Olivia Carvajal; Isabel Castellanos; Mr. and Mrs. Ramón Cernuda; Reinaldo Raimundo "Papo" Chaguayceda; Tom Concordia; Donald Cosentino; Pedro Cosme Baños; Daniel Crowley; Joanne Crudgington; Antonio Martín de Armas Arredondo; Omaira De la Torre; Lauren Derby; Robin Evanchuck; Antonio Elígio Fernández ("Tonel"); Ariel Fernández; Pilar Fernández; Ruddy Fernández; Ysamur Flores-Peña; Raisa Formaguera; Lisa Freiman; Henry Louis Gates; Annette Gilsdorf; Jesús González Funes Hernández; Julian González Pérez Sr.; Julián González Jr.; Juan Gutiérrez Boza; Alberto Gutiérrez; Juan Carlos Gutiérrez; Zenaida Justíz; Katherine Hagedorn; John Howett; Dr. Nikolaos Kaltsas; Elliot Klein; Mr. and Mrs. Melvin Knyper; Elliot Leib; Julie Levin; María Teresa Linares; Alberto López; Natacha López; Rafael L. López Valdés; María de Guango; Sara McPhee; Michael Atwood Mason; Caitlin Miller; Claudia Mola Fernández; Concepción Morales; Keith Nicklin; Ester Nicle; Robert Orsi; María Fernanda Ortiz Herrera; Luis Alberto Pedroso; Melba Pérez; Monica Lea Pérez; Jane Rehl; Renee Romano; Norge Romero Cordiés; Nicholas Spitzer; Gregory Svitil; Jessica Taplin; Krista Thompson; Robert Farris Thompson; Nong Tumsutipong; Carlos Torrens Vega; Jesús Varona Puente; and Francisco Zamora Chirino ("Minini"). I thank as well Duke Johns, Scott Mahler, Gregory McNamee, Emily Sollie, and Janice Wheeler of Smithsonian Books for helping see this book into print.

I would like to thank the following institutions for their support: Albertina Grafische Sammlung, Vienna; Art Museum of the Americas of the Organization of American States; Artists Rights Society; La Casa de Africa; the Center for Folklife Studies of the Smithsonian Institution; Efí Embemoró of Havana; Efori Eñongo of Regla; Eforikamá of Regla; Eron Entatí Ibionó of Guanabacoa; the Estate of Lydia Cabrera; Irionda of Regla; the Metropolitan Museum of Art; El Museo Criminológico de la Catedra de Medicina-Legal de la Universidad de la Habana; El Museo Etnográfico de Guanabacoa; El Museo Nacional de Bellas Artes, Havana; El Museo Polívalente de Regla; Museum of Arts and Sciences, Daytona, Florida; National Archaeological Museum, Athens; Orú Papá of Guanabacoa; Uriabón Efí #1 Hijos de la Caridad of Matanzas; and the W. E. B. Du Bois Institute for Afro-American Research, Harvard University.

I conducted preliminary research for this work as a postdoctoral fellow at the Center for Folklife Studies of the Smithsonian Institution in 1989. La Casa de Africa, under the directorship of Claudia Mola Fernández, aided my research in the Fernando Ortiz Collection in 1992. I wrote the manuscript while a Non-Resident Fellow of the W. E. B. Du Bois Institute for Afro-American Research in spring 2000. Early versions of portions of this book were presented as papers at the "Imaging the City in the Americas: The Formation and Display of Urban Identity around 1910" symposium at the Getty Center for the History of Art and the Humanities (Santa Monica, California, 8 May 1995) and the "Spirited Discussion 1" panel at the American Folklore Society annual conference (Lafayette, Louisiana, 12 October 1995). I had the opportunity to develop part two of this book in my fall 1996 graduate seminar "Afro-Caribbean Arts and Cuban Secret Societies" at Emory University.

I am especially grateful to Stephan Palmié for his generosity in sharing ideas, historical documents, and his own unpublished papers with me during the course of my research. I remain indebted to Jesús Nasakó, Perico Abasonga, and the late Juan Mokongo; without their support, this book could not have been written.

I owe special gratitude to Morris, Sylvia, and Alan Brown.

1

"The Light Inside" Abakuá Society Arts and Modern Cuban Cultural History

The whites put the [Abakuá] sacred attributes on [the] *Kende*, altar, but in the Catholic style. It was Andrés [Petít] who put the crucifix in the lodges, in order that everyone would be convinced that [the Abakuá] were not savages; it was he who suggested that they put their saintly devotion on the altar and who devised, along with his white boys [*blanquitos*], the spending of a day *asanga makotero* [in a *ñáñigo* procession] before the doors of the church, in order to demonstrate to the priest that they were devotees, Christians, and not unbaptized. . . . They came out on Jesús María Street. They stopped before the very door of the Sacristy. Upon seeing them with their drums, carrying a crucifix, a clay water vessel, and the head of a goat, [the priest] asked them:

—Who are you? What do you want?

—We are Abakuá. We want you to bless us.

—But do you believe in God?

—We believe in the Father, the Son, the Holy Spirit and in the Holy Mother Church.

The priest prayed over them and blessed them.

(Cabrera 1970:55)

The *Reforma* of [Andrés] Petít within the [Abakuá] and in *Mayombería* definitively tied the African-borns with the creoles and the Cuban blacks, the mulattos, and the whites, all in the same group of common beliefs, rites, recreation, interests and solidarity. For this reason, such social phenomena, which, before were simply "black things," became what today are "Cuban things," in which blacks, mulattos, and whites participate personally and intimately; and not only Africans and creoles, but also Chinese and Spanish. And, what is most curious, some Jewish Poles become possessed by the [*orichas*] just like an African from Guinea. These episodes help one to understand the very complex Afrocuban transculturation, which had, and continues having, an effect in every aspect of life.

(Ortiz 1954:70–71)

[The *bricoleur*] interrogates all the heterogeneous objects of which his treasury is composed to discover what each of them could "signify" and so contributes to the definition of a set which has yet to materialize.

(Lévi-Strauss 1966:18, 21)

1 Introduction

Meanings, Methods, and the Cultural Biography of Things Abakuá

In 1979, the Nasakó grade of a Havana Abakuá lodge, which I will call Eforí Eñongo,[1] refurbished its altar objects (plate 1). Originally fabricated for the lodge's founding on April 9, 1916, the objects were, and continue to be, "renovated" *(renovado)* regularly. Some had been worn through repeated ritual handling and humid storage conditions. Others were simply considered unattractive by rising authorities within the lodge. "Jesús Nasakó," as I will call him, is known by his Abakuá brethren as learned, creative, and resourceful. In 1979 he redecorated the altar's cylindrical staffs and stout drums with diverse adornments. They included items that he had salvaged, bought for a bargain, borrowed from his personal cache of family heirlooms, and even stolen: leopard skin, pieces of red velvet, furniture tacks, silk upholstery cords and tassels, African cowrie shells, mass-produced metal key fobs, rooster feathers, a custom-welded crown of chromed sheet metal, a rainbow of beads, broom fringe, brass fishing connectors, house paint, an American Roosevelt dime, Roman Catholic saint medallions, a nineteenth-century Italian-made crucifix, and a vintage American automobile hood ornament. Subsequently, in the late 1980s, the lodge's Mokongo grade, whom I will call "Juan," added another layer of adornment. Though known as an erudite master of Abakuá liturgy, Juan was not an artist, and he lacked quality materials. He applied ungainly designs and symbols on the staffs with inadequate brushes and commercial paint in gold and green. Jesús Nasakó was disappointed that this subsequent renovation had "ruined" his earlier handiwork. Soon after I was permitted to photograph the objects in 1992, they were renovated once again, thanks in part to a foreign visitor's donation of hard currency to the lodge. They gained, among other things, spectacular new plumage for the altar's drums.

The periodic renovation of Abakuá altar objects maintains their beauty and spiritual radiance. New adornment expresses the collective well-being and esteem of a lodge. It is also intended to impress spectators, including visiting dignitaries from other lodges when they enter a group's secret temple, as well as the public when the officers "come out" into the walled compound's courtyard in a dramatic procession. Renovation may also include the "recharging" of the contents of some objects with spiritually imbued substances. The altar objects are considered to be the permanent living repositories of ancestral presences; the quality and effect of adornment indexes their spiritual force, radiating "the light inside."[2]

The quantity and quality of adornment, its particular aesthetic "taste" *(gusto),* and the meanings it expresses have changed over the course of Abakuá history (the Abakuá Society was founded in 1836). Innovations by one lodge have been adopted by others, and, in this way, have become "traditionalized" in Abakuá circles (Kirshenblatt-Gimblett 1983; Schoemaker 1994). Because many innovations have been taken from other ritual systems, Cuban popular culture, and the imagination of makers, periodic renovations draw from wide-ranging domains. These include, on one extreme, individual experience and artistic creativity and, on the other, Cuban social and cultural history.

This book looks closely at the altar objects of one lodge in order to identify not only changing styles of Abakuá arts at a general level of form and meaning but also the intentions and agency of particular makers. I have limited my fieldwork to two principal sources, both of whom are members of Eforí Eñongo: the late guardian of the objects, Juan Mokongo (ca. 1935–1997), and Jesús Nasakó (b. 1945), the most recent significant renovator of the objects. Ethnoaesthetic and ethnohistorical attention to a single integrated altar assemblage reveals levels of significance that may be opaque to more general iconological and symbolic interpretation alone (see Brown 1996).

Previous treatments of Abakuá art and ritual have limited their interpretations to the level of generalized symbolic meanings.[3] These tend to be abstractions, enabled by the observer's constitution of changing historical practices as synchronic or synoptic representations. Meanings at this level are assumed to be "shared" by the members of a territorialized "culture," and they can be elicited through "symbolic" or "iconological" interpretation such as that found in the 1960s and 1970s works of Victor Turner, Clifford Geertz, and art historians influenced by Erwin Panofsky's iconological method (see Brown 1996; Turner 1967; Geertz 1973, 1983; Panofsky 1955; Wescott 1962; see also Bell 1992). In studies of the Abakuá of Cuba, as in many anthropologically based works on African religions, Abakuá objects and practices are interpreted by referencing the Abakuá "mythical charter" as if it were a fundamental and historically prior "text" (see Apter 1992:13–14). For example, students of the Abakuá have typically treated objects and practices as the realization or execution of a single dramatic "tragedy of the Ñáñigos" (Ortiz 1950b; León 1964). The Abakuá *plante* (ceremony) appears as a "theatrical" representation or "commemoration" of the founding myth, cast against the scrim of a light historical backdrop. "In reality," writes Cuban folklorist Israel Moliner Castañeda, "the *plante,* which is the festival or principal ceremony of the Abakuá, *is nothing more than* a commemoration or reconstruction of the myth of the death of Sikana, only that here, the goat substitutes for the woman. As [Fernando] Ortiz would say, this reproduction of the myth acquires the dimension of a truly theatrical representation, where the participants assume the roles of the old protagonists of the myth" (Moliner Castañeda 1988:16; see also Ortiz 1954:1–85, 1950b; Cabrera 1970:144–145, 1954 (plates); Thompson 1983:237, 258, 262–266).

In the African and African Diaspora scholarly literature, specific art makers, objects, and ritual actions have often become "transparent" to a set of timeless cultural values or "core principles," which characterize a bounded ethnographic group—for example, "The Yoruba," "The Lucumí," "The Nagô" (see Omari 1984; Thompson 1983; Dallas Museum of Art 1989; Drewal, Pemberton, and Abiodun 1989:26; Lawal 1974, 1996; see also Mintz and Price 1992; Price and Price 1980:194–215; M. Drewal 1992; Brown 1996;

M. Mason 1997; Giddens 1976; Arens and Karp 1989; Hardin 1993).

It has also become conventional in African Diaspora studies for writers to locate art objects as the essential descendants of their African source cultures, however much "creolization" has apparently changed them. Though assumed to have been modified formally by some innovation, for example, as old wine in new bottles, they are still supposedly traceable, like isotopes, to a set of African morphological prototypes within a relatively uniform and stable transatlantic semantic field. For example, in the "Cuban Yoruba" and "Cuban Kongo" religions (Lucumí and Palo Monte, respectively), adornments from the Catholic Church were "fused" or "blended" with African elements extant and stable since time immemorial, and which remain legible. Clearly, as the investigations of Fernando Ortiz (1954), Lydia Cabrera (1970), and Robert Farris Thompson (1983) show, "foreign" or "Western" objects, such as the Catholic crucifix, were added to the Abakuá altar in response to formidable sociopolitical stress from at least the early 1860s onward. Still, such "syncretisms" or "creolizations" are typically believed to result from the encounter and dialogue of two "bodies of belief" (see Mintz and Price 1992:18). Ortiz believed such syncretisms to be relatively superficial (see Ortiz 1954:70–71), as did Alfred Métraux (1972:323–358), Karl Reisman (1970), Thompson (1983:18), John Mason and Gary Edwards (1985a), and Ernesto Pichardo (1984:20–28). Where African and Catholic icons are taken to have a more thoroughgoing and interdependent "symbiotic" relationship (Desmangles 1992; Murphy 1988, Bastide 1972), the monstrance and crucifix upon the Abakuá altar might represent a reconciliation of the Christian God and "Abasí," the "Supreme Being" of the Abakuá.

Such interpretations virtually float within mythopoetic or superorganic cultural fields, high above practices on the ground. Monstrance, crucifix, and Catholic saint statues come to mark the "encounter" of African and Catholic "religions" or "cosmologies." Still, as this investigation reveals, the "meanings" of such "Roman Catholic" adornments can be much more particular, subtle, personal, and idiosyncratic. They may register very specific "social meanings," as opposed to "iconographic" and "iconological" meanings (see Price and Price 1980:194–215; Brown 1996). As Jesús Nasakó insisted when I wanted to discuss the Catholic significance of the religious medals he employed in his altar renovation, "No one besides me would be able to explain to you the meaning of these things, because they come from my personal experience and family history." Jesús Nasakó had so recontextualized and reinscribed the "Catholic" objects as mementos of personal and local identity that one could never look at a St. Christopher's medal in the same way again. Nasakó's history and experience simply exceed the "bodies" of Catholic, African, and "religious" belief. As Michael Atwood Mason insists, "syncretism," as hitherto conceived, obscures questions of individual "agency" and "experience" in the making of meaning, that is, culture (M. Mason 2002: 87–89).

African Diaspora studies of "syncretism" or "creolization" might benefit from recent writings in historical anthropology. The social and cultural productions, or "symbolic practices," of subaltern groups within hegemony, are, in effect, "struggles for possession of the sign" (Kelly and Kaplan 1990:133). Such "struggles" pervade the thoughts, actions, and imaginations of individuals, groups, and state administrators. As a result, the Abakuá in Cuba, or the Zionist churches of South Africa studied by Jean Comaroff, perpetuate and accommodate in relation to dominant discourses as much as they resist. This is because all symbolic innovations, as Comaroff writes, "are *bricolages,* concoctions of symbols already freighted with significance by a meaningful environment." Where such "symbolic reconstructions" have been called "syncretistic" and "subversive," *bricoleurs* "struggle to control key signs and to construct an order of practice that might domesticate the divisive forces that have come to pervade their environment." Necessarily, their reconstructions are "both expressive and pragmatic," as they seek to transform the world. However, because "signs are never transparent and innovations are always partial . . . subversive *bricolages* always perpetuate as they change" (Comaroff 1985: 197–198; see also Hebdige 1979). Therefore, Abakuá objects and signifying practices, no less than those of any other group, are produced as the ongoing outcomes of struggles and exceed the "results" of any imagined initial "encounter" of "Europe" and "Africa."

Many Abakuá objects and beliefs have been individually illustrated, analyzed, and interpreted in several classic studies (e.g., Ortiz 1954:1–88; Cabrera 1970; Thompson 1983:236–267). However, they have never been documented in situ—their altar context—as integral "sets," "series," or "ensembles" (Preston 1985; see also A. Rubin 1974; Blier 1995; Rush 1999). As Robert Farris Thompson's important exhibition *Face of the Gods* (1993) demonstrated, attention to the altar as a complex artistic unit overcomes the limitations of the modernist focus upon single, "autonomous" artworks, underscoring the "ecumenical . . . additive, eclectic, non-exclusivistic" character of the Afro-Atlantic artistic and religious imagination (Thompson 1993:14). Few have been able to phrase it better.

Whether they acknowledge or dismiss the significance of Roman Catholic meanings, ethnographic and art-historical accounts of Afro-Cuban religion have usually emphasized this single influence as central to African Diaspora visual traditions in the Caribbean and Latin America. A great virtue of the accounts of Robert Farris Thompson (1983, 1993) and Donald Cosentino (1995a, 1995b), following the pioneering African studies of Marilyn Houlberg (e.g., 1983), is that they assume the formative role of popular and mass culture in transformations of sacred artwork. For example, in his analysis of the Afro-Cuban Ósun staff, Thompson writes, "The new forms had absorbed Western industrial or cultural fragments—the hubcap of an automobile, a metal rooster from a weather vane or discarded garden furniture, store-bought jingle-bells—and invested them with new meaning. The rooster replaced the flattened bird of the elders, the hubcap sometimes became the base, and the jingle bells recalled the *agogo* gongs" (Thompson 1983:48). Donald Cosentino celebrates the improvisatory "postmodern" use of found objects in the creation of meaningful, cosmologically appropriate, and beautiful religious objects, the "origins" of which may be overdetermined and indeterminate (see, e.g., Cosentino 1995a, 1995b, 1998; see also Polk 1995). Altars are examples of "synthetic" knowledge production and aesthetic creativity par excellence, assemblages from fragments or streams of multiple cultures as opposed to direct representations of nature. As Michele Anderson astutely notes, "authentic voodoo is synthetic" (Anderson 1982; see also Cerny and Seriff 1996).

In sum, Afro-American and African Diaspora comparative ethnography of the sort that the anthropologist Melville Herskovits practiced, emphasizing the analysis of New World objects against the African background, has tended to flatten history and "process." The question of discontinuity, as opposed to an assumed historical continuity based on visual similarities, is skirted (see Mintz and Price 1992; Price and Price 1980; Palmié 1993); as well, an object's meaning and value, which are contextual, not essential, change with changing discursive formations. For example, Abakuá things and meanings putatively derive from the Ngbe/Ekpe societies of the Cross River Delta region of West Africa. Still, questions remain as to what happened in the Cross River itself in 1836, or 1863, or 1902, or 1925, or 1983, and we should ask *what* forces shape and situate, and *whose* meanings and values *constitute,* things Abakuá in any given historical setting.

The "Abakuá Society," in practice, has always involved a shifting set of constituencies or factions, which have debated practices and meanings among themselves, including what it has meant to be an "Abakuá" in Cuban society. Over time, from the perspective of the Spanish and Cuban government authorities, the creole planter aristocracy, the middle classes, and the Abakuá themselves, the "meaning" of things Abakuá or *ñáñigo* changed significantly over time. To observers early in the nineteenth century, *ñáñigo* "meant" curiosity of exotic, albeit frightening, custom, as reflected in the period's journalism and *costumbrista* arts and letters (see Ortiz 1960; Landaluze 1881). In general, as *cosas de negro* ("n-word things"), though they caused some repugnance, during the license of carnival their excesses were tolerated as a necessary evil, a safety valve to release social pressure—including among bourgeois families themselves, as the "devil's dances" vicariously afforded them light amusement and leaps of imagination in a theater of social classes enacted between the rough street and the genteel balcony.

After the great slave rebellions of the mid-nineteenth century, and with the specter of western Cuban cities teaming with African freedmen following emancipation in the last third of that century, things *ñáñigo meant,* and *derived* in essential ways from, "delinquency," "vagrancy," "promiscuity," "homicidal criminality," miscegenation, and evolutionary "atavism." Abakuá objects and performances, read as symptoms, found their referents not in a charming African or folkloric mythical charter. On the contrary, their ground and referent was the contagious Afro-Cuban "underworld" and pathologically evil lifeways (*la hampa cubana* and *la mala vida,* respectively; see Saco 1946 [1832]; Ortiz 1973; I. Castellanos 1916).

From a late twentieth-century liberal-left analytical standpoint, of course, what it "meant" to be Abakuá between the 1860s and the 1940s can be located partly in the phenomena of gendered Cuban social identity, *barrio* identity, mutual aid, and proletarian organizing and self-defense. These phenomena, in turn, articulated with the contradictions of emergent global capitalist modes of production, Cuba's peculiar forms of racism, classism, and sexism, and U.S. imperial domination of the island's political economy. Abakuá members struggled in union for the island's independence in two wars, but they also fought against each other along racial lines for wharf jobs and resources (see López Valdés 1985; Palmié 1993; Kutzinski 1993; Pérez 1988:195–199; Scott 1985:227–278; Helg 1995). Many young white Abakuá recruits came from wealthy families that owned slaves, detested blacks, and benefited from capitalist expansion from the north. Yet these enthusiastic recruits sought Abakuá membership in order to demonstrate their *hombría* ("real manhood") partly in compensation for their lack of heroic participation in the wars of independence (see Robreño 1925:7–28).

Beginning in the mid-1920s and continuing through the 1940s, *ñañiguismo* and other things Afro-Cuban could mean, and derive from, the mystical, the transcendent, and wholesomely primitive renewing forces of human creativity—not least as located in the African and the indigenous. To the avant-garde, these forces could, if effectively tapped through artistic representation, effect a transvaluation and modernization of Cuban aesthetics, culture, and society. This was particularly true beginning during the years of the dictator Gerardo Machado's brutal and corrupt rule (1924–33). Such ideas were at the heart of the avant-garde Afro-Cubanismo literary, artistic, and folklore movements, which were also linked, at different levels, to Euro-American surrealism and Francophone Caribbean negritude. In the formation of modern Cuban society and cultural identity, images of the Afro-Cuban, the peasant, and the landscape offered cultural "antidotes to Wall Street" (Kutzinski 1993; Martínez 1994; Blanc 1992).

The Cuban Revolution since 1959 has gone further. In place of a minority cultural avant-garde, the government itself has elevated things Afro-Cuban to the status of national folklore on the model of Third World socialist ideas of popular culture's seminal role in national formation (see Franco 2001; *Caribbean Quarterly* 1956). In Trinidad, given the great influence of socialist prime minister Eric Williams, "traditional" black carnival offered a "mandate for a national theater" (Hill 1972). In Haiti, the former ethnologist "Papa Doc" Duvalier, appropriating *noiriste* ideas, created a populist facade for his dictatorship around the majority religion, Vodou (see Ferguson 1987:32–54; Apter 1991). In the late 1960s and 1970s, one of Cuba's specific intentions was to use "folklore" in order to define the island as an "Afro-Latin" nation, and thus legitimate its political, military, and commercial interests in Africa (C. Moore 1988; Hagedorn 2001).

Museum and other forms of cultural "display" embodied and expressed these shifting discourses on the Afro-Cuban and the Abakuá. Whereas Abakuá objects were first featured in Havana's anthropology and criminological museums, as of the mid-1960s they would occupy entire salons of the Ethnographic Museum of Guanabacoa, "The Africa House," and the National Museum of Fine Arts. In the historiography, whereas Fernando Ortiz, Lydia Cabrera (1954, 1970), and Harold Courlander (1944, 1976:20–25) studied the Abakuá as "folklore," Robert Farris Thompson boldly announced Abakuá objects as "art" and repositories of moral "philosophy" on par with that of other classical civilizations (1983:225–268).

Each of the foregoing discursive formations constitutes a layer in the "stratigraphy" of Cuban and Abakuá cultural history in very specific ways (see, e.g., Barnes 1989:7). Igor Kopytoff aptly uses the term "biography" to register an object's shifting "identity" and trajectory, particularly as it moves between distinct social contexts and semantic domains over time (Kopytoff 1986). In James Clifford's terms, which are appropriate to the circulation of things Abakuá through time and space, objects "graduate" between different categories of cultural function and regimes of value and may become "art" only at a particular historical conjuncture (1988). This was clearly the important message of Susan Vogel's clever exhibition *ART/Artifact: African Art in Anthropology Collections* (1988). Distinct types of display were seen to constitute the meaning of objects in historically specific ways. Objects were mounted in four different display contexts: the nineteenth-century "cabinet of curiosities," the natural history "diorama," structural-functional "ethnic" or "culture" classification, and as modernist "art." In the last display context, individual "functional" pieces were constituted as autonomous, objets d'art exhibited in vitrines within the modernist white gallery cube.

This book respects Abakuá objects by paying close attention to them as one would in any other scholarly art-historical or material-culture study. At the same time, it does not take for granted their rather recent classification as "art." Instead, I combine close looking, analysis, and interpretation with attention to the genealogy of ideas. Rather than consider the objects and their meanings as essential and continuous through time, I want to see these things Abakuá as protean objects of ongoing reconstitution. I do this by devoting the book's first part to close readings and historical treatment. The book's second part excavates the stratigraphy of changing discourses that constituted and located things Abakuá in Cuban time and space.

2 The Abakuá Society and the African Diaspora

The Abakuá Society, a system of men's lodges *(juegos, tierras),* first emerged among Afro-Cuban island-born (creole) slaves who had established connections with the colonial-era religious brotherhoods *(cabildos)* of particular African "nations." These *cabildos de nación,* composed of African-born slaves, had reconstituted, distilled, and differentiated a spectrum of "ethnic" identities in Cuba among the subject populations. For example, the *cabildos de nación* system organized and divided the Lucumí (Yoruba), Congo (Kongo-Angola), Arará (Dahomey), Carabalí (Cross and Niger Delta regions, and "Old Calabar") and their numerous subgroups.

The creole founders of Cuba's Abakuá lodges sought out the Carabalí *cabildos,* whose various constituent peoples had been governed by local gerontocratic "leopard societies" on the continent. The "Carabalí" meta-ethnonym broadly encompassed Africans taken to Cuba from the borderland regions of present-day eastern Nigeria and southwestern Cameroon during the eighteenth century. Thus, the Carabalí rubric subsumed many subgroups, including the Ibo, Ibibio, Ijo, Ekoi, Efik, and Efut, who had voluntarily migrated to the Cross River Delta or had been forcibly marched by Aro and Efik traders from the hinterlands to be sold in the Delta's bustling slave-trading center, "Old Calabar."[1] The Efik (pronounced EH-fik) of Old Calabar, an Ibibio-speaking people, for example, had originally migrated southeast by canoe to found riverside villages on the Cross River estuary, where they lived mainly as fishermen. They founded settlements upriver in the Enyong region and downriver at "Creek Town" (ca. 1650). Later settlements were established at "Old Town" (Obutong), and then in "Duke Town" (Orok) after 1748 (Forde 1956:vii, 1–4).

These Efik divided themselves into seven "wards" or "houses" controlled by trader-chiefs, each with its own settlement or "town" (Lovejoy and Richardson 1999:340–341; n.d.:16). This territory, crosscut by Cross River loops and meanders, as well as the

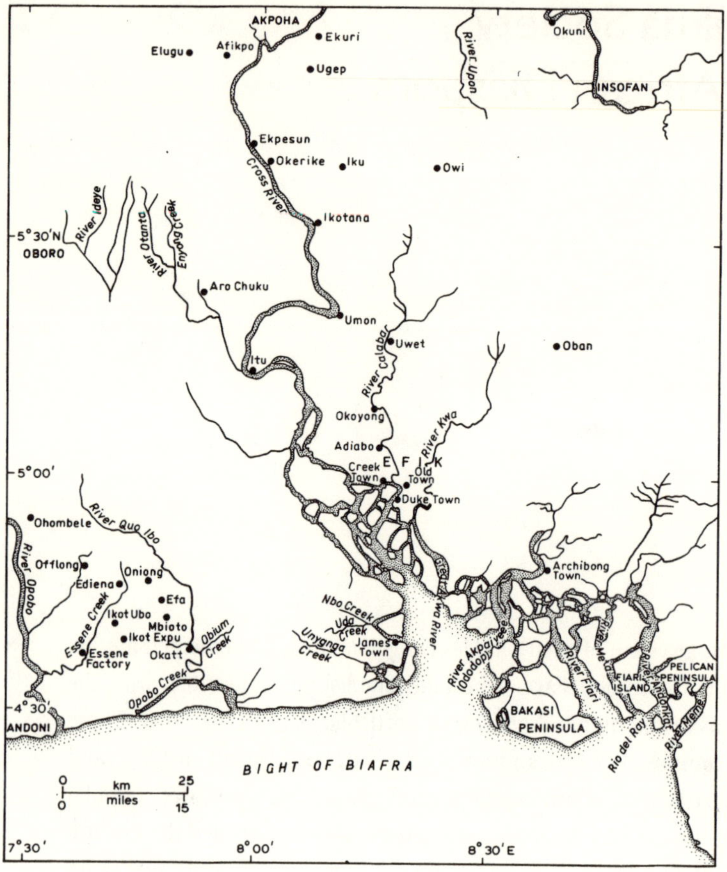

Map 2.1. The Bight of Biafra, Old Calabar, the Cross River, and hinterlands, nineteenth century. Redrawn by Keith Scurr, School of Geography, University of Hull, after a map in Kannan K. Nair, *Politics and Society in South Eastern Nigeria, 1841–1906: A Study of Power, Diplomacy, and Commerce in Old Calabar* (London: F. Cass, 1972).

Calabar and Kwa river estuaries, would become known as "Old Calabar" (see map 2.1). Duke Town, for example, sat on an eastern loop of the Cross River estuary a few miles downriver (southeast) from the mouth of the Calabar River. It occupied rising terrain surrounded by a steep hillside, over a beach that the Efik fortified with cannon (Forde 1956:68, 72).[2]

At Creek Town, farther upriver and just northwest of the mouth of the Calabar River, the newly arrived Efik encountered a small village of earlier settlers, the Efut. The Efut are a Bantu group that had migrated from southern Cameroon, where numerous Efut towns still cluster around the Rio del Rey area. There they are also known as the Balondo (Forde 1956:3–4; Nicklin 1991).[3] Indeed, well before the arrival of the Ibibio-Efik, the Efut had occupied what later came to be known as "Old Calabar" around the late fifteenth to early sixteenth centuries (Nicklin 1991:12). Apparently, they also settled in Cobham Town (Akabom), which is southeast of Duke Town (see maps 2.1 and 2.3).

As Daryll Forde, and more recently, Paul Lovejoy and David Richardson have outlined, the early slave trade at Old Calabar was dominated by Efik traders based at Old Town (Obutong), which sits between Creek Town and Duke Town on the same Cross River loop. By the late 1760s, the Old Calabar trade had shifted directly to Duke Town and Henshaw Town (see maps 2.1 and 2.3) (Lovejoy and Richardson 1999:331, 340; n.d.:16).[4] Other neighboring peoples that had migrated to the Old Calabar area included the Ibibio, Oron, Kwa, Efiat, Okoyong, Uwet, Enyong, and Arochuku Ibo. As Forde (1956:2) noted in the 1950s, "The Ibibio and Oron live on the west side of the lower Cross River [see map 2.2], and the Kwa in several villages east of Duke Town, having originally migrated from the Ejagham Ekoi of the Oban Hills

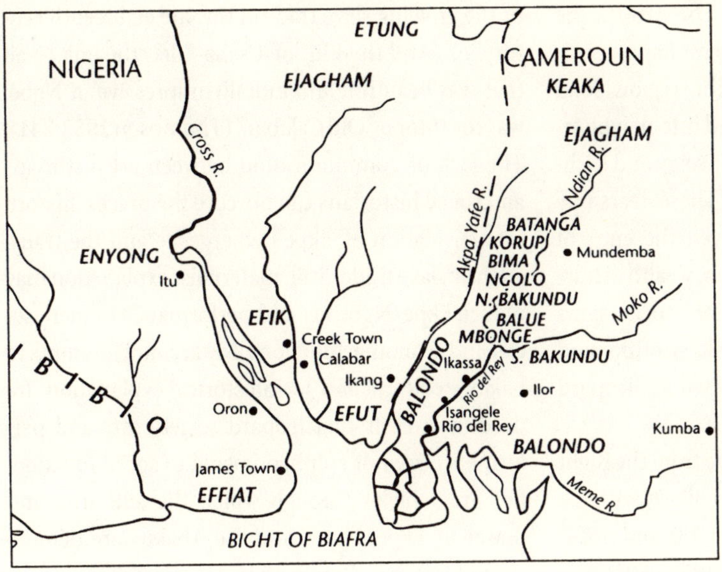

Map 2.2. Ethnic groups of Old Calabar and the Rio del Rey region. Note old Ejagham hinterlands to the north and northeast and the Balondo to the southeast of Old Calabar.

district" deep in the hinterlands to the northeast (see Oban, upper middle right in map 2.1). Many of these people, along with Efik themselves, were sent to Cuba as slaves. A dispassionate look at the historical record makes it indisputable that the "Efik enslaved those of their own people who were guilty of theft or adultery, and also captured or purchased slaves from neighboring groups, such as the Igbo-Aro" (Forde 1956:7). The Efik also conducted concerted and far-flung war expeditions to enslave the inhabitants of other villages (Forde 1956:69).

The Efik Ekpe Society, a graded association of males, was established at least by the mid-eighteenth century. It was dominated by wealthy merchants who had purchased the highest grades of the society. Ekpe's functions were multifold. Ekpe regulated the rivalry among the different "wards" of the Old Calabar area, as well as the particular locales where Ekpe had spread into the hinterlands. Most directly, it is widely known that Ekpe organized, sanctioned, helped spread, and economically profited from the transatlantic slave trade (Lovejoy and Richardson 1999:348–49; n.d.:17). In what was never merely a reaction to an already developed external European slave trade, the Efik Ekpe society propelled and expanded the trade. More specifically, as historians note, the very foundation of the Old Town (Obutong) slave center in the second half of the seventeenth century, for example, "was associated with the introduction of Ekpe into Old Calabar, and may have represented an attempt to manipulate the secret society to advance the commercial interests of the [Efik and other] settlers at Old Town" (Lovejoy and Richardson 1999:347). As A. J. H. Latham hypothesizes, if Ekpe was "an elementary capitalist institution . . . of entirely African origin" (quoted in Lovejoy and Richardson 1999:347), it was also a commodity in and of itself. It could easily be transferred through sale, and, therefore, was distributed to many ethnic groups far and wide (see also Palmié 1993, 1994, 1997). Specifically, "Ekpe spread into areas where

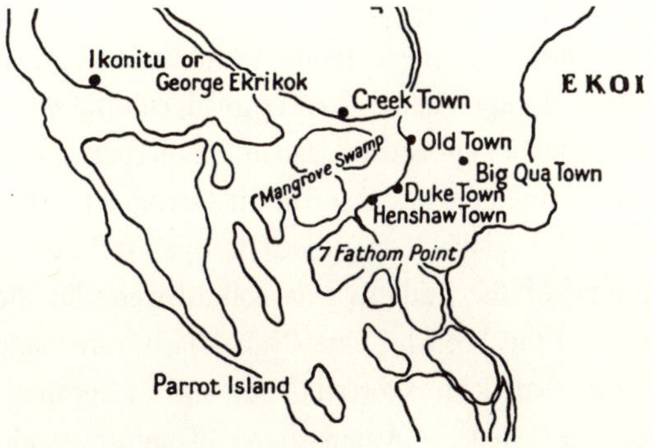

Map 2.3. Close-up of Old Calabar, showing most of the major towns (Forde 1956:vi).

Old Calabar merchants traded. . . . The Aro [to the northwest] maintained their own secret Ekpe association, and Ekpe also spread to the Ibibio region along the Cross River [southwest/west] and into neighboring Cameroon [to the southeast]" (Lovejoy and Richardson 1999:349) (see map 2.2). These fearsome Ekpe "palaver houses,"[5] which served the ends of local government, property protection, wealth extraction, debt recovery, judicial execution, social sanction, recreation, and, among the Efik, Aro-Ibo, and others, slaving, were commonly known as "leopard societies" (see also Forde 1956:vii, 16).

The British transatlantic slave trade from the Bight of Biafra (see maps 2.1 and 2.2), particularly with the Efik, was most intensive between 1700 and 1807, when it was abolished (see Forde 1956; Eltis and Richardson: 1997:29–31; Chambers 1997:75–79; Morgan 1997:129–131; Palmié 1993:343–345). Ekpe was central to the operation of the trade's local economics of exchange: trust, collateral, and debt. By the nineteenth century, the "European-Efik credit system depended upon the ability of Ekpe to invoke its sanctions against those who defaulted on their debts" (Leib and Romano 1984:48). Trust and credit were crucial factors in the success of this trade. Thus, some British traders were initiated into Ekpe during the period for that very reason. For example, by 1820, one "Capt. Burrell of the ship *Heywood* of Liverpool held the rank of Yampai [Nyankpe? Iyamba?] and he found it exceedingly to his advantage as it enabled him to recover all debts due to him by the natives" (quoted in Forde 1956:141).

In contrast to the foregoing sociohistorical explanation of Ekpe's function and spread, cultural interpretations of Ekpe and its Ejagham counterpart, Ngbe, tend to stress the moral and aesthetic characteristics of the Old Calabar leopard societies against the background of the trade as externally driven. "In the name of this Voice [of Ekpe/Ngbe], laws were made or canceled, debtors forced to pay, and European arrogance defied. . . . A new source of authority and moral insight had entered the world of Calabar precisely when the area was heating up under the impact of the growing slave trade in the late eighteenth century. . . . And the Efut of Usaha-Edet, the link to all that was beautiful and morally impressive in Ngbe, was the tutor of Old Calabar" (Thompson 1983:241). The lack of communication between art historians and social historians can obscure the precise historical articulation of Ekpe's emergence and the transatlantic slave trade. Still, materialist explanation may reduce Ekpe/Ngbe art and performance to mere social and economic functions. My account attempts to balance cultural and sociohistorical explanation. Indeed, it is clear that leopard society arts and performance are not epiphenomenal to social function, but are vehicles through which the authority and power of Ekpe, Ngbe, and the Abakuá are demonstrated (see, e.g., Brown 1996; Hardin 1993).

The origins of Ekpe are debated by scholars and are contested among the groups historically in possession of the society. Origin narratives are contested for the same reason that Ekpe arts and performance are vehicles for social power. As Andrew Apter demonstrated in the Yoruba case, origin claims in oral founding narratives are ideological; they enhance one group's authority as they seek to undercut that of another group rhetorically (Apter 1992). Basing his account in local Efik diaries and fieldwork, Daryll Forde writes that the Egbo (Ekpe)[6] society of Old Calabar was derived from the neighboring Kwa (or Qua), who claimed that they brought it with them from their Ekoi-Ejagham homeland in the northeastern hinterlands (see maps 2.2 and 2.3). More recent writing suggests something else. The Efik themselves sent out a "delegation" from Old Calabar to purchase the "secrets" from the Efut people in order to found an Ekpe Society. This enabling event occurred, according to less than disinterested oral sources, not in Old Calabar at all, but at Isangele, in a place called Usaha-Edet (also Usak Edet). Drawing on his own fieldwork and the earlier accounts of Latham and Thompson, who were preceded by Fernando Ortiz in this question, Keith Nicklin attempts to demonstrate that Usaha-Edet was located at Isangele in the Rio del Rey region southeast of Old Calabar. Isangele is found in the Efut/Balondo-inhabited territory of southern Cameroon (see map 2.2) (Nicklin 1991:12; Thompson 1983:241; see also Ortiz 1955:241–242).[7] According to Latham's sources, "Esien Ekpe Oku, grandson of Oku Atai, one of the first Efik founders of Creek Town, Calabar, bought the secrets of the leopard spirit cult from Archibong Ekundo of Usak Edet in the mid-eighteenth century. The first head or *Eyamba* of *Ekpe* in Calabar was thus Esien Ekpe Oku of Creek Town, who in due course passed on his title to Ekpenyong Ekpe Oku, also of Creek Town. Thereafter the *Eyamba* title in Calabar passed through the Duke Town rulers, while the deputy headship, *Obong Ebunko,* passed through those of Creek town" (quoted in Nicklin 1991:13).

Notwithstanding the specificity and persuasiveness of this piece of oral history, each group clearly maintains its own origin story that corresponds to its local sense of historicity and its strategies for claiming authority when push comes to shove. Western fieldworkers undoubtedly provide a forum for the vociferous expression of origin claims, and, hence, a chance to gain attention, potential resources, and a plug in the anthropological transcript. For example, each of three Rio del Rey subgroups interviewed by Nicklin claimed that the society's secret originated with them: none had bought it from anyone (1991:10–11).

The Carabalí in Cuba: If You're Not Efó, Then You're Efí

The diverse Africans sold in Old Calabar to British traders between 1700 and 1807 were known under the Cuban colonial rubric *Carabalí.*[8] Under the umbrella of the Carabalí "nation" were found the many subnations, or "ethnicities" *(étnias),* of the Ibo, which included the Isuama, Olugo, Isieque, and Briche; the Bibí (Ibibio), which included the Orú (Oron) and Efí (putatively the Efik of Old Calabar, who were also called Appapá Chiquito, or "Little Appapá"); the Iyó (Ijo, also known as Ijaw), which included the Bras and Carabalí (Kalabari) proper; and the Ekoi or Ekoy, which included the Cuá (putatively the Kwa/Ejagham Ekoi of Calabar). Finally, various Efut groups were redistilled in Cuba as the subnation variously called Efor, Eforí, Efó, Efok, and Brícamo, as well as "Appapá Grande" ("Big Appapá"; see Sosa Rodríguez 1982: 71–72).

In Cuba, the leopard societies of the Cross River region, as Thompson notes, following Forde, became "known by the creole name Abakuá, after Abakpa, a term by which the Ejagham of Calabar are designated" (Thompson 1983:228; see also Forde 1956: 66).[9] This Cuban fraternal order, historically maligned as the despotic, brutal, and homicidal *ñañiguismo* "clans," regained its more proper denomination "Abakuá," at least in scholarly discourse, with the mid-twentieth-century publications of Lydia Cabrera and Harold Courlander (see Cabrera 1954, 1958; Courlander 1944). The many local West African branches of Ekpe and Ngbe, and the numerous "leopard societies" regionally derived from them, were "compacted," Thompson astutely notes, into two principal Cuban "branches" *(ramas),* the Efí and the Efó (Thompson 1983:248).

Until recently, scholars have tended to essentialize the neo-African ethnonyms of Cuba: "Lucumí," "Arará," "Congo," Carabalí, Efí, Efó, and so on. It is tempting, for example, to attribute Cuba's "Efí" branch to the direct influence of West Africa's Efik. Indeed, it is likely that the name of the first Cuban Abakuá lodge, Efik Buton (pronounced eh-FEE-kee BU-ton), derives from "Obutong," the early, powerful Efik settlement in Old Calabar, which was anglicized as "Old Town" (Cabrera 1975:342; Sosa Rodríguez 1982:119). Moreover, the denominations "Efó" and "Efor" (pronounced Ef-OH), are possibly derived from "Efut." Doubtless, however, both Cuban "branches" *(ramas)* drew on a range of available "resources," as leopard society knowledge was regathered and "incubated" within Cuba's Carabalí *cabildos* in Havana and Matanzas (Palmié 1993:341). Not least, Cuban men entered Abakuá lodge membership through initiatory rituals from the very beginning, not through "ethnic" criteria. Therefore, the "Efí" were no more limited to direct Efik descendants than the Abakuá society was to the "Abakpa," that is, to the Ekoi-Ejagham from Old Calabar who ended up in the western Cuban ports of Havana and Matanzas. Finally, although the West African groups arriving in Cuba spoke a variety of languages (Ibo, Ibibio, and Bantu varieties), a single ritual lingua franca, with some lexical variation, spread to all Abakuá. One of several terms for a single Carabalí subgroup, originally a "Bantu" group, the Efut, came to name the most common Abakuá ritual language: Brícamo.[10]

In sum, as Stephan Palmié persuasively argues, though ethnic and linguistic terms, as well as place names, might continue to carry powerful West African referents, ethnonyms such as "Efó" and "Efí" were redistilled in Cuba as local institutional denominations, which the Abakuá diasporic imagination, not to mention the scholarly imagination, projected back across the Atlantic and mapped onto the African continent. In terms developed by Fredrik Barth and put to use in the Cuban case by Stephan Palmié, the "Efí" and "Efó" ethnonyms, and the local practices that have distinguished them, were institutionally and performatively "marked" or "bounded" in relation to one another, within the specific historical setting of western, urban, coastal Cuba (see Palmié 1993; Barth 1969). Therefore, Palmié concludes, it is perhaps hazardous to reify these terms as legible West African ethnic identifiers that have existed *as such* from time immemorial. Moreover, African history and ethnicity have always been diverse, dynamic, and changing (see Palmié 1993, 1994, 1997).

The Spread of the Abakuá in Cuban Port Cities

In the 1830s, West Africans and their creole (island-born) descendants, free and enslaved, elaborated and reinvented aspects of the palaver houses of Ekpe and Ngbe as walled lodges *(juego, tierra, potencia)* in and around the port cities of Havana (Havana the capital, Regla, Guanabacoa, and Marianao), Matanzas, and Cárdenas. The system of lodges greatly expanded in the mid-nineteenth century, during the apogee of Cuba's sugar and slaving fortunes (1820–1860). Subsequently, the number of lodges grew exponentially during the last third of the century, as proletarianization changed the face of the urbanizing workforce in the teeming ports of these cities, where the Abakuá Society came to control stevedore, transportation, and local manufacturing labor between the 1870s and 1942 (López Valdés 1985).

During the somewhat more permissive government of Cuba's Captain General Don Miguel Tacón (1834–1848), the first Abakuá lodge, Efik Buton (also called Efique Butón, Acabatón, and Acuabutón), was founded in 1836 in Regla with the "help and protection" of that town's Cabildo de Nación Carabalí Brícamo Appapá Efí.[11] This *cabildo* was an officially registered religious fraternity for African-born people claiming origin from among ethnically reconstituted Old Calabar groups. Though the *cabildos de nación* were reserved for enslaved Africans, this seminal "Efí" *cabildo* was a notorious gathering place for large numbers of black creoles, who were able to become members after having paid the requisite entry "contribution" and monthly "dues" (Rodríguez 1881: 1; Roche y Monteagudo 1925:4; see also Moliner Castañeda 1988:14; Sosa Rodríguez 1982:19–131; Ortiz 1987:45–47; Palmié 1993:343–344; Cabrera 1970: 50) (see figure 2.1 left).

According to the detailed July 1881 account of one Alejandro Rodríguez, containing the first substantial information on the "Ñáñigos" (see Cabrera 1970: 11),[12] the number of creoles requesting membership had swelled so alarmingly that the Cabildo Carabalí Brícamo Appapá Efí leadership opposed further admission. The African elders were apparently concerned to prevent the widespread "discovery of the secret," in other words, the sacred resources that undergirded their visible social power. As a result, the secret itself emerged as a premium, though restricted, commodity, as it continued to be in coastal West Africa (Palmié 1993, 1994, 1997). The Cabildo Carabalí of Regla "proposed that if the creoles wanted to form their own lodges apart, by means of payment

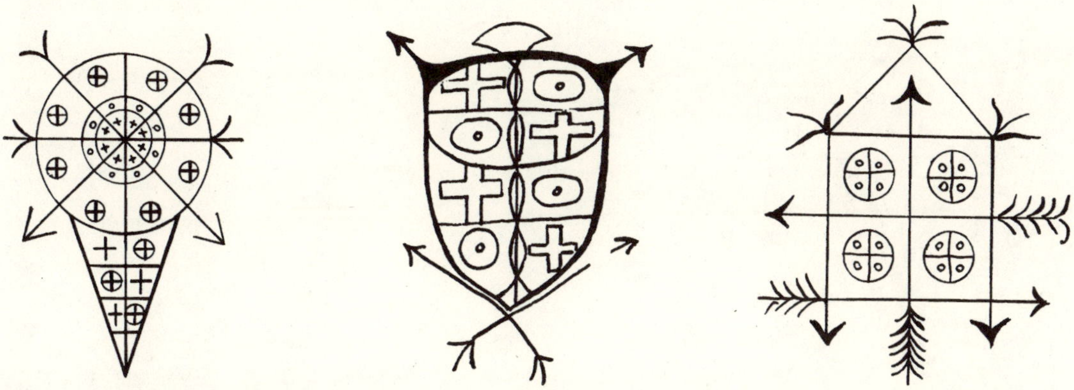

Figure 2.1. Signs for three Abakuá historic landmarks: Cuba's first lodge, Efik Buton (left), founded in Regla (1836; from Cabrera 1975:342); Awana Bakokó Efor (center), the lodge of Andrés Facundo Cristo de los Dolores Petít (Cabrera 1975:323); and Akanarán Efó Ocobio Mukarará (right), the first "white" lodge, founded in 1863 in central Havana (Cabrera 1975:314). Courtesy of the Estate of Lydia Cabrera.

of 100 pesos in gold [the Cabildo] would baptize them in the manner of the Coast of Africa. . . . [The creoles] acceded, forming, thusly, their [own] lodge, composed of 25 black creoles, all of them from a Havana *barrio* within the [Old City *intramuros*] walls, being slaves of wealthy houses [see maps 2.4 and 2.5]. The first lodge that was formed in Regla [gained] the name 'Acuabuton' [Efik Buton, comprising] various [creole] slaves of Doña Josefa Aguiar y Díaz, a resident of San Ignacio Street" (Rodríguez 1881:2–3).[13]

The members of Efik Buton, which grew through the subsequent initiation of other black creole slaves of counts and *marqueses* from the same rich *barrio* of Old Havana, Belén, were called the "Belenistas." According to Alejandro Rodríguez's account, which reflected official Havana's view of *ñañiguismo,* the Belenistas committed every sort of "misdeed" under the cover of their "renown" and the protection of their wealthy owners (1881:3).

Within a short time, a matter of two decades, according to the Rodríguez report, as many as "forty [Abakuá] corporations [*juegos*] sworn in by the Carabalies and [first black] creoles existed in the *intramuros.* . . . So numerous were they that the *juegos* began to outnumber the *cabildos*" of the African "nations" themselves. Eventually, "every neighborhood of the Capital" claimed its own *juegos.* The laws of supply and demand evidently had their way. In order to form a new *juego* in "whatever *barrio* of the population," any prospective group of twenty (to twenty-five) men would now have to pay two hundred pesos. They would also have to deliver a series of small tributes *(derechos)* to their "godfathers" of initiation, and be recognized by other extant lodges (Rodríguez 1881:4; see also Trujillo y Monagas 1882:365).[14] By the year of Rodríguez's writing—forty-five years after Efik Buton's founding—seventy-seven *juegos* populated the nine districts of Havana. Six populated the nearby municipalities of Regla and Guanabacoa, making for a total of eighty-three for all of Havana (see tables 2.1 and 2.2 and maps 2.6 and 2.7).[15]

Along with the *cabildos* of the African "nations" themselves, each *juego* would "come out" onto the street annually to process and petition for *aguinaldo* (gratuities) on the "Day of Kings" festival of Epiphany (January 6; see Rodríguez 1881: 3–4; Ortiz 1960: 12, 25, 31; Moliner Castañeda 1988:14; Brown 1993a: 52, 54–56, 61–63, 69–70, 75–76). It is during this period, 1836 through the shutting down of Carnival in 1884, that the "Ñáñigos" became publicly visible, as their supposed characteristics and crimes echoed throughout the city's police blotters and rumor mills.

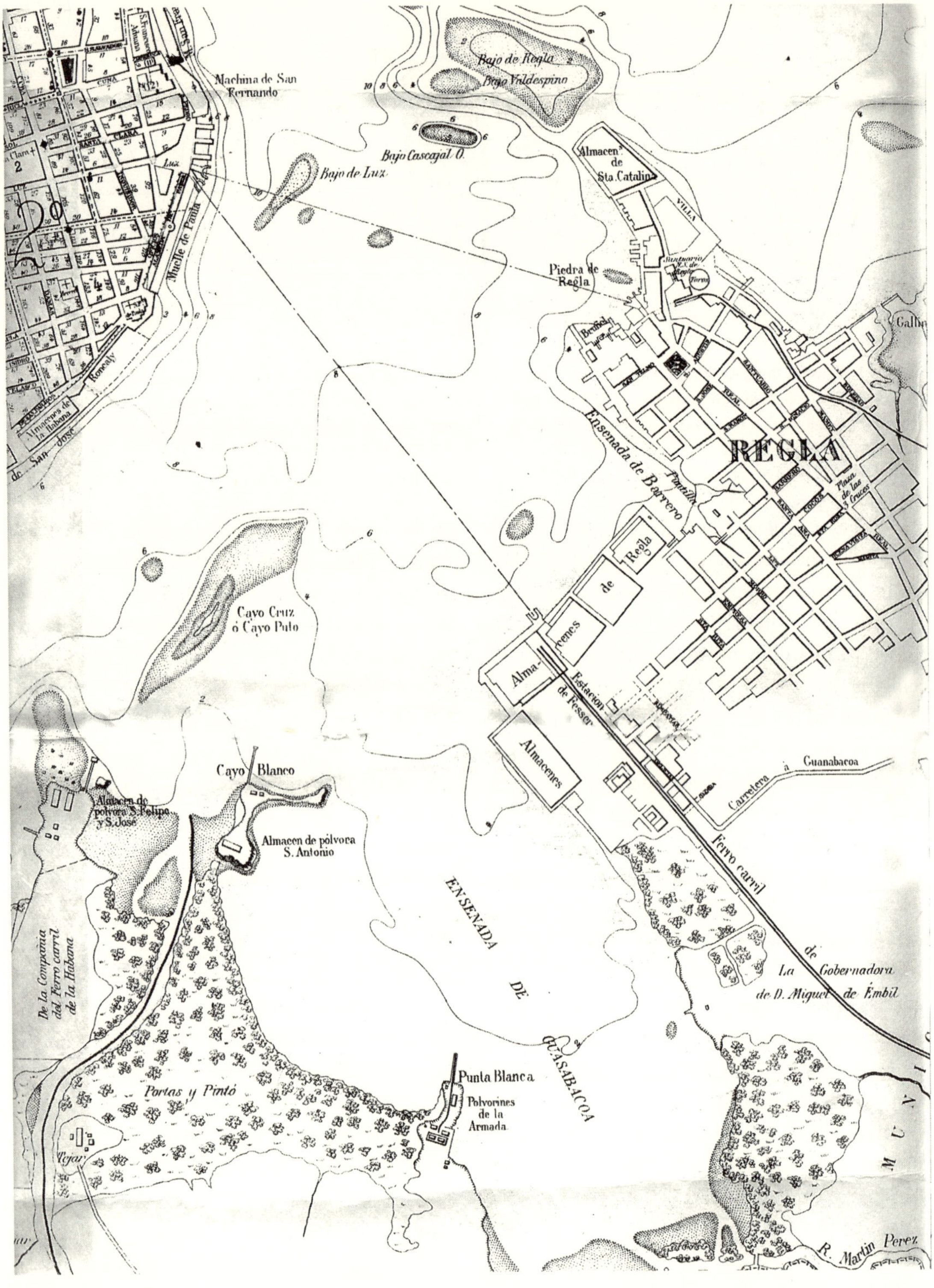

Map 2.4. Map of the Bay of Havana and Regla, detail, 1874. Guanabacoa would be to the lower right. See Cuba, Havana (city), 1874, 1:10,000, D. Esteban T. Pichardo, Geography and Map Division, Library of Congress.

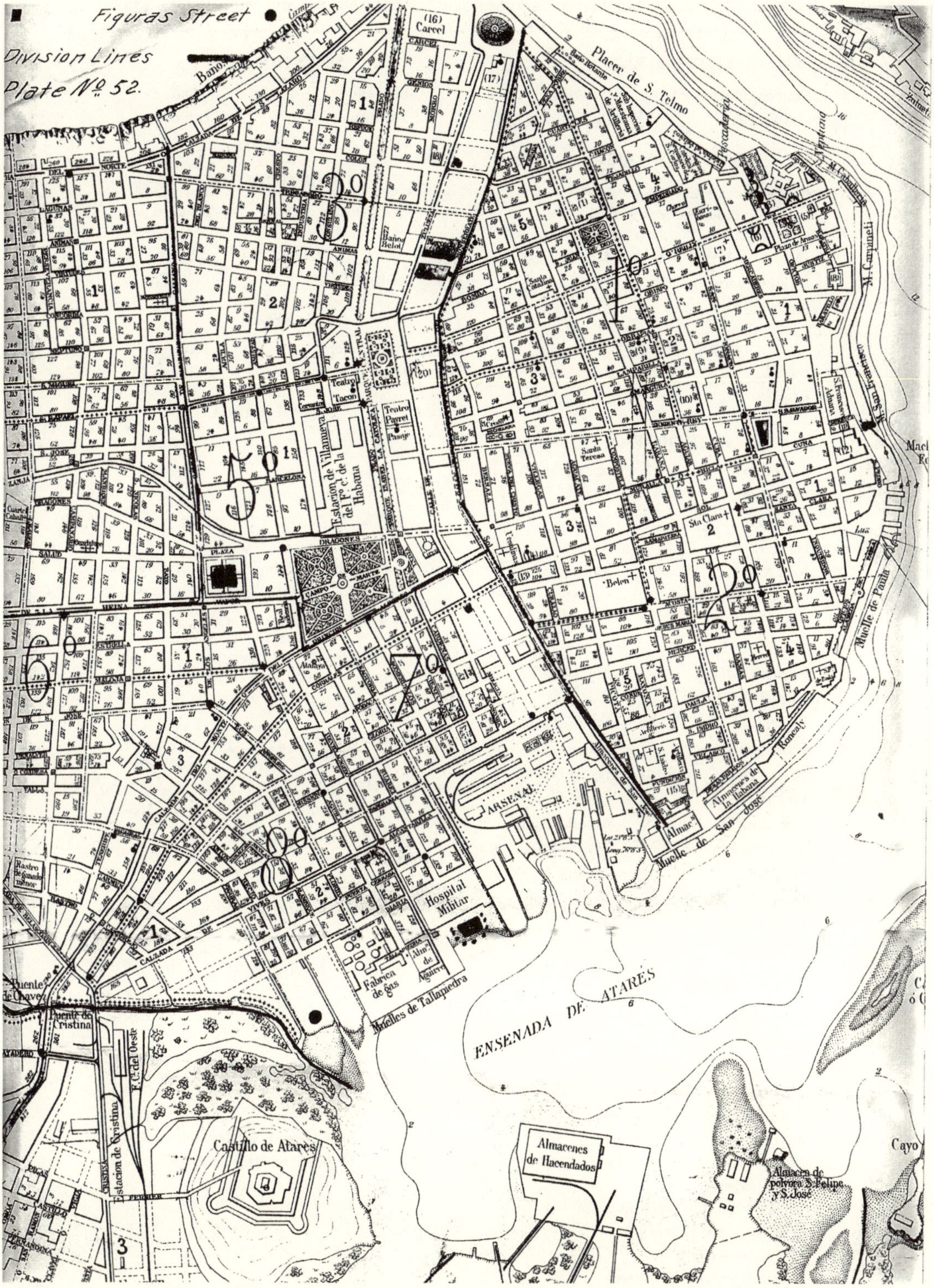

Map 2.5. Map of Old Havana, detail, 1874. The *extramuros* (working-class neighborhoods outside the former fortress walls, districts 3, 5, 6, 7, and 8) are to the west of the lozenge-shaped old city (districts 1 and 2). Numbers represent administrative districts, 1874; Library of Congress Map Collection. See Cuba, Havana (city), 1874, 1:10,000, D. Esteban T. Pichardo, Geography and Map Division, Library of Congress.

Table 2.1

Havana, Regla, and Guanabacoa Abakuá Lodges Listed by District and Municipality, 1882

FIRST DISTRICT

Otiabanga Muñón	Ibiocó Efí
Orú Apapá	Uruá Abacuá

SECOND DISTRICT

Iriabán #1	Araucón
Bacocí Mobandú Efór	

THIRD DISTRICT

Efí Embemoró	Eforí Encomó
Ecoria Efó #1	Iriabón #2

FOURTH DISTRICT

Umocué Apapá	Efí Ibondó
Betongó	Urianabón

FIFTH DISTRICT

Barando #1	Isagaré #1
Barando #2	Efión
Ororó #1	Ubané
Ororó #2	Anglona
Icoreguao	Moirondé
Obiabangá Petinaroco	Odan Efí
Iriabón #3	Odan Efor
Eforí Bondad	Efori Isun #1
Betongó Naroco	Efor Isun #2
Ecuerepón	Efiá
Berocobebá	Erube Abacuá
Ecuerepon #2	Eutomiñón
Naroco Efor	Ecoria Efor #2
Efí Efiqueremó	Ecoria Efor #3
Indiagumé Efí	Mocaldó Efor
Macumba Efor	Efor Acanarán
Iando Efor	Efietete
Mucundu	Guaná Nongó
Ebutón	Baraqueñón
Efí Ebruitón	Ordán Efí #2

SIXTH DISTRICT

Enchemillá	Buburán Efor
Nandibá	Acuabutón
Efor	

SEVENTH DISTRICT

Efori Eucamó	Eutati
Muãnga	Eutati #2
Eterenón	

EIGHTH DISTRICT

Eforimoteque	Nandibá

NINTH DISTRICT

Jordán Efí	Cobió Efor

REGLA

Efí Camarón	Efí #1
Eron Efí	Abakcuá Efor

GUANABACOA

Efí Acanirán	Erube Efor

Between all of them, they add up to eighty-three "of color," and they are found distributed in the following manner:

In the first	district	4
In the second	"	8
In the third	"	4
In the fourth	"	4
In the fifth	"	42
In the sixth	"	5
In the seventh	"	6
In the eighth	"	2
In the ninth	"	2
In Regla	"	4
In Guanabacoa	"	2
		83

SOURCE: Trujillo y Monagas 1882:370–372.

AUTHOR'S NOTE: The writer has named, in his list, in fact, only 75 lodges for the nine districts and Regla and Guanabacoa. All of these are evidently lodges "of color." In the original, just above the table, he had noted five additional "lodges of whites," including:

Aranará Efor (4th district) [Akanarán Efor]
Ecoria Efor (third district)
Efor Abakuá (Regla)
Narocó Efor (barrio of Carraguáo)

There may or may not be some overlap in the two lists, given that the "white lodges" may have taken on the same or similar names in several cases, as the lodges "of color." In any event, only 80 lodges are accounted for. Either he miscalculated or is accounting for some for which he lacks names. The sum of the number of lodges listed under each district and the calculation then done are inconsistent. For example, he lists eight in the second district whereas only three names appear for that district.

Table 2.2

Esteban Pichardo map detail, Havana districts broken down as judicial, municipal, and gubernatory divisions, 1874

DIVISION JUDICIAL

de la Catedral, comprende el		*1º Municipal*	
Belen	"	*2º*	*Idem*
Monserrate	"	*3º y 4º*	*Idem*
Guadalupe	"	*5º y 6º*	*Idem*
Jesus Maria	"	*7º y 8º*	*Idem*
Pilar	"	*9º*	*Idem*
Cerro	"	*10º*	*Idem y Marianao*

DIVISION MUNICIPAL

Distritos	Nº de los barrios	Nombres	Distritos	Nº de los barrios	Nombres
1º	1	*Templete*	7º	1	*Arsenal*
	2	*San Felipe*		2	*Séiba*
	3	*Santo Cristo*	8º	1	*Jesus Maria*
	4	*S. Juan de Dios*		2	*Vives*
	5	*Angel*		3	*San Nicolas*
	6	*Casa blanca*	9º	1	*Chavez*
2º	1	*San Francisco*		2	*Pilar*
	2	*Santa Clara*		3	*Atarés*
	3	*Santa Teresa*		4	*Pueblo nuevo*
	4	*Paula*		5	*Vedado*
	5	*S. Isidro*		6	*Principe*
3º	1	*Punta*		7	*Villanueva*
	2	*Colon*	10º	1	*Jesus del Monte*
4º	1	*Monserrate*		2	*Luyanó*
	2	*S. Leopoldo*		3	*Arroyo Apolo*
	3	*S. Lazaro*		4	*Cerro*
5º	1	*Tacon*		5	*Puentes grandes*
	2	*Guadalupe*		6	*Arroyo Naranjo*
6º	1	*Marte*		7	*Calvario*
	2	*Dragones*			
	3	*Peñalver*			

LA DIVISION GUBERNATIVA comprende los mismos barrios, agrupados en 9 Distritos y ordenados asi:

1er. Distrito	1	*Templete*	5º Distrito	1	*Arsenal*
	2	*San Felipe*		2	*Seiba*
	3	*Santo Cristo*		3	*Jesus Maria*
	4	*S. Juan de Dios*		4	*Vives*
	5	*Sto. Angel*	6º Distrito	1	*S. Nicolas*
	6	*Casa blanca*		2	*Peñalver*
2º Distrito	1	*San Francisco*		3	*Chavez*
	2	*Santa Clara*		4	*Pilar*
	3	*Santa Teresa*		5	*Atares*
	4	*Paula*	7º Distrito	1	*S. Lázaro*
	5	*San Isidro*		2	*Pueblo nuevo*
3er. Distrito	1	*Punta*		3	*Principe*
	2	*Colon*		4	*Vedado*
	3	*Tacon*	8º Distr.	1	*Jesus del Monte*
	4	*Marte*		2	*Luyanó*
4º Distrito	1	*Monserrate*		3	*Arroyo Apolo*
	2	*Dragones*	9º Distr.	1	*Villanueva*
	3	*Guadalupe*		2	*Cerro*
	4	*S. Leopoldo*			

Puentes grandes, Arroyo Naranjo y Calvario estaban como Pedanias, no inclusas en los 9 Distritos.

Source: Pichardo 1874.

Lessons in Abakuá Demographics

For more than twenty years after its founding in 1836, Efik Buton and other descendants in the same genealogical lineage ostensibly followed a strict criterion of membership and deference based on color. In "obedience" to their "godfathers" in Regla's Cabildo Carabalí Brícamo Appapá Efí, they officially refused membership to whites and mulattos—who were said to lack "pure blood." Still, though such protoracialist classification figured into the criteria of early Abakuá rosters, the identity of Efik Buton's members remains "unclear" (see Palmié 1994, 1997). The stated criterion of "pure blood" was undoubtedly based on phenotype, as well as, perhaps, individual professions of genealogy. In the colonial period, "pure blood" translated into the official terms of Cuban social and legal classification, which were based on color: *moreno* (African descent), *pardo* (mixed descent), and *blanco* ("white"). The official term *moreno* belied, of course, the subtly calibrated racial nomenclature to describe combinations of hair texture, skin complexion, facial and bodily features, and so on. *Pardo* or *mulato* was as, or even more, complex; for there could be *jabaos* and *jabas* (men and women, respectively, who mixed black and white and had "bad"—that is, kinky—hair) and *mulato blanconazos* (*mulatos* with "good"—straight—hair). *Moros* had relatively dark complexions but aquiline facial features and softer, wavy hair.

As important, it is worth caution in assuming any smooth association of racialized denomination and what is now called "identity." Though people were legally ascribed as *morenos* and self-ascribed as of "pure blood," it remains to be researched what other factors influenced identity formation among "black" creoles in Cuban urban settings. How much relative social weight did other probable factors in ascribed and self-ascribed identity formation carry? These might have included people's "ethnic" association with one or more neo-African nations, their ownership by particular slavemasters, their residence in particular *barrios,* their membership in particular *juegos,* their trades, their marital partners' status, and so forth. Evidently, the members of Efik Buton were not only recognized but also apparently self-identified as "The Belenistas," and many of them moved under the specific protection of "Josefa Aguiar

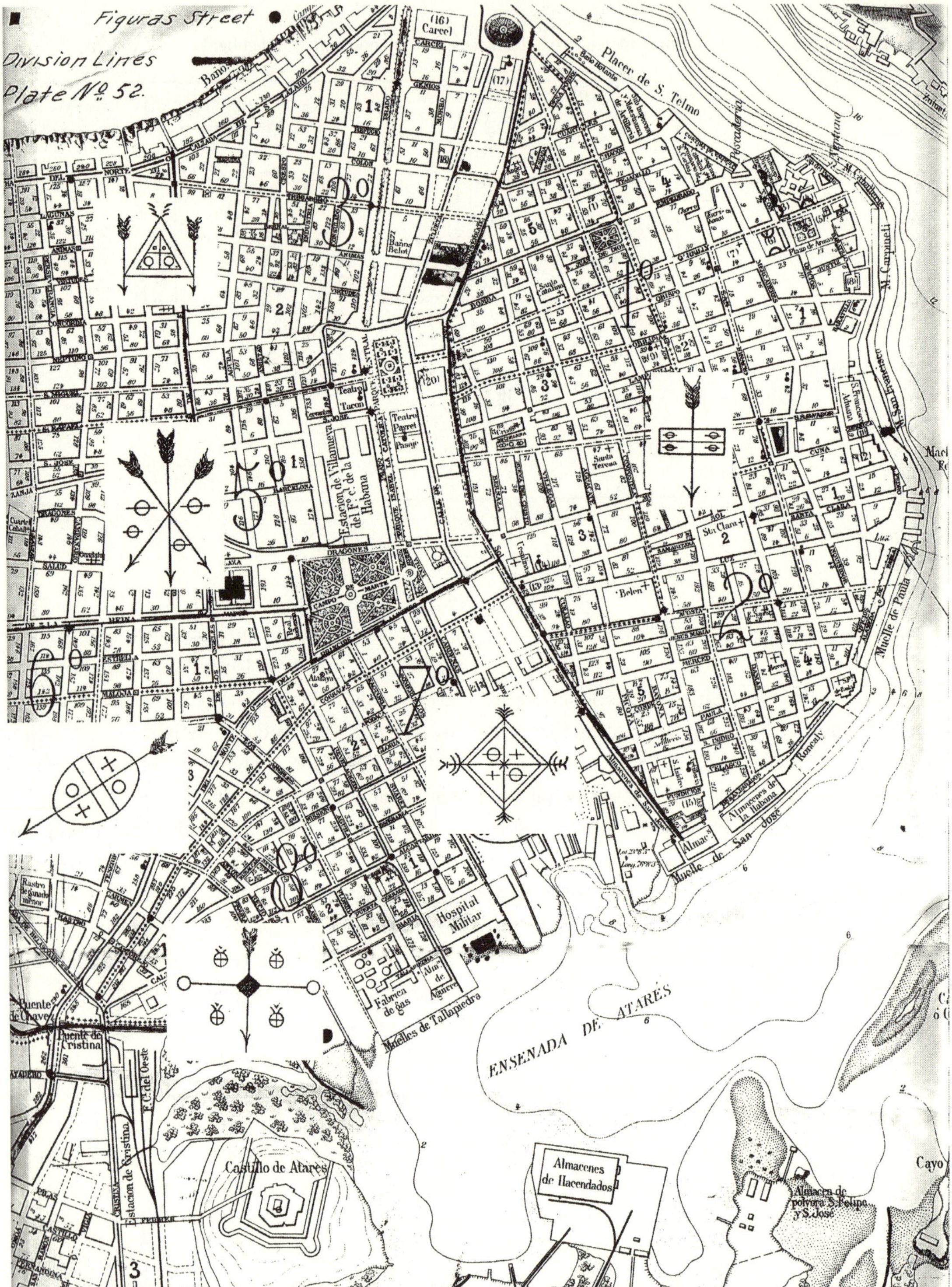

Map 2.6. Map of Old Havana showing numbered districts with this author's superimpositions of signs identifying these same districts for the Abakuá Society. Note that the sign for district 3 (now Central Havana) is just southwest of where the "whites" of Akanarán Efó were initiated on Christmas Eve 1863.

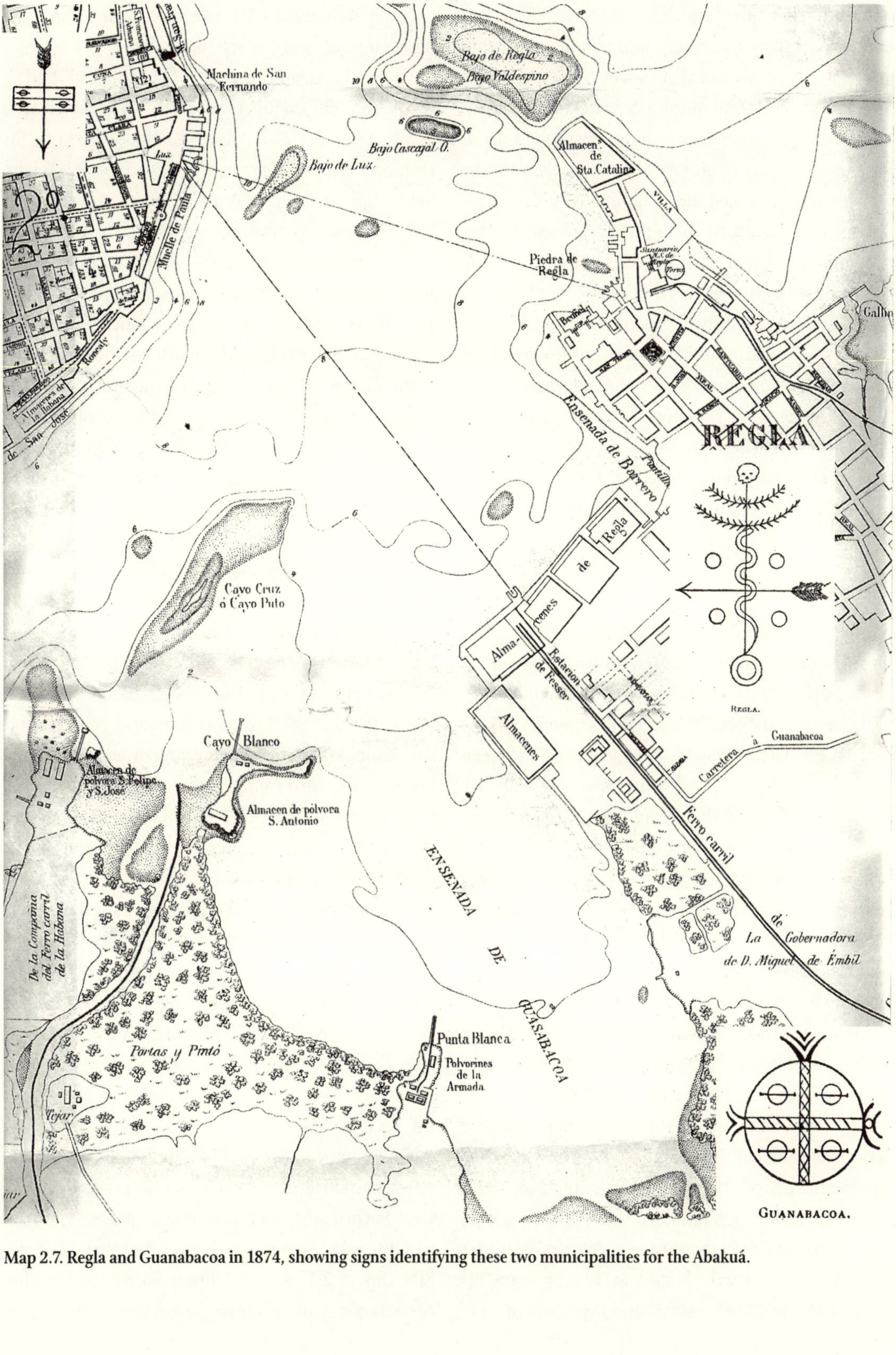

Map 2.7. Regla and Guanabacoa in 1874, showing signs identifying these two municipalities for the Abakuá.

y Díaz, a resident of San Ignacio Street." They evidently used their ownership and residence, if only strategically, to protect themselves from arrest and attack. Moreover, Efik Buton's members were island-born—creoles—who may have descended from parents belonging to different "nations." How many of them also practiced the Lucumí and/or Congo religions, and did any of them internalize and profess the Catholic faith of their official baptism, as many Abakuá have for more than 165 years? How many of them substantively adhered to the cultural and racial canons of Cabildo Carabalí Brícamo Appapá Efí of Regla, and how many professed them nominally, but had other plans for building their self-presentation and authority? These are important questions that may only be partially satisfied by further research, inasmuch as the historical record is thin.

"White" Abakuá?

Dramatic nineteenth-century changes in the economics and social contours of western Cuban cities shaped demographic shifts within the Abakuá's membership and vice versa (López Valdés 1985; Cabrera 1970:31–46, 51–62; Ortiz 1954:55, 69; Moliner Castañeda 1988:14). By 1863 one of the two principal branches ("Efí" and "Efó") of the young Abakuá society had openly begun to initiate Cubans of diverse backgrounds. Until that point, the extant lodges ostensibly maintained their *moreno* profile with African and creole members of "pure blood." In an apparent ethnic and racial sea change, the Havana Efó branch became flush with "whites" as of 1863. This trend among the Efó branch as more "mixed" or "integrated" than the Efí has continued down to the present day in Havana and Matanzas (Moliner Castañeda 1988:14).

The new members of the Efó branch included large numbers of Spanish-descended "whites"—predominantly of the working class, but also not a few aristocrats, high military officers, politicians, and young gentlemen born to wealthy families (Ortiz 1954:81). The Efó branch, and, eventually, some Efí lodges, also initiated *mulatos* and members of burgeoning immigrant and creole groups, including Chinese, Filipino, and Canary Island men.

Evidently, Afro-Cubans not of "pure blood" had already attained membership in the Efó branch well before 1863. In 1857, Andrés Facundo Cristo de los Dolores Petít, a fair-skinned *mulato* (figure 2.2) who held high office in Havana's Awana Bakokó Efor lodge, began assembling personnel for the first "white" Abakuá lodge, Ocobio Mukarará (also called Akanarán Efó #1). The complete name of the lodge, adds Jesús Nasakó, a ritual descendant of Petít, was Akanarán Efó Ekobio Mukarará. In his gloss the name means "the Efó mother of the brothers of the white skin." With the founding of Akanarán Efo #1, "so began the question of initiating *blancos* into the Abakuá. And all of those they swore in were rich."[16] Indeed, archival accounts and oral history show that this new "white" lodge, and some of its immediate offspring (table 2.3), included not only young working-class men but also a number of dissipated youths from Havana's wealthiest families. They frequented the famous Acera de la Louvre café on the Prado and Parque Central next to the Hotel Inglaterra. Though it was the seat of Havana culture and government, the Prado was also a complex interzone, sandwiched between the Afro-Cuban *barrios* of Central Havana to the west and the Old Havana mansions of big slaveholders, not to mention neighborhoods of emerging tenements *(solares)*, to the east. There these gentlemen of the easy life *(vida alegre)* spun out their desires for manhood and female conquests in the presence of their working-class white, black, and *mulato* street-tough acquaintances *(guapos)* of the *hampa cubana* (Ortiz 1954:81–82; see also Robreño 1925). The house in which some of these men would be "sworn" as *ñáñigos* stood a mere six blocks west of the Acera de la Louvre.[17]

On Christmas Eve of 1863, in a house in what is now Central Havana, Akanarán's twenty-five officers were "sworn in" *(jurado)* under the "godparenthood" or ritual sponsorship *(apadrinación)* of Petít's Bakokó Efor (figure 2.1 center).[18] Immediately the reigning Abakuá old guard of the capital accused Petít of "sell-

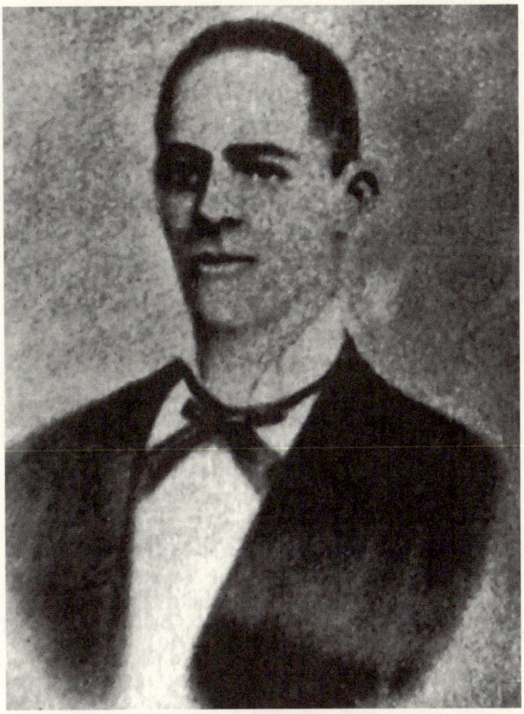

Figure 2.2. Andrés Facundo Cristo de los Dolores Petít, Isué of Awana Bakokó Efor and founder of La Regla Kimbisa del Santo Cristo del Buen Viaje and the first "white" Abakuá lodge, Akanarán Efó. Courtesy of the Estate of Lydia Cabrera.

ing the secret" to the whites for profit. As a result, "the blacks [of Bakokó] were suspended and punished," Rodríguez reported (1881:14–15). Others professed Petít's explanation that the revenue gained from these initiations, and, presumably, the rich patronage relationships implied, served to buy Abakuá brethren out of slavery under the Spanish policy of *coartación* (see Ortiz 1954:69; Cabrera 1970:24–62; Sosa Rodríguez 1982:141–144). "The cost of the secret was thirty ounces of gold," reported Rodríguez, "and was delivered to the first chief of Bakokó, with which he bought the freedom of members of that lodge" (Rodríguez 1881:14–15; see also Trujillo y Monagas 1882:369). The "thirty ounces" of gold, undoubtedly a potent metaphor in the oral history of Petít's detractors, underscores the perceived severity of Bakokó's offense, for it recalls the amount gained in Judas' betrayal of Christ.[19]

The binary notion of "black" versus "white" lodges deserves scrutiny in a critical treatment of Cuba's complex social and cultural history. "Racial" identity in Cuba historically turned on complexities of phenotypical "color," "legal color," and social position and was not rationalized in terms of pseudoscientific notions of "race" until well into the second half of the nineteenth century (see Martínez-Alier 1974: 15, 71–81; Palmié 2002:223). The possession of "the secret" by *blancos* and *pardos* had been prohibited in Carabalí *cabildo reglamentos* since long before the birth of Efik Buton in 1836. Yet, Bakokó Efor, likely a

Table 2.3
Selected Genealogy of the "White Branch" of the Abakuá

I.
Bakokó Efor
(Andrés Petít, Isué)

- ➜ **II.**
  Akanarán Efó Ocobio Mukarará
  1857, personnel gathered; born Christmas Eve, 1863
  Querino Valdés initiated as *obonekue*
    - ➜ **III.a.**
      Ekobio Efó #1
      1874, founded, Havana
    - ➜ **III.b.**
      Abakuá Efó #1
      1875, founded, Regla
      Querino Valdés, Abasonga
      Juan Gutiérrez Montojo, Aberiñán
      1902, Manuel de Jesús Capáz ("Chuchú") initiated as *obonekue*
        - ➜ **IV.**
          Efori Eñongo
          9 April 1916, founded by Juan Gutiérrez Montojo, Isué
    - ➜ **III.c.**
      Enyegueyé
      1882, founded
      1909, Chuchú Capáz installed as Iyamba

Source: Interviews with Jesús Nasakó and Juan Mokongo, 1992–97.

The table shows Petít's Bakokó Efor, the first "white" lodge in Akanarán Efó (Ocobio Mukarará), the latter's first three offspring, and Efori Eñongo.

generationally close descendant of Efik Buton,[20] had already quietly broken a long-standing taboo against diluting the desired homogeneity of Abakuá "pure blood." Andrés Petít simply could not have attained the third highest Abakuá grade of Isué by 1857, just twenty-one years later, without having passed considerable time in Bakokó or another *juego*—likely Bakokó's parent lodge, which would have been even a step closer to Efik Buton.

On the other side of the coin, the notion of "white Abakuá" is also complex. For example, a man by the name of Quirino Valdés (1859–1937), who later gained national fame as a revolutionary combatant in the Second War of Independence (1895–98), was initiated before 1875 into Akanarán Efó.[21] Quirino Valdés was a Cuban creole of Chinese-Filipino descent (Cosme Baños 1998:51), with some apparent African phenotypical features (figure 2.3).[22] His presence in Cuba and membership in the Abakuá undoubtedly reflected the "white immigration" movement at mid-century, which entailed the encouraged migration of workers from around Spain's empire, as well as the importation of Chinese (Cosme Baños 1998:11–23; Pérez 1988:115–119).[23] Therefore, it is perhaps more interesting to interrogate the politics and classificatory criteria of color during the middle third of the nineteenth century than it is to assume anything about the composition of a given Abakuá branch or lodge. The binary rhetorical construction of "white" and "black" lodges belies the process by which Chinese, Filipinos, and Canary Islanders "became white" Abakuá through the social and cultural "alchemy of race" (see, e.g., Jacobson 1998:91–170). Given such diversity, it is also worth wondering about when in its history, and under what criteria, would a lodge or branch be seen to become "mixed."[24] It also belies the process by which Abakuá men considered "white" or as part of "mixed" lodges in one context, founded their own lodges and marked them along particular lines of identity. For example, members of the Akanarán Efó lineage today consider their tradition and their ancestors to be "African." Another case is equally complex. Contemporary Havana Abakuá remember the existence of a "Chinese" lodge in Matanzas, yet always note that one of its most prominent members was the famed West African Yoruba priest Ño Remigio Herrera, who passed perhaps twenty years in that city following his enslavement on a sugar plantation halfway between the two provincial capitals.[25]

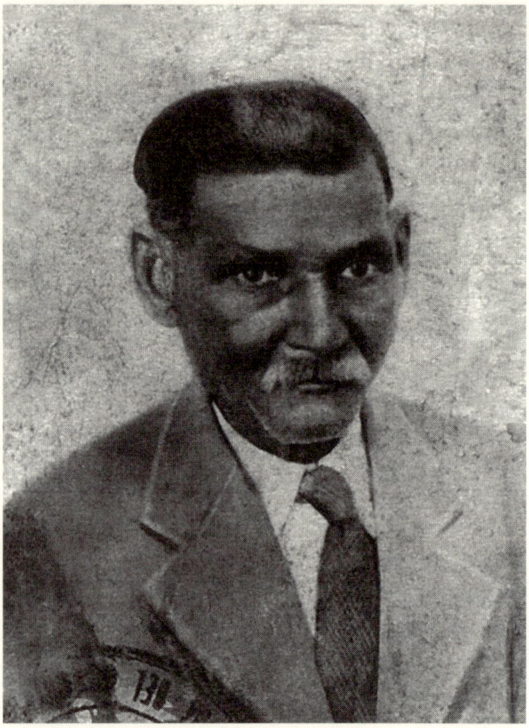

Figure 2.3. Quirino Valdés, wharf boss, *mambí, obonekue* of Akanarán Efó, a founder and the Abasonga of Abakuá Efó #1 of Regla (1874), and sponsor of Efori Eñongo (1916); from Cosme Baños 1998. Courtesy of Pedro Cosme Baños and the Museo de Regla.

A brief summary of the tumultuous events of this middle third of the nineteenth century provides some explanatory context for the dramatic growth and diversification of the Abakuá from 1836 through the 1870s. As well, it helps explain the colonial government's hysteria about the Abakuá's spread and the repressive police responses to *ñañiguismo* as of the mid-1870s. As Louis Pérez notes, Britain and France had already illegalized the slave trade (1807) and abolitionism was in the air. The Cuban creole planter class had grown weary of Spain's rigid economic and political administration of the island. And, during this period, U.S. interest in the annexation of Cuba soared, giving the planter class hope of preserving the system of slavery under U.S. control. A sharp dilemma of alliance arose for the creoles when the Spanish imperial authorities announced that any challenge to their rule would be met with a decree of emancipation. In response to the dilemma, a creole reform movement emerged, based on certain liberal ideas, including a gradual emancipation—yet only through indemnification from Spain for the anticipated loss of slave fortunes (Pérez 1988:105–107, 111–115).

Eventually, the creoles agreed to the suppression of the slave trade (1865) in return for reforms to adjust the economic and political balance in their relationship with Spain, though they did so only by guaranteeing themselves alternate sources of labor. Thus, between the 1840s and early 1870s, approximately 125,000 Chinese contract laborers were imported to Cuba. This, and continuing pressure for white immigration to offset the specter of an Afro-Cuban majority (the "Africanization of Cuba Scare"), radically changed the demographics of the island, particularly in the west. During the middle decades of the century (1846–61), the white population increased by 86 percent. As Louis Pérez summarizes, it "more than doubled (230,986 to 468,107), while the number of white males of economically productive ages (16 to 60) increased even more dramatically, from 132,738 to 300,926). Of these 300,926 males, almost 86 percent were located in the west" (Pérez 1988:115–116). In the cities, the "increase of white workers augmented the ranks of the urban wage labor force, arguably one of the fastest-growing sectors in Cuban society. . . . It is clear that white workers were extending their control over urban jobs at the expense of free people of color" (Pérez 1988:117), especially in Havana. In addition to these sheer demographic changes, labor activism boomed, particularly in response to instabilities in the labor markets, especially for cigars. Cigarworker unions mostly took the "form of mutual aid societies, organized along national and racial lines, providing members accident, sickness, and death benefits" (Pérez 1988:119). Such organizations increased throughout the multifarious labor sectors and geographical regions, as did labor militancy. Threatened by increasingly organized labor power and a number of strikes *(huelgas)*, the government began to suppress the expanding labor movement, in particular, reformism, in general, during the second half of the 1860s. Repression increased throughout the island. Military over civilian authority was reasserted, the government moved against critics, and taxes and tariffs on Cuban products were raised by Spain. Crushing economic recessions and general discontent from worsening island conditions paved the way for the 1868 *Grito de Yara*, or Ten Years War against Spain (1868–78) (Pérez 1988: 119–121).[26]

It is worth hypothesizing that the explosion in the "white" urban male labor force, the surge in mutual aid societies—in lieu of other institutions of support—and conflicts between free black creole labor and the soaring non-black sector contributed to the advent and exponential growth of the "white" lodges, particularly among workers in the cigar, shipping, warehouse, meat, outdoor agricultural market sectors (see López Valdés 1985; Palmié 1997:44–50). Still, Abakuá lodges were not merely "labor unions" *(sindicatos)* or substitutes for them. Tight local collectives of men sworn to protect the "secret" to the death provided the socio-spiritual foundation for the assertion of invincibility, self-defense, and advancement. What Palmié astutely theorized for "Africans in a slave society" is equally applicable to "white" immigrant working men: they could "manipulate one of the few sources of power open to them: superhuman resources that could only be tapped by the possession of secrets bound to priestly titles" (1993:345–346).

Palmié's most important insight is that the transatlantic, portable Abakuá/Ekpe "model of corporate aggregation" could "unite men not on the basis . . . of tribal affiliation, but economic power." In western Cuba, as in Africa, though Ekpe/Abakuá "seems to have started off as an 'ethnic' phenomenon, its built-in capacity for the assimilation of 'strangers' via cultic initiation quickly effected its diffusion across even the most deeply entrenched social cleavages" (1993:344). Still, as Palmié would insist, Abakuá membership, as well as its ritual system and arts, do not reduce to social function any more than culture reduces to economics; "superhuman resources"—including dazzling processions of regalia and masquerades—mediated social struggle within and between "black," "white," and "mixed" groups, as well as in relation to the power and authority of state and foreign interests. "Symbolic capital" and "social capital," not easily teased apart analytically, serve as currencies, effectively circulate, and can be exchanged for one another.

Questions of Identity: Cultural Geography, Ethnicity, and the Abakuá Habitus

The worldviews, identities, and bodily practices of men of diverse connections and backgrounds, including not a few wealthy notables, were transformed in the social and ritual habitus of the Abakuá Society. The system of Abakuá lodges both reflected and transformed the myriad terms of urban Cuban social identity—class, color, occupation, neighborhood, and gender. Membership in the *juegos* of the Abakuá articulated with the marked, and often conflicting, identities of men in urban *barrios* and their labor relationships with particular coastal Cuban industries (López Valdés 1985; Palmié 1993, 1994:5–6, 1997:38–50; Ortiz 1986:14–15). The identities of "white," "black," "mixed," rich, poor, island-born creole, enslaved, free/freed men, and immigrant alike were constituted, conjoined, differentiated, and set in conflict as they "swore" their lives to the "secret" *(ekue)* of their respective lodges. In common patterns, they sang prayers in the Brícamo ritual language—learned by rote from hand-copied *libretas*—and donned hooded costumes to dance in the angular feline movement language of the *íreme* masquerade. Yet they fought in pitched street battles and competed for work, struggles that were figured through the codes of Abakuá male reputation, respect, and revenge. The colonial era street "dispute between the ñáñigo juegos 'Muñanga' and 'Taiba' in the barrio of Jesús María" depicted by Roche y Monteagudo (figure 2.4) conceals as much as it reveals. Used by Rafael Roche y Monteagudo as a straightforward illustration of *ñáñigo* delinquency, particularly because a looming *íreme* orchestrates a murder, the drawing carries a kernel of truth. In one more recent case revealed to me by an Abakuá living in Miami, Sebastian Gil, the Mokongo of the Usagaré lodge of Matanzas killed one Hilario Rodríguez of Cárdenas "because of problems over the *fundamento,* in other words, over his second mother"—the secret *sese* drum, considered to represent the "Mother of the Abakuá."[27] Some show of disrespect caused this conflict, which is expressed in the Abakuá sacred idiom. "Superhuman resources that could only be tapped by the possession of secrets bound to priestly titles" had to imply "superhuman" sanction for breaches of Abakuá codes of behavior; and we will likely never know the more global dimensions of the "problems" between these men from two of three Abakuá port cities in western Cuba. In a better-known case, the famous black port boss and labor leader Aracelio Iglesias was killed in a Havana wharf dispute in 1948. Iglesias was an Abakuá officer, a priest of Shangó, and a *babalawo.* Though a worker-hero of the Revolution today, with a wharf in Old Havana named after him, Iglesias surely can neither be reduced to a poster boy for *ñáñigo* delinquency nor socialist struggle. His violent death on the wharf raises questions about how the articulation of race, class, contemporaneous social conditions, and the "superhuman resources" of his Abakuá membership positioned him in his career trajectory and put him on the wharf that day. How much of the dispute revolved around "labor" issues and how much revolved around his "second mother" may never be determined. Indeed, Havana *babalawos* believe that he was killed because of "disobedience": he disobeyed the

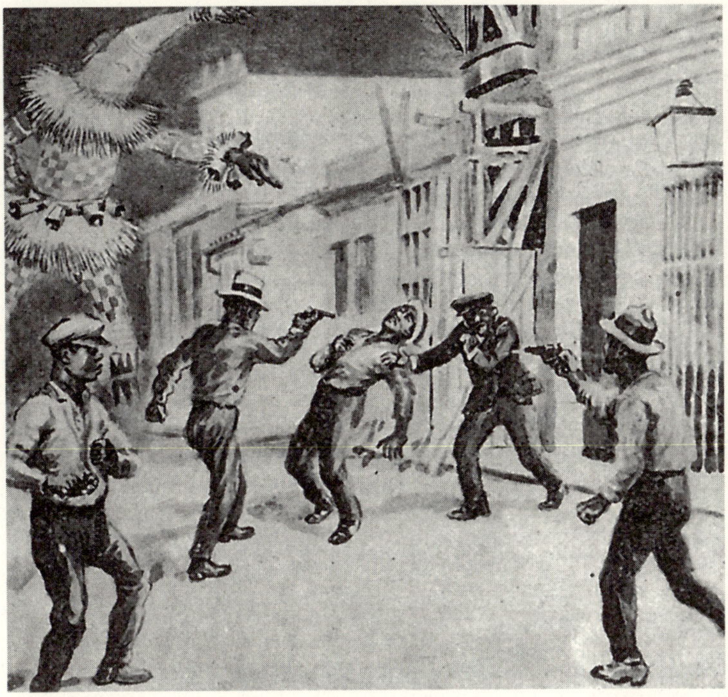

Figure 2.4. Street fight between the Muñanga and Taibá lodges in the Jesús María neighborhood of Havana during colonial times. The sensationalist document suggests that the *diablito* fingers the victim. From Roche y Monteagudo 1925.

thunder god Shangó's warning that he give up labor organizing.

Drawings of separate white, mixed, and black processions turned up in the private notebooks of Abakuá by the beginning of the twentieth century (see figures 2.5 and 2.6). Yet lodges had been "mixed" for at least fifty years. The American folklorist Harold Courlander (1908–1996), who had previously done intensive fieldwork among black Vodouists in Haiti (see Courlander 1990), was taken quite by surprise when he visited Cuba in 1941. "Something bothered me a little, and I sensed it only vaguely," Courlander wrote in his field notes about his first experience of an Abakuá *plante,* which took place in Guanabacoa. "It later came to me with a shock that many of the spectators and *ocobios* were white. White men singing Carabali songs. When I closed my eyes there was no way of distinguishing who was white and who was black. The white *ocobios* were as completely 'African' as the Negroes. Their singing gestures and postures, too, were African. I have a great admiration and respect for those white 'brothers' who have somehow leaped the great gap between the *gua[j]íro* or Castilian attitude of mind and that of the direct and legitimate heirs of Africa" (Courlander 1944:465).

On balance, did such demographic and cultural transformations point to the "whitening" of an original and essential African Abakuá of "pure blood" (i.e., Ekpe or Ngbe in Cuba), the "Africanizing" of non-blacks, or the "Cubanizing" of diverse individuals and groups? Applying his "transculturation" theory to the Afro-Cuban ritual systems, Fernando Ortiz posited what scholars in the 1970s would articulate as "creolization": "social phenomena, which before were simply 'black things,' became what today are 'Cuban things'" (*cosas de negro* vs. *cosas de cuba;* see Ortiz 1954:70–71).

Still, within the category of *cosas de Cuba,* such transformations were much more specific. The Spanish-descended "white" Abakuá brother was not "Cuban" in any simple sense of a homogenous "national identity." As Fernando Ortiz's sociological classifications suggest, did not the Abakuá brother's personhood come to embody and objectify a histori-

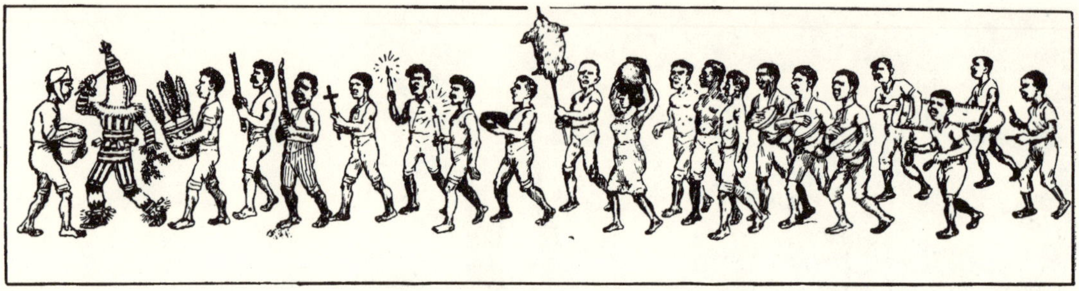

Figure 2.5. Drawing of a procession of a "white"/"mixed" Abakuá lodge and three new initiates, late nineteenth or early twentieth century; from Roche y Monteagudo 1925.

cally specific, emergent male social type—the *ñáñigo* (see Brown 1993a)? For example, the criteria of a *juego*'s exhaustive *investigación* of a prospective candidate's background, and the rules to which he would swear his life, were intended to select out, constitute, and engender a particular subset of hypermasculine men. As officially inscribed in the Abakuá *reglamento,* the *okobio* (alternately *ekobio,* lodge brother) had to be "a good son and a good father," with an unblemished history of respect toward his mother; he should have the self-control to avoid sexual involvement with his lodge brother's wife or sister. Within the already macho gender matrix (Butler 1990, 1997; Lumsden 1996) of Cuban society, which was honed to a science within the Abakuá, the *okobio* had "to be a full man . . . brave, not effeminate" and could never "let [him]self be struck by anyone, above all, by a woman," or the consequences would be dire for the perpetrator of any blow against him before the tribunal of his lodge and in the subsequent violent payback. In defending his honor, and that of *ekue* and the *sese* drum—his "second mother"—he might have to kill for his *potencia,*[28] just as other "real men" in Cuban society would defend the honor of themselves and their families (Sosa Rodríguez 1982:180–181).[29]

In the society at large and its performative rituals of gender (Butler 1997), there was little middle ground in a starkly binary gender configuration (masculine/feminine); therefore "males" were heterosexually "real men" *(hombres),* those who had relationships with other men but acted out the "active" *macho* role *(bugarones, goodmen)* and therefore did not consider themselves "homosexuals," and openly effeminate "passive" males *(afeminados, maricones)* who paro-

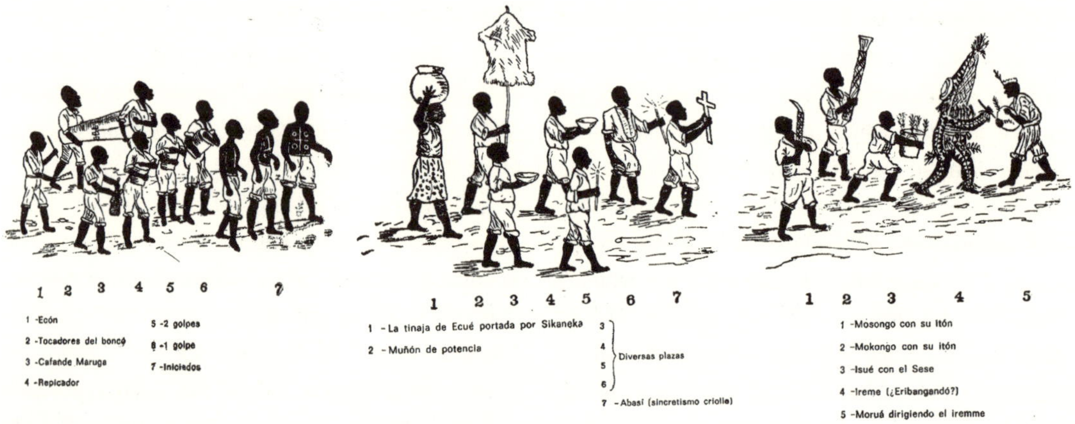

Figure 2.6. Abakuá procession of black lodge; from Sosa Rodríguez 1982.

died the feminine gestural set of Cuban women (see Lumsden 1996). In the performance of Abakuá power and efficacy, through secrecy, background "investigations," solemn processional, the muscular displays of the *íreme*'s leopard dance, gender restriction, homophobia, labor assertion, and, sometimes, displays of violence and revenge, the Abakuá "real men" played before an "audience" consisting of social and sexual "others" who, in effect, were collectively feminized: women, children, mothers, non-initiates, homosexuals, as well as the police, the colonial government, and the corporate officials of large economic enterprises, such as cargo lines.[30] Still, the relationships enacted between these groups remained complex and complicated, even contradictory, particularly between the "white" and "black" Abakuá.

As one of Lydia Cabrera's mid-twentieth-century Abakuá sources put it, black and enslaved Abakuá could not, logically and ethically, be "other" to "white" Abakuá. Admittedly an advocate for Andrés Petít's ecumenical vision, this source linked the fraternal attitude of the Abakuá with the ethos of abolitionism: "The white abakuá [member] would have to consider a black abakuá as his brother, and, as in those days the whites were really hard on the blacks; [but] those who were initiated as *ñáñigos* could not mistreat their brothers. It meant also that even those whites who weren't *ñáñigos* mistreated blacks less. That idea was called abolitionism . . . as Andrés Petít explained—How great Petít was!" (Cabrera 1970:53).

Still, for years following Petít's *Reforma* (beginning with the Akanarán Efó "white" branch), serious conflict characterized relations between the black lodges and the new white or mixed ones. This resulted as much from the displacement of social and class conflict onto color lines, as from any essential enmity between branches, lodges, and individuals. Clearly, the infamous street battles in Havana's *barrios* during the 1860s and 1870s were not always, and not merely, "blood feuds" acted out between "white" and "black" lodges over the "betrayal" of the secret, or, as the police later thought, as the result of *ñañiguismo*'s barbaric, homicidal tendencies (see Castellanos 1916: 13; Roche y Monteagudo 1908:39, 1925:51–52). As Palmié and López Valdés suggest, lodges with opposed labor interests came into conflict, for example, when a group of white Regla Abakuá crossed the bay of Havana to break *(rompehuelga)* a dockworkers' strike on the Havana City wharves in the 1910s in order to "take jobs away 'from the blacks of Havana'" (López Valdés 1985:172; Palmié 1997:50–51). As Palmié astutely observes, "many of the violent skirmishes different 'potencias' fought out on Havana's streets . . . may have been struggles over access to resources of employment and economic power," organized around the Abakuá system's distribution, defense, and debate over *barrio* and labor turf (1994: 6). Such class and racial conflict, embodied within local inter-"ethnic" or "territorial" enmity (see Bastide 1978:114), suggests just how layered and complex this Cuban male Abakuá "identity" was in the nineteenth century. When Abakuá groups engaged in pitched battles with each other or with the police, was it, as the authorities imagined, a war of the "savage" against the "civilized" order, or was it a stunning manifestation of the social, political, and economic contradictions of Cuba and the Atlantic "unit" as a whole (see Roche y Monteagudo 1925:50–55; Palmié 1993, 1994, 1997:11–12)? As the tone and content of criminological treatises demonstrate, the authorities located the source of Abakuá violence in its "supreme incarnation," the *diablito*, or "little devil," which Ortiz early identified as a "fetish priest" (1960:32). Arguably, the authorities themselves "fetishized" the *diablito* by displacing onto this figure a host of imponderable cultural anxieties, thereby deflecting the reality of modern social conditions (see Palmié 2002). For example, in figure 2.4, a drawing from the colonial period, the *diablito* is shown fingering the target of an assassination.

The growing ports of Matanzas and Cárdenas, approximately 90 and 120 kilometers to the east along Cuba's northern coast, respectively, witnessed the Abakuá's appearance twenty-five to fifty years after Havana. As historian and folklorist Israel Moliner Castañeda reports, Matanzas officially opened its

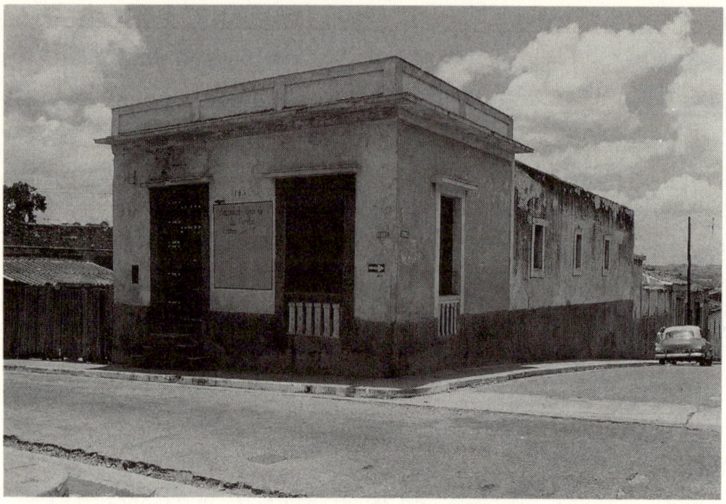

Figure 2.7. Sociedad Hijos de la Caridad, Uriabón Efí #1, Matanzas, 1989. The name of this famous Matanzas lodge derives from the first Abakuá *juego* founded in Matanzas, Uriabón Monson Efín, which emerged from the Cabildo Brícamo del Niño Jesús in the second half of the nineteenth century. It is not clear whether the lodge is the same as the first Matanzas lodge or a reorganized descendant. Photograph by David H. Brown.

capacious port in 1795, and immediately began to "enjoy the benefits . . . of slave commerce. . . . Some 236,599 slaves passed through this port between 1790 and 1820" (1988:13). Still, as in Havana, the "birth" of discrete Abakuá *juegos* from the womb of selected African *cabildos* required a number of decades to emerge, a process that was related to the demographics of the slave trade, the opportunities and constraints of the emerging port systems, and the regathering of personnel and cultural knowledge within the *cabildos* (see Palmié 1993:341). Thus, on Christmas Eve of 1862, the "men of the *Cabildo Carabalí Bríkamo Niño Jesús* authorized the formation of the first *juego ñáñigo*" in Matanzas. It was called Uriabón Monson Efín, whose temple is venerated as the "cathedral of Cuban *ñáñigos*" even today (figure 2.7). Three more lodges were then founded, which, along with Uriabón, are considered to be the "four pillars" of the Abakuá of Matanzas.[31] Then, "toward the end of the 1890s, the two first *ñáñigo* groups of the city and port of Cárdenas appeared" (Moliner Castañeda 1988:14). Though little is known about the Abakuá of Cárdenas, the demographics of the Abakuá lodges of Matanzas apparently were, and remain, different from Havana's, that is, more heavily staffed by members of apparent African descent. The Matanzas lodges did not begin to emerge until five years after Andrés Petít began to gather the "white" personnel (1857) for Akanarán Efó #1. Therefore, Petít's "reform" seems not to have affected Matanzas with the same intensity in terms of its membership's complexion until much later. At the same time, some of its lodges eventually adopted important ritual and artistic innovations that Petít introduced.

3 Abakuá Altar Arts: Ekue, Representation, and the Banner of Regla's Efori Eñongo

Significant changes in Abakuá sacred artwork and ritual reflected and embodied social conflict and change in Cuba and within the Abakuá Society itself. The reportedly austere, and sometimes rustic, "African" aesthetic of the society's first thirty or more years (see Ortiz 1954:70–71) was significantly modified after 1863. This was the moment of Petít's Reform—that is, his creation of Akanarán Efó #1 and his successful resolution of the fierce opposition of old-guard "pure blood" lodges to the initiation of "whites." The "peace" achieved between the Bakokó Efor/Akanarán #1 branch and the old guard followed at least half a decade of interlodge war. White Abakuá seeking participation in black Abakuá ceremonies were denied entrance, resulting in brawls and deaths—another ingredient in the street "disputes" mentioned in the preceding chapter. In view of the crisis, an "extraordinary session" of elders, convened of blacks, whites, and mulattos in Marianao, resolved that in lodge ceremonies no "mixing" would occur, but in public all would be respected as "sworn" Abakuá "brothers" *(ekobios, ocobios)* in order to avoid arguments and fights *(disgustos* and *peleas).* A motto was coined to encapsulate the reconciliation of the special session, *"La amistad a un lado y el ñáñigo separado"* (essentially "friendship on the one hand and separation on the other"; Roche y Monteagudo 1925:5). Nevertheless, this voluntary separate-but-equal clause was, it seems, mooted over time. Havana's *juegos* eventually became more "mixed," and Petít's formerly disputed innovations spread through much of Cuba's Abakuá by the twentieth century.

At least three distinct but related kinds of aesthetic and ritual changes occurred initially among Petít's Bakokó Efor/Akanarán #1–descended lodges. The first, commonly addressed in works on African Diaspora religions and arts, is often described as "syncretism," entailing the "borrowing" and "blending" of Roman Catholic objects within the Abakuá iconographic repertoire, such as crucifixes and monstrances. Fernando Ortiz saw such changes principally as strategic responses to state persecution in the last quarter of the nineteenth century. They marked "an episode of defensive process, through syncretic mimesis, [*mimetismo sincretista,* which the Abakuá] began adopting in order to sustain their ancestral religions and rites."[1] This "syncretic mimesis" provided a "licitness" *(licitud)* to Abakuá religious practice (Ortiz 1954:79; see also Cabrera 1970:55).

Second, Petít imported into Bakokó Efor and its offspring a number of ritual forms and practices from the religious movement he had earlier innovated, called La Regla Kimbisa del Santo Cristo del Buen Viaje (The Kimbisa Order of the Holy Christ of the Good Voyage). Kimbisa was Petít's self-conscious mixture of Lucumí, Congo, Spiritist, and popular Catholic elements. Within the Bakokó Efor/Akanarán lineage, for example, Petít wedded Kimbisa's Congo-Cuban-derived *nkisi* medicines to the Carabalí-derived Abakuá repertoire of sacred forms (see Ortiz 1954:70).

Third, the range of sources, decorativeness, texture, and semantic content of Abakuá altar objects shifted. Adornments apparently became more varied and eclectic. For Ortiz, a range of "adornments in the creole taste" *(adornos a gusto criollo)* characterized this new aesthetic (Ortiz 1954:55, 69–70, 79). In short, as the membership diversified, and as the social and political investments of individual lodges expanded, so did the resources and expressiveness of its object makers and artwork. The meanings of altar objects became more multilayered, or polyvocal, as new adepts added adornments in relation to their own experiences. New kinds of adornments were imported from diverse domains.

Following shifts in practices established during the Abakuá's first two decades or so (1836–57/63), and with Petít's powerful example of innovation and self-conscious Kimbisa syncretism, altar makers may have felt freer to improvise and personalize objects. Moreover, within the "social drama" (Turner 1986: 33–71) of the Abakuá on the urbanizing Cuban landscape, which increased in its intensity following 1863, lodges began to compete against one another artistically. Art, patronage, and entrepreneurship became enmeshed. Thus, aesthetic elaboration apparently became more marked and valorized as a sign of well-being, power, and success. Early on in the 1860s and 1870s, the wealthier new members of the "white" lodges—the sons of the rich and a few nobles, generals, and politicians—could support, in many cases, lavish altar and lodge renovations. Given the visibility, economic power, and voting-block influence of the Abakuá by the early twentieth century, candidates for local office began to court the votes of Abakuá constituencies. Political messages in the Brícamo language appeared on handbills. It is not unimaginable that during election periods, innumerable greased palms enlarged Abakuá coffers (see the plates to Sosa Rodríguez 1982).[2] The following section offers a close look at the altar objects of one lodge, Eforí Eñongo, in order to open up the question of aesthetic change and multiple meanings in altar adornment.

The "First Sanctuary": Abakuá Mythico-Historical Narrative and Iconography

On July 2, 1992, Juan Mokongo of Efori Eñongo carefully unpacked his lodge's objects from their capacious cedar storage box and mounted them in the living room of his ramshackle house in Regla. Juan lived there with his wife, María. Their sons, both of whom had recently married and moved out, were also members of Eforí Eñongo. The three families were feeling the strain of the height of Cuba's "special period" of economic austerity (officially 1991–97). Juan Mokongo, a wiry ex-stevedore and barber, was an honored *combatiente* who had fought alongside Fidel Castro in the Sierra Maestra. An erudite practitioner, he had belonged to the Abakuá for more than forty years. He was also a dedicated priest of two other Afro-Cuban religions, Palo Monte and Santería.[3] Juan had inherited the guardianship of the lodge's objects from his father, Juan Gutiérrez Montojo, a late nineteenth-century pioneer of Regla's "white" and "mixed" Abakuá branch. Juan Sr. was an intimate *ekobio* of the objects' original maker, Quirino

Valdés, perhaps Cuba's most famous Abakuá after Isué Andrés Petít and Iyamba Manuel de Jesús "Chuchú" Capáz (1881–1963?) (figures 2.2, 2.3, and 3.1; see also López Valdés 1985:170–171). Juan Mokongo Jr. was convinced not only of the beauty and cultural importance of the *religión Abakuá,* as he called it, but also that it should be seen and studied by scholars in the most positive light. To him the Abakuá Society was an institution of mutual support and economic self-defense; its members were all *gente humilde* ("humble folk"), workers.

Without any direct expression of personal *interés* in remuneration, Juan Mokongo meticulously set up the altar for me to photograph (plate 1). He was careful to assemble the many objects atop the storage box in the same manner in which he would "fabricate" *(fabricar)* the altar within the temple *(fambá)* for an Abakuá ceremony *(plante).* Juan was a shrewd man. He quietly reveled in, and sought to protect, his relationship with a North American ethnographer; this was not unique. During the Special Period, the benefits a "friendship" with an *extranjero* could potentially bring were not lost on any Cuban. In a larger framework, Juan had become a self-conscious, recognized spokesman for the Abakuá—an articulate and motivated representer of his own culture within the program of Cuba's own self-presentation to the worlds of cultural tourism and international politics. In other words, Juan was something of a "professional informant," as Chuchú Capáz had apparently been before him. Juan worked closely with the curator of Havana's Fernando Ortiz collection in the Casa de Africa (Africa House), Claudia Mola Fernández, and with the director of Regla's municipal museum, Pedro Cosme Baños. Juan installed exhibitions of collected Abakuá objects and acted as an indispensable historical source. His exchange relationship with Regla's museum had developed so well by 1992 that its director regularly led foreign ethnographers to Juan's house for interviews. Finally, Juan was connected within the Abakuá and was respected by the police. Highly recognized among the Abakuá throughout western Cuba, Juan fomented the Abakuá bureau of elders, which regularly met with the authorities to negotiate permission for ceremonies to take place free from police interference. Thanks to Juan and his social preparation to negotiate, as well, the "fieldwork" relationship (see Rabinow 1977), this is the first time, to my knowledge, that an active lodge's altar, as a whole, has been photographed and published.

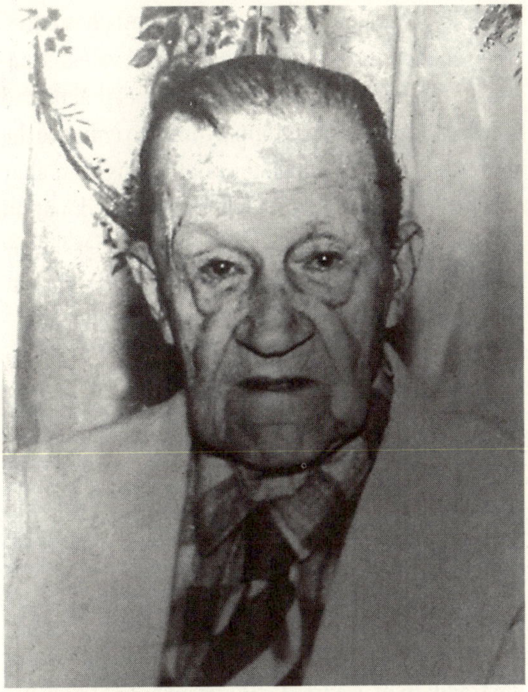

Figure 3.1. Manuel de Jesús Capáz, nicknamed "Chuchú," was a powerful wharf boss, politician, and Abakuá. Early on an *obonekue* of Abakúa Efó #1 of Regla, he became the Iyamba of the Enyegueyé lodge in 1909, also in Regla. Photograph taken ca. 1962–63 in Miami, where he died. Chuchú is believed by some Abakuá to have been one of Lydia Cabrera's most important "informants." Courtesy private collection, Regla.

Though encouraging of my work, Juan and his sons were nevertheless concerned to maintain discretion and avoid reprisal, as well as to gain recognition as go-betweens for lodge patronage. In order to skirt the problem of potential suspicion for "revealing Abakuá secrets," they asked me to change the name of the lodge and erase the lodge's name from the altar's banner. They had me draft a document of gratitude and make a small donation to the lodge in order to demonstrate that they had not personally sold secrets; on the contrary, they had created a valuable patron of the lodge by exchanging what the Abakuá had to teach the world for the opportunity to enhance the lodge's reputation through the renovations of its altar objects. In fact, Juan immediately used the donation to commission seven spectacular new plumes for the altar's drums and staffs. The donation, of course, helped the foreign ethnographer to write a book.

The group of objects, elevated upon their 3.5-foot high altar (the storage box itself), consists of four plumed drums, four 2.5-foot cylindrical staffs (Br. *itón,* Sp. *bastón*), which are mounted on a tiered wooden stand *(bastonera)* painted in red and gold leaf, an antique cast bronze Jesuit monstrance symbolizing the Holy Sacrament *(Santísimo Sacramento),* and a realistically carved and painted wood statue of Christ on the Cross with his head deeply inclined. In the tradition of Andrés Petít and Akanarán Efor #1, the lodge has mounted the monstrance and the Christ statue on the altar since its founding. A simple white cloth covers the altar's top surface. A lavishly embroidered, fringed Prussian blue velvet banner *(pañuelo* or *bandera)* is tacked to the altar's front face (see plate 1). The banner was designed and commissioned by Juan Gutiérrez Montojo Sr. in 1918, two

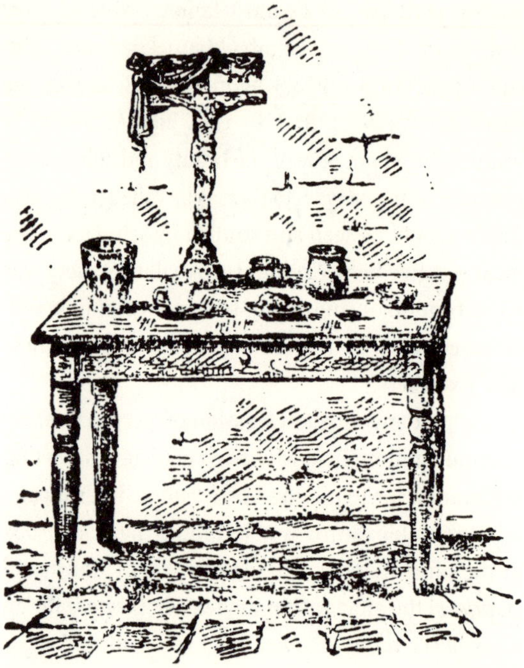

Figure 3.2. Drawing of altar table in house of an alleged "sorcerer" *(brujo),* late nineteenth century; from Ortiz 1973:63, fig. 10. Courtesy of María Fernanda Ortiz Herrera, Representante Sucesores de Fernando Ortiz.

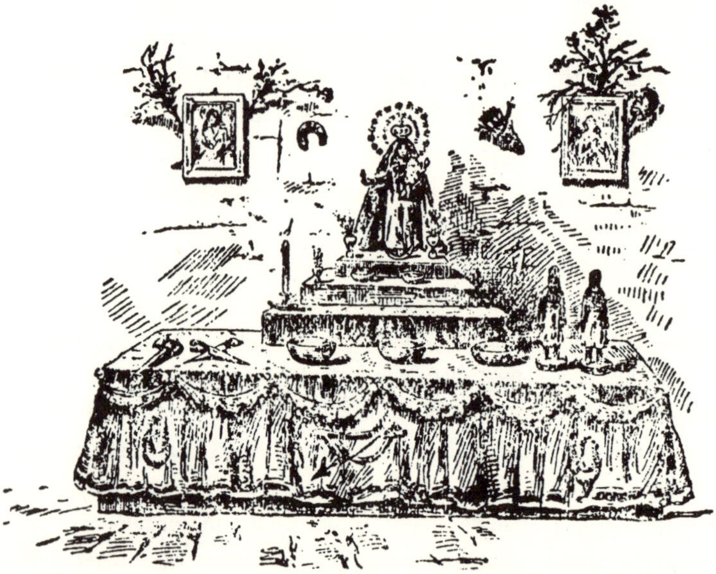

Figure 3.3. Drawing of altar table with lavish tablecloth, bowls, twin statues, tiers supporting statue; from Ortiz 1973:64, fig. 11. The draped tablecloth carries iconographic adornments on its *frontal.* It is likely that the wall pictures are of deceased ancestors. Courtesy of María Fernanda Ortiz Herrera, Representante Sucesores de Fernando Ortiz.

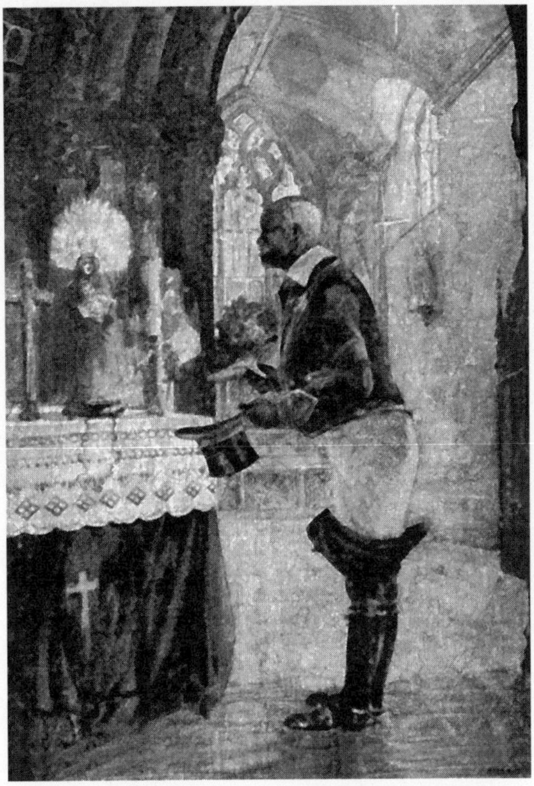

Figure 3.4. Víctor Patricio de Landaluze, *El Místico del ángel*, n.d. Pencil and watercolor. The piece depicts an Afro-Cuban nineteenth-century *calesero* (coach driver) in supplication before a side altar in a church. Landaluze painted the faint figure of an angel praying above. A white lace cloth drapes the rectangular boxlike altar, and a darker *frontal* bearing the crucifix drapes the front. The table supports a statue of the Virgin and a crucifix; from Corporación Nacional del Turismo 1950.

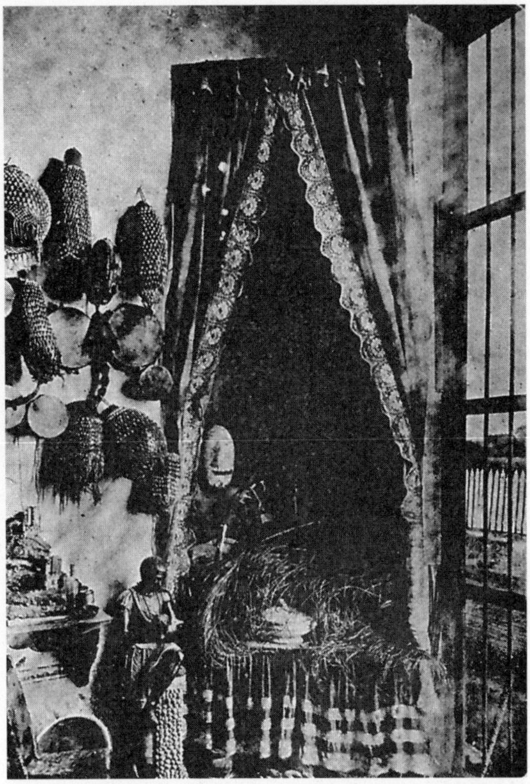

Figure 3.5. Lucumí *capilla* (shrine) and proto-"throne" for Oshún/La Caridad del Cobre in the Cabildo de Santa Rita de Casia of "Papá" Silvestre Erice, ca. 1904, showing rectangular altar table with canopy, curtains, and decorative cloth *frontal;* from Roche y Monteagudo 1908.

years after the lodge's founding. The ensemble of box-altar, white cloth cover, and banner reproduces the overall form of colonial-era domestic and church side altars, found both in popular Catholic and Afro-Cuban religions. This time-honored presentational device, which elevated crucifixes, monstrances, saint-statues, and vessels upon more or less simple tables, was typically dressed with decorative skirts featuring religious iconography in color and symbolism (see figures 3.2, 3.3, 3.4, and 3.5) (Ortiz 1973:63,64; see also Roche y Monteagudo 1908:79; Bascom 1950). Here, the banner, which functions as the altar's *frontal* or *delantal* (literally "apron" or "skirt"), serves as the *juego*'s coat-of-arms. It is a powerful blazon that reminds members of Abakuá history; it also lends meaning to the altar objects and liturgical practices around them. As set up in Juan's house, the altar stands against a bare cinderblock wall. In the temple setting during a ceremony, the wall would be covered by a maroon satin dossal covered with hand-drawn yellow ideographic signs (Br. *anaforuana,* Sp. *firmas*) representing the lodge's officers.

When the altar is set up in the temple (Br. *fambá*) of the walled compound belonging to the Irionda lodge, which Eforí Eñongo uses, the altar faces the double front doors. As exemplified in the famous compound of Erón Entatí Ibionó of Guanabacoa, the *fambá* is a roofed masonry building within the larger compound, which is filled with plants; benches; a large cement platform for sacrifices, initiations, and dancing; and a series of trees, including the sacred palm and *ceiba* (see figure 3.6; see also Cabrera 1970: 279; Sosa Rodríguez 1982:451, fig. 3; Moliner Castañeda 1988:18). Just inside the heavily guarded front doors hangs a second physical barrier in the form of a curtain that closes off the main room and its altar, so that the public in the courtyard may not see inside the temple when officers enter and exit.

The altar's banner, its intricately adorned plumed objects, and the satin dossal typically hung behind are intended to impress visually, as well as to evoke and invoke ancestral forces. The altar's principal function is to be the embodiment and engine of the lodge's *potencia* (potency). *Potencia* refers to the manifest, efficacious, authorizing, spiritual power, or "secret"—in short, its "superhuman resources"—summed up by the Brícamo term *ekue*. As lavishly adorned, the altar marks and honors *ekue*'s royal presence.

Ekue is a polyvocal term. *Ekue* with a small *e* can refer variously to God's "Divine Voice" *(Voz Divina)*, the Abakuá's mystical ancestral foundations and sources in nature from which spiritual power is drawn, the unique, invincible "potency" in the emblems undergirding the graded hierarchy of the lodge's corporate group, and its complex liturgy. *Ekue* reproduces itself in the world through the consecrated objects, initiatory brotherhood, self-sacrifice, obedience, and oath-sealed loyalty-to-the-death of Abakuá men, who occupy ancestrally sanctioned offices. For the purposes of this discussion, *Ekue* with a capital *E* refers to the hidden Ekue friction drum that reproduces the "Divine Voice."

The small-e *ekue* is expressed in a repertoire of objects and materials that bespeak the nobility, authority, valiance, and great force of the "leopard" and other powerful beings at the heart of the Abakuá narrative. These include staffs and drums adorned with leopard and goat skins, cowrie shells, silk cords and tassels, silver and gold regalia, and the feathers of the rooster. The objects' adornments recall royal, ecclesiastical, and military iconography and make organic references to the human body, flora, fauna, and the natural landscape, as seen in the banner and the objects' animal skin and feathers. Indeed, the highly worked Abakuá regalia, which blends natural and human-made prestige elements, marks the domestication within the corporate *fambá* of raw power from the outside, drawn from "nature" and its "otherworld" associations *(la naturaleza* and the *más allá)*.

If the altar makes the "secret" visible in some way, it also indexes the ineffable, restricted, fearsome, and dangerous. A dimension of *ekue* is "seen" by lodge officers in the form of the altar, and by the rank-and-file and visitors when the officers make formal processions outside the *fambá* in the semipublic court-

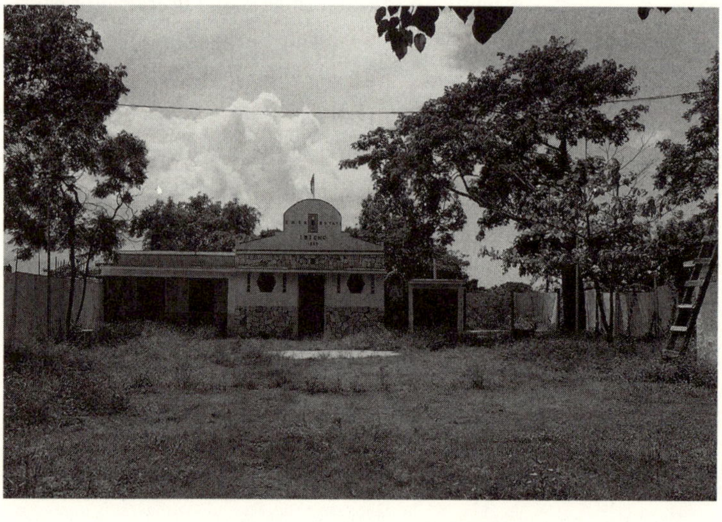

Figure 3.6. Walled *tierra* (compound) of the Erón Entatí Ibionó Abakuá lodge, Guanabacoa, founded 1888, showing *fambá* temple, grassy grounds *(solar)*, cement pad for sacrifice of *mbori* (center), and ceiba tree (right). Photograph by David H. Brown, 1986.

yard and sometimes the street. In its most profound, or "deepest," dimension, *ekue* is invisible; it is heard only. The organ of the secret and its "Voice" are ensconced within ever-more restricted recesses: within the *tierra*'s walls is the *fambá*. Immediately within the *fambá* is a curtain. Beyond the curtain is the altar. In the corner of the temple's main room, behind another curtain, is a highly restricted secret inner recess, a holy of holies *(fo-ekue)*. Beyond this curtain is the Ekue drum, which sounds the "Voice" of *ekue*, also known as *uyo*. Inappropriate "seeing" or other disrespectful behavior is condemned and could be punishable by death; the "Voice," as it is heard from deep within the temple, creates and recreates the secret and the power it implies. In this sense, *ekue* is an "acoustic mask," which constitutes hierarchical power relations between a social institution and the determinate "audiences" it excludes from membership and participation, but also before which it strategically performs (see Kasfir 1988:5; Barber 1981).

The Banner of Eforí Eñongo

The Eforí Eñongo banner depicts the advent or "birth of the Abakuá in Africa." The embroidered landscape arrests the dramatic moment in which the Efó princess, Sikán, unwittingly captured a strange, fish-like creature in her water gourd at the bank of the Oddán River. The fish was Obon Tanze, a principal avatar of God (Abasí) and organ of the Divine Voice. As Sikán raised the gourd to her head, Obon Tanze roared, bellowed, and shrieked *(chillar)* like a leopard (plate 2).[4] This first major sounding of "the Voice" remains the anchor of Abakuá mythico-historical narrative. During every ceremony it provides an aural variant of the phenomenon Mircea Eliade defined as *hierophany*, a divine manifestation in which "something sacred shows itself to us."[5]

Tanze's roar marked the immediate presence of *ekue*, which Jesús Nasakó defines as "'mystery,' 'God,' and 'manifestation of God on the Earth'"—a definition similar to Eliade's. *Ekue* derives from the Ejagham and Efik terms, *ngbe* and *ekpe*, respectively, for "leopard" or "leopard society." *Ekue* condenses many layers of meaning. *Ekue* is grounded in two principal mysterious creatures of the wild, the "fish" and the "leopard." They are denizens of two powerful natural domains (river and forest, respectively). In nature, and in the banner's visual space, river and forest are represented as distinct domains. At the same time, they are spiritually related to each other and to human experience through themes of ancestorship, royalty, and reincarnation. "Obon Tanze," Jesús Nasakó explains,

> was a king, a chief of the leopard society in Africa, who died many years before. . . . There circulated a great legend about . . . the advent of a mystery that would be important for the Efó tribe. . . . The tradition recognizes that the king's spirit was reincarnated as a fish. Thus, when we say "Obon Tanze," we mean, "King Fish." . . . Animated by the spirit of Obon Tanze—the chief of the leopard society—the fish emitted the roar of the leopard. . . . Ekue [the drum] reproduces [nothing less than] the sound of a beast, a cat [*fiera, felino*]. . . . The leopard society itself already existed and was distinguished. But it was *reborn* with the Abakuá.[6]

Nasakó's narrative nuances the commonly understood "birth" of the Abakuá as a momentous "rebirth." Following the ancestral King Tanze's reincarnation, Sikán's capture of Tanze led to the special reorganization and consecration of an extant governing "leopard society." This would be realized, as narrated in subsequent mythical episodes, through an unprecedented achievement: a secret *fundamento* that was created to store, and an enduring *fundamento* to sound at will, the *Voz Divina* or *ekue*. Upon these material foundations could then be consecrated a new "leopard society" for purposes of commerce, social control, and spiritual transformation.

Space and the "Geography of Sacred Memory"

The banner's landscape paints a geographical "space" transformed into sacred "place" (see Brown 1999; Tuan 1977:6, 149–160; Kirshenblatt-Gimblett 1988: 551). This "oriented" place is sacralized by the hierophany of *ekue* and its subsequent ritual and iconographic elaboration (Eliade 1959:21–22). The embroidered image depicts the mystical ecology of the secret's origin, as imagined, remembered, and recreated by generations of Cuba's Abakuá. Notable is its dramatically rolling terrain, punctuated by sacred hills and impressive trees, crosscut by meandering rivers and creeks, all of which evoke the terrain of the Cross River region (see plate 1, map 2.1).

The Abakuá believe Obon Tanze's capture and sounding occurred "in Africa" at the bank of the winding "River Oddán." The Oddán, according to the Abakuá "geography of sacred memory" *(geografía del sagrado recuerdo),* divided the "tribes" of the Efó and Efí (see Cabrera 1970:63–64; Sosa Rodríguez 1982:452). This elaborated landscape, which corresponds to other, albeit simpler, "maps of sacred memory" drawn by many an Abakuá, locates Sikán and the Efó (Efor) territory on the picture's left, and the Efí on the right (figure 3.7).[7] Still, Cabrera's sources revealed that the river coursed through at least seven territories populated by various Efí and Efó groups, including Obane, Efori Isun, Bekura, Ibondá Efó, Ibondá Efí, and Ibondá Kuririón (Cabrera 1970:79). Indeed, in Abakuá narrative, remote echoes of the same "Voice" had been heard in Efí Kondó by Bibí-Efí (Ibibió-Efik) fishermen before Sikán's discovery (Sosa Rodríguez 1982:192; Cabrera 1970:80).[8]

Glossing an early twentieth-century line drawing virtually identical to the banner's embroidered image, an elderly informant of Rafael Roche y Monteagudo elaborated upon this landscape's toponyms. He related that "the [Oddán]-Ororó was a navigable river between two hills . . . the right [being] Uban [Efí] and the left hill [being] Ororó Efó."[9] The picture, according to Roche, was "drawn by [this] 86 year old [African] native before he died . . . [and was] the only picture made by an African in Cuba" (Roche y Monteagudo 1925) (figure 3.8).[10] Like the banner, it locates the Efó on the left and the Efí on the right. Uban (sometimes Ubani, Obane, Oban, or Owane), according to Abakúa tradition, refers to one or more Bibi/Efí territories around Old Calabar, but, most important, to the "capital" of Efí culture (see Sosa Rodríguez 1982:287, 409;

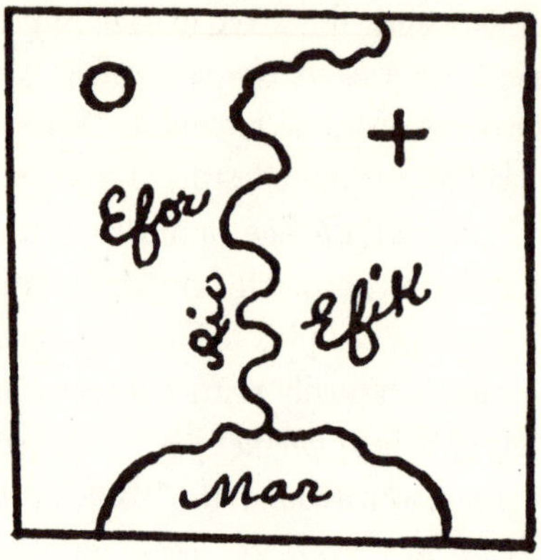

Figure 3.7. Line drawing of "Geography of Sacred Memory," showing the Efor and Efik on either side of the Oddán River in Africa, drawn by Lydia Cabrera's informant Saibeke ca. 1940s–1950s (1970:64). Courtesy of the Estate of Lydia Cabrera.

Cabrera 1970:65, 73; 1988:434–435, 501).[11] Abakuá songs that honor the Efí branch in Cuba, for example, as sung by Havana's Grupo Yorubá Andabo, explicitly associate Ubane with the Efí branch: *Owane, Owane, Owane//Ekue (E)fi, Okobio [O]wane* (essentially, Owane, Owane Owane, the *ekue* of Efí of the Owane Abakuá brother; Grupo Yorubá Andabo 1998, track 2). Just as Abakuá have always nuanced maps of sacred memory and narrative to include other "tribes," Juan Mokongo and Jesús Nasakó do not fail to point out the origin of one other important Abakuá branch in Cuba, the Orú. They locate Orú territory just beyond and slightly to the left of the hills in the landscape's background around the river's bend (plate 1, figure 3.8).[12]

The two landscapes, one embroidered and one drawn, construct a putatively original scene, which mythically condenses space and time—a space become cultural place via hierophany and the production of a past, present, and narrative future. The scene economically delineates a "world" of the potent figures, or tropes, of *ekue*'s advent and homeland: its riverine, canoe-dependent lifeways; its spirit-imbued natural and supernatural creatures, and its legendary human actors, who have been elaborated through Abakuá hagiography. The stunning hierophany of *ekue* irradiated and transformed all of these elements

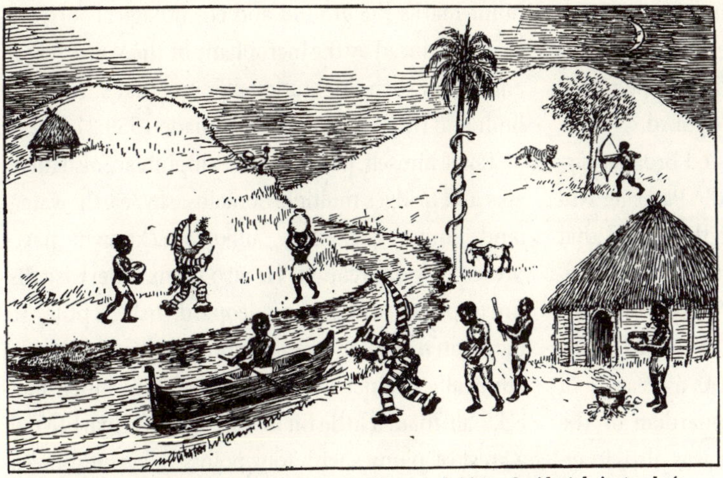

Cuadro que simboliza el nacimiento del ñañiguismo en el Africa Occidental, junto al río "Oldan-Ororó", donde se descubrió el misterio de Ecue.

Figure 3.8. "Picture symbolizing the birth of Ñañiguismo in West Africa, next to the Oldan-Ororó [Oddán] River, where the mystery of Ecue was discovered." Supposedly drawn by an "86 year old [African] native before he died" (Roche y Monteagudo 1925:99).

and actors within its proximity into "witnesses" *(testigos)*. Each became a figure of divine mediation. And each—the river, hills, trees, night sky, moon and stars, mammals, reptiles, Sikán, the Bibí canoeman, the masquerades and their entourages—form the dramatis personae of the Abakuá mythico-historical drama.

Because this seminal Abakuá icon has never been fully glossed, it is worth taking time to address each figure and its relationships. Pictured near the river's left bank (as oriented by the landscape scene) is the crocodile (Akanúman Kuari, Macombe, or Ekokominandubé; see plate 2, figure 3.8). In Abakuá legend the crocodile is a principal "guardian of rivers and lagoons." The Efó people, according to Cabrera's sources, "poisoned the water of the [Oddán] river [and] magically prepared a crocodile" in order to impede the aggressive Efí in their repeated efforts to cross the river and conquer the Efó (Cabrera 1988:37, 347; 1970:134).[13] An equally important spiritually imbued water guardian is the serpent *(majá)*, called Ñangabión in Brícamo.[14] The iconographic importance of Ñangabión, as well as the royal palm tree (Ucano Mambré) it entwines, is marked by their position in the exact center of image (plate 1). By virtue of their proximity to the river, Sikán, and the water gourd, these two sentinels at the river's edge are key "witnesses" of *ekue*'s discovery. They also embody and generate Abakuá visual forms and spiritual meanings encountered throughout the iconography and liturgy. At the center of the image, they bridge and unify the composition's natural forms and figures.

The capacity of serpent and crocodile to mediate distinct domains is highlighted by their amphibious nature. They can traverse water and land. In their fluid positionality "between" categories, they become mysterious, and represent the potential for transformation (see Douglas 1978:55). Ñangabión, the serpent, keenly hears and "sees." He swiftly and elegantly traverses space like an electrical arc, catalyzing, and then protecting, sacred phenomena. For this reason, Ñangabión is the indispensable companion of the "sorcerer," magician, diviner, and healer: the archetypal Nasakó.[15] In one version of the discovery narrative, just as Sikán lifted the gourd containing Tanze to her head, Jesús Nasakó relates, "the palm tree [that] stood at the foot of the river, around which the *majá*—Ñangabión or Añanga—had entwined itself, was the first witness present [along with] the *majá*, which was there *at that moment!* When Sikán discovered the secret, the *majá* went to the gourd . . . and [*ekue*] sounded. Stunned, Sikán put the gourd at the foot of the palm, and the snake coiled itself around the gourd." That is why, according to Jesús, the Isuama [Carabalí] proverb goes: *amalogró kurité newán añánga itiá awaneróneri.* Jesús translates the proverb as: "The first witness before whom sounded the Voice of *ekue* was the *majá,* which dropped from the palm and coiled itself around the gourd."[16]

Cabrera's Abakuá sources attributed broader significance to Ñangabión in the Middle Passage. Not only was the serpent a "Divinity of the River" that was "offered goats, roosters, and bushrats as sacrifices," but Ñangabión was also a "protector of many inhabitants of Calabar who came to Cuba" in the holds of ships (Cabrera 1988:424). As a creature of water and movement, and as the guardian of the gourd-envesseled secret, Ñangabión was also, in effect, the mobile protective charm of African Carabalí in the belly of the slave ship.

Structurally, the palm tree is an *axis mundi,* inasmuch as it vertically bisects the landscape composition. As such, it bridges and mediates at least three critical domains of the Creation: sky, earth and its living dependents, and water. The palm also acts as an earthly foil and transmitter for natural and heavenly forces, in particular, the energies of the sun, the moon, and the stars. Between the sky and the canvas of the land, the palm etches the contrasted values of light and dark—which become symbolic values. In the embroidered composition, a subtle shadow, cast by the palm, darkens and delineates the spot of *ekue*'s discovery (the shadow falls obliquely and can be seen on each bank, and it bridges the river's two banks). Abakuá typically characterize the site of *ekue*'s first sounding as "beneath" or "at the foot of" the royal palm tree (Br. *Ukano Mambre*), in other words, in its shadow (Cabrera 1954:277). Shadows represent spiritually imbued spheres in many of the Afro-Cuban religions, and can carry connotations of mystery, danger, and the presence of often potentially disturbing spiritual beings.[17] Here, the tree's shadow creates a portal or threshold to the other world, which exists just the other side of this one. Indeed, as the palm takes a perpendicular relationship to the river, a crossroads is formed at the very center of the composition, wherein the shadow is a third dimension. This point marks the ground and cosmological "orientation" produced by the hierophany of the Voice. It is at, and upon, such orientational points that shrines are built and ritual is enacted (see Eliade 1959:21–22).

Tanze himself, part fish, part amphibian, also mediates and bridges multiple domains: sky/earth, water/land, forest/settlement, unknown/known, past/present, God/Creation. He also spans otherwise distinct species and groups: leopard, fish, reptile, reincarnated human beings, and geographically and ethnically distinct riverine "tribes." Tanze was "half-eel, half toad, a little bit of fish, with a tripartite tail, a crest of plumes with four points . . . grotesque extremities . . . and a roar" (León 1964; see also Cabrera 1970:86). Thus, Tanze was a strange, disfigured hybrid, and, therefore, like his serpent and crocodile colleagues, falls between classifications (see Douglas 1978:55). In Abakuá narrative, the fish periodically sounds "the Voice," which is heard as a remote echo as he circulates through the seven aforementioned territories—thereby linking their inhabitants in a common destiny. However, the major revelation of the Voice occurs in one particular territory along the Oddán, Awana Bekura Mendo, which becomes the origin, font, and elder authority for the dissemination of the secret to other groups. In this sense, the secrets of Tanze, along with Sikán, will also come to mediate the relations of hierarchy in space and time. It is only there, in Awana Bekura Mendo, that Tanze realizes his ancestral essence—as Obon Tanze, or Lord Tanze, the reincarnation of a Leopard Society King. It is there that Obon Tanze offers *ekue*'s potential to humankind when landed and contained by a particular woman, Sikán. And it is there that Tanze, along with Sikán, is subsequently transformed into a *fundamento* through the ritual work of Nangobié Nasakó. It is there that the first Abakuá society was born, and from there that it disseminated.

As the spiritually imbued shadow of the palm generates within and between distinct domains, so Obon Tanze's sound also mysteriously generates from the polar opposites of water and land, depth and surface, clear swift midstream water and turbid, growth-infested water along the riverbank. Jesús Nasakó sang to me an Abakuá chant about Obon Tanze's sounding, which poses a question that marks not merely the Voice, but the conditions of its revelation, as a deep mystery:

Akuriñanga sene, akurien yene tini awon bibí
And it is a strange creature
That the woman and the Bibí heard [repeat].

Akuriñan diba-a-a, anandiba fisi e-e, Ororopa kufon namfocó? [repeat].
Was it in the middle of the river,
Where weeds do not grow, or at the bank of the river where thistles grow?[18]

Abakuá narrative is thus deeply dynamic, evoking its forces and the philosophical conditions of their creation as complex relations within nature, between nature and society, and between the past and the present. The figures that flesh out Abakuá narrative are encountered in chants such as this one and in oral legends. Equally important, they are encountered in realistically rendered imagery, such as the embroidered banner landscape, as well as in relatively more abstract ideographs and more figurative pictographs, which will be treated in their turn.

Sikán, Nasakó, Ekueñón, and the First *Fundamentos*

In sacred discovery narratives it is often a solitary, liminal, or marginal character—the indigene, boatman, woman, black, or Amerindian—who is the witness of hierophanies and the discoverer of sacred icons. This character is also a threshold figure, who mediates between domains of power but is not ultimately granted sole or permanent possession of the priceless discovery. The find is typically appropriated by a dominant institution, and the humble discoverer becomes a spiritualized attribute, or metonym, of the icon itself (see, e.g., Taussig 1987:188–189).[19] The Abakuá banner's embroidery pictures a Bibí canoeman, a fisherman, in the middle of the river (plate 2). As Jesús Nasakó relates, the Bibí (an Ibibio) "was the first human being to hear the mysterious sound of the Voice when the fish, Tanze, was still free in the waters."[20] Whereas the Bibí fisherman had heard Tanze's bellowing sound from time to time in his travels up and down the river, Tanze's presence would be fully revealed only before Sikán. This narrative strand highlights Sikán's status as special, though also marginal, liminal, gendered, and ambivalent. Sikán is a young woman, and she has a "troubled life." Her social status is ambiguous and still debated (was she married, single, a virgin, the daughter of Mokongo or Iyamba? [León 1964]). The Bibí, a male of age, freely and independently moves up and down the river. Though Sikán is a privileged princess, she is a royal daughter; therefore, imaginably, she is circumscribed by her father's court, until the "fattening house" institution and marriage presumably transfer her to another man; and, though a princess, she is an African woman, who typically draws and carries water. Thus, Sikán might be read as more or less passive in this narrative version, and the object of forces bigger than her and beyond her control. Not by design, but only unwittingly, Sikán discovers Tanze and the Voice. In turn, the Voice is a powerful force in a region thoroughly controlled by kings, male sorcerers, hunters, and male secret leopard societies. The secret she discovers is swiftly taken away from her, and she meets an untimely end—at least as a living, breathing woman.

In one more conflict-laden version of the myth, Sikán's discovery of the "Voice" resulted in a struggle of politico-religious authority, which ultimately led to her death. A Bantu sorcerer by the name of Nangobié Nasakó had traveled northwest to the "Carabalí" delta region of Awana Bekura Mendo from his homeland, Etié-tié Poripó Corombán, on the coast of "Congo." Nangobié Nasakó immediately became powerful in his new home by imposing on the local people the cultic authority of a prophesied sacred "Sound," or "Voice," which only he could interpret through his magical "Instrument." This instrument consisted of a charged pot, called *mañongo umpabio* in Brícamo, and a divining mirror, called *ntubikán* (*mpaka* in Congo; see figures 3.8 and 3.9, lower right). Nasakó was essentially a Kongo *nganga*, or ritual expert and divination priest (*ngangulero* in Cuba) (see figure 3.10).[21] He had predicted that an "animal," the organ of this "Sacred Sound," would soon appear among men. In preparation, Nasakó surrounded himself with "seven servants" *(kunansa)* of his instrument, forming an incipient secret society. Thus, the banner's image depicts Nangobié Nasakó standing before his sacred temple *(fambá)*, holding his *mañongo umpabio* pot.[22] According to the foregoing version of the myth, given a kind of Marxist, protofeminist spin by Fernando Ortiz's student Argeliers León, Sikán's capture of Tanze and discovery of the "Voice" threatened Nasakó's monopoly on power and authority. For Obon Tanze "appeared as just the kind of strange and frightening animal that was predicted to be the mouthpiece of the Supreme Being" (Abasí; see León 1964).

Nangobié Nasakó hence becomes a key dramatic link in the Abakuá discovery legend. The roles of the Bibi, Sikán, Tanze, and Nasakó and a series of other important characters are marked spatially and narratively in the banner's composition. Several clusters of figures in distinct locations flesh out the legend's roles and distinct episodes: (1) in the center, Sikán, following the Bibí's glimpse of the Voice, discovers Tanze within the radius of sacralized agent-witnesses: the snake-entwined palm tree; the "star" and the "moon" *(lucero* and *luna)*, two astral bodies regarded as the "witnesses of the night" (top).[23] Their presence in the midnight blue sky is the otherworldly correlate to the spiritualized "shadow" cast by the palm tree; (2) the solitary, half-hidden hunter called Ekueñón. This itinerant "Congo" personage,[24] ready with bow drawn, spies the hierophany from beneath the spreading, spirit-embracing branches of the Silk Cotton tree (Br. *Ucano Beconsí*, Sp. *Ceiba*). The hunter, the *ceiba*, and the fierce "tiger" (Br. *yevengo*, the leopard)[25] metonymically figure this distinct sphere within the composition as remote, mysterious, undomesticated "forest," *el monte*. The *monte* is recognized in all the Afro-Cuban traditions as a principal source of spiritual power. The *monte* resides beyond the threshold of the "house" and the "town" (see Cabrera 1954: 149–220; Brown 1999).

Just as the palm, the river, and the radius of *ekue*'s sound distinguish and unite spaces and experiences, so does Ekueñón—through proximity, the theme of itinerancy, the bowman's media and technique, and implied sightlines within the composition (plate 1, center). Ekueñón, a liminal denizen of the "outside," acts as a key mediator between deep forest *(monte adentro)* and settled territory. From his vantage point

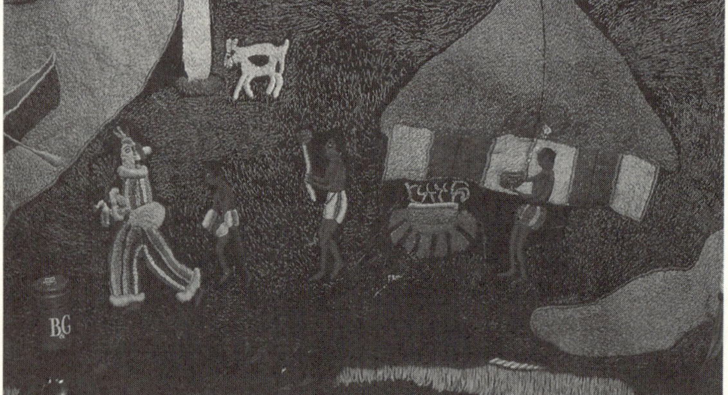

Figure 3.9. Efori Eñongo banner, detail: Nasakó in front of his *fambá* holding his gourd of *mokuba* or *mañongo umpabio* magical pot and a smoking pipe, with other Abakuá *plazas* and *íreme*. *Mbori*, the goat, is tied to the royal palm by the river, awaiting sacrifice. Photograph by David H. Brown.

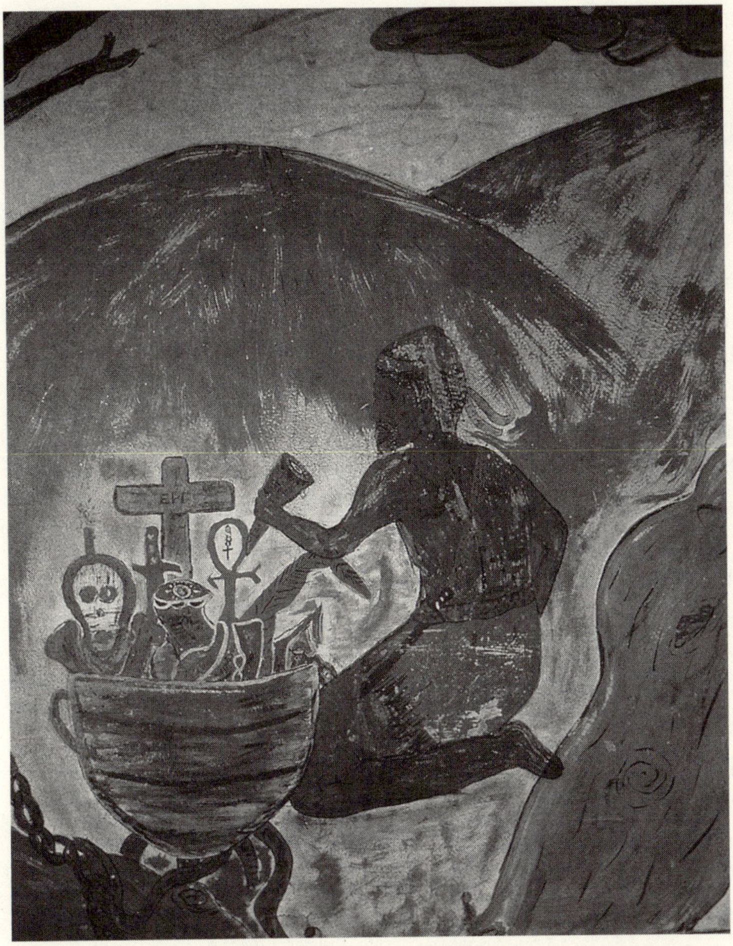

3.10. Ariel Fernández, ***Francisco Siete Rayos*** **(detail), ca. 1980, tempera on paper, Guanabacoa, Havana. The full painting is approximately 12 × 14 inches. Fernández painted this work to represent the principal** ***palo*** **spirit of his brother Adolfo. The painting depicts Francisco, a spirit of the dead, who, "in life," was a Congo who worked with the sacred cauldron** ***(nganga, nkisi, prenda)*** **of Siete Rayos. Francisco kneels before the iron pot in the** ***monte,*** **the sacred forest of medicinal plants and spirits. The "countryside" setting is marked by mountains and a traditional rustic** ***bohío*** **dwelling. A candle burns atop the cauldron's principal relic of its animating spirit of the dead, the skull** ***(kiyumba),*** **indicating "work" in progress, as Francisco divines with his** ***mpaka vititi mensu*** **horn. The sacred elements of the "charged" pot and the divining horn are cognate with the spiritual tool kit of the "Congo sorcerer" Nasakó of the Abakuá lodge and the supposed contents of the Efó goblet-style** ***sese.***

at the threshold of forest and settlement, Ekueñón "kept vigilance over the river and all its happenings," relates Jesús Nasakó. "He knew the advent of *ekue* . . . of the great event that had occurred, and, thus, he became a [mythic] personage himself."[26] As a "hunter," like Oshosi in the Lucumí religion, Ekueñón bears the marginal vocation of tracking and killing; he does not live permanently, like others, within the town, but moves back and forth between the town and his secret places in the forest. Like Oshosi, Ekueñón's deadly arrow swiftly and accurately traverses space with great force, killing instantly, in order to supply sustenance to society (see, e.g., Mason and Edwards 1985a; see also Armstrong 1989). Like the snake, so is Ekueñón's arrow a swift vehicle and vector of spiritual current. This will be seen again and again in Abakuá drawn signs of ritual invocation, which revolve around sinuous lines and straight vectors tipped with arrow points and flanked with symbolic feathers. In this sense, the sinuous snake and the straight arrow reiterate the traversing forms and mediating roles of the river and the palm. Ekueñón's vocation as hunter, mediator between settlement and bush, and archer whose arrow always reaches its target, would continue in the elaboration of Abakuá ceremonial. At the start of every Abakuá *plante,* Ekueñón leads a procession out of the temple into the "forest," often just a round of the outer courtyard. In his "search for the Voice" *(búsqueda de la Voz),* he "captures" *(prender) ekue* in his small plumed drum, and returns with it to the temple's inner sanctum, so that Iyamba can sound the Ekue friction drum.

The Consecration of the Secret: Nasakó, Ekueñón, and the "Sacrifice" of Sikán

Narratively, Nangobié Nasakó and Ekueñón form the bookends of what might be read as a male-centered, patriarchal Abakuá narrative. Nasakó's role as sorcerer and prophet of the "Sacred Voice" and Ekueñón's vocation as hunter and executioner connect the opening and closing episodes of the myth: the capture of Obon Tanze by Sikán and their common fate in the "birth" of the first Abakuá *fundamentos.* Sikán finds herself, in effect, caught in the middle, just as she has caught the potent fish-king in her gourd—which might be read as the incipient womb of this embryonic secret society. Ultimately, Nasakó and Ekueñón become top hierarchs of the Abakuá Society, along with Iyamba, Mokongo, and Mpegó, who authorized Sikán's death. Sikán and Obon Tanze become the hidden, magical attributes of the *ekue* secret, something like the spiritual mother and father of the Abakuá, respectively. Still, Sikán remains embodied as a silent vessel, which guards and nourishes the "Voice"/*ekue,* whereas the "Voice" of Obon Tanze itself becomes the central, authorizing expression of all Abakuá practice, expressed through the Ekue drum in the hands of Iyamba.

Several variant stories explain Sikán's fate, and all carry an ideological and political load. In one story, Sikán's capture of Obon Tanze "caused an opposition to Nasakó's hegemony . . . for she would have competed with him by manipulating . . . the sacred 'Voice'" (León 1964). This gloss carries the germ of a more feminist and socialist rereading of the Abakuá myth. As a woman hemmed in by patriarchy and male gerontocracy, Sikán could neither approximate nor possess the "secret," which was eagerly sought by the politico-religious governing societies of Awana Bekura Mendo, including Nasakó and his *kunansa.* In a simpler and more misogynistic gloss, which reflects intrinsic suspicion of woman's character and rationalizes the Ekpe/Ngbe/Abakuá logic of female exclusion, Sikán was killed because "no woman is capable of keeping a secret." In another, related version that is equally politicized, Sikán was condemned to death for "betraying" the Efó by revealing the secret to her father, Mokongo, the king of the opposing tribe, the Efí (see Moliner Castañeda 1988:15–16; León 1964).[27] Finally, a kind of classical "tragedy" narrative constitutes one of the most common myth variations (see Ortiz 1950b). Here, Sikán was "sacrificed," or "gave her life," for a higher principle: the greater "good of the Abakuá."[28] This version bleeds into the Christian narrative of Christ's sacrifice. Without her spiritually charged blood, bones, head, and hair, *ekue* could not live on for lack of reinvigorating blood consecrations and relics for embodying *ekue*'s potency with such ingredients. The sorcerer Nangobié Nasakó would confect an enduring medium for conserving the "Voice," which enabled him in turn to consecrate the first chiefs of the "reborn" Abakuá society. Fertilized by the generative power of the fish/*ekue,* as it were, Sikán, correspondingly, became immortalized as the "Mother of the Abakuá."

Complementing Nasakó's role in Sikán's fate and *ekuê*'s consecration, Ekueñón, the Carabalís' sanctioned killer, graduates from hunter to formal executioner *(verdugo).*[29] Ekueñón killed Sikán at the insistence of Nangobié Nasakó, though with the legal sanction of Mpegó, the Efó tribe's Arbiter of the Law, and, depending upon the version, with the "authorization" of Sikán's father, either Iyamba or Mokongo. Sikán's unused remains were then entombed beneath the sacred *ceiba* tree—some say the palm. In the banner's image, the goat (Br. *mbori*), which would later become Sikán's sacrificial substitute, quietly awaits its fate just as Sikán herself awaited execution there.

Enter Nangobié Nasakó once again. As the archetypal sorcerer and monopolist of ritual power, he was the original confector not of one but two *fundamentos*—spiritually embodying material foundations—at the heart of the incipient Abakuá society: (1) a portable vessel that would contain and guard the power of *ekue*/Tanze. At first, it was a simple bottle gourd (Br. *ibóbora,* Sp. *güira*) modeled after Sikán's which, since then, would be guarded with great secrecy" (León 1964; see also Cabrera 1970:106).

As depicted in the banner, Nangobié Nasakó is a key "witness" by the river Oddán (figure 3.9, right), yet one with a keen technological edge. For a long time, the sorcerer saw, heard, and tracked the fish through his oracular instruments. He "stayed up night and day, alone with his *mañongo umpabio* and his *ntubikán*, observing the ample and swift movement of the Fish, now here, now there, in the River Oddán" (Sosa Rodríguez 1982:193). Following Nasakó's appropriation of Obon Tanze from Sikán, Nasakó sought to

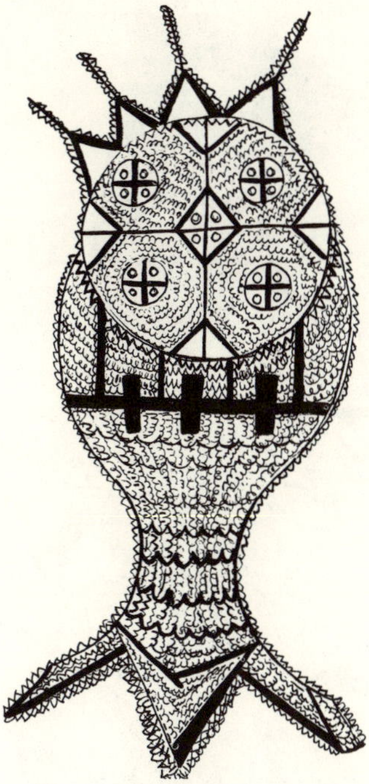

Figure 3.11. Drawn sign *(anaforuana)* of "Tanze transforming into the Ekue drum." Shown are a stylized three-footed drum with a skin marked with invocatory signs and the drum body's wedge-tuning system (Ekue). Its surface retains Tanze's scales, the three feet represent Tanze's three-part tail, and the drumhead sprouts Tanze's four-plumed crown (Cabrera 1975:110, fig. 37). Courtesy of the Estate of Lydia Cabrera.

water vessel, which contained the selected potent remains of Sikán and Tanze, among other ingredients. Ultimately, it took the form of an urn-shaped or a squat open-bottomed "symbolic drum." Hewn from wood, it was adorned with four upright plumes of rooster feathers—modeled after the crest of Obon Tanze's head (see figures 3.11, top, 5.6, 6.5, plate 1, center)—and called *sese* or *seseribó* (Cabrera 1970:106, 148–149; 1975:78; (2) an enduring and efficacious means of reproducing the "Divine Voice," which, ultimately, would take the form of a three-footed wood friction drum called Ekue (figures 3.11, 3.12, and 6.4; see also Cabrera 1975:108–110; 1954 [plates]; 1970: 83–109; Sosa Rodríguez 1982:193–300; Thompson 1983:241–242; Roche y Monteagudo 1925:33–37).[30] Sikán's blood "served to consecrate [this] drum,

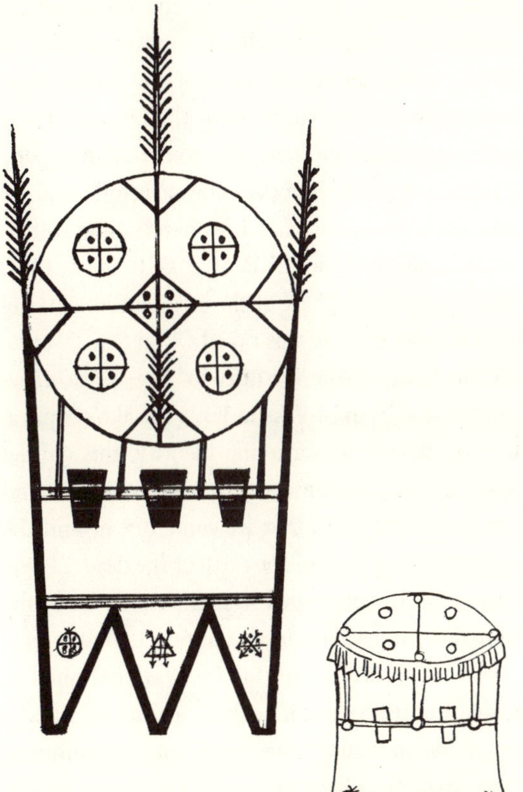

Figure 3.12. Drawings of the three-footed Ekue friction drum, one symbolically depicted with four *plumeros* (which it does not actually have), though Tanze had a crest of plumes (Cabrera 1975:108, fig. 36). The three feet of both drums feature the signs of Mokongo, Isué, and Iyamba. Courtesy of the Estate of Lydia Cabrera.

care for him in the woman's original water vessel. Still, Tanze remained silent, and eventually died. Nasakó and his *kunansa* desperately conducted numerous experiments to revive Tanze magically. For example, using Nasakó's spiritually charged cruciform rattle, called *erikundé* in Brícamo, they tried to "call" the Voice back to Tanze's dried skin, which they had marked with invocatory chalk signs (Br. *anaforuana,* Sp. *firmas*) and consecrated with blood over three stones by the river. Nasakó then ordered them to fashion a special wooden "bell" or clapper, called *ekón,*[31] to call the Voice—but to no avail (figure 3.13; León 1964). Still, the ambitious and persistent Nasakó forged ahead, utilizing the mute, proto-*fundamento* in order to "initiate . . . over the skin of Tanze . . . the Seven Sons of Ekue, the Seven First, representing the Seven Tribes of the Efor. . . . These the Seven Heads, or Chiefs, who were born in the Beginning, [were] the Founders, the ancestors, who are present in the seven sacred feathered plumes [*plumeros, muñones*] of the Cuban Abakuá" (Cabrera 1970: 93).[32] In this early phase of the incipient Abakuá Society in Africa, Tanze was called Obón Séne Moruá, literally "King of the Territory [of the] Voice" (*Rey-Tierra Voz* in Spanish). As in Jesús Nasakó's explication of Tanze's transforming identity, this epithet refers to Tanze's reincarnation of a great ancestral presence: "The earth that we come out of and the earth that we return to. The earth of the dead. . . . Because what is worshipped were the dead. We [came from dust] and will be dust" (Cabrera 1970:93–94).

Nangobié Nasakó and his *kunansa* continued in their attempts to resuscitate the Voice. Surely, Nasakó was under pressure, since his claims to authority rested significantly on the existence of the "Sacred Sound." Thus, they tried to mount over a resonating vessel Tanze's own skin, those of other animals, and even the skin of sacrificed Ibibio and Congo men, but they failed. Finally, Nasakó succeeded with the skin of the royal goat, which had belonged, like Sikán herself, to the King of the Efó tribe, Iyamba (León 1964). Sikán and goat were metonymically connected via the rules of property to each other and to Iyamba.

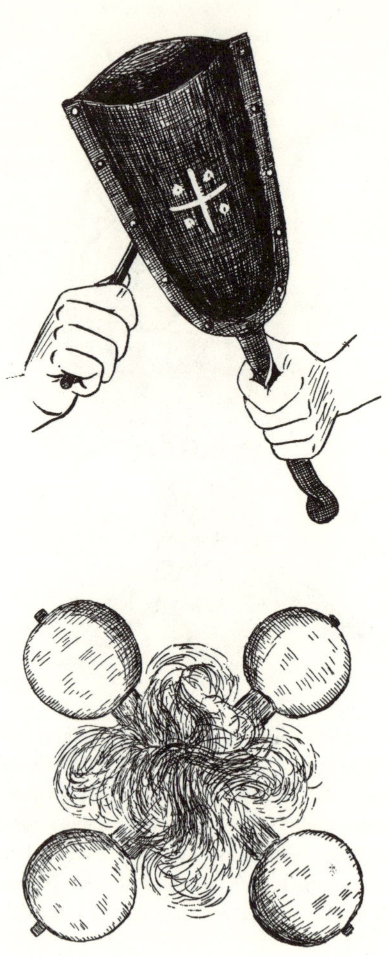

Figure 3.13. ***Ekón*** **(top) and** ***erikundé*** **(bottom). The** ***ekón,*** **marked with the "four winds" in chalk, top, and the** ***erikundé*** **cruciform rattle were first used by the helpers of Nasakó to call spirit of** ***ekue*** **to the** ***fundamento*** **they were constructing in order to preserve the sound of the Divine Voice. Originally, the** ***ekón*** **was a kind of wood clapper. These two instruments are still used to call forth spiritual energy; the officer called Moruá Yuansá uses the** ***erikundé,*** **constructed of crossed wood handles with small gourds filled with seeds at the extremes, to communicate with the** ***íremes.*** **Courtesy of María Fernanda Ortiz Herrera, Representante Sucesores de Fernando Ortiz.**

Sikán and the goat became metaphorically connected inasmuch as the goat became Sikán's symbolic substitute. In short, Nasakó effectively "converted the goat into Sikán. . . . It was sacrificed just like he [had her] sacrificed by the river, in order that its blood reanimate Tanze" (Cabrera 1970:113). At last, with the skin of *mbori,* Nasakó had found a medium that "finally, and perfectly, resonated the Divine Voice"

(Cabrera 1988:339; 1970:92–95; see also Thompson 1983:243).[33] The result was "a strange drum, which stood on three legs reminiscent of Tanze's tail" (figure 3.11). "Atop the drumhead [*parche*], Nasakó rubbed a rib of wood [*yín, güín*], which he took from the very palm where Sikán had leaned to recover from the fright of hearing the Voice, and at the foot of which she had placed the water jug" (León 1964; see also Cabrera 1970:116; 1975:110–111).

A metonymic magical logic links the sound, all the figures of the discovery event, and the drum that would embody and reproduce the Voice/*ekue*, including Sikán, Tanze, the palm, the goat, Iyamba, and the *ceiba*. As noted, the remains of Tanze, and Sikán's head, were incorporated as the principal relics of the *sese*, the first *fundamento* produced by Nasakó. Sikán's blood consecrated the Ekue drum, which was hewn of palm or *ceiba* wood. Like the other drums of the Abakuá, it was mounted with a drumhead *(parche)* of goatskin. This first drum's tuning system consisted of cords of gut and shims of tibia bones from Sikán's body. It would be played *(fragayar)* with a rib from the palm. Among the Efó, this drum would be called Ekue, and among the Efí, Bongó.[34] As an "old adept" explained, "*From the union of tree and victim was born the Voice of the Mystery* in Usagaré; the organized religion of the Society" (Cabrera 1970: 120, emphasis added). Usagaré, in Cuban Brícamo pronunciation, refers to the territory *(tierra)* within the Awana Bekura Mendo region in which the first Abakuá lodge was founded and consecrated, also called Usagaré.[35]

The Ekue or Bongó, as receptor, medium, and amplifier of the Voice, produces its sound as Iyamba rubs a blood-moistened palm rib stood vertically upon the drum skin. Ekue is thus a classic West African "friction drum" (*tambor fricativo;* Ortiz 1955: 125–265, 203–242). Within West Africa's Ekpe society, as Daryll Forde has noted, "the roar of the leopard is simulated by a secret noise-making apparatus called *mbok*" (Forde 1956:18). Within the Cuban Abakuá society, the Ekue and Bongó also issue a "roar," though its pitch and timbre are modified according to the ceremonial event at hand. The drum bellows, powerfully vibrating in one's stomach and chest, during life-giving initiation ceremonies. In contrast, the drum "cries" at a high pitch, vibrating in one's neck and head, during funerary ceremonies (Br. *ñámpe,* Sp. *llanto*). Such sonic variations of register and timbre should be familiar to anyone who has heard the low groan and high shriek of the Afro-Brazilian *cuica* friction drum in samba (see Forde 1956:18; Leib and Romano 1984:50; Ortiz 1955: 203–254).[36]

Conclusion

The Eforí Eñongo embroidered velvet banner represents in realistic, narrative, and symbolic form the society's founding myth. All of its figures—the landscape, the sky and its astral bodies, the river, the forest, the flora and fauna, the human and supernatural protagonists—collectively embody *ekue.* Still, *ekue,* as a generative principal, encompasses but is not exhausted by this cluster of metonyms or attributes, including the "sublime" Voice itself, which "pants, roars, [and] wails" (Cabrera 1970:121). The voice of *ekue* carries a distinct descriptor, *uyo,* which, depending on context, is not always interchangeable with the more elusive *ekue* concept. As Barbara Browning astutely notes in the case of the Afro-Brazilian Candomblé gods *(orixás),* "Divinity cannot be represented mimetically . . . but only contiguously or metonymically. The manifestation of the orixás is pure presence" (Browning 1995:44).[37] Indeed, this is what makes spiritual power a mystery. In the Abakuá case one of *ekue*'s approximate definitions is "mystery." As Leib and Romano observe about the Ejagham Ngbe society, Ngbe-as-mystery constitutes and links, but also transcends, each individual aspect of the society. All of the society's objects, masquerades, policies, and activities metonymically figure and flesh out Ngbe. Thus, members "'play' . . . Ngbe . . . 'cook' . . . Ngbe, and 'drink' and 'chop' Ngbe" (Leib and Romano 1984:48). Likewise, the content and process of knowledge acquisition within the graded initiation process "are" Ngbe. In short, in Leib and Romano's terms, the West African Ngbe and Ekpe, as well as the Cuban Abakuá, can be defined as, but not limited to,

> 1) the corporate group, that is, the association itself, its established principles of organization, and the politico-juridical functions it encompasses; 2) the cult agency, meaning the body of religious beliefs belonging to Ngbe and the set of ritual means to enact them; and 3) the icon, the venerated image of the leopard in its numerous manifestations [e.g., drawn signs, material objects, etc.]. . . . There is nothing secret about the existence of Ngbe. What is secret is the knowledge the initiate can "see" (understand), and the powers, both social and spiritual, afforded him through this knowledge. (Leib and Romano 1984:48)

Nasakó's ritual work following the sacrifice of Sikán and the production of the first *fundamentos* or *potencia* (that is, generative *sacra*) created the conditions for the consecration of the "first" Abakuá lodge in Africa, called Nyenisón Usagaré Nandió (Usagaré for short), located in the territory of Awana Bekura Mendo.[38] Awana Bekura Mendo, the Efó region of Tanze's discovery, Sikán's death, and Nasakó's confection of the Abakuá's first *fundamentos / potencia,* was considered the "Potencia-Owner of Tanze" *(Potenciá-Dueña de Tanze).* For this reason, Usagaré was "the only *potencia* [i.e., lodge] that possessed the actual relics of Tánze and Sikán and for which Nasakó Nangobié Efor constructed the first attributes" (Cabrera 1970:107). Sikán, who was sacrificed beneath the palm, had become, in effect, the "first initiate" to give her life to *ekue* in Bekura Mendo. In turn, *mbori,* the goat, became not only the sacrificial "substitute" for Sikán and an "initiate" in his own right; as well, he became the sacrificial substitute for every subsequent initiate, who would "swear" *(jurar),* that is, give, his life to the society.

According to Abakuá mythico-historical narrative, Nyenisón Usagaré Nandió gave birth to two immediate offspring, Bakokó and Eforisún.[39] As one of Cabrera's informants explained, "the Progenitor, Usagaré Nandió [was] mother of all the nations that worship Ekue" (Cabrera 1988:104; 1970:124–131). Subsequently, the "secret," *ekue,* would be transferred to the Efí, following the cessation of violent conflict, thus constituting the second major trunk of Abakuá tradition in Africa. According to the Cuban Abakuá, though the Efó triumvirate of Usagaré, Bakokó, and Eforisún constituted the root *potencias* of *ekue* in Africa, it would be the secondary recipients of the secret, the Carabalí Efí, who would give birth to the Cuban Abakuá in the form of Efik Buton of Regla in 1836.

4 Cloth and Signs

West African Ukara *and the Iconography of Regla's Efori Eñongo*

The iconographically rich banner of Efori Eñongo might be seen as a realistic version of the more abstract *nsibidi*[1] designs of Ibo-derived Ejagham and Efik *ukara* cloth, as well as the Cuban Abakuá Society's own *anaforuana.*[2] *Ukara* cloth is a resist-dyed medium of highly contrasting blue and white designs. *Anaforuana* are hand-chalked line drawings, "signatures" *(firmas)* that combine geometric and figurative elements. Many of the banner's principal characters, particularly its reptile avatars and hooded *íreme* masquerades, are typical of *ukara*'s more figurative *nsibidi* (plate 3; see Leib and Romano 1984, figs. 2, 3, and 4; Picton and Mack 1989:151; Thompson 1978). At the same time, the abstract patterns of *ukara*'s *nsibidi* designs (check, right triangle, sawtooth, stripe, and pinwheel), seen as well in the Ekpe, Ngbe, and Cuban Abakuá masquerade costumes,[3] make reference to the "paw print" (Leib and Romano 1984:54) or checked pattern of the leopard (figure 4.1) (see also Thompson 1983:228, 244–260). Though the banner's *íreme* masquerade characters limit their designs to one of these variations—multicolored stripes (plate 2)—numerous historical Cuban examples display a range of variations on the "pawprint" theme (plate 4). Although the iconography of *ukara* cloth and the Abakuá velvet banner share much in common, including form and semantic reference, they serve different ends.

In their practical function, the large rectangular bolts of West African *ukara* cloth protect the pillar-supported, open-sided architecture of the Ngbe/Ekpe society lodge from the sight and ingress of the uninitiated (the lodge is *ekat-ngbe* in Ejagham, *ikot-ekpe* in Efik). At a formal and semantic level, *ukara* encodes the secret initiatory knowledge and history of the Ekpe/Ngbe (see Forde 1956:18).[4] In this sense, *ukara* cloth presents an intriguing double entendre. It physically prevents "sight," and the cloth's designs are, in effect, "unseeable" by the uninitiated and lower society grades, who do not "understand" its *nsibidi* symbols (Leib and Romano 1984:50–51). Both of these functions maintain the social power of the lodge through the performative construction

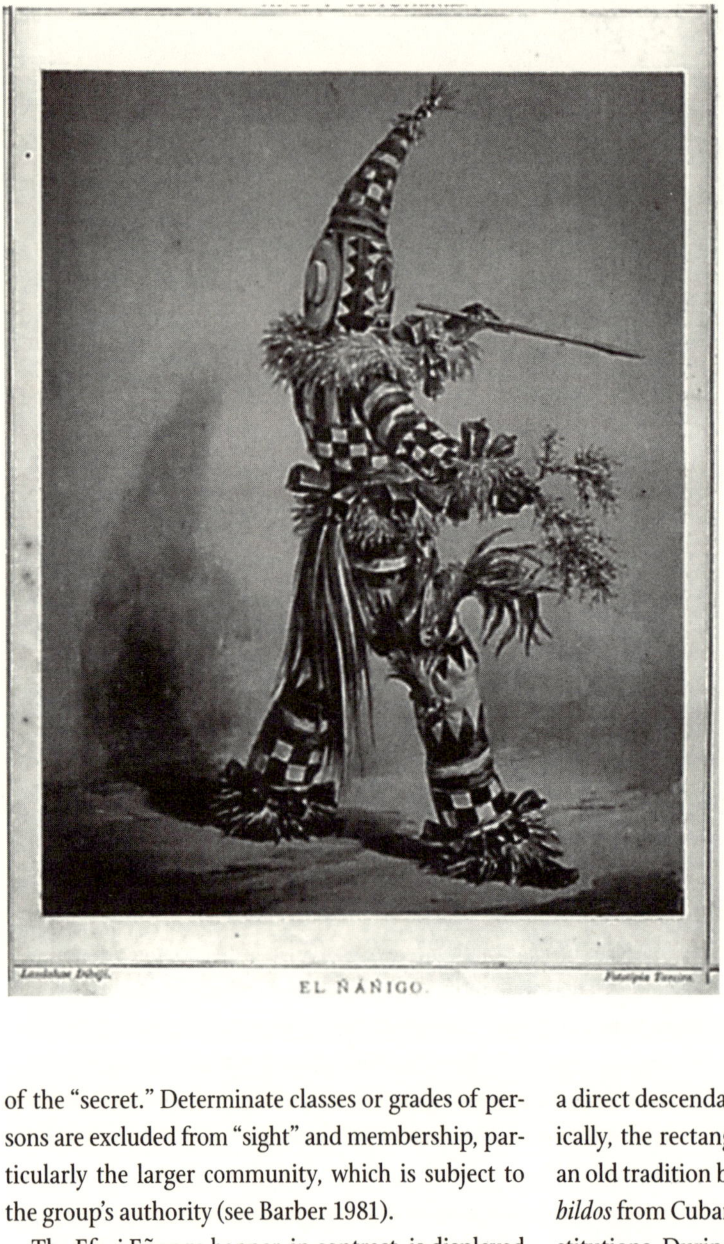

Figure 4.1. Víctor Patricio de Landaluze, *El Ñáñigo,* lithograph, approx. 11.5 × 8.5 inches, from *Los tipos y costumbres de la isla de Cuba,* 1881. The nineteenth-century *íreme*'s mask may have been modeled after the rare masquerade called Embema, which features an articulated face and carries a rooster (see figure 7.3).

of the "secret." Determinate classes or grades of persons are excluded from "sight" and membership, particularly the larger community, which is subject to the group's authority (see Barber 1981).

The Efori Eñongo banner, in contrast, is displayed deep inside the secret lodge *(fambá),* rather than outside. The *fambá* is typically a masonry building with a single, highly guarded front door, and small windows above eye level (figure 3.6). The banner's "audience," consisting exclusively of the lodge's own and visiting *plazas* (dignitaries), is clearly more restricted than *ukara*'s, because the Abakuá rank and file and outside *obonekues* are not allowed to enter the *fambá.* The "banner" genre, therefore, would not seem to be a direct descendant or cognate of *ukara.* Morphologically, the rectangular banner reproduces aspects of an old tradition borrowed by the African nations' *cabildos* from Cuban government, military, and civil institutions. During the colonial period, the *cabildos de nación,* including those of the Carabalí, flew fringed banners *(banderas)* of colorful prestige cloth during all ceremonial occasions (see Roig de Leuchenring 1950:14–15; Aimes 1905:22; Deschamps Chapeaux 1968:50; Brown 1989:39–42; see also Polk 1995). These banners typically bore the name and founding date of the *cabildo,* along with iconography relating to the institution's spiritual patron. Undoubtedly, Regla's Cabildo Carabalí Brícamo Appapá Efí and

Matanzas's Cabildo Bríkamo del Niño Jesús owned banners similar in form to one documented in the town of Bayamo in 1836 (figure 4.2).

Still, the Efori Eñongo banner carries multiple functional and aesthetic dimensions, as well as multiple historical and cultural references. It clearly functions and communicates as a "banner" in a way consistent with those of the historical *cabildos,* particularly given its embroidered *anaforuana* signature/coat-of-arms of the lodge, the lodge's founding date, and its name (erased for purposes of publication here). Beyond any role served by *cabildo* banners, it also serves functional and aesthetic purposes as an altar *frontal* of popular Catholic provenance. For example, Landaluze's nineteenth-century *El Místico del ángel* depicts a black carriage driver before a Havana side-chapel altar. Like Efori Eñongo's altar, a white mantle and dark *frontal* cover the high, box-like altar, which supports a crucifix, a saint statue, a candelabra, and other objects (see figure 3.4). Upon the *frontal* is an appliquéd or embroidered crucifix. It would seem, therefore, that *ukara* cloth finds a more compatible Cuban counterpart in the *anaforuana*-covered satin curtain that hangs just inside the *fambá*'s front door. This highly guarded curtain obstructs the view of the lodge interior when the door is opened for dignitaries to enter and exit.

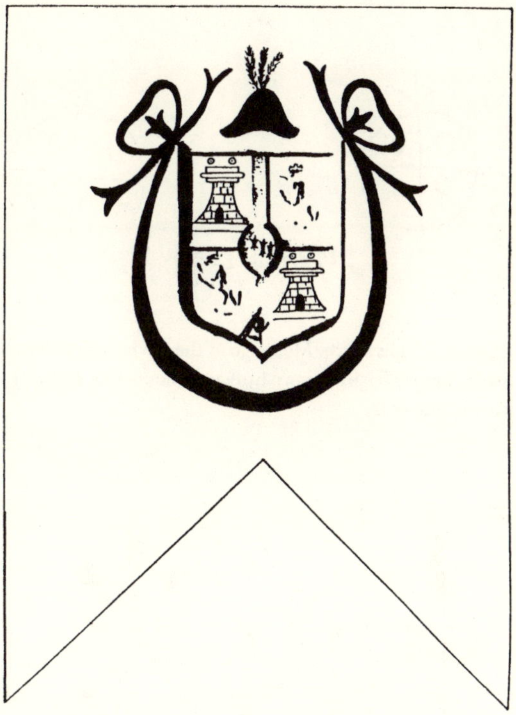

Figure 4.2. Carabalí *cabildo* banner *(bandera)* from the town of Bayamo, 1836. The *bandera* was carried in *cabildo* processions at festival time. From Deschamps Chapeaux 1968.

Abakuá *Anaforuana:* Formal Elements

The principal dramatis personae of the banner's discovery narrative also manifest more abstractly in Abakuá chalk-drawn signs, called *firmas* in Spanish and *anaforuana* in Brícamo (figures 4.3–4.9). *Anaforuana* putatively derive from Cross River ideographic and pictographic systems, such as the *nsibidi* of the Ejagham. Scholars' formal comparisons between the Cross River and Abakuá representations have provided persuasive evidence of this transatlantic genealogy of secret "writing" systems (see Thompson 1978, 1983:244–260). Both Cross River *nsibidi* and Cuban *anaforuana* vary in their media and design. However, where Cross River *ukara* boldly combines a variety of *nsibidi* design types, the Abakuá system tends to confine high-contrast geometric surface design (i.e., check, sawtooth, pinwheel) to its *íreme* masquerade costumes and uses line drawings alone as invocatory and identifying signs during ritual events; these are mostly abstract, though they occasionally use figurative elements. At the same time, the geometric "pawprint" design appears, albeit subtly, in the very quartered circles, squares, and triangles of *anaforuana* line drawings (see, e.g., figures 4.3–4.5). Moreover, as evinced in the velvet banner and its line-drawn contemporaneous counterpart, Abakuá representations of mythical narrative are expressed not only in *anaforuana* but also in Western-influenced realistic genres of picturing, which may combine with West African narrative appliqué traditions (compare plate 1 and figure 3.8 with plate 3) (see, e.g., Vlach 1978:44–55; Wahlman 1993:60–67).

The most basic Abakuá drawn figure is a cross *(cruz)* within a circle, square, or triangle; each of the

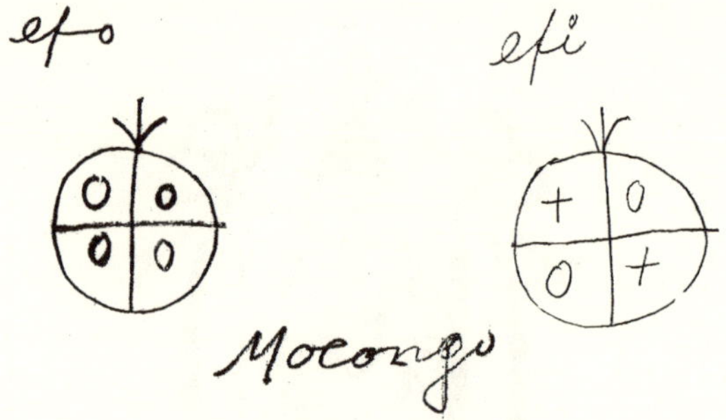

Figure 4.3. Signs for the Mokongo of the Efó branch (left) and the Efí branch (right), drawn by Juan Mokongo for David H. Brown, July 1993.

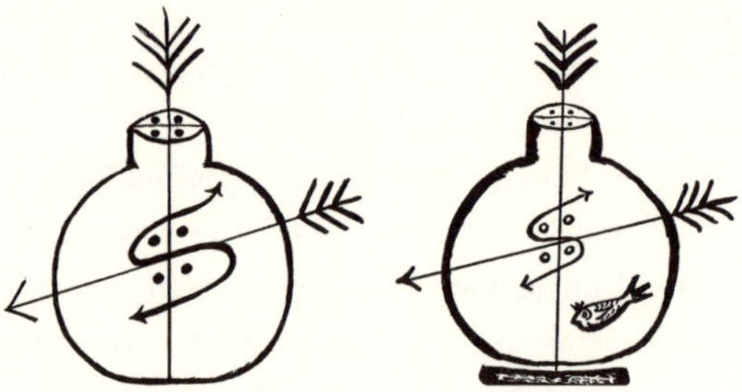

Figure 4.4. Signs of Sikán, depicting her water gourd, with and without the image of Tanze captured inside. The standing palm rib and the arrow form the cross within the circle, and a sinuous S for Sikán contains the eyes of Sikán and Tanze; from Cabrera 1975:76 and Cabrera 1970, first sign after page 90, respectively. Courtesy of the Estate of Lydia Cabrera.

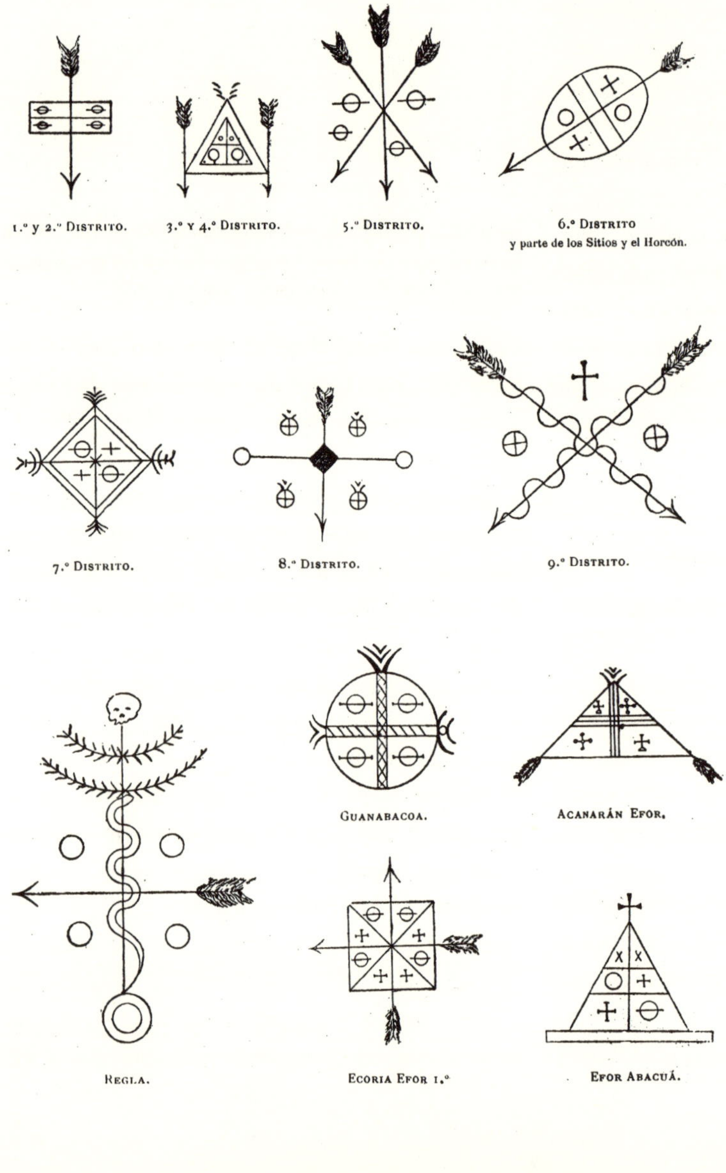

Figure 4.5. Abakuá signs assigned to the City of Havana's nine districts, and those of the municipalities of Guanabacoa and Regla, along with the signs for two lodges (Trujillo y Monagas 1882:371).

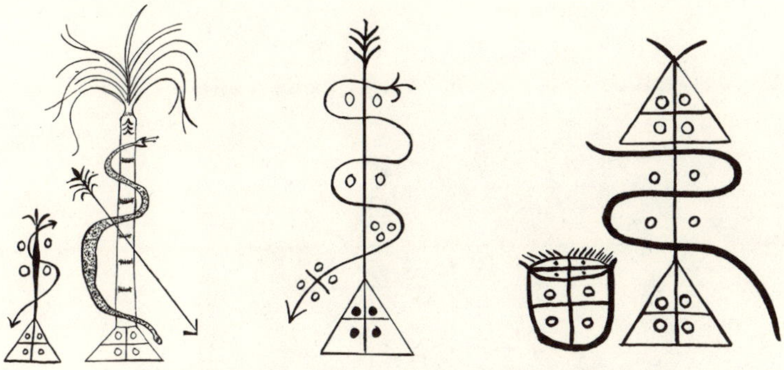

Figure 4.6. Signs of Nasakó, relatively more and less abstract. The two leftmost signs more representationally reference the palm and the serpent Ñangabión. The triangular bases reference the three founding stones and the three feet of Ekue (Cabrera 1975:223); the central sign is spare and abstract (Cabrera 1975:224); the rightmost emblem is specific to the original Nasakó of Bekura Mendo, the "sorcerer who consecrated the first potencia" (Cabrera 1975). This sign of Nasakó shows the vessel of the first *fundamento* made by him. Courtesy of the Estate of Lydia Cabrera.

four quadrants produced thereof is occupied by a dot, a tiny circle *(óvalo),* or a cross. Four dots—two over two—represent the "eyes" of Tanze over the eyes of Sikán (see Thompson 1983:249). *Óvalos* predominate among the Efó, and alternated crosses and *óvalos* distinguish Efí *anaforuana* (figure 4.3). Some early Efó lodges, including Andrés Petít's Awana Bakokó Efor, maintained the alternated *óvalo* and *cruz* pattern apparently to acknowledge their roots in Efik Buton (see figure 2.1, left and center). The basic figure of the cross within the circle generates an array of formal and semantic possibilities as it is reshaped, multiplied, shot through with arrows and sinuous lines, and refined with featherlike finials.

In its most literal and referential gloss, the basic sign positions Tanze within the gourd atop Sikán's head—two eyes over two eyes. The sign for Sikán, which revises the basic figure as a legible bottle gourd, may also include Obon Tanze himself with a realistic drawing of this odd fish with a tripartite tail (figure 4.4). Cabrera's sources make the foregoing references explicit. Upon Obon Tanze's death and Sikán's sacrifice, they told Cabrera, Nasakó "took [Sikán's] eyes—*okorio*—in order to accompany those of Tanze, [as] *symbols of the Society*" (Cabrera 1970:106–107, emphasis added).

The basic sign of the cross within a container (circle, square, or triangle) is more than an ideographic evocation of mythological and historical figures. *Anaforuana* are integral to performance. They are chalked at particular times and places so the brethren can invoke the spirits of Tanze and Sikán and an array of other forces—collectively, *ekue*—into presence for the ceremonial work at hand. The cross is said by Abakuá to represent the "Four Winds" *(los cuatro vientos),* that is, the four cardinal points.

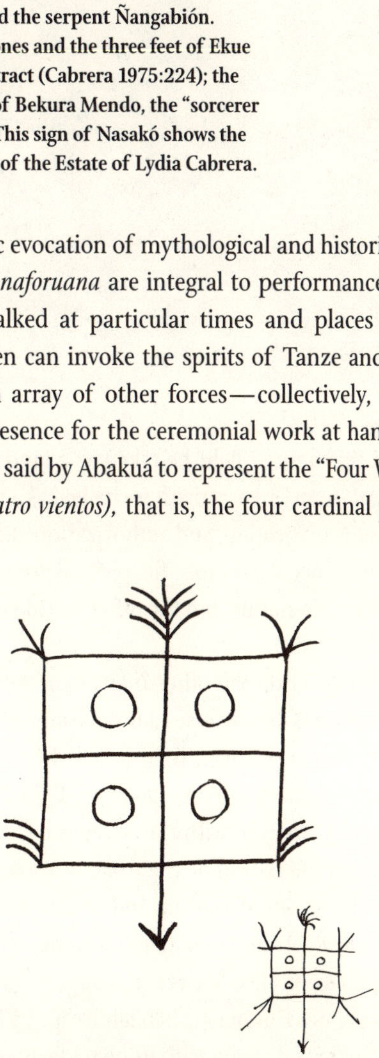

Figure 4.7. "Sign of the first Sanctuary": Kufón Abasí Fambá Nitangá (Cabrera 1975:122, fig. 46). The sign makes reference to the "Four Winds," to the space of the temple, to the palm tree (the vertical line), and to the eyes of Sikán and Tanze (the four circles). Courtesy of the Estate of Lydia Cabrera.

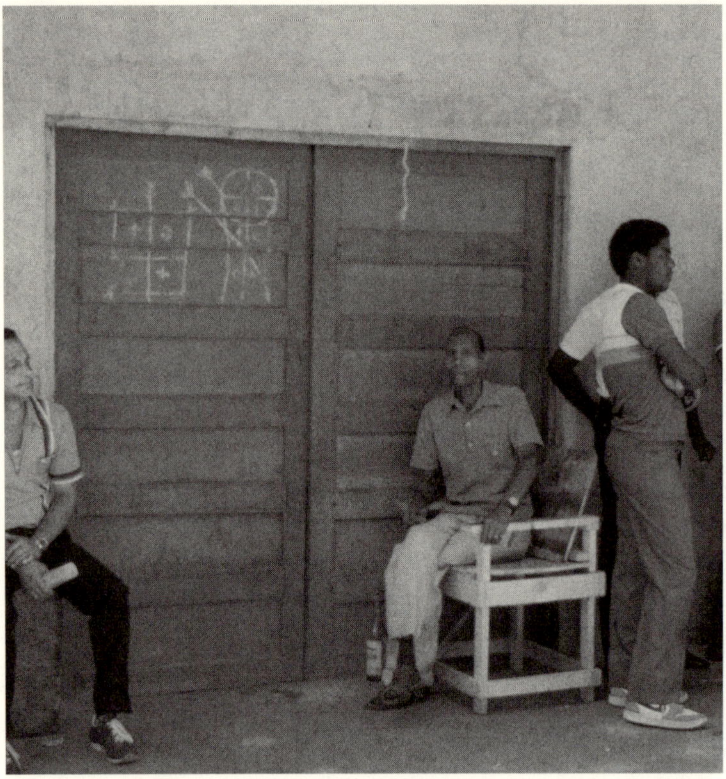

Figure 4.8. Doors to the *fambá* of the temple used by Havana *juego* Efí Embemoró for a ceremony in June 1986. The Efí sign of the sanctuary (note circles and crosses) is chalked on the left door, along with the sign of the ceremony, which refers to the three-footed Ekue drum. Photograph copyright © Annette Gilsdorf 1986; all rights reserved.

Though this figure might be taken as a kind of cosmological "map," in practice it is chalked as a point of orientation, invocation, and authorization; it actively draws and concentrates specific spiritual powers from their sources in nature and the other world (see Cabrera 1975:67–68).

Each lodge and each office *(plaza)* and ceremony within the Abakuá possesses a unique signature and prayer (*enkame;* see, e.g., figures 2.1, 4.5, and 4.6) (see, e.g., Cabrera 1970:350–374; 1975:91–300, 392–492). Moreover, with the advent of Efik Buton in 1836 and the spread of the Abakuá Society, each district of the city of Havana and outer municipalities such as Regla and Guanabacoa came to have its own sign. The Abakuá Society "remapped," or appropriated, greater Havana's urban landscape by inscribing each official division with its own ideographic toponyms (see figure 4.5 and superimposed maps 2.6 and 2.7; see also Brown 1989:41, 346; Brown 1999). That a specific sign marked each district and municipality suggests members' consciousness of an Abakuá *society* greater than the sum of its parts—the individual lodges and the *barrios* in which they were situated. Just as the chalked signs of individual lodge members were not merely identifiers but authorizations for specific ritual actions, the signs of lodges, districts, and municipalities may have had larger practical significance. In 1839, Margarito Blanco inscribed the sign of his *plaza,* (M)ocongo, on an official document next to his signature (Deschamps Chapeaux 1964:99). Mokongo's sign and the authorization it spiritually invokes predicates and confirms the identity of the individual, not the reverse. Similarly, the "taking out" of a new lodge has always required the explicit, written consent of the representatives of elder lodges, who have historically served on high commissions of Abakuá authorities. Lodge and district signs may have served to authorize "public" actions concerning more than one lodge, as well as serving as protective seals of specific urban terrains *(tierras),* which would be jealously defended vis-à-vis codes of respect, ritual practice and carnival partici-

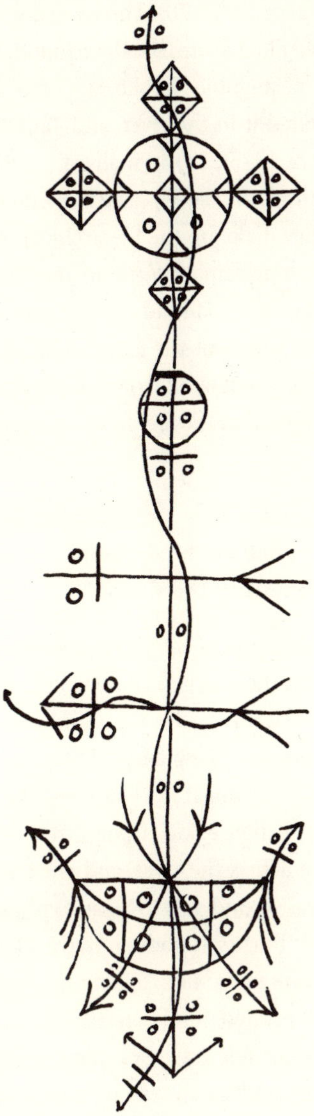

Figure 4.9. The *gandó* sign called Itiarongomenta. It is drawn across the floor of the *fambá* from its threshold to the curtained corner where Iyamba plays Ekue. It carries the "Voice" from nature to the drum. Cabrera 1975:128, fig. 51. Courtesy of the Estate of Lydia Cabrera.

pation, labor relationships and economic resources, and Abakuá judicial proceedings.[5] Within the terms of Abakuá mythico-historical and practical categories, how much difference was there between the specific location of Old Calabar's Usagaré precinct/lodge within the Awana Bekura Mendo territory and the location of the Ecoria Efó #1 or Efí Embemoró *tierras*/lodges within Havana's Third District in 1882? One major difference, of course, was that within the terms of official categories, Havana's district map also organized Trujillo y Monagas's police surveillance grid, used to monitor and destroy the Abakuá lodges within it (table 2.1; see Trujillo y Monagas 1882:370–372; Cabrera 1975:282–283). In a real sense, the colonial authorities found themselves party to an ideological and practical "struggle over possession of the sign," or flag, for that matter, with the Abakuá vis-à-vis the meanings and control of urban terrain.

Containers of Power and Vectors of Ekue: Anaforuana's Generative Elements

Embroidered in yellow silk thread on the Eforí Eñongo banner, the basic Sikán-Tanze/Four Winds signature expands to form twelve Efó *óvalos* within twelve squares, which, together constitute an apparent rectangle (plate 1). The sign is an ideographic coat-of-arms. Jesús Nasakó believes that the "twelve *óvalos* represent the twelve first *potencias* that were established in Regla."[6] For Juan Mokongo, whose father designed the banner in 1918, the multiple *óvalos* represent selected dramatis personae of the birth of the Abakuá, including Iyamba, Mokongo, Nasakó, Sikán, and Tanze; as a whole, the sign ideographically reiterates the lodge's name, which signifies powers of *brujería* ("witchcraft").[7]

However elaborated, Abakuá lodge signs tend to revolve around dominant container-like forms: circles, squares, triangles, gourds, schematic boats, drum bodies, thick animal horns, and combinations thereof. This is not surprising, since the building blocks of *anaforuana* often reference Sikán's gourd container, the Ekue drum, and the temple space (see figures 2.1 and 4.3–4.7; Cabrera 1975:334–376). In this sense, lodge signs might be read as references to ritualized vessels, such as Sikán's gourd or Nasakó's *mañongo umpabio*. These forms might also be read as markers of socialized space, for example, the ritual space of the lodge, its corporate group, and the force of *ekue* contained and manifested therein, not least within the *barrios* and wharves as historically influenced by specific Abakuá lodges. Indeed, the dominant form of Efori Eñongo's sign is not precisely a standing rectangle. The rounded corners of its base, when contrasted against the right angles of its upper corners, suggest the form as a vessel. Inasmuch as the lodge's name signifies the powers of *brujería*, the lodge's sign appears to reiterate the magical vessel form found in the emblem of the first Nasakó of Bekura Mendo, the "sorcerer" *(hechicero)* who "consecrated the first *potencia* and transmitted the Voice of Ekue to the skin of the goat" (see figure 4.6, right) (Cabrera 1975:90).

Two tall, vertical, downward-pointing arrows and three crossbars structure Efori Eñongo's grid, which is filled with *óvalos*. Sets of fringe add flourish to the upper corners and the lower sides, echoing the arrowlike feathers above, which rise like new growth or finials. Each of these elements is polyvocal. The tall arrows recall the erect trunk of the palm tree and its gently curving leaves, not to mention the feather-topped *güín* used to sound the Ekue drum. The fringes on the sign's border come in sets of three and seven, which echo each of the arrows' seven sprouts, while the rectangle itself is structured by three columns of four *óvalos*. Beyond palm leaves—which cast their shadow over *ekue*'s discovery—fringe can also reference the feathered plumes associated with Tanze's crest and Sikán's hair. Seven plumes can reference the "Seven Sons of Ekue," that is, the "Seven Heads" or "First Chiefs" *(Cabeceras* or *Jefes)*, whom Nangobié Nasakó consecrated in Awana Bekura Mendo. Each chief in turn represents one of the first "Seven Tribes" of the Efó in West Africa. Seven also references the "Seven Founders, [the] ancestors who are present in the seven feathered plumes"of the Abakuá altar. These are the seven top grades of the Abakuá: 1. Iyamba, 2. Mokongo, 3. Isué, 4. Isunekue, 5. Mpegó, 6. Ekueñón, 7. Nkríkamo (see plate 1; Cabrera 1970:145–146).[8] According to Cabrera's sources, three, as in three plumes or the quartered triangle, can refer to the concept of "beginnings" and "foundation": for example, the first three Abakuá lodges consecrated to the religion (Usagaré, Bakokó, and Eforisún; see Cabrera 1970:24–30; 1975:318; Sosa Rodríguez 1982:176). Three can also refer to the three-footed Ekue drum, the three foundation stones upon which Nangobié Nasakó supported Ekue when he consecrated it in the river, and Tanze's tripartite tail (Cabrera 1975:224).[9] Finally, though the numbers four, three, and seven have individual referents, together they make up the hierarchical constituents of the "seven principal" *plazas* of the "fundamental thirteen" required to found a lodge. The *sese* drum's four plumes represent the lodge's four *obones;* three additional single-plumed drums represent the three chiefs who follow in the hierarchy—seven grades altogether.

Nasakó's Signature, Ñangabión, and the Genesis of the *Gandó*

The basic elements of *anaforuana* would be incomplete without the charged sinuous line. Its most literal referent seems to be the rapidly moving amphibious serpent, Ñangabión. Entwined vertically about the palm, Ñangabión witnessed the capture of Tanze (plate 1, figure 3.8). Upon dropping from the tree, gliding across the river, and encircling Sikán's gourd, he was second only to Sikán as physically closest to Obon Tanze's sounding of the Divine Voice. Through contiguity, like Sikán, the serpent was thereby consecrated, made sacred. Like an electrical arc, the sinuous line traverses space, bridges events and domains and catalyzes *ekue*'s immediate presence in sacred sound. Three brief examples illustrate the operations of the sinuous line, and flesh out the foregoing discussions of how *anaforuana* evoke, and serve to invoke, powerful spiritual happenings, in particular, the sounding of *ekue*.

Ñangabión is the inseparable companion of Nasakó. Ñangabión's reptilian body, as entwined about the tree, appears in more or less abstracted form in the sorcerer Nasakó's *anaforuana*. The sorcerer's signs come as variations on the spiral-entwined vertical line, which recalls the universal symbol for medicine. Gently curving leaflike fringe surmounts the straight vertical, and one or both ends of the sinuous line is an arrow. Typically, the principal vertical line bisects a triangular base; the quadrants of the base, as well as the spaces created by the dance of sinuous and vertical lines, feature four *óvalos.* These forms also appear in more realistic representations as the Royal Palm entwined with the serpent atop a trapezoidal base (figure 4.6, left; see Cabrera 1975:224–228). A mid-twentieth-century informant's gloss of an abstract Nasakó sign (figure 4.6, center) highlights a critical combination of all the basic elements discussed so far: "The vertical line is the sacred tree, the palm of the consecration." The "undulating line," representing a subclass of *anaforuana,* is called *gandó sambaka.* The *gandó* "winds about the [straight vertical], and represents the serpent belonging to Nasakó." At the top extreme of the serpent, three little branches symbolize three of the first Efor lodges consecrated by Nasakó. The sign at the lower end of the serpent represents "the first Obonekue [initiate], who was the woman Sikán herself—consecrated by the first sound uttered by the supernatural Fish within the gourd she had carried on her head." The three *óvalos* "in the last curve of the serpent are the three stones over which Nasakó placed Ekue in the river" during his efforts to consecrate the drum. "The triangle at the base of the emblem represents the [three-footed] Ekue, the Mystery, and the great power that the Efor tribe took possession of." The four *óvalos* within the triangle, and between the undulating *gandó* and the vertical line "are the eyes of Tanze and Sikán that Nasakó put over the drumskin of Ekue in order to carry out the magical operations [necessary to] attract their spirits to the drum" (Cabrera 1975:224).

In short, in the drawn sign of Nasakó, the serpentine *gandó* unifies and activates a critical mass of actors and events in the realization of Ekue as an enduring *fundamento,* the possession of which projects "great power." These actors and events include the first sounding of the fish in the shadow of the palm and in contact with Ñangabión; Sikán's "initiation" as she raised the gourd to her head and through her the subsequent sacrifice; and the ritual use of Sikán's blood and bones, along with the skin of the fish, in order to consecrate the *fundamento* of Ekue over three foundational river stones. In turn, the first consecration and empowerment of three Efó "tribes" was enabled. In this sense, Nasakó's sign assembles, connects, and activates the ritual hardware and software of *ekue,* the components of which are drawn from nature and carefully guarded within the Abakuá sanctuary *(fambá)* and its inner sanctum of the Ekue drum, called *iriongo* or *fo-ekue.*

The "First Sanctuary" and the "Second Sanctuary"

The strong vertical line, or "palm tree" surmounted by "leaves," also appears prominently in the container-like signature of the *fambá* itself. Called by Cabrera's sources *kufón Abasí fambá nitangá,* the sign is chalked directly on the temple's door. It is the "sign of the sanctuary." In preparation for Abakuá ceremonies, which are called *plantes,* a second sign is chalked next to it. Appropriately, this second sign references the tapered cylindrical shape and flaring tripartite feet of the Ekue drum, which is guarded inside the temple (figures 4.7–4.8). In the *kufón Abasí fambá nitangá,* the "palm" bisects a quartered square, the quadrants of which bear the eyes of Tanze over Sikán. Cabrera learned that the "square with the circles of Efor *represents the temple* with its 'Four Winds' or corners. In the center [is] the palm of the consecration . . . *which was the first sanctuary, Fambá Nitangá*" (Cabrera 1975:122, emphasis added). In other words, in Cabrera's reading, the enclosed physical space of the Abakuá temple, typically a square building or covered room set within a walled compound, is the "second sanctuary." It reconstitutes in masonry and tile the "first sanctuary" in which the Voice first sounded within the shadow of the Palm (Cabrera 1975:75–76, 122). As the palm, its shadow, and the river formed a veritable crossroads of orientation and spiritual container, so does the temple room. Still, the chalking of *kufón Abasí fambá nitangá* on the door does merely illustrate the formal correspondence of the Ur-sanctuary and its typological second sanctuary; it actively *constitutes* the second as the first by invoking and reiterating the force of the past in relation to the specific intentionalities of the present.

The signs of Nasakó, the sanctuary, and the *plante* evoke and help to invoke the presences more realistically limned in the embroidered banner. In this sense, the banner lends a self-reflexive dimension to the altar. The banner evokes the originary scene of *ekue*'s advent and iconographically marks the "second sanctuary" space as a typological reproduction of the "first sanctuary." The altar objects themselves, as well as the Ekue drum, of course, are enduring material embodiments of actors and events related to the "first sanctuary." The realistic banner image describes and narrates what the altar does. Conceptually, the banner's image becomes a powerful chronotope—a spatio-temporal figure that condenses epochal time and transatlantic space, as it predicates the present as the past and the past as the present. Given that the "first sanctuary" was in "Africa," the banner, the sign of the temple, the physical temple, the altar, the compound and its sacred foliage (including palm and *ceiba*), constitute the *habitus,* or practical embodiment of the Abakuá diasporic imagination in Cuba.[10]

As Leib and Romano astutely noted in their visit to an Ejagham village, the temple of the Ngbe society, called *ekat,* is the symbolic counterpart or double of nature, in particular, as the space was charged with the spiritual power of the "secret." The direction of their interpretation might be equally applicable to the Afro-Cuban "second sanctuary": "the *ekat,* the secret recesses of the Ngbe lodge, reproduces the natural domain of the leopard in the forest within the confines of the lodge. Secrets learned during initiations in the bush have their material and ideographic representations concealed in the *ekat.* It is here that the leopard spirit is kept in captivity with a 'chain around (his) neck to lock him [up] while sleeping.' The leopard spirit emerges from the *ekat,* where he has been ritually prepared, passing under the starch-resist, blue-and-white dyed *ukara* cloth to the sounds of the Ngbe voice. Numerous *nsibidi* signs on the [*ukara*] cloth depict what is to be found in the secret chamber, among them the pictographic symbols learned during initiation" (Leib and Romano 1984:54).

In the case of the Abakuá sanctuary, as the banner conveys, "a river runs through it," to borrow the title of Norman Maclean's novel. There, river meets palm as Iyamba sounds the Ekue drum with his *güín.* As Leib and Romano's interpretation suggests, the physical temple is a demarcated shadow space, which has been domesticated within human settlement and its governing institutions. Via the space of the temple, the *potencia,* officers, sacrifices of *mbori,* and initiations of *obonekues, ekue* maintains its relationship to this world. Still, the symbolic conditions for *ekue*'s explicit manifestation must be actively prepared and "fabricated" each time through ritual performances.

The Temple, Ekueñón's "Search for the Voice," and the *Gandó*

The temple's guarded door is the threshold between the second sanctuary and the charged ecology of the first sanctuary (figure 4.8). Something must be *done* in order to connect them, make them one. Not least, just as more than Obon Tanze's roar by the river was required to possess the means to produce the Voice artificially, ritual work is required to sound it once again. In the first case, Ekueñón executed Sikán; Nasakó "called" the spirits of fish and woman to a drum made of wood. In the second case, the critical work of Ekueñón and Nasakó, among other *plazas,* is required to enable the Abakuá *plante.* Nasakó prepares the herbal *wemba* and *mokuba* concoctions of spiritual cleansing and the physical incorporation of *ekue,* respectively. The lodge's dignitaries must "fabricate" the altar and insert the seven *plumeros* into its drums while verbally invoking the presences of the Seven Founders in prayer.

As a prerequisite to the sounding of the Ekue drum and the commencement of the *plante,* the hunter Ekueñón leads a procession of officers from the temple to "search for the Voice" of *ekue* in the "forest" *(la búsqueda de la Voz).* Along with the Mokongo,

Mpegó, Enkríkamo, and others, Ekueñón "conjures the spirits of the other world until the Voice is attracted from [Sikán's possession]. . . . Ekueñón transports the Voice of *ekue* in his drum, enters the [sanctuary] . . . and transfers the Voice from his drum to Ekue" (Moliner Castañeda 1988:17). Only then can Iyamba, hidden with the friction drum behind a curtain in the *fo-ekue,* sound the Voice.

The undulating line, the serpentine vehicle of spiritual invocation and transmission, appears once again in a specific *gandó,* sometimes called Itiarongomenta. This complex sign is formed by the undulating line wound over a straight, very long central arrow (figure 4.9). Itiarongomenta reiterates Ekueñón's journey and connects the poles of "forest" and "sanctuary," thereby hard wiring, as it were, the Ekue drum. Itiarongomenta, chalked on the ground, begins at the temple's threshold to the outside, shoots across the floor, and terminates in the curtained *fo-ekue,* where Iyamba manipulates the friction drum with his *güín.* Itiarongomenta is a composite sign that conjoins significant spaces and inscribes temporality, key episodes, authorizing personages, and spiritual unfolding. It begins with the sign of Sikán's execution (a gourdlike crescent figure crosscut by arrows and punctuated with *óvalos*). It proceeds through the sign of *ekue*'s consecrator, Nasakó, and continues through Sikán's executioner, Ekueñón. Along the way, it marks the presence of Mokongo, the authorizer of Sikán's sacrifice, and it ends in an elaborate quartered circle chalked directly beneath the Ekue drum itself. Itiarongomenta, explains Cabrera, is the (magical . . . *gandó* for the manifestation of the Divine Voice. The Spirit accedes, through the medium of the . . . rituals, through the central line to the sacred Drum [Ekue], and is installed in [its] skin *(parche);* (Cabrera 1975:127–132, 143; see Sosa Rodríguez 1982:226; Ortiz 1955:229–237).

In the *plante*'s sequence of preparatory events, the inscription of this *gandó* is followed by Ekueñón's chanted *rompimiento*—the "breaking open" of the path. The Congo hunter, Ekueñón, stands just outside the door to the temple with his plumed drum. He calls all present to attention with a ritualized tap of his drum: *tan, tan, TA-TAN,* and chants a dramatic prayer of opening, the *enkame de rompimiento.*

> *Jeyeí bariba bacongo!*
> *Jeyeí bariba bacongo!*
> *Osoiro encaño suabasí* (Chorus: *yayó!*)
> *Osoiro encaño suabasí* (Chorus: *yayó!*)
> *Usoiró crucoro indiobón obonécue orominãn*
> *Sancantión manantión ara asere banurán*
> *entión en bariye chene pon cheneneri otrogofocó*
> *Macuairén asucuaracuantiyén un barino abasí*
> *abome* . . . etc.[11]

During Ekueñón's *enkame,* Iyamba begins to rev up Ekue *(vrrrrrrrrrrr . . . vrrrrrrrrrrrr . . . vrrrrrrrrrrr)* from within the temple. In great anticipation, the *íreme* Eribangandó, standing within the temple, rhythmically rotates his hips, sounding the cowbells belted around his waist *(enkaniká).* In so doing, he "expresses joy" at the imminent revelation of the Voice.[12] Suddenly, right at the end of Ekueñón's *enkame,* a spectacular flash of gunpowder ignites at the threshold of the temple, illuminating the blue pall of twilight just before sunrise. Immediately Ekue commences in earnest its bellowing, otherworldly roar. The Voice reverberates within the temple walls, and radiates outward, filling the courtyard and neighborhood with its mysterious sound. With the great flash and Ekue's roar, the Abakuá orchestra, accompanied by *íremes,* "comes out" *(salir)* in procession onto the semipublic *patio,* makes a brief appearance on the street outside the walls, and then returns, wherein the *ekobios* ("brothers") sing in call-and-response fashion and the *íremes* dance (plate 5).[13] Ekue continues to sound all day, as other ceremonial phases proceed, including the felling of the goat *(mbori)* by the "twin" *íremes,* Aberisún and Aberiñán, the initiation of new members, the cleansing of participants by *íreme* Eribangandó with his rooster, and the preparing of a communal meal by the *plaza* called Ecandemo at the termination of the *plante* (see Ortiz 1955:218–235; Cabrera 1975:15–65).

5 Altars, Offices, and Multiple Meanings

Juan Mokongo regularly walked the hilly mile from his old house in one of Regla's *barrios abakuá* to the temple of *juego* Irionda at 2:00 in the morning. Juan's Efori Eñongo, along with Eforikamá, another "mixed" *juego* in the *rama* of Akanarán Efó #1, have used the Irionda compound for many years. Irionda, walled in by rusting corrugated steel, sits on a rise at the rim of the town, overlooking the vast shipping and industrial complexes in the reclaimed lowlands that now separate Regla from the southeastern rim of Havana Bay (map 2.4, right). In the two or three hours before Ekueñón's *rompimiento* at the temple's door, the old men of Efori Eñongo would "fabricate" the altar in preparation for the *plante.*

On a hot afternoon in July 1992, Juan removed each altar object from a large cedar chest.[1] He spread a white cloth over the top surface and then tacked the blue velvet banner across the front. He carefully removed the urnlike *sese* drum from its protective five-gallon metal can and placed it front and center atop the white surface. He securely inserted each of its four *plumeros* into their marked slots around the chromed crown: Iyamba, Mokongo, Isué, and Isunekue. He then unpacked and inserted the impressive staffs *(bastones)* into a tiered wood stand *(bastonera)* that he had placed against the altar's back wall: Iyamba on the far left; Mokongo on the far right; Mosongo and Abasonga in the middle. The *bastonera* is painted bright red. Its front face bears a delicately painted set of radiations in gold leaf. The carved, foot-tall statue and crucifix of Christ on the Cross is placed at the center of the *bastonera*'s highest tier.[2] It stands directly behind the *sese.* In its most general symbolic role, the Christ statue represents Abasí, the Abakuá "Supreme God" (see Cabrera 1988:18). Next to the *sese,* Juan placed the lodge's antique Jesuit brass monstrance. The drums of Mpegó, Ekueñón, and Enkríkamo followed: Mpegó on the right corner, Ekueñón on the left corner, and Enkríkamo just to the left of Mpegó. Juan carefully inserted each of their *plumeros* in the same order. Fabricated as such, the altar radiates energy. As seen frontally, it is bilaterally symmetrical. A dense constellation of attributes in many media, colors, and textures centers on the soaring *sese.* The four staffs also dramatically angle upward and outward, echoing the gold radiations painted on the *bastonera* and the symbolic emanations of divine light from the crucifix and the monstrance (plate 1).

Juan's arrangement took place in the living room of his home, where he stored the objects on the lodge's behalf. In an actual fabrication in preparation for a *plante,* formal arrangement of the objects is inseparable from the invocation of their power. First, Mpegó would mark each object with the basic invocatory quartered circle and four *óvalos* in yellow or white chalk *(ngomo)*—yellow for ordinary ceremonies and initiations, white for funerary ceremonies. Mpegó is the Abakuá officer of "Order." Each action in the fabrication would be accompanied by a chant of "authorization" *(enkame),* uttered by the officer responsible for each action. For example, because each *plumero* represents the presence of its corresponding ancestral chief, its insertion is accompanied by an *enkame* of invocation and authorization. The ceremony, one of many preparatory steps, is called the "authorization of the *plumeros*" *(autorización de los plumeros).* The *plumeros* are initially laid obliquely across their respective drumheads. Nasakó "washes" each of them, using a basil branch wetted with the purifying herbal infusion, called *wemba;* he fumigates them with cigar and incense smoke; and they are sprayed with *aguardiente* and *vino seco* (cane rum and dry cooking wine). Meanwhile, the chanted *enkame* prayers of the *plumeros* are intended to "call the spirit to them."[3] In order of seniority, each officer chants his own *enkame* and inserts his *plumero* into the drum that represents his office within the lodge: Iyamba, Mokongo, Isué, and Isunekue atop the *sese,* and Mpegó, Ekueñón, and Enkríkamo atop their respective drums.

Arranged about the elevated altar, the grouping of objects organizes and displays the consecrated attributes of the seven Abakuá highest grades *(plazas),* plus those of three additional *plazas:* Abasí (Christ statue), Mosongo (staff), and Abasonga (staff). These "attributes," or *piezas,* along with the three-footed Ekue drum, which resides in the guarded *fo-ekue,* as well as some of the masquerade costumes *(sacos)* of the numerous *íremes,* embody the collective *potencia* of the lodge. *Potencia,* literally "potency," might be defined as the spiritual power of *ekue:* tapped, materialized, contained, guarded, and prepared for transformative practice within the hierarchical corporation of the individual Abakuá lodge.

The Altar, the *Potencia,* and the "Collective Pact"

The objects of the *potencia* are produced months in advance of the "birth" *(nacimiento)* of a new lodge. They are produced by a single artist or a series of them. Typically, a principal artist is commissioned, though he may contract out specialty tasks, such as lathe turning, metalwork, and the construction of the *plumeros.* Often the wives or female relatives of *plazas* or members sew the *íreme* costumes. For nearly two decades, a single artist in Regla has produced or repaired a large proportion of lodge objects in the country. He is a master craftsman, specializing in skin, cloth, and bead adornment; his work can be expensive, and sometimes prohibitive to impoverished lodges, which must rely on the ad hoc talents of members, who may or may not be skilled in the trades.

A new lodge is "born," or "taken out" *(sacado),* from an extant sponsor lodge—its "godfather" *(padrino)*—just as Bakokó and Eforisún were born from Usagaré Nandió in Awana Bekura Mendo. The new objects are consecrated during extensive ceremonies intended to transfer *ekue* to them from the objects of the elder, sponsoring lodge. These ceremonies are carried out by the officers of the elder lodge. At the culmination of the ceremonies, according to Jesús Nasakó, "the old attribute is put on top of the new one, or next to it, and then they [both] are placed atop the *fundamento* [the Ekue drum]; the *fundamento* transmits to them the sound of life, *ekue.*" By this means, "the *grácia* [spiritual power] of the old attributes is 'transmitted' to the new ones. . . . Each [old] attribute gives birth to the other [new] one, and [thus] is born the new *potencia.*" For example, the staff of the extant, elder Mokongo gives birth to the new Mokongo staff; Ekueñón's plumed drum gives birth to the new Ekueñón drum, and so on. Lodge-founding consecrations, called *baroko fundamento,* are oriented around a large, circular ground design, sometimes called *orunakuá abasí rirí.* The complex chalk drawing consists of the signs representing each of the top thirteen *plazas* that are required to found a lodge. Each pair of attributes, old and new, are placed atop their respective invocatory signs (see also Cabrera 1975:133–136).[4]

Abakuá initiation draws on the metaphors of "birth," spiritual descent, and "sponsorship" *(apadrinación)* found in the other Afro-Cuban ritual systems (Santería, Ifá, Palo Monte, Kimbisa, and Arará). Genealogically, each new lodge forms another shoot on the "branch" *(rama)* to which the senior sponsoring lodge belongs. The sponsoring lodge is the "godfather" of the new "godchild" (Sp. *padrino* and *ahijado*). For example, Awana Bakokó Efor, of the Efó *rama,* gave birth to Akanarán Efó Ocobio Mukarará (1863), which gave birth to Abakuá Efó (1875), which gave birth to Efori Eñongo (1916). However, unlike the other ritual systems, the birth of a new lodge is not entirely an individual affair. One Abakuá member does not a lodge make. The birth of a new lodge is a "collective pact" or "oath" *(pacto colectivo* or *juramento).* Once the *potencia*—the sacred attributes of thirteen *plazas*—has been consecrated, the candidates for the new lodge's hierarchy are sworn during a single complex ceremony wherein they accept the attributes of their office.

Though some Abakuá initiatory steps appear to be patterned after aspects of Yoruba-Lucumí initiation, membership is constituted more by the moral, juridical, and social terms of "pact" and "oath" than by the kind of spiritual embodiment that characterizes the *kariocha* ceremony of Santería. True, members undergo an Abakuá "consecration" or "baptism" that utilizes pan-Afro-Cuban religious media and methods, but these men are "sworn" as occupants of an office *(plaza)* or as part of the rank and file (the *obonekues*). Their *juramento* (swearing-in) does not make them priests of a deity, but endows them with the faculty and capacity *(facultad* and *capacidad)* to act authoritatively, responsibly, and efficaciously within the office or as a rank-and-file member.[5]

Though the terms *juego* (corporate group), *tierra* (land, homeland, terrain, compound), and *potencia* (power, potency) are often used interchangeably, the particular referents and connotations of *potencia* are clear to learned Abakuá. Jesús Nasakó explains that "the *potencia is* the attribute [*pieza*], because men go on dying and being born. The *piezas* last always. Men pass through the Abakuá. The Abakuá [Society] endures."[6] Unlike the other Afro-Cuban ritual systems, initiates do not receive and own their personal set of consecrated attributes, such as the multiple porcelain soup tureens *(soperas)* of Santería (see Brown 1993b). Each newly initiated *plaza* holder, or, for example, a replacement following the death of a Mokongo or Iyamba, inherits the original attribute (e.g., of Mokongo or Iyamba) fabricated when the lodge was born. Each of these objects, integral components of the *potencia,* embodies an ancestral office; the candidate is "sworn" *(jurado)* to, and to uphold, the office, receiving its appropriate attribute as an emblem of his authority to act on behalf of the Abakuá Society, the *rama,* and the *juego.* Jesús Nasakó elaborates that each staff or plumed drum, "represents the spirit of the deceased [for example] the first *Iyamba* that lived. The staffs are symbols, just as the *plumeros* are, of the spirits of the first *plazas,* or the First Chiefs of the Abakuá in Africa. This is their meaning."[7]

The *Plazas* and Their Attributes

Seven of the thirteen Abakuá *plazas* are the "chiefly" offices, which are ascendant among the thirteen "fundamental" grades. As Jesús Nasakó encapsulates this organizational principle, there are *siete principales, trece fundamentales:* seven principal, thirteen fundamental, grades. At the same time, the highest four *plazas* within the top seven are considered "kings," *obones* among the *principales.* As many as twelve to twenty additional *plazas* follow the fundamental thirteen. After the "founding" collective pact[8] *(baroko fundamental),* the next twelve to twenty *plazas* are initiated individually, or in small groups, over time, in ceremonies called *baroko normal.*[9]

Nine of the thirteen fundamental *plazas* are represented by altar drums, *plumeros,* and/or staffs, which, together with Ekue and the masquerade costumes, make up the *potencia.* The top four "kings" or *obones,* Iyamba, Mokongo, Isué, and Isunekue, own *plumeros,* which rise from the *sese* drum. Isué is the special custodian of the *sese,* while Iyamba is the principal authority over the Ekue drum, though they, and the other top *plazas,* have one or more assistants (see table 5.1). Three *plazas* possess squat, tapered altar drums; each carries its own *plumero* marking its owner's "chiefly status": Mpegó (The Law), Ekueñón (Hunter and Executioner), and Nkríkamo (Chief of the Íremes). Iyamba and Mokongo among the top four, and Mosongo and Abasonga, who list among the fundamental thirteen, have staffs. Finally, at least thirteen *plazas* perform their major duties dressed in *íreme* masquerade costumes, three of which rank among the top thirteen fundamental grades: Eribangandó, Enkóboro, and Enkanima. Other *plazas* include the Moruá Yuansá, who carries a cruciform rattle *(erikundé)* to communicate with the *íremes,* and the *Abasí,* who leads Abakuá processions with the statue of Christ, often placed atop his head (figure 5.1).

Meanwhile, the lodge's rank and file, the *obonekues* (alt. *abanekues*), is augmented by periodic initiations of perhaps three to six individuals. Yet, along with the collective initiation of the first thirteen fundamental *plazas,* a single, "first" *obonekue* must be initiated to lead and inspire the rest. This "first son" *(primer hijo)* of the new *potencia,* though not technically a *plaza,* functions like one. The first "son" of Ekue has as much value as the other thirteen *plazas,* because he was born in the *baroko fundamento.* . . . He is called the *obón-obonekue,* "the king of the *obonekues.*"[10] During the colonial period, he was also called the Capitán Obonekue (Rodríguez 1881). As such, the *obón-obonekue* retains the right to occupy whatever *plaza* becomes vacant through the death or absence of its officeholder.

The only *plaza* within the fundamental thirteen that does not have attributes represented in the altar or in the *íreme* costumes is Nasakó. He is an exceptional case among the hierarchy and membership of the Abakuá Society. Often ranked among the fundamental *plazas,* the Nasakó is the only officer who is not sworn into the Abakuá lodge through the same initiation ceremonies as the other *plazas.* Nasakó is considered a Congo sorcerer, a *brujo.* He is specially consecrated in a formal ceremony and conducts much of the lodge's most critical ritual work, but technically he is separate from the *baroko fundamento.* His "attributes," the *mañongo umpabio* and divining equipment, correspondingly, are identified with the "Congo" nation, not the "Carabalí." Indeed, his ritual toolkit, along with his herbal *wemba* and *mokuba* liquids, are analogous in form and substance to the ritual media of the Palo Monte priest *(palero, mayombero, ngangulero),* which, in effect, he is. In 2000, for example, Jesús took on the *plaza* of Nasakó to replace a deceased Nasakó. He was chosen for the office precisely because of his extraordinary capacity as a Tata Nkisi of the Regla Kimbisa, a religion similar to Palo Monte that revolves around the use of the *nganga* or *nkisi* and the mirror-embedded *mpaka* divining horn.

As in the case of Jesús Nasakó, and in the case of Juan Mokongo's son following Juan's death, if a *plaza* occupant dies, his office may be filled through the elevation of a lodge *obonekue.* Another common way that *obonekues* become *plazas* is when new lodges are born. *Obonekues* and *plazas* from an extant lodge may choose to go independent and "take out" a new lodge, usually elevating themselves to higher or different *plazas* in the process. Thus, one may be sworn into more than one lodge over time at different levels. For example, Quirino Valdés began as an *obonekue* of Akanarán Efó #1 after 1863 and went on to found and become the Abasonga of Regla's Abakuá Efó #1 (1874). Valdés's *ekobio,* Juan Gutiérrez Montojo, began as the *íreme* Aberiñán grade of Abakuá Efó #1

Table 5.1

The Abakua Hierarchy of *Plazas*

The Top Thirteen Grades (4 + 3 + 6)

The Four First: The Obones

Iyamba	"Highest King"; sounds the Ekue drum (*bongó* in Efí), carries an *itón* (staff)
Mokongo	"Supreme Chief," "Military Chief"; sometimes the "Father of Sikán"; carries *itón*
Isué	"The Bishop"; Custodian of the *sese/seseribó* plumed drum
Isunekue	"Husband of Sikán," "Owner of the Parche" (drumskin)

Three That Complete the First Seven "Principals"

Mpegó	"The Law," "The Scribe"; owns Mpegó drum and the sacred *ngomo* (chalk)
Ekueñóñ	"Hunter," "Executioner," "Guardian of Ekue"; owns the Ekueñóñ plumed drum, "searches for the voice"; "breaks" open the path for the ceremonies in his *enkame* prayer of the *rompimiento*
Enkríkamo	"Chief of the Íremes"; owns the Enkríkamo plumed drum, which commands the *íremes*; guards the *fambá* (temple)

The Six That Complete the Thirteen "Fundamentals"

Mosongo	"Owner of Heads" (i.e., all Abakuá initiates), "Father of the Religion"; guardian of the *güín/yín* (palm ribs that sound Ekue), which he stores inside his *itón*
Abasonga	"Religion, Justice, Order"; helper of Iyamba and Mosongo, carries the *ekue* secret across the Oddán River from the Efó to the Efí; carries *itón*
Enkóboro	*Íreme,* master of initiations; helper of Isué, never leaves the temple
Eribangandó	*Íreme;* with the river as his origin, he is master of cleansings
Enkanima	*Íreme,* master of the forest; *íreme* of prayers and cleansings
Nasakó	"Sorcerer" (*brujo*), "Ritual Doctor," creator of the *fundamentos* (the Ekue and *sese* drums), the sacred herbal fluids used in all consecrations *(wemba, mokuba),* and the secret *carga* of Ekue

The Next Twelve *Plazas* That Make up Twenty-Five

Emboko	*Íreme,* "Guardian of the Offerings," and delivers them to the *obones* (high chiefs) when required; "mboko" can refer to "sugarcane," which is one of the ingredients of Nasakó's *mokuba,* and the sugarcane can be used as a rod to punish delinquents
Embakará	*Íreme;* For some, he is the son of Isué, whom he helps care for the *plumeros* (feathered plumes from the rooster) of the *sese.* He is also the custodian of the victim of the sacrifice bound to a palm or ceiba (i.e., archetypally, Sikán, herself, or Sikán's substitute, *mbori* the goat)
Anamanguí	*Íreme;* He is "The Dead that carries the Dead"; plays significant role in funerary ceremonies (*llantos*)
Ekoumbre	*Íreme,* helper of Nasakó
Moruá Yuansá	Represents his "nation" before the music. "Enchanter of the Íremes," singer, carries the *erikundé,* a cruciform rattle with which he communicates with the *íremes*
Aberisún and Aberiñán	*Íremes,* "The Twins," responsible for preparing and enacting the public sacrifice of the goat by immobilizing him and knocking him out with a blunt rod; thus, they are "Íremes of the Festival"
Kundiabón	*Íreme;* helper of Mokongo; cares for ritual tributes, and carries out the functions of treasurer; he collects and administers the funds of the society
Ibandí	*Íreme;* deals with sacrificial practices and offerings
Enkandemo	*Íreme;* "El Cocinero," responsible for preparing the open fire and cooking the sacrifices and food for the ceremony *(plante)*
Koifán	*Íreme;* "The "Sweeper," he cleans off the dining table and cleans the temple at ceremonies; he "sweeps out" all bad influences to the outside
Abasí	Represents the "Supreme Being," Abasí is represented by the crucifix bearing the "Sad" or "Dead" Christ
Moni-Fambá	also Famballín; *íreme* who guards the door to the *fambá*

Table 5.1 *Continued*

Other *Plazas* That Not All Lodges Have	
Moni-Bonkó	"Chief of the Drummers" and the music
Sikán	Sometimes represented by a postmenopausal woman and sometimes a cross-dressing man, who carries the lidded clay *tinaja* water vessel or gourd in which Sikán captured Tanze
Akuaramina	*Íreme;* represents the spirit of Sikán; distinguished by its helmetlike, inverted calabash headpiece bearing four white *plumeros;* an extinct mask
Embema	*Íreme;* considered a kind of grotesque, or "monster" figure; an *íreme* of special festivals, particularly funerals; an extinct mask
Efimeremo Moko	*Íreme;* "Prince of the Dancers"
Moruá Ngomo	Helps Mpegó with the chalk and drawn signs *(anaforuana, gandó)*
A Special Class of Lodge Member	
Obón-Obonekue	The first initiate (*obonekue*) of any lodge, considered a de facto *plaza;* the captain of all the other initiates; one first initiate is consecrated in the *baroko fundamento,* the ceremony that founds the lodge, after the first thirteen officers; he leads and inspires the other *obonekues* subsequently initiated

Sources: Sosa Rodríguez 1982; Moliner Castañeda 1988; Jesús Nasakó, Juan Mokongo 1992–2000

(founded 1875) and later founded Efori Eñongo in 1916, becoming its Isué. Chuchú Capáz began as an *obonekue* of Abakuá Efó #1 and went on to become the Iyamba of Regla's Enyegueyé in 1909 (table 2.3). Jesús, unlike some Nasakós, was already sworn as an *obonekue* of Efori Eñongo when he took on the *plaza* of Nasakó. In 2002, Jesús will advance in the new lodge from *obonekue* and Nasakó to the *plaza* of Iyamba, and his close *obonekue* and *plaza* confidants will advance to other *plazas.*

Renovations of Efori Eñongo's Altar Objects

One day in late 1979, Jesús Nasakó, a highly motivated, learned, and creative member of Efori Eñongo walked two dusty miles from the lodge's home in Regla to Guanabacoa to borrow a car. He drove back to Regla to the house of an Efori Eñongo member who had temporarily stored but then abandoned the lodge's objects when he split with his wife. The objects, which had been owned and celebrated with great pride for sixty-three years, languished in the house for much of the 1970s without regular use or care. Jesús prevailed upon the woman to turn the objects over to him. He loaded the old car with dented cans and tattered boxes and returned home. "When I opened them in my house, they were filled with bugs. I removed the damaged parts and washed the objects. I began to accumulate shells, beads, and adornments—in sum, everything that you see today, including the leopard skin, which I came across and stashed away. From that point, and for a year, I dedicated myself to giving the pieces the new design they have."[11]

Periodically, a lodge, or, in this case, a solitary member, chooses to refurbish *(renovar)* the objects of its *potencia* for restorative or aesthetic reasons. Over time, the objects suffer from their conditions of handling and storage. During *plantes,* the objects are displayed upon altars, where they are sprayed with liquids (e.g., *wemba, aguardiente,* and *vino seco*) and smoke (cigars and incense), and marked with chalk. They are held and danced in processions. During *barokos* they stand atop one another. Stored in humid tropical conditions in cans and crates, their cloth, wood, and feathers are destroyed by insects, mold, and water damage. It has not been uncommon for the emblems to remain in storage for long periods without ceremony, cleaning, or renovation. Many lodges were destroyed or forced deep underground between 1875 and the 1920s; if their objects were not confiscated by the police, they were hidden for long periods.

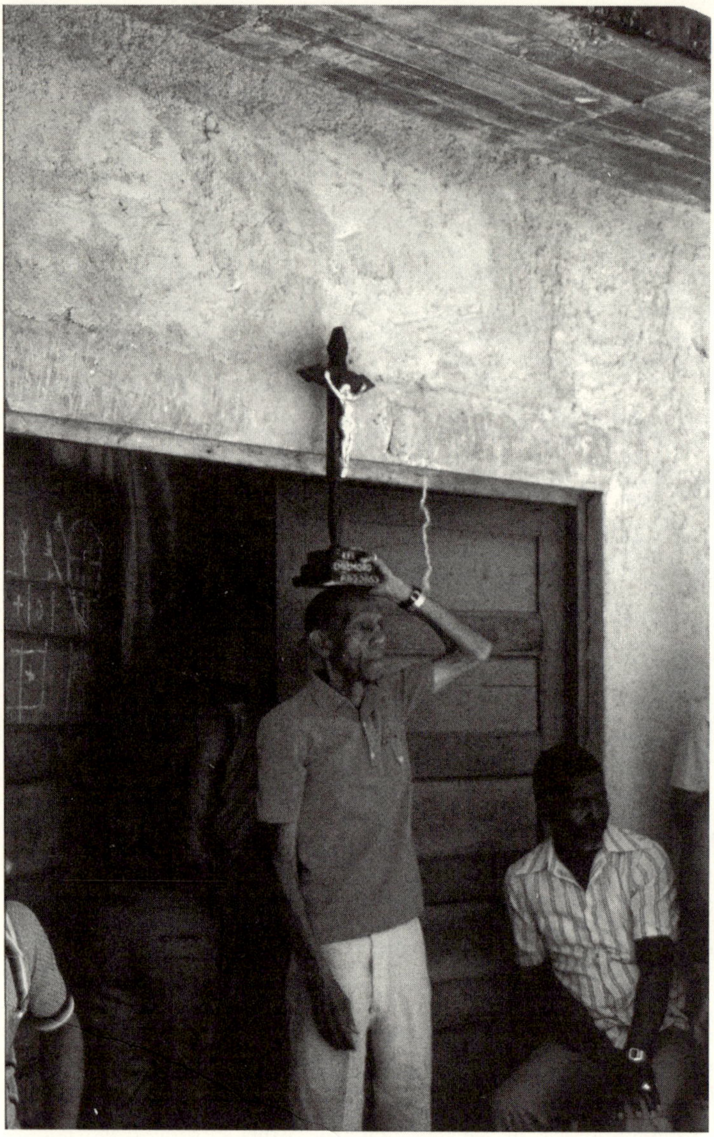

Figure 5.1. The *plaza* of Abasí of Efí Embemoró emerging from the *fambá* at the head of a procession, bearing the crucifix of Christ on his head. Abasí is considered the Abakuá "High God" in Cuba. Just inside the heavily guarded double door the satin curtain, a second barrier to ingress, is visible. Photography copyright © Annette Gilsdorf 1986; all rights reserved.

More recently, many lodges lost *plazas* and members in the second two exoduses from Cuba (1965–73, 1980). Though substitutions could be made, there were not always enough members, or members in agreement, in order to fulfill obligations. Police restrictions up through the first three decades of the Revolution often made ceremonies difficult to carry out, and economic austerity, particularly during Cuba's "Special Period" (1991–97), made renovation difficult for lack of resources. For example, as Jesús Nasakó relates, during the late 1960s and early 1970s, Eforí Eñongo of Regla experienced "shifts" and "misunderstandings" among the leadership. It was a "transitional period," because some members had died and others had migrated to the United States.[12] For a time, the rest of the members were powerless to resolve the situation. Meanwhile the altar objects languished.

By 1979, Jesús Nasakó was exceptionally equipped to take on the task of renovating the lodge's altar objects. His sketch of his artistic experience and the setting of his work illuminates the ways that some Abakuá have learned to make altar attributes, as well as the conditions under which they continue to be made in contemporary Cuba. "I already had experience as an artisan since my childhood, especially because of my old godparents [in Kimbisa]; all of them knew how to adorn, sew, and create. Among everything I know of the African liturgy, I know much about its artisanry." Jesús served as the apprentice of Abakuá *plazas* and artisans who, themselves, had been mentorees of the luminaries of the Akanarán line's founders and its descendants in Regla's Abakuá Efó, Enyegueyé, and other lodges. Jesús apprenticed with Vicente Puebla, the Iyamba of Regla's Obon Tanze lodge and Máximo, the Mosongo of the town's Muñongo lodge. He had grown up in Old Havana around Francisco Hurtado de Mendoza ("Yenequita"), the Isué of Usagaré Munankebé. All three knowledgeable elders specialized in altar attribute making and renovation, especially Máximo, who had adorned the pieces of many of Regla's lodges. Máximo was a specialist in *plumeros* and metalwork, including silver-plating the finial caps *(casquillos)* of the staffs. Jesús taught himself to illustrate, and his notebooks are filled with meticulous drawings of Abakuá attributes, designs for adornments, and *anaforuana.* At the same time, having grown up on the rough streets of Old Havana, he specialized, like many Cubans have had to, in recycling castoff materials, which is most impressively seen in the miraculous maintenance of Havana's pre-1959 American automobiles. Many of the adornments he eventually employed in 1979 were from salvaged materials. Jesús's artmaking experience, thus, nicely illuminates the conditions and possibilities of domestic, virtually underground ritual artmaking, outside of any formal institutional setting in which materials, not to mention training, would be provided.

The following discussions, enabled by Jesús's intensive commentary on his work, closely explore the altar renovations of one Abakuá *potencia* and artist. My discussions so far of Abakuá objects have relied upon the Eforí Eñongo altar objects as illustrations for generalizing symbolic interpretation. That approach has been useful for heuristic purposes, in helping build a composite picture of Abakuá art and iconography. What follows is a different kind of account. I look closely at the particular aesthetic choices, stories, and interpretations of a single maker, focusing especially on his thought process and experience in selecting adornments in the renovation of the lodge's emblems as of 1979. This might be called an "ethnoaesthetic" or "experience-near" approach (see Geertz 1983:57; Brown 1996).

As glossed by Jesús Nasakó, the lodge's altar objects reveal many layers of meaning. Jesús's interpretations range from expected symbolic or general Abakuá (or, at least, Bakokó Efor/Akanarán lineage) references to idiosyncratic and personal references to his life experience, including his personal religious history. Still, it may be difficult to tease apart the former and latter extremes, in that any putatively "shared" set of Abakuá references, as well as Jesús's "experience," are mediated and crosscut by different currents and fragments of oral and textual sources. In his interpretations, Jesús responds to and remembers things seen, heard, read, thought, and reevaluated. He has stored away twice-told tales and retold them seamlessly as part of his own narrative. He has shored up and filled in his interpretations and definitions with selective readings, foremost of private, shared, and inherited Abakuá notebooks *(libretas),* and of Roche y Monteagudo (1925) and Lydia Cabrera (1954, 1958), which he keeps faithfully on his bookshelves. Undoubtedly, much he learned afresh. For example, does he define the "leopard" as *yevengo* because he learned it from his *libretas,* the mouths of his brethren, or from Cabrera's *Lengua sagrada de los Ñáñigos* (1988)? If Jesús's narratives and explanations are idiosyncratic, they also reflect the imaginative and practical conditions of the Abakuá men around him and their historical conditions. Therefore, my choice to focus on the intentions and interpretations of a single maker does not limit their usefulness in making generalizations about "the arts of the Abakuá." Since the founding of the first lodge—a group of creoles whose experience and memories were filtered by the discursive currents of colonial Cuban cultural history—individuals who joined "collective pacts" have told and exchanged stories and have imaginatively produced objects for their practice. The Abakuá artmaking tradition is not static, but changing. It has been influenced not only by people of diverse experiences within the Abakuá, but also by other Afro-Cuban artistic traditions and Cuban cultural and sociopolitical contexts. These include, not least, the transatlantic history of the slave trade, slave society and the African nations in colonial Cuba, the building of the republic, and the Cuban Revolution.

Abakuá Staffs I: Form and Adornment in Iyamba's *Itón*

A close look at the altar's four staffs opens up discussions of form, changing adornment styles, the assemblage aesthetic, and multiple layers of meaning: personal, cultural, and historical.

Two altar objects represent Iyamba, considered to be the "Highest King" *(Máximo Rey)* and Elder of the *potencia.* Iyamba possesses his own plumed staff *(itón)* (figures 5.2 and 5.3). Like the three other *obones* (Mokongo, Isué, and Isunekue), Iyamba is also represented by one of the four feathered plumes (Br. *muñon, beromo,* Sp. *plumero*) that constellate upon the altar's central and most important object: the goblet-shaped *sese* drum (plate 11). Iyamba is the mythico-historical king of the Efó "tribe" of the Awana Bekura Mendo region, where the "secret" was discovered and the Abakuá society was born. As king and ruler of this Efó *tierra* in the Carabalí homeland, the father of Sikán, and the owner of the sacred goat *mbori,* Iyamba has the authority to sound (Br./Sp. *fragayar*) the Ekue drum. He remains within the *fo-ekue* inner sanctum during all initiations and festivals.[13]

Form and Materials

All but one of the staffs are similar in form and construction. Iyamba's *itón* is a 2.5-foot-long solid cedar cylinder. It was turned on a lathe, though the earliest staffs in Cuba were hand-hewn with machetes or drawing knives. Cedar, a "male wood," as Jesús Nasakó describes it, is ideally employed for all Abakuá objects, including the altar and orchestra drums. Cedar is a pan-Afro-Cuban medium, particularly for objects representing and used by males and male deities. Jesús Nasakó gives the example of the Lucumí (Cuban-Yoruba) *orisha* Shangó, a macho warrior-king, whose attributes are made of cedar, for example, his six wooden "tools" in the form of miniature axes and knives, handheld thunderax dance wand, mortarlike initiation stool *(pilón)* that supports a cedar vessel *(batea)* containing his thunderstones, and *batá* drums. Consecrated *batá* are handled and played exclusively by men, as are, of course, the drums and attributes of the Abakuá. Within the Lucumí tradition, attributes of a "red" hue symbolize the principles of ("action, struggle, and war."[14]

Botanical and historical data lend support to cedar's practical and stylistic use in the Afro-Cuban religions. Cedar *(Cedrela mexicana),* is a tall tree, reaching as high as fifteen meters and as large as two meters in diameter. Its relatively soft and porous, but resilient, character provides an ideal medium for turning, carving, and finishing. In Cuba, as elsewhere, the elegance and richness of its grain and color made it a preferred wood for fine furniture, as well as for the beams and finishings of Cuba's oldest houses. Cedar is considered to be "incorruptible," not least because its aromatic and somewhat bitter odor resists insects (Rodríguez-Herrera 1958:318). Cedar ensures the longevity of drums and attributes. As a prestige material, it lends them distinction, identifying the attributes of spirits and deities with the finer things.

Shiny metal caps *(casquillos)* and goatskin make up the two dominant elements that encase and finish the staff's cylindrical form; metal and goatskin, sharply contrasting against one another in surface texture, also provide dramatic canvases for further adornment. Worked sheet-metal caps have been typical of Abakuá staffs since at least the end of the nineteenth century, if not before (plate 6). Iyamba's *casquillos* are chrome plated. They were custom-made for the staffs between 1940 and 1950. Because twentieth-

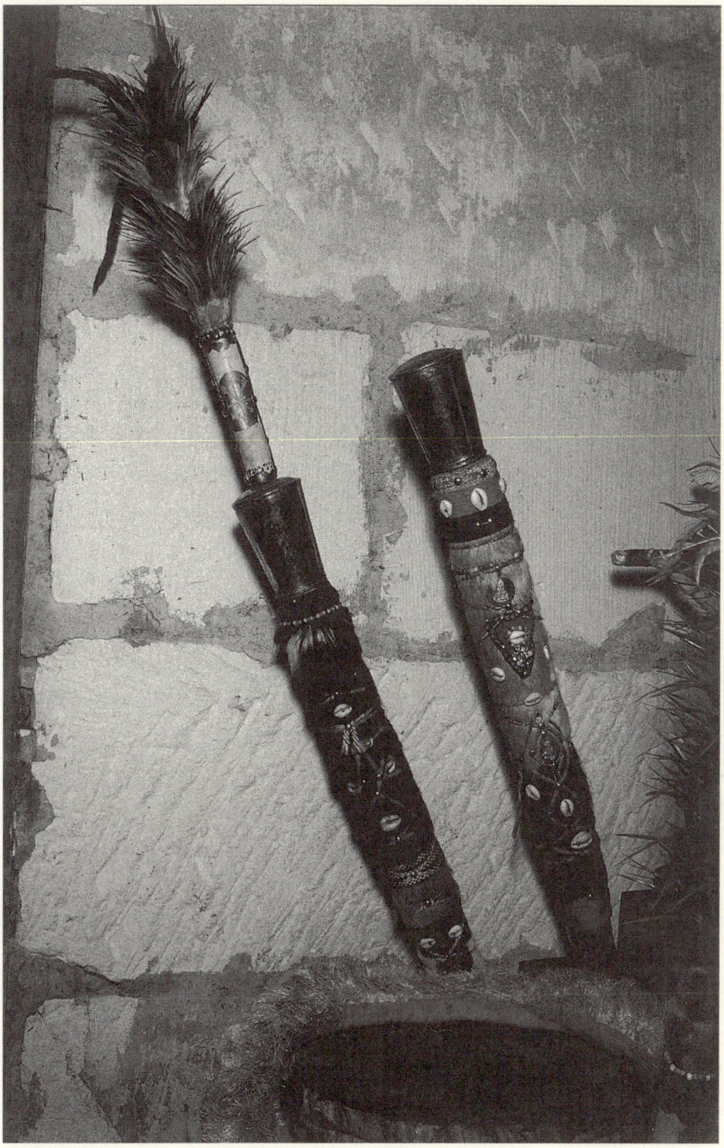

Figure 5.2. Staffs *(itones)* of Iyamba and Mosongo, altar of Efori Eñongo, Regla, 1992. Iyamba's staff carries its own *plumero.* Mosongo's staff is hollow and guards the sacred sticks *(yín)* used to sound Ekue. Photograph by David H. Brown.

century, prerevolutionary Cuba was always flush with American cars, and because post-1959 Cuba learned to maintain generations of Detroit bumpers and trim, it seems there have been plenty of specialists around for the chrome plating of ritual attributes. Sheet metal, particularly stainless steel, is among the preferred materials stolen from Cuban industries, and it is bought and sold on the black market. Similarly, though quality cedar is found only in the countryside, a clandestine industry has developed in Havana for the manufacturing of fine cedar cigar boxes for the vast black market in *tabacos;* recently, some Abakuá altarmakers have gotten broad, unblemished blocks of cedar from this source for drums and staffs.

Goatskin sheathes the entire surface of Iyamba's staff between the upper and lower *casquillos,* exemplifying a time-honored Abakuá artistic convention that dates to the earliest Cuban forms. Carefully removed from goats sacrificed in Abakuá *plantes,* the skin is meticulously cleaned, dried, and softened; the artist uses a razor to shave back the hair so that it lies flat and even. Segments bearing black, brown, and

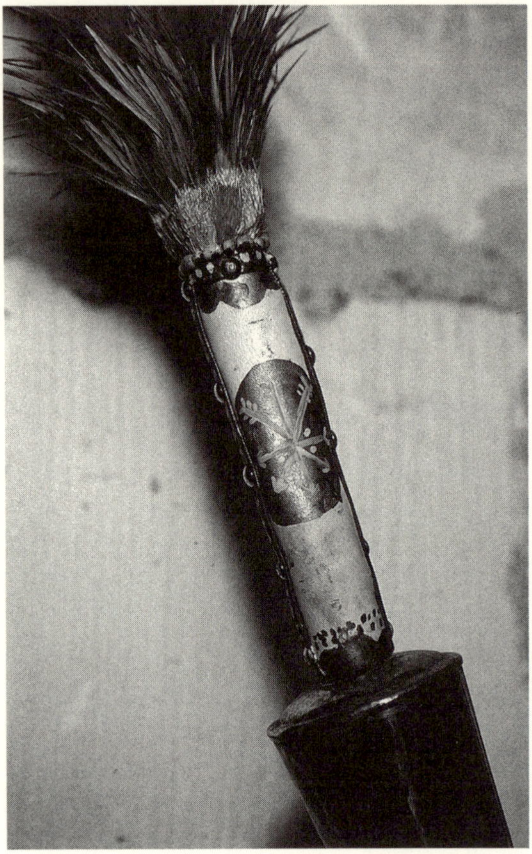

Figure 5.3. Detail, *plumero* of Iyamba showing leather covering, painted signature, tackwork, vegetal fringe, and rooster feathers. Photograph by David H. Brown.

white hair, and combinations thereof, are selected for aesthetic effect. Though the four altar staffs vary in the degree of contrast between colors and/or values, Jesús's creation of alternating bands using *mbori*'s own color markings registers a tradition established during the nineteenth century (figure 5.4). The staffs of Iyamba and Mosongo, for example use converse proportions of black and brown skin; light brown with wisps of white characterize Abasonga's staff, and Mokongo's alternates brown, black, and white. Such goatskin is highly prized and is considered integral to the materials that comprise the Abakuá *fundamento.* The goat, *mbori,* is, of course, the Abakuá Society's principal four-legged sacrificial animal. The first *mbori* belonged to the archetypal King Iyamba and remains the symbolic substitute for the "first initiate," Sikán, as well as for all *obonekues* initiated after her. In this sense, the skin of *mbori* condenses the Abakuá myth-history, liturgy, principal narrative characters, and socio-ritual hierarchies; it remains the most revered and sacred medium within the society. Goatskin, used for the *parche* of Ekue and all the other drums, embodies the spirits of Sikán and Tanze, and carries the Voice of *ekue,* which is "transmitted" intergenerationally.[15]

The stories of Cabrera's old, mid–twentieth-century sources suggest that the sheathing of Abakuá staffs with the skinlike remains of *ekue*'s earthly embodiments has its mythico-historical origin in the earliest Abakuá adornments—those of the Usagaré lodge in Awana Bekura Mendo. Many of Sikán's body parts, such as her eyes, head, and hair, were used to "charge" the first *fundamentos.* In contrast, her intestines, in particular, were used to "adorn a staff [*itón*] . . . for Mokuire [Mokongo], as an immortal memento of [Sikán] and symbol of command" (Cabrera 1970:107). The staffs of Abakuá dignitaries retain these two central significances: they are embodiments of ancestral presences that signify authority and command.

In Abakuá myth and practice, skin or tissuelike human remains for ritual and aesthetic purposes found their substitute in goatskin. Among the peoples of Old Calabar and the hinterlands, many, particularly the Efut and Ejagham, have a tradition of animal skin–covered *Ikem* masks, which represent the "fattened" girl/"beautiful maiden" with an elaborate coiffure. Human sacrifices allegedly were performed before 1842, but British colonial laws against the practice were instituted with the help of the Ekpe society (Nicklin and Salmons 1988:128, 126; see also Jones 1988). It would not be surprising if research were to reveal some historical, formal, and semantic relationship between these elegant, skin-covered sculptural bust portraits of a coiffured royal female and the Abakuá tradition of the goatskin-covered *sese* with its upright feather *plumeros,* which is, in effect, a bust portrait of the Efó princess Sikán. Sikán's "vessel" is, of course, the womb of *ekue,* and it is not unimaginable that Sikán would have passed through the "fatting house" as a young maiden (see Thompson 1983:230; Nicklin and Salmons 1988:125–126, 178–179).

The bright, smooth, flared chrome *casquillos* and their borders of colored and textured materials frame and set off the staffs' segments of adorned goatskin, and they unify the whole object as a strong vertical with an upward thrust. Still, if cedar provides the foundation, and chrome and goatskin the dominant surfaces, of the staffs, these objects are, clearly, more complex assemblages. Their multifarious exterior adornments stand as discrete, miniature emblems and tableaux with their own significances within a larger unity. Dominant and repeated elements in varied materials, such as tacks, cowrie shells, beads, coins, medals, ribbons, cords and tassels, velvet and leather, paint, and vegetal fringe produce aesthetic density and visual complexity. At the top of Iyamba's staff, a dyed band of vegetal fringe cinched by a

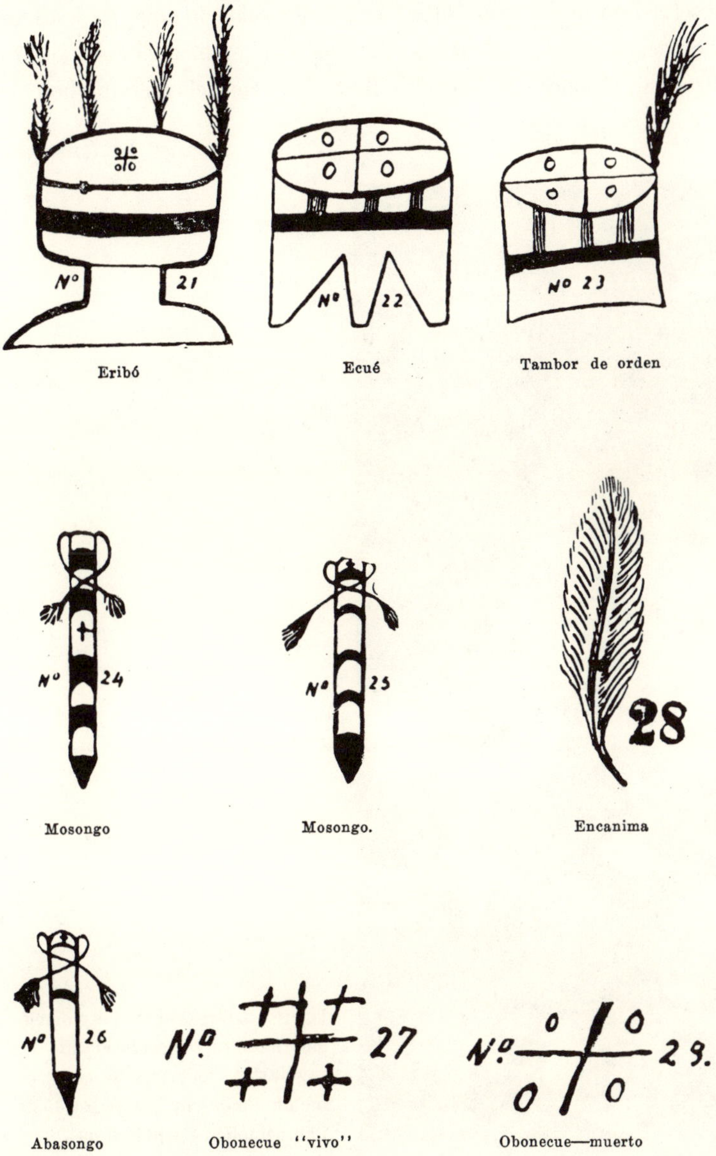

Figure 5.4. Drawings of Abakuá attributes, taken from private notebooks confiscated by the police in the late nineteenth or early twentieth century (Roche y Monteagudo 1908:47).

strand of multicolored beads borders the *casquillo*'s bottom (figure 5.3). On other staffs, Jesús bordered the *casquillos* with alternating horizontal bands of gold, red, and black cord punctuated by tacks and cowries (Mosongo), a combination of red cords and white satin ribbon along with cowries and red and white beads (Mokongo), and a thick red corduroy band featuring miniature appliqués of contrasting materials (Abasonga).

Between the high-affect, texturally contrasting *casquillo* borders, Jesús Nasakó arranged the tacks, patches, cords, and tassels in ways that recall state and military regalia as might be observed on regiment standards and the chests and shoulders of dress uniforms. The winding of cords horizontally around the cylinders, and in crisscross fashion, creates visual dynamism out of the interplay of solidity and lyrical expression (figure 5.2). This approach to Abakuá adornment was apparently an established tradition when Rafael Roche y Monteagudo had drawings made of confiscated attributes for his 1908 first edition of *The Police and their Mysteries* (figure 5.4).

Jesús tacked down the oblique cords—red, orange, yellow, green, gold, candy stripe, and black—over the goatskin to form significant spaces and repeated geometrical frames. These, in turn, serve as canvases for iconographic appliqués and features that compose "little faces," he explains. In doing so, Jesús not only creates the regalia of command; he also anthropomorphizes the ancestral officeholders to whom the

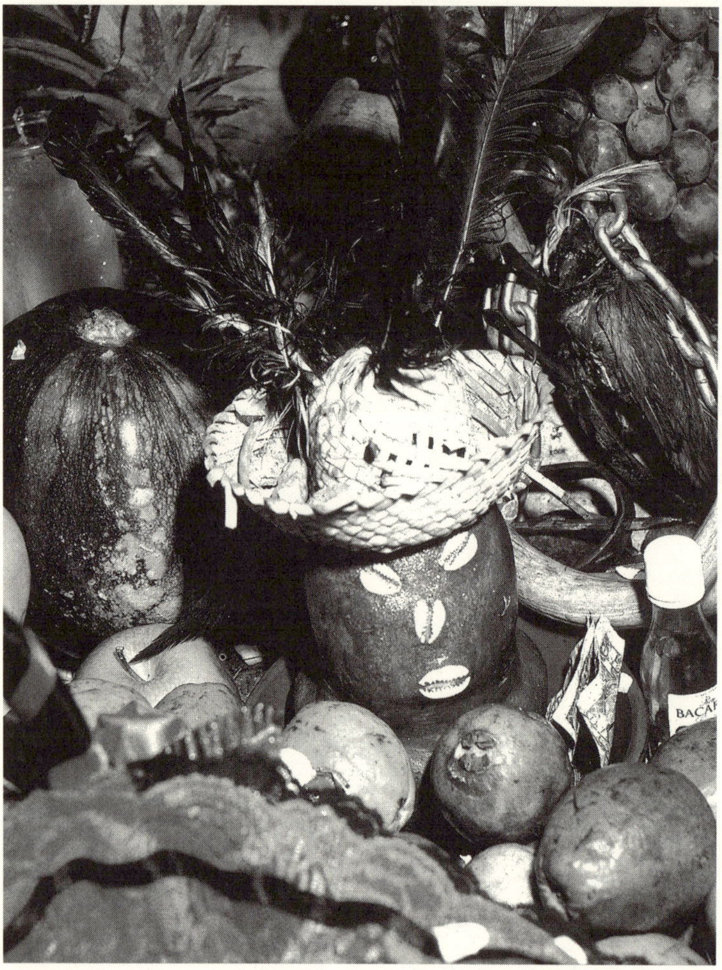

Figure 5.5. Eleguá of the Lucumí religion: a conical cement head with cowrie shells for eyes, nose, and mouth, Union City, New Jersey, 1989. Photograph by David H. Brown.

regalia belong. Thus, "Iyamba's face" appears just below center as two cowrieshell eyes with red cord borders, a nose formed of a long diamond of tacked down cord, and a cowrieshell mouth within a horizontal diamond. The two stacked tapered spaces above the "eyes," punctuated with an emblemlike single cowrie and draped with two tassels, respectively, form headgear above the face. Cowries are a generalized African adornment found in all Afro-Cuban ritual arts (see Thompson 1993; Brown 1993b). Jesús Nasakó likes cowries for aesthetic reasons, because they add textural and value contrast—smoothness and white luster—against the natural goatskin and darker cloth materials. Still, for the Iyamba and Mokongo staffs, Jesús adapted the formation of "little faces" with cowrie features from the cement head of the Lucumí *orisha* Eleguá (figure 5.5). This is intuitive for him, since Eleguá is Jesús's tutelary *orisha* in Santería.

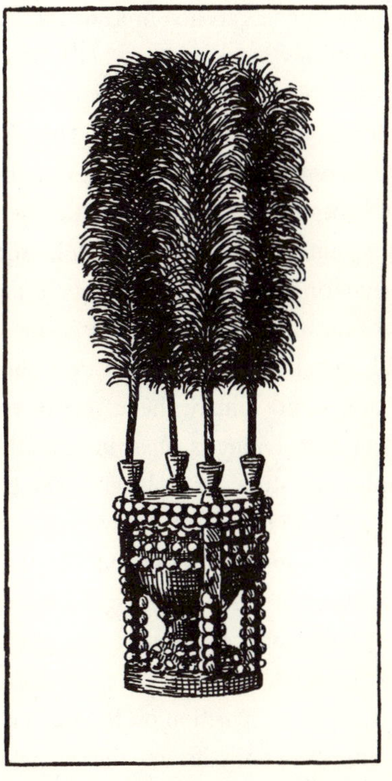

El "Sese Eribó".
El "Santísimo Sacramento" de los ñáñigos

Figure 5.6. Drawing of "El 'Sese Eribó': El Santísimo Sacramento de los Ñáñigos" (The Holy Sacrament of the *ñáñigos*); Roche y Monteagudo 1914, 1925. This *sese* was confiscated from the Efore Muna Tanze lodge of Pogolotti by the Marianao police on May 20, 1914.

Like the metal caps, goatskin, and wrapped cords, cowries are a time-honored adornment of Abakuá objects. Yet, Abakuá, Palo Monte, and Santería artists debate the proper use and meaning of the cowries as attached to ritual objects. Jesús nailed the cowries "mouths up," which is typical of the Lucumí practice, where this position signifies the "speaking" or "revelation" of oracular wisdom, as in the Yoruba-Atlantic cowrie divination system called *dilogún* in Cuba and *jogo de buzios* in Brazil. Eleguá's cowrie facial features, "mouths up," correspond to his role as the "speaker" *(vocero)*, messenger, and interpreter. In contrast, some practitioners insist that within Palo Monte, Abakuá, and Ifá, shells should be applied mouth-down, toward the surface of the staffs and pots. This is particularly important in the case of ritual pots, such as the *ngangas* of Palo Monte, the *sese* of the Abakuá, and the Olokun vessel of Ifá, because the shells in the "down" position signify and enable the "guarding" of secrets within. Palero and Abakuá Julián González Pérez Sr. applies cowries in this way, and for this reason, to his *ngangas* and the miniature *seses* he produces for tourists. A magnificent *sese* (figure 5.6), densely incrusted with cowrie shells, which was confiscated by the Cuban police in Marianao in 1914, suggests that this tradition is time-honored.

The *Plumeros*

Iyamba's *itón* is exceptional within the *potencia* for having its own *plumero* (also known as Br. *muñón, beromo*), though most lodges employ the customary seven. For Juan Mokongo and Jesús Nasakó, Iyamba's *plumero* on his own staff marks his unique role as the *bandera de la potencia*—the "banner" of the lodge's sacred identity and foundational power—though others attribute that role to Mokongo (Sosa Rodríguez 1982:156). This variation might depend upon whether the lodge identifies Iyamba or Mokongo as the "father" of Sikán, since the *plumero*'s feathers represent not only chiefliness but also the princess's "hair."

Like the *potencia*'s other chiefly plumes, Iyamba's consists of densely layered feathers, which aspire upward as if in flight. These relatively short curved feathers from the back of the rooster are painstakingly bound with a tight spiral of thread and glue to a stalk of *caña brava.* This tall, hard, bamboolike cane *(Bambusa vulgaris)* grows at the banks of creeks, rivers, and lagoons, watery terrains that correspond to the symbolic ecology of Tanze's discovery by Sikán. In Cuba, *caña brava* has served many common uses, including rods for flags (Roldán 1940:292). Accustomed to improvising, Abakuá have as often used three-eighths-inch-diameter wood dowels and the rods of old-style wood clothes hangars. The *plumero* aesthetic among master altar makers requires a thin cane and spreading feathers that give the impression of fullness. These makers are disgusted by recent examples that seek fullness on the cheap, using thick cane with fewer and poorer quality feathers.

Though the Abakuá have always produced their own *plumeros* by hand, before the 1970s import vendors on Zanja Street in Havana's Chinatown provided a handy, perfect alternative. There Abakuá regularly sought out feather dusters made in China. At 2.5 feet in length, supported by a similar bamboolike cane, and sprouting gorgeous feathers of consistent color and length, they were, and remain, ideal. Following the 1968 state "intervention" that banned private enterprise, these imports ceased to be available. Therefore, Havana Abakuá now depend on a couple of specialists in Matanzas to make the *plumeros.* Curiously, among all of the other vital necessities that Cubans ask friends and relatives to carry or send from abroad, like shoes, shaving kits, and electronics, Abakuá regularly appeal to foreigners for this precious item in sets of seven. The feather dusters cost between three and four dollars in the Chinatowns of New York, Toronto, and California.

The *plumero* as a whole is in fact a complex object. The plumes/dusters are often slotted into thick cylindrical bases up to seven inches long, which, themselves, are mounted upon strong metal tangs with screw threads *(toquillos).* This permits the whole *plumero* to be securely screwed into the top of Iyamba's metal *casquillo,* and the other seven into the four slots around the *sese*'s crown and the brackets or wedges of the three other chiefs' drum bodies (see plates 11 and 12).[16] Some earlier *plumeros* were evidently simpler. Those of the elegant *sese* confiscated from a Marianao lodge in 1914 (figure 5.6) were simply inserted into four jigger-shaped cups welded to the drumhead's rim at the four cardinal points. In contrast, the *plumeros* of Efori Eñongo are highly finished. Leather or crimson velvet is tightly tacked in upholstery fashion around cylindrical cedar bases. The tacked leather and velvet produce a level of elegance and richness with which the Akanarán line honored its kings and chiefs (plate 11). Further finish and symbolic appropriateness are accomplished with an intermediary band of vegetal fringe cinched by thick beads, between the feathers and the leather (figure 5.3). This vegetal fringe, in material and form, corresponds to the sashlike *beromos* or *muñones* that ring the drumheads of Mpegó and Ekueñón and the fringe that encircles the joints and hood of the *íreme* masquerades. The vegetal fringe maintains the symbolic and material link of the inner sanctum's *potencia* objects to the powerful domain of *ekue* in the forest outside the temple compound. Finally, the leather or velvet upholstery of Efori Eñongo's *plumeros* bears the raised ideographic signature of its owner. Jesús scored the signs into the underside of the wrapping material before tacking it down. Later, Juan Mokongo enthusiastically smeared these low-relief signs with gold paint (plate 11). Each stored *plumero* needs to be identified, as a practical matter, when taken from storage, so it may find its correct position on the staffs and symbolic drums. More significant, the low-relief ideographs are enduring signatures of ownership, just as other objects of authority, prestige, and office might be marked with coats-of-arms. During Abakuá ritual the embossed signs, permanent, inscribed versions of chalked drawings, also serve to invoke, along with prayer, the ancestral owners of each *plumero.*

"Sikán's Hair" and Rooster Feathers

Feathers carry a double, even paradoxical, set of references. Most directly, they represent Sikán's royal "hair," as Abakuá regularly say, as well as the chiefliness of the top Abakuá *plazas,* or dignitaries (Ortiz 1954:43). "History tells us," Jesús Nasakó relates, that "when Sikán was sacrificed, the first *sese* was formed with her head, along with thirteen feathers of *nkikomo tangrí,* the first rooster that was [fed] directly to her head [i.e., skull], in order that her spirit would not abandon the material world."[17] Intriguingly, if the feathers are intended to evoke the princess Sikán's coiffure, the feathers themselves come from the iconically macho species of fowl in all of the Afro-Cuban ritual systems, the proud cock *(gallo),* called *nkiko* for short among the Abakuá.[18] Thirteen feathers represent, of course, the thirteen fundamental *plazas* required in the birth of an Abakuá lodge. Another apparent basis for this sign of chiefliness lies with Tanze himself. The fish also bore plumelike sprouts upon his head, undoubtedly because Tanze reincarnated an archetypal leopard society king (figures 3.11 and 4.4, right). Similarly, the rooster claims its own special crown in the form of a bright red articulated crest.

In Abakuá ritual practice, just as the rooster's sacrifice was crucial to the first consecration of *ekue* in Awana Bekura Mendo, it remains important to the reinvigorating of *ekue* within the *fambá* in preparation for ceremonies. More subtly, according to Jesús Nasakó, the rooster also acts here as a symbolic "substitute" for the premier sacrifice that occurs later in major Abakuá events: *mbori,* the goat. Additionally, *nkiko* also functions as a spiritual brush, with which the *íreme* Eribangandó "cleans" initiates and members; bad influences are absorbed into the bird's body. In this sense, feathers refer not only to royalty, authority, and Sikán's hair, but also to spiritual purity and healing. Thus, not surprisingly, during the semipublic processions of the *plazas,* the *plumeros* upon Sikán's "head" and *nkiko*'s own head "come out" together. Isué, the *sese*'s guardian, emerges from the *fambá* carrying the plumed *sese* in his hands and the head of *nkiko* in his mouth—the rooster's bright red crest between his teeth. As Jesús Nasakó relates, within the *fambá, nkiko* has just been sacrificed, and his head "put on top of the *sese,* the Mother of the Abakuá. *Nkiko*'s head belongs with the *sese,* and it is carried with it in procession"[19] (figure 5.7).

Nkiko thus forms one important link in a chain of sacrificial substitutions. In one ceremonial phase, *nkiko* can apparently stand in for *mbori,* the goat, and *mbori* for Sikán. The woman Sikán was the first "initiate" to give up her life for *ekue.* The male goat became the second, symbolic "initiate" to give up his life to *ekue,* in order that the Voice be reproduced with the Ekue drum. Subsequently, *mbori* would be the recurrent sacrificial substitute for every living male initiate, who would give up—"swear"—his life to *ekue* not through literal sacrifice but symbolic identification with *mbori* in the oath-taking process. He could face death, or "social death," for betraying *ekue,* and might also have to kill to protect his "second mother," that is, the *sese.*

Intriguing symbolic contrasts arguably come into play, particularly between masculine and feminine, and between speech and silence. In the founding Abakuá myth and its iconography, *nkiko* stands uncooped and "free" upon the hill overlooking the Oddán's banks in Awana Bekura Mendo (plate 2, right; figure 3.8). From his high vantage point, he gloriously "sings of liberty, about the force of *ekue,* and about the solid independence that the knowledge of the secret brings."[20] In a bold parallelism, *nkiko* "sings" as Tanze "roars." Yet Sikán is silent. As the "Mother of the Abakuá," she remains, in effect, the patient vessel and womb of this rebirth event, which is fertilized, as it were, by the Divine Voice, *ekue,* in effect, the Word *(el Verbo),* while the male figures, *nkiko* and Tanze, "sing" and "roar," respectively. As well, in the chain of sacrificial substitutions, *mbori,* the male goat, symbolically replaces and regenders the first, female "initiate" with a male "initiate," who becomes an *obonekue* and *ekobio* of the lodge. In the course of Abakuá practice, of course, only human males become *ekobios.*

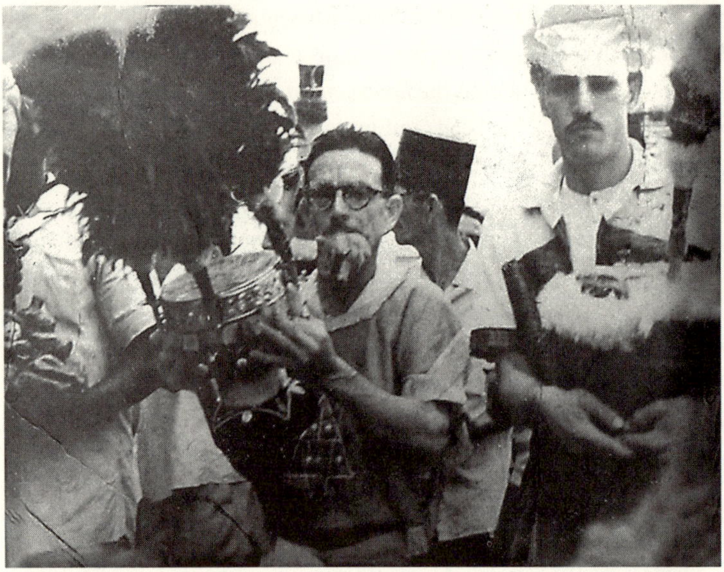

Figure 5.7. Pedro Ferrer, the Abasonga of Regla's Otán Efó lodge, substituting for Isué, 1952; he wears the honorific vest or sash with Isué's sign and carries the *sese efó* in his hands and the head of *nkiko* in his mouth. The multilodge procession heads toward the cemetery of Regla to celebrate a mass in memory of a deceased Iyamba of an Efí lodge and an Iyamba of an Efó lodge. Photograph courtesy private collection, Regla.

These symbolic links and paradoxes demand further scholarly attention: Sikán's head and female coiffure are recreated in the *sese* drum and *plumeros,* respectively. Interestingly, the *plumeros* are made from the reddish, black, and white feathers from the rooster's mane, not from its stiff, long wing feathers. As Sikán's "head," the *sese,* too, remains silent. Still, while the live *nkiko* epitomizes garrulous speech, responding to Tanze's roar—later produced by *mbori*'s skin—*nkiko* as sacrificed is silent, and placed atop the silent *sese.* Though, as held between Isué's teeth as a veritable "mouthpiece" of *ekue,* it is worth hypothesizing, nevertheless, that *nkiko* marks the difference between what is authorized to happen among the male *plazas* within the secret *fambá* and what may happen in the semipublic space outside. Though *nkiko* "sings" freely in response to the Voice within the "first sanctuary" and may crow within the "second sanctuary" (the *fambá*) as Ekue is sounding, he ultimately gives up his life, and in the public demonstration of Abakuá potency, the procession, *nkiko* becomes a "sign of silence, discretion," in the words of Jesús Nasakó. *Nkiko,* with his royal red crown and assertive voice, is something of a miniature male Abakuá chief, who, outside the *fambá,* nevertheless acts in accordance with the exigencies of the secret's preservation. For public discretion and aggressive exclusion undergird and protect the power of the secret. In sum, *nkiko* paradoxically both provides the iconography and character of male chiefliness and, through his feathers and ultimate silence, represents Sikán and her hair. Correspondingly, he is both the voluble announcement of the secret's force, *ekue,* and signals the limit of the secret's revelation.

Abakuá Staffs II: Slavery, the "Father of Heads," and Syncretism

Mosongo combines the roles of sacred patriarch and defender of secrecy oaths. In an apparent paradox, he is both an intimate of *ekue* and Ekue—which lie at the heart of Abakuá fraternity—and a feared *negrero* (slaver) who sent boatloads of Carabalí leopard-society members across the ocean into dreaded New World slavery. Mosongo's role as "slaver" begs the question of the Abakuá member's new destiny and the stakes of belonging: initiates "give up" their lives to be incorporated into the secret, *ekue,* just as their core sacrificial models do, Sikán and *mbori.* Ekue (small *e*) is their liberator, who has also radically constrained them within a tribe, which is protected by stringent taboos. The *ekobio* might have to kill for *ekue.* At the same time, treason against the secret can mean capital punishment, death.

Using a pan-Afro-Cuban, if not also, a universal, idiom, Juan Mokongo identifies Mosongo as the "Father of the Religion" *(Padre de la Religión)*—the "Abakuá religion." Elaborating, Jesús Nasakó and Cabrera's sources have defined Mosongo's name as "divine, sacred, holy, supernatural power" (Cabrera 1988:358–359). In this way, Mosongo is rather like the Lucumí arch-*orisha,* Obatalá, who is the "Father of the Pantheon" and the "Owner of All Heads." Correspondingly, Mosongo, as founder and *obon,* is the "Father of the Heads of the Abakuá." "Owners of Heads" in the Afro-Cuban religions possess the authority to condemn, as well as "rule," the "bodies" of the initiated. Tutelary *orishas* rule individuals and collectives—the "houses of Ocha." In the Abakuá Society, Mosongo seals and sanctions, vis-à-vis *ekue,* the *juramento* and standing of members: he ensures their oath-based fidelity to the secret. Mosongo "contains the life of the initiate in his *itón:* there 'as in a trap,' are [the initiate's] breath, his word, his blood, [and] his being . . . so that if the [initiate] betrays the oath, [Mosongo] can destroy him" (Sosa Rodríguez 1982:164).

Mosongo's role as Owner of Heads and guardian of secrecy is enabled by the kind of attribute he carries. His *itón* is as much a powerful "charged" *fundamento* as regalia of office (see figure 5.2, right). In its construction, Mosongo's staff is the single exception among those belonging to the Abakuá dignitaries. It is hollow. Though often made of hollowed cedar, the Mosongo staff of Eforí Eñongo is made from a wide-diameter tube of *caña brava.* As a result, his metal *casquillos* become more than decorative; sacred materials can be capped within the staff. They are reported to be of two kinds. First, Mosongo controls members' fidelity to *ekue* through metonymy. The hollow staff supposedly contains the name, and hence the being, of each initiate written on a tiny piece of paper. Second, Mosongo's vigilance and enforcement mechanisms derive from a magical power *(brujería),* which is built upon concrete metonyms of oath-taking and oath-witnessing: the "tongue" and the "ear." Mosongo's *brujería* is said to contain the *tongue* of the rooster and the *ear* of the sacrificed goat. The rooster's tongue "symbolizes the initiate's own tongue, which made the oath" (Cabrera 1988: 358), and the goat's ear "heard the oath of the *obonekue.*" Echoing *nkiko*'s role in Isue's mouth, Mosongo's *brujería* is the guarantee that the initiate be loyal to the oath and never divulge Abakuá secrets (Sosa Rodríguez 1982:164). "As the ñáñigos say . . . 'in the Mosongo . . . the life and death of the *obonekue* is kept'" (Cabrera 1988:358). Might the fear of death as a deterrent to oath-breaking draw resonance from the fear of slavery's darkness and "social death" (Patterson 1982)?

Mosongo's institutional authority, derives, in great measure, from his intimate relationship with *ekue* and the Ekue drum vis-à-vis relationships of protection, identity, and kinship. Physically, Mosongo's hollow staff guards the sacred ribs of palm or cane *(yín/güín)* used by Iyamba to sound the voice of *ekue* with the Ekue drum.[21] The Mosongo, in effect, is the protector of the Ekue drum's indispensable kin. "The Brícamo word for *yín,*" explains Jesús Nasakó, "is *saekue.* It means 'brother of *ekue,*' because, without the *yín, nothing can be done.*"[22] Without the *yín,* the sound of the Divine Voice cannot be produced by Iyamba, and Ekue is the engine behind all major Abakuá endeavors: the *yín,* as placed over Ekue, reproduces Tanze's roar in the first great hierophany by the River Oddán.[23] Symbolically, it seems, the *yín* is to the Ekue drum in the second sanctuary as the palm was to the sounding of Ekué in the first sanctuary. On the level of identity, the term *mosongo* has been used interchangeably with *ekue* (Cabrera 1988:358).[24]

The foregoing mythological themes and liturgical functions provide crucial background for a reading of Jesús Nasakó's adornments. However, these themes and functions do not exhaust the very specific meanings, mnemonic evocations, and personal experiences registered in his renovation work. It is worth commencing this level of interpretation with the Catholic religious medals that Jesús Nasakó mounted on the Mosongo staff and two others. Their appearance is conventionally interpreted as evidence of thoroughgoing "syncretisms" on one hand, and merely overt, nominal adornment on the other. Jesús mounted a brass circular medal of Our Lady of Charity of the town of Cobre (La Caridad del Cobre) and a silver medal of a robed, preaching Jesus—apparently an icon depicting events in his "public ministry," such as the Sermon on the Mount (figure 5.8, top and bottom; see Apostolos-Cappadona 1994:178, 304–305). At one level, the adornments are clearly Roman Catholic in origin and play a conventional role in Jesús Nasakó's life experience: they elaborate his given name and identity as a baptized Catholic and serve protective purposes. At the same time, apart from any referential value they carry, they serve clear aesthetic purposes. The medals add luster and textural contrast to the staffs—shiny metal against darker goat hair. Still, the meanings that emerge upon a close reading based on Jesús's own narrative are much richer, especially when attention is paid to the specific reasons he made use of these objects.

The religious medals form the kernels of overlapping, hybrid narratives spun out by Jesús Nasakó, an artist, theologian, and historian of Abakuá and Kimbisa. "Every adornment calls up a memory," Jesus relates. "The medals have their symbolism, but at the same time, they have their personal history."[25] Jesús affirms the presence of general meanings tied to ever-wider horizons of theological interpretation; yet, such meanings encounter a parallel, if not opposed, set of intimate, even private references in his life as lived. *No one besides me would be able to explain to you the meaning of these things, because they come from my personal experience and family history.*

Near the top of Mosongo's staff, Jesús nailed an old brass religious medal of La Caridad del Cobre, the patron saint of the island of Cuba since 1916

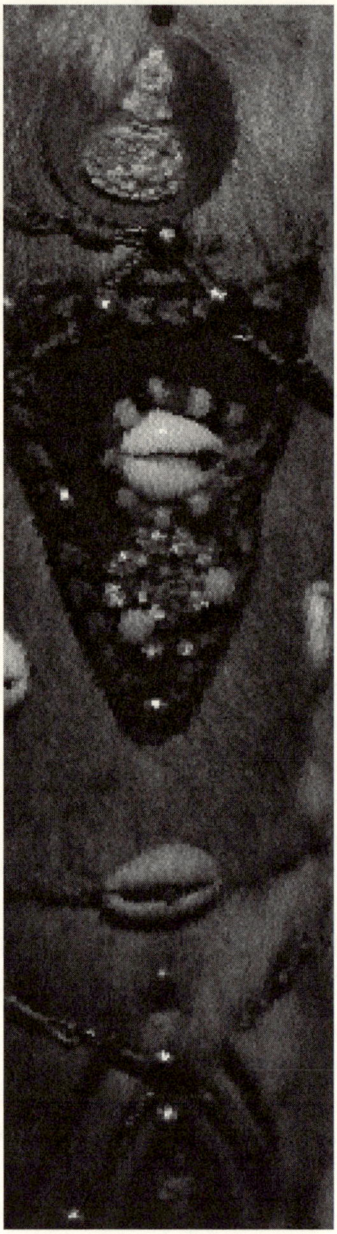

Figure 5.8. Detail of Mosongo's staff, showing brass religious medal of La Caridad del Cobre (top), an abstract decorative patch (center), and linked brass fishing connectors used to bind the body of the staff. A medal depicting Christ preaching is seen at bottom. Photograph by David H. Brown.

(Cabrera 1980:56–57) (figures 5.2, right, and 5.8, top). He chose this particular medal in order to reference the transatlantic historical conjuncture that produced the Abakuá on the island of Cuba. The common low-relief icon pictures the momentous seventeenth-century appearance of the Virgin Mary to three fishermen in a rowboat in the Bay of Nipe in eastern Cuba. This group of men, conventionally identified as two *mestizos* and one black slave, all carry the name Juan. "The Three Johns" *(los Tres Juanes)* became permanent attributes of this icon (see Brown 1993a:77; Cabrera 1980:57). However, Jesús Nasakó has always interpreted the three men as "black slaves" *(esclavos negros)*, who figure within a complex black Atlantic narrative. For Jesús, the boat, the blacks, and the water reference Mosongo's own mythico-historical vocation as a "slave trader" *(traficante de esclavos)*. The role of active slave kidnapper and trader was, in fact, played by Efik and Aro men, with the help of their "leopard societies." As Jesús explains, via the iconography of black men, boats, and water, the Caridad del Cobre becomes not merely the patron of Cuba, but also represents "all the Africans who were slaves and came here in ships and boats."[26] The copper mines of the town of Cobre were manned by slave labor. Jesús elaborates his story with further adornments. He tightly bound the Mosongo staff with little chains made of brass fishing connectors. These refer, at once, to the river's nourishment (fishing connectors), "slavery" (chains), the Middle Passage, and the central Abakuá figure of Africa's Oddán River. Jesús also intended the brass connectors to reference the sacred metal, representing sweet water and wealth, that is prized by the Virgin's counterpart, the *orisha* Oshún, the Yoruba Lucumí "Owner of the River." Oshún's vocation and meanings are clearly seen in a Lucumí proverb linked to her: "blood that runs through the veins." The proverb refers not only to biology and kinship, but also to the role of waterborne movement in connecting lands and civilizations. In one dimension of his identity, Mosongo is fleshed out as a figure linked to global historical relationships, movement, and economic fortunes, utilizing, in part, cognate religious vocabularies borrowed from Roman Catholicism and Lucumí liturgy.

Jesús Nasakó further elaborates Mosongo's biography with another religious medal. Two thirds of the way down the staff, Jesús attached an antique silver and brass medal depicting Jesus Christ standing in robes with hands to his chest. "Why do you think I put that there?" he asked me. I waited for the answer. The slaver Mosongo, Jesús explained, was an *horro*—a free or freed African—who, ironically, was an *albino*, "an African with white skin." Thus, with this medal, Jesús Nasakó added more layers of significance and thickened the plot. First, and most directly, Jesús transvalued the medal in order to elaborate a legendary hybrid character, marking Mosongo's "white" complexion with the icon of the putatively white Jesus. Second, he registered *ekue*'s metaphorical association with the story of Jesus Christ. Some Abakuá draw a parallel between God's sacrifice of his own son and Sikán's "sacrifice" with the assent of her own father. In the words of Jesús Nasakó, "Sikán gave her life, her body and blood, so that *ekue* might live, just as Christ gave his life so that Christians might live."[27] Third, Jesús Nasakó draws on the Christ metaphor to elaborate Mosongo's high spiritual rank as the "Father of Abakuá Heads,"[28] just as many Lucumí drew upon the Christ metaphor to elaborate Obatalá, the pure arch-*orisha* of the pantheon, the son of Olofin (God), who "owns all heads."

Jesús's narrative goes further, of course, as it implicitly theorizes color, race, and the long-debated issue of Africanness in Cuba. Mosongo as *negrero* reiterates Ekpe's historical responsibility for the slave trade, making the profile of this beloved Abakuá ancestor as well as Abakuá historical consciousness much more ambivalent. At the same time, Jesús's narrative destabilizes the signifiers of race and color that developed within Cuba's colonial social history, wherein pseudoscientific notions of "race" became more powerful and institutionalized as the nineteenth century came to a close. Mosongo was a "white" African who sold slaves, not a slave himself, thereby rhetorically disconnecting "African" from "slave" as an essential status. The relationship of skin color to social status is fluid and reversible. There are Africans who are "white" slave traders on one side of the Atlantic and Cuban whites who are sworn members of the African-derived Abakuá Society in a Cuba obsessed with its racial identity. Given the implications of the mid-nineteenth century's "Africanization of Cuba scare" (see Martínez-Alier 1974:27–41), the politics of race and color clearly crosscut, and constituted, the demographics and ideologies of the emerging Abakuá branches. In turn, the Abakuá of the Akanarán Efó #1 lineage—seen by the public as whites "dragged down" into African primitive savagery—threatened in the 1870s the racial gains only recently achieved in recreating a "white" majority on the island just after mid-century by importing working-class Spaniards, Filipinos, and Chinese.

One wonders how widespread Mosongo-as-albino-slave-trader has been among Cuba's different Abakuá branches, and what conceptual labor it has performed for Bakokó/Akanarán's "white" and "mixed" (i.e., *pardo*) offspring. Arguably, this Mosongo story version forms one kernel of a Bakokó/Akanarán "creole" historical hypothesis, which resonates with modern Cuban *mestizaje* nationalism. In this sense, the Bakokó/Akanarán construction of its past seeks to revise older stories about "pure blood," expounded, albeit in different ways and for different reasons, both by Cuba's white elite and the old-guard Efí and Efó lodges that have retained the "pure blood" prescription of their Carabalí *cabildo* ancestors. Without doubt, the nineteenth-century personage that most powerfully figures a Bakokó/Akanarán modern "creole" or *mestizaje* nationalism is Andrés Petít, the *mulato* who "sold the secret to the whites" (see also Mosquera 1996a:227, 256 n.3).[29] In this charged phrase converge the economics, racial politics, and "erotics" of modern Cuban national identity in the context of slavery's decline and the increasing penetration and domination of northern capital on the island (see, e.g., Kutzinski 1993).

Indeed, Jesús Nasakó redoubles the resonance of Mosongo's Christ medal in a narrative bridge from the albino slave trader of Old Calabar to Abakuá's complex, post-1863 history in Havana via the figure of Petít himself. Jesús relates that he used this medal especially because "our founder was Andrés Petít, who was [also] the founder of our Order of Santo Cristo del Buen Viaje and the initiator of the white Abakuá." Earlier in the nineteenth century, Andrés Petít, a free Cuban *mulato,* had created a self-consciously syncretic religion called La Regla Kimbisa del Santo Cristo del Buen Viaje (The Kimbisa Order of the Holy Christ of the Good Voyage), incorporating Lucumí (Yoruba), Palo Monte (Congo), spiritist (derived from the European-American spiritualism of Allen Kardec), and popular Catholic elements. Cabrera's mid-twentieth-century informants aptly called the Regla Kimbisa an *ajiaco,* a rich stew of diverse ingredients typical of Cuban cuisine. The *ajiaco,* of course, was precisely the "stew" metaphor Fernando Ortiz used to describe the supposed give-and-take process of "transculturation" in Cuban history that produced a unique Cuban national identity (Cabrera 1986a:3; Ortiz 1939:155; Moore 1997:42; see also Mosquera 1996a:226).[30]

Andrés Petít, vis-à-vis the Christ image, is crucial to Jesús Nasakó's Abakuá aesthetic, historical, and religious perspective—what Cubans would call his *cosmovisión* (worldview). First, Jesús has been a practitioner of La Regla Kimbisa del Santo Cristo del Buen Viaje ("Our Order") for half a century, initiated as a boy in Old Havana during the early 1950s.[31] As Jesús reckons his ritual genealogy, he is two to three generations from Andrés Petít in the Regla Kimbisa, as his godfather was a Petít godchild and heir. For Jesús, the medal stands not only for Christ but also for Petít and the religion he founded, which carries Christ's name. Petít himself, as does Jesús Nasakó, also carries Christ's name. Petít's baptismal name was Andrés Facundo Cristo de los Dolores Petít (Andrés Facundo "Christ of the Sufferings" Petít). For Jesús, Petít amounts to a personal saint. Andrés Petít became a widely feared Kongo-Cuban ritual expert *(brujo),* and an exemplar of creole ritual appropriations. For example, Petít transformed the personal Roman Catholic silver crucifix into a Kimbisa *nkisi* charm[32] by embedding sacred medicines in it, and had each of his followers carry one as a protective amulet. In his tenure as Isué of Bakokó Efor, Petít incorporated similar *nkisi* principles into the most important *potencia* objects of his lodge and the Akanarán Efó #1 lineage (the *sese* drum) in order to protect its controversial "white" initiates (plates 9 and 10). For Jesús Nasakó, Petít is "our founder" because his Abakuá creation, Akanarán Efó #1 is the genealogical root, and "grandfather," of the lodge to which Jesús Nasakó and Juan Mokongo belong, Efori Eñongo of Regla (see table 2.3). The significance of Petít's specific connection to the Abakuá objects of Eforí Eñongo, which were renovated by Jesús Nasakó, are fully illuminated only in relation to Jesús's ritual and family history, as well as the history of Regla.

Sometime before 1875, a Cuban creole of Filipino-Chinese, and possibly African, descent was initiated as an *obonekue* of Akanarán Efó #1. This famous figure of Cuban social history, Quirino Valdés (1859–1937), worked as a wharf boss *(dirigente porturario)*, rose to prominence as a dock labor leader, and is recognized as a heroic *mambí* fighter in the Second War of Independence (1895–98). His memory is close to Regla's heart. A town native, he was a veteran of Regla's Ejército Libertador, or Liberation Army (Cosme Baños 1998:51).[33] Valdés's lifespan is coterminous with the period of Abakuá control of labor around Havana Bay, where numerous *contratistas* (labor contractors) occupied high ranks in local lodges (see López Valdés 1985). Regla, which overlooks the bay, was a stevedore's town, and it contained many *juegos*, particularly of the "white" working-class Efó branches. The Regla *barrios* of Ledice, La Colonia, and Pati Larga are still considered to be *"barrios abakuá."*

Quirino Valdés participated in the extension of Petít's Akanarán Efó Ocobio Mukarará as it gave birth to three new "white" lodges in Havana and Regla during the late nineteenth century: Ekobio Efó #1 (1874, Havana), Abakuá Efó #1 (1875, Regla), and Enyegueyé (1882, Regla).[34] Valdés cofounded Abakuá Efó #1, emerging from its *baroko fundamento* as the Abasonga grade. There, he became the *ekobio* of the lodge's Íreme Aberiñán grade, Juan Gutiérrez Montojo, who was Juan Mokongo's father. In turn, Juan Gutiérrez Montojo founded Efori Eñongo from Abakuá Efó on April 9, 1916; Gutiérrez rose to become the new lodge's Isué grade. As the sponsor and "godfather" of Eforí Eñongo, the multitalented Quirino Valdés fabricated the new lodge's altar objects, its *potencia*. In addition to his occupations as wharf boss, labor leader, and guerrilla fighter, he was also a carpenter and skilled *tornero*—an artisan of the lathe, with which he turned the Efori Eñongo's staffs and drums. Two years later, in order to enhance the altar's adornment and commemorate the lodge's inauguration, Juan Gutiérrez Montojo designed the lodge's blue velvet banner, which features the embroidered Birth of the Abakuá image, Eforí Eñongo's name, coat-of-arms, and the date of its founding.[35]

Abakuá Assemblage: Patronage, Aesthetic Competition, and "Syncretic Mimesis"

Until the era of Andrés Petít's Akanarán Efó #1 branch, Abakuá altar attributes were, apparently, relatively austere.[36] A permanent Havana museum exhibition of nineteenth-century altar objects displays staffs and drums with little external adornment beyond hemp cord *(cáñamo)*, goatskin, some cowrie shells, and plain metal caps. These objects, from the Casa de Africa's Fernando Ortiz Collection, were mostly confiscated by the Cuban police at the beginning of the twentieth century, if not before (plate 6). Though they probably do not historically precede the *potencias* of Akanarán Efó's first offspring lodges (1874–82), they nevertheless exemplify the most austere extreme on a scale of adornment.[37] Jesús Nasakó believes that in the nineteenth and early twentieth centuries, and in some impoverished cases down to the present, "the adornments were simpler." Indeed, as he and Juan Mokongo note, Efori Eñongo was founded in 1916 by "humble workers." Its objects were "more rustic, more common." Notwithstanding, major aesthetic changes in Abakuá display were well underway by the founding of the first three offspring of Akanarán Efó #1.

Among the Abakuá, Akanarán Efó and its descendants are credited with raising the ante on altar artistry because of their increased resources, as well as the rise of a form of conspicuous consumption driven by interlodge competition. Given Akanarán Efó's patronage and the powerful positions of its offspring's founders within local economic and political machines, the sky was the limit. Drums and staffs were richly adorned with leopardskin, elaborate beadwork, imported cloth, trimmings, and tassels, gleaming European-style crowns, and silver- and gold-plated *casquillos.*

Alejandro Rodríguez reported in 1881 on an Abakuá altar featuring staffs with handles and finials of silver *(plata).* Mosongo's staff, in particular, was "decked out" *(engalanado)* with velvet in a pleasing color. Rafael Roche y Monteagudo's 1908 work presents sketches of Abakuá staffs adorned with artistically contrasting horizontal bands and cords with tassels (figure 5.4; 1908:47). Roche y Monteagudo's revised 1925 edition features detailed drawings and photographs of the exquisite attributes confiscated by the police on 20 May 1914 from the "ample *fambá*" of a well-appointed godchild lodge of Ebión Efó #1, called Efore Muna Tanse of Pogolotti, Marianao, Havana. The objects are adorned with skins, velvet, and silver *casquillos.* Each staff features a silver figurated finial, such as a rooster, a cross, and a quartered circle. Even Roche y Monteagudo, the twentieth century's most ruthless warrior against *ñañiguismo,* was enchanted by the lodge's *sese* drum. It "had a certain artistic form, and its four feathered plumes that adorned it were splendid." The goblet-shaped *sese,* mounted within four vertical columns ending in lyrical finials, was incrusted with African cowrie shells. All of these riches were "facilitated by [Efore Muna Tanze's] patrons, or sponsors, [in] the Ebión Efó lodge" (Roche y Monteagudo 1925:70–71) (see figures 5.6 and 8.1).

Lydia Cabrera's mid-twentieth-century sources suggest that voluptuous and expensive Abakuá adornment articulated with creole social aspirations. The new "white" *juegos* were despised by the Havana old guard for the same reasons that Petít was attacked for "selling the secret to the whites." The Akanarán Efó #1 offspring were "seen to enrich [themselves] and institute innovations"—read exploitative self-interest and violation of tradition through unwarranted inventions. Such "enrichment," expressed in lavish displays, was enabled by the initiation of many "dissipated" sons of Havana's "best families," who hung out at the elite Acera de La Louvre Café on the grand Prado in Old Havana, along with wealthy and influential elder whites, such as politicians and generals (Ortiz 1954:69). Still, the comments of the Akanarán line's detractors suggest that "white" may have referred as much to the privilege and resources that the relatively elastic social category "white" made possible (even for recent immigrants who had "become white"), as to any narrower breach of the established "pure blood" principle. In other words, "white" could reference the socioeconomic domination and arrogance of the powerful upper stratum and new self-fashionings among emerging local elites within the immigrant-descended, as opposed to slave-descended, working class. Some of Cabrera's sources went so far as to suggest that the Akanarán Efó line inspired not merely class resentment but also social "jealousy." At the same time, as might be expected among this emerging "white" Abakuá elite, particularly in Regla, intensive symbolic competition ensued, driving rivals to produce unprecedented numbers of offspring lodges and ever-greater levels of display (Cabrera 1970:54).

Akanarán Efó #1 apparently set the tone by arrogating to itself a kind of superiority, demonstrated through the supposed procreative capacity and lavishness of its *potencia.* According to Fernando Ortiz, "*Okobio Makarará* was so prosperous in its proselytism that it was able to create and sponsor seven other lodges . . . for which reason its name was changed to *Akanarán Efó.*" Though Ortiz and his early twentieth century sources may not be entirely correct in their translation, they believed that "Akanarán Efó," in the "Efik language . . . means 'the ancient and superior *Efó* men'" (Ortiz 1954:81–90). One of Lydia Cabrera's mid-twentieth-century sources recalled that the staffs of the older black lodges "used to be made of wood covered with animal skin, and caps equally of skin." In contrast, "the whites adorned them with *casquillos* of gold and silver on their ends. If Abakuá Efó had them with *casquillos* of silver and of gold, those of Nyegueyé made all of them of gold" (Cabrera 1970:54). Abakuá Efó #1 and (E)nyegueyé were, of course, the politically connected direct descendants of Akanarán Efó #1. Enyegueyé came under the control of the famous Reglano Manuel de Jesús "Chuchú" Capáz, a member of Abakuá Efó #1, where he was the *ekobio* of Quirino Valdés and Juan Gutiérrez Montojo. Chuchú Capáz became the Iyamba of Enyegueyé in 1909. Having founded Abakuá Efó #1 of Regla in 1875, Quirino Valdés and Juan Gutiérrez Montojo, as noted, then founded Efori Eñongo. Chuchú Capáz, Valdés, and Gutiérrez acted as mentors or models for the generation of men who would later lead Efori Eñongo, principally Juan Mokongo and Perico Abasonga.[38]

Though they initially opposed the "innovations" wrought by the descendants of Akanarán Efó #1, many of the Efí, and older Efó, lodges, according to Ortiz, eventually adopted the *adornos al gusto criollo* of the "white" Abakuá (1954:49–84). Given evidence that Abakuá altar styles remained relatively plain until the last third of the nineteenth century, it may be that *potencia* adornment as such may have been added as a currency within the already long-standing genres of competition in costume, music, and dance among African-descended social institutions (the "clubs" and *cabildos* of the colonial period throughout the African Diaspora). In the face of what Ortiz identified as the "prosperity" resulting from Akanarán's "proselytism"—foremost, the spawning of new lodges and patronage relationships—it may be that many lodges took up the challenge of marked aesthetic competition, especially on public festival days and Abakuá *plantes* in order to gain reputation and recruits (see Bastide 1978:114; Ortiz 1960:10–17; Deschamps Chapeaux 1968:50; Omari 1984:27–28; Brown 1996:119–128).[39]

During the same period of the Akanarán lineage's expansion and the adoption of the *adornos al gusto criollo* (1870s–1880s), the Abakuá Society, in particular, the "white" lodges, came under heavy fire from the authorities. In response, the "reformer," Andrés Petít, apparently sought reconciliation with his detractors and persecutors: the older Efí and Efó lodges, the authorities, and the society in general. This included his incorporation of Roman Catholic objects and styles into the Abakuá altar. Fernando Ortiz would later interpret this aspect of Petít's reform as a strategy of "syncretic mimesis," intended to lend "licitness" *(licitúd)* to the face of the Abakuá, countering stigma from the church, State, and society (Ortiz 1954:70). For example, Andrés Petít is credited with introducing the "Catholic style" altar, which the old Abakuá called *kendé*. "At the beginning of the Abakuá all the attributes in the African *cabildos* were put on a table. [Then] five lodges of white ñáñigos created altars of Catholic design, which they placed in all the *fambás* [of] Akanarán Efó [and its offspring]" (Cabrera 1975:55). A painting from about 1878 by Victor Patricio de Landaluze of a supposed *fambá* interior (plate 8) includes a small, low table on which attributes are placed. If the picture at all accurately reflects what Landaluze saw, the table may represent something of the earlier *kendé* form. Second, Cabrera's sources remembered, it was also "Andrés [Petít] who put the crucifix in the lodges, in order that everyone would be convinced that [the Abakuá] were not savages" (Cabrera 1975:55). In 1881, half a decade after the founding of Havana's Ebión Efor and Regla's Abakuá Efó and one year before the birth of Enyegueyé, Alejandro Rodríguez documented an Abakuá altar featuring not only drums and staffs but also a "crucifix," "a crystal goblet of holy water," and a "censer" (Rodríguez 1881). Rodríguez's description of this lavish, Catholic-accented altar type first appeared in an 1882 issue of the widely read *Correspondencia de Cuba*[40] and in Trujillo y Monagas's massive police chronicle of the same year. This suggests that not only the authorities but also a significant Havana reading public were informed about these "Catholic" furnishings among the Abakuá, which could already claim a nearly twenty-year tradition since the birth of Akanarán Efó #1.

Despite Petít's attempts to achieve "licitness," and despite the demographic fact that all or most of the new Abakuá—black, white, and mulatto—were baptized and raised in the church, Catholic objects on the altars of Abakuá temples apparently did not sway the police or the public positively. Cuban colonial and republican society increasingly regarded *ñañiguismo* as antithetical to Christian civilization. Roche y Monteagudo, undoubtedly reflecting the majority view by 1908, denounced such objects as "practices . . . introduced . . . [by] the creoles . . . which have given the character of a ridiculous profanation of Catholicism, casting [as well] to the ground the mysterious idolatry of their [African] progenitors in this country" (1908:31; 1925:37–38).[41] Cubans evidently forgave the African-borns for being Africans—"mysterious idolatry" was expected of them—but Cubans could not bear the thought of their own white countrymen as *ñáñigos.* As products of promiscuous breeding, they respected no tradition, "casting to the ground" even that of the Africans.

Cuban contempt was extremely virulent toward *ñañiguismo* and *brujería* at the dawn of the republic, given the islandwide hysteria over alleged ritual kidnappings and murders of white children by Africans and Afro-Cubans (see Chávez-Alvarez 1991). Irene Wright, an otherwise sensitive and observant visiting American writer during the twentieth century's first decade, sanguinely parroted a police official's misunderstanding that the remaining African *cabildos* descended from the "old ñanigo clans." The legal Lucumí religious events she witnessed in El Cerro were just the tip of the iceberg, "the threshold beyond which lie their nefarious mysteries and the trickery of witchcraft." Seconding police official Roche y Monteagudo during the same period, Wright saw a benign drum celebration and a series of hybrid altar installations as "a demonstration of fanaticism and ignorance it would be hard to equal anywhere. It was the most astounding confusion of heathenish and Catholic worship one could imagine" (1910:150). Still, though Roche was clearly not persuaded that the white *ñáñigos* were merely pious, "humble workers" belonging to benign fraternities of mutual support, he occasionally lapsed into neutral comparative analysis. In effect, he textually legitimated and normalized for readers Petít's "mimetic" strategy, utilizing a rhetoric of simile that continues to mute Catholic and African differences in discourse today. In dispassionate ethnographic style, Roche describes "*Ekue as like a representation of the Eucharist among the Catholics;* but without making of it the use that is effected with the Host; its manifestation is in the sound produced by a special drum" (1925:33, emphasis added). Similarly, though Wright condemned African "ignorance," she noted dispassionately that the Lucumí *orishas* dressed in costumes that "seemed to imitate the robes altar images of the Virgin and saints wear. . . . In honor of these [deities, members] wear copper, silver, bead, and coral trinkets. The local Catholic church recognizes this same symbolism in color and ornament" (Wright 1910:149–150).

Abakuá Assemblage II: Sacred Stories, Biography, and Mass Culture

The Staffs of Abasonga and Mokongo

The staffs of Abasonga and Mokongo exemplify ritual art assemblage amid the circulation of symbolically resonant objects between different cultural domains (figure 5.9). The "appropriation" of objects from one domain and recontextualized in another is a term of contemporary criticism. "Appropriation," from the Latin *appropriare,* means "to make one's own," and, as used in art history, "pertains to artwork's adoption of preexisting elements" (Nelson 1996:117–119).[42] As assembled on and around core Abakuá attributes—drums and staffs—icons from Catholic practice and mass-produced objects from home and abroad find themselves as the kernels of multilayered narratives.

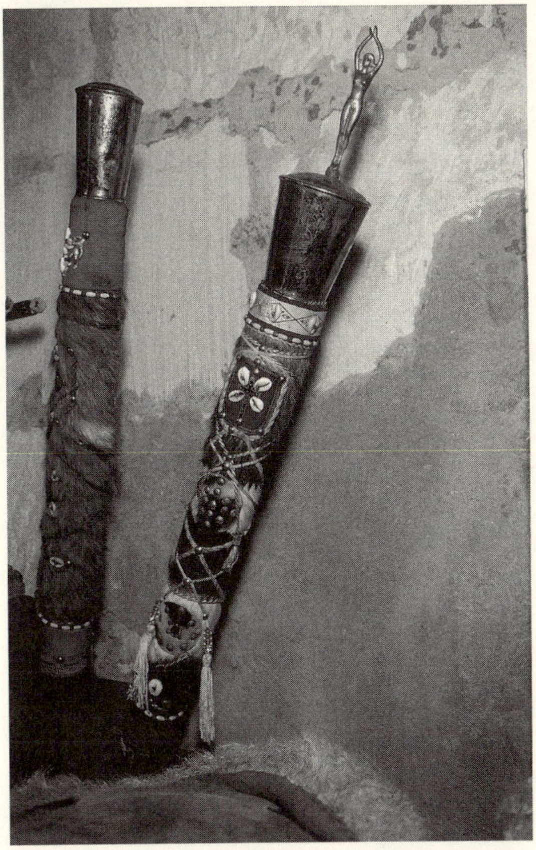

Figure 5.9. Efori Eñongo altar detail. Staffs of Mokongo (right) and Abasonga (left). Mokongo's staff is surmounted by a stolen hood ornament of a nude woman with raised arms ("Sikán"). The quartered circle sign of Mokongo is incised on the chrome cap's surface. Below are three iconic patches: a crucifix and a four-cowrieshell assemblage reiterating Mokongo's drawn sign, the same pattern below in furniture tacks, and then a cameo of "Mokongo" using a Roosevelt dime. The Abasonga staff features a medal of Saint Christopher and two brass key fobs in the form of *íremes* (top). Photograph by David H. Brown.

Though religious "syncretism," "merging," "mélange," "symbiosis," "reconciliation," and "masking" have been discussed at great length with respect to other African Diaspora arts, including those of the Abakuá Society (Thompson 1983:241, 1993:28; Ortiz 1954: 50–83; see also Baron 1994:327–341, 449–554; Bastide 1978:260–284; Cosentino 1995:25–55, 243–263), the "encounter" of "African" and "Catholic" objects is typically regarded in overly general terms (Mintz and Price 1992). Jesús Nasakó's personal narratives offer an example of Michael Mason's contention that individual agents working within and against cultural structures are responsible for what is far too generally called the "process of syncretism" (M. Mason 2002:87–89).

Abasonga's staff represents, at a very general level of interpretation, "seniority of age" within the *potencia.* Abasonga stands for the lodge's "independence, merits, and responsibilities," as well as the collective principle of "Religion, Justice, and Order" (Sosa Rodríguez 1982:164–165; Cabrera 1970:135–136, 194). A key assistant to Iyamba, Abasonga is also the "brother of Mosongo, [providing] Mosongo with a calabash of water" when he performs his duties.[43] Through eclectic adornments, Jesús Nasakó fleshes out Abasonga's complex identity in itself, and as it articulates with his own biography. Intriguingly, the juxtaposition of a religious medal with a peculiar form of mass-produced Cuban tourist souvenir permits Jesús to weave an extraordinary story of the mythico-historical "transmission" of *ekue* from the Efó to the Efí in Africa. In doing so, he spatializes two icons from radically distinct historical and cultural domains: Roman Catholic practice of prerevolutionary Cuba and the atheism of state-controlled postrevolutionary Cuba. As assembled and transvalued within Jesús's narrativized adornments, the two icons are both semantically "nourished" by and resist their conventional historical assignments (see Barthes 1972:118; Comaroff 1985:197–198).

One third of the way down Abasonga's brown and white staff, Jesús tacked a brass Saint Christopher's medal. It is enclosed by a hexagonal frame of red cord and tacks, and sandwiched vertically between two bright white cowrie shells (figure 5.10). In Christian hagiography, the third-century Saint Christopher was a "ferryman," whose job it was to carry travelers, ostensibly pilgrims, across a wide, rushing river. In his Christian iconography, as in the brass relief medal, he is often depicted as a large, muscular, bearded man with a staff, who bears the burden of carrying the Christ child on his shoulders across the

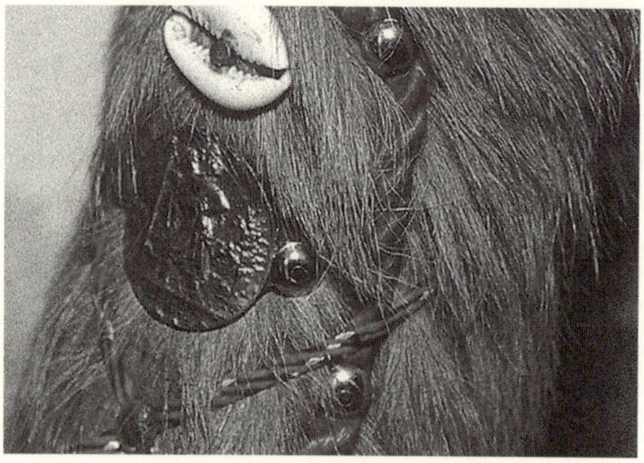

Figure 5.10. Detail, Abasonga staff. Roman Catholic brass medal of Saint Christopher. Photograph by David H. Brown.

river (figure 5.11). Christopher's name derives from the Greek for "Christ-bearer" (Apostolos-Cappadona 1994:79–80). Thus, Christopher became the patron of travelers, particularly over water, in the Christian world, including its age of exploration and its consequent colonial expansion. Christopher Columbus and his perilous journey from Spain to the New World are associated with this saint, and the full name of Havana is named after him: San Cristóbal de la Habana.

As Abakuá oral history relates, the Efó, the original owners of *ekue,* transmitted the "secret" to their former enemies, the Efí, with whom they had made a "pact." Upon payment of a "tribute" of money by the Efí, the Efó performed a preliminary ceremony in Awana Bekura Mendo. There they consecrated an Efí

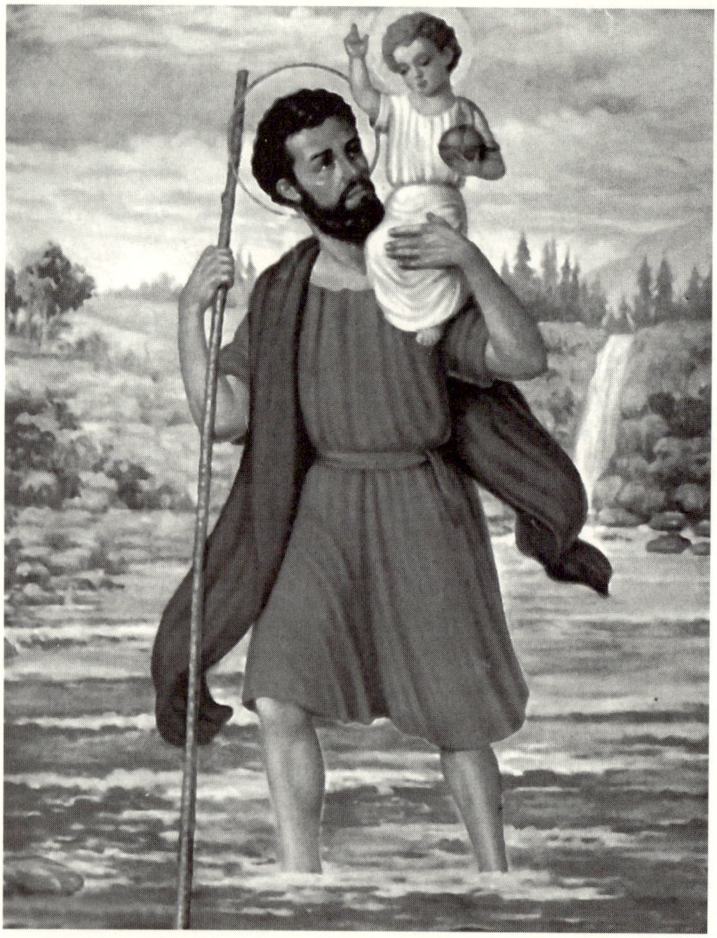

Figure 5.11. Popular chromolithograph of Saint Christopher, the "ferryman" who carries the Christ child across the river on his shoulder. Jesús Nasakó identifies Saint Christopher with Abasonga, the Abakuá officer who carried "the secret" *(ekue)* across the river from the Efó to the Efí.

prince, Otowá Nbéke, initiating him to the Abasonga grade within the Abakuá Society. Otowá Nbéke Abasonga was in turn charged with delivering the secret of *ekue* to the Efí. His initiation and deeds resulted in the Efó sponsorship of the first Efí lodges. As the first Efí person to be formally consecrated by the Efó in Awana Bekura Mendo, and as the vehicle by which the secret was transmitted to the Efí, the staff of Abasonga is said to "be as great in Efik as in Efor" (Cabrera 1970:135–138).

In the narrative tradition Jesús Nasakó learned within the line of Akanarán Efó and Andrés Petít, "Abasonga is the Saint Christopher of the Abakuá." For him, the Saint Christopher medal depicts Abasonga crossing the River Oddán, which divided the Efó and Efí territories. Wading through the rushing water, Abasonga carries the great spiritual power, *ekue*, on his shoulder. Jesús elaborates: "The child represents the religion, Christ, on the shoulder. Abasonga carried the religion from one side to the other."[44] At the same time, as one might expect from a seasoned storyteller, Jesús places himself at the center of the narrative. Christopher is Jesús's personal patron saint, from birth. Later, Jesús worked as a stevedore on Regla's docks for many years. Christopher has been the patron of many a dockworker, as well as sailors, whose livelihoods depend on maritime travel, literally the crossing of water. It is worth noting, of course, that *ekue* was carried across the water in transatlantic slave ships; in Cuba itself, *ekue* resurfaced in an old fishing village and port town on Havana Bay, Regla, in the Cabildo Carabalí Brícamo Appapá Efí. With Efik Buton in 1836 it crossed the bay once again to the barrio of Belén in Old Havana, and in 1875 it crossed the bay again in the founding of the town's first Abakuá lodge, Abakuá Efó #1, from which Efori Eñongo was born (1916). Finally, this particular Saint Christopher medal is a memento of one of Jesús's most cherished relationships. He received it as a gift from his baptismal godfather in 1958, when he was thirteen and living in Old Havana. These last two levels of the medal's significance described by Jesús resist general iconographic or mythological glosses of "African-Catholic syncretism." Perceived similarities in popular story versions of Abasonga and Saint Christopher clearly substantiate the medal's presence, which is usefully approached through iconological interrogation. Still, the staff's significance is more fully seen when Jesús's agency in making meaning through cultural practice is considered (see Mason 2002).

Saint Christopher does not stand alone in the elaboration of Abasonga; Jesús's 1979 renovation would simply not be complete without another icon both appropriate to and transcendent of its time. Jesús created a charming little tableau near the top of the staff to narrate Abasonga's "double" identity, as Efó and Efí, and his role as mediator in carrying *ekue* over water. In the center of the red corduroy band below the upper *casquillo* Jesús attached two detailed tiny brass *íreme* figures (plate 7). The two *íremes* placed side by side make reference to Abasonga's double identity as Efí and Efó. To weave the scene together narratively, Jesús nailed four cowries to the staff in the form of a cross between the two figures. The cross sits atop another cowrie, which is surrounded with multicolored beads in soapy white, black, yellow, and red; thus, the cross's two vertical shells become three. The ring of beads reproduces the necklace pattern of the Lukumí religion's strong *orisha* called Agayú, the "ferryman" associated with Saint Christopher in the syncretic perspective. The cross of four cowries evokes the orientational "four winds"/quartered circle Abakuá ideograph; with this cross atop the bead-adorned fifth shell, the assemblage takes on the shape and proportions of a vessel surmounted by a cross, that is, Sikán's sacred water gourd and the *sese* drum. Still, the cross, which is formed by two horizontal and three vertical cowries, retains the proportions of the Christian crucifix and the "world-ball" in the child's hand, a multiple reference to the Christ child/*ekue* that Christopher/Abasonga carried across the river. Of course, the three vertical cowries that divide the two *íremes* also delineate the Oddán River itself, bridged by the two horizontal cowries. Thus appears Abasonga-doubled, one in Efó territory and one in Efí territory on the two opposing sides of the River; *ekue* is captured in its movement between them.

Two assemblages narrate Abasonga's biography. One is a framed antique brass Saint Christopher medal, which, in 1958, passed intergenerationally within the baptismal kinship network of the church. The second assemblage's brass figures emerged in 1970s socialist Havana from a new kind of Cuban shrine. The two tiny *íreme* figures came from brass key fobs, mass-produced souvenirs that the government sold to tourists through the system of Intur "dollar stores," based on the Soviet bloc's novel mechanism for providing diplomats and tourists with commodities in exchange for hard currency. These stores became the most immediate showcase for goods unobtainable by Cubans in pesos and on the ration book from the neighborhood *bodega*. Ironically, this central and ambivalent symbol of Cuba's Abakuá since the early nineteenth century, appropriated by the state in the cultivation of its touristic folklore industry, was officially unavailable to the Abakuá themselves. Still, the key fobs were highly sought and could be obtained on the street by the *ekobios*, including Jesús.

In 1979, though optimism still reigned among Cubans for a better life, Intur marked the glass ceiling to individual betterment and comforts. Until 1993, Cuban citizens were prohibited from carrying American dollars and entering Intur stores unless accompanied by a foreigner, who would pay on their behalf with crumpled bills eked out of the daily *lucha* (struggle, hustle) by needy Cubans. A year before Jesús's acquisition of the key fobs, through the *diálogo* established between the Carter administration and the Castro government, Cubans who had fled the island after 1959 were permitted to return to visit their relatives for the first time. The *diálogo* experiment found ostentatiously dressed exiles walking around Havana with gold watches and stories of prosperity in Miami, and it is credited as a significant cause of the 1980 Mariel exodus, in which the poorest Cubans thus far crossed the water to the United States, many Abakuá among them.

Mokongo's Staff: *Anaforuana* and Symbolic Play

Jesús Nasakó chose Mokongo's staff as his canvas for ingenious elaborations of the Abakuá ideographic system, its *anaforuana* (figure 5.9, right). Jesús transposes Mokongo's sign from its more typical chalk-drawn or embroidered form to a series of tiny multimedia collages. The staff incorporates found and customized objects from local and international culture, thus making meaning in and through the stuff of ever-wider domains. In Mokongo's staff, Jesús Nasakó demonstrates his critical awareness of the morphological and semantic codes of multiple reference systems and the effects produced by their confrontation in the form of art assemblage.

Mokongo is the "Supreme Chief" *(Jefe Supremo)* of the Abakuá *potencia*. In some cases he is seen as its lodge's "Military Chief" and "Standard Bearer" *(Jefe Militario* and *Abanderado)*. Mokongo's staff is called the "Vara de la Justícia"—the Staff of Justice—for Mokongo is responsible for vigilance over everything that occurs in the lodge.[45] In some lodges and some myth cycles, Mokongo is the father of the princess Sikán, the first possessor of the "secret," and authorized her sacrifice.

Over alternating bands of brown, white, and black goatskin, Jesús organized yellow and candy-striped silk cords into a vertical series of three diamonds. The contiguous diamonds create framing devices for three tacked-on patches of velvet and goatskin. The patches boldly stand out against their backgrounds. Moreover, as set in their diamond frames, the patches sharply stack up along the staff's central vertical axis—which culminates in the staff's figurative finial (plate 9; figure 5.9).

The staff's upper silver *casquillo* features the most direct representation in content and formal means of Mokongo's signature. Mokongo's quartered circle, with its four *óvalos* and three little fringes sprouting from the top, is scored into the chrome surface. Of all

Abakuá signs, Mokongo's is closest to the basic quartered circle organizing "eyes" of Tanze over Sikán (figure 4.3; see also Cabrera 1975:183–184; Thompson 1983:248–249).[46] Mokongo's signature here, drawn with a sharp metal instrument, forms a point of departure, or baseline, for a series of three visual puns elaborated beneath it.

Below the *casquillo*'s border of white and red satin ribbon and beads, Jesús centered a modular velvet rectangle, to which he tacked an antique silver crucifix with cowrie shells nailed into each of its quadrants (plate 9, top; plate 10). In quartering the crimson rectangle with the crucifix and nailing the four cowries into the resulting quadrants, Jesús reiterated Mokongo's *anaforuana* sign in a mixed-media collage. Whereas cowrie shells represent the *orishas'* "mouths" in the Lucumí religion, here they represent the "eyes" of Tanze and Sikán. The series of tacks rising vertically from the crucifix and the oblique yellow cords they bisect form the three sprouting leaves/feathers that distinguish Mokongo's sign. In this way, this diminutive Mokongo collage visually puns upon the incised *anaforuana* above it, which follows more straightforwardly from drawn signs and their West African sources.

Just below the crimson-backed collage appliqué, Jesús reiterated the incised Mokongo *anaforuana* in what we might call a ritual upholstery medium, which is often seen in the construction of rustic Cuban straight-backed chairs: goat hide and tacks. The quartered circle, the eyes of Sikán and Tanze, and the sprouting leaves/feathers are accomplished with thirteen round-headed tacks over the black and off-white skin (plate 10, center).

Having limned Mokongo's firma three times—drawn (incised), wrought in an assemblage of crucifix and cowries, and formed from a more abstract organization of tacks—Jesús presents Mokongo a fourth time, though figuratively in cameo. Near the bottom of the staff, within the third diamond frame, he attached another circular patch of goatskin with eight tacks. Using four brads, Jesús mounted a silver American Roosevelt dime, which presents in profile Franklin Delano Roosevelt. While the tacked outer circle and the four central brads continue to play with Mokongo's drawn sign, the dime cameo intends to represent not precisely the thirty-second president of the United States, but Mokongo Moküire himself. Recontextualized in the staff's semantic field, the commander-in-chief of the United States from the Depression to World War II becomes the supreme military chief of the Abakuá.

Mokongo, Filial Sacrifice, and Andrés Petít's "Dead Christ"

Observers of Abakuá objects since the late nineteenth century have noted the frequent presence of "crucified Christs." Early twentieth-century observers saw this as a "ridiculous profanation," and late twentieth-century anthropologists glossed it as a manifestation of a syncretic "Abakuá Christianism" (Roche y Monteagudo 1908:31; Sosa Rodríguez 1982:156). The cultural bias of the former characterization and the generality of "Abakuá Christianism" do an interpretive disservice to a historically specific and quite subtle use of the crucifix by the Bakokó/Akanarán Efó lineage. Indeed, the Mokongo staff's crucifix is a very particular icon within Christology. Its use by Andrés Petít and his followers is inextricably linked to transformations within the Afro-Cuban practices and their relationship with the emergent "white" Abakuá as of the mid-nineteenth century.

Apparently versed in some of the finer points of Christology, Andrés Petít chose a particular icon to represent the essence of the Regla Kimbisa del Santo Cristo del Buen Viaje. This icon figures Jesus on the cross with his head inclined, in some cases leaning heavily toward the right shoulder. In the Efori Eñongo altar, this icon is seen in the antique silver crucifix of Mokongo's staff (plate 10) and in the carved representation of Abasí (figure 5.12). These Christ figures upon the cross are neither the living nor the resurrected Jesus. As Kimbisero Jesús Nasakó explains,

"The Christ with his head toward the heavens is still alive. . . . He is the *Santo Cristo de Limpias* [Holy Christ of Purification].[47] The Christ with his head on his right shoulder is the Holy *Santo Cristo del Buen Viaje* [the Christ of the Good Passage]. . . . Here Christ is already *dead* on the Cross [*el Cristo Muerto*]." This is the liminally dead Christ, who supposedly walked through the underworld between Good Friday and Easter Sunday—between the Crucifixion and the Resurrection.[48]

In Christology, as Diane Apostolos-Cappadona explains, the iconography of the inclined head began as a function of changes in Byzantine art, in which "the Crucifix was transformed by the aspects of the *Christus Dolor* ('Sad Christ'), whose body was covered only by a loincloth thus exposing his humanity and his wounded torso side. His head tilted to the side, his arms drooped, and his eyes began to close. Two streams poured from his wounded side." Later, in the early medieval period, Christ's head sagged down on his chest (*Christus Patiens,* "Patient Christ"). Finally, in the late fourteenth and early fifteenth centuries, the *Christus Mortuus* ("Dead Christ") developed, particularly in northern Renaissance Europe. This figure was elaborated proto-expressionistically by artists such as Matthias Grünewald. In this last icon, the "body of Jesus reflected all the aspects of *physical death* and *tremendous suffering*" (Apostolos-Cappadona 1994: 93, my emphasis).

The "sad," "suffering," and "dead" Christ cycle perfectly served Petít's ritual and iconographic program for the Regla Kimbisa. Not least, the iconic tradition of the Christus Dolor constituted Petít's own baptismal identity: he was, of course, Andrés Facundo *Cristo de los Dolores* Petít. Like Palo Monte, Kimbisa works spiritually in the otherworld through the relics of deceased intermediaries *(muertos),* including their skulls, tibias, and other bones. Frequently, the relics of persons who suffered great torment in life, such as the African slaves or murder victims, permit their recaptured spirits to perform difficult, fierce, and very "material" work for their human contractors. At the same time, as noted, the crucifix could create the aura of "licitness" and protection with which Petít intended to shroud his beloved Kimbisa religion. Around the middle of the nineteenth century, the resourceful Petít commissioned three to four thousand of these crosses, which were manufactured for him in Milan, Italy, according to his ritual descendant Jesús Nasakó.

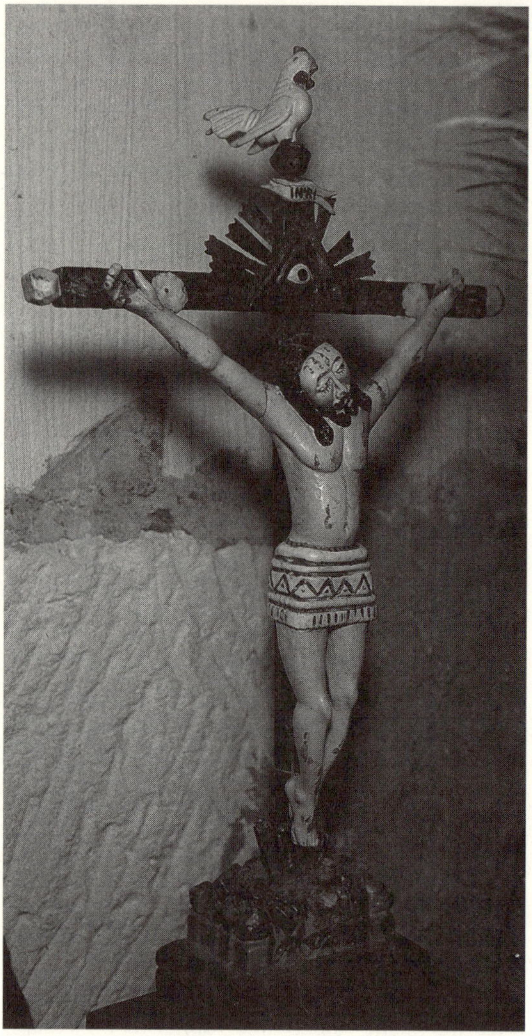

Figure 5.12. Efori Eñongo altar detail, Crucifix of the "sad" or "dead" Christ surmounted by a rooster. About twelve inches tall and of polychromed wood, the crucifix symbolizes "Abasí," the Carabalí High God, as well as the syncretic heritage of Andrés Petít's Regla Kimbisa del Santo Cristo del Buen Viaje within the Akanarán Efó lineage. Photograph by David H. Brown.

Strictly speaking, Mokongo's Dead Christ is not entirely a "found" or "appropriated" "foreign" object.

Petít specifically customized the silver crucifix following Kimbisa form and function. Each crucifix featured a tiny skull and crossbones at Christ's feet. Called *carabela* by Afro-Cuban practitioners, the skull-and-crossbones refers to the spirits of deceased *Africanos esclavizados* (enslaved Africans), most often Congos, who endured the Middle Passage and the brutality of slavery and who died on Cuban soil. The *carabelas* form one of the most important groups of *muertos* in Afro-Cuban ritual work with the dead. Their spirits may be called to cemetery relics placed within the Kimbisa or Palo Monte/Mayombe priest's sacred cauldron *(nganga, nkisi, prenda),* along with graveyard earth and other potent ingredients (see Cabrera 1986a:7, 1954:118–146; Brown 1993a:20–21). Most important, Petít designed the silver crucifix with a tiny *hueco* (aperture) in the back so that it could be embedded with *nkisi* medicine substances.

It is perhaps less useful to debate where on a syncretic scale of "Africanization" and "Christianization" Petít's use of the crucifix lies. Theoretically speaking, if it is a form of self-conscious "bricolage" or "syncretism," it became a fully integrated, traditionalized practice that resists a teasing apart of its elements. The Regla Kimbisa crucifix-*nkisi* is an Afro-Cuban achievement that responded to a set of colonial social and cultural conditions with clear historical precedents. It is useful to recall the similar revision of Portuguese Roman Catholic crucifixes and other icons by the "Christianized" kings of Kongo-Angola as early as the late fifteenth century, which converted them into *minkisi* (Kikongo, plural of *nkisi;* see Balandier 1968; Consentino 1995a:31). In Cuba, in the words of Cabrera's sources, "Andres Petít learned with the congos. . . . We call the Santo Cristo [an] *Nkisi.* This crucifix that you see, which has its *brujeria* inside, accompanies us always. . . . There is no Kimbisa [priest] who doesn't carry it on him. It is obligatory; without Him we are nothing, it is our power, [our] everything" (Cabrera 1986a:4–5).

Upon the Mokongo staff, the Cristo Muerto figures a central episode in the Abakuá founding narrative. For Jesús Nasakó, the Cristo Muerto is an allegory for the role of Sikán and her relationship to Mokongo, her father in one important myth cycle. Mokongo "had to sacrifice his daughter Sikán for the good of the religion. . . . The daughter was sacrificed for the tribe, just as Christ was sacrificed for the Christians—in other words, both are events of filial sacrifice." The Abakuá narrative of "filial sacrifice," becomes, in effect, a dramatic tragedy form, in which a life is given up for a higher principle. As God the Father sacrificed his son, so Mokongo sacrificed his daughter. The shining result was the birth of the Abakuá Society, just as Christ's crucifixion and its subsequent episodes resulted in the birth of Catholicism.

Drawing from, and reinterpreting, the story of Christ in Kimbisa terms—Kimbisa works with relics that embody potent spirits of the dead—Jesús Nasakó understands "Christ as the first *muerto* [deceased] of the Christian era."[49] Similarly, Sikán was the first *muerto* of the Abakuá era, as it were. Within Catholicism, Christ's body and blood would become the essence of the Eucharist, the Holy Sacrament upon the altar. Within Kimbisa, Christ became a leading *muerto,* and the iconography and relics associated with the Cristo Muerto would become powerful *nkisi* media. Within the Abakuá, Sikán-as-*muerto* and her associated iconography and relics (e.g., head, bones, blood, hair, eyes, gourd, feathers, and crown), would form the basis of the first Abakuá altar and its generative *fundamentos:* the *sese,* as well as Ekue. Upon the Mokongo staff, the silver *nkisi*-crucifix becomes a central element in Mokongo's assemblaged *anaforuana,* which thematically encompasses all of these linked narrative pieces and invokes them into presence. As an *nkisi,* this crucifix exemplifies the ritual technology and *cosmovisión* that Kimbisa and the Bakokó/Akanarán Efó lineage share.

Of course, in Bakokó/Akanarán Efó lineage practice, the *potencia* of the altar and the *fo-ekue* (room of Ekue) take center stage in Abakuá ritualizing but do not eclipse the iconography Andrés Petít incorporated into Kimbisa during the mid-nineteenth century. Apart from Jesús Nasakó's use of the Christ figure for Mosongo, Mokongo, and the narrative of "filial sacrifice," the realistic, polychromed wood crucifix of the *Cristo Muerto* also represents the Abakuá "High God" (Abasí), and belongs to the *plaza* by the same name, Abasí. Second, the Christian Holy Sacrament is represented conspicuously in the altar's antique brass monstrance (plate 11, left). The staffs and drums of the altar and the monstrance and crucifix both stand alone and mutually define one another for many Abakuá.

The "monstrance," or *ostensorium,* is a Roman Catholic altar object developed in the fourteenth century to display the consecrated Host for adoration and meditation. From the Latin for "show," the *ostensorium* could be placed on the altar for the veneration of the Sacrament and carried in procession (see Hemeldonck 1995:299; Apostolos-Cappadona 1994:244). In common versions of the *ostensorium,* its flat circular form surmounting the sacred chalice is called the *paten.* It stands vertically, for display purposes, before the flock and is seen frontally as a disk. It represents the gold plate used to hold the Host. It also stands for the Last Supper and the plate used to serve the Eucharistic bread.[50] In the antique brass monstrance upon Efori Eñongo's altar, the *paten* bears the Jesuit symbol for the name of Jesus: the three letters IHS are based on the "abbreviation of the Greek form of the name of Jesus" (Howard 1995: 508). This monstrance form is very common in Cuba; the Jesuit order played a formidable role and had a lasting influence in Latin America, including the Spanish possessions (Frazer 1995:513–514).[51] Among Cubans, the monstrance is referred to as the *Santísimo Sacramento,* the "Holy Sacrament." One of the two principal polyvocal references to Christ and Abasí, the monstrance, remains on the altar during celebrations. The other, the sculpture of Christ, is carried at the lead of the Abakuá procession by the Abasí *plaza,* sometimes atop his head (figure 5.1). In this context, particularly when the early Akanarán Efó–descended lodges made their way past the church, the sculpture provided a double entendre: it signified both the reign of the Carabalí God, Abasí, over the procession and the baptismally legitimate place of Abakuá members within the Christian fold. Whether or not individual members internalized their place within the Church and the Christian belief system, Petít and his followers apparently intended such displays to "guarantee themselves," in the words of Alfred Métraux, "immunity from the insults addressed to the non-baptized" (1972:331).

Abasonga's brass key fobs and Mokongo's Roosevelt dime exemplify another domain of appropriation in the service of Abakuá iconography and narrative. Together with Jesús Nasakó's brilliantly wrought finial of Mokongo's staff, the three adornments highlight the treasure house of mass and official cultures as a fertile source of artistic possibilities—beyond the iconography of the Church. The first circulated within the early Cuban Intur commercial system, requiring American dollars for its purchase; if some of these *íreme* brass key fobs ended up in the hands, and on the altars, of the Abakuá, countless others must have ended up abroad, attached to the ignition keys of Italian, Spanish, German, and Canadian tourists. The second, a Roosevelt dime, undoubtedly also entered Cuba through the foreign-currency pipeline, inasmuch as all tourists had to pay in U.S. dollars, which continued to circulate between Intur and hotel cash registers and the hands of ordinary Cubans, not least as they received tips from foreigners. Many American bills and coins have circulated for years in Cuba; through the mid-1990s, one could still find 1935 silver certificates in one- and five-dollar denominations, along with buffalo nickels and Indian-head pennies in Havana cashiers' tills. If the Roosevelt dime marks, albeit in a general way, the relationship between the U.S., Cuban, and global economies, it also marks a more specific bit of ironic historical conjuncture. Originally struck with the engraver's initials, J. S., for John Sinnock, though probably based on a relief of Roosevelt by the African American sculptor Selma Burke, the dime began as a memento of this beloved president and hero of liberty. Soon afterward, with the Cold War and Communist conspiracy in the air, and given the ideological color perceived in Roosevelt's New Deal, so many Americans believed that J. S. stood for Josef Stalin that the "Mint was forced to issue a statement identifying the coin's creator, and refuting the claim of 'Reds' being harbored within its venerable walls" (Numismatic Guaranty Corporation 2001). The finial atop Mokongo's staff carries an equally ironic and intriguing "biography" (Kopytoff 1986).

A slender nude female figure rises from Mokongo's upper *casquillo* (figure 5.9, right). She gazes upward toward her cupped skyward hands. Five inches tall, the cast and chromed metal figure was a hood ornament that Jesús Nasakó stole in the 1970s from a 1959 Ford Edsel, one of the innumerable pre–Castro era car models that continue to prowl Cuba's streets.[52] Ford had launched this bloated symbol of American mass cultural fantasy, which immediately became a nightmarish lemon, in 1957, two years before American economic and cultural dominance in Cuba came to an end with the triumph of Fidel Castro, Ché Guevara, and Camilo Cienfuegos. Not the Edsel's original hood ornament, the romantic female figure was, undoubtedly, one of countless begged, borrowed, or stolen improvisations of global car culture, which Cubans, in particular, have mastered, in order to conserve and beautify their *cacharros* (big old cars). In contemporary Cuba, against the crumbling background of Havana's baroque architecture, the boatlike *cacharro,* as in a movie set, poignantly calls up a romanticized, bygone era for the foreign visitor. In truth, most Cubans would rather have a smaller, more gas-efficient Russian Lada. Upon Mokongo's *casquillo,* itself a bulky chromed metal ornament that reminds one of a car bumper, the figure represents none other than Mokongo Mokuire's daughter, Sikán. Sikán's figure used to hold between her cupped hands a tiny articulated metal fish, an old Chinese import item, representing Tanze. Jesús had recreated, in found mass-produced assemblage, the moment in which Sikán lifted Tanze above her head.

Though the *íremes* of Abasonga's staff more narrowly reference a mythico-historical personage within the Abakuá universe, Jesús Nasakó's explanations of his working process and the events around such prize found objects constitute a meta-narrative that conjoins, in significant ways, ostensibly separate domains. The finial, the key fobs, and the dime compound their significance from previous contexts of production and distribution with their recontextualized significance within Abakuá assemblages.

6 "Symbolic Drums"

Innovations and Inventions

The Abakuá altar's drums,[1] with seven elegant *plumeros* distributed among them, embody the seven principal grades of the lodge: Iyamba, Mokongo, Isué, and Isunekue in the *sese,* and Mpegó, Ekueñón, and Enkríkamo in three additional drums. As integral to the lodge's *potencia,* these drums authorize each officeholder's role and duties, as well as symbolize and evoke the personas of each of the seven archetypal officeholders. In short, they condense the ancestral history and liturgy of the lodge and the Abakuá Society. The drums, as consecrated emblems, compound all of the Iyambas, Mokongos, Isués, Isunekues, Mpegós, Ekueñóns, and Enkríkamos, as well as all of the *obonekues,* who, over time, were sworn to *ekue*—the living and those who have passed. They are, like the staffs, living repositories and generators of a specific diasporic history, practice, and imagination.

Abakuá altar drums, as Fernando Ortiz defined them, carry a "symbolic and ritual" function. They are mounted with a consecrated goatskin *parche,* and all but the goblet-shaped *sese* carry the cord-and-wedge tuning system like the four drums of the Abakuá orchestra *(biankomeko).* Though the individual drums of Mpegó, Ekueñón, and Enkríkamo are regularly tapped in calls to attention, they are not played musically (plates 1, 11; figures 6.1, 6.2).[2] Instead, as Ortiz wrote in 1954,

> each one has a specific mystic function. They represent the respective supernatural entities and, in turn, in their worldly interventions. . . . [These] spirits are represented . . . by high dignitaries, ministers or priests, who carry their name and perform with those drums in their hands, [tapping] their respective instruments in order to vitalize their sacred potency, and speaking in their name. This "personification" of a superior entity, through the medium of a drum that emits its voice, is very frequent in Africa. We have already said that among its various peoples the term that signifies *drum* is synonymous with "king," "chief," or "command." (Ortiz 1954:42)

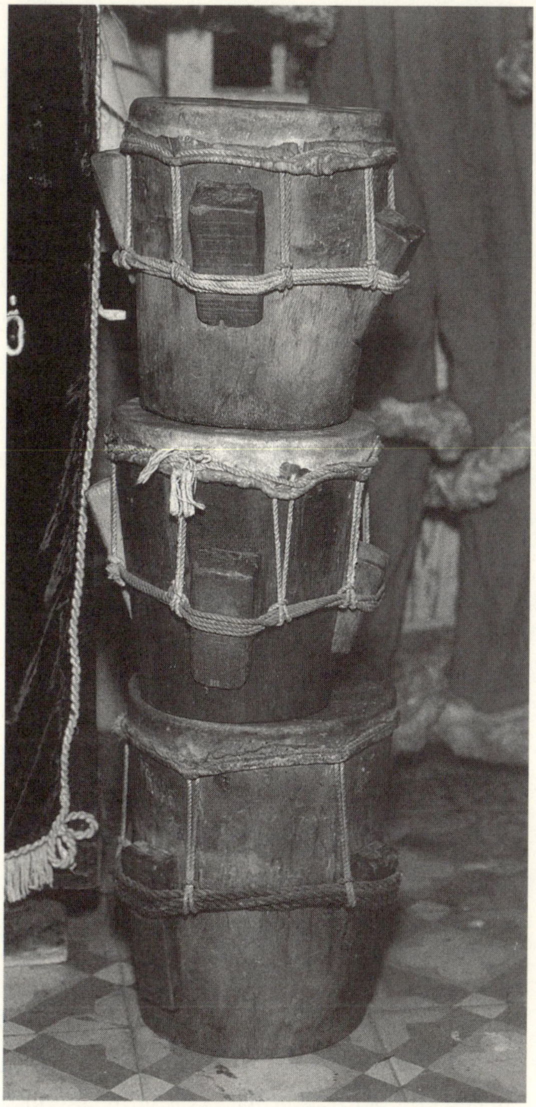

Figure 6.1. The three *enkomos* of the Efori Eñongo musical orchestra *(biankomeko);* from top to bottom, Kuchi Yeremá, Arobapá, and Biapá. They are tuned with a system of cords and wedges *(cuñas),* which are driven downward to tighten the skins. The fourth orchestra drum, the *bonkó enchemiyá,* is a tall tapered drum (not pictured; see figures 2.5, 2.6, and plate 1). Photograph by David H. Brown.

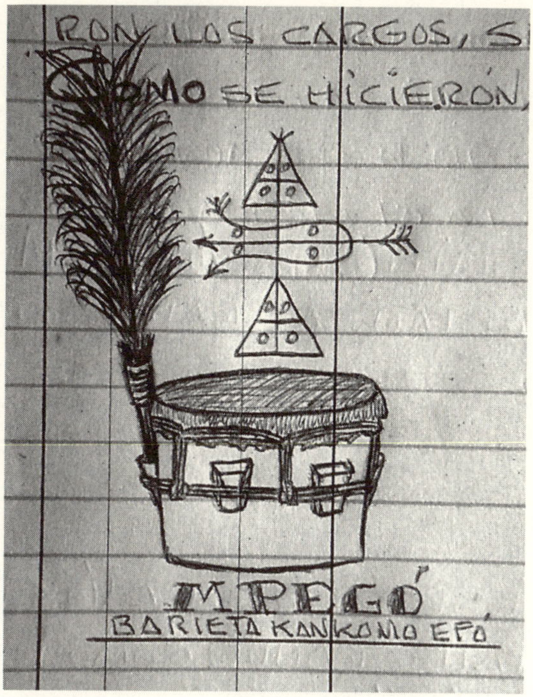

Figure 6.2. Jesús Nasakó, *Mpegó Barieta Kankomo Efó.* Blue ballpoint pen drawing of Mpegó's drum and his sign in Jesús's private Abakuá ledger book. The drum is in the *enkomo* or *kankomo* style, which features the same wedge-tuning system as the orchestra drums. Mpegó represents the principles of "Order" and the "Law" in the lodge. Photograph by David H. Brown.

As representatives of high dignitaries and bearers of a "vital . . . sacred potency," Abakuá altar drums possess a form of subjectivity and agency, a characteristic of consecrated vessels and drums in African and Afro-Cuban religions (see, e.g., MacGaffey 1988:203; M. Mason 2002). They are animated through their initial consecration and reinvigorated by regular ritualizing.

The "vitality" of Abakuá drums especially revolves around the drumskin, the *parche,* taken from *mbori,* which, through consecration, embodies *ekue.* The *parche* is the most crucial link of sacred transmission across space and time between different generations of *potencias* and geographically separated *tierras.* Theoretically, any given *parche* could trace its origin to the skin of the first *mbori* sacrificed in Awana Bekura Mendo. Any skin used, Jesús Nasakó explains,

> must come from a goat that was sacrificed in an Abakuá consecration ceremony, in which [*ekue*] was transmitted [to it] and the *fundamento* [the Ekue drum]. Those skins also serve to mount any of the drums or to cover any of the staffs. The skin does not

come from just any goat. If it was not part of the consecration, it's useless; it is not sacred, and cannot be used for a drum or staff. After the consecration, the skin is cleaned, dried, and stored. For example, the skin of Ekue can break, and in order to replace it, you must have another goatskin that has eaten [blood] with the *fundamento,* that is, which came from a goat that was killed [to feed] the *fundamento.* When the skin breaks, and it is replaced with a new one, the old one is placed inside the Ekue [drum]. It is stuffed in there, and left there. It is piously guarded. We have old skins put away, and although those old skins are not functioning, they are regularly fed and attended to, *because in those skins reside the ancestral spirits of those who were sworn [initiated] atop that Ekue drum skin. There, in them, is the transmission of all the old ones that died and passed into those skins.* For that reason, no one person can say that they know all there is to know about [any given] consecration, because such knowledge cannot fit within a single head. This secret knowledge is distributed [and held collectively; emphasis added].[3]

The "piously guarded" goatskins of Abakuá consecrations (e.g., *baroko fundamento* and *normal*) comprise a store to be used not only in the remounting of Ekue, but also in the mounting of the symbolic and musical drums, as well as in the adornment of the staffs. Therefore, "every *pieza* [drum or staff]," says Nasakó, "*is* a *fundamento,*" an earthly material support with indwelling spiritual power.[4] An Abakuá *fundamento* represents not only the particular ancestral presence associated with it—Iyamba, Mpegó, Ekueñón, and so on—but also the entire sacred genealogy, the corporate group, and the collective secret knowledge of the Abakuá—*ekue,* in the broadest sense.

Four *Obones* in the *Sese* and Three Chiefs in Mpegó, Ekueñón, and Enkríkamo

The *sese* drum supports the leadership edifice of the *potencia,* the four ancestral personages, the *obones:* Iyamba, Mokongo, Isué, and Isunekue. Edifice is an apt metaphor, inasmuch as the *plumeros* of the *sese,* Juan Mokongo explained, are the "Four Columns of the *potencia.*" Iyamba, as noted, is the "Highest King." Mokongo is the "Supreme Chief." Isué is the "Bishop" of the Abakuá (see Cabrera 1970:161–176). He is the "priest" of all "baptisms"—consecrations and initiations. As the "bishop," Isué is also the primary custodian of the lodge's *sese* itself, the "Holy Sacrament" of the Abakuá Society. Isunekue, the "husband of Sikán," is Sikán's principal male representative in the Abakuá hierarchy, though some lodges also reserve an honorary Sikán *plaza* for a postmenopausal woman. Isunekue, as Sikán's "husband," is also, interestingly, the "owner of the *parche*" of *ekue,* the sacred skin that mounts all drums, including the *sese* and Ekue. It seems that the husband owns his wife's "skin," which, in its "substitute" form, is the skin of *mbori.* For this reason, apparently, Isunekue is also considered the "confidant of Iyamba," and, is permitted to substitute for Iyamba in producing the Voice (Cabrera 1970:16–97,174–179).[5]

Mpegó, Ekueñón, and Enkríkamo, the three chiefs *(jefes)* directly beneath the four *obones* stand for law and order, authorized execution in the name of *ekue,* and guidance of the Abakuá Society's distinctive spirit messengers, the *íremes,* respectively. In contrast to the goblet- or urn-shaped *sese* of the Bakokó Efor/Akanarán Efó line, the individual drums of Mpegó, Ekueñón, and Enkríkamo possess the squat, tapered, open-bottomed *enkomo* (alt. *kankomo*) form of the musical drums of the Abakuá orchestra in both the Efó and Efí branches, as well as the open-bottomed *sese* of the Efí branch. Each of the three altar drums features an adorned *plumero,* which is marked with the *firma* of its respective owner (figure 6.2; plates 11, right, and 12). Made of cedar, each drum is typically encircled with a *beromo* or *muñón,* a sashlike piece of regalia made of stiff vegetal fringe, often from the palm. Such fringe on all Abakuá attributes, including *íreme* suits, is called *empitá* or *belemé.*[6]

Mpegó's principal emblem of office is sometimes called the "Drum of Order" and "Drum of Respect."[7] As Juan Mokongo explained to me, Mpegó represents "the Law," or better stated, he continued, the juridical consequences of oath-taking. "Mpegó is the one who confirms the initiation of everyone. The day you slip up, Mpegó authorizes your punishment," which is preceded only by Mosongo's deliberation. Therefore, Mpegó's drum is called *Ekue Mpegó Barieta Kankomo Efó.* This means, as Juan elaborated, "The Drum of the Law of Efó, the one that sentences you to punishment. The first Mpegó gave three beats to his drum, *bap, bap, bap,* and condemned Sikán to die as a sacrificial victim" (see figure 6.2).[8]

During ceremonies, Mpegó maintains order in the temple and authorizes the most important activities. As the "scribe" and "director of the religion," a master of ceremonies, Mpegó traces *anaforuana* in yellow or white chalk (Br. *ngomo,* Sp. *yeso*)[9] on all of the objects, initiates, offerings, and on the temple's floor. Mpegó is extremely close to the Ekue drum. It was precisely through Mpegó's legal condemnation of Sikán that the fabrication of Ekue could be realized by Nasakó. Mpegó's drum, therefore, logically, existed before Ekue and therefore can act as Ekue's substitute. Played with the *güín,* Mpegó is converted into a friction drum (see e.g., Cabrera 1954, plates) (figures 6.3 and 6.4).[10]

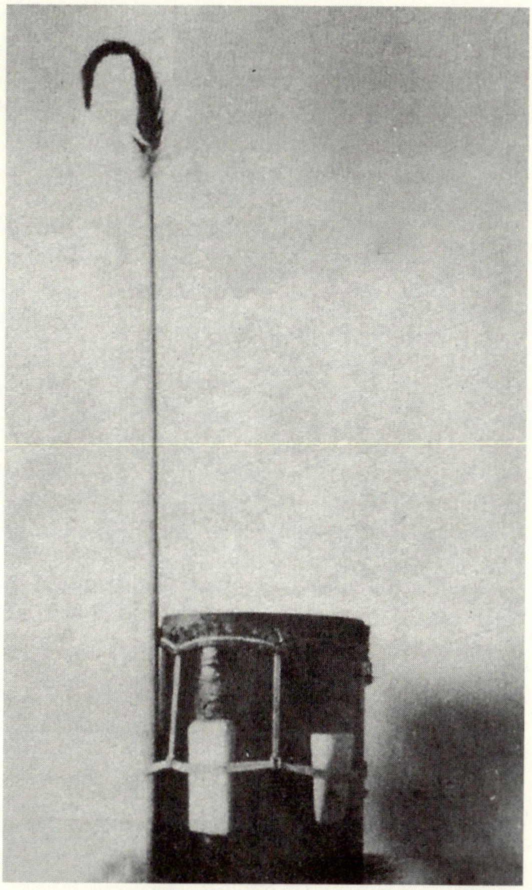

Figure 6.3. ***Mpegó Mbibó Muna. The Mpegó drum substituting for Ekue.*** **1957. The photograph shows the feather-surmounted *yín* or *güín,* which is otherwise stored in the staff of Mosongo and used primarily by Iyamba to sound the Ekue drum. The Mpegó drum can substitute, as a friction drum, for Ekue if necessary, as shown here. (From Cabrera 1958, third plate after p. 144. Courtesy of the Estate of Lydia Cabrera.)**

Ekueñón is the pathfinder and precursor of Ekue's sounding. Above all, he is responsible for sustaining the vitality of the *potencia.* Without Ekueñón, the hunter and executioner who acts with the legal sanction of Mpegó, there would be no blood for purposes of consecration. In this sense, he is very much like the hunter Oshosi of the Lukumí religion, an itinerant who tracks the path, brings sustenance to the community. In Jesús Nasakó's etymology, "Ekueñón" derives from "Ekueñong": *ekue* is the *fundamento,* or foundation; *ñong* is the "action of killing." Thus, "Ekueñón means executioner on behalf of *ekue,* that is, Ekueñón sacrifices in order to nourish the sacred attributes" and the initiated sons of *ekue.* In his role as the "hunter," Ekueñón "searches for the Voice" in the forest (i.e., in the courtyard outside the *fambá*). He "captures" *ekue* in his drum and returns to the temple so that Ekue can sound in the inner sanctum. Because he is intimate with the spirit of *ekue* as it permeates the forest and manifests in the leopard, Ekueñón's drum is typically covered in leopardskin (plate 12). Following his transmission of *ekue* across the threshold of the *fambá,* Ekueñón emerges once again in an indispensable role. Standing just outside the door to the temple, he "breaks open the path" for the ceremony to begin with his chanted *enkame de rompimiento,* followed by a burst of gunpowder.[11] Ritual bursts of gunpowder to clear obstacles and, veritably, shoot spiritual forces in carefully chosen directions, are

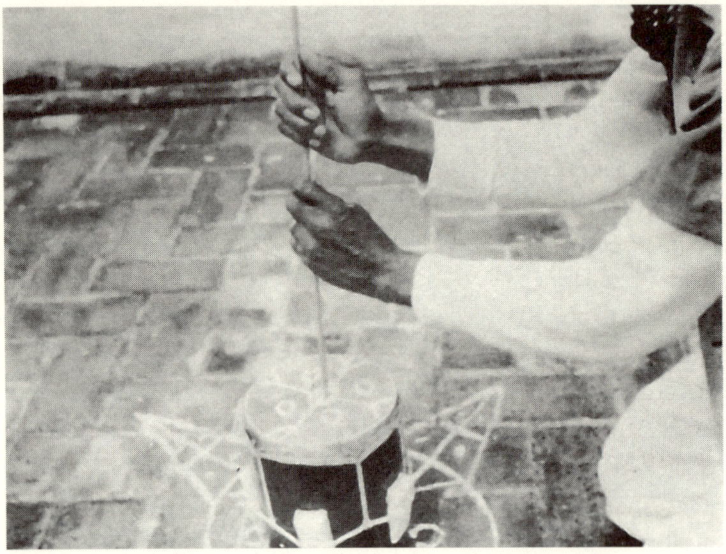

Figure 6.4. *Fragayando. Orotoyín oroto apana wa.* 1957. Sounding Ekue with the *yín* over the *gandó* sign. Here Cabrera's informant sounds Ekue in a demonstration on a *patio*, possibly of the lodge itself or in Cabrera's own Quinta San José, where it was photographed by Pierre Verger, who was visiting Cuba in 1957. (From Cabrera 1970, eighth plate after page 144.) Courtesy of the Estate of Lydia Cabrera.

central to the talents and skills of hunters like Ekueñón and Ochosi and the warrior spirits of Palo Monte.

As "Chief of the Íremes," Enkríkamo commands the hooded masqueraders in order that they perform their duties within and without the *fambá.* He calls them out of the temple into the courtyard to dance to the music of the orchestra and to assist in tasks such as preparing *mbori* for sacrifice. When necessary, he calls them back into the temple. Enkríkamo carries his diminutive plumed drum—he is called "the smallest son of Ekue"[12]—wherever *íremes* are present, directing and controlling their actions (plate 11, right). Most of his commands are gestural, as he elegantly "dances" his drum in step with the agile *íremes.* However, Ekueñón may speak to the *íremes* in Brícamo if they are not following his orders. For example, he may firmly say: *"Íreme! asokaká tié tié bonkrí bongó butame"* ("Respect everything that is here") or *"Íreme akamanyere bonkrí bongó butame"* ("Respect this attribute [drum] because it controls you"). The *íreme* must respond immediately with a gesture of respect, a genuflection, which is called *entumitiá* in Brícamo (plate 13). Exemplifying the great authority and agency of the altar drums themselves, Enkríkamo's drum can continue to command the *íremes* without the presence of the *plaza*-holder himself. The Enkríkamo officeholder might reenter the temple and place his drum on the floor. This obligates the *íremes* to return inside and kneel before it. Enkríkamo can then leave to perform another duty, and the *íremes* must guard the drum while he is gone. If anyone else inappropriately approaches the drum, they *entregarle palos* ("deliver a beating") to the transgressor.[13]

Sese *Namokimbán* and Sese *Eribó*: The "Charged" and "Empty" Sese

Because striking differences in drum form, contents, and connections to specific interests and institutions within the Abakuá Society are amply documented, the *sese* is a valuable study in historical, religious, and artistic change. Two different *sese* types are found on Abakuá altars today: a goblet- or urn-shaped cedar vessel sealed with a goatskin head. It is called the *sese de copón* ("goblet *sese*"); there is also the open-bottomed cedar drum form. Cylindrical in shape, and squarish in its profile, this drum form resembles the three small orchestra drums (*enkomo* or *kankomo* form). Both versions, the *sese de copón* and *sese de kankomo,* feature four *plumeros* and may be covered in

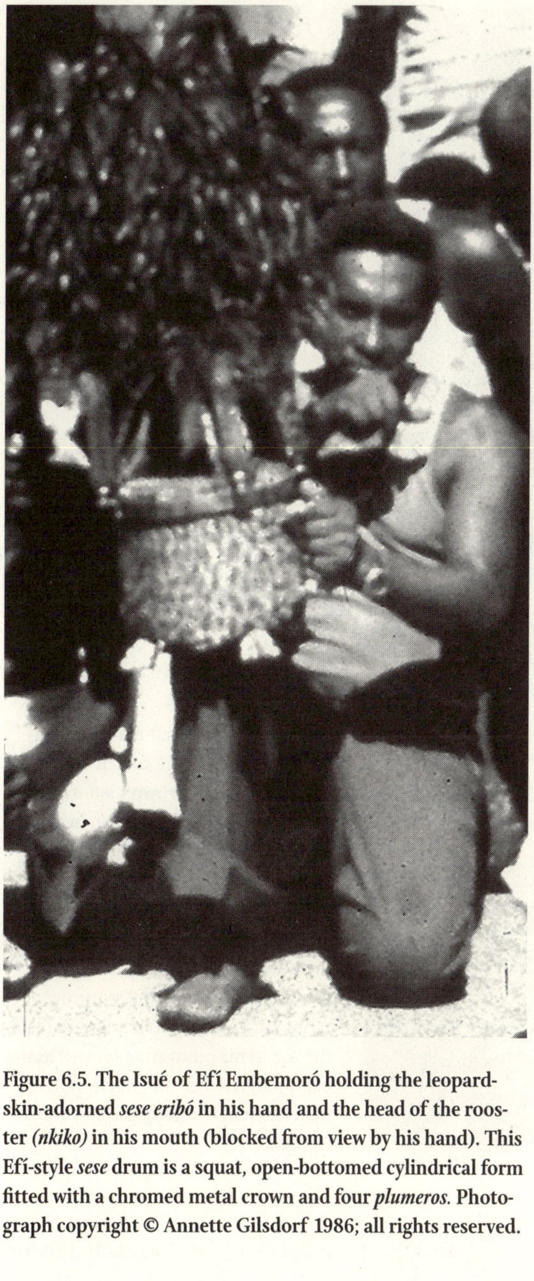

Figure 6.5. The Isué of Efí Embemoró holding the leopardskin-adorned *sese eribó* in his hand and the head of the rooster *(nkiko)* in his mouth (blocked from view by his hand). This Efí-style *sese* drum is a squat, open-bottomed cylindrical form fitted with a chromed metal crown and four *plumeros.* Photograph copyright © Annette Gilsdorf 1986; all rights reserved.

leopardskin (compare plate 11 and figures 6.1 and 6.5). With its institution within the Akanarán Efó line by 1863, the *sese de copón* came to be associated with the Efó branch in general, while the *sese de kankomo* remains a distinguishing attribute of the Efí branch.

Historically, the emergence of the *sese de copón* form corresponds directly to Andrés Petít's "reform" of the Abakuá Society with Akanarán Efó #1, his innovations utilizing Catholic and Kimbisa elements, and the harsh response the new "white" branch received from the established Havana Efí and Efó lodges. The goblet-shaped *sese* provoked intense conflict among the two principal Abakuá branches, including aggressively contested truth claims over the "authenticity" and "origins" of the two forms among practitioners and scholars. Observers have referred to Akanarán's *sese de copón* as the *forma criolla de copón,* "*creole* goblet form" (Ortiz 1954:64, 77) because it was associated with the *mulato* Andrés Petít's reformist "innovations" as opposed to a presumably older, African-based open-bottomed drum form. Not to be trumped, however, members of the Akanarán line from the beginning responded with their own claims to their *sese*'s authenticity.

The *sese de copón* of Eforí Eñongo is a lathe-turned, hollow cedar goblet approximately ten inches in height with a drumhead of about nine inches in diameter (plate 11). This *sese,* fabricated in 1916, follows the pattern set by Petít's Akanarán Efó *sese,* produced in 1863. As Petít intended, the goblet form served a crucial function. The vessel was and is believed to have been "charged" with secret ingredients and then sealed by the goatskin drumhead over its aperture. In his 1979 renovation of Efori Eñongo's *sese,* Jesús Nasakó relates, he "refreshed" the contents, encircled the drumhead with a yellow and white silk fringe, and covered the urn in leopardskin, beads, and cowrie shells. Efori Eñongo's *sese* also wears a chrome-plated metal crown surmounted by a crucifix (plate 11). Its four *plumeros* are inserted into tubular slots at the base of the crown's arches (figure 6.6).

"Charged" *(cargado)* with potent materials from which its force derived—beyond the *parche* itself—the goblet-shaped *sese* earned the Brícamo praise name *sese namokimbán* (alt. *namoquimbán*). This term has been translated as *"sese* of *brujería,"* or "witchcraft" in common Cuban parlance (Ortiz 1954:75; Cabrera 1988:482). Scholars might now translate *namokimbán* as pertaining to sacred "medicines," that

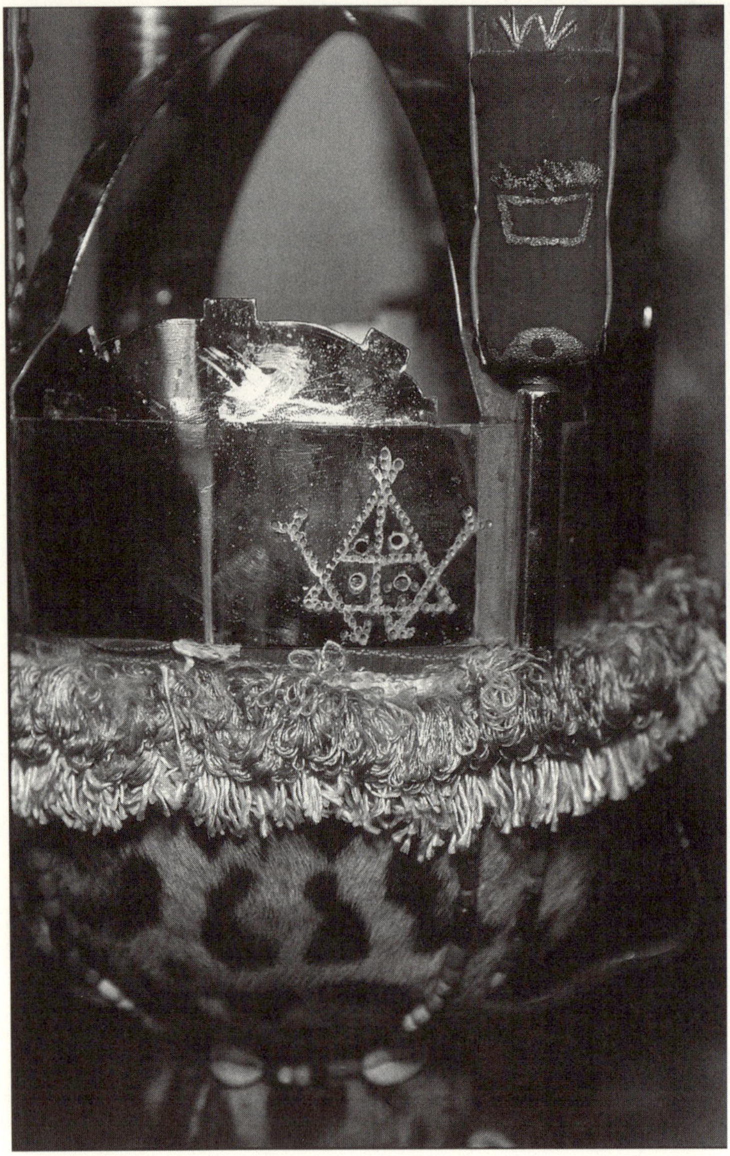

Figure 6.6. Detail, *sese* drum of Efori Eñongo, showing the sign of Isué punched into the crown's band next to Isué's *plumero.* Also shown in close-up is the crenellated, cutout dome flanking the arches, a version of the arch-and-miter combination appropriated by European kings to signify their divine rule. Also visible are the two bands of yellow and white decorative fringe Jesús Nasakó applied to the *sese* in his renovation, as well as the hand-painted designs later applied by Juan Mokongo. Photograph by David H. Brown.

is, charged with "spirit-embodying" ingredients, including relics (see Thompson 1983:117; MacGaffey 1983:117; 1988). The first *sese namokimbán* or its prototype is believed to have belonged to Bakokó Efor before the birth of Akanarán Efó, and its first exponent is believed to have been none other than Andrés Facundo Cristo de los Dolores Petít, the founder of the Regla Kimbisa and the Isué of Bakokó (see Ortiz 1954:74–75; Cabrera 1988:482).[14] The Isué grade is the principal custodian of the *sese.*

For Abakuá of the Bakokó Efor/Akanarán Efó lineage, the visual appearance of the *sese namokimbán* gives iconic form to its supposed secret contents. For them, the *sese*'s goblet-profile "represents the head and neck of Sikán." The crown further elaborates this anthropomorphized bust-portrait of the Efó princess (plate 11). According to Jesús Nasakó, "In Africa, Nangobié Nasakó made the first *sese* with Sikán's head. . . . [Every *sese namokimbán*] represents her head, as such, and, for that reason, the *carga* inside carries the hair and . . . the *kiyumba* [cranium or] . . . a piece of bone of a deceased woman, as well as a fish . . . recalling Tanze. . . . Every *sese namokimbán* must contain this. Furthermore, every *sese* [*namokimbán*] contains the hair and nails of the *plazas* and *ekobios* [officers and brothers of the lodge] . . . [all of] which recalls all the *brujería* that Nasakó made for the first time." Following the sacrifice of Sikán, Nangobié Nasakó, the Congo sorcerer, it is believed, confected the *sese*'s *brujería* in preparation for the first Abakuá consecrations in Awana Bekura Mendo. Similarly, prior to the *baroko fundamento* of every new Efó *potencia* and the initiation of its officers, the reliquary-like *sese namokimbán* is prepared by the Nasakó of the sponsoring lodge. In the case of Eforí Eñongo, Jesús Nasakó is charged with this responsibility.

The *sese namokimbán* is "charged like an *nganga*," Jesús explains.[15] The *nganga*, of course, is the sacred "cauldron" or "pot" (figure 3.10) of the Congo-Cuban Palo Monte and Kimbisa religions and is also known as *caldero, prenda, nkisi,* and *nkiso* (see Cabrera 1954: 118–146; 1986a; 1986b; Thompson 1983:117–124; 1993:60–69). By extension, the Nasakó grade, in his capacity as the confector of the *brujería* of the *sese de copón,* performs in ways similar to a Palo Monte or Kimbisa priest. In this case, Jesús is a life-long Kimbisero, and he understands his role in relation to the work Petít performed within Kimbisa and the Abakuá lineage he founded.

The *sese de copón* is, in effect, a Kimbisa *nganga* inserted into the Abakuá *potencia.* Efó *sese* ingredient lists documented by Cuban scholars Fernando Ortiz and Enrique Sosa Rodríguez closely resemble the principal contents of the *nganga:* human and animal relics, sacred earths (e.g., from the cemetery), plants, and diverse liquids (water, holy oil, and holy water from the Catholic Church; see Sosa Rodríguez 1982: 178).[16] Hence, Ortiz concluded, "the goblet form [uses] a practice common to the Kongo *nganguleros* [priests], among whom Petít was initiated." In a rare display of levity, Ortiz commented that the *sese* was "like a bomb prepared in secret by African science" (1954:76–77).

The *sese de copón* serves not only to embody and invoke the spirits of Sikán and Tanze, and by extension, the force of *ekue.* Because the Abakuá corporate structure, particularly its junta of four *obones,* was built atop the "foundation" of Sikán and Tanze's relics, an important part of the goblet's *brujería* is charged on behalf of the four men who occupy the top *plazas* of a new lodge.[17] The goblet's differentiated interior compartments or the bases of the *plumeros* themselves, as Ortiz found, are charged with ingredients that empower and protect each of the four *obones,* Iyamba, Mokongo, Isué, and Isunekue. According to Ortiz, this *brujería* enables "each *obon* [to] unite . . . his force with that of the other three *obones* for the defense of the secret fraternal group." When one of the four *obones* is replaced, "the *sese* must be opened in order to renovate the *carga* with the fetish [*fetiche*] of the new *obon,* upon his being named and sworn" (Ortiz 1954:75). In contemporary terminology, "fetish" would refer to an assemblage of metonymically resonant materials with indwelling force, such as the hair and nails of each *obon.*[18] In short, like an *nganga* or *nkisi,* the ingredients provide ancestral energies (such as Sikán and Tanze) with appropriate material supports or foundations in the world, arrested and contained within a bodylike vessel (see MacGaffey 1983:17, 1988; Thompson 1983:117–124).

Like the *nganga* or *nkisi* of Palo Monte or Kimbisa, the *sese* could be utilized for defensive and offensive ritual work on behalf of the *juego* or its individual members. As Ortiz argues, initially, the goal of the "charged" *sese namokimbán* was to protect the "white" Abakuás "against the blacks and orthodox, who disagreed with Petít's *Reform* . . . [i.e., the] whitening of their secret society . . . [though they] would not dare to attack the 'new *ñáñigos*' for fear of the witchcraft given them by Andrés Petít, who was one of the most feared sorcerers Cuba ever had" (Ortiz 1954:74).

Conflict over Petít's introduction of the *sese de copón* manifested in rhetorical, as well as physical, struggle. Rhetorical contest has taken the form of ideological and analytical debates over the definition, naming, and significance of the Efó and Efí *sese* forms, as well as a genre of ritual insult characteristic of the more macho Afro-Cuban practices such as Palo Monte. For example, though scholars and practitioners alike typically refer to all *sese* drums as *sese eribó* (alt. *seseribó, eribó*), Jesús Nasakó insists that the *sese* of the Efí line, which bears the *kankomo* form, should be called *sese eribó,* strictly speaking. *Sese eribó,* he explains, means "sacred-hollow" or "empty" *sese.* For Jesús and members of the Akanarán Efó line, the open-bottomed *sese* of the Efí derives its status by negative definition: it is merely "uncharged," an "empty" *sese (sese vacío)* with four *plumeros.*[19]

Whether the Efí *sese eribó* is actually "empty" and whether the *sese efó de copón* is actually "charged," as Akanarán advocates claim, has been vociferously debated. In response to Efí denunciations of the Akanarán Efó lineage, the latter fired back with a Congo-Cuban form of ritual insult called *puya* or *mpuya,* which had entered Afro-Cuban religious performance and popular Cuban discourse (see Castellanos 1977: 141–160). As Ortiz notes, the Efó liked to "throw the *puya,*" *kimbán umón ayenirén,* in order to rib the Efí for their inadequacy. The Brícamo phrase means: "'the *brujería* or magical force of the *efí* is like the water of the river,' that is, its pure, clear water, [but] without 'carga,' and [thus] inoperable" (Ortiz 1954:75). The Efí of Cuba had thrown their own *puyas* at the Efó. These undoubtedly included the accusation that the *sese* of Petít the "traitor" was no more than a mere *invention,* a Cuban reference to groundlessness and inauthenticity, and a matter of *negocio* (business), rather than religion.

Jesús Nasakó, no detractor of the Efí line, concedes that the Efó *puya* denies that the Efí *sese eribó,* though not a charged and sealed goblet, in fact carries small protective magical packets, or *makuto,* attached to the inside.[20] Most important, the ritual efficacy of the Efí *sese eribó* derives not from sealed *brujería,* but from its spiritually imbued *parche,* the drumskin itself. In the *baroko fundamento,* which grounds a *potencia, ekue* is "transmitted" from the sponsor's extant *sese parche* to the new lodge's *sese parche.* During initiations, where the Efó *sese* is placed atop the neophyte's head, the Efí *sese* goblet is lowered over the neophyte's head, helmetlike, so that the head's crown comes into direct contact with the sacred *parche.*

At the same time, recent interviews reveal, revisionist members of the Akanarán Efó line in Regla argue that the sealed, goblet-shaped *sese* is inauthentic. For them, the existence of a "charged" goblet *sese* is more rhetorical than real, more myth than reality. The foremost maker and renovator of Abakuá attributes for lodges in Havana and Matanzas, whom I shall call Pablo, a loyal member of the Akanarán lineage, argues that the *sese de copón* of Andrés Petít was *mere syncretic invention;* it simply "did not exist in Africa." The only "true" *sese,* he believes, continues to be that of the Efí line, the open-bottomed symbolic drum in the *kankomo* form. Having renovated nearly forty goblet-shaped Efó *seses* in his career, many of which were older than eighty or ninety years, he found no more than a handful that contained anything, and just two among those that contained anything significant. This large sample, making up a sizable proportion of all the Efó *sese* drums in Cuba, includes several of the earliest descendants of the Akanarán Efó lineage, lodges founded from the last third of the nineteenth through the first two decades of the twentieth century. As Pablo related to me in March 2002, "from time to time you find two little chunks of chalk, yellow and white, or merely a mix of yellow and white powder. In one I actually found a small dead mouse, and I have no idea how it got in there." In only one *sese* he found a *makuto,* a little bag of powders and ingredients, and in another he found a small mass of dried herbs. "Do you think," he asked me rhetorically, that the members "really open up the *sese* every time a *plaza* dies in order to replace the herbs and relics? And even if they wanted to, how could they identify the particular herbs and hair that needed to be replaced," given that materials from multiple men are assumed to be contained in the vessel?

In short, if only two of nearly forty *sese* drums, representing a large proportion of the Efó lodges in Cuba, do not have secret contents within them, which *seses* do, if at all? Might it be that this "secret," is, in fact, a socially efficacious myth, as Karin Barber found in her research on the Yoruba concept of the "secret" (*awo*):

> It is by being made into a "secret" that a spiritual being gets its authority. It has been said [among the Yoruba], "If something we call *'awo'* has nothing in it to frighten the uninitiated, let's stop calling it *'awo'*; but if we put a stone in a gourd and make a couple of taboos to stop people looking into it, it's become an *'awo'*. The face of a denizen of heaven [ancestor masquerade] is *'awo'* for the very reason that if you removed its costume you might find nothing there." Human collusion to keep the "secret" endows the object with spiritual power. (Barber 1981: 739–740)

In short, it may be that credible claims, which are rhetorically performed at many levels, including principled statements and hearsay among Abakuá and to ethnographers, have been as crucial in maintaining Efó power as the existence of an actual indwelling "fetish," as early writers liked to say. The classic Efó *puya* on the "empty" and thus "inoperable" Efí *sese* provides a perfect historical example of how rhetoric functions among contenders for power within a determinate social and cultural arena. Ideologically motivated claims by situated agents seek to create hierarchies of knowledge, power, and prestige (see Apter 1992).

These findings do not suggest that dedicated researchers such as Fernando Ortiz and experienced practitioners such as Jesús Nasakó misconstrued or misrepresented the Efó *sese.* They simply may have overgeneralized from the particular *sese* examples they worked on, enchanted, as it were, by longstanding "myths" of Efó potency. Clearly, Ortiz found complex *carga* in at least two *sese* drums, one of which belonged to a descendant of Akanarán Efó, called Efore Muna Tanze. And, much of Jesús's knowledge of Efori Eñongo's *sese* comes from his reported renovation of it, as well as his apprenticeships with veteran Abakuá. It is likely that Petít did "charge" the *seses* of Bakokó Efor and Akanarán Efó, but that the charging of subsequent *seses* in the lineage may not have been universal and was generationally discontinuous. For example, while Efore Muna Tanze's *sese* was charged, Pablo found, surprisingly, that the *sese* of a lodge older and more prestigious in the same line—Abakuá Efó #1 (founded in 1875), a direct descendant of Akanarán Efó—"had nothing in it."

As a researcher, Fernando Ortiz amply documented and engaged the debate over the status and origins of the two *sese* types. Attempting to place the two in historical perspective, following study and interpretation of confiscated specimens and the extant African ethnography, he concluded that the open-bottomed, "empty" *sese* was *the* original "African type." As such, it was the "oldest" and first Afro-Cuban form. The *sese de copón,* in contrast, fully emerged as a defensive resource of the Efó against the Efí during the fallout from Petít's "reform" or "selling of the secret to the whites." Still, Ortiz, who sought to leave no stone unturned, was not ready to conclude that the *sese de copón* had no origins earlier than Havana's Bakokó Efor in the mid-nineteenth century. Ever the philologist and comparative ethnologist, Ortiz looked for an "origin" of the goblet form, conjecturing that the goblet had its own precedents in Africa. For example, he argued, the Yoruba have long utilized the mortar-shaped drums of the thunder god (Shangó), which have their formal counterpart in actual gobletlike mortars for pounding grain. He speculated that similar drums might have been used among the Africans of Old Calabar (Ortiz 1954:77–78).[21]

Still, Ortiz's interest in African precedents did not obscure his larger, subtly theorized framework for situating Afro-Cuban artifacts within processes of "syncretism," "transculturation," and what has come to be called "creolization." Was the goblet *sese* form, he asked, an ancestral type that was lost in the Middle Passage? Or was it a Cuban invention that attempted to unite the island-born "creole goblet" with the original open-bottomed "African" *sese* form? Ortiz was careful to frame his ethnohistorical questions of continuity and change with reference to Cuban sociopolitical conditions and the kinds of resources the Abakuá had available in order to adapt and survive. The *sese de copón* not only served as defensive ammunition in the struggle between the two Abakuá branches, but, Ortiz argues, the specific goblet form adopted by the Cuban Efó was also integral to Andrés Petít's "licitness" strategy during an era of increased persecution. The *sese de copón* "signified an episode of defensive process"—which Ortiz calls "syncretistic mimesis" (Ortiz 1954:79). Given the onset of intense police persecution by 1875, the "creole" *sese de copón* tactically took on the mask of *Copón Divino* (divine goblet). As Roche y Monteagudo described the object, it became the "Holy Sacrament" of the Abakuá.

The *sese de copón* form does indeed resemble the goblet of the Eucharist, particularly as it appears in the stylized display form of the *ostentorium* (monstrance, the stemmed goblet-and-Host ensemble that sits prominently on the Roman Catholic altar [see Hemeldonck 1995:295–301]).[22] The resemblance remains not merely an abstract similarity. In juxtaposing the *sese* and the monstrance itself in the center of the altar, the Bakokó/Akanarán Efó Abakuá line self-consciously incorporated into its presentation a morphological and semantic homology, a kind of visual proof of status and intentionality—the Abakuá are benign and good as well as powerful (plate 11). On the altar, the monstrance throws into relief the form of the *sese de copón*, just as the repetition of visual elements in a composition can elaborate, if not constitute, a work of art's significance. Repetition, of course, can amount to "revision" and what Henry Louis Gates introduced to contemporary criticism as "signifying" (Gates 1988:44–88; Apter 1992:8–10, 210). Within this family resemblance, the *sese de copón* "is," is "like," revises, and is different from, the Santísimo Sacramento. Jesus Nasakó suggests the basis for the comparability of the *sese* goblet form and the monstrance. The comparison was "*natural*, because the monstrance represents the Host. The priest of the Church offers it on the altar. He is making an offering of the body and blood of Christ, making Communion. And it is the same with the *sese*. When the [Abakuá] initiation takes place [*juramento*], communion is made with Sikán, represented by the *mbori*"—the sacrificial goat.[23] That the *sese copón* supposedly contains human relics and sacrificial blood amplifies the comparison. Of course, as a Kimbisero and the lodge's Nasakó, Jesús should know better than anyone precisely what differentiates the Eucharist and the *sese de copón*, not to mention the *nganga* of the Congo-Cuban religions.

I asked Jesús his opinion of Fernando Ortiz's ethnohistorical argument. Was Andrés Petít, who "introduced" the *sese namokimbán*, also its "inventor"? On the whole Jesús Nasakó seconds Ortiz's argument, which he has thoroughly read and digested, but elaborates his own story of the Cuban *sese*. A proud Kimbisero and Akanarán descendant, Jesús bristles at the suggestion that the Efó *sese* could be a mere "invention"—in the sense of a creation without "logical" or "historical" basis. He argues that the "original" African form of the *sese*, which belonged to the Efó, was, in fact, a charged and sealed vessel fabricated by Nangobié Nasakó, the *sese namokimbán*, lending reinforcement to some of Ortiz's speculations. Jesús relates that the first Efí lodges consecrated in Africa by the Efó received, in contrast, a *sese eribó* in the *kankomo* form: its *parche* was charged with *ekue*, but it was "empty" of the *carga* of *namokimbán*. In his own theory of diaspora and its creole implications, Jesús argues that, in the Middle Passage, only the Efí *sese eribó*, not the Efó *sese namokimbán*, made it to Cuba with Africans from Old Calabar. "The first form to come to Cuba was that of the Efí branch." They were able to transport something of their *fundamentos* across the Atlantic. Indeed, Jesús believes that Efik Buton, the New World's first lodge, was the "only *potencia* that made it to Cuba. They were able to carry their attributes with them."

With the formal establishment of Efik Buton, the proximate origin of the Abakuá on the island of Cuba, the Efó nation immediately became dependent upon the Efí for the recovery and reestablishment of their own *potencia*, their ritual attributes. For this reason, argues Jesús, including himself and his Akanarán Efó lineage colleagues in the equation, "all of the Efó of Cuba—we are children of the Efí. This is the reverse of Africa. There, the Efí are the children of Efó"—that is, the Efí received the secret from the Efó across the Oddán River.[24] Logically, however, Jesús qualifies, the first *sese* received by the Efí in Africa could not have contained the same *carga*—the blood and bones of Sikán and Tanze as fabricated by Nasakó—"because the Efí did not possess Sikán." The Efó fabricated a "representation" for the Efí, and this is what they carried across the water to Cuba: a *sese eribó* (empty *sese*) possessing a charged *parche* but neither the form nor the charged contents of the *sese namokimbán* itself. In Jesús's diasporic hypothesis, in Cuba the Efó received their *potencia* from Efik Buton, but were able to recreate—"reafricanize"—their own African-based *sese namokimbán*. They combined the *ekue*-imbued *parche* of the Efí with the knowledge of *brujería* they carried through the Middle Passage in their heads. In short, Jesús argues, Andrés Petít did not "invent" the *sese namokimbán*, though he may have introduced the particular "creole goblet form" in the kind of strategic "syncretistic mimesis" Ortiz speculated about, as well as his knowledge of Congo medicines. In other words, Petít "recopied" *(recopiar)* the *sese namokimbán*, the "*sese* of *brujería*" that the Efó sorcerer Nangobié Nasakó had originally confected in Africa.[25]

Though the *sese de copón* emerged as the distinguishing attribute of the Akanarán Efó line, as opposed to the established Efí and Efó lodges, it did not remain so. By the beginning of the twentieth century, many Efí lodges had adopted the goblet form, such as Efí Etete of Cárdenas (Ortiz 1954:289). Ortiz astutely explained the diffusion of this form in relation to sociopolitical conditions. He hypothesized that state persecution of the Abakuá produced different "reactions," which were reflected in the *sese*'s form over time. "The old African lodges, survivors of the *Efí* branch, maintained their *eribó Africano*, conserved also by some blacks of the *Efó* branch," while "all the lodges of whites" have their goblet form. At the same time, some black lodges, which reorganized themselves after the persecution and the police confiscation of their sacred objects, "reformed" their own *potencias:* "instead of returning to the *eribó* of the African type, and with the intention of mimesis and deafricanization, they adopted the creole form" (Ortiz 1954:81–82).

Prominent Efí lodges proudly maintain the tradition of the open-bottomed *sese*, such as Efí Embemoró, one of Havana's oldest Efí *juegos*. During a *plante* in 1986, the brethren proudly displayed their leopardskin-adorned *sese* (plate 14; figure 6.5; see also Trujillo y Monagas 1882:370). Still, as evidence suggests, the processes that produced the *sese namokimbán* are not linear; and the "empty *sese*" cannot at all be considered simply a survival of an older tradition. For example, in the 1960s a movement was afoot among some Efó members of the Akanarán Efó line, which produced a curious shift in traditions. One of Jesús Nasakó's principal Abakuá mentors, Francisco Hurtado de Mendoza ("Yenequita"), the Isué of Usagaré Munankebé of Regla, founded a new lodge called Asoiro Bekura Ibondá. Though the sponsor and new lodge were of the Akanarán Efó line, Yenequita wanted to "fix" the received tradition and recreate the *sese eribo kankomo* out of respect for Efik Buton, the root of Cuba's Abakuá. Yenequita thus recreated an Efí-style "empty *sese*" for his new Efó lodge. Within the last decade or more, a more self-consciously antisyncretic movement has emerged within all of the Afro-Cuban ritual systems, in which practitioners not only reject the iconography of the Catholic Church, but also identifiably "creole inventions."[26] Thus, Pablo, the revisionist designer and renovator of Cuba's Abakuá objects, though he produces the *sese* goblet form upon commission, nevertheless rejects it as a "mere invention" proffered by Andrés Petít, and insists upon the open-bottomed *sese* as the only original and authentic form.

The conflict between the Akanarán Efó line and the old guard, the specific debate over the two *sese* types, the subsequent conversion of many Efí lodges to the *forma criolla de copón*, and the reversion of more than one lodge more recently to the "traditional" *kankomo* form, suggests a process of change and exchange, which some scholars have identified as "traditionalization" and others as the ideological dynamic of syncretism/antisyncretism (see Kirshenblatt-Gimblett 1983; Schoemaker 1994; Shaw and Stewart 1994; Palmié 1995).

"The Light Inside": The Renovation of Efori Eñongo's *Sese Namokimbán*

In 1979, Jesús Nasakó focused his artistic attention and resources on the adornment of Efori Eñongo's *sese,* in order to project its grace and potency. For him, external adornment has the potential to radiate "the light inside"—the invisible in and through the visible. This was his intention.

The "power" of Bakongo *minkisi* objects, anthropologist Wyatt MacGaffey argues, lies not only in the "complexity" of their assembled contents and social investments but also in the "visual astonishment" they are intended to produce. Aesthetically marked display, through artistic elaboration, projects an awe-inspiring, even fearsome, presence, and compels respect (see MacGaffey 1988; MacGaffey and Harris 1993). The same could be said for the *sese.* An Ortiz anecdote tells of two colonial-era policemen out to entrap and arrest Abakuá. They carried out to the street a confiscated *sese* partly cloaked in cloth. Two men approached, and, upon seeing the *sese,* "doffed their hats and kneeled as if the Eucharist had passed in procession." Given such "proof of their ardent faith," the policemen arrested them (Ortiz 1954:51).

The Efó *sese namokimbán*'s iconic goblet form—as a container—indexes and announces its supposed *brujería* contents. For the *sese namokimbán* is considered an *nkisi* of Kimbisa provenance within the Bakokó/Akanarán Efó lineage. In its anthropomorphized outward display, it is a bust portrait of Sikán, the "Mother of the Abakuá," who supports and nurtures four kings (the *obones* of the *potencia*) and the group as a whole. In its contents it is indeed a "bomb prepared in secret by African science." As Efori Eñongo's Nasakó, Jesús "renovated" both the *sese*'s contents and its external appearance.

Jesús Nasakó covered the cedar goblet with leopardskin, and, like the staffs, with multicolored beads, cowries, tacks, and patches of leather. He encircled the drumhead with an elegant double fringe of yellow and white silk. The yellow and white fringe makes the object "beautiful," but these are also the "colors of life and death" respectively (figure 6.6 and plate 11).[27] He made new *plumeros* with red velvet covering their cylindrical bases. Jesús believes that the *sese* and the Ekueñón drum should be covered with leopardskin. Ekueñón, the hunter, is intimate with this mysterious beast of the forest—a kind of spirit double on the land of the riverine Tanze—and Ekueñón transfers *ekué* from nature into the controlled confines of the temple. The *sese,* through the medicines and relics of Nasakó the sorcerer, embodies the spirits of Tanze and Sikán, and acts as a permanent repository or *fundamento* of the Voice of the "leopard." The *sese*'s leopardskin stands as a "sign of nobility, of force and power" (Sosa Rodríguez 1982: 178). The *sese* thus reiterates its double reference to Sikán's hair with its *plumeros,* which also honor the four highest chiefs of the "leopard society" (see Ortiz 1954:75), and to the leopard, with the animal's skin. Not least, the "nobility, force, and power" of the *sese* derive from the fact that this emblem is the visible counterpart to the invisible: both the fish and the leopard remain hidden in their respective domains and are known mostly through their sound, an index of their veiled presences. Likewise, the Ekue drum, veiled within the *fo-ekue,* is known through its sound only. The *sese* is visible as it takes up its place on the altar and in public processions, yet it remains silent. "From the *sese,* say the [Abakuá], Ekue was born, because its fabrication by Nasakó preceded that of Ekue. [Indeed, the *sese*] received [the Voice] first. After the Divine Voice goes quiet in Ekue, it returns to the *sese,* into the *brujería* it contains inside, which permits the Voice to express itself" (Sosa Rodríguez 1982:178).

Over the *sese*'s leopardskin Jesús applied a series of

cowrie shells, both out of "traditional concerns" and in order to create vibrant visual "contrasts." Cowrie shells, he says, are "the most traditional adornment merited by the *sese*, used since colonial times. Some use fewer, some use more, but all lodges adorn the *sese* with cowries"[28] (see, e.g., Roche y Monteagudo 1925:35, 73; Ortiz 1954:66–67). Jesús mounted four cowries on each of the two beaded bands cinching the goblet's stem. He then arranged four sets of four cowries around the base. Each grouping on the base forms a cruciform pattern set within an appliquéd disk of black leather, which is framed with a red border surrounded by tacks. Juan Mokongo later painted the tack heads yellow. Cowrie shells in sets of four register multiple levels of meaning, Jesús explained. Each is similar to an "eye," and four together represent "the eyes of Tanze and Sikán." Formed as a cross, they represent the "Four Winds"—the cosmological figure that draws spiritual energy from the four cardinal points. Set into circular frames, they give over to the shape of the basic *anaforuana* pattern, Sikán's gourd, and the *sese* vessel itself. Finally, the number four, and the equidistant placement of four sets of cowries around the base reiterate the four cardinal points and "the four *plumeros* of the *sese*," which mark the presence of the four highest grades of the society.[29]

The overall aesthetic effect of Jesús's adornments is the outward visual and emotional expression of the object's spiritual power—whether it be an altar staff or drum. With cowries against black leather, for example, Jesús created a high-contrast value effect: porcelain-white cowries against textured black. "The shells and tacks should stand out" *(resaltar)*. To many Abakuá, Jesús explains, "the aesthetic is very important," and therefore the object must be "interesting" and "pleasant to the eyes" *(interesante* and *agradable a la vista)*. Still, his work is not merely a formal exercise. These effects were intended precisely to "give life to the piece" *(darle vida a la pieza)*. "The aesthetic recreates—how can I explain it to you?—'the light inside' [speaks in English], *la luz interior*. Do you understand? The interior light . . . comes to reflect from [the adornments], giving spirituality to the piece [*darle espiritualidad a la pieza*]." The outward "reflection" of "light"—the appearance of a projection from within—along with a high contrast color and value scheme, suggest to the beholder the object's internal power. In short, though external adornment does not substitute for internal ritual ingredients, it projects the object "as a *fundamento*," a seat of grace. Still, the "dark of night, veiling perpetually the brilliant light of the sun" was all the authorities could see of the *ñáñigos*, not the "light inside."

Sese Namokimbán Crowned

The crowned *sese* is an innovation—some say "mere invention"—introduced along with the goblet form during Andrés Petít's era. Atop the *sese*, the crown is multivocal. Insofar as the charged goblet anthropomorphizes Sikán's head, the crown marks Sikán as a royal and sacralized presence. Before the advent of *ekue*, Sikán was an Efó princess. When she raised the gourd containing Obon-Tanze to her head, she was, effectively, "crowned" as a divine queen: a moment doubly figured as an "initiation" and a "marriage" to the reincarnated "king" of the leopard society. Alternately, as Thompson observes, "by mere contact with the presence of the Voice, Sikán became in essence the bride of God" (Thompson 1983:243).[30] Atop Sikán's "head," the crucifix-surmounted crown visually captures this moment. Of course, as figured here in overt Roman Catholic iconography, Jesus on the Cross references Sikán and the rebirth of *ekue* via the episode of "filial sacrifice."

The crowned Sikán evokes other important associations that correspond to Abakuá institutional organization, as well as an array of "creole" religious references that Sikán embraced within Petít's social and ideological orbit. The crown redoubles the signs of royalty already present in the *sese*'s four *plumeros*, which represent the princess's "hair" and the kingliness of the lodge's four *obones*. Sikán's "head"—as

Abakuá *fundamento,* Kimbisa *nganga,* and ancestral reliquary—provides the generative foundation for the Abakuá leadership edifice of the *potencia's* "Four Columns"—Iyamba, Mokongo, Isué, and Isunekue. Centered on the Abakuá altar, Sikán's "head" is both altar and throne in itself. Surmounted by the crucifix, this crowned "Mother of the Religion" cannot escape suggestive association with the Virgin Mary in her cycle as the "Queen of Heaven," an important icon painted in Havana church frescoes (plate 15).

The crown of Efori Eñongo's *sese,* made somewhat crudely of cut, welded, and chromed sheet metal, was fabricated by a now deceased *obonekue* of Efori Eñongo lodge, Napolís. The circular crown features two arches, perpendicular to one another, which form a cross. At the apex of the arches stands a silver crucifix. The four *plumeros* are inserted into tubular slots, which are welded to the base of each arch. The four open quadrants produced by the arches feature crenellated domical arches (plate 11, figure 6.6). In Abakuá terms the two crossed arches reiterate the cosmological "four winds" and institutional "Four Columns" motifs, which are echoed in the four sets of four cowries on the goblet's base. Each *obon's plumero* corresponds to one of the four arches/four winds, his place marked by his unique signature formed out of a matrix of dots punched into the crown's surface with a nail.[31] Each of these seminal signs appears twice upon the fully assembled *sese,* once as inscribed into the crown, and again, as embossed upon the red velvet surface of each *plumero's* handle (figure 6.6).

Toward an Art History of the Napolís Crown: The Royal and the Divine

Napolís undoubtedly drew on his familiarity with local examples of *sese* crowns, most directly, those within the Akanarán Efó line in Regla. For example, the crown of the *sese* of Efori Eñongo's "godfather," Abakuá Efó #1, similarly is a silver, double-arched, and crucifix-surmounted crown. Made for Abakuá Efó's *baroko* in 1875, it was improvised from an elegant circular hanging lamp with double arches.[32]

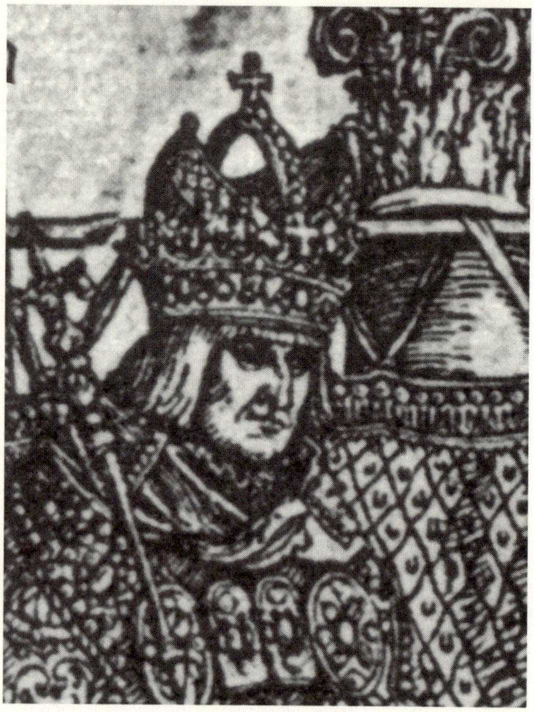

Figure 6.7. Single-arched crown with miters, surmounted by crucifix. Detail from Albrecht Dürer, *Assembly of Princes at Vienna,* 1515 (reproduced in Goodall 1995:79). Courtesy of The Albertina, Vienna.

Both crowns—a simpler double arch style and the more elaborated double arch-and-miter style of Efori Eñongo—draw on time-honored conventions of European-derived royal and ecclesiastical regalia.

As art historians reckon the development of European crown styles, a crucifix-surmounted, single-arched crown form, with miters flanking the arch, emerged with the fourteenth-century rule of Holy Roman Emperor Charles IV (1355–78).[33] The miter "stressed the sacral powers claimed by the Holy Roman Emperors." Divine kingship was thus signified through hybrid iconography. This form spread far and wide, and soon, it set the mold for imperial crowns in Austria, Russia, and other states (figure 6.7). The arched crown was taken up in France in the sixteenth century, becoming standard royal regalia there. Though two-arch crowns came to dominate in England, crowns across Europe often featured four arches (Goodall 1995:79–80).[34]

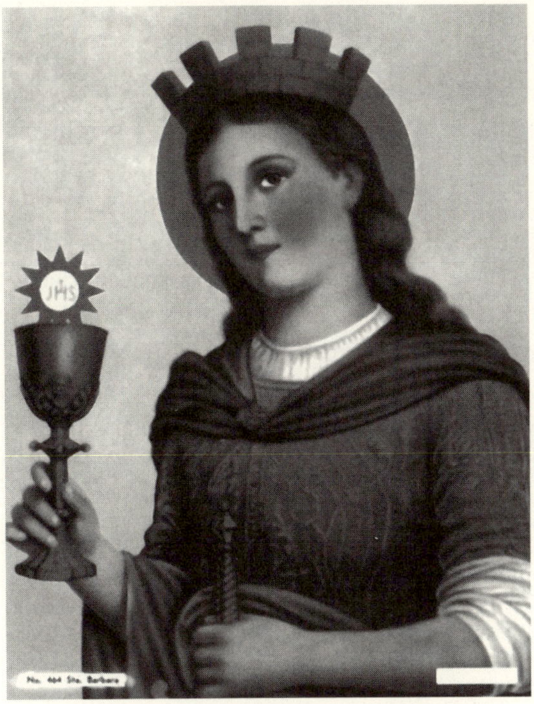

Figure 6.8. Popular chromolithograph of St. Barbara, carrying the Eucharist and sword and wearing a crenellated crown. The crown indicates her status as a "royal saint," and its crenellations represent the castle tower in which she was imprisoned by her father, Nicodemus, in the third century.

Though the domical, crenellated forms that flank the arches of the Napolís crown do not precisely mirror the typical profile of the tall peaked miter, they strongly recall this feature in their prominence and position. By choice or chance, the Napolís crown appropriately makes reference to the royal and ecclesiastical roles of the *potencia*'s *obones:* for example, Iyamba is a "king," whereas Isué is a "bishop." Insofar as the *sese*'s crown signifies Sikán's head and her "royalty" through birth, initiation, and marriage, it is comparable to the European "coronation crown [form] . . . often regarded as a relic of a sainted ancestor [and] reserved for investiture alone." At the same time, insofar as the *sese* is an *nganga* and a reliquary vessel, the crown recalls another, related, role played by European-style headgear. "Some crowns were kept in churches as votive offerings, and those having relics set in them were preserved as reliquaries" (Goodall 1995:80).

The foregoing formal and iconographic analysis of royal crowns seeks not to document the artisan's sources in a self-conscious "European" tradition, but to provide suggestive context for more proximate influences that likely shaped his choices. Crown regalia, as utilized within Afro-Cuban practices, dates to the Cuban colonial period—perhaps as early as the late sixteenth century—among the African nations' *cabildos,* and continues today (see Brown 1993a, b, 2003). Beyond more narrowly conceived "traditional" and "traditionalized" sources within the Abakuá, sources for the Napolís crown could be found in historical paintings of the Spanish Bourbons in Havana, popular renderings of European royalty in the Cuban vernacular theater, in the regalia of the other Afro-Cuban ritual systems,[35] and upon the heads of Vir-

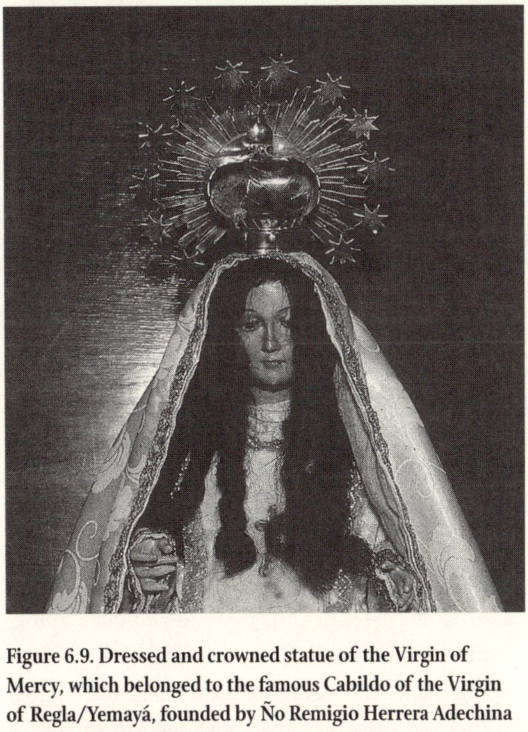

Figure 6.9. Dressed and crowned statue of the Virgin of Mercy, which belonged to the famous Cabildo of the Virgin of Regla/Yemayá, founded by Ño Remigio Herrera Adechina and led by his daughter Eshu Bí Pepa Josefa Herrera. The virgin wears a simple silver double-arched crown snipped from metal sheeting, surmounted by a crucifix. The *cabildo* carried this hand-carved icon through the streets to celebrate the double feast day of the Virgin and Obatalá. The statue is now in the collection of the Museum of Regla. Photograph by David H. Brown.

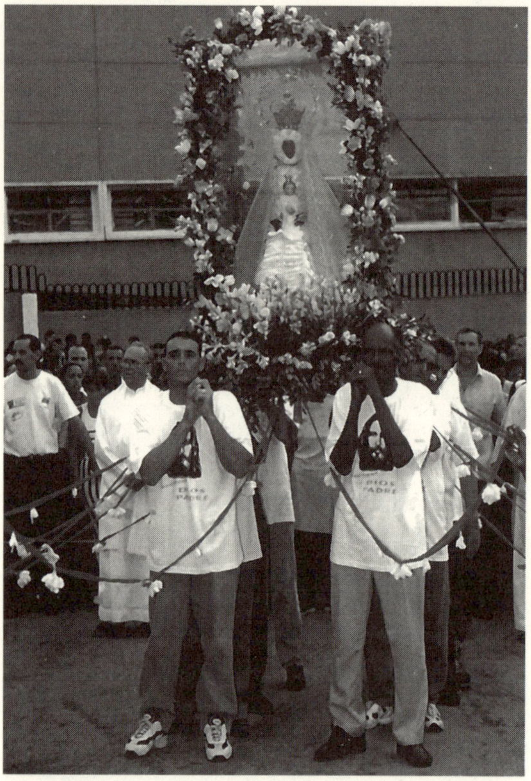

Figure 6.10. Head of the procession of the Virgin of Regla, 7 September 1999. This is the first time that the church procession carrying the icon of the Virgin was permitted since it was banned in the early years of the revolution. Note that the Virgin's elaborate openwork silver crown is double-arched, surmounted by a crucifix. Photograph by David H. Brown.

gins and royal saints in churches and homes. For example, double-arched metal crowns appear atop the ubiquitous Lucumí *orishas'* lidded vessels. The Napolís crown's blocky crenellations recall those often used in crowns for the Lucumí *orisha* Shangó. Of course, this crown style was adopted from the crenellated crown and castle tower motifs of the royal Saint Barbara (figure 6.8). Closer to home—Napolís's hometown—the statue of the Virgen de Regla, which is carried annually in procession, wears a double-arched silver crown. Similarly, the Virgen de la Caridad del Cobre icon of Regla's church wears a double-arched crown, as do a number of the Virgin statues that belonged to Regla's African Cabildo of Yemayá. All of these crowns are surmounted by crucifixes (figures 6.9, 6.10). Fernando Ortiz, who took great interest in the "transculturation" of African objects, was fascinated with the crown gracing the *sese de copón* of Efí Etete of Cárdenas (figure 6.11): it was a crucifix-surmounted "regal crown of gold, in the high and pompous style of the Spanish Bourbon Dynasty." Ortiz's informant, a lodge member, who was a "sergeant in the national army," unabashedly described Efí Etete as "progressive," a term that equally characterizes the offspring of Andrés Petít's Reform in Havana. In other words, these Abakuá strove to project themselves as "licit" modern religious practitioners, humble, law-abiding workers, not criminals, and patriotic citizens personally invested in the nation as of the establishment of the Republic (1902). Ortiz observed that Efí Etete demonstrated its "progressive" profile through a "profusion of adornments in the

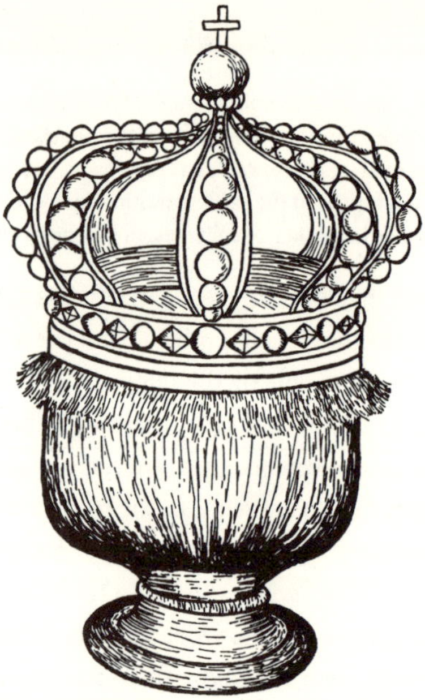

Figure 6.11. Drawing of the *sese* of Efí Etete of Cárdenas, featuring a bejeweled, double-arched crown surmounted by the "world-ball" of Christ. This is an example of a lodge of the Efí branch having adopted the Efó convention of the sealed *sese* instead of the customary Efí open-bottomed *sese.* Ortiz described the crown as like those of the Bourbon dynasty. (From Ortiz 1954:59, fig. 289; courtesy María Fernanda Ortiz Herrera, Representante Sucesores de Fernando Ortiz.)

creole taste and its Lucumí-Christian [style] syncretism on its altar, with images of the Virgen de la Caridad del Cobre (Ochún), Santa Barbara (Changó), etc., along with the Crucifix and the Custodia del Santísimo [monstrance or ciborium]. They adopted the Bourbon crown as yet another symbol of 'progress'" (Ortiz 1954:55). An array of references—Roman Catholic, Lucumí, and "creole"—a peculiar Caribbean baroque fusion—came together as a seamless display of Cubanness *(cubanidad),* a homegrown *mestizaje* nationalism in the "creole taste" among the "progressive" and "reformed" lodges.

Sikán, Christ, and the Virgin Mary: Some Interpretations

Jesús Nasakó and Juan Mokongo use two similes to explain Sikán's destiny. In an "episode of filial sacrifice," Sikán "gave her life, her body and blood, so that *ekue* might live, just as Christ gave his life so that Christians might live." At the same time, Sikán is the "Mother of the Religion." In the first simile, a Christ-like Sikán, as embodied in the *sese* drum, bears formal comparison with the Host and the Goblet, the "Holy Sacrament" of Christ's "body and blood," most directly represented in the altar's monstrance. In the second simile, as in a second cycle of legend, Sikán, as "Mother of the Religion," emerges more as a generative vessel for the "birth" of the "secret," *ekue,* which, like Christ, is subsequently carried across the River Oddán on Abasonga/St. Christopher's shoulder. To push the likeness further, an iconic New Testament subtext might be seen in Sikán's motherly role: her proximity to the secret in the form of a "voice" recalls the Annunciation, the announcement by the Archangel Gabriel to Mary of the miraculous conception of the Son of God (see Apostolos-Cappadona 1994:28–30). It is perhaps not coincidental that the fish, contained within Sikán's vessel as Tanze, is also a "primary early Christian symbol for Jesus Christ, and, among other things, the Eucharist" (Apostolos-Cappadona 1994:132).

Centered on the altar table, the *sese* becomes *ekue*'s seat and throne (plates 1 and 11), as the body of Mary cradles and supports the Christ child following his birth and his sacrifice, represented in the Pietà and its devotional variation, the Lamentation (Apostolos-Cappadona 1994:278). In Christian iconography, Mary, draped in rich cloth and holding the Christ child beneath the altar baldachin *(baldachino),* is interpreted by some art historians as a visual homology for the Eucharist upon the cloth-covered altar. The crowned *sese* reiterates these relations insofar as Sikán's head supports the crucifix-mounted crown. It may come as no surprise that Jesús Nasakó and Juan Mokongo consider the altar's banner to be the "apron of Sikán" (Br. *bakariongo,* Sp. *delantal*). In this sense, the velvet-adorned altar is a gendered assemblage. Surmounted with the radiant bust portrait of the crowned Sikán, the "mother who gave birth to the religion,"[36] the altar box is a cloth-draped female body, throne to *ekue* and to the Abakuá hierarchy. Every Abakuá member, in general, is a "son of *ekue.*" Members' specific identities revolve around the particulars of their "birth." When a member of Efori Eñongo is asked, *"enewé akanarán Abakuá?"*—"Who is your mother of Abakuá?"—he answers, *"añene mio akanarán momí seseribó ekobio Eforí Eñongo garima saquenti birő"*—"My mother is the *sese* of the Eforí Eñongo lodge." The answer addresses not just which lodge but specifically points to one's birth "mother"—the *sese* of the lodge. Abakuá have been known to kill for their (second) mother, the *sese,* when they or their lodge have been disrespected. Sikán/*sese* is thus the mother of a lodge's incorporated sons of *ekue* as Mary is the mother of Jesus of Nazareth, and, by extension, the Church. Of course, the crowned *sese* evokes subsequent scriptural episodes. Mary becomes the "Queen of Heaven" when she is crowned by Christ upon her Assumption (Apostolos-Cappadona 1994:231–233).

Sikán's "apron"—the lodge's honorific banner—depicts the episode of Sikán's "discovery" of *ekue* in the form of the fish and, in its depiction of Nasakó, his temple, and various Abakuá *plazas,* evokes the establishment of the Abakuá as a sacred institution. The banner's image, with which this chapter opened, is thus a multivocal and self-reflexive representation. The banner visually narrates in the form of mythico-historical legend what it concretely performs as altar furnishing.

Not to be forgotten is the Ekue drum, which remains apart from the altar in the holy of holies, the *fo-ekue* or *iriongo.* The three-footed Ekue drum reproduces Lord Tanze's body, in wood and goatskin (figure 3.11), and, thus, his sound, the "Voice" of God, Abasí. In effect, Ekue is the "father" of the "sons" to whom Sikán/*sese* gives birth. In a gendered logic, "The *sese* represents Sikán as mother; the *sese* consecrates man and the Ekue confirms it."[37]

Abakuá Altar Objects and Their Ritual Function

As the *potencia,* or collective *fundamento* of the lodge, the altar objects together form an enduring embodiment of *ekue* in its broadest sense: as the socially situated and gendered corporate group, past and present (a men's "secret society"), and the transformative cult agency, which is both a repository and vehicle of social and symbolic capital vis-à-vis its ritual and belief system.[38] The *potencia,* embodied in the altar and the Ekue drum, is the sine qua non of the individual *juego* or *tierra* Abakuá, which occupies a determinate place in a line of descent and upon a sacralized landscape of other *tierras,* that is, the landscape of urban, western, coastal Cuba. The *potencia,* which outlives a lodge's mortal officeholders, constitutes the set of authorizing emblems of authority and the means to manifest and deploy the "secret" for mutual benefit and protection.

The *potencia* is consecrated in the *baroko fundamento,* a "collective pact" that establishes a lodge. A minimum of thirteen grades are initiated together. Subsequently, initiation of the other twelve to twenty *plazas* and groups of *obonekues* takes place. The "oath-taking," or "swearing in," is the controlling concept of individual and group Abakuá initiation *(juramento).*

All Abakuá ceremonies *(plantes)* commence with the purification of the *fambá* (temple) and all its sacred attributes. According to Jesús, the Nasakó officeholder utilizes a basil branch dipped in the *wemba* herbal concoction for this purpose; Mpegó chalks the attributes, drums, initiates, sacrificial animals, and the floor with their appropriate *firmas;* together, the men "fabricate" the altar. Central to the *fabricación* is the "authorization of *plumeros*" ceremony, a protocol of activating these emblems of chiefly office through invocatory prayer and consecration. A procession led by Ekueñón "searches for the Voice" outside, and returns with it to the temple. The grand *gandó* of the voice's transmission is chalked across the floor of the temple. Ekueñón's *enkame de rompimiento* chant breaks open the way for the sounding of Ekue and the festive phase of the *plante.* A procession of the *plazas* with their attributes, the *íremes,* new initiates, and the orchestra comes out of the temple into the semipublic *patio* space and street. The public phases of initiation and sacrifice occur at this time.

According to Jesús Nasakó, when initiations of rank-and-file members *(obonekues)* take place, the neophytes take their places in a line on the semipublic *patio;* they are marked with yellow chalk by Mpegó, and spiritually cleaned by Nasakó's *wemba* and the rooster wielded by the *íreme* Eribangandó. Blindfolded, they enter the *fambá* in a line for the secret phase of the initiation, in which their lives and fortunes are sworn to *ekue* through a solemn oath-taking upon each of the *potencia*'s objects.

Jesús related the following outline of the initiation's sequence of events. The neophytes first swear before *nkalú* and Abasí in many, but not all, lodges.[39] *Nkalú* is a candle that represents the "soul" and "life" of the initiate, Jesús explains. Abasí, the Supreme Being, is represented by the altar's crucifix. Then the initiates must make the *juramento de los bastones*—the oath-taking of the staffs. Each initiate swears before the staffs of Mosongo, Mokongo, and Abasonga, in that order, via a series of ritualized questions and answers. Mosongo, for example, instructs the blindfolded initiate kneeling before him to "take the staff." He puts the staff in the hand of the initiate and says, "Do you know what you have in your hand?" The initiate answers, "No." Mosongo identifies it and makes a brief explanation of the purpose of this oath-taking step: "The staff that you have in your hand is that of Mosongo, and with it you swear your fidelity to *ekue.*" Mosongo then chants his *enkame* prayer, giving faith to the initiate's *juramento.* When Mosongo finishes his *enkame,* the initiate is asked to kiss the staff. Mosongo then proceeds to the next initiate and repeats the sequence. Then come the staffs of Mokongo and Abasonga, which proceed in similar fashion. The candidate thus makes a specific series of oaths before the fundamental *plazas* and attributes of the lodge's *potencia.*

A more complicated and dramatic series of events follows, some of which Jesús Nasakó related to me. Isué, the custodian of the *sese,* conducts an oath-taking session first by placing the *sese* drum in the initiate's hands. He identifies the object, explains the neophyte's obligations to *ekue,* and chants his *enkame.* While the *sese* is being held, Isué says to the candidate: "This is the Mother of Our Religion, which we swear to defend, take care of, and protect, albeit, in danger of our own lives. Do you agree?" The neophyte must say, "Yes." Then Isué makes a second prayer, this time lifting the *sese* high above the initiate's head. He makes a third prayer, lowering the *sese* closer to the head. Then he makes a fourth prayer, this time having placed the *sese* directly upon the kneeling initiate's head.[40] This phase varies depending on the class of *sese* the lodge possesses. When the lodge possesses the goblet-shaped Efó-style *sese,* the drum's flat base rests atop the head. When the lodge possesses the open-bottomed drum of the Efí, it is placed, helmetlike, over the head, in order that the head's crown, or *coronilla,* touch the sacred drumskin from the inside, where *ekue*'s power resides. "Nasakó intended that the powers of the *sese* [*namokimbán*] were materially inside the [sealed] drum. For that reason, when they swear you into the Efí [in contrast] the drum is put around the head."[41]

At this point, all the elders present and the neophyte chant a version of the *Credo del Padre Nuestro* ("Creed of God Our Father") in the Brícamo ritual language. Abasonga is then called to "give faith to the *juramento,*" and Nkóboro, the *íreme* of consecrations, stands behind the kneeling initiate, and "reaffirms" the oath in a dramatic way. While the Brícamo prayers are being chanted, Enkóboro rhythmically rotates his waist so that the bells attached to his belt *(enkaniká),* now directly at the level of the initiate's head, produce their sound. "The bells transmit to heaven that this man has sworn with the *sese.* . . . They produce a transmission, which lets Abasí [God] know that this man is being consecrated into the Abakuá. . . . Isué *confirms* the oath, and Nkóboro *reaffirms* it," Jesús explains.

Mpegó then steps forward with his drum—the "Drum of the Law"—or, better, the drum that represents the principle of "swearing before the law." Mpegó affirms that "the day you slip up, Mpegó condemns you to punishment," just as he condemned Sikán to her death. Mpegó has chalked a sign over the skin of the Mpegó drum. In doing so, he affirms that, as the "Law of the Religion," he is always going to condemn and sentence whoever is not faithful to *ekue.* As with the other objects, the initiate is instructed to kiss the skin of the Mpegó drum. Then Ekueñón comes forward and presents the calabash or goblet containing Nasakó's herbal *mokuba* liquid.[42] Just before that, the head of *nkiko,* the rooster, had been severed by the executioner, Ekueñón, and placed atop the *sese* drum. Isué, the *sese*'s custodian and "bishop" of the Abakuá, dips the head of the rooster in the *mokuba,* and the initiate is instructed to put his mouth to its neck, thereby incorporating the spiritual essence of the *mokuba* and the blood together—in a word, *ekue.* Ekueñón then offers the initiate the vessel of *mokuba* to drink.

The culmination of the secret phase of the initiation is the most dramatic. *Enkames* are sung, and the initiate, with the *sese* still atop his head, walks on his knees toward the *fo-ekue,* the curtained holy of holies where the Ekue drum is being sounded by Iyamba. Blindfolded and kneeling, the initiate enters the *fo-ekue.* His head is placed directly atop the *parche* of the Ekue drum. With the *sese* above and Ekue below, the head is sandwiched, as it were, between the two great *fundamentos.* "Ekue then is sounded more strongly, and it is as if a current of electricity enters your body. . . . It is a moment that you never forget, never. It is the most marvelous moment in the Abakuá," Jesús vividly recalls from his own initiation as an *obonekue* of Efori Eñongo many years ago.

The *juramentos* of the staffs, the *sese,* and contact with the sounding Ekue employ pan-Afro-Cuban ritual patterns: a series of ritualized questions in order to predicate rhetorically the candidate as a subject belonging to the religion (see e.g., Castellanos 1977: 81–101; M. Mason 2002); "washing" the body with and drinking herbal liquids in order to incorporate sacred essences; the placement of *fundamentos* atop the head in concert with invocatory prayer and bell tones, a form of spiritual coronation that brings the seat of the initiate's consciousness into direct communication with the sacred through metonymy.

Following this intensive phase of the initiation, the candidate leaves the *fo-ekue* to rest in a side room of the temple, and another initiate is called. The blindfold is taken off and the candidate awaits the final performance, a semipublic procession outside the secret temple (figures 2.5 and 2.6). Having finished their *juramentos,* the initiates are taken outside because they must "salute the celestial bodies [*astros*] and salute the sun. . . . In the procession, each *plaza* carries his attribute. Isué is near the head of the procession holding the *sese,* dancing it." Here Isué carries the rooster's head between his teeth (see figure 5.7). Two, three, or more *íremes* may participate, including Eribangandó, Aberiñán, Aberisún, and Mbóko, while Nkóboro carries out his responsibilities entirely within the *fambá.* During this phase, joyous drumming, singing, dancing, and the prodigious consumption of *aguardiente* (cane rum) take place (plate 5). The sacrifice of *mbori* is enabled by the *íreme* "twins," Aberisún and Aberiñáñ, who immobilize and render the goat unconscious with a blow to the head. *Mbori* is then sacrificed over a cement slab in the center of the courtyard, and communal food is prepared over an open fire by the *plaza* called Encandemo—the cook, *el cocinero.*[43]

7 The *Íremes* and Their *Sacos*

The *íremes* have been described by scholars as spirit "messengers." With their angular movements—silent kinetic communications—they look to be "*anaforuana* in material form," as Thompson eloquently writes (1983:260–262). Jesús Nasakó understands the term *íreme* as "manifested, materialized, or represented spirit. . . . When a man dons the suit of the *íreme,* he is representing a spirit of the other world [*más allá*]." Like the sacred drums and staffs of the other *plazas,* the masquerade costumes embody the personages of the Abakuá's "birth": "the first Eribangandó, the first Nkóboro, or the first Mbóko," and all those who have occupied these important *plazas* since their time.[1] As Enrique Sosa Rodríguez writes, the *íremes* "endow the ceremonies with transcendental importance." This is so not merely in their appearance alone but in their practical functions as well. The *íremes* "act as witnesses and supervise [ceremonies], they conduct purifications, they execute punishments" (Sosa Rodríguez 1982:173). Where the Ekue drum poignantly expresses *ekue*—"speaks"—in its bellow or cry, the *íremes* are also *ekue*'s vehicles. They "'speak' with bodily movements, but do not emit sounds. . . . Their pantomime is incessant, expressing itself in the steps and gestures of their dance—a system of symbols, in which participate their staff and branch held in the hands, and the bells about their waists, shaken to sound in diverse ways" (Sosa Rodríguez 1982:173). For example, the belt of multiple cowbells *(enkaniká)* is shaken to express "joy" at the manifestation of *ekue* during the opening *rompimiento* phase. Nkóboro sounds his *enkaniká* during the initiation to inform God that the consecration phase is complete. One of the most important roles played by the *íremes* is to control and protect the lodge, its ceremonies, and its personnel, execute punishments, and facilitate aspects of ritual. They also constantly work to "send away evil influences. When shaken the bells emit a vibration that expels maleficent spirits." During ceremonies, one of the primary functions of the *íremes* is to "insure that no problems or arguments occur," which may be caused by external spiritual agents, including *brujería*.[2] Following the fulfillment of their primary duties within and without the temple, for example, Eribangandó's purification of the initiates and Nkóboro's supervision of their consecrations, the *íremes* are encouraged to animate the public festivities in dance. The dance style of each class of *íreme* is different. Yet, the quality of the movement depends upon the ability of the dancer. Some *íremes* "dance beautifully, others badly [yet] every gesture signifies something." During the fulfillment of their duties, or during their dance, an *íreme* may be called by the Enkríkamo or Moruá Yuansá to modify its behavior, including returning to the *fambá* or punishing an out-of-line member or visitor.

Íreme Masquerade Costumes

Sacos I: Hoods, Masks, and Faces

The masquerade costume of the *íreme* consists of a close-fitting, comprehensive, hooded suit, which is entered through an opening in the chest. The hood's front, its "mask" *(careta)*, and, sometimes, more of the suit, are constructed of jute, made from the principal material used for agricultural shipping bags called *saco* or *yute* in Cuba. The material may be left to show its natural burlap color or painted black, red, or other colors (plates 4 and 13). *Saco* was, of course, plentiful and free for the taking around the wharves where many Abakuá members historically worked. In Cuba, *saco* evidently replaced the hand-knitted fabrics worn by West African masqueraders (plate 3; figure 7.1) (see Talbot 1912:44; Leib and Romano 1984:54).

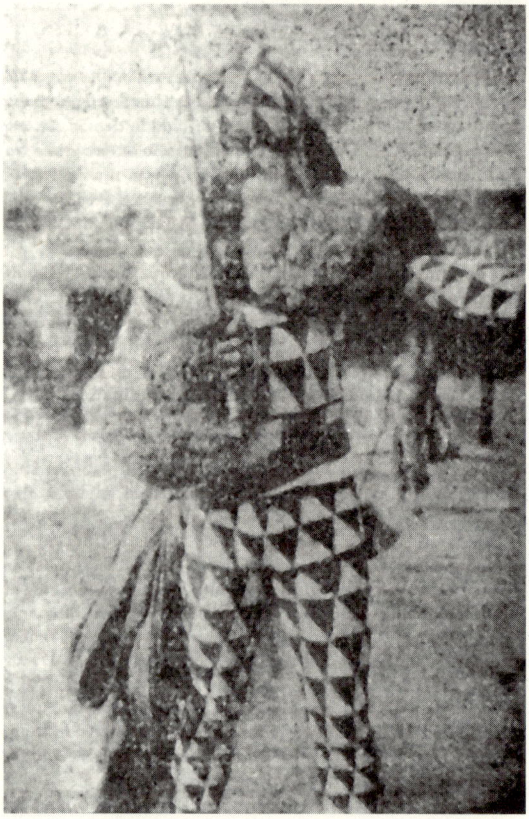

Figure 7.1. Comparative illustration used in Ortiz 1985 and incorrectly identified as a Landaluze painting from Cuba. In fact, it is a photograph of an "Nkanda image" taken around 1912 in the Old Calabar region (see P. Amaury Talbot, *In the Shadow of the Bush*). With his conical hood, high-contrast, sawtooth patterned suit, fringed joints, circular hat, and rod in one hand and branch in the other, he bears an uncanny resemblance to Landaluze's 1881 lithograph *El Ñáñigo* (figure 4.1). Courtesy of María Fernanda Ortiz Herrera, Representante Sucesores de Fernando Ortiz.

The *íreme*'s tall triangular "mask" most often appears as an abstract, faceless visage, except for a pair of outsized eyes, which float high upon the hood surface at a level just at or above the dancer's head (plates 4, 13, 16, and 17; figure 7.2). The open weave of the *saco* permits the dancer to see. Though the eyes are most often constructed of white or white-painted cloth stuffed with batting and sewn to the jute, they may consist of flat ovoid cutouts (plate 16, right). In either case, they stand out in high contrast against the mask. Bright white, outsized eyes set high upon and in sharp contrast to a solid, featureless background emphasize the *íreme*'s keen faculty of vision—spiritual sight—but not speech. The *íreme*'s specialties are vigilance, silent gestural communication, agile movement, and decisive action. This makes the *íreme* rather like the leopard, though the roar of this beast comes not from within the *íreme*'s costume but from the roar of the Ekue drum, a powerful universal spiritual agency grounded in cosmology, nature, and the secret inner recesses of the *fambá*.

Though all *íremes* represent ancestors and mytho-

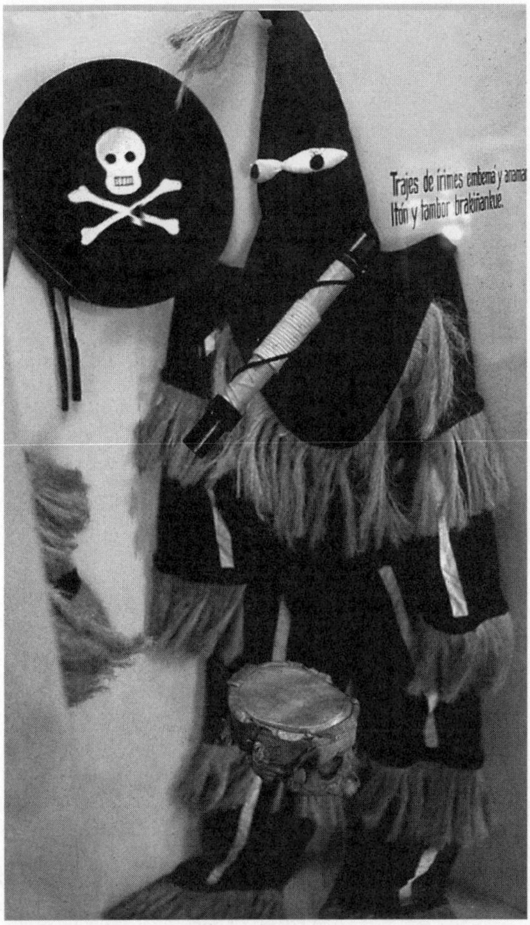

Figure 7.2. Vitrine in the Abakuá salon of the Ethnographic Museum of Guanabacoa, titled "Suits of írimes embemá [not visible] and anamangüí. Itón and brakiñankue drum." Anamangüí is a funerary *íreme* whose suit and *sombrereta* are black. The white appliquéd stripes on the suit are schematic references to a human skeleton, and the graphic skull and crossbones on the hat refers to his identity. The *itón* is a staff carried by Anamangüí. The *brakiñankue,* or Bakri Ñámpe drum, used in funerary ceremonies *(ñampe),* consists of a human skull with the calvarium removed and a drumskin attached to the aperture. The vitrine presentation is one of several ethnographic styles of display used in the Guanabacoa Museum, including a diorama-like facsimile of a *santero*'s sacred room and realistic Palo Monte altar. Photograph by David H. Brown.

logical characters, some historical masquerades distinguished themselves in other ways. With their elaborated facial features, they were representatives of legendary humans, though transfigured by the hooded *saco,* which gave their spirits corporeal form. For example, Victor Patrício de Landaluze's famous 1881 lithograph *El Ñáñigo* depicts an *íreme* with articulated facial features (see figure 4.1). Two little-known and now extinct *íremes,* Akuaramina and Embema, featured fully articulated, three-dimensional anthropomorphic faces.[3] Akuaramina represented the spirit of Sikán, and, like her embodiment in the *sese,* carried four lavish *plumeros* upon her headpiece—fashioned from an inverted calabash representing her water gourd (plate 18). In some historical examples, Embema's facial features were delineated by high-contrast cutout appliqués upon the hood's surface (plate 4, second from left). The most famous Embema remembered by Regla's Abakuá was Janus-faced, with another visage projecting from the circular "hat" *(sombrereta)* at the back of his head. In surviving documents, he appears with cutout eyes, an articulated nose, tribal markings, and, most notably, the white hair, eyebrows, moustache, and beard of an old man, made from palm fringe (figure 7.3). Apparently, as embodiments of legendary humans, these two *íremes* claim not only anthropomorphized faces but also more elaborate hagiographies than the other *íremes,* whose identities derive more from their particular functions and ecological origins (see e.g., Cabrera 1970:208–236). Embema, like Sikán, was less an *íreme* "spirit messenger" than a royal presence with a complicated life history. As Perico Abasonga related to me in March 2002, Akuaramina Mendo, as she was known, was a "troubled person," like Sikán. Embema was mistreated as a child and fled into the *monte* (forest), where he grew old and became a fearsome "monster." Enkríkamo, Chief of the Íremes, though initially frightened by him, gently guided Embema out of the forest and into the Abakuá temple, where he was crowned king. Embema returned to the *monte,* where, apparently, he remained something of an elder among the *íremes* who mediate between the temple and the bush.

Sacos II: The *Íreme* Suit

The body of the *íreme* suit typically has been assembled in patchwork fashion, sewn of a continuous

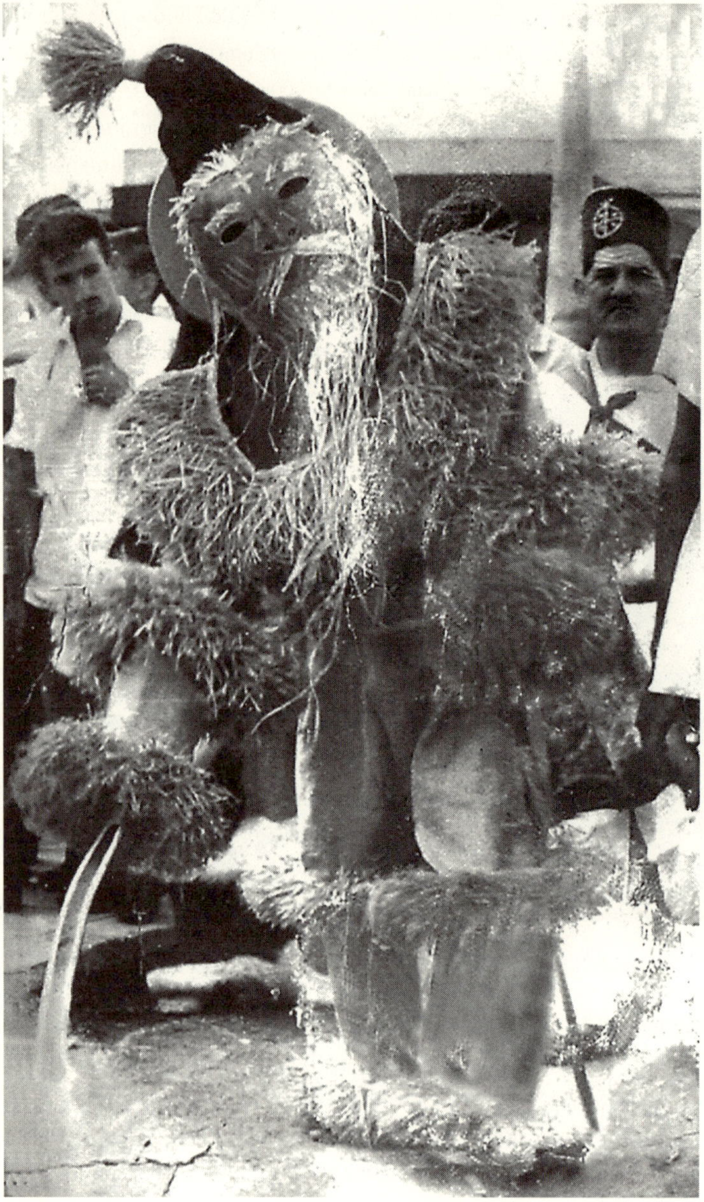

Figure 7.3. Íreme Embema, photographed in situ during a ceremony given by Regla's Otan Efó on 16 June 1953. Embema, who represents a kind of "monster"-king of the forest, features an articulated face. He carries a rooster and a staff. Embema is a now-extinct masquerade. The famous Francisco Hurtado de Mendoza ("Yenequita") is seen in the right background, acting in the capacity of Mokongo for the purposes of this ceremony. Courtesy private collection, Regla.

patterned industrial cloth type, which provides its own designs (e.g., stripes, paisley), or composed of a solid background adorned with contrasting geometric appliqué (see plate 4, second, third, fourth, and fifth from left; plate 16, lower right). The kinds of cloth used have included the common *saco de yute,* industrially produced dyed cotton, and prestige fabrics such as satin, velvet, and various brocades (e.g., plate 4, fourth from left; plate 16, center). Israel Castellanos, who compared *íreme* costume examples from Havana's Criminological Museum of Legal Medicine, found that some of the most "primitive" suits, made in Cuba by the first lodges (mid-1830s–1850s), used striped cotton cloth ticking called *cotí,* which was commonly employed in pillows and mattresses (1928: 32) (plate 4, third from left; plate 16, lower right).

Castellanos concluded that more expensive prestige cloth came later, with demographic changes in Abakuá membership, specifically in the "white" lodges.[4]

By the early twentieth century, if not before,[5] Abakuá artisans had produced gorgeous suits employing contrasting appliquéd bands and patches over expensive cloth (plate 4, left and first and second from right; plate 16, left and center). In contrast, some suits supplanted the classicizing geometric aesthetic with the entirely decorative, for example, paisley cloth—though this design could also be a whimsical reference to leopard spots. Though the *íreme* repertoire counts a few monochrome suit styles, such as the sober black of Anamangüí, a funerary figure, and the white of Akuaramina (figure 7.2; plate 18), most costumes are notable for their sharp contrasts of values, colors, materials, and textures.

Many costumes mark the particular identity of the *íreme* with color and iconography. For example, Eribangandó typically wears costumes in shades of blue, for he is associated with the "River" and the cleansing properties of water (see plate 5). Anamangüí's mostly black suit is broken up only by spare vertical white stripes delineating the human skeleton, along with crosses and/or skull and crossbones on the back of his "hat" *(sombrereta)* (figure 7.2). Suits marked by identifying features such as color, specific *anaforuana,* the appliquéd name of the particular *íreme,* or an articulated face comprise one general class of costumes; these are owned by, and exclusive to, the particular *íreme plaza* in question (figure 7.3, plate 5). Another generic class of suits does not carry specific identifying iconography. It can be extremely festive in color and varied in design. This class of costumes consists of *trajes de baile* (dance suits), which any member of the lodge may don in order to dance during the semipublic portion of the *plante* (e.g., plate 4, second, third, fourth, and fifth from the left; plate 13, right; plate 17, according to Jesús Nasakó).

The *íreme* masquerades, as characteristic of most Abakuá objects, are fitted with palm fringe *(empitá, belemé,* or *irome),* which creates an impressive textural contrast against cloth. The apex of the *íreme*'s conical hood and the joints (neck, elbows, wrists, knees, and ankles) may feature *empitá,* linking these mysterious figures with the forest. Still, the tightly cinched finial of fringe surmounting the *íreme*'s hood is called *pon-pon,* suggesting that Abakuá see such features partly as decorative adornment. Indeed, one conspicuous feature of *íreme* costumes is apparently intended as a whimsical and beautiful adornment. The *íreme*'s *faldeta,* a ruffled, layered, colorful "apron," is tied about the waist and drapes the rear. The *faldeta* moves to and fro when the *íreme* dances. Landaluze's nineteenth-century *íremes* do not wear *faldetas,* and, it seems, older costume examples do not feature them—though these tied-on accessories could have been excluded by Landaluze or lost in Cuba's mostly chaotic museum storage conditions. In any event, the cloth *faldeta* might have derived from a prominent feature of the *negrito* tradition of the nineteenth- and early twentieth-century Cuban vernacular theater *(teatro vernáculo)* (figure 7.4), which produced the instantly recognizable *guarachera* stage dress of twentieth-century Cabaret Rumba performance, still in use today among "folklore" performers (figure 7.5). Still, the *faldeta*'s earliest ancestor in Cuba may lie in the flamboyant attire of a nineteenth-century Afro-Cuban festive street subculture, Los Negros Curros—attire that was later heavily stereotyped in the popular theatrical media (see R. Moore 1997:53–60, 148–149, 160; Landaluze 1881:129–134; Ortiz 1986). It might be hypothesized that this latter fixture of popular Afro-Cuban sartorial performance presented itself to the Abakuá as a festive resource for their semipublic *plante* celebrations.

Each of the *íreme* masquerade's accessories carries specific functions in gestural expression, ritual duties, such as punishment of offenders, and self-protection. For purposes of spiritual communication and self-expression, *íremes* wear a series of square cowbells attached to a leather belt *(enkaniká),* which encircles the waist. They can rotate their waists back and forth,

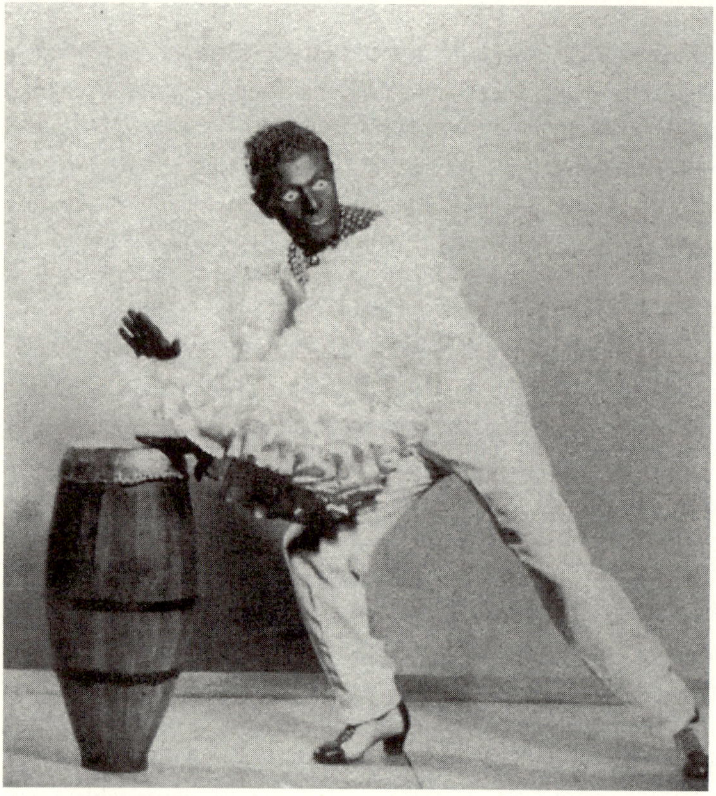

Figure 7.4. ***Negrito,*** **probably Paquito Rodríguez, from "cabaret rumba" style performance with whites in blackface, 1920s–1930s. The *negrito* wears the *guarachera*-style ruffled blouse (R. Moore 1997:148).**

typically in 4/4 time. As noted, *íremes* express joy at the sounding of *ekue* and communicate particular messages to Abasí. A circular, hatlike disk called the *sombrereta,* tied to the back of the *íreme*'s hood, fulfills both mystical and beautifying functions (plates 5, 13, and 16; figures 4.1, 7.2, and 7.3). As an embellishment, the *sombrereta* makes the costume stand out or shine *(lucir);* formally, the *sombrereta* enriches the density and geometry of the costume as it provides harmonious circular background for the conical hood and bright white eyes from a frontal vantage point. The *sombrereta,* if it is painted or appliquéd with the *plaza*'s *anaforuana,* serves to identify the *íreme,* and, like any other signature, to invoke spiritual energy. The *sombrereta* also stands as a sign, a warning, a limit, marking a strong protective taboo. The *sombrereta* (i.e., the head) should not be touched by anyone who is not a member of the lodge. "A lodge member can rearrange it if it becomes unfastened. But everyone else must keep away from it; somebody might just try to introduce a *polvo* [spiritually malevolent "powder"] to inflict damage on the one who is working [i.e., dancing the costume]."[6] Among all of the Afro-Cuban ritual practices, malevolent forces are widely believed to creep up from "behind" *(detrás)* or "through the back door," as it is often said. In this sense, the *sombrereta* contributes to the *íreme*'s spiritual sight and is dedicated to watching the *íreme*'s back. In particular, when the *sombrereta* is elaborated with an additional "double sight" or visage to produce a Janus-faced hood, it suggests clairvoyance.

The *íreme* is a transformational figure between domains: the human, the natural, and the otherworldly.[7] His power and effect are produced through an apparent performative paradox. Though his costume is virtually comprehensive, what it does *not* cover goes far in highlighting the *íreme*'s modus operandi and function. The human dancer's hands and feet are the only features to remain exposed (plates 13 and 17).[8] That the costume masks all but the hands

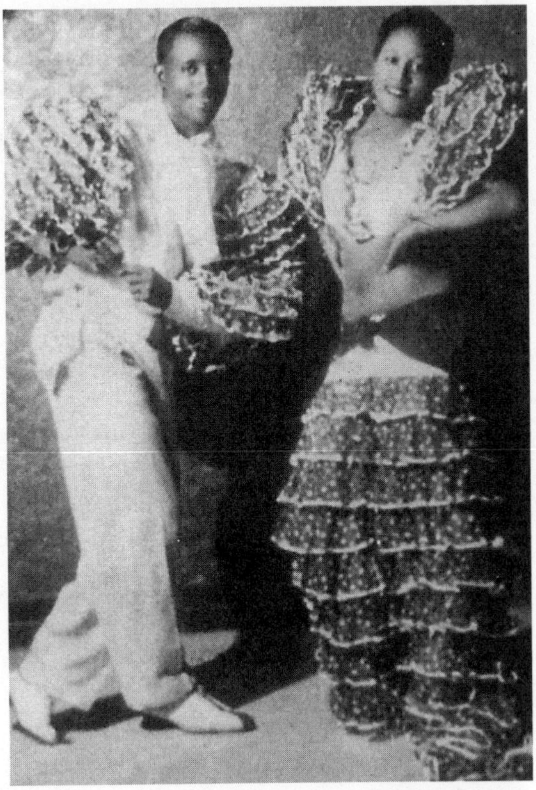

Figure 7.5. ***Guarachera*** **costumes from a 1930s-style stage rumba performance. Dancers are René (Rivero) and Estella (Ramona Ajón). Photograph dated 1933 (from R. Moore 1997:199). The** ***guarachera*** **costume features layered, puffed-out, white-bordered sleeves for men and shoulders and dresses for women. In the 1930s, because of tourist demand for authenticity, Afro-Cubans replaced whites performing in blackface, a tradition dating from the nineteenth-century "vernacular theater" or** ***teatro vernáculo.***

and feet, combines materials of human dress with a profusion of palm fiber, and radically revises the head and its features, produces the effect of ontological in-betweenness. The suit deforms and refigures the body as a creature, a kind of beast, with its conical head, outsized eyes, and no other facial features (in most cases). Still, the *íreme* continues to depend on two key organs of human quotidian and ritual action—the hands, with their opposable thumbs—which neither disincarnated human spirits nor leopards have. And *íremes* have two feet, not four. Though they do occasionally get down and crawl (figure 7.6), only Anamangüí—"the dead that carries the dead" (Sosa Rodríguez 1982:169)—assumes this attitude as a defining feature of his movement repertoire. During funeral ceremonies Anamangüí swiftly scoots across the courtyard's grounds like an agile feline or crocodile.[9] Therefore, Anamangüí, as a master of horizontal and four-footed, rather than upright, locomotion is the exception, not the rule. Though all *íremes* tend to move in a cool, angular style consistent with the feline, the referents of their movements are specific. *Íremes* communicate in legible, articulate ways with symbolic gesture—a feature of human culture, not nature. Handheld attributes—in a word, human-made tools—move in concert with dance steps, bodily twists, mudra-like hand positions, and struck poses, which form responses to the prompting speech and gestures of Enkríkamo or the Moruá Yuansá. Ortiz saw this variety of Afro-Cuban performance as "an incessant pantomime." As an Abakuá member most cogently explained to him, "the mouth of the *diablito* is in his hands and feet" (1951: 471). Indeed, the *íreme*'s only sound is produced by its *enkaniká,* a sound that is neither vocal, as in human speech or animal sounds, nor musically "vocal," like the variable and elastic tone and timbre of the "Voice" of the Ekue friction drum and other instruments. The *íreme,* as a masquerade, gains its power not in any simple suspension of disbelief that a spirit, not a man, dances within the costume. It does so by fashioning, through physical disfiguration—including shades of the grotesque—and specific performance codes, a paradoxical interstice between the human, natural, and spiritual, which can only be experienced as awesome and revelatory. This is why, of course, nineteenth-century non-Abakuá observers found the *íreme* fascinating, frightening, and very much a "devil" *(diablito).* It is also why the modernist, surrealist avant-garde found the *íreme* so compelling as a mystical figure of transformation between domains, which they had so earnestly pursued in their arts.

The *íremes* carry out many of their ritual duties with two hand-held implements, a cloth-adorned wood rod (Br. *itón,* Sp. *vara*) and a basil branch or

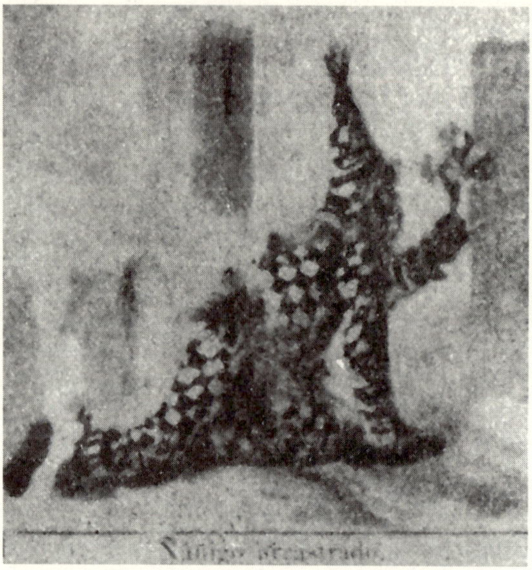

Figure 7.6. *"Diablito" Ñáñigo of Havana* (1870), with the title *Ñáñigo arrastrado* within the document's outer border (Ortiz 1951:471, fig. 105). This *costumbrista* drawing, which goes unattributed, shows an *íreme* crawling *(arrastrado)* and apparently making a gesture of cleansing or offering with a basil branch, perhaps in exchange for *aguinaldo* during Carnival. Courtesy of María Fernanda Ortiz Herrera, Representante Sucesores de Fernando Ortiz.

little broom (Br. *ifán tereré,* Sp. *escobilla*). One is a sign of force and the other a sign of salutation and healing. As commanded by Enkríkamo, the *íreme* wields his *itón* to "attack" and "punish" offenders. For example, those who have disrespected an elder, shirked responsibilities in the lodge, or acted badly toward their families must kneel before the *íreme* and receive blows about the body, particularly on the shoulders—though they are not so harsh that severe physical damage is done. When the *íreme* is commanded to kneel, he inverts the *itón* by placing its tip against the ground, consistent with the constraint and respect signified by his genuflection (plate 13). In contrast, the *ifán* broom is used to "greet, as well as purify, in communication with Enkríkamo."[10] John Dumoulin astutely interpreted the angular sweeping and cutting gestures of the broom across the body and joints as "cleaning" motions (Dumoulin 1962). The identity of one *íreme,* in fact, thematizes this task. Koifán is known as the "sweeper *íreme*" *(íreme barrendero),* whose function it is to clean the temple in preparation for *barokos:* he "sweeps all the bad influences outside," employing basil as well as an herb called "bitter broom" *(escoba amarga)* in similar activities (Sosa Rodríguez 1982:170). Using a different medium, Eribangandó wields a live rooster to "clean" away bad influences.

Changes I: *Íreme* Adornment, Masquerade Dynamics, and Change

Several important changes have characterized *íreme* costumes over time. The earliest visually documented *íreme* costumes seem to closely resemble West African patterns. Fernando Ortiz was the first to directly compare the now-famous 1881 *El Ñáñigo* lithograph by Landaluze and a ca. 1900–1912 photograph of the "Nkanda" grade of "Egbo" (i.e., Ekpe/Ngbe) in southeastern Nigeria by P. Amaury Talbot. Ortiz and more recent writers have assumed the direct continuity of the former and the latter—that is, the putative source.[11] Landaluze's 1881 *El Ñáñigo,* as in other works he produced in the previous several years, features high-contrast black and white geometric patterns: repeated triangles, checks, and stripes—designs that seem to resemble the Talbot example. Both carry a rod in one hand and a leafy branch in the other (see Ortiz 1951:466–467; Talbot 1912:42). The two were so similar to the editors of the 1985 reprint of Ortiz's 1951 text that they mistakenly entitled the Talbot photograph "Figure of 'diablito' ñáñigo. (*Painting by Landaluze* [!])" (1985:466, emphasis added) (figures 4.1 and 7.1).

That the presumed result of transatlantic transfer, the Cuban *íreme,* was captured in paint and lithograph more than two decades *before* Talbot's example, presents methodological challenges. In lieu of African documentation earlier than the Landaluze works, an argument for the direct derivation of the Cuban masquerade style from Talbot's "image" would have to assume the prior, enduring, and "traditional" standing of the Nigerian masquerade documented in 1912. This is a risky proposition for historically rigorous anthropologists, who caution that visual similarity does not amount to historical continuity (Price and Price 1980:204–215). Still, it would be unwise to discard the kinds of formal evidence with which art historians are often left to work in lieu of written documents (see Thompson 1969b, 1983).

Similar as they first appear, a closer look might reveal that within a general family resemblance, the Cuban and African examples diverge significantly, depending on the level of abstraction or specificity one is comfortable in presenting as evidence. Both examples depend on high-contrast, black and white, repeated geometric forms. The Talbot example makes its forceful impression and gains its unity through a disciplined sawtooth pattern, based upon diagonally divided square patches, with all of the resulting repeated right triangles registered in the same direction. Clearly, this *nsibidi*-based pattern, seen also in Ejagham *ukara* cloth, is open to infinite revision, so that sawteeth, pinwheels, checks, and other forms might be produced from the same basic visual elements (plate 3). The Landaluze *El Ñáñigo* and *Diablito Mongo* (plate 8) feature black and white checks, like the *ukara* cloth example, but they do not employ the sawtooth pattern based upon diagonally divided squares and right triangles. Its triangles are interlocking black and white isosceles forms (see the suits' arms, head, and knees). The only other patterns present consist of black and white stripes or checks. Intriguingly, the opposed repeated isosceles triangles result in larger and diametrically opposite patterns produced by their negative spaces—for example, two opposed crowns or pork-pie hats, or a teeth pattern. These are seen at the knees and the side of the head. Between the two rows of "teeth" results a more whimsical and decorative accordion pattern, not the kind of hard repetition produced in the sawtooth pattern.

To my eye, the impression of the high-contrast geometry in both costumes can obscure hypotheses about processes of change. The Cuban example might be seen to attain a certain "family resemblance" with its presumed African source via formal similarities with harlequin-like patterns, as much as anything else: particularly in the *Ñáñigo*'s whimsical, opposed triangles and the stylized manner in which they rest upon horizontal stripes and a foundation of checks at the ankle. Harlequin-like patterns, which may have appeared in Cuban street carnival and on the popular stage, were felicitously adopted by Lucumí artists in their costumes for the *orisha* Eleguá, for example. Unless one presumes an objective "original scene" set before the artist in 1878 or 1881, we will never know fully enough what formal conventions and prior visual experience Landaluze brought to his *El Ñáñigo*—particularly as he, undoubtedly, transferred his ideas from sketched notes done rapidly on the street, or memory, to paintings and lithographs. Conceivably the "real" *íreme* looked more like Talbot's later documented examples than Landaluze's.[12] In any event, that Landaluze stylized his *El Ñáñigo* based on conventional formal patterns gains support in their repeated use in virtually all the other *diablitos* he painted; and a similar figure appears in a variety of settings (see e.g., plates 8, 19, and 20).

Is it worth carefully parsing the two costumes—the presumed African source and its transatlantic result—or is this merely a zealous formal exercise in splitting hairs? Clearly, if formal analysis can produce evidence of similarity, it can also produce evidence of difference. Differences may usefully suggest intervening discontinuities and encourage revision of seamless, linear historical narratives. Aside from the more conspicuous issue of anachronistic transatlantic comparison, the particular stylization, lavishness, and refinement of Landaluze's *El Ñáñigo* suit raise questions about the trajectory of Afro-Cuban *íreme* costumes themselves. If Israel Castellanos is at all correct that many of the earliest Cuban Abakuá costumes (1830s–1860s) were made of cheap, plentiful *cotí* (not to mention *saco de yute*), surviving examples of which admit of minimal elaboration and aesthetic refinement, then whence comes Landaluze's *El Ñáñigo* as the presumed and generalizable result of direct transatlantic transfer? Moreover, Castellanos, who was well aware of Landaluze's much-published *diablitos* (e.g., in Roche y Monteagudo 1908; and see I. Castellanos 1937), presents no examples in his "ethnographic analysis" (1928) of *íreme* masquerades that are anything like Landaluze's classic *diablitos.* Indeed, no such examples show up in any of the extant Havana historical collections, except for the rare Embema-like example in Havana's Casa de Africa, whose lower leg designs compare favorably with Landaluze's 1881 lithograph (plate 4, second from right). It may be that fact by published repetition has produced the impression of their ubiquity in nineteenth-century Havana, when, in fact, like the Embema example, Landaluze's *diablitos* might have been based upon a single rare or specialized costume. For example, Landaluze might have gained access to a unique, possibly "older," Carabalí costume type conserved within a particular *cabildo* or lodge, which he generalized in his artwork. Or it may be, as some have boldly argued, that some traditions on both sides of the Atlantic developed independently, in parallel fashion, given similar cultural principles and conditions—alleviating altogether the need to fashion linear diffusion arguments (see Palmié 1994). Only such logic could solve the problem of an assumed "source" that is newer than its assumed transatlantic result, unless Talbot's Egbo society members had been paging through Landaluze's *Tipos y costumbres de la isla de Cuba* in 1881. It should be noted that the selective comparison of Landaluze and Talbot skews the transatlantic comparison to begin with, obscuring the fact that West African Egbo "images" have appeared in many forms and styles historically, including the use of large swaths of dark solid cloth with minimal surface elaboration (see Nicklin and Salmons 1988; Jones 1988). Solid and nongeometric suit designs are as, or more, abundant in the extant Cuban collections than geometric designs (see plate 4).

Another transatlantic process presents itself as a possibility. Even a cursory look at extant examples shows a great range in the Cuban designs. Some Cuban examples, without doubt, go far in reproducing the hard-edged, high-contrast, geometric impression of the "leopard paw" or "spots" of Talbot's Nkanda "image," though they may come to it through an alternate stylistic vocabulary, for example, the harlequin. In other words, if the least elaborate and most pedestrian *cotí* at all dominated the early suits, it is possible that Abakuá *íremes* later "reafricanized" themselves following a temporal "gap," through a synergy of older stylistic conventions and new resources previously unavailable (for a similar case, see Price and Price 1980:60–80, 194–202). Certainly "new resources" could have included new sources of patronage among the "white" lodges, an increased diversity among imports of foreign cloth, and increased technical, aesthetic, and iconographic refinements in suitmaking, given the coalescence of liturgical and artistic knowledge within the Abakuá over a number of decades.

Changes II: Ritual Technique and Semantic Range in *Íreme* Suits

Beyond variations and changes in suit materials and surface adornment, Jesús Nasakó points out two other significant changes in costume construction, adornment, and their liturgical implications. Early in the Abakuá Society's history, Jesús argues, the *saco* was spiritually closer to other "charged" objects of the *potencia.* It used to be that two parts of the *íreme*'s costume were "charged with a magical load," the *sombrereta,* the circular "hat" tied to the back of the conical hood, and a structural feature within the hood. When an Abakuá member put the suit on, "he would fall into trance. . . . Truly, in trance, as in the other religions. But today, the suits are not charged, and this custom has been lost. Now they dance consciously. Some dancers are so impassioned that, at times, they almost fall into trance. For example, there are people who possess great capacity as spirit mediums—they have the spiritual grace for it. . . . In the case of the *íreme,* an ancestral spirit is always going to manifest in the suit. But, since the *sacos* are no longer charged, no trance occurs."[13]

According to Jesús Nasakó, an internal feature of

the *íreme* hoods of old functioned in concert with the charged *sombrereta* to bring on trance. In all costumes, the conical hood *(capucha)* sits firmly and erectly upon the dancer's head because of a stiff circular support inside it known as the *rodela.* The *rodela* maintains the conical fullness of the hood and, thus, an upright *pon-pon.* It also helps support the sometimes bulky *sombrereta.* The difference between "today" and years ago lies in the composition of the *rodela.* "Now the *rodela* is made of twisted cord [*soga*]. . . . Before, however, the *rodela* was also made from corn straw, and it was twisted with *quimbanza;* [that is], a charge made of the herb called 'hen's claw' [*pata de gallina*], among other things. Thus, the *rodela* carried *brujería,* and when it was seated on the head of the dancer, he fell into trance."[14]

Second, apart from their overall surface design patterns, many of the old *sacos* were distinguished by embroidered or appliquéd signs, particularly on the *sombrereta,* which identified the grade of the *íreme:* Eribangandó, Nkóboro, Mbóko, and so on. This typically took the form of the grade's *firma,* or *anaforuana.* Occasionally this is seen today, though more spectacular, bannerlike forms of identification have been added. In sparkling gold braid, Eribangandó's sign appears upon the flat circular surface of the *sombrereta.* Below, upon the *íreme*'s back—like the team blazon of a soccer jersey—are the names of the lodge and the *plaza,* with a cutout of a rooster between them (plate 5). It used to be, according to Jesús, that not only each individual *íreme* owned his own *saco* with an identifying sign; as well, some lodge members who liked to dance owned their own specially commissioned costumes, which they took home after the ceremony was over. This may have lent more variety, idiosyncrasy, and personal meaning to the *íreme* suit genre. Nowadays lodges own many fewer individualized *sacos* and more generic ones. Instead of a particular *plaza*'s identifying sign, the *saco*'s *sombrereta* might carry simply a quartered circle with *óvalos,* or the appliquéd image of a rooster. Thus, any *plaza* or *obonekue* could wear the costume. Certainly, this more informal arrangement might be useful in the case of lodges in which *plazas* remain empty and other members or visitors substitute during ceremonies.

Conclusion

The foregoing discussions locate Abakuá Society altar attributes and *íreme* costumes within a Cuban and African Diaspora historical and cultural context. Though such a contextualization seems natural or intuitive, the "historical" narrative I have written—narratives have beginnings, middles, and ends—begins in Africa, follows Africans to Cuban shores, and traces the development of the Abakuá on the island. This is partly a pragmatic choice, inasmuch as it facilitates introducing a complex subject with many levels of analysis rather than reinventing the wheel with new writing strategies. Of course, it also serves heuristic purposes, for it rehearses a more conventional narrative of diffusion from Africa in the book's more descriptive first half precisely in order to launch a critique in the book's second half. Second, these descriptive ethnographic and art historical discussions of the Efori Eñongo altar begin with the lodge's iconographic banner as a kind of prism for looking at various aspects of Abakuá liturgy and art. This approach tends to reinforce a conventional way of situating the referents of Abakuá ritual in a prior mythical text. However artificial, this approach serves didactic purposes; a retelling of the Abakuá origin myth facilitates familiarity with Abakuá categories, characters, and meanings for the reader.

Despite the historical and cultural contextualization provided, the art historical and ethnographic discussions of the Abakuá here assume the legitimacy of the subject for neutral, if not also celebratory, scholarly discussion. More directly, these are post-1970s kinds of discussions that assume an Abakuá practice already valorized as "culture" and "art." That the Abakuá Society is a set of wholesome social, cultural, and artistic practices is a relatively recent idea. Outside of avant-garde and scholarly circles, the Abakuá Society only very recently became socially redeeming—and only in the narrowest sense of "folklore"—and still remains a misunderstood practice. Though Cuban scholars have written neutrally about the Abakuá since the 1950s, and cultural institutions began to present Abakuá performance as early as the mid-1960s, a host of pressures to blunt, dilute, and co-opt the institution and its visual arts has been at work. For a good part of the Cuban population, for many of the Cuban exiles, and with respect to the actual agenda of the state—behind the folkloricized facade—the Abakuá Society is still regarded ambivalently, if not reviled.

Since the mid-1940s, particularly within American ethnography, the Abakuá Society has become a focus of ethnographic (Courlander 1944) and art historical (Thompson 1978, 1983) study. Robert Farris Thompson's majestic *Flash of the Spirit: African and Afro-American Art and Philosophy* locates Afro-Cuban and other African Diaspora ritual forms—including those of the Abakuá—on a transatlantic continuum. They are seen to originate in five West African classical civilizations, and, as the book's subtitle indicates, they constitute "art" and "philosophy." The book's title more dramatically locates African Diaspora art and philosophy as incarnations of powerful, positively construed, spiritual continuities with Africa.

The positive and celebratory evaluation of African and Afro-American-descended cultural products began at least as early as the Harlem Renaissance, manifested in important local and regional ethnographies in the 1930s and 1940s (Herskovits 1941), and continued in the 1960s and 1970s with the civil rights and black cultural nationalist movements. The academic field of African Diaspora art history has grown rapidly since that time. Still, the assumption of Abakuá objects *as art,* and as a valid object of study in papers, theses, and books, requires its own historicization. This means a close look at the ways in which Afro-Cuban "arts" in general, and those of the Abakuá Society specifically, have been constituted as objects of study within institutionalized discourses over time, including the techniques and categories with which they have been observed and evaluated. The second part of this book, therefore, explores the discourses within which Abakuá attributes gained their meanings within shifting regimes of knowledge and power, in tension and dialogue with meanings that were maintained and created by the Abakuá themselves. In short, Abakuá Society attributes might be seen as shifting or "graduating," over time, between emergent contexts that have their political, social, and cultural dimensions.

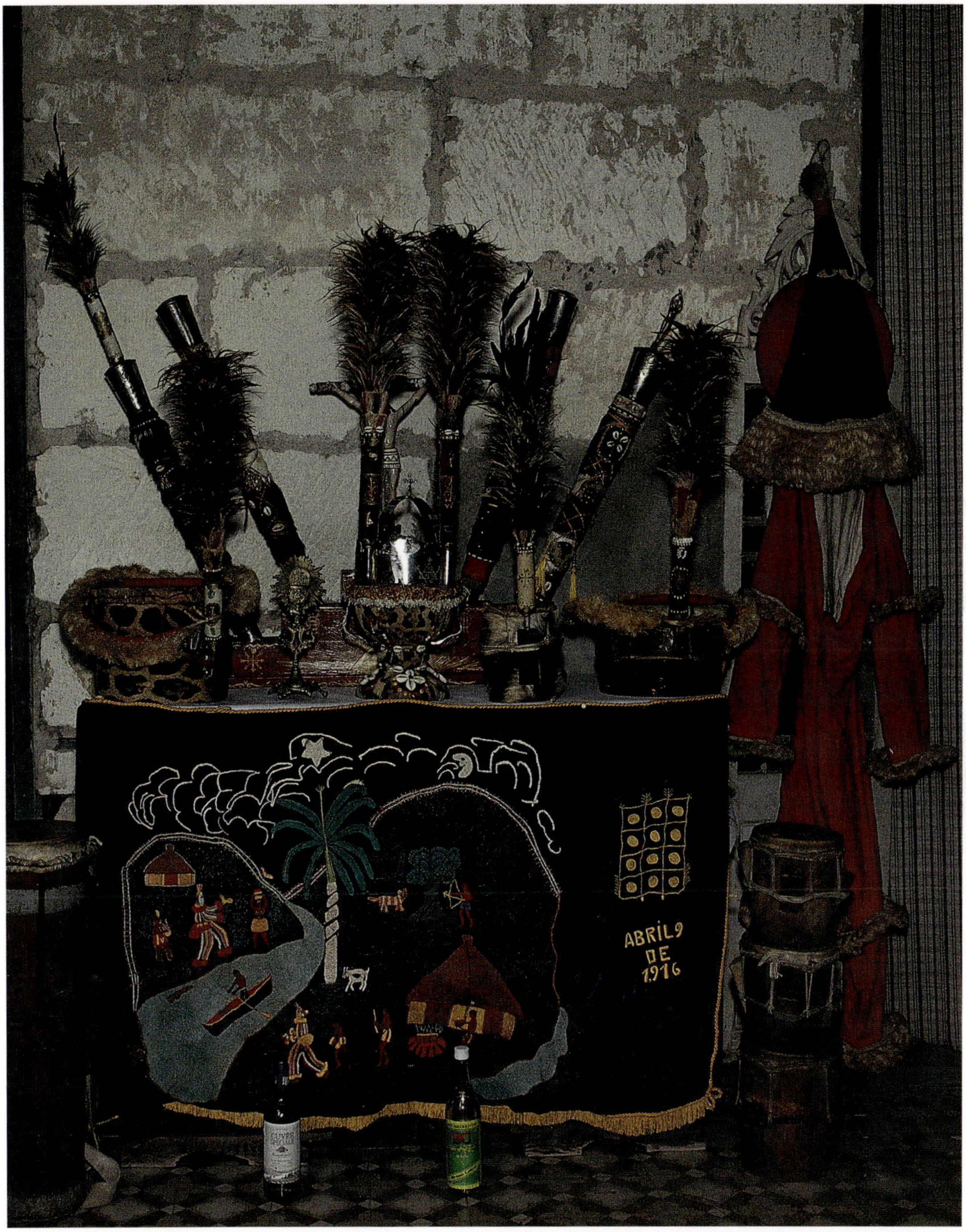

Plate 1. Altar, Efori Eñongo, 1992. Silk thread embroidery on velvet. The altar "apron" *(delantal* or *frontal)* of Efori Eñongo depicts the "birth" of the Abakuá in Africa. The altar objects were made in 1916 and last renovated in the late 1970s while the velvet, embroidered, yellow-fringed apron was made in 1918. Photograph by David H. Brown, 1992.

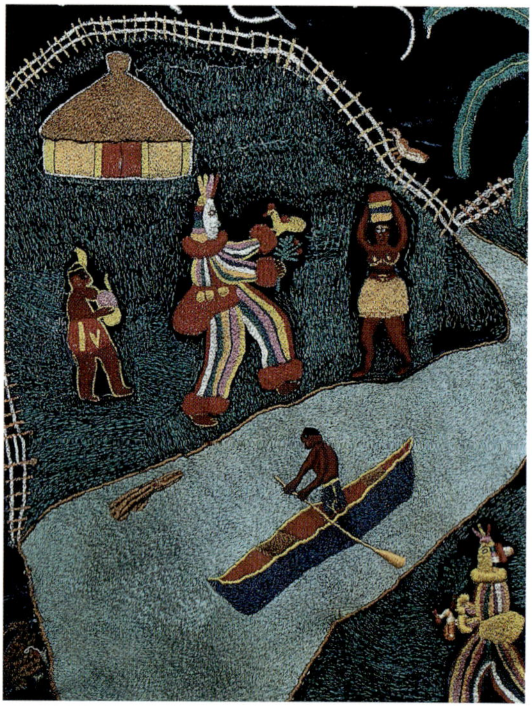

Plate 2. Efori Eñongo banner, detail, Sikán with gourd atop head by the Oddán River, along with the "Bibí" fisherman, Ñangabión (crocodile), and Íreme Eribangandó, guided by Enkríkamo. Nkiko "sings" at upper right. Photograph by David H. Brown, 1992.

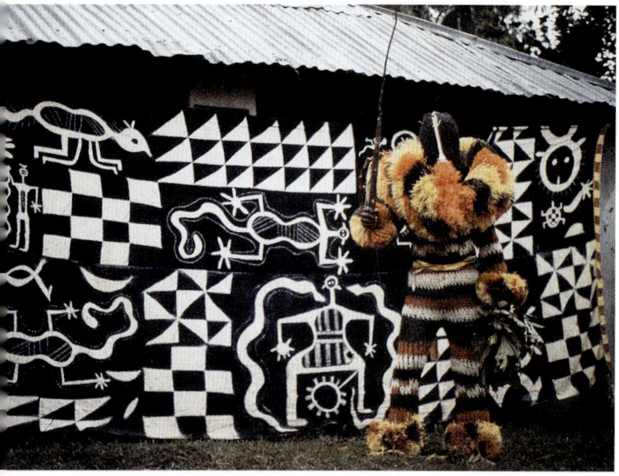

Plate 3. *Ukara* cloth around the *ekat*, the Ejagham Ngbe Society lodge in Africa. The Nkanda grade of the society, a masquerade, stands before the lodge. The resist-dyed *ukara* cloth features diverse figurative and abstract *nsibidi*—the leopard's "paw print," reptiles, snakes, and the masquerade figure himself, center (from Leib and Romano 1984). Courtesy Elliot Leib and Renee Romano.

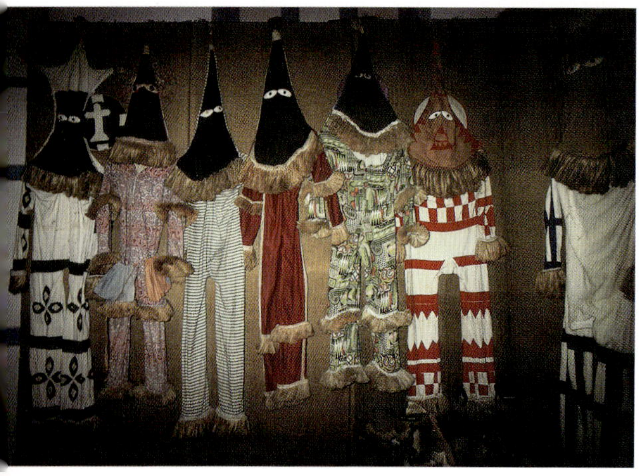

Plate 4. Seven *sacos de íreme* as exhibited in the Abakuá salon of the Fernando Ortiz Collection, La Casa de Africa, Old Havana, 1992. The suits, of diverse materials, colors, and masquerade identities, were confiscated by the police in the early twentieth century. Photograph by David H. Brown.

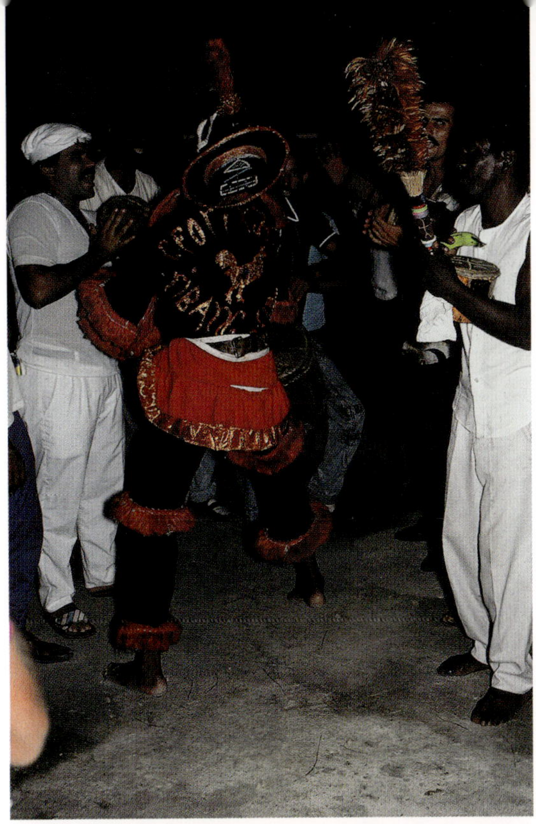

Plate 5. *Íreme* Eribangandó dancing with the orchestra in the courtyard of Irionda in Regla, with Enkríkamo at his right. The adornments on the masquerade's back include a rooster, this *íreme*'s name (below), and the name of the lodge (above), Eforikamá of Regla. The *íreme*'s *sombrereta* (hat) bears the sign of Eribangandó. The decorative red *faldeta* falls below the leather belt, which holds a series of cowbells. Photograph by David H. Brown.

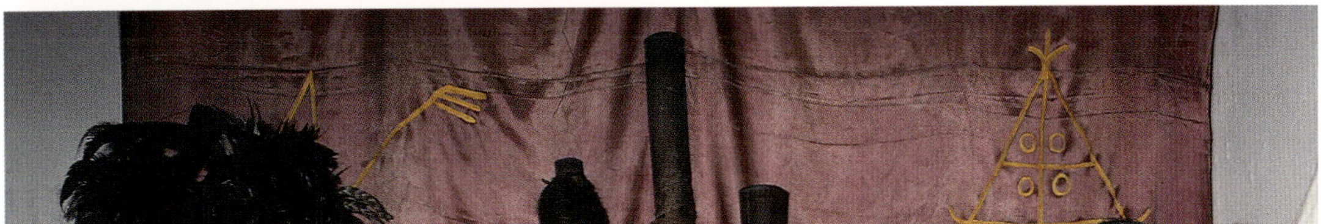

Plate 6. An altar as assembled in the Abakuá salon of the Casa de Africa, Havana, 1992. The altar's staffs are adorned very simply with rope, some goatskin, and plain metal caps. It was installed by Juan Mokongo. Also included are the drums of Mpegó and the *sese* (left), Ekueñón and a *sese de pandero* (right), Nasakó's magical horns, and the crucifix representing Abasí. According to Juan Mokongo and Jesús Nasakó, the altar bears the style of the smaller Orú branch of the Abakuá, because there are seven, rather than four, staffs. Photograph by David H. Brown.

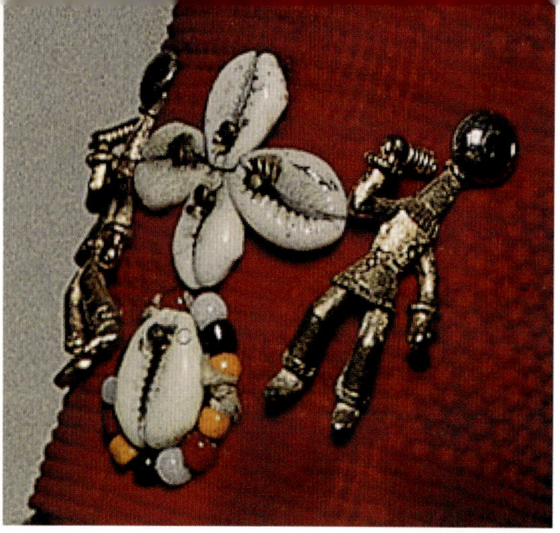

Plate 7. Detail, Efori Eñongo's Abasonga staff. Two mass-produced brass key fob *íremes* separated by a cross formed by cowrie shells and beads. Photograph by David H. Brown.

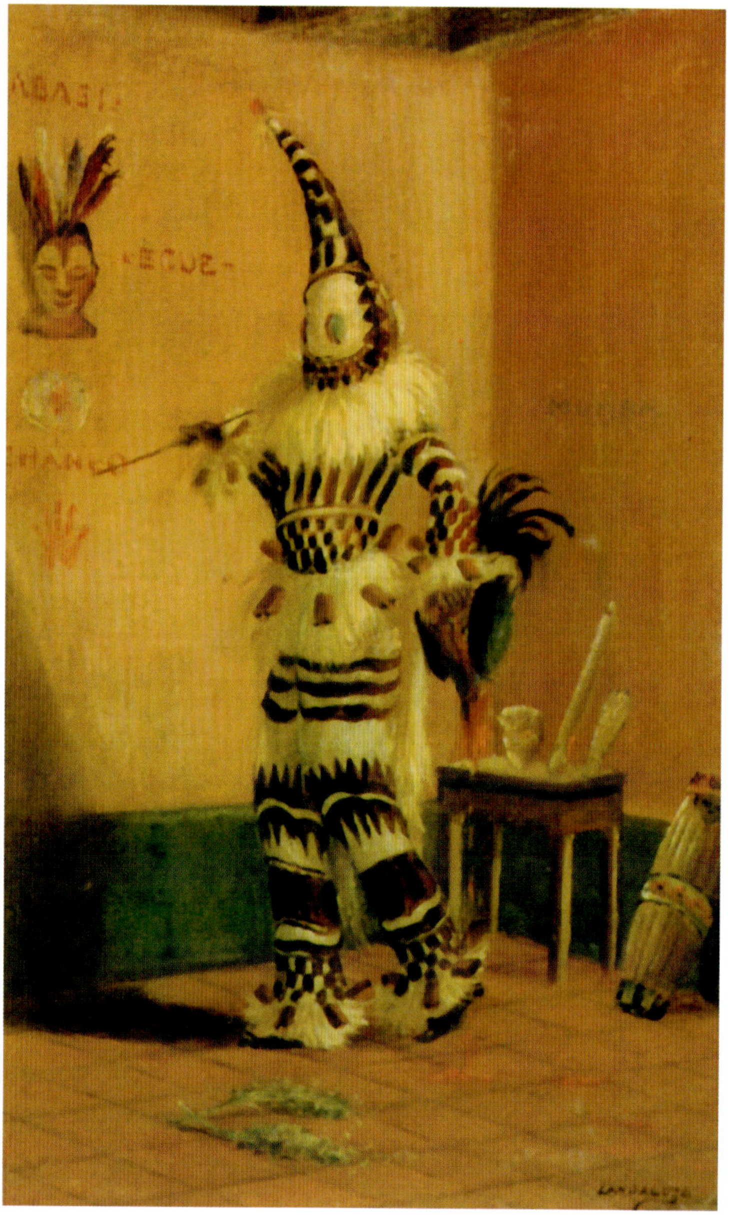

Plate 8. Víctor Patricio de Landaluze, *Diablito Mongo* (in Fambá), ca. 1878, oil on canvas, 11.25 × 7.5 inches. Courtesy Museo Nacional de Bellas Artes, Havana.

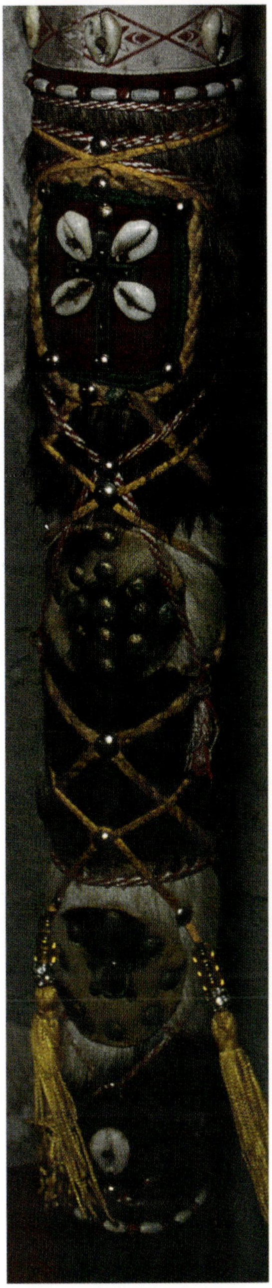

Plate 9. Detail, Efori Eñongo's Mokongo staff, showing three appliqué patches and the decorative windings of silk cord with tassels over contrasting pieces of goatskin. Photograph by David H. Brown.

Plate 10. Detail, Efori Eñongo's Mokongo staff. Red velvet patch with four cowrie shells nailed into the quadrants of the crucifix featuring the "Dead Christ" with inclined head, reiterating the drawn sign of Mokongo. The silver crucifix of the Dead Christ was carried by all followers of the Regla Kimbisa. It is among several thousand commissioned in Milan, Italy, by Andrés Petít in the nineteenth century as an *nkisi* charm to protect members. Photograph by David H. Brown.

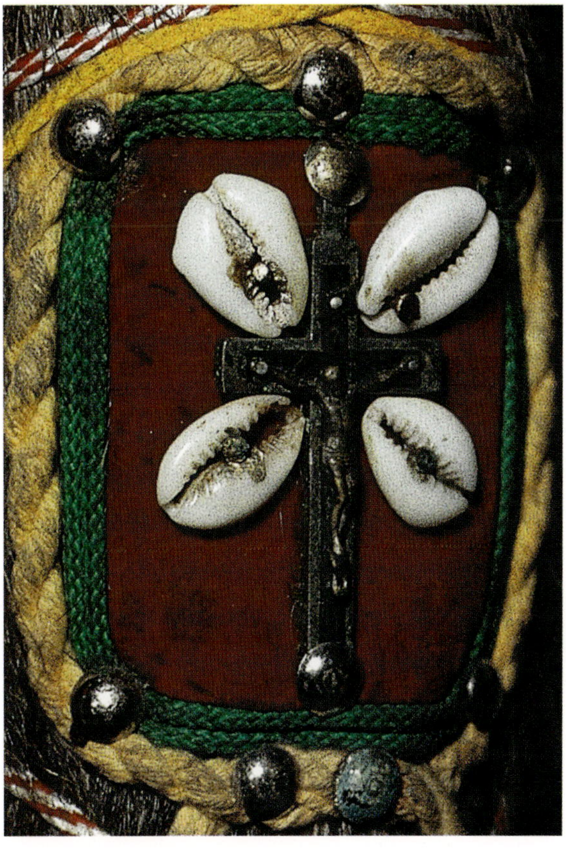

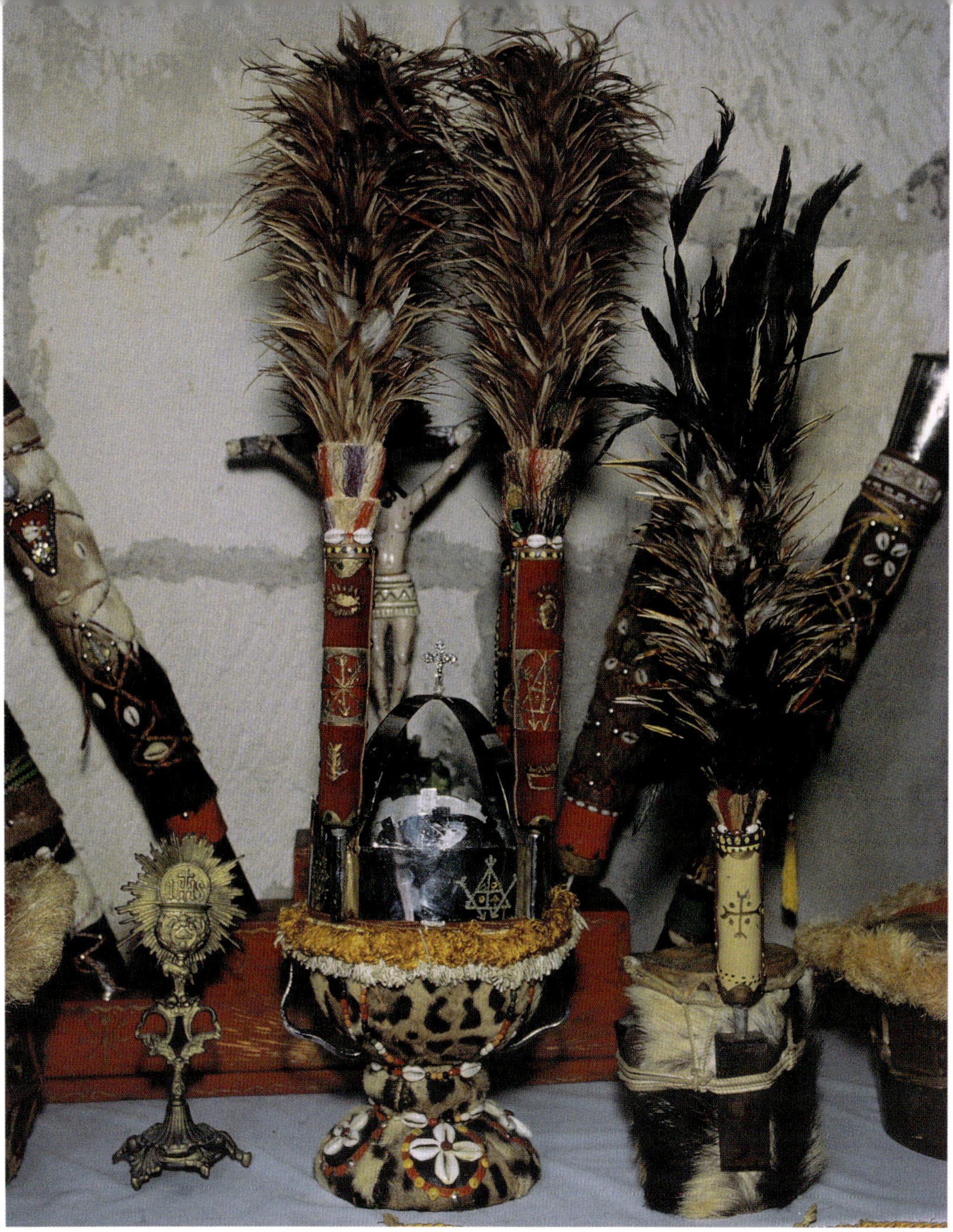

Plate 11. Detail, Efori Eñongo altar surface: The Sese of Efori Eñongo (center), the Santísimo Sacramento or monstrance (left), and Enkríkamo (right). The *sese,* topped with a crucifix-surmounted, double-arched chromed crown, is a sealed cedar urn, a symbolic reliquary for Sikán and Tanze. Adorned with leopardskin, silk fringe, and cowrie shells, it also supposedly contains *brujería* protecting the four highest officers of the lodge, each of whom is represented by a *plumero,* which is inserted into slots at the crown's four cardinal points. Anthropomorphized, the *sese* is a bust portrait of Sikán, and the rooster feathers represent her "hair." Each *plumero* is inscribed with its owner's sign. The Isué officer grasps the two metal handles when he carries it in procession. To the left is the monstrance, representing the Eucharist—the goblet (blood), the upright circular paten, and the Host (body) of Christ, which bears the Greek initials of Christ as used by the Jesuits (IHS). A fixture of Roman Catholic Church and domestic altars, the monstrance was added to the Abakuá altar in the second half of the nineteenth century by Andrés Petít for purposes of "licitness." This monstrance marks the widespread presence of the Jesuits in Latin America. This representation of the "Holy Sacrament" is regularly compared to the *sese efó* as the "holy sacrament" of the Abakuá. Behind is seen the red *bastonera* holding the lodge's four staffs. Photograph by David H. Brown.

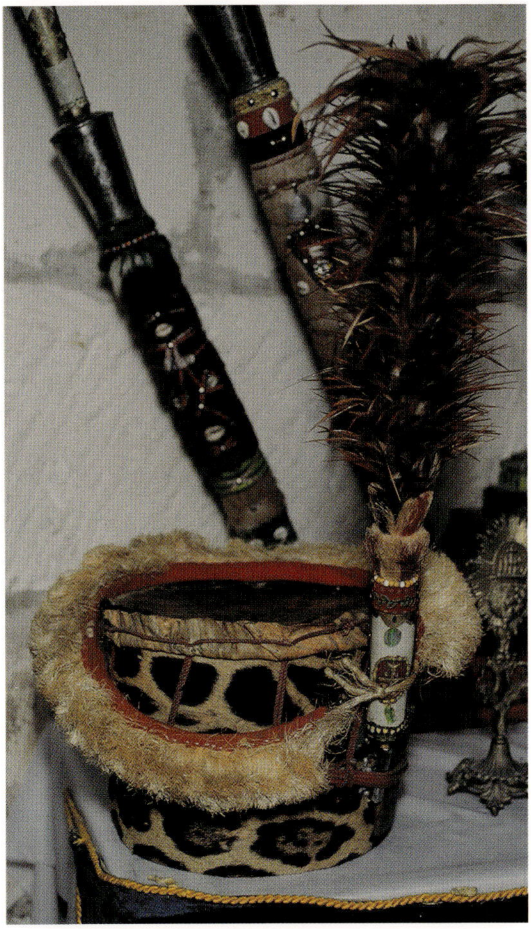

Plate 12. Detail, Efori Eñongo altar surface. Drum of Ekueñón, covered in leopardskin. Ekueñón, the forest hunter, is the Abakuá's "executioner" *(verdugo).* The circular *beromo* or *muñón* of fringe adorns the drum. Photograph by David H. Brown.

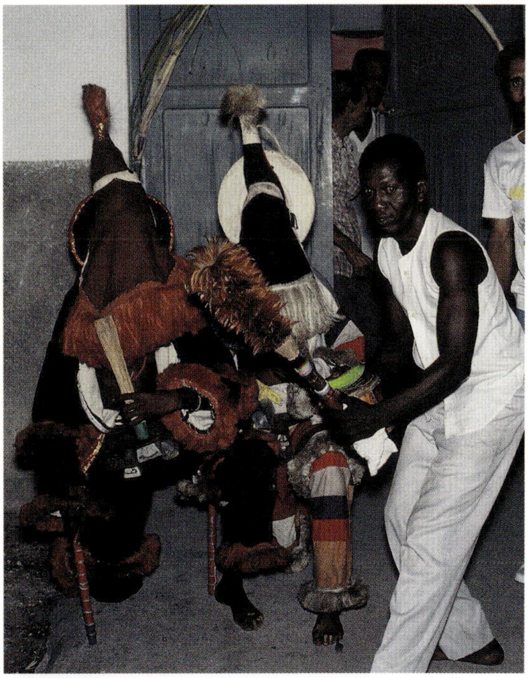

Plate 13. The Enkríkamo *plaza,* with his small plumed drum, commanding two *íremes* to kneel outside the *fambá* of the Regla Irionda lodge, 1992. The kneeling gesture of respect and control is called *entumitiá.* Eribangandó is to the left. Photograph by David H. Brown.

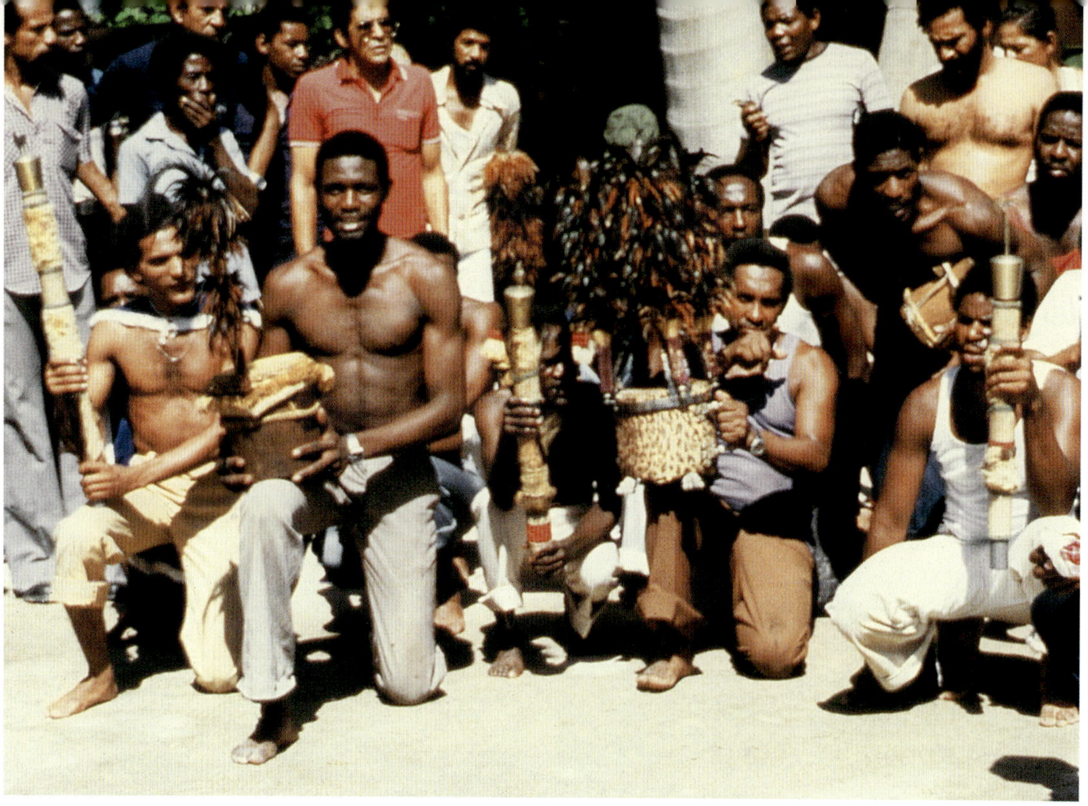

Plate 14. The procession of the *plazas* of the Efí Embemoró lodge of Central Havana, which uses a *tierra* in Párraga, stops to pose for a photograph in the courtyard, 1986. The Isué (right center) carries the Efí lodge's *sese eribó* in the *kankomo* form: the open-bottomed drum that the Efó branch mocked as "empty." Photograph copyright © Annette Gilsdorf 1986; all rights reserved.

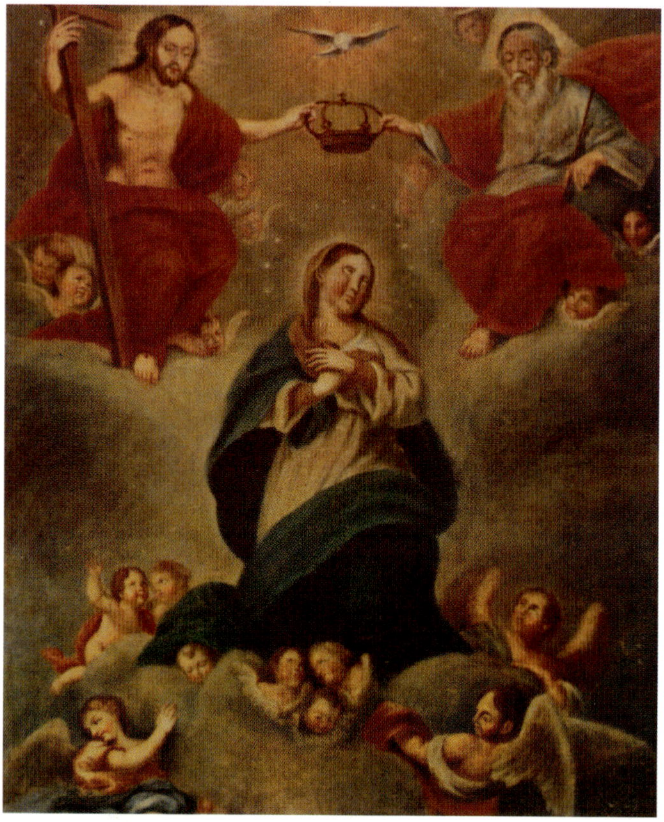

Plate 15. José Nicolás de la Escalera, *Coronation of the Virgin by the Trinity,* eighteenth century, Santa Maria del Rosario church, Havana. Courtesy of the Museum of Arts and Sciences, Daytona Beach, Florida.

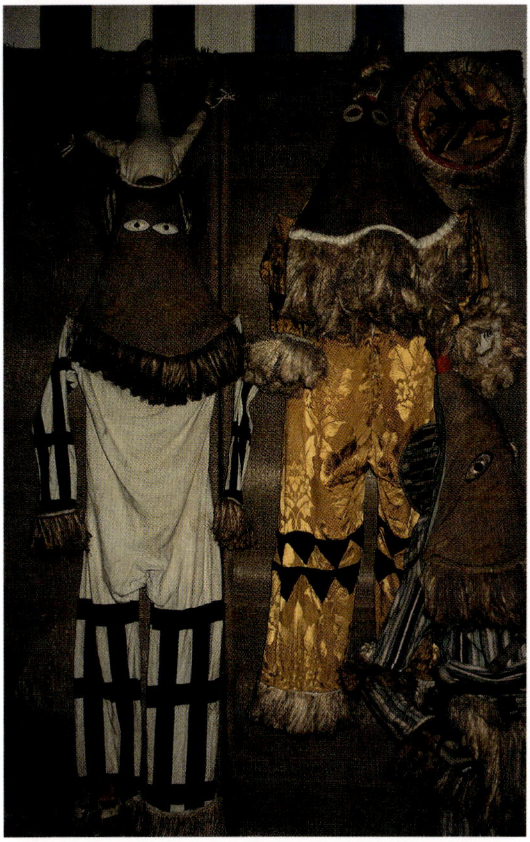

Plate 16. Three *íreme* masquerades in the Casa de Africa's Fernando Ortiz Collection, 1992. The central *íreme* is constructed of a gold satin floral brocade with an appliquéd repeated triangle pattern in black. The suit at front right is made from a striped *cotí* in pink, turquoise, black, and gray, typically used in mattress ticking. Blue velvet geometrical designs over satin adorn the left suit with its tripartite hood. This suit belonged to the Museum of Legal Medicine and was studied by Israel Castellanos (1928). (See figure 9.6, left.) Photograph by David H. Brown.

Plate 17. *Íreme* posing for a photograph at *plante* of Eforikamá, Regla, 1992, exemplifying a typically angular body style, with one arm crossing the torso with a staff held obliquely between the fingers, the other raised, with the palm turned out and the broom dangled vertically. One leg, in shifting, padding steps, crosses the other. This *íreme* suit is referred to as a *traje de baile,* a "dance suit," which may be donned by any Abakuá brother in order to dance. It is brightly colored and features a plaid, layered *faldeta,* or "apron," which is bordered in white. It is tied around the waist and falls to the rear. Photograph by David H. Brown.

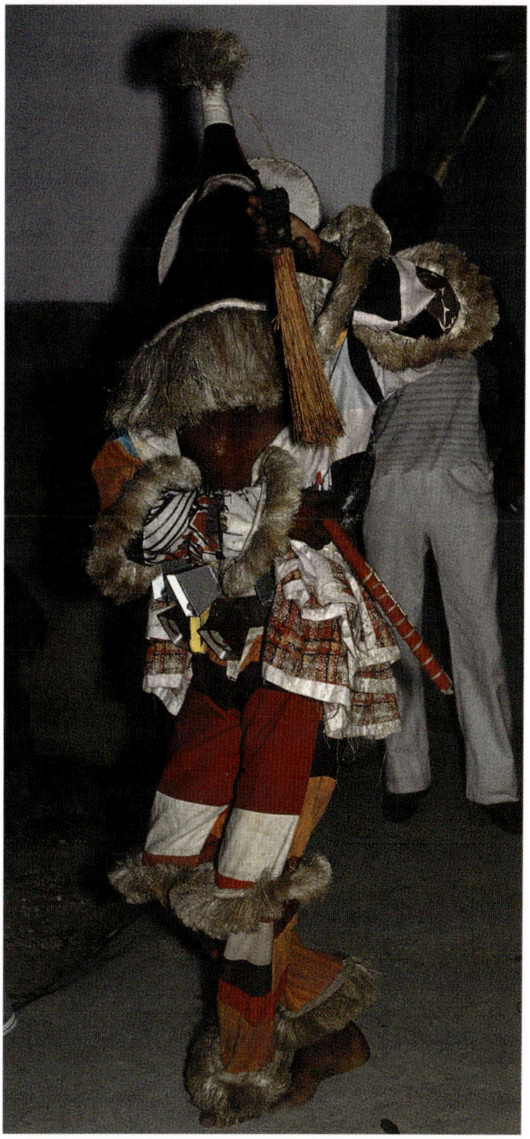

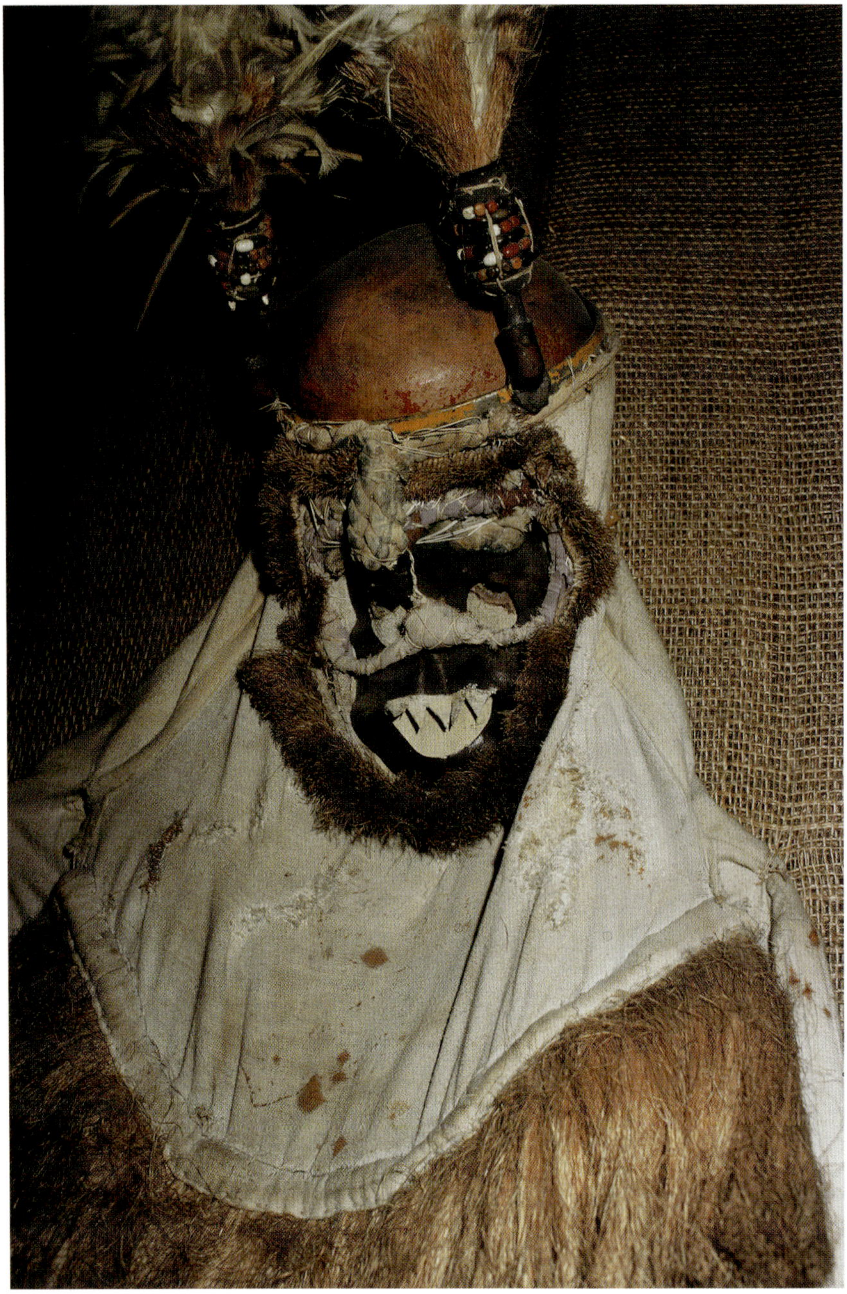

Plate 18. *Saco* of Íreme Akuaramina as exhibited in the Casa de Africa, 1992. Akuaramina, a now-extinct masquerade tradition, represents Sikán. It is distinguished by a solid white suit. Recalling both Sikán's water gourd and the *sese* drum, it features an inverted calabash headpiece with four *plumeros* representing her "hair." Articulated facial features are apparently confined to two classes of *íreme,* this one and Embema (see figure 7.3). Photograph by David H. Brown.

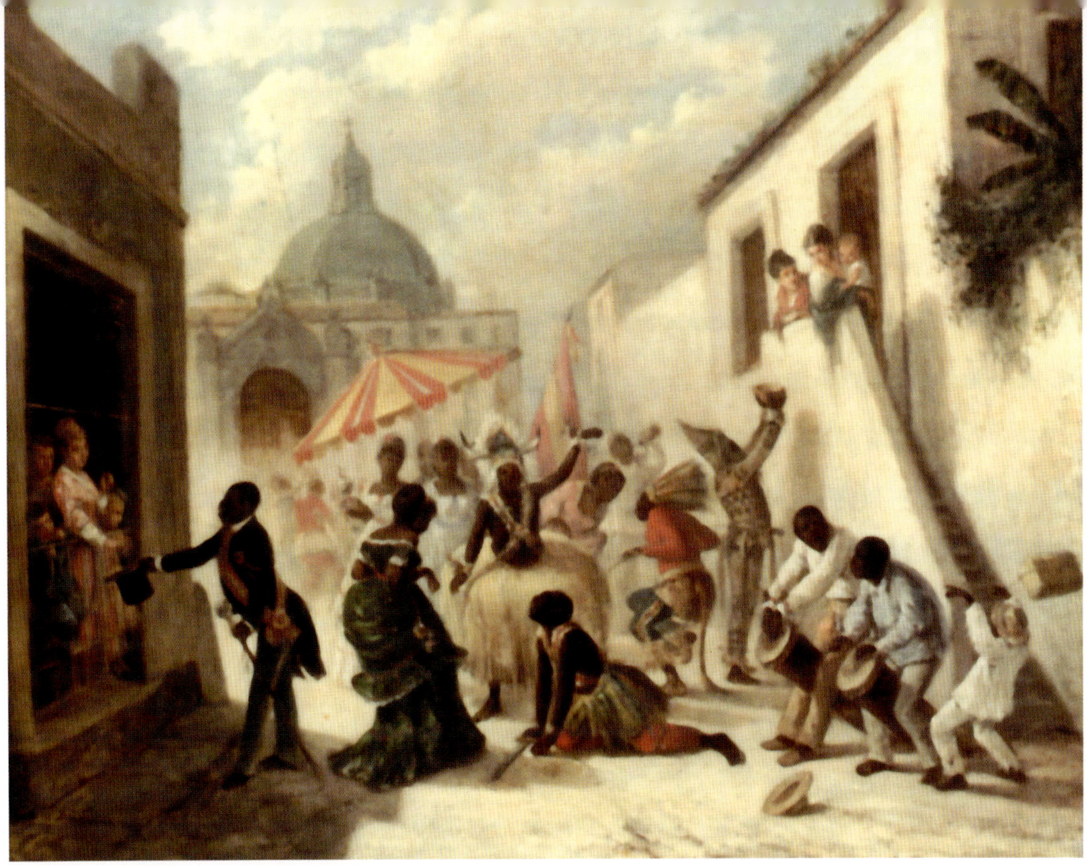

Plate 19. Víctor Patricio de Landaluze, *El Día de los Reyes,* ca. 1878, oil on canvas, 24 × 20 inches. Landaluze depicts a *cabildo* carnival group in a street by the Plaza de San Francisco in Old Havana. The *cabildo* captain solicits *aguinaldo* (left); queens and entourage process beneath umbrellas. They are preceded by three dancing and mugging *diablitos,* one of whom entreats a fancily dressed, perhaps free, woman of color. The *cabildo*'s red and yellow banner appears at right rear center. An *íreme* solicits *aguinaldo* from a family above (right). Two drummers play rhythms while a child dances. The composition is likely a composite of different characters. Landaluze used the same *íreme* over and over, as well as the groups of bourgeois onlookers. Courtesy of the Museo Nacional de Bellas Artes, Havana.

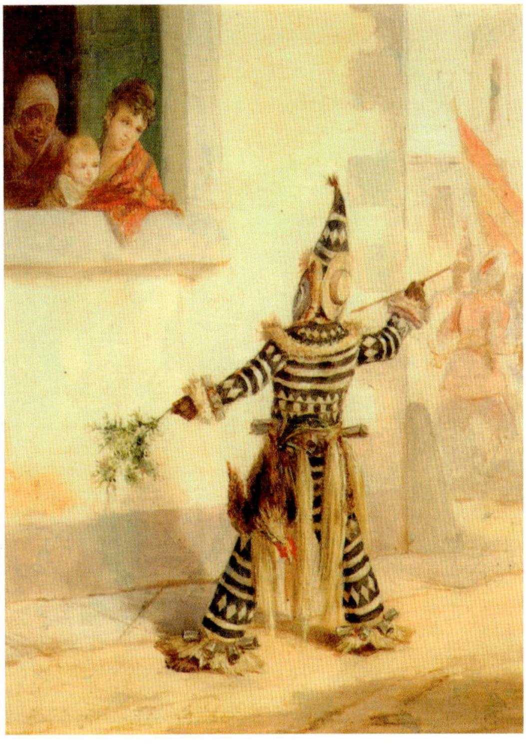

Plate 20. Víctor Patricio de Landaluze, *Diablito,* ca. 1878, oil on canvas, 14 × 10.75 inches. A variant on a section of his "Day of Kings" painting (plate 19), the artist depicts an intimate scene of performance before a charmed audience, consisting of a young white woman, her child, and an older Afro-Cuban woman, likely the *criada* (maidservant, nanny). Landaluze placed similar figures in different exterior and interior scenes. This *diablito* figure was later cut out as a specimen and illustrated by Israel Castellanos as his frontispiece (1937) (see figure 10.1). Courtesy of the Museo Nacional de Bellas Artes, Havana.

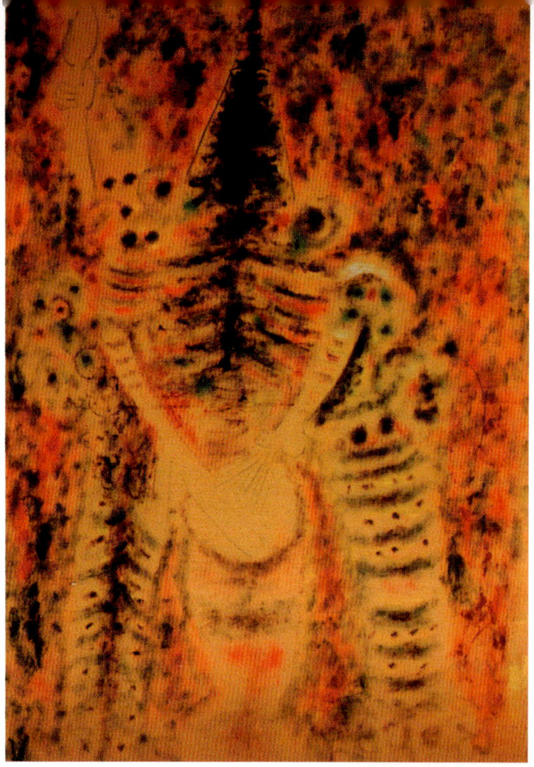

Plate 21. Wifredo Lam, *Untitled* (*Ñáñigo*), 1943, oil on canvas (Blanc 1992:119). Lam schematically depicts a standing *íreme* playing a goblet-shaped drum in atmospheric flat space, with the impression of other figures behind him in procession. Copyright © 2002 Artists Rights Society (ARS), New York/ADAGP, Paris.

Plate 22. Victor Manuel García, *Carnival,* ca. 1940, oil on canvas. An *íreme* holding a scorpion dances before a multiethnic Carnival crowd as *farolas* (lanterns) are held aloft. Courtesy of the Collection of Mr. and Mrs. Ramón Cernuda, Miami.

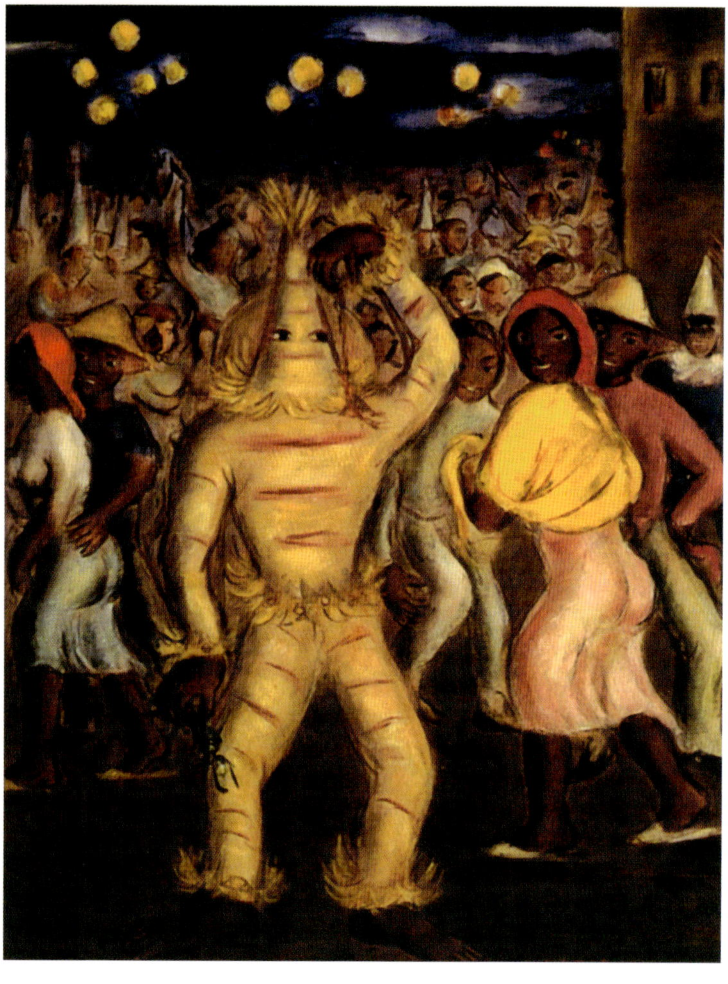

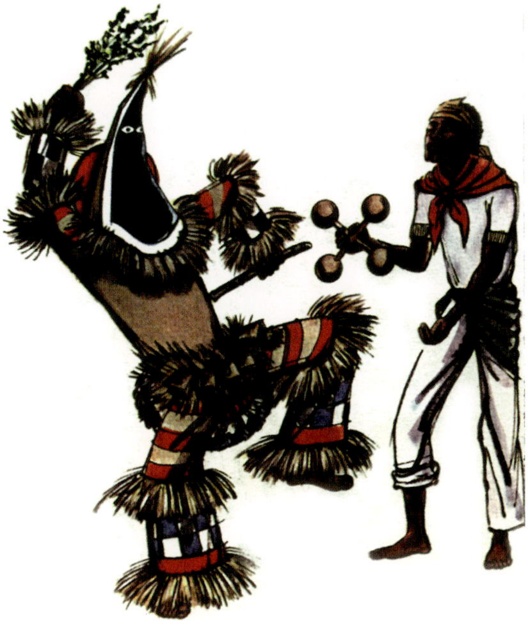

Plate 23. *Íreme and Moruá,* illustration of Abakuá performance dress *(vestuario)* in Lamerán's 1982 teacher's manual for folklore and dance study.

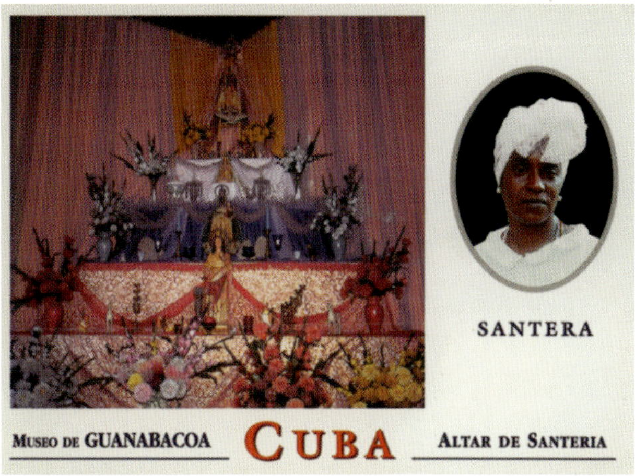

Plate 24. Tourist postcard showing the tiered syncretic Santería altar *(Altar de Santería)* in the permanent exhibition of the Ethnographic Museum of Guanabacoa, along with a cameo inset of a typical *santera.*

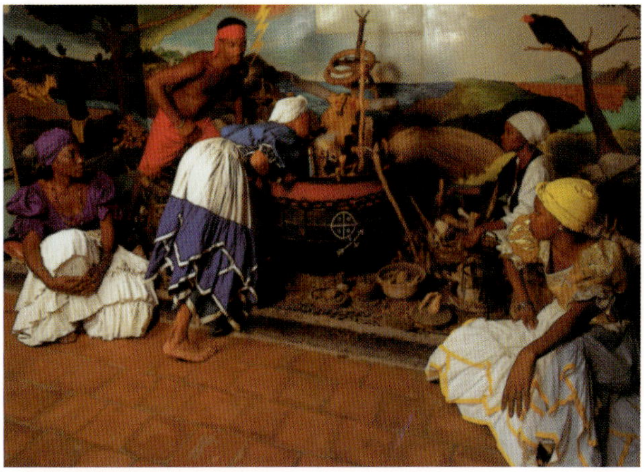

Plate 25. Tourist postcard showing facsimile of Palo Monte altar, with mural behind it, along with folklore performers in "congo" dress in the Ethnographic Museum of Guanabacoa. The smaller cauldron, directly to the right of the large one, is believed to be "Buey Suelto," which belonged to Arcadio Calvo of Guanabacoa.

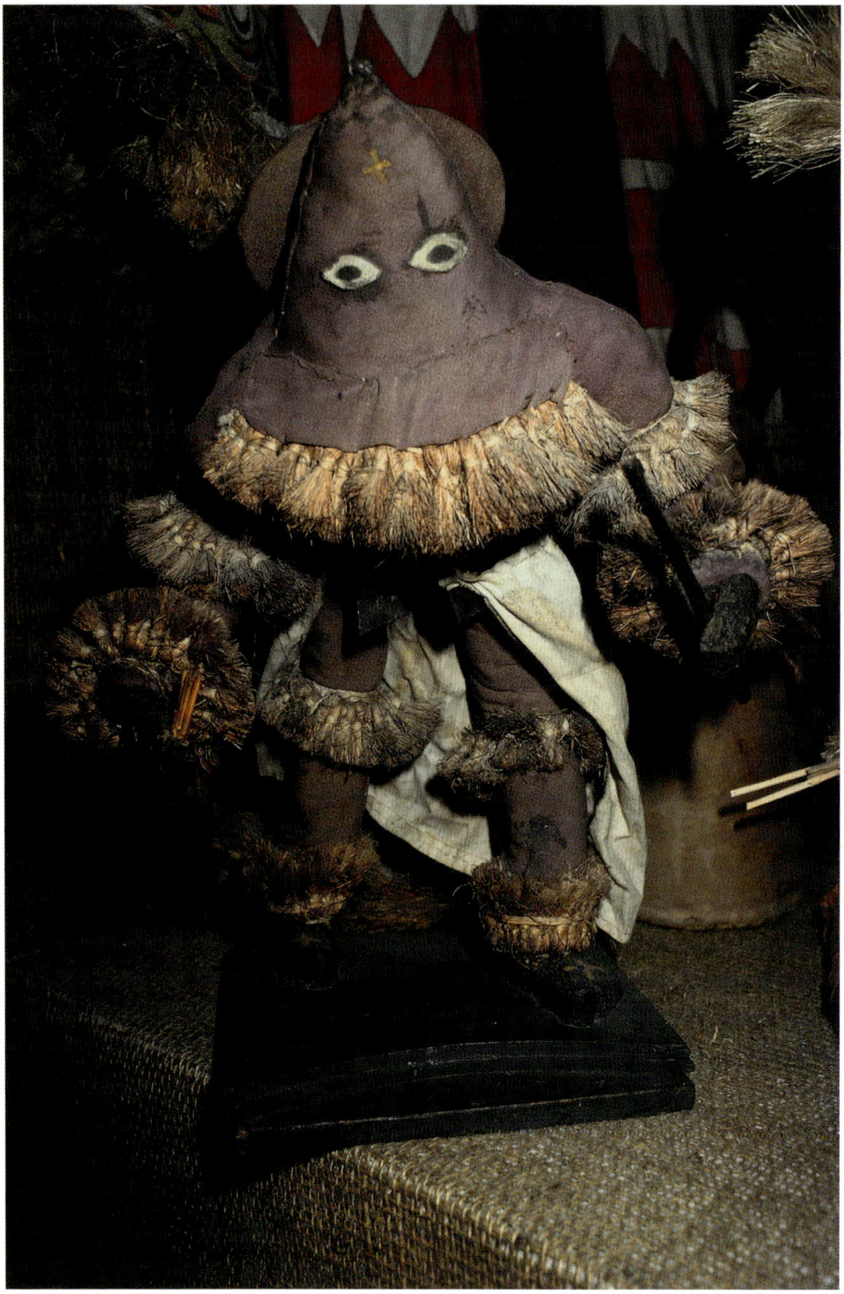

Plate 26. *Íreme* doll in the Fernando Ortiz Collection of the Casa de Africa, n.d. Abakuá members have produced *íreme* dolls for sale to tourists for perhaps half a century or more. With the exception of the wood-carved feet and hands, note the similarity to J. González's *íreme* in the construction of the rings of fringe at the joints (cf. plate 27).

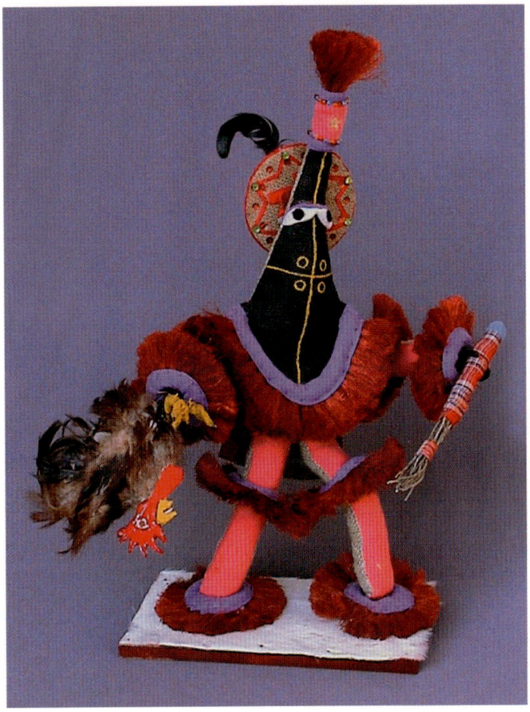

Plate 27. J. González, miniature Íreme Eribangandó figure, 22 inches tall, burlap, cloth, broom fringe, goatskin, sequins, beads, paint, Havana, 2000. This handmade *íreme* in the tradition of Abakuá miniatures is sold on the street in Havana. It is made from cloth glued and sewn over an armature of wire, which has been wrapped tightly in cotton batting and sewed down with a canvas under layer. The rooster carried by Eribangandó is a construction of rooster feathers, cloth, and paint over cardboard.

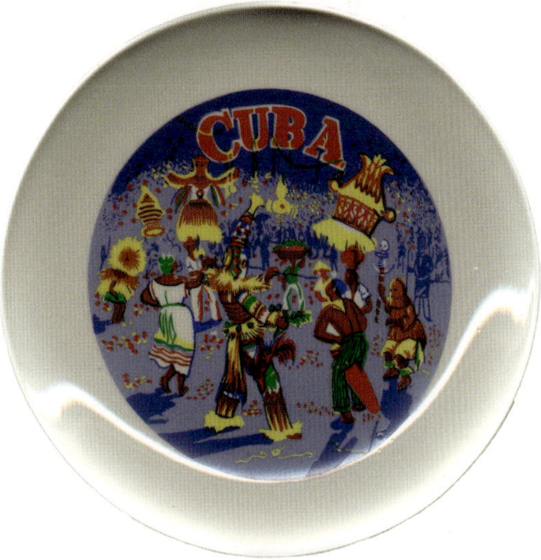

Plate 28. Tourist plate purchased by the author at the José Martí International Airport in Havana, 1999, featuring a version of Landaluze's 1881 *El Ñáñigo* set in a carnival scene recalling the "Day of Kings" scenes of Landaluze and Miahle. Photograph by David H. Brown.

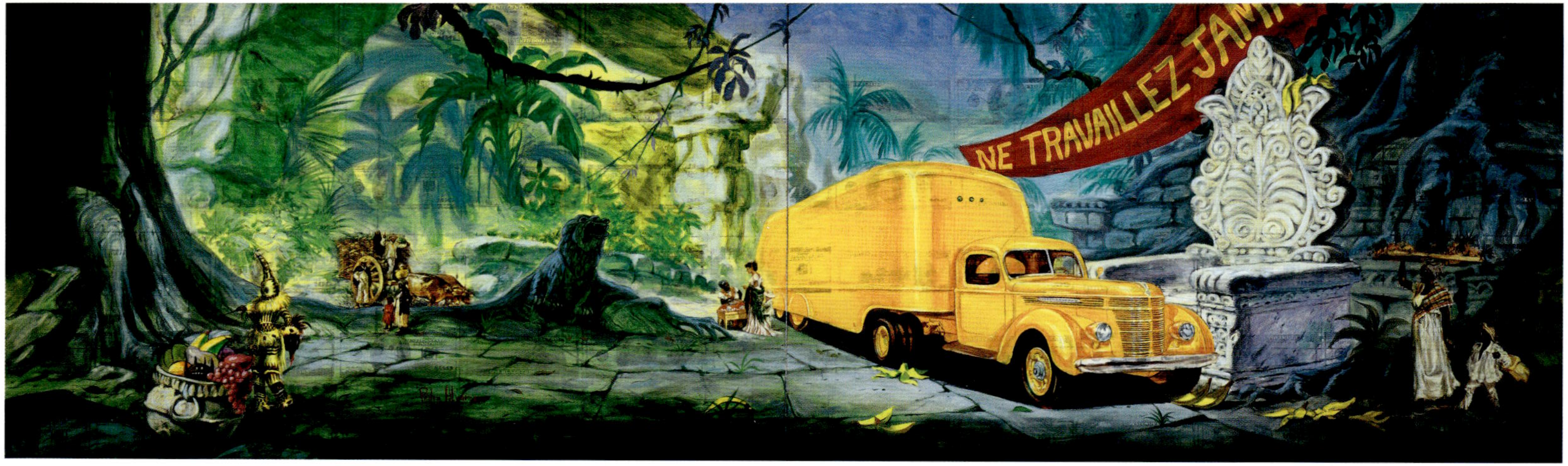

Plate 29. Pedro Álvarez, *Site (Homage to Wifredo Lam)*, 1998, collage and oil on canvas, $45\frac{5}{8} \times 74\frac{1}{4}$ inches. Through the appropriation of Landaluze's *costumbrista* arts, including *Diablito Mongo* (see plate 8), socialist sloganeering, images of modern American neo-colonialism, and tricky references to Wifredo Lam, Álvarez presents an epic counternarrative of Cuban art, history, and politics, producing a trenchant critique of the island's history. Courtesy of Pedro Álvarez and the Arizona State University Art Museum. Photograph by Damian Johnson.

2 *El Ñáñigo* "Graduates"

8 Pictures, Performances, and the Police

Changing Contexts for Costumbrista *Arts*

An elegant *íreme* stands before a neutral background, stilled by the artist's fastidious eye. His close-fitting suit, all dramatic checks, bands, and triangles, features a conical pointed hood, mask with articulated facial features, small *sombrereta,* and bristling fringe at the joints. Bells sprout from around his waist, wrists, and ankles. He wields a thin rod in his left hand, as if pointing or conducting an orchestra, and a leafy branch in his right hand. A rooster dangles at his belt. The *íreme* stands barefoot in relief against the neutral seamless background, which admits of nothing but the figure's shadow and transforms this central character of Abakuá Society celebration into a larger-than-life monument of Cuban popular "types." Víctor Patricio de Landaluze's realist lithograph *El Ñáñigo* has commanded the attention of police inspectors, forensic pathologists, ethnologists, folklorists, art historians, and artists for its presumed verisimilitude since it was published in 1881 (figure 4.1). First appearing prominently in Landaluze's *Tipos y costumbres de la isla de Cuba* (Types and Customs of the Island of Cuba), a *costumbrista* study now counted among the greatest works of Cuban arts and letters, *El Ñáñigo* would soon reappear in another important genre of Cuban literature, the police chronicle. There, in Rafael Roche y Monteagudo's *La policía y sus mistérios* (The Police and Their Mysteries), *El Ñáñigo,* reduced in size and framed in black, served as the early twentieth century's principal emblem of *ñañiguismo* deviance, rampant street crime, and all that was wrong with Cuba (Roche y Monteagudo 1908:16). As republished during the second American occupation of Cuba (1906–9),[1] *El Ñáñigo* was now the equivalent of physical evidence on the police blotter. In Roche y Monteagudo's book, along with the mug shots of one or two *brujos* (sorcerers) charged with ritual murder, *El Ñáñigo* functioned as the Cuban Willie Horton in a great rhetorical and legal campaign to extinguish any and all obstacles to the modern nation's progress, including the political organizing of the island's workers and people of color. In this cultural moment, *El Ñáñigo* could not be Art, because it was the antithesis of Civilization—just now being aggressively forged with the help of the U.S. military and sugar industry. By 1964, however, the *íreme* of the Abakuá Society had been rehabilitated as a nearly wholesome icon of Cuban national culture via countless artists' canvases and scholars' ethnographies. In the United States, *El Ñáñigo* was on its way to becoming a principal icon of the Black Atlantic visual tradition by the early 1980s in the American academy and was rapidly and rightly gaining parity with the great works of Western art. As Robert Farris Thompson lyrically writes of Landaluze's *tipo*, this "nineteenth century Abakuá masker," a paragon of "richness of mediation and spiritual embodiment," with its "Janus of mystic vision, checkerboard of feline strength, soft conical headdress [of the] female dimension of Ngbe, the mother of all leopards . . . is a marvel of cultural reinstatement, a fusion of sartorial and ideographic means" (Thompson 1983:265–266). Within the celebratory explosion of African Diaspora studies during 1980s multiculturalism and 1990s transnationalism, in which Cuban art played a central role, the *íreme* was transcending even its firm assignment as art; it was, perhaps rightly deserved, becoming a messianic emblem for the coming "black planet" (see Thompson 1999:8).

"The Social Life of Things": Biographies and Histories

In the early 1980s, the altars, objects, and performances of the Abakuá Society, along with those of the other Afro-Cuban ritual systems, decisively "graduated"[2] to the status of "art" in the American academy and the international art world (see Clifford 1988). By the 1980s in Cuba, they had reached unprecedented visibility as "national folklore," and, within emerging artistic movements in the Cuban academy, had become profound models of and models for artistic achievement, transnational identity, and spiritual connection. This was not always so in terms of their social value and meaning. Indeed, the Abakuá Society had graduated within Cuban hierarchies of social normalcy and aesthetic "distinction" many times since 1836 (Bourdieu 1984). Before the mid-nineteenth century in Cuba, things Abakuá and other *cosas de negro*, sighted most prominently once a year during Carnival, were exotic, if not also frightening, curiosities of the "customs" of the African "nations." Early delegated the "savage slot" (Troulliot 1991), they could be amusing from afar, but terrifying for the "immoralities [that] lay behind many of the suggestive details we noticed," as Irene Wright would later write about another Afro-Cuban ritual practice and its supposed connection to the "*ñáñigo* clans" (1910:149–150).

By the mid-1870s, during the tense period of revolution and abolitionism portending slave emancipation, the Abakuá Society and its attributes had been formally criminalized. The Abakuá were ferociously persecuted by the Spanish colonial government. By the twentieth century's first decade, the period of Roche y Monteagudo's 1908 police chronicle, the Abakuá Society was considered not only a mafia-like, homicidal secret society but also a scientifically diagnosed pathogen—a "center of infection" on the body politic—that had to be wiped out for the sake of the new nation's health (Ortiz 1973:1–22, 223, 230). Between the 1920s and the 1950s, the Abakuá Society and its attributes graduated once again, in the eyes of Cuba's scholarly community and cultural avant-garde, as a formative historical feature of Cuba's ethnic and emotional landscape, a key "folkloric" expression of Cuba's creole stew, and a vital artistic source of creative and spiritual renewal. Though Fidel Castro's socialist state (1959) intermittently persecuted Afro-Cuban practices until the Special Period of the early 1990s, Afro-Cuban "folklore" would take center stage before the world as a sign of national identity and unity. Here was the *íreme*'s apotheosis as an icon of Cuban national culture, albeit mediated by an emerging tourist-based economy.

In the United States, with the publication of Robert Farris Thompson's magisterial *Flash of the Spirit: African and Afro-American Art and Philosophy* (1983), the ritual objects and practices of black populations in the Western Hemisphere were proposed as continuous transatlantic extensions of five classical West African civilizations. Following ethnoaesthetic and ethnophilosophical approaches to African art developed during the previous twenty years, Thompson's work insisted that things Abakuá were to be studied as "art and philosophy" (see Lawal 1974; D'Azevedo 1973; Thompson 1969b).[3] Thompson's timely gesture prefigured the vociferous, politically incensed revisionism in the aftermath of MOMA's *Primitivism in 20th Century Art,* cast as it was in terms of Western, colonial, and modernist aesthetic hierarchies. Where *Primitivism* had subordinated non-Western, or "tribal," arts as sources for modernist projects, a later exhibition presented Western and non-Western works side by side, in nonhierarchical fashion, as a kind of antidote (see W. Rubin 1984; McEvilley 1984; *Magiciens de la terre* 1989).[4] Ironically, many attempts in the field of African and Afro-American art history question Western canons but nevertheless reproduce their logics of purity and pedigree—that is, African art, too, proceeds from a "classical tradition." Moreover, though African and other "non-Western art," via modern principles of cultural relativism, can surely claim and deserve parity with Western art, such warm humanistic approaches have tended to skirt critical discussions of power and authority: who gets to represent "non-Western" art and make what comparisons?

Like the legion of American scholars studying "Afro-American" cultures in the post–civil rights era 1970s,[5] Robert Farris Thompson's work in art history was inspired by the pioneering research of Melville J. Herskovits, his students, and, indirectly, by the Harlem Renaissance: Afro-American arts, considered broadly, from Suriname to Haiti to New York, were expressions of evolved philosophical and aesthetic systems that had resisted the shock of slavery. This liberal historiography forcefully took up Herskovits's charge to regard "New World Negro" cultures as "tenacious," "resilient," and salutary continuities of West African practices, not vestigial fragments or pathological symptoms of slavery's legacy (see Herskovits 1941; Thompson 1969b; Szwed 1969; Abrahams and Szwed 1983; Jackson 1986).

The moral premise that things Black Atlantic and Afro-Cuban were dignified contributions to world art served important institutional interests within the academy (e.g., program development, hiring, expansion of the literature) and larger political objectives during the culture wars of the 1980s. Still, the mostly celebratory approach to this classically based art tended not to reflect upon how the emergent discipline of Black Atlantic or African Diaspora art had constituted its object of study *as art,* just as Herskovits's comparative ethnography had constituted its object of study around the need to prove the existence of black *culture* and disprove arguments for black "pastlessness" (D. Scott 1991).

Mirroring both Herskovits's achievements and stumbling blocks in African/New World Negro comparative ethnography, the scholar could now conceive of historical continuity between classical and contemporary black art producers. Diasporically, academic and popular accounts could "cut" between pure African art—mostly conceived within the ethnographic present on the eve of colonialism—to Afro-Cuban and Afro-American art and back again. Such epic master narratives were cast against the light historical scrim of the "Middle Passage" and "slavery" (see Palmié 1993; D. Scott 1991). Because of the liberal/left moral burden of "New World Negro" culture study, black artists *had* to have resisted oppression by creating psychologically "autonomous" spheres during slavery, just as Afro-Cubans must never have internalized any aspect of Catholicism (see Blassingame 1972; Palmié 1993). Otherwise, they could not be mobilized as heroic figures on the cultural battlefields of post–civil rights American racial and cultural politics. Ironically, the then-Marxist historian Eugene Genovese, applying a Gramscian hegemony model to antebellum American slave culture, was attacked for hypothesizing that blacks "accommodated," as well as resisted, within Southern American paternalistic social relations (Genovese 1976), an idea that is now central to cultural studies and historical anthropology (see Hebdige 1979 and Comaroff 1985).

Before the 1970s, the principal models for writing about the Afro-Cuban practices, including object-making and performances, had been mostly criminological, ethnological, ethnographic, and folkloristic.[6] Within the later writings of Fernando Ortiz and his students (1952–55, 1973; León 1964), Lydia Cabrera (1954, 1958), and the first works of Herskovits's students (Courlander 1944; Bascom 1950, 1952), things Afro-Cuban were not necessarily "art," though they may have been "artful." Early ethnology and modern anthropology and its subfields constituted things Afro-Cuban as objects of study according to these disciplines' respective boundaries. Indeed, the objects sanguinely studied today as Abakuá Society arts had graduated from exotic curiosity to criminal evidence and scientific pathological specimen. They then became valuable "objective" ethnographic data subject to rigorous scientific classification, "folklore," and formal foil for modernist primitivism—all within the sociopolitical context of Cuban progressive republican nationalism. With the 1959 Cuban socialist revolution, things Abakuá began to become icons of national folk culture and important documents of Cuba's "Afrophilic profile" in the politics of "Afro-Castroism." As well, they once again became useable and legitimate artistic sources for several generations of trained artists that had grown up under the Revolution.

An ahistorical comparative ethnography and art history, in its cinematographic cuts between West Africa and the Caribbean, leapfrogs historical processes, including changing discursive formations and modes of knowledge production that have constituted and differentially valued things Abakuá. As agents, Abakuá members and groups produce culture and make meaning within social contexts of opportunities and constraints. Whether or not any or all members have personally considered their work as "art," they have always actively made meaning in response to changing historical contexts. Making objects is making history, participating in and shaping, as well as being shaped by, the historical process. It could be said that any signifying practice, particularly within hegemony, actively participates in complex loops of resistance and accommodation (see Comaroff 1985). Abakuá members, far from being the anonymous producers of superorganic "folk culture," have been slaves in the struggle for liberation, workers, anti-imperial soldiers, criminals, deportees, politicians, professional folkloric "informants," and both performers in and audiences of state cultural displays. For example, though colonial and early republican Abakuá practitioners undoubtedly viewed their practices as artful and beautiful *(lindo, chévere)*, they were also aware that their productions were culturally controversial and illegal. The public dissimulation tactics of Abakuá members during crises, including "syncretistic mimesis" and the creation of "false" attributes to deliver up to the police, evince their critical awareness of the different and contradictory values and meanings their objects could take on. To the Abakuá, if their objects were "art," they were also, in part, *brujería*—witchcraft, which they consciously and enthusiastically mobilized to fight fire with fire, among themselves and against the state. To them, then, their objects constituted symbolic capital—embodying socioreligious investments in local power and economic relations—as much as they were art. Their objects were illegal for much of Abakuá history, and they knew it. This knowledge convinced some humble Abakuá to give up the business altogether and others to produce self-consciously limited editions of artful forgeries for public consumption. Finally, and most important, Abakuá objects could not be "art," at least in any modernist sense, because they were *fundamentos*, the living embodiments of moral structures, ancestral presences, and kinship relations. In short, a close look at intentionality and context tells us that Abakuá objects have always complicated and exceeded the category of art to the makers themselves.

The first part of this book reproduces aspects of modern comparative ethnographic, ethnohistorical, and ethnoaesthetic models of investigation. In part, this permits the development in the second part of this book of an argument about kinds of "meaning" in art historical study in relation to the agency of art producers, in particular, imposed versus derived meaning. The first part serves as something of a heuristic exercise for launching the kind of historicized account I suggest in this introduction to part two. Thus, the following discussions track classes of Abakuá objects, and in some cases particular objects themselves, as they "graduate" between different and contested status assignments, as if narrating their "biographies" (Kopytoff 1986). Put another way, part two tracks how knowledge of such objects is produced and how the objects are constituted differently by changing institutionalized discourses. After all, comparative ethnography and art history engage not simply in the contrast and comparison of *practices,* but in the contrast and comparison of representations of practices: for example, the knowledge produced and inscribed within the discourses of colonial proto-ethnography by administrators, missionaries, and travelers, the social scientific anthropology of the 1920s, and the art historiography. Contemporary comparative ethnography and art history are based in good measure on already "written" or "textualized" cultures: ethno-graphy. Thus, part two asks not whether Abakuá Society objects are or are not "art and philosophy"; it asks what historically situated truth claims were made about and around objects in order to constitute their particular status at a given moment; and it asks how individuals, groups, and institutions have appropriated things Abakuá and *cosas de negro* in order to make cultural meaning and further local, national, and international agendas.

First Epiphany: Representations of the *Ñáñigo* in the Nineteenth Century

The first public sightings of Cuba's Abakuá occurred early in the middle third of the nineteenth century, during Havana's annual "Day of the Kings" *(El Día de los Reyes)* celebrations. Most knowledge of Afro-Cuban nineteenth-century practices derives from journalistic, *costumbrista,* and police accounts, from later scholarly writing often based on those accounts, and, to a much lesser degree, from oral history (see e.g., Ortiz 1960, Landaluze 1881; Cabrera 1954:24–5). On January 6, Epiphany on the Catholic sacred calendar, the African "nations" marched in lavish costume from their marginalized *barrios extramuros* to the governor's palace in the Plaza de Armas of the walled Old City of Havana.[7] On the way, in periodic "stops," the groups formed circles and broke out into energetic nation dances, accompanied by drums and singing. The groups' "Captains" and masquerade dancers requested *aguinaldo* (tips) from onlookers (Ortiz 1960) (plate 19, far left and right, respectively).

Before 1836, the members of the numerous Carabalí subnations marched with their respective *cabildos de nación.* According to one report, the Carabalí nations' masquerades consisted of "animal skin costumes as they used in Africa," with "rounded hoods" (Rodríguez 1881:2). With the birth of Cuba's first Abakuá *juego,* Efik Buton of Regla in 1836, and the swift establishment of scores of others throughout Havana, the *juegos* gathered, marched, and danced in Havana's streets independently of the Carabalí *cabildos.* Each lodge's Mokongo carried a banner *(bandera)* or wood emblem *(madero)* and led in procession the other Abakuá chiefs, the rank and file, families and neighbors, and the masquerade dancers, known popularly and pejoratively as *diablitos,* "little devils" (Ortiz 1960:31; Fernández Carrillo 1881:144). Of course, these *diablitos* were the *íremes,* or stylized representations of them, who wore pointed, conical fringed hoods of *saco* and bells about the waist (see plate 19, right). These peculiar *íreme* costumes were evidently distinct from the nation masquerades of the Carabalí *cabildos,* which were made of skins and featured hoods "not [like those] of the *criollos,* [as the] part covering the head was rounded" (Rodríguez 1881:2).

The reception of the *juegos* of *ñáñigos* by Havana's authorities, bourgeoisie, journalists, and newspaper readerships was different in degree, if not also in kind, from the more amused reception given other performing groups. The other "tribes . . . picturesque and exotic," provoked curiosity and wonder by their "songs, costumes, and dances." The *ñáñigos,* aside from occasional charmed responses to the *íremes,* as a whole provoked fear and disgust. The performances of other groups could be more easily appropriated aesthetically as quaint custom; on the whole, the performance of the *ñáñigos* could not. Looking back, the well-known Cuban writer Ramón Meza y Suárez Inclán (1861–1911) remembered in 1891,

> The ñáñigos took to the extreme the crude and barbarous imagination of the African tribes. Their institutions, signs, costumes—everything was repugnant to the highest degree. It was a sight to see: the ferocious enthusiasm with which the mobs of the lowest class of the population, without regard to age, sex, or race, followed that ridiculous feathered wood emblem [*madero*],[8] the symbol hoisted up by every one of those savage groups, all gorged with cane rum [*aguardiente*] and rooster blood. According to public hearsay, they all had sworn an oath [to deliver] a fatal wound to the chest of anyone at all. . . . Replete with daggers and knives, the horde marched slowly, not in formation, but pressed together behind the dancers, who never stopped their offensive convulsions, agitating the bells that they carried tied about the waist. And when two groups met, usually being enemies, they would always declare war . . . a battle would ensue, and they would ferociously and cruelly wound and kill one another (Meza 1891 quoted in Ortiz 1960:12; see also Roldán 1940:958).

The only rival to *ñáñigo* performance as narrated by Meza might be Hieronymus Bosch's *Garden of Earthly Delights.* It was a hellish nightmare of evils: mob irrationality and disorder, class/racial/sexual promiscuity, drunkenness through the consumption of *aguardiente* (a strong cane rum associated with slaves and the urban lower classes), animal sacrifice and savage blood-drinking, grotesque bodily contortion, evisceration and murder with fists and knives. It seemed the antithesis of moral order and civilization. As the famous lawyer, historian, journalist, and *costumbrista* folklorist Emilio Roig de Leuchenring (1889–1964) noted, "as a consequence of the frequent and bloody brawls that continued among the *juegos de ñáñigos*—for, they all waited for that very day [of license] to take out their revenge [on each other]—the authorities continued to restrict them little-by-little, until their coming out on the Day of Kings was completely prohibited" (Roig de Leuchenring 1923 quoted in Ortiz 1960:31; see also Roldán 1940:1000–1004). Still, somehow, *ñáñigo* street performance was, in Meza's words, "a sight to see."

By the time of Ramón Meza's account in 1891, the Abakuá Society, or *ñañiguismo,* had been high on official Havana's watch list since at least 1839, when Margarito Blanco, a creole Mokongo (or Ocongo) officer of the "Ultán *cabildo,*" and six others were arrested for "suspicion of clandestine assembly" (Deschamps Chapeaux 1964:97–98). As the high chief of an undoubtedly powerful and well-known organization among Havana's Africans and Afro-Cubans, Blanco was no small catch. Indeed, it is possible that "Ultán" was a nickname for the old institutional Carabalí root of Efik Buton itself.[9] The charge of "unlawful assembly" was part and parcel of the limited Spanish colonial means to regulate African and Afro-Cuban society and culture. For example, the *cabildos* and their activities were restricted by a string of "Decrees of Good Government and Order" between 1792 and 1884—when the boisterous Day of Kings carnival was banned altogether (see Ortiz 1921: 16–22). Still, the social and *cultural* repugnance that middle-class and elite Havana felt toward the *ñáñigos,* evident in Ramón Meza's writing, did not manifest as criminalized activity and focused persecution—complete with systematic surveillance, raids, confiscations of property, court trials, imprisonment, and deportations—until the last quarter of the nineteenth century (1875).

Government officials linked the increase in alleged *ñáñigo* "crimes" during the 1850s and 1860s, particularly during the Carnival period, to the exponential growth of the *juegos* in the twenty to thirty years after 1836. As Inspector Roche y Monteagudo later noted, there was observed an increase in adepts of *ñáñigos,* "so much so that the streets in the *barrio* of Jesús María [in Havana] were turned into a battlefield" (see figure 2.4). *Ñañiguismo,* represented by its most fearsome incarnation, the *diablito,* was credited with the murder of a police guard on Christmas Eve 1853, murders during the 1865 carnival, and continued violence through 1866, at which point the island's captain general, Don Francisco Lersundi, deported many people of "bad conduct," "generally ñáñigos—to the island of Fernando Poo." The turning point came on March 12, 1875, when *ñáñigo* assembly was definitively outlawed. Regular raids, arrests, and confiscations of sacred attributes continued with great vigor through 1889, and did not wane until the second decade of the republic (est. 1902; see Roche y Monteagudo 1925:24, 56–58) (figure 8.1).

Though the police and observers laid much street violence directly at the door of *ñañiguismo,* there were many factors at work during the second half of the nineteenth century, a period of great social distress and revolution. The violence associated with the *ñáñigos,* it now seems, must have formed one part of a larger sociopolitical picture of "disorder." Following the government's grisly repression of the 1844 *Escalera* slave insurrection in Matanzas, carried out by determined coalitions of Africans and creoles, whites, blacks, and *mulatos*, slaves and free people, workers and intellectuals,[10] there was, Inspector Roche y Monteagudo reported, a "lapse of violence." Perhaps it was that state terror produced its intended

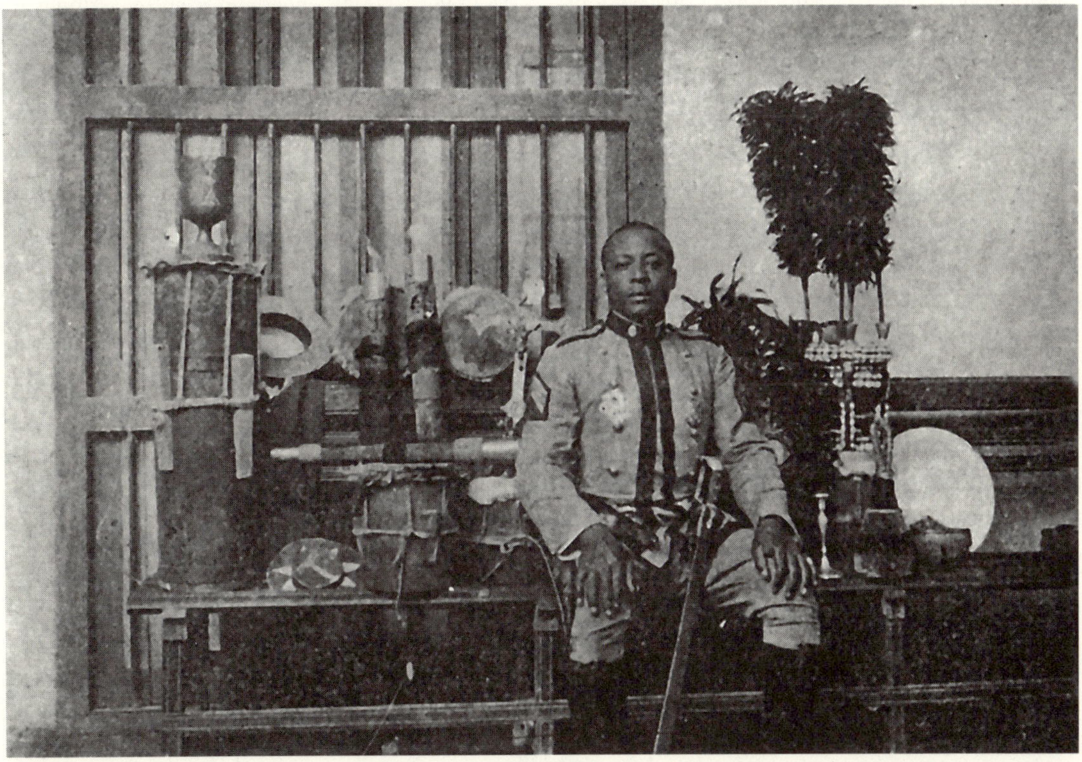

Figure 8.1. "Attributes surprised in the Fambá room, in a festival that was celebrated in the Barrio of Pogolotti, on the 20th of May of 1914. The service that the now Chief of Police of Marianao, Captain Estanislao Mansip was excellent." This is a unique document of the most notorious and fruitful police raid on the Abakuá during the Republican period. All or most of the objects, following their analysis in the Bureau of Identification under Juan Francisco Steegers, were donated to the Criminological Museum of the Faculty of Legal Medicine at the University of Havana by Israel Castellanos. The cowrie-encrusted *sese* (right) and staffs (center left), were later studied in the museum and illustrated by Ortiz (cf. figures 9.7, 9.11, 9.13). Roche identifies the lodge as Efore Muna Tanze, which was born from the Ebion Efó of the Akanarán line (from Roche y Monteagudo, 1914, 1925).

effect in the cities, however temporarily, following the crushing of the well-organized and widespread insurrection. Increasing violence following this "lapse" may have given the appearance of its "increase"; in turn, increased applications of "unlawful assembly" laws helped to constitute *"ñañiguismo"* (a rather vague social category of deviancy)[11] and its public legibility as much as responded to it; and acts of "disorder," always subject to official interpretation, may have been rooted as much in antislavery, anticolonial, and anti–local government resistance as Abakuá activity in any essential way.

Indeed, fear of disorder and street violence in the western cities could not have escaped connection with larger concerns of official Havana. *Ñañiguismo* was outlawed in 1875 for its "crimes" (see Roche y Monteagudo 1925:51ff). Still, during this same period, the Ten Year's War (1868–78) against Spanish rule had been raging in the east for seven years and was threatening to overcome the west. For this reason, a great trench *(trocha)* was dug across the island in the countryside in order to halt the westward movement of revolution. A corollary to spreading revolution was "race war." "The specter of race war continued to haunt the west, as planters feared that a separatist revolt [against Spain] would expand into a slave rebellion" (Pérez 1988:122). Finally, it appears that the social mixing ("promiscuity") within *ñáñigo* circles was just one facet of a larger perceived disorder in Cuban society. To Cuba's government, the revolutionary army itself had become "a vast social amalgam" of peasants, workers, poor whites and blacks, and former slaves (Pérez 1988:123). At the same time, economic crises plagued the island, leading to a full-blown, countrywide depression by the 1880s. Cuba "lost two-thirds of the value of its total wealth between 1862 and 1882" (Pérez 1988:134).

Thanks to recent historical research, it is now clearer that official justification of the war against the "homicidal" and "mafia-like" *ñañiguismo* from 1875 through the 1910s, as were the witch hunts against Afro-Cubans for their supposed *brujería,* significantly lay in sociopolitical control along lines of class and color. Following emancipation, and with radical ethnic and class transformations in the west's demographic landscape, the state sought to crush emerging counterhegemonic cultural identities, alternative revolutionary agendas, institutional independence, political organizing, and labor control among Cubans of all racial and ethnic stripes. Such state repression paralleled the discrediting of black entitlement to full rights after slavery (1880), despite this group's contributions in the two Cuban Wars of Independence (Helg 1995:91–139; R. Scott 1985:264–278). Aline Helg has shown that *ñáñigos, brujos,* and ordinary Afro-Cubans crystallized as "icons of fear" in the tumultuous twenty-year period between the era of emancipation and the first decade of the new republic, 1880s–1912 (Helg 1995:107).

By the late 1890s, emerging scientific writings by Cuban scholars provided the rationalizing discourse for continuing *ñáñigo* persecution after independence. For example, drawing on Italian sociologist Cesare Lombroso's medico-criminological model of deviancy and social hygiene, as well as the analogy of the Cuban yellow fever epidemic—which plagued the island between 1900 and 1902—the lawyer and ethnologist Fernando Ortiz identified the "houses" of Afro-Cuban practitioners as "sores" and "centers of infection" that needed to be wiped out (Ortiz 1973: 20, 223, 230; Ortiz 1939:86; Mullen 1987; I. Castellanos 1916; Helg 1995:96ff; Palmié 2002:210–224, 233–241).[12] *Ñañiguismo* and *brujería* thus figured in new ways into Cuban national fantasy. Now the *ñáñigos, brujos,* and blacks were not merely "promiscuous" and violent. They were pathologically contagious forms of African savagery undermining the "health" of the incipient Cuban nation.

Though the most recent scholarship on state repression between 1880 and the early years of the republic focuses upon discrimination against Afro-Cubans, which led to the "race war" of 1912 (Helg 1995), official fear of a certain class of "white" Cubans nearly exceeded that of blacks. It seems that fears of social promiscuity, miscegenation, disorder, and violence—threats to the colonial, and later, national, order and its codes of color and class—had long taken concrete shape in the religious reform agenda of a Cuban *mulato,* Andrés Facundo Cristo de los Dolores Petít. Not only had Petít's Havana *juego,* Bakokó Efor, and its offspring, the Akanarán Efó line, initiated nonblacks into the Abakuá, but some of its members had also apparently participated in anti-Spanish revolutionary activity (see Quiñones n.d., 1998). The specter most fearful to the authorities was less black *ñañiguismo* than the initiation of Cuban "whites" into the Abakuá Society beginning in 1863 and continuing with great rapidity through the 1910s. The "white *ñáñigos*" became as fearsome, or more so, because they seemed to presage the slippage of the nation in general into the vortex of contagion, atavism, and Africanness.

I paint the foregoing picture, albeit in broad strokes, of Cuban history between 1875 and ca. 1915 in order to contextualize late nineteenth-century and early twentieth-century representations of the Abakuá. Landaluze's *Tipos y costumbres de la isla de Cuba* was published and widely distributed one year after the abolition of slavery on the island, and five years before full emancipation was decreed in 1886. Landaluze's lithographs were printed thanks to a sophisticated Cuban industry of mechanical reproduction, which had rapidly expanded since its founding in 1824 by the Dominican Juan de Mata y Tejada. Some of the most notable early productions were Frédéric Mialhe's *La isla pintoresca de Cuba* (The Picturesque Island of Cuba) in 1838–39 and Eduardo Laplante's stunning engravings of pastoral scenes of sugar mills in 1857, as well as the stereotyped depictions of blacks in tobacco advertisements *(marquillas cigarreras)* and trade dress from the 1840s through the turn of the century (Kutzinski 1993:43–60) (figures 4.1, 8.2, and 8.3).

The contrast between the stilled, elegant *íreme* of Landaluze's *Tipos y costumbres* and Ramón Meza's disturbing description ten years later highlights two distinct perspectives on the Abakuá during the second half of the nineteenth century: the outsider Basque artist's sensitivity to unique creole customs and the island-born journalist's reflection of moral

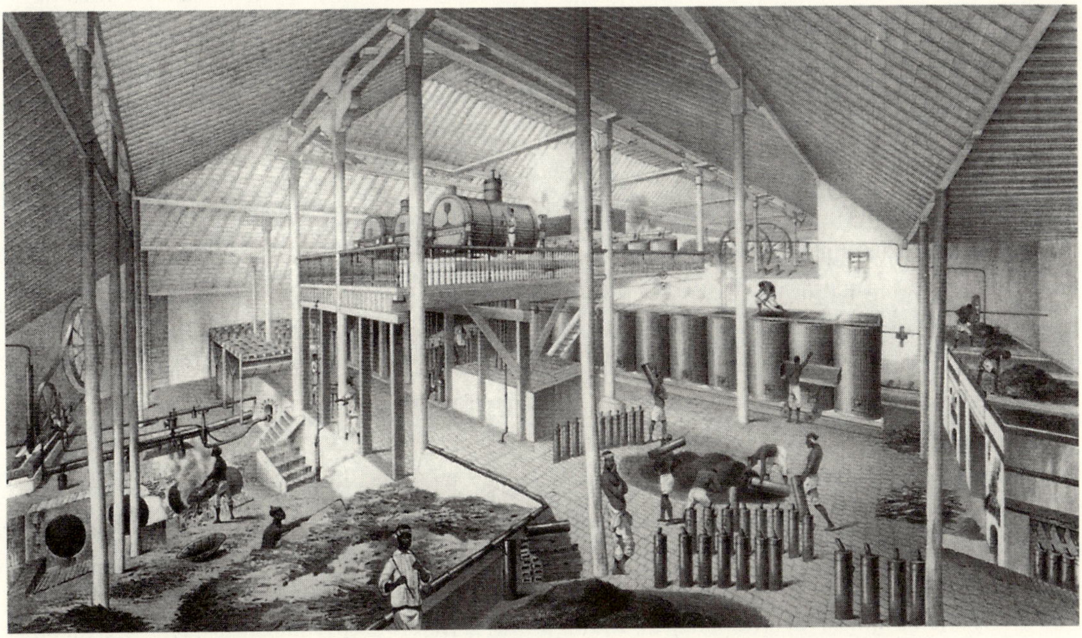

Figure 8.2. Eduardo Laplante, *Casa de Calderas del Ingenio Asunción,* from the series *Los Ingenios,* 1855–57; lithograph, 208 × 360 mm. Courtesy of the Museo Nacional de Bellas Artes, Havana.

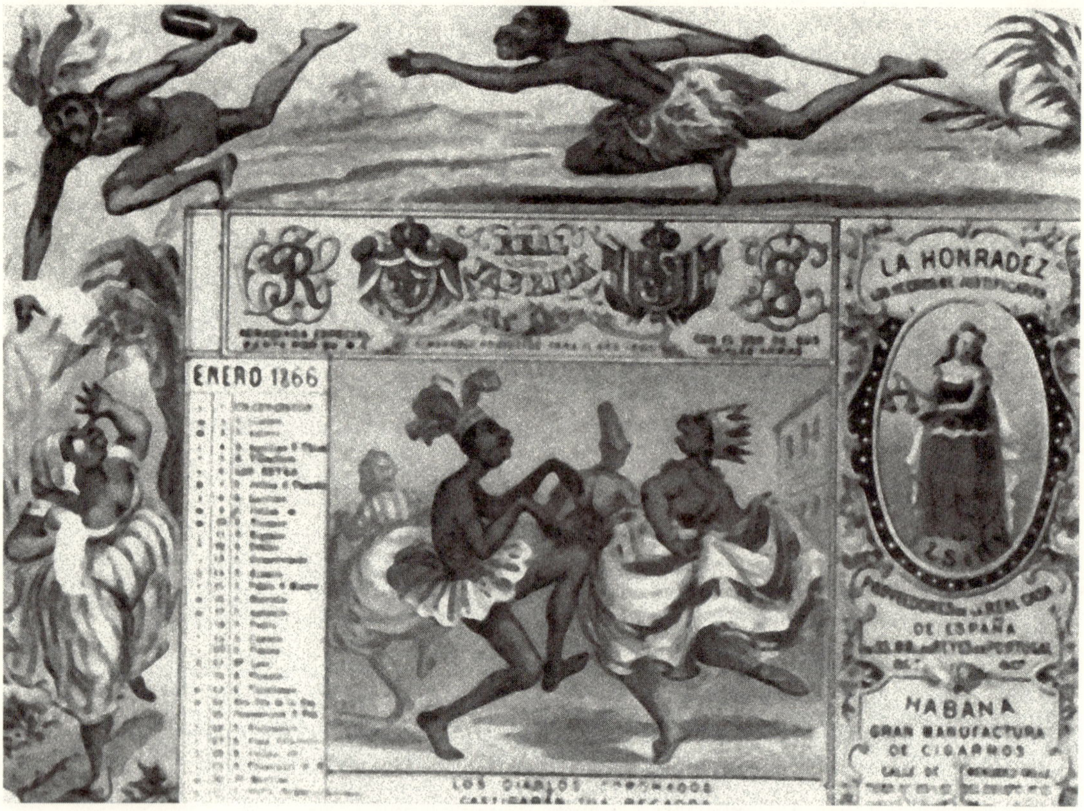

Figure 8.3. ***Los Diablos Coronados Castigarán Tus Pecados*** **(The Crowned Devils Will Punish Your Sins), 1866** ***Marquilla Cigarrera*** **tobacco trade dress of Havana cigar company, showing a** ***cabildo*** **male dancer and a Carnival queen dancing in the street. They are presented in racially grotesque form.**

trouble at home. In the late nineteenth century, Meza's outrage on behalf of civilization would resonate with the public moral condemnation substantiating juridical discourse on *ñáñigo* criminalization. Meanwhile, Landaluze's aesthetic wonder at dazzling exotic surfaces would quickly give way to the wonder of heroic police work in a pitted struggle between law and chaos in Roche y Monteagudo's *The Police and Their Mysteries* (1908). In striking contrast to Meza's narrative, Landaluze's *El Ñáñigo* suggests no "offensive convulsions." Against the neutral background, as if on a stage, the *íreme* remains isolated. Meza's drunk, blood-drinking "horde . . . pressed together behind" is conspicuously absent. Indeed, in numerous depictions of similar figures, likely all drawn from the same model or composite sketches, Landaluze paints the *íreme* alone, or separated from other carnival participants absorbed in festive enjoyment. In two now-famous pieces, the *íreme* stands pacifically before the members of white bourgeois households. For example, in Landaluze's oil painting *Día de los Reyes en la Habana* (1878), an *íreme* benignly reaches upward toward women and a baby on a balcony for *aguinaldo;* he certainly doesn't kill for it. In *Diablito,* a white mother, her infant, and a conventional black mammy betray neither fright nor disgust, only charmed contemplation, before a similar *íreme* that poses in an unthreatening, open-armed gesture, as if proud of his suit and grateful for audience attention (plates 19 and 20).

Within the pages of Landaluze's *Tipos y costumbres, El Ñáñigo* keeps company with thirty-eight other benign, charming images of Cuban genre "types" and their "customs," that is to say, the figures and social phenomena of everyday life, realistically rendered by this Spanish traveler/reporter/artist. Landaluze (1828–1889), who worked in Cuba between 1852 and his death, lived in the Havana village of Guanabacoa. He produced stunning oils and black-and-white and color lithographs of rural *guajíro* dances, traveling doctors, *curanderas,* and urban images of *mulata* demimondaines, black volante drivers, Havana's exotic black gypsies *(los negros curros),* firemen at work, and pathetic drunks in a *bodega.* Like his well-known French counterpart Frédéric Mialhe (1810–1881), Landaluze also seriously documented the Day of Kings celebrations of the African nations in pencil, pen, watercolor, and oil. Landaluze's *El Ñáñigo* and *Día de los Reyes en la Habana* demonstrate the artist's meticulous attention to the details of African and creole costume, the diversity of "types," and expressive cultural gestures small and large. Few of his figures suffer from the grotesque and stereotypical representations that characterized the *marquillas cigarreras* of the same period (figure 8.3), though Landaluze is known to have indulged in this mode (Kutzinski 1993:43–60).

Landaluze's lithographs were not valorized as true artistic contributions to Cuban culture by the institutions of taste until the middle third of the twentieth century, when the avant-garde "recast" popular Cuban subject matter in modernist approaches (Martínez 1994:85). Moreover, Landaluze's works would not fully transcend their narrower definition within the *costumbrista* genre until perhaps the late 1980s and early 1990s, when the Basque's works looked to be the very foundation of the Cuban national ethos, if not also emblems of great transnational conjunctures (see Blanc 1992; Royal Museum of Fine Arts 1992). At mid-century, observers at home and abroad clearly agreed upon Landaluze's verisimilitude and sensitivity and sometimes his greatness on par with other artists of his period. One Cuban critic praised him in 1950 as "the most complete and defined artistic personality of the many who worked in Cuba in the nineteenth century."[13] The same year, in response to an exhibition of Landaluze's work in Havana, an American critic praised the work in romantic tones for its ability to "reproduce" the authenticity of Cuba's heart. Landaluze's "personal and incomparable contribution, is his penetration into the creole soul, his grasp of tropical light, the inspired reproduction of the happiness, passions and artfulness, the customs and jokes, the prejudices and superstitions of genuine Cubans, whether they be whites or blacks. The comparison with any other *costumbrista* suffices to verify [his] enormous superiority in realism and emotion" (Museo de Bellas Artes de Bilbao 1998:20–21).

The American critic's 1950 gratitude to Landaluze for providing a cheerful visit with Cuba's "happy" folk may have been shared by some Cubans, but it most certainly keeps fine company with the island's growing touristic profile in the three decades before 1959. Still, neither his sentiments nor the recent revival of interest in Landaluze should obscure Fernando Ortiz's keen observation during the same period. Though Landaluze's work was widely seen in its time and beyond in Cuba, Europe, and the United States, his depictions of the *diablitos* were stigmatized by the Cuban middle class as *cosas de negro* ("'n-word' things"; see Ortiz 1953). No one in 1953 but select members of the intelligentsia would have touched them. With some exceptions, many of Ortiz's mid-century avant-garde artist contemporaries continued to think of Afro-Cubans as "noble savages" (Martínez 1994:81–82).

In his time, Landaluze, a foreign observer enchanted with the island's bustling creole life, was apparently immune to the disgust with which elite Havana regarded *las cosas de negro*—something still detectable among the Miami exile community and the Havana socialist hierarchy, not to mention Havana hoteliers, restaurateurs, cabdrivers, and police. During the colonial period, and at least through the 1910s, blacks and most expressions of Afro-Cuban culture were virtually excluded from dignified public representation. Africans and Afro-Cubans appeared as anonymous slaves in the backgrounds of rural and urban views, as criminals in mug shots, and in tobacco advertisements. On the stage, Afro-Cuban expressive

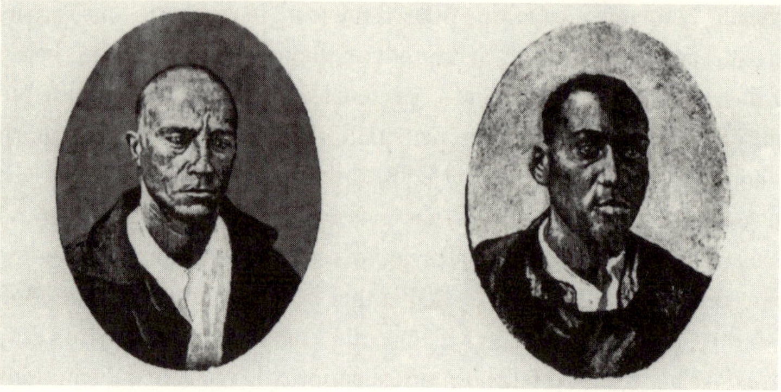

Figure 8.4. ***Núm. 167. Pardo Domingo Vicente Barrios; 168.—Negro Slave Ricardo Benedit,* drawn police mug shots from Cases #167 and #168 (from Trujillo y Monagas 1882:73).**

culture was appropriated, diluted, and performed by whites in blackface in the often minstrel-like *teatro vernáculo* and the "cabaret rumba" until the 1930s. Thereafter, foreign tourists, coming in increasing numbers through the 1950s, demanded the genuine article, and Afro-Cubans themselves returned to the stage (R. Moore 1997:182–183) (figures 7.4, 7.5, 8.2–8.4). As we will see, Cuban fears had as much to do with class as race, that is, contaminated working-class whites.

The earliest institutions of high art in Cuba created an inhospitable atmosphere for the representation of "low" subjects. In the nineteenth century the tradition of popular painting, such as tavern and domestic murals, was scorned by the Europe-ward view of the San Alejandro Academy, founded in 1818. First directed by the French neoclassical painter Juan Bautista Vermay (1784–1833), San Alejandro "provided solid training based on European antecedents and produced artists interested in conventional treatment of mythological, religious, and historical subjects and in portraiture" (Blanc 1992:54; see Martínez 1994:2–3; Roldán 1940:1030). More to the point, Sybille Fischer argues, the very outlook and admission process of San Alejandro were directed at countering the influence of a widespread popular painting movement, which included numerous Cuban artists of color (Fischer 1997). The passage of time, the weight of class and race prejudice, and inadequate conservation obscured important early contributions of popular artists. The gorgeous baroque church frescoes of the *mulato* José Nicolás de la Escalera (1734–1804) were not recovered and widely appreciated until the early 1940s, when avant-garde artists and writers such as Wifredo Lam and Lydia Cabrera raised money to restore colonial buildings, including the Church of Santa María del Rosario (see plate 15) (see Blanc 1992: 52, 94; Intar Gallery 1984:14).[14] Academy-trained Cuban artists were little interested in anything having to do with artists of color and the lower classes in general. This interest was circumscribed, as noted, to *costumbrista* artists, mostly foreign.

El Ñáñigo and Landaluze's "Discipline"

Víctor Patricio de Landaluze was credited for his "ethnographic realism" by his mid-twentieth-century admirers, including Fernando Ortiz (see Ortiz 1953). Landaluze is now heralded as the father of sympathetic and culturally meaningful Afro-Cuban artistic and popular representation. To scholars, his lithographs and paintings serve as virtual photographic documents (Roche y Monteagudo 1908:17; Ortiz 1951; Cabrera 1958:236; Thompson 1983:264; Bettelheim 1993:200). Still, as an artist trained in Madrid and Paris in the first half of the nineteenth century, Landaluze brought more than just emotional sensitivity and realist technique, considered in the narrowest sense, to Cuba. Clearly, *El Ñáñigo* avoids grotesque representation with its realist representation. However, perhaps not unwittingly, Landaluze "disciplined" the bodies and gestures of the *íreme* through classical figuration and the views he offered to beholders (see Foucault 1979:135–169). Most conspicuously, the artist transforms the *íreme*'s zigzag movement vocabulary into rational stasis. Even when posed during a ceremony, the bodily disposition of an Abakuá *íreme* is typically all counterpoint and angularity. Limbs cross one another, and slice diagonally across the torso; implements are held obliquely. And the *íreme* moves with a stylized falter in his step (see plate 17). In contrast, Landaluze organizes *El Ñáñigo*'s bodily set with a classical pose of a particular kind: the *íreme*'s stance is wide, with the right leg dramatically thrust forward and the arms extended, gestures one might see on the classical stage. Clearly, the *íreme*'s pointed hood, extended limbs, and implements do boldly penetrate into the surrounding space. Yet, however dramatic the figure's gestures seem, they do not suggest dynamic bodily movement, such as the hallmark counter-torsion of baroque naturalism exemplified by Bernini's *David* winding up to slay Goliath (1623) (figure 8.5). *El Ñáñigo*'s pose arguably compares more favorably with the stiff Greek Severe style than later developments in true *contrapposto* during the Greek classical period, in which flexion and relaxation are set in dynamic tension along the body's central vertical axis. If Ramón Meza's Eurocentric pen could describe the street *diablito*'s movements only as "convulsions," the putatively sympathetic Landaluze nevertheless turned *El Ñáñigo* into the Greek Zeus bronze of ca. 460 BCE (compare figures 8.5–8.8). We will never be sure whether it was the *costumbrista*'s intention to transform *El Ñáñigo* into a Greek god.

Official culture's particular response to Landaluze's elegant *El Ñáñigo* is suggested, ironically, in the very text chosen to accompany the lithograph in 1881. In the text, the *diablito* is evolutionary atavism par excellence on the nineteenth-century vertical scale from savagery to civilization. It seems that Cuban writers were beginning to develop not only a vocabulary of description, as in Meza's account, but also one of deeper explanation. In *Tipos y costumbres de la isla de Cuba,* short articles by well-known Cuban writers accompanied groups or individual plates of Landaluze's thirty-eight lithographs. Antonio Bachiller y Morales (1812–1899), one of Cuba's nineteenth-century renaissance men, wrote the introduction. Enrique Fernández Carrillo was a logical though "reluctant" choice for Landaluze's *El Ñáñigo.* He was evidently an official in the office of the famous Don José Trujillo y Monagas, the Second Chief of the Havana police, the most venerated warrior to date against *ñañiguismo,* as well as the subject-to-be of the voluminous police chronicle *The Criminals of*

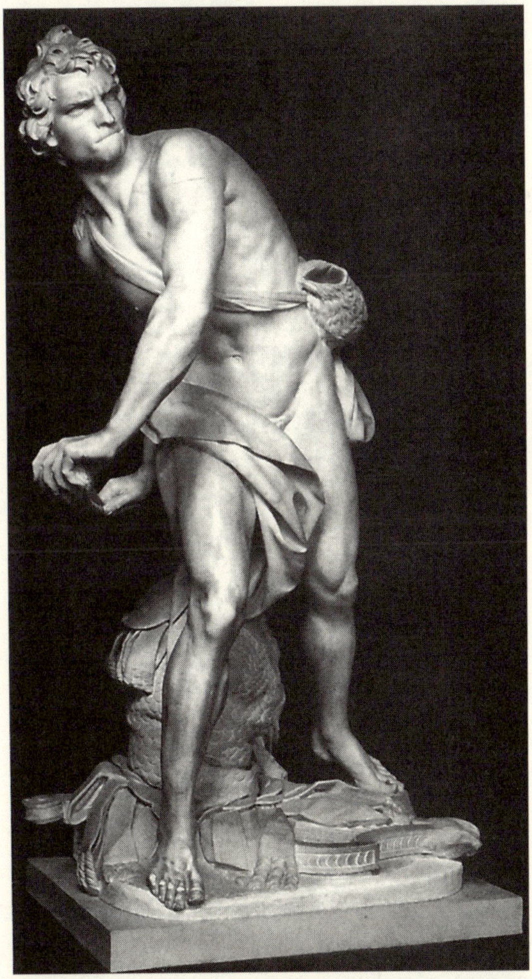

Figure 8.5. Gianlorenzo Bernini, *David,* 1623, marble. Bernini's baroque-period work demonstrates dynamic naturalism in the body's countertorsion and emotion, as well as the drama of the cloth as he winds up to slay Goliath. Courtesy of Galleria Borghese, Rome.

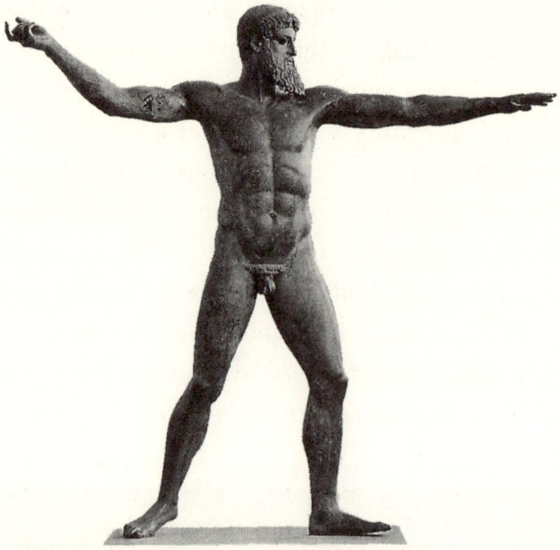

Figure 8.6. *Zeus* or *Poseidon*, ca. 460 B.C.E., bronze, 82 inches. The figure exemplifies the Greek Severe style. It is a dramatic but static figuration, prior to the development of *contrapposto* during the Greek classical period. Courtesy of National Archaeological Museum, Athens.

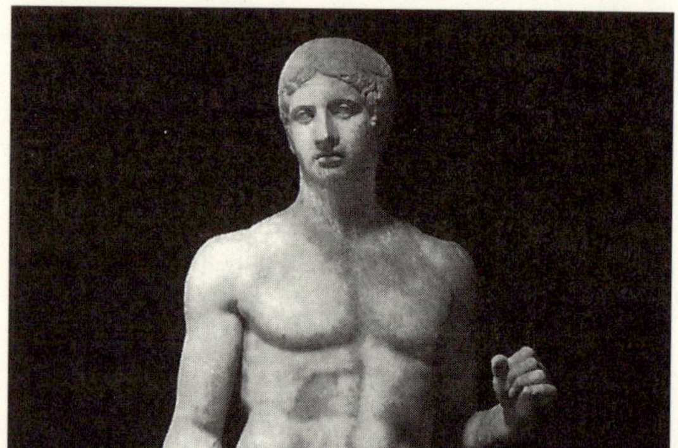

Figure 8.7. Polykleitos, *Doryphoros*, ca. 450–440 B.C.E. Roman copy of Greek original from the Greek classical period, exemplifying the *contrapposto* pose of dynamic tension and relaxation. Courtesy of National Archaeological Museum of Naples.

Cuba y Don José Trujillo y Monagas: A narration of the services given in the Havana Police Force by D. José Trujillo y Monagas . . . History of Criminals Imprisoned by Him, in Different Periods (1882). Casting his introduction in epistolary form, Fernández Carrillo chides Landaluze for asking him to depart from his "usual reserve" and compromise restricted case information. Still, Fernández does present some of the first published information on the Abakuá, which was, at the time, being systematically assembled in Trujillo y Monagas's office (Trujillo y Monagas 1882:360–374; A. Rodríguez 1881). Ortiz himself would later draw on Fernández Carrillo's article in writing about the Day of Kings carnival (Ortiz 1960:31), complete with the same misspellings.[15]

Though ostensibly a reluctant contributor, Fernández not only distills the chestnut that would dominate discussions of the artist down through the present—Landaluze's verisimilitude—but he also notices what no one else has been able or willing to say about Landaluze's generic and formal control of his subject matter. With tongue only partly in cheek, Fernández foregrounds his own inherent inadequacy to represent what his "friend don Victor Patricio [has already] so perfectly painted, which needs only to move or talk in order to come to life, and [which] my boss don José Trujillo would like to get a hold of to see if it declares just . . . what keeps it quiet" (Landaluze 1881:141–144). Fernández catches the foreigner Landaluze at his aesthetic game of calming and quieting *El Ñáñigo*, a luxury the reality of the streets hardly permitted to the writer's warrior-boss. At the time, and down through the 1950s, no one else in Cuba wanted to get a hold of *El Ñáñigo* and his

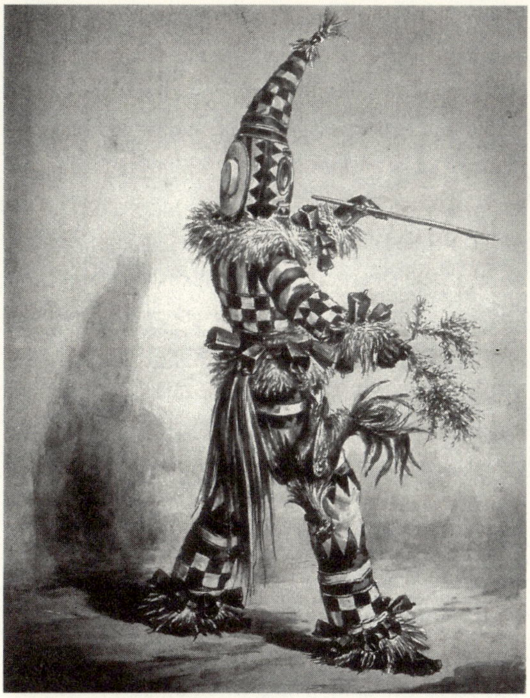

Figure 8.8. Victor Patricio de Landaluze, *El Ñáñigo,* 1881, lithograph from drawing.

cronies as much as Trujillo y Monagas and his successors. Insofar as Fernández's article resonated with official and elite views, it demonstrates Landaluze's representations both as anathema in their own time, and deconstructs—from a historically situated position, of course—Landaluze's supposed verisimilitude. *El Ñáñigo* really was convulsive, not to mention fiercely carnivorous; Landaluze merely soft-pedaled a social delinquent and criminal. The police chronicle was certainly more real than Landaluze's *costumbrista* realism, just as cop reality shows are more real than TV cop dramas.

By 1881, official Havana was convinced that *ñañiguismo* was a violent and "idolatrous religion . . . a reflection of the barbaric customs of the African soil . . . [and] contains a constant danger for the society by its aspirations and tendencies" (Fernández Carrillo in Landaluze 1881:142, 145). Still, the Africans themselves were not seen as the core social problem. The problem lay with Cuba's most vulnerable flank, which it had struggled to nurture and expand from the mid-nineteenth century: whiteness. As Inspector Rafael Roche y Monteagudo would later write, the African nations were already recognized as inherently "crude, idolatrous, savage, backward, [and] ridiculous," though "fraternal, charitable, and moral"—in their own way. In an inimitable logic, a kind of racialist tautology, Roche y Monteagudo postulated that "the whites cannot be ñáñigos because the ñáñigos are the black African Carabalí Brícamo nation" (Roche y Monteagudo 1925:118–119). The practical problem was that a certain class of "whites" was acting badly, in a double sense. They were acting against their nature, and they were bad actors. In racially essentialist terms, *whites* simply cannot be black Africans of the Carabalí Brícamo nation. To do what these black Africans instinctively do, one has to be constitutionally weak, susceptible to disease and evolutionary atavism, or be an impostor. Perhaps white *ñañiguismo* was a combination of both. In any case, something had to be done.

Trujillo y Monagas, Fernández Carrillo, Roche y Monteagudo, and the governor of Havana, not to mention a brilliant young specialist in penal reform, were desperate to stem the deviance of wayward members of their own "nation": the white *ñáñigos. Ñañiguismo*'s "mix of crude superstitions," José Trujillo y Monagas asserted, "proves its very rudimentary and backward stage in the scale of civilization" (1882:363). In terms absorbed from social Darwinist discourse, these white *ñáñigos,* consequently, were being *arrastrado*—"dragged down"—in their level of evolution.[16] Subverting their own racial and cultural development, including their proper verbal and bodily discipline, these *arrastrados* "spoke *ñáñigo,*" and adopted the "roguish and boastful" *(guapo)* behavior of the blacks, all this, predictably, in order to seduce black women. As a result, these susceptible white bodies—literally and figuratively weak in the flesh—and the inevitably mongrelized offspring of their miscegenation, would, consequently, *arrastrar* the progress of Cuban society and the Caucasian race as a whole. Férnandez Carrillo dramatically sums up the case:

> The love of the flesh is the tie that binds; the disordinate appetite is the feed that drags it along. Ñañiguismo desires the degradation of a superior race in order to elevate the inferior races. That is, my friend [writing to Landaluze], its supreme aspiration. Man has disordinate appetites, and if the intelligence has not been developed, if he doesn't possess the education that regenerates humankind, there are no obstacles to contain it. The longing for woman fills it [the disordinate appetite], and the black woman, drags it lower [i.e., to feed at the bottom]. There it begins, and I don't have to tell you where it ends. . . . The ñáñigo is not political. He aspires to the union of the Caucasian race with the African race, but through the absorption of the former by the latter. (Fernández Carrillo in Landaluze 1881:144)

In a curious mix of social Darwinism, Catholic bodily disdain, and racist hysteria, Fernández imagines the "eating" of the white race by the black—a metaphor that carries lurid and terrifying sexual connotations. The yawning specter of racial disorder, mixture, and demographic change must have been particularly disturbing to official Havana during the period era of emancipation. By 1886, not only had the plan for gradual emancipation through the *patrocinato* been aborted,[17] but Cuba had also suffered the Ten Years War, which had threatened to let the Africans loose. The island had only recently averted its mid-century "Africanization of Cuba Scare" through the immigration of Spaniards, workers from Spanish colonies such as the Canary Islands and the Philippines, and the importation of Chinese "coolies" in the second half of the century (see Pérez 1988:106, 115–116; Martínez-Alier 1974:27–30; Suchlicki 2001:97). Ironically, these were apparently the "white" groups most susceptible to the pull of *ñañiguismo,* apart from a few rich, young, dissipated braggarts with a taste for the sporting life and a couple of swaggering generals who had been initiated into Akanarán Efó Ocobio Mukarará. Cuba's demographic success, its de-Africanization, would surely be set back if these "whites" were to sink into the muck and mire of *ñañiguismo.*

The police continued to raid Abakuá *juegos* through and beyond the period of Landaluze's publication, desecrating temples, confiscating altar objects, and jailing and deporting groups of suspected *ñáñigos* to Ceuta (Roche y Monteagudo 1908:38–53). These were heralded as great deeds of public service, in which Fernández Carrillo was surely involved. Curiously, though, Fernández publicly cast the solution to the grave social problem of *ñañiguismo* in the rhetoric of progressivist reformism, part and parcel of the ideology of emergent Cuban nationalism in the late nineteenth century. In 1881, before the systematization of criminal sociology study under Ortiz at the University of Havana, Fernández Carrillo could marshal this early sociological vocabulary of human progress: *Ñañiguismo,* a primitive form of social organization on the evolutionary scale, was "despotic," "personalistic," and "absolutist." It "desires the domination of the dark of night, veiling perpetually the brilliant light of the sun." Therefore, the solution could never be the application "of violent measures to suppress [it]. Because, it is clear, that being the fruit of ignorance and superstition, it is not remedied with violence, but with that panacea of the present era, that which reaches it, modifies, and cures it, and that is called education. . . . Strangle with the iron arm of teaching the mythical hydra, the ignorance, the superstition, and everything will be saved" (Fernández Carrillo in Landaluze 1881:145). Opposition to *ñañiguismo,* whether it be through police raids and deportations, or "education," represented a positive, progressive stance in favor of a wholesome future.

The Police and Their Mysteries

The only "education" the white *ñáñigos* would receive was a program of punitive treatment and coercive reeducation, which entailed stripping them of their powerful attributes in concert with public recantings of faith. Beginning in 1882, the police began their most intensive, coordinated raids on the Havana *juegos,* resulting in numerous arrests and the confiscation of sacred objects.[18] The first raids, mostly in and around what are now Old Havana and Central Havana, were undoubtedly the result of recently acquired surveillance. The raids produced further information, which, in turn, enabled more raids. In this sense, the greatest beneficiaries of "education" with respect to *ñañiguismo* were the authorities themselves. Social control and enforcement were to be strengthened by focused police study of *ñañiguismo*'s internal workings and specific bases of operation: the temples and private domiciles of their members.

As his biographer explains, Don José Trujillo y Monagas "worked tirelessly . . . to obtain all the information [necessary] for the authorities to arrive at an understanding of that pernicious group, the *ñáñigos* . . . taking into account their beginnings, their beliefs, customs, and the language they have adopted" (Trujillo y Monagas 1882:363). Who would disagree that "the Police [have an] obligation . . . to know everything there is to know about [the society's] groups, and ascertain their ends"? (1882:363). Hence, Trujillo's professional biography, otherwise an exhaustive compilation of his law-enforcement successes during sixteen years of service through 1881, contains a special section entitled "The Ñáñigos: Their History, Their Practices, Their Language (with a facsimile of the signatures that each one of the *juegos* or groups uses)." Originally written by Alejandro Rodríguez and first published in the journal *La Correspondencia de Cuba* in 1882, it is a thorough, compact account of *ñáñigo* history, grade organization, liturgy, and altar making; it provides the locations, district by district, of Havana's lodges and their individual ideographic signs, as well as a lengthy glossary of *ñáñigo* vocabulary (figures 8.9 and 8.10).[19] It traces in detail the birth of the first "white" *ñáñigo* lodge, Ocobio Mukarará Akanarán Efó #1, from Bakokó Efor in 1863. Rodríguez's data was undoubtedly enabled by information gleaned through prior raids, interrogations, and the confiscation of attributes and private Abakuá notebooks. Investigators found the last resource indispensable. For example, on October 22, 1882, the police raided an initiation taking place at Akanarán Efó Ocobio Mukarará itself, arresting "seventeen whites" and confiscating their attributes and their "archive" (Roche y Monteagudo 1908:40). Such troves of documents and letters not only permitted the publication of secret *ñáñigo* prayers, signatures, and vocabulary; in this case, records in the Akanarán Efó archive permitted the police to solve an alleged *ñáñigo* murder, as well.[20] *Los Criminales de Cuba*, an example of the police chronicle genre, was not merely a vanity exercise. It was intended as a primer for current and future warriors.

Their "Most Sacred Effects"

The renewed and intensified focus upon the confiscation of *ñáñigo* objects at the dawn of the republic goes far in revealing historically specific definitions of what Abakuá attributes meant to official Havana, as well as to the Abakuá themselves. Rafael Roche y Monteagudo (figure 8.11), a detective and police inspector for the provincial government of Havana, surpassed Trujillo y Monagas in analysis as much as descriptive content. As never before, Roche explicitly articulated the relationship between police intelligence gathering and the specific problem of *ñáñigo* tenaciousness. "For years," he wrote, "their behavior remained shrouded in the most impenetrable mystery." Undoubtedly, the Alejandro Rodríguez account had been useful in a general way. Still, the raison d'être of Roche y Monteagudo's 1908 chapter on the *ñañigos*[21] was precisely this: "the selection of the most adequate means to the complete extinction of Ñañiguismo, which inflicts grave damage on our culture, *follows from their practices becoming public domain*" (1908:3, emphasis added). In theory, the public revelation of the "secret" would logically render the "secret society" extinct. This project would entail not only arrests but also the exhaustive confiscation of *ñañiguismo*'s enabling "fetishes"—something many believed the colonial governor of Havana had already done. So why were the *ñáñigos* still around? The very appearance of Roche y Monteagudo's 1908 work suggests a reason, which Fernando Ortiz would keenly articulate almost half a century later. The governor,

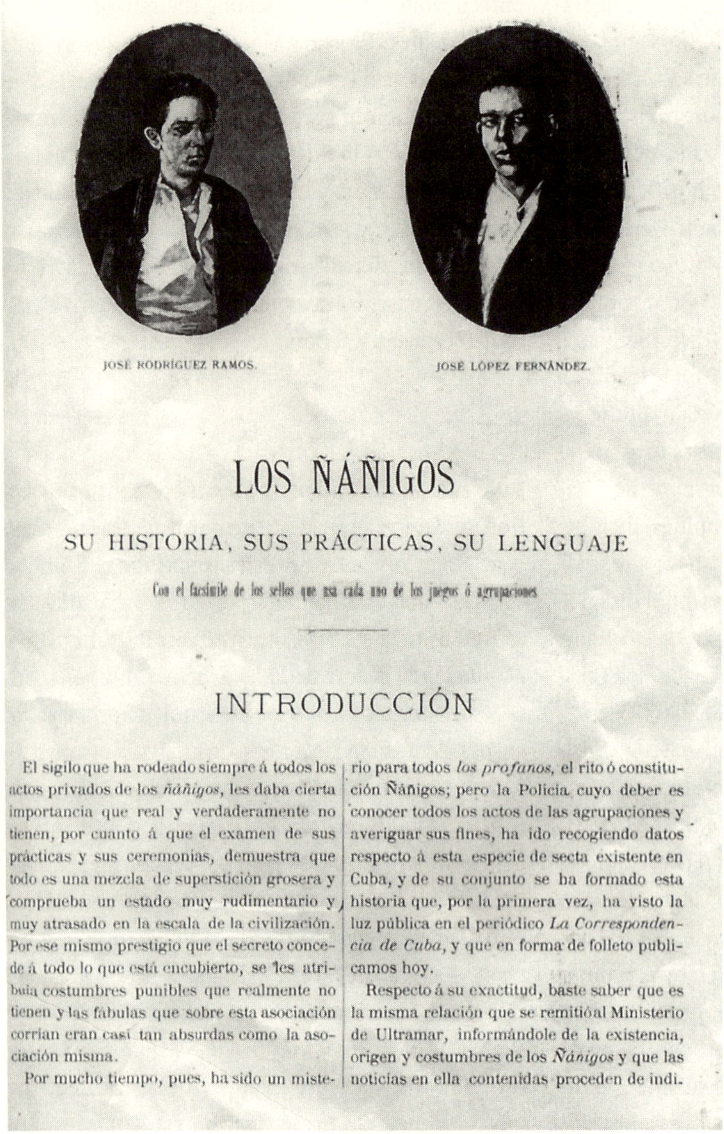

JOSÉ RODRÍGUEZ RAMOS.

JOSÉ LÓPEZ FERNÁNDEZ.

LOS ÑÁÑIGOS

SU HISTORIA, SUS PRÁCTICAS, SU LENGUAJE

Con el facsímile de los sellos que usa cada uno de los juegos ó agrupaciones

INTRODUCCIÓN

El sigilo que ha rodeado siempre á todos los actos privados de los *ñáñigos*, les daba cierta importancia que real y verdaderamente no tienen, por cuanto á que el examen de sus prácticas y sus ceremonias, demuestra que todo es una mezcla de superstición grosera y comprueba un estado muy rudimentario y muy atrasado en la escala de la civilización. Por ese mismo prestigio que el secreto concede á todo lo que está encubierto, se les atribuia costumbres punibles que realmente no tienen y las fábulas que sobre esta asociación corrían eran casi tan absurdas como la asociación misma.

Por mucho tiempo, pues, ha sido un misterio para todos *los profanos*, el rito ó constitución Ñáñigos; pero la Policia cuyo deber es conocer todos los actos de las agrupaciones y averiguar sus fines, ha ido recogiendo datos respecto á esta especie de secta existente en Cuba, y de su conjunto se ha formado esta historia que, por la primera vez, ha visto la luz pública en el periódico *La Correspondencia de Cuba*, y que en forma de folleto publicamos hoy.

Respecto á su exactitud, baste saber que es la misma relación que se remitió al Ministerio de Ultramar, informándole de la existencia, origen y costumbres de los *Ñáñigos* y que las noticias en ella contenidas proceden de indi.

Figure 8.9. ***Los Ñáñigos: Su historia, sus prácticas, su lenguaje;*** **the first page of J. Trujillo y Monagas's chapter on the Abakuá Society in** ***Los criminales de Cuba*** **(1882), based on police investigation and the unprecedented 1881 reporting of Alejandro Rodríguez, which was first published in an 1882 issue of** ***La Correspondencia de Cuba.*** **The premise of its publication was that "the Police [have the] duty to understand all of the behavior of groups and discern their purposes."**

under whose mandate local authorities could force lodges to give up their attributes, not only failed, but he had also obscured the fact that he had failed, making a hasty retreat for the Peninsula in 1899 following the Spanish-American War. There had been much public hoopla, but nothing substantial to show for it.

Back in 1889, under a special mandate of the civil governor of the island—a Reglano by the name of Don Carlos Rodríguez Batista—the legal strategy toward the *ñáñigos* shifted decisively from a focus on individual violent crimes to "conspiracy against the public order of the colonial government" (see Ortiz 1954:80). As Roche y Monteagudo noted, "it [was] a step so significant, that . . . *mutuo propio,* [it] would deliver up the most sacred effects of ñañiguismo, and by this method, finish them off once and for all" (Roche y Monteagudo 1908:33, 43). Under political and police duress, a council of top Regla Abakuá leaders de-

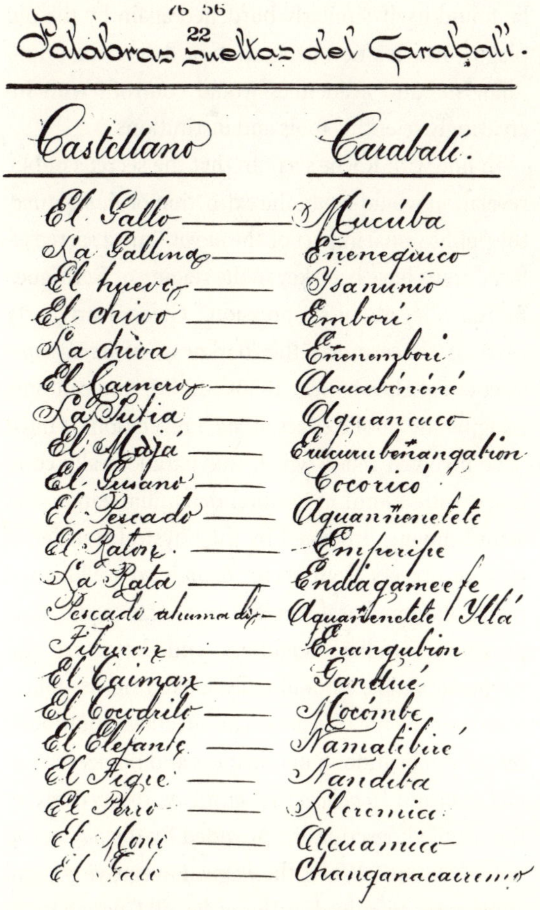
76 56
22
Palabras sueltas del Carabalí.

Castellano	Carabalí
El Gallo	Mucúba
La Gallina	Eñenequico
El huevo	Ysanunio
El chivo	Embori
La chiva	Eñenembori
El Carnero	Acuabiriné
La Jutía	Aguancuco
El Majá	Eucurubeñangabion
El Gusano	Cocórico
El Pescado	Aguañonetete
El Raton	Emperife
La Rata	Endiagameefe
Pescado ahumado	Aguarenetete / Yllá
Tiburon	Enangubion
El Caiman	Gandué
El Cocodrilo	Mocómbe
El Elefante	Namatibiré
El Tigre	Nandiba
El Perro	Eleremica
El Mono	Acuamico
El Gato	Changanacauremo

Figure 8.10. ***Palabras sueltas del Carabalí;*** **the first published Spanish-Carabalí glossary, from police-confiscated Abakuá documents, from A. Rodríguez 1881, later published in Trujillo y Monagas 1882.**

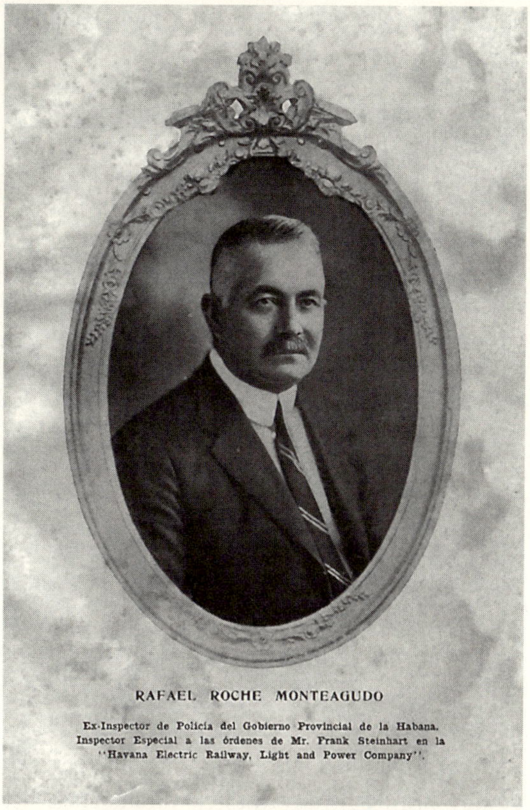

Figure 8.11. Rafael Roche y Monteagudo, police inspector of the provincial government of Havana and special inspector under the command of Mr. Frank Steinhart of the Havana Electric Railway, Light, and Power Company, an American corporation in Havana. (From Roche y Monteagudo 1925.)

clared in a letter of "clarification" to the editor of *La Lucha* (5 January 1889)[22] their "resolution" to "terminate once and for all membership in an association that . . . is illegal under the law." They promised never again to form such organizations. And they agreed to comply, including giving up all their attributes to the chief of police, despite the fact that they had been mischaracterized, suffered "constant police persecution," and were nothing more than "peaceful" organizations of workers dedicated to "bettering their individual condition" through "honorable work."[23] Their attributes were beloved, priceless possessions; but they resigned themselves to give them up for the sake of their survival. Still, they reported, "though the majority [of members] have seen the way out by these means, an ignorant minority continued to be reluctant, to the point of tears, to let go of objects that were very dear to them." The letter enumerates in detail the attributes from their *fambás* handed over on January 3, 1889, including Ekues, *seses,* Mpegós, and orchestra drums, Mokongo and Mosongo staffs, *íreme sacos,* yellow chalk, metal crucifixes, and silver candelabras (Roche y Monteagudo 1908:45–46). They were not even allowed to keep the last two object types, which, in another worship context, would be common Catholic sacred attributes. In a resigned tone, the letter summed up the current state of affairs:

> Today it can be said that in Havana the *white ñáñigo no longer exists.* Whoever continues as such is wretched. The Macaró, Ecorio Efó #1, Ecorio Efó #2, Ecorio Efó #3, and Ebión *juegos* have been destroyed. [Previously] there were those that had not been destroyed, and they continued functioning, [despite] the deportations and other methods. . . . Yet today is something else altogether. We repeat: not a single white ñáñigo exists in Havana, and we expect that the two [white] *juegos* "Enlleguelle" #1 and #2 of Guanabacoa and Regla, as with the *juegos* of color that still exist, following our example, and as would be most convenient for the interest of Havana, cease as ñáñigos and [cease] carrying the sad distinction of being the authors of so many murders. (Roche y Monteagudo 1908:45)

What does one make of this apparently obsequious and contrite letter, which communicates extreme gratitude to the civil governor and the police for destroying its authors' lifeblood? Undoubtedly, their gesture was, in part, an earnest clarification that they were "peaceful," law-abiding "workers." Still, there is evidence to suggest that their response to the governor's *auto-da-fé* was a remarkably successful tactic of survival through dissimulation, perhaps only to be matched by the governor's own grand dissimulation. One might say that the late colonial period's war against the *ñáñigos* was a war of relatively more or less efficacious performances, complete with handy props and trophies.

Writing sixty years later, a skeptical Fernando Ortiz noted that "still [today] the legend of the suppression of *ñañiguismo* is maintained." In fact, Governor Rodríguez Batista's "suppression of the 'potencias' of *ñáñigos* was nothing more than the ostentatious *simulation of a great police service.* Rodríguez Batista had hardly stepped down as governor before the 'juegos,' supposedly disintegrated, [began] functioning anew, just as before" (Ortiz 1954:81, emphasis added). Though *ñañiguismo* was forced deep underground for a time, the Cuban government of the new republic found itself similarly burdened again by the old plague, which a new generation of detectives, criminologists, and academics would confront with increasingly scientific tools and institutions.

In line with Roche's axiom that the secret's public revelation would mean the extinction of *ñañiguismo,* the public visual impact of the *juegos*' "most sacred effects" must have been key to the staging of Rodríguez Batista's "legend of suppression." Given nearly forty years of concern over the "darkness" of *ñañiguismo* in colonial Havana (ca. 1850s–1889), one can only imagine the public effect of such revelation. It must have involved relief, which was paradoxically combined with a kind of cultural defamiliarization and astonishment, produced by the physical transfer of strange objects from secret *fambás* to well-lighted police stations, local bastions of vigilance and state presence. Families, neighbors, and detractors and supporters alike undoubtedly looked on as policemen oversaw the transfers. The effect was multiplied by the publication in newspapers and books such as *La Lucha* and *La policía y sus mistérios,* respectively, of the detailed descriptions provided by the *juegos* and police blotters. When the *juegos* Enyegueyé #2 and Taibá were dissolved at the order of Guanabacoa's mayor, detailed descriptions of the objects were published. For example (referring to one *sese* and both groups' *plumeros*), a description read: "a goblet of a half yard in height, by a palm and one half in diameter, of fine wood, covered in blue corduroy, [encircled] with a silver ring, with four handles and nails of the same metal; and eight *plumeros,* of two kinds and colors, that served the two *juegos* for the celebration of all their ceremonies" (Ortiz 1954:81). Roche y Monteagudo would later present photographs and detailed drawings of such objects to lay bare, and thus, complete, the intended illumination and deflation of the *ñáñigo* secret. Of course, though the legend of suppression was reinforced by the visual impact and appropriation of Abakuá Society "effects," evidently they were merely effects both of Abakuá shrewdness and state propaganda.

9 Struggle over Possession of the Secret

The Museuming of the Ñáñigos' *"Most Sacred Effects"*

Many of *ñañiguismo*'s "most sacred effects," delivered up as of 1889, did not remain in police custody for long. At first radically recontextualized as confiscated criminal evidence within the profane hands of "The Law," *La Justícia,* as Cubans say, the objects were soon transferred once again, in publicized fashion. "Upon leaving [Cuba] for the Peninsula [Spain, in 1899] Sr. Rodríguez Batista carried with him some of the *ñáñigo* attributes, among them a *saco* or suit of a *diablito,* which can be seen in the Library-Museum of Ultramar in Madrid" (Roche y Monteagudo 1908:49). Ultramar was a proto-ethnographic museum for objects from Spain's overseas possessions (see Pacheco de Amorim 1934).[1] As recontextualized once again, *ñáñigo* objects graduated from case evidence to imperial booty, now-dead artifacts of supposed imperial successes in bringing order and civilization to the colonies.[2]

Late nineteenth-century ethnographic museum exhibitions dedicated to the material culture of primitives or aborigines typically served to illustrate the anthropological stages of evolution through which mankind had passed in its advancement to "civilization" (see Chapman 1985; Clifford 1988). Ethnographic museum display has widely participated in discourses on the nation, constituting the boundaries of national identities precisely through delineating cultural "others" in space and time (Karp and Lavine 1990:2; Fabian 1983:xi, 7, 15–16). A museum dedicated to material "collected" (or looted) from an empire's colonies would, on a hierarchical scale, mark the contrast in "civilization" between the governing peoples of the imperial center and the "natives" of the periphery, rationalizing, in turn, the colonization of far-flung lands and subjects. It is not difficult to understand how such a museum's artifacts—in the Abakuá case, the "fetishes"—might index the fate of their former owners, and, by extension, the status of the exhibitions' sponsors (Clifford 1988:201–202, 217, 225–226; Chapman 1985).

Object display in eighteenth- and nineteenth-century exhibitions tended toward the "cabinet of curiosities" mode—eclectic arrays of heterogeneous and far-flung artifacts, jumbling together the utilitarian and aesthetic, along with flora, fauna, and so forth. Even with subsequent updating to modern anthropological standards, objects might remain mostly as dry scientific specimens collected from "remote areas."[3] Alternatively, they might be displayed in realistic dioramas (complete with dressed mannequins), which nevertheless remain as frozen material-culture capsules from the past.

In contrast, the most recent ethnographic exhibitions thematize the agency of culture bearers through varied contextualizations, for example, the representation of the faces and "voices" of makers who are reflective subjects. Through exhibition design and interactive displays, authors and audiences are spatialized; they meet, as it were, albeit in mediated and choreographed fashion. Thus conjured into virtual presences via "stories," the objects exhibited might graduate from, for example, dead taxonomic presentation to indexes of living, contemporary persons and cultural groups with substantial historical pasts. The objects' meanings, theoretically at least, might be apprehended as multilayered, self-reflexive, and derived rather than imposed (see Arnoldi, Kreamer, and Mason 2001).

As artist Fred Wilson has persuasively argued, if ethnographic exhibitions have referenced their target peoples at all, they also signify colonial history from the standpoint of imperial powers. In Wilson's revised, ironic ethnographic exhibition displays, some African masks are blindfolded, and African voices and agencies are silenced. The visitor looks into the eyes of other masks and sees videos of troop movements in imperial adventure movies. As expressed in many an anthropological museum display, for example, the "noble" indigenous populations of this continent in official nineteenth-century narrative could not but fall before the advance of American civilization's Manifest Destiny, just as Mexico City's contemporary anthropological museum puts to rest living indigenous populations, which are still around and converse in their ancient languages. Native American objects in "Natural History" museums may conjure wonder, even pity, but explicit reference to genocide, for example, has not always been well received by donors and politicians (see Truettner 1991; Limerick 2002).

In sum, *ñáñigo* objects in the Museum of Ultramar apparently intended to celebrate the death of the fetish and the extinction of a peculiar, pesky colonial group. The great difference between the *ñáñigos* and "native" peoples of "remote" areas, of course, was their presence in the thick of urban Cuban society. More significantly, not entirely "other," except through class distinction, the white *ñáñigos,* many of whom were of Spanish extraction, represented not simply the remote primitive but the specter of horrific mixture at home. As Roche y Monteagudo insisted, they could not be black African ("natives") because they were "white"—an argument with which the Carabalí *cabildos,* ironically, would have agreed. They were part evolutionary throwbacks, part social deviants; and they were either set straight or crushed through the heroic efforts of imperial civilization's defenders, such as Governor Rodríguez Batista.

Fakelore and Forgery in the Blink of an Eye

In the end, as Fernando Ortiz concluded in the 1950s, Governor Rodríguez Batista's "victory" was a hollow one, more rhetorical than real. For the white *ñáñigos* had shrewdly devised their own rhetorical and performative displays. Their public revelation of *ñañigo* objects was calculated and scripted indeed. As Ortiz concluded, "Not a few 'juegos' only apparently dissolved, having hidden their 'attributes.' Others, more shrewdly, constructed, in the blink of an eye, drums and fake attributes that were unconsecrated [*judío,* "unbaptized"], in order to preserve the real ones in hiding. It is said that the *ñáñigos Muñanga* had their real attributes hidden for years in the house of a Marquis of Havana, where . . . their *iyamba,* an ex-slave of this aristocrat, [continued to work] as a favored cook.

Meanwhile, the fake attributes embarked for Spain to figure [into the collection of] the . . . Museum of Ultramar" (Ortiz 1954:81).

The "shrewdest" of the Abakuá *juegos* must have been aware of the level of their primary audience for these critical performances. Given ten or more years of prior police "education" about what *ñáñigo* objects looked like, the *ñáñigos* needed to create authentic-looking, visually impressive facsimiles. They accomplished this swiftly, if they had not already prepared substitutions in advance. They must have used the most appropriate and attention-grabbing materials for their props: fine wood and cloth, including velvet, silver and gold hardware, and stately feathered plumes. Their only sins of omission in their preparations were the all-important *carga,* the consecration of the goatskins, and the required invocatory prayers. Undoubtedly, the *ñáñigos* simply prayed that their ruse would work. These attributes were perfectly disingenuous: dazzling on the outside but truly *vacío* ("empty").

Imaginably, the in-camera meetings among Abakuá leaders that led to the delivery of their "most sacred effects" to mayors and police chiefs were not all tears and hand wringing. They must have included discussions of how to build false objects and script and stage public performances of compliance, complete with letters bearing the appropriate contrite, resigned, and obsequious tone. As in the early twentieth century's activist labor ethos, they would not mourn but organize. Ironically, many of the "darkest" objects escaped Fernández Carrillo's "brilliant light of the sun" in their hiding places within the very bosom of Havana "civilization"—its very own thousand points of light. Who would have thought to search the glistening palaces of Marqueses for savage fetishes? At the same time, "profane" but pretty objects, fabricated on the sly, were marched in a unique variant of Abakuá procession. Their downcast and humiliated owners went to meet the inquisitors in a public arena of dissimulation and artistic forgery. The objects' official recipients and exhibitors-to-be were apparently satisfied, self-deceived, or cynical: police pickers, mayoral dealers, governor-collectors, and imperial museum curators. Of course, no few pickers, dealers, collectors, and curators have been fooled by fakes, or else further seduced into the disingenuous hawking of such forgeries. As a result, the Ultramar Museum collection itself was mongrelized and thereby destabilized from within relative to its claims of imperial truth. How could inauthentic, faked booty connote anything but the emperor's new clothes? Rafael Roche y Monteagudo, one of the greatest *ñáñigo* artifact connoisseurs of his time, despite his years of intelligence gathering, apparently remained none the wiser as a member of the viewing audience when he visited the Ultramar Museum himself in 1920 (1925:63). In this sense, the 1889 *ñáñigo* performances, obviously enduring and efficacious even behind glass as late as 1920, redoubled, rather than ruined, the Abakuá "secret." For who would ever know but the "sworn" confectors of *seses,* Ekues, Mpegós, Ekueñóns, Enkríkamos, and *sacos* themselves what was "real" and what was "fake"? The "secret" could be "something," or it could be "nothing," and it would still achieve its social and political effect (see Barber 1981).

The Abakuá had, of course, engaged in prior public dissimulations. Andrés Petít advocated the "defensive process" of "syncretic mimesis" during the mid to late nineteenth century, but his attempts at *licitúd* through additions of Catholic iconography did not entirely succeed. Yet, Petít's shrewd Acanarán Efó offspring utilized another kind of defensive process of mimesis, which might be labeled an early form of folklorization. Still, in Cuba "folklore" presentations depend on the notion of the authentic and the genuine, albeit, as executed by professional, paid, "informants" (see Hagedorn 2001:141–150). In their competent reproduction of facsimiles from consecrated originals for profane public consumption, yet with the intention of dissimulation, the *ñáñigos* created objects and performances that might better be known as early "fakelore."[4] Of course, the story is more complicated, as it contains deeper levels of ambiguity. That many "real," supposedly "charged" objects were in fact empty in the first place, as the renovator of forty Efó *seses* found, begs the question of just what this secret consisted. As Karin Barber found, the "secret" is inextricably bound up in, indeed constructed by, political struggle; through institutional exclusion, rhetoric, and performance, the "secret" can operate successfully whether it contains "something" or "nothing." In this sense, it is a "fetish," a socially invested repository of symbolic capital, something both sides somehow knew all along.

El Ñáñigo, Crime, and the Police Chronicle

Having graduated in 1875 to the status of illicit goods, the *sacos* and attributes carried to Spain by Governor Rodríguez Batista were transvalued, once again, this time into museum relics of the bad old days and into signifiers of imperial order—despite, of course, the ignominious loss of the colonies to effective U.S. control. Landaluze's *El Ñáñigo*, a 12.25 × 9.75–inch lithograph, underwent analogous morphological and semantic transformations. Whereas Landaluze produced *El Ñáñigo* as *costumbrista* art, Havana Police Inspector Rafael Roche y Monteagudo turned this lithographic print into a mass-produced illustration for the sake of the heroic police chronicle and its hagiography of crimefighters.

El Ñáñigo boldly appears as the second visual document in Roche's 1908 *La policía y sus mistérios*, preceded only by the obligatory photograph, in three-quarter pose, of Sr. General Emilio Nuñez y Rodríguez, the successor to Rodríguez Batista as provincial governor of Havana.[5] Reduced in size, framed with a black border, retitled, and left unattributed, Landaluze's impressive lithograph now emerges in stark halftone (figure 9.1). Captioned "Ñáñigo outfitted with the *saco*," the figure no longer stands on its own or as an equal to literary creation. It now derives meaning from a descriptive, rather than the former iconicizing, title—*El Ñáñigo*. As disengaged from authorship—the "name of the artist"—the figure is subordinated to the sober police narrative as an illustration of the "attributes" of "Official *Ñáñigo* Personnel." Thus, in the text opposite the figure, Roche writes: "In order to constitute a *juego*, it is necessary to complete the thirteen *plazas* that form the *potencia* or *Junta* of permanent government. . . . Each has his particular name that designates his office, responsibilities, and place he occupies in the association, [also] having a sign—signature or attribute, which is illustrated in the reproduced plate we [provide]" (1908:16–17). *El Ñáñigo*, an 1881 artistic monument to Cuban "types and customs," has become the two-dimensional visual cognate of the *sacos* in police evidence lockers and colonial museum vitrines. Yet, by the time of Roche's expanded 1925 edition, the *costumbrista* figure had apparently lost its currency as illustrative material. With a new surge in police raids, masses of drawn and photographic illustrations of actual crime-scene evidence—seized attributes, the contents of private Abakuá notebooks, and naked white *ñáñigo* convicts covered with tattoos[6]—became a more efficacious means of extinguishing *ñañiguismo* through the revelation of the secret.

Ñañiguismo, New Sciences, and Museum Display

Though more analytical than his predecessor's *Criminales de Cuba*, Roche y Monteagudo's *La policía y sus mistérios* was obsolete by the time of its 1925 republication. The modern moment of the professional scientist had already arrived. Just as professional anthropologists edged missionaries, colonial administrators, and travel writers out of ethnography's domain between around 1900 and 1922 (see Stocking 1983:71–74; Clifford 1988:24, 26–30), the institution of forensic science and modern penal theory in Cuba seized analysis, identification, and interpretation out of the hands of cops. A group of scientists and lawyers, Israel Castellanos and Fernando Ortiz (1881–1969; figure 9.2) among them, stood as the professional vanguard of the new fields of legal medicine, forensic pathology, dactyloscopy, anthropology, penology, and criminal ethnology. Social-science scholars covered the last three, while the first three,

PERSONAL OFICIAL ÑAÑIGO

Para poder constituir un juego, es necesario que estén completas las trece plazas que forman la potencia ó Junta de gobierno permanente, en la cual cada una tiene su denominación particular, que designa su gerarquía, cargo y lugar que ocupa en la asociación, teniendo un signo, firma ó distintivo que figuran en la lámina de facsimiles que acompañamos.

Los cuatro miembros primeros se estiman como jefes superiores, y los demás, aunque considerados como tales, se denominan en conjunto *abanecúes* (vocales), teniendo, con arreglo á las funciones que ejercen, su nombre particular:

1er. Jefe: Illamba.	Ecueñón.
2° Idem, Isué.	Nasacó.
3° Idem, Mocongo.	Aberiñán.
4° Idem, Empego.	Mesongo.
Insunecue.	Mosongo.
Encricamo.	Encoboró.
Anaonangui.	Embocó.

Se compone de plazas secundarias también, como son los cuatro Diablitos, figurando una mujer, única á la que se permite entrar en el cuarto *fambá*, donde se llevan á cabo las ceremonias, dándosele el nombre de *Casicanecuá ó Ibana*, poseedora por lo tanto del secreto de la potencia ó partido, concediéndosele el honor de portar sobre la cabeza la vasija que usan en el juramento.

El *Illamba* es la representación del Obispo; *Nasacó* es el brujo del juego, siendo su misión, al participársele el asesinato de un individuo, reconocerlo, para lo cual le propina con un palo tres golpes en el vientre, llevando de esta manera al ánimo de sus compañeros el convencimiento de que no pertenece al partido; *Monifambá* es el portero ó conserje del *butamú* ó *fambá*, cuya entrada está terminantemente prohibida

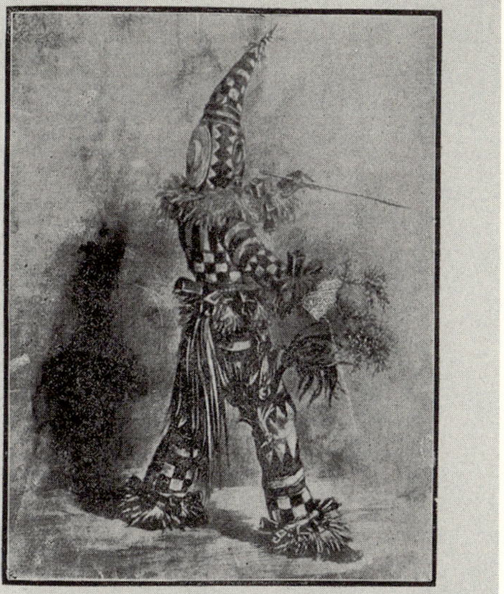

ÑÁÑIGO CARGADO CON EL SACO.

Figure 9.1. Víctor Patricio de Landaluze's 1881 *El Ñáñigo* as it appears in the 1908 first edition of Roche y Monteagudo's *La policía y sus mistérios* (p. 17), captioned "*Ñáñigo* fitted with the *saco* [costume]"; for illustrative use, it provides an example of the "attributes" of the "Official *Ñáñigo* Personnel"; see opposite page.

among others, were connected to burgeoning state institutions of forensic "identification." The *íreme* would undergo further morphological and semantic transformations within the new institutions. The principal figures in the new fields were trained in, or drew heavily on, European scientific discourse and recent technological discoveries and applied their knowledge to the Cuban case, that is, *ñañiguismo, brujería,* and the problem of the nation's health.

Having studied neocorrectionalist penal theory as well as anthropometric and anthropological science in Barcelona, Fernando Ortiz published scholarly and journalistic articles on the growing field of criminal ethnology between 1903 and 1906, first under the tutelage of the famous Cesare Lombroso[7] (1835–1909) and Enrico Ferri (1856–1929) in Turin, Italy, and then in Cuba on two brief return trips. This groundwork formed the basis for his first major publication, *Los negros brujos: Apuntes para un estudio de etnología criminal* (The Black Sorcerers: Notes Toward a Study of Criminal Ethnology; Ortiz 1973; Ortiz 1939:86; Rubin 1998:26). *Los negros brujos* was the first installment in a projected five-volume series that would cover all aspects of *negro* "delinquency." His plans included a never-to-be-published volume on *los negros ñáñigos,* "that African secret society that abundantly exists even in the twentieth century in various Cuban cities" (Ortiz 1924a:xiii). Ortiz's teacher, friend, and colleague Lombroso wrote the brief but effusive prologue to *Los negros brujos,* and Ortiz cited Lombroso's work in this study of *la mala vida cubana* (literally the "bad life," or the underworld of Cuban delinquency). A recent bibliographer of Ortiz's writings characterizes *Los negros brujos* as a momentous work that "marks the beginning of anthropological and sociological studies of criminality in Cuba

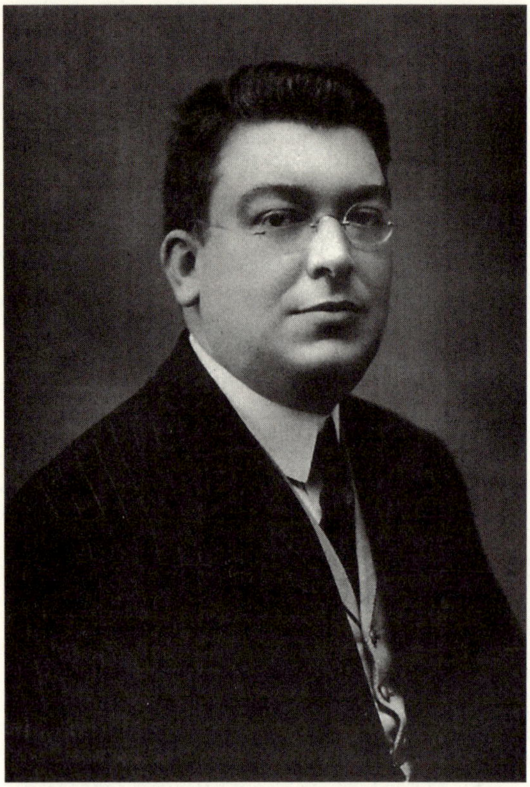

Figure 9.2. Fernando Ortiz y Fernández, ca. 1910. Lawyer, penal theorist, pioneer of Cuba's criminal ethnology field, folklorist, statesman, and diplomat. Courtesy private collection of María Fernanda Ortiz Herrera.

and the criminological study of Afro-Cuban male delinquents" (Rubin 1998:26). Through Ortiz and his publications and teaching, Lombroso's influence was decisive on a generation of Cuban anthropologists, criminologists, and forensic pathologists. Briefly put, Lombroso's works postulated that criminals manifest a higher percentage of physical and mental "anomalies" than do noncriminals. These anomalies owe partly to "degeneration" and partly to "atavism," that is to say, reversion to a primitive evolutionary stage. Criminals, Lombroso believed, could be identified by certain outstanding physical characteristics or "stigmata." Cuban scholars applied Lombrosian theory to the study of Afro-Cuban *brujos, ñáñigos,* and other "delinquents" (see, e.g., Castellanos 1916).

Ñañiguismo and *brujería* were now subject to intensive laboratory study by Ortiz's scientific contemporaries. This included gruesome approaches (e.g., dissection) to the bodies of convicted delinquents following execution. For posterity and further study, for instance, the brains of Domingo Boucourt and Victor Molina (an African and a black creole garroted following their conviction in the supposed ritual murder of the "Child Zoila," *la Niña Zoila;* see Chávez Álvarez 1991) were preserved in formaldehyde at the National University's Anthropology Museum of Dr. Luis Montané Dardé. Montané had, like Ortiz, studied at the University of Barcelona, and he went on to establish the field of anthropology at the University of Havana. The forensic pathologist Dr. Israel Castellanos, following Lombroso, was obsessed with the anomalies and atavistic traits of *brujos* and *ñáñigos.* He hypothesized that the brains of the Afro-Cubans Boucourt and Molina—insufficiently studied by Montané, he argued—were "simian-like" (1916:22). Castellanos studied their garroted bodies in an attempt to uncover their stigmata and prove their physical anomalies, with uneven success (I. Castellanos 1916:31–32; see Palmié 2002:244–248; figure 9.3). Montané himself, who wrote his doctoral thesis under Paul Broca[8] in Paris on the "anatomy of microcephalic craniums," had published a turn-of-the-century book titled *The Cranium of Antonio Maceo,* the *mulato* hero (1845–1896) of the two Wars of Independence (Roldán 1940:961). By that time, former slaves and other Afro-Cubans who had fought in the Second War of Independence for a free Cuba were subject to the equivalent of Jim Crow laws after the fall of Reconstruction in the United States.

Given renewed police scrutiny and prosecution of *ñáñigos* early in the republic, it was not long before Abakuá attributes and *sacos* would once again begin their journey from *fambás* to police stations to museum vitrines. Yet, this time around, the material traditions of the "black African Carabalí Brícamo" would no longer recross the Black Atlantic to Ultramar. *Ñáñigo* objects were no longer just concomitants of illicit assembly by *ñáñigos* or state trophies of conquest; they became specific kinds of forensic evidence within rationalized criminal procedures. Fol-

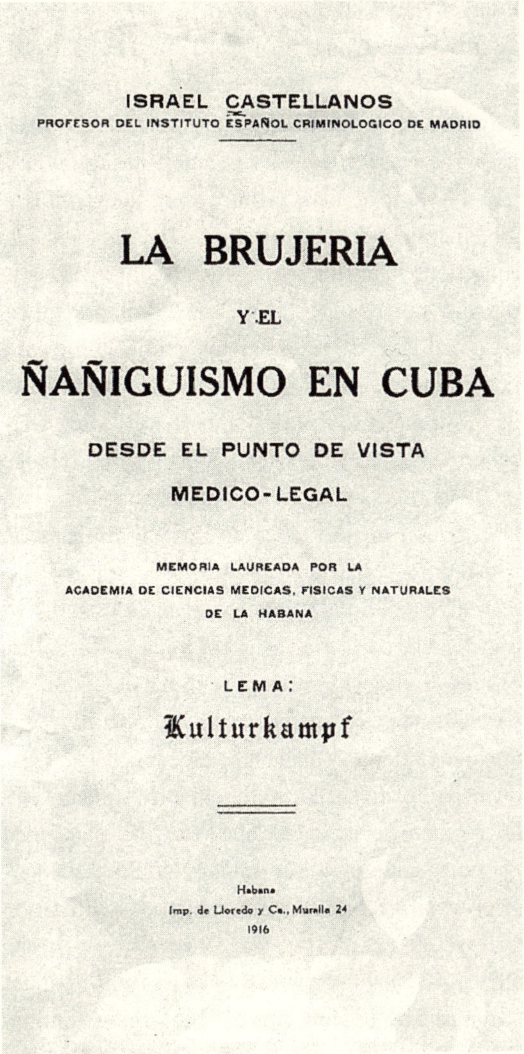
ISRAEL CASTELLANOS
PROFESOR DEL INSTITUTO ESPAÑOL CRIMINOLOGICO DE MADRID

LA BRUJERIA

Y EL

ÑAÑIGUISMO EN CUBA

DESDE EL PUNTO DE VISTA

MEDICO-LEGAL

MEMORIA LAUREADA POR LA
ACADEMIA DE CIENCIAS MEDICAS, FISICAS Y NATURALES
DE LA HABANA

LEMA:

Kulturkampf

Habana
Imp. de Lloredo y Ca., Muralla 24
1916

Figure 9.3. *La Brujería y el Ñañiguismo en Cuba: Desde el punto de vista médico-legal* (Witchcraft and Ñañiguismo in Cuba from a Legal-Medicine Perspective) with the German motto *Kulturkampf* (culture struggle), 1916, by Israel Castellanos, then professor of the Spanish Criminological Institute of Madrid; he took over Cuba's National Bureau of Identification after Juan Francisco Steegers.

lowing their seizure by the republican police, *ñáñigo* objects would now move through a series of new institutions.

With the efflorescence of criminal forensic science at the dawn of the nation, the social lives of *ñáñigo* objects beyond the *fambá* and the police station would develop within the emergent bureaucracy of "Identification." Little known outside of Cuba, Juan Francisco Steegers y Pereira (1856–1921) may have been the greatest republican collector of *ñáñigo* attributes, among other things, long before Don Fernando Ortiz, the twentieth century's dean of Afrocubana. Beginning soon after the republic's founding, within the new Office of Criminal Identification in the Prison of the Republic, Steegers combined the increasingly versatile medium of photography with anthropometry. Having helped organize the Bureau of National Identification, practically built around the Galton-Henry science of fingerprinting (dactyloscopy) developed in Europe, Steegers patented a photographic dactyloscopic method that utilized transparent paper. Steegers diligently "collected" the *ñáñigo* and *brujo* objects that came his way from police raids and had them "conserved" within the Bureau and with its scientific resources.[9]

Just after the mid-1910s, *ñáñigo* and *brujo* objects, hitherto guarded within the criminal identification bureaucracy, made another transition, this time to the burgeoning University of Havana, where they would be studied by generations of anthropology and medical professors and students. Many warehoused, as well as some newly confiscated, objects were deposited and put on view at the anthropological museum, which was founded in 1899 by Dr. Luís Montané y Dardé (1849–1936). The objects collected and conserved by Steegers were donated to another academic faculty by his successor at the Bureau of Identification, none other than Dr. Israel Castellanos. The Steegers Collection formed the basis of a small museum within the University of Havana School of Medicine's Faculty of Legal Medicine and Toxicology.[10] The collection has migrated at least three times between the lower and upper floors of various buildings in the sprawling medical complex behind the great Beaux Arts University of Havana building, and it still functions as a study collection under the direction of the sober and hard-working Dr. Francisco Ponce Sequiera, who uses it to teach courses on "legal and ethical medicine."[11] Recently, the biographies of the objects, having accumulated the grime of years, were burnished by a professional museologist from the Museum of Regla, Luís Alberto Pedroso, who conserved and reinstalled them with typed labels in two well-lighted rooms.

Still, the Museum of Legal Medicine collection strikes one as odd today. Its content and organization reflect the early Lombrosian intimacies of racialist, anthropometric, and hereditarianist anthropologies with the criminal identification practices of a fraught new nation and former slave colony. As reinstalled in ways that reflect its earlier incarnations, the museum juxtaposes glass cases filled with *ñáñigo* and *brujo* attributes, myriad weapon types (pistols, razors, blackjacks, and brass knuckles), and jars of hydrocephalic and otherwise deformed fetuses in formaldehyde. The objects of *brujería* include carved Lucumí *orisha* statues, Ifá divining equipment, beaded necklaces, and iconographic attributes confiscated from the houses of suspected *brujos*, along with the black and white transparencies of Domingo Bocourt published by Ortiz and Castellanos (Ortiz 1973: figures 3–5, 19–21, 26–28; Castellanos 1916: figures 11, 12, 23).

The small but impressive display of Abakuá objects includes three altar staffs, a cowrie-encrusted *sese*, an Ekue, four orchestra drums, an elaborate crucifix and monstrance, two large *maruga* shakers, an *ekón* bell, and a lovely carved wood goblet, all gathered around an extraordinary *saco de íreme* with a tripartite hood.[12] Installed in a museum today, the exhibition would form a dazzling, perhaps celebratory, display of Black Atlantic art and philosophy or transnational history and culture. Back then, however, deviance, evolutionary atavism, physical anomaly, crime, and what we now know as the Abakuá Society simply went together in this peculiarly Cuban cabinet of curiosities. If the father is the child of the man, then *ñañiguismo* was the child of hydrocephalic fetuses and degenerated white working-class bodies fated to criminality. My entree into the museum, an extremely bright medical student, who had recently attended legal-medicine lectures based on the study collection, confided to me that she "didn't understand a single thing that was said."

Police Work, Scholarship, and Museum Collections

Virtually all of the Abakuá objects studied by Fernando Ortiz and Israel Castellanos during the first half of the twentieth century were housed in the aforementioned anthropology and legal medicine collections following their accession there, likely in the mid- to late 1910s. At the same time, several exceptional objects, among many confiscated by the police during the presidency of the Conservative Party's General Mario G. Menocal (1912–20), were collected by the National Museum of Cuba, founded in 1913. This new institution represents an important variant on the range of Havana museums in which Afro-Cuban objects were collected and displayed. By the 1920s, the National Museum had transformed itself from a kind of nineteenth-century cabinet of curiosities writ large into a more disciplinarily, though still idiosyncratically, organized system of "sections." The heterogeneous collection was divided into archaeology, ethnography, lapidary, eminent Cuban personages, "Fine Arts" (which included painting, sculpture, numismatics, and antique jewelry), furniture, natural history, and books. Fernando Ortiz reveled in parts of this collection between the 1920s and 1960s, particularly as it was refined under the museum's second director, the painter Antonio Rodríguez Morey (1872–1967; Rippe 2001). The Afro-Cuban objects prized by Rodríguez Morey included perhaps the most spectacular African-derived piece of all the ethnographic collections on the island, a tall, exquisitely carved drum of the Dahomean-descended Arará group (see Moreno 1988), seized from a *cabildo* in Matanzas between 1913 and 1914. This drum, because of its visible Africanness and great beauty, apparently made the otherwise sober Fernando Ortiz smile, as revealed in a photograph taken with the diminutive Rodríguez Morey in the late 1940s or early 1950s. Undoubtedly, the artist Rodríguez Morey and the ethnologist Ortiz generated some of the first discussions about Afro-Cuban objects—otherwise considered dangerous fetishes and social pathogens—as artful and culturally significant, if not as "art" proper.

The Anthropological, Legal Medicine, and National Museum collections played an important practical role in the works of Fernando Ortiz and Israel Castellanos, particularly in the former's huge organological essays on Abakuá, Arará, Lucumí, Congo, and popular musical instruments, many of which essays were written over the course of decades, from the 1920s through the 1950s (1954:1–85; 1955:203–261). These writings were intimately linked to Ortiz's lifelong preoccupation with *ñañiguismo* and *brujería*, but they decisively revised formerly pejorative evaluations of the objects with objectivizing scientific treatments. Ortiz's colleague Israel Castellanos relied upon the collections' *íreme* suits for an important 1928 article on *ñáñigo* material culture. Still, in their utilization of confiscated objects-cum-museum specimens as primary research material, Ortiz and Castellanos worked, in effect, one side of the same street on which police Inspector Roche y Monteagudo had walked his beat.[13] The overlap of contents in the published works of Roche, Ortiz, and Castellanos reflects the complementarity of their respective professional missions; between Cuba's founding and the 1920s, one hand washed the other. Police confiscations enabled scientific research on the relation of penal systems, delinquency and its profiling, and national health; in turn, these publications by recognized lawyers and doctors undoubtedly offered scientific rational and justification for further police prosecution and confiscation (e.g., Ortiz 1906).

Thus, by 1916, through his close study of the bodies of *brujos* and *ñáñigos* and their objects housed in the Bureau of Identification, Israel Castellanos formulated his scientific distinction between two principal forms of Cuban delinquency, *ñañiguismo* and *brujería*.[14] Armed with additional documents from emerging literature and Havana museum collections, the persistent Dr. Castellanos continued to reiterate his criminological theories and conclusions as late as 1937. The *brujo*, Castellanos argued, is a religious "fetishist" who uses charms *(embó)*[15] and conjures evil, but only rarely murders, and who does not stand in self-conscious, organized opposition to society's rules and government institutions. In contrast, the *ñáñigo* is, by nature, brutal and homicidal. Consciously opposed to the law and morality, the *ñáñigo* belongs to a despotic, mafia-like secret society organized by the sociopathic members of Cuba's evil underworld *(la hampa cubana/mala vida)*, that is, "*by the true microbes of the criminal world*, [conjoined] for the defense and vengeance of their brothers of association" (I. Castellanos 1916:10–15, emphasis added). *Ñañiguismo* was clearly a pathogen. Such classificatory schemes to distinguish *brujería* from *ñañiguismo* and other forms of delinquency also preoccupied the lawyer, penal theorist, ethnologist, and rising statesman Fernando Ortiz, though he was eventually taken to task by Afro-Cuban scholarly colleague Rómulo Lachatañére (1906–1952) for continuing to refer to the Yoruba-Lucumí Santería religion as *brujería* (see Ortiz 1939; Lachatañeré 1938, 1942, 1961).

The Missing Link

The first critical links between police confiscation and the appearance of *brujo* and *ñáñigo* objects in Cuban museums were Juan Francisco Steegers, the collector, and Israel Castellanos, the donor. For example, many of the key research examples used by Ortiz and Castellanos in their most important works on the Abakuá came from a single police raid. On May 20, 1914, the Marianao police, under the command of Sergeant Estanislao Mansip, raided a "celebration" in progress at the Efore Muna Tanze lodge in the poor neighborhood of Pogolotti. Confiscated were all of the *fambá*'s "indispensable attributes," including the *sese*, the Ekue, four altar staffs, the four orchestra drums, a carved ceremonial goblet used for *mokuba*, numerous *sacos de íreme* and their *sombreretas*, and other objects, such as a candelabra and crucifix (see figure 8.1; Roche y Monteagudo 1925:71; 1914:85, 89).[16] This was apparently the most successful raid in the entire history of *ñáñigo* prosecution. A police photograph taken at the scene places the proud *mulato* sergeant, outfitted in a uniform complete with epaulettes and a saber, sitting erect in the desecrated *fambá* before the collection of confiscated objects, including a gorgeous cowrie-encrusted *sese de copón* (figures 8.1, 9.4, and 9.5). Such "excellent service" apparently gained the sergeant a promotion to chief of police of Marianao (1925:73–74).

Juan Francisco Steegers held on to the Efore Muna Tanze objects pictured with Sergeant Mansip. Perhaps Steegers was convinced of their value for forensic science or was something of a police trophy buff; it would not be surprising if he did not keep selected objects on informal display in his Bureau of Identification offices, representing, in effect, the earliest exhibition of confiscated *brujería* and *ñañiguismo* pieces outside of the sacred temples themselves. In any event, the Efore Muna Tanze objects would form an important component, if not the core, of the *ñáñigo* donation that Israel Castellanos later made to the

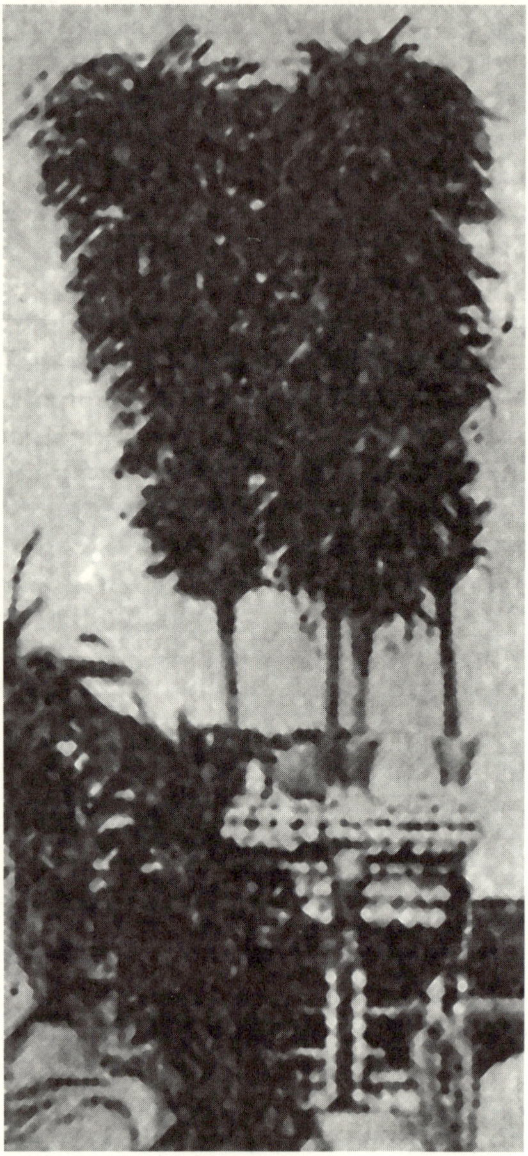

Figure 9.4. Enlargement for comparative purposes of the Efore Muna Tanze *sese* when confiscated by the police on 20 May 1914 in Marianao. The same *sese* appears in Roche y Monteagudo's 1914 edition of *La policía y sus misterios* (see figure 8.1) and was closely studied by Fernando Ortiz. This *sese* was studied in the Legal Medicine Museum by Fernando Ortiz (see figures 9.7, 9.11, 9.13).

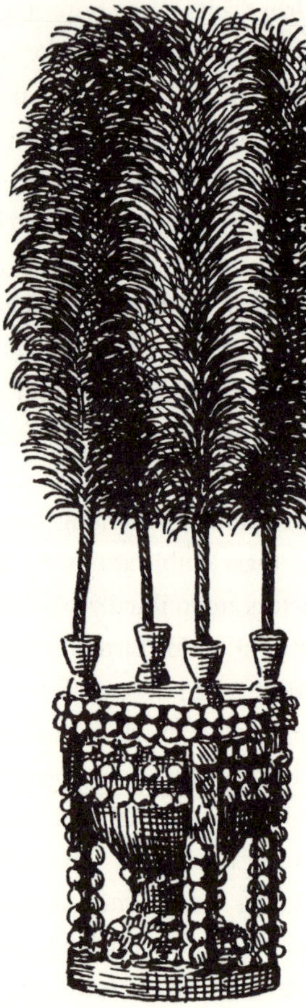

Figure 9.5. Thumbnail for comparative purposes of *El "Sese Eribó": El "Santísimo Sacramento" of the Ñáñigos.* Drawing of Efore Muna Tanze *sese* as it appeared in Roche y Monteagudo's 1914 and 1925 editions of *La policía y sus misterios.*

Museum of Legal Medicine. Clearly, the objects first pictured with Mansip in 1914 figured directly into this museum's earliest installations, which Castellanos and Ortiz illustrated in their 1928 and 1954 works, respectively: For example, Castellanos (1928) reproduces the extraordinary *saco de íreme* with the tripartite hood, possibly confiscated from Efore Muna Tanze (figure 9.6, left). Ortiz illustrates a museum-like tableau displaying the same gorgeous Efore Muna Tanze cowrie-encrusted *sese* with its "splendid" *plumeros,* as Roche y Monteagudo had noted (see Roche y Monteagudo 1925:71), along with the lodge's three symbol-topped staffs (Mokongo, Mosongo, Abasonga), the carved wood *mokuba* goblet, and the three-footed Ekue drum figure (Ortiz 1954:65–66; compare figures 8.1, 9.4, 9.5, and 9.7). Castellanos concentrated on five *ñáñigo* suits altogether, which had been confiscated by the authorities and exhibited in the Museum of Legal Medicine, in the first systematic study of Cuban *diablito* masquerade (1928:31–33; compare figure 9.8, first and second suits from right, with figure 9.9; see also figure 9.10). Many of these pieces have been on regular display at the Museum of Legal Medicine, apart from intermittent closings and relocations, for three-quarters of a century. All of the Efore Muna Tanze objects and another *saco de íreme* with a tripartite hood continue to be exhibited there today.[17]

Dr. Castellanos, the Laboratory, and *El Ñáñigo:* The Death of *Costumbrista* Arts

Though Israel Castellanos, as well as Fernando Ortiz, had published the Bureau of Identification's *brujería* objects before their subsequent donation and exhibition (see Ortiz 1973: figures 3–5; Castellanos 1916: figures 11–13), it was the collection of *íreme* suits displayed at the Museum of Legal Medicine, and perhaps at the National Museum, that appear in the literature's first scholarly analysis of this Abakuá genre. Characteristic of the kinds of cloistered scientific analyses that would, in many cases, plague Afro-Cuban studies until very recently,[18] Castellanos's 1928 "ethnographic"[19] investigation took place entirely within the laboratory and library setting. He apparently conducted very little fieldwork (see Moreno 1988; Sosa Rodríguez 1982; Quiñones 1994). Castellanos's careful documentation of the suits, in

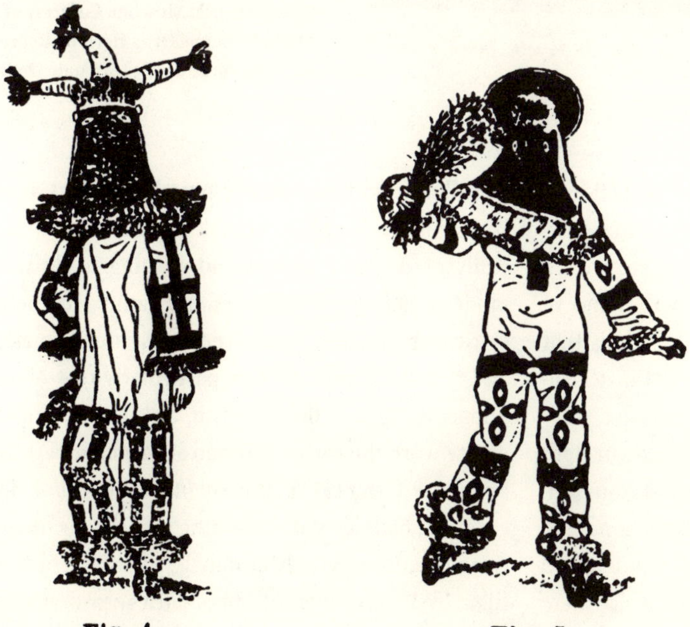

Fig. 4. Fig. 5.

Figure 9.6. Two arguably more "modern" *íreme* suits studied by Israel Castellanos (1928) in the Criminological Museum, now exhibited in the Casa de Africa Fernando Ortiz Collection (cf. plate 4, extreme right and left, respectively; see also plate 16, left). Castellanos concluded that these two suits were worn by "criollos," not Africans, because they were smaller in size and were more aesthetically elaborated. The constellations of four diamonds in Castellanos's figure 5 suggest the eyes of Tanze and Sikán and the Four Winds.

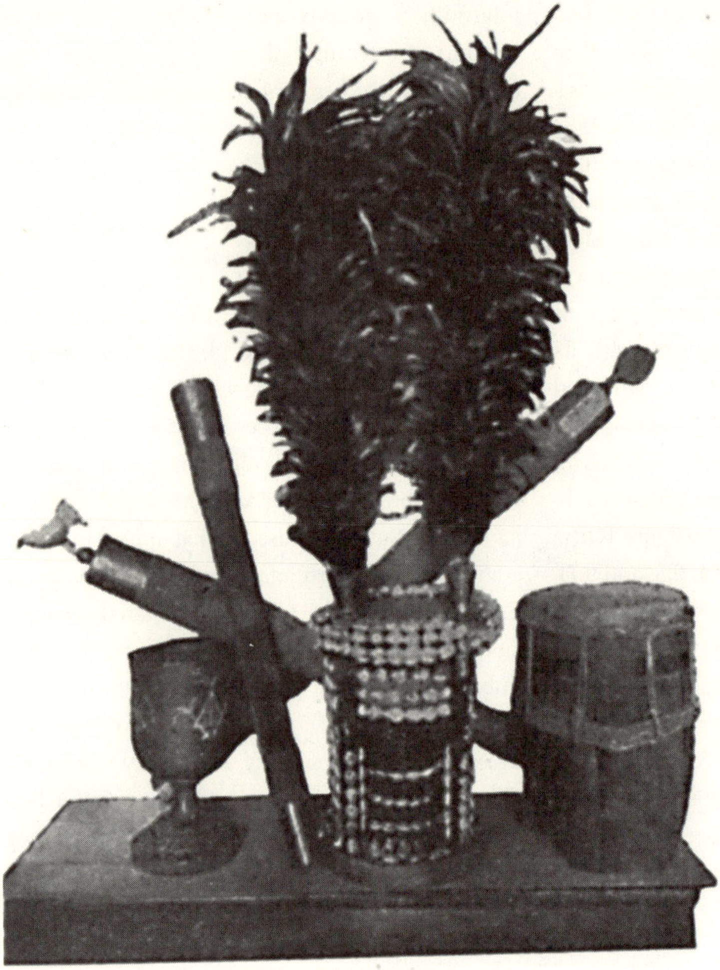

Fig. 293 — Un *eribó* con lujosa ornamentación de cauris, junto a otros utensilios rituales.

Figure 9.7. *"Fig. 293—An* eribó *with luxurious cowrie shell ornamentation, with other ritual implements."* These *sese* and Ekue drums, three altar staffs, and the wood *mokuba* goblet, here illustrated by Ortiz (1954:66, fig. 293), were likely displayed and photographed in the Criminological Museum, if not also before in the Bureau of Identification. The *sese,* staffs, and goblet (and possibly the Ekue drum) derive from the raid on Efore Muna Tanze on 20 May 1914. They were first published in the 1914 edition of Roche y Monteagudo's *La policía y sus mistérios.* The photograph was taken early on, likely in the 1920s, before the disintegration of the *sese*'s *plumeros* and the damaging of the finials by the time Ortiz studied the *sese* for his 1954 work (figure 9.11). The three staffs, the Ekue, and the goblet remain on exhibit today in the Criminological Museum. Courtesy of María Fernanda Ortiz Herrera, Representante Sucesores de Fernando Ortiz.

their distinct cloth types, measurements, patterns, and adornments, complete with analytical line drawings (figures 9.6, 9.9, and 9.10), has much to recommend it and remains consistent with the kind of close material culture description and analysis that undergirds ethnographic or art-historical investigation. Castellanos usefully sought to establish a chronology of suit types and changing emphases in cloth and adornment. Moreover, he discovered from diligent measurement of constituent suit sections that the costumes were typically based on standardized patterns, that is, cutout paper "molds," which were shared across Havana (Castellanos 1928:30–33).[20]

Still, the guiding methodological basis for Castellanos's ostensibly postcriminological "ethnographic" study of museum objects had nothing to do with modern, cultural relativist ethnography. His methods turned on nineteenth-century anthropometric and racialist pseudoscience, particularly that of Alphonse Bertillon, Rudolf Martin, and Henri Dumont, whose work the early Ortiz had studied and written about (see Ortiz 1914). Atavism indeed! Bertillon, for example, had devised a scientific method for identifying people, especially criminals, in 1879. The Bertillon System records anthropometric measurements and personal characteristics, including physical de-

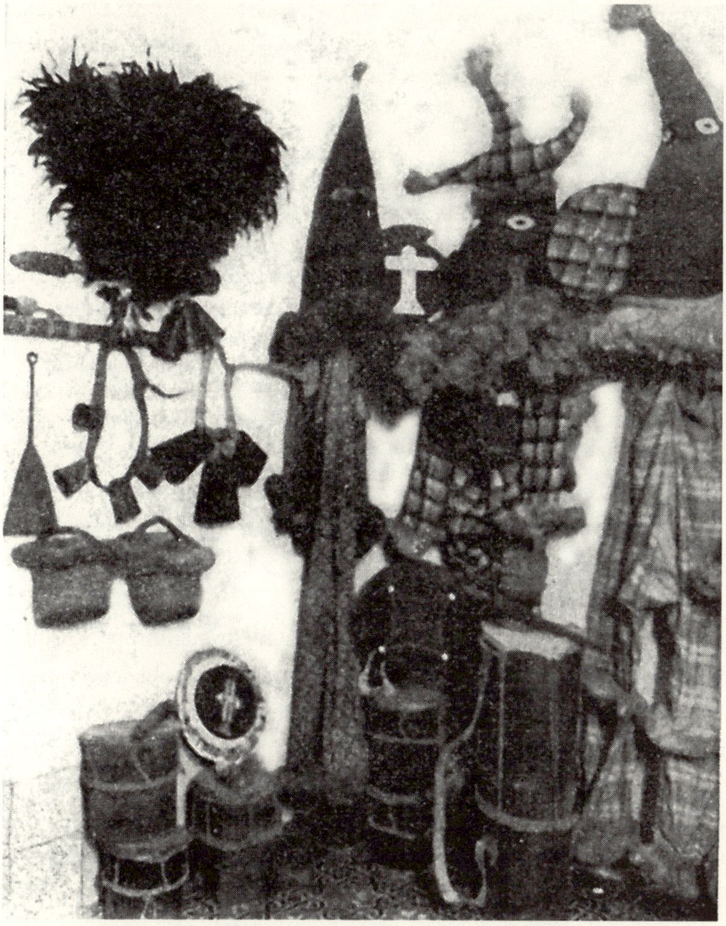

Figure 9.8. *Ñáñigo musical instruments confiscated by the authorities,* as illustrated in Ortiz 1954:16, fig. 272. Castellanos used these three *íreme* suits and all of the *sombreretas* in his 1928 study of "Diablitos Ñáñigos." From Castellanos's captioning, it is evident that these objects were in the Criminological Museum of the Faculty of Legal Medicine (see figure 9.9). The middle and right suits in the photograph correspond to Castellanos's figures 1 and 2, respectively (figure 9.9). The *sombreretas* with a large white cross, plaid cloth, and diamond design correspond to Castellanos's line-drawn figures 6, 7, 8, 9 respectively (see figure 9.10). The two cylindrical *maruga* shakers and the *ekón* iron bell likely also came from Efore Muna Tanze, if not also the other objects. Most are on display today in the Criminological Museum. Courtesy María Fernanda Ortiz Herrera, Representante Hererderos de Fernando Ortiz.

formities. Body measurements are made of the standing height, the reach from fingertip to fingertip, the length of the trunk and head, the length of the left foot, and so on. These are recorded on cards that are classified according to the length of the head. Unfortunately, the Bertillon System was seen as inexact, given the fact that changes in physical dimensions occur over the life cycle of a person, among other things. Therefore, fingerprinting methods, among them, the Galton-Henry method used by Steegers, decisively superseded Bertillon's anthropometry as the principal means of identification in American and European police systems. Still, in order to forge an historical argument about changes in *diablito* costumes, Castellanos relied on the same, already antiquated, Bertillon-like method, or some equivalent, along with the nineteenth-century anthropometric premise that each of the "races" of men is distinguished by significant bodily measurements. Thus, Castellanos worked backward from the *diablito* suits-as-material evidence to the supposed wearers and their respective races. Castellanos claimed to be able to distinguish between the "primitive suits" of "pure negro fabrication" and the "adulterated" suits of creole Cuban modification. The scientific method was Bertillon-like, but the lynchpin, in its racialized application, evidently owed to the work of Henri Dumont, a French doctor and anthropologist who treated and studied black slaves for many years on the plantations of the Oriente Province in Cuba. For example, Castellanos discovered that the height, waist, and inseam dimensions of particular *íreme*

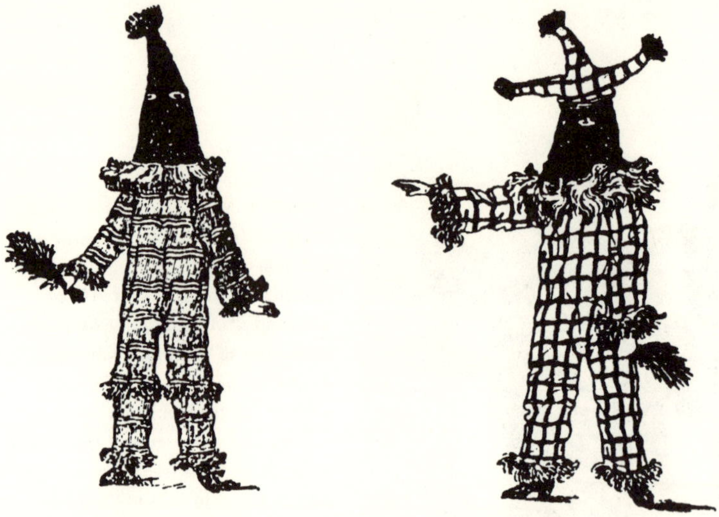

Fig. 1. Fig. 2.

Figure 9.9. Two arguably early *íreme* suits studied by Israel Castellanos: suit of *cotí* (cf. figure 9.8, right); the suit of white wool crisscrossed with blue, black, and yellow stripes is seen in figure 9.8, middle. The hood has three fringed points. Castellanos considered these to be "primitive" suits of the Africans, as they supposedly conformed to "negro" body size, based on the racialized anthropometric literature. Both were deposited in the Criminological Museum of the Faculty of Legal Medicine of the University of Havana.

suits corresponded to certain "negro body dimensions" that Dumont had published in an article in the famous Ortiz-directed journal *Revista Bimestre Cubana* called "Comparative Anthropology and Pathology of the Negro Slaves" (Dumont 1915–16; see also Dumont 1922). In contrast, "the newer suits . . . were smaller, and appear to have been made for subjects of smaller height, and for our studies, about the height of the races in Cuba. . . . We know that the *negro* adult is taller than the *mestizo* and the white adult is shorter than both of them. . . . Thus . . . even though the suit is shorter and is made through an African pattern, the height is adjusted to a *mulato* and *blanco,* and if it is put on a *negro* it will be too small" (I. Castellanos 1928:35–37). By 1928, Castellanos had become an expert in Dumont-style anthropology, having translated Dumont's major book-length work from French into Spanish in 1922.

Still, Castellanos was apparently unaware of or ignored the seminal work of anthropological revisionists Franz Boas and Melville J. Herskovits at Columbia during this period. With the intention of disengaging "race" and "culture," they demonstrated, partly by using anthropometry itself, that the head is infinitely plastic; there was no single "negro" physical type demonstrable through consistent body measurements. And, therefore, one could not assume that determinate sets of (inferior) socio-psychological characteristics corresponded to The Negro, in particular, and "races" in general (see Jackson 1986; see also Ap-

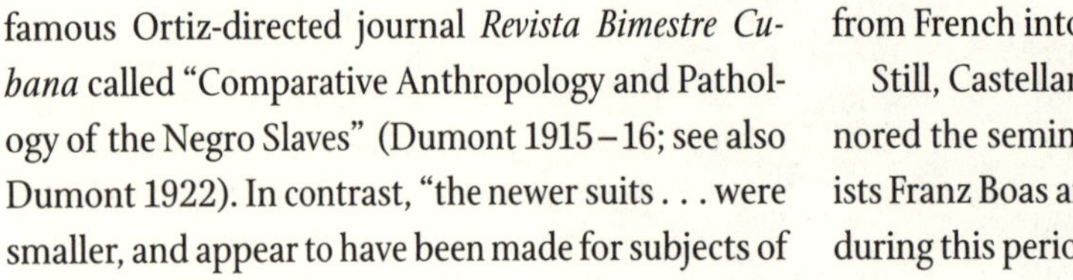

Figs. 6, 7, 8 y 9.

SOMBREROS DE DIABLITOS

6. Copa de cartón, cubierta de género, con una cruz en el interior de un triángulo.—7. Sombrero de cartón, revestido de lana blanca, con rayas negras.— 8. Cartón cubierto de tela negra. En la copa una gran cruz blanca.—9. Sombrero negro adornado con cordón y borlas.

Figure 9.10. *Sombreretas de Diablitos.* Illustrations of the *íreme* masquerade "hats" from the Criminological Museum studied by Israel Castellanos (1928; cf. figure 9.8). Fig. 6: Cloth-covered cardboard hat, with a cross inside a triangle; Fig. 7: Cardboard hat dressed in white wool, with black crossed stripes; Fig. 8: Cardboard covered with black cloth [with a] large white cross in the center; Fig. 9: Black hat adorned with cord and tassels.

piah 1992:28–84). In any event, one might be hard-pressed to apply Castellanos's measurement typologies to the extremely diverse Cuban population, let alone to the diverse West African peoples from which Cuba's African groups were constituted.

Still, despite its fatal scientific flaws, from an empirical point of view, Castellanos's 1928 piece remains not only an important primary document for marking Cuban scholars' shifting methodologies used to approach the Carabalí presence in Cuba; it also helps reveal shifts in the conceptual labor that the figure of the *ñáñigo*, in particular Landaluze's *El Ñáñigo*, played in the intellectual and popular imagination. Castellanos explicitly demarcates his scientific study from the *costumbrista* descriptive paradigm of the nineteenth century. Referring specifically to the *diablito* lithographs and paintings of Víctor Patricio de Landaluze, he writes, "the flamboyant diablito, *the supreme incarnation of ñañiguismo*, through its various colors, inspired literary and artistic focus and produced images of exquisite beauty. *But the pen, the pencil, and the brush would not give the solid ethnographic notion that flows from clear and scientific observation*" (1928:37, emphasis added). What Landaluze could capture only in pen and brush from fleeting glimpses on the street, Castellanos could rigorously submit to specimen analysis, thanks to the *diablito*'s literal capture by the police, its conservation in the Bureau of Identification, and its subsequent collection by the Museum of Legal Medicine. Of course, Castellanos compares apples and oranges, since the Basque's mission was artistic and his results served the exotic purposes of the *costumbrista* genre for elite, peninsular, and larger international readerships. Castellanos's institutional positionality, disciplinary concerns, and ostensible methodology were different in form and substance. Landaluze marked Cuban creole difference with his pen and brush; as an artist, he lived and let live. In 1916, Castellanos had marked the island's internal otherness with racialized, identificatory methodologies, in order that the Cuban nation live, while the others—in but not of the nation—might die, or at least spend their degraded lives in prison or exile. In contrast, in the 1928 "ethnographic" piece, Castellanos is concerned not with documenting quaint "types and customs," but with "ethnography" based in specific material evidence—clothes—that indexes innate differences between racial types. Secondly, Castellanos's claim to scientific rigor also implicitly distinguishes his methodology, and the conceptual labor performed by *El Ñáñigo*, from the writings of Roche y Monteagudo and his predecessor in the police chronicle genre, Trujillo y Monagas. For these two policemen, *El Ñáñigo* and other attributes served as a kind of evidence, but within the narrower agenda of extinguishing a group whose behavior was illegal under laws of unlawful assembly and conspiracy. *Ñáñigo* objects were, in one sense, simple indexes of the conditions and consequences of delinquent behavior. If you get together with a group of men and are caught with particular kinds of objects, you will be charged with illegal assembly, labeled a *ñáñigo*, and made to suffer tremendously. At the same time, as keys—secret fetishes—in *ñáñigo* hands, altar objects and *diablito* suits enabled "militant" criminal actions. As confiscated, along with the jailing and deportation of their owners, the objects indexed the extinction of *ñañiguismo* and the restoration of the status quo.

In sum, Castellanos's approach—already an atavism itself in 1928—excludes certain categories of cultural and artistic representation as interesting or legitimate, as exotic to the scientific enterprise; Landaluze's realism is of no use to the descriptive ("ethnographic") project, though Ortiz would later have disagreed (see 1953). Moreover, former street cops turned administrators such as Roche y Monteagudo and Trujillo never got to know the real possibilities of the objects they confiscated—they weren't professional scientists; they never looked beyond the surface. It may be, in fact, that Dr. Castellanos himself sensed his own obsolescence in 1928. His article "El Diablito Ñáñigo" was published not in a legal-medicine journal but in Ortiz's *Archivos del folklore cubano*, perhaps his way of arguing for the value of forensic science when *ñañiguismo* and other things *afro* had already shifted from criminal evidence to "folkloric" artifact. Perhaps it was only through the good graces of his old friend Fernando Ortiz that he got to publish at all.

Fernando Ortiz: The *Sese de Copón* and Transculturation

The confiscated Efore Muna Tanze *sese de copón* is probably the most complexly built and richly adorned example anywhere in the literature (figures 9.5 and 9.7). Through the works of Roche and Ortiz, it also has become the most studied and published. The Pogolotti raid enabled Roche y Monteagudo to add a new chapter, along with more illustrations and photographs, to his 1914 and 1925 editions of *La policía y sus mistérios* (1914:85, 89; 1925:36, 70–73). Roche titled his 1925 chapter "The Profanation of May 20th" for the great blow the raid had supposedly dealt to *ñañiguismo.* This same raid and confiscation furnished Fernando Ortiz with such abundant data that he was able to launch a global comparative argument about changes in the form and content of the *sese* drum, a keystone of his historical account of Abakuá altar objects and creole changes in Cuban society (1954:66–80). Theoretically informed by his idea of "transculturation," Ortiz was able to compare the Museum of Legal Medicine's Efore Muna Tanze "creole goblet-*sese*" with an "archaic" *sese* of the squat and cylindrical "African form" along with examples observed during his fieldwork in Cárdenas and Guanabacoa—indeed, at a *plante* at Efore Muna Tanze's own godfather lodge, Ebión Efó, on August 13, 1927 (1954:55–59, 62–64; figures 6.11, 9.7, 9.11, and 9.12). Ortiz studied the "archaic" African *sese,* a marvelous piece adorned with purple velvet, silk fringe, and cowrie shells, at the Montané Museum of Anthropology (figure 9.12). It had been confiscated by the police during the first year of the new nation, 1902, and was used as evidence by the "Court of Havana in criminal case number 285/1902, prosecuted for the crime of illicit association" (Ortiz 1954:64).

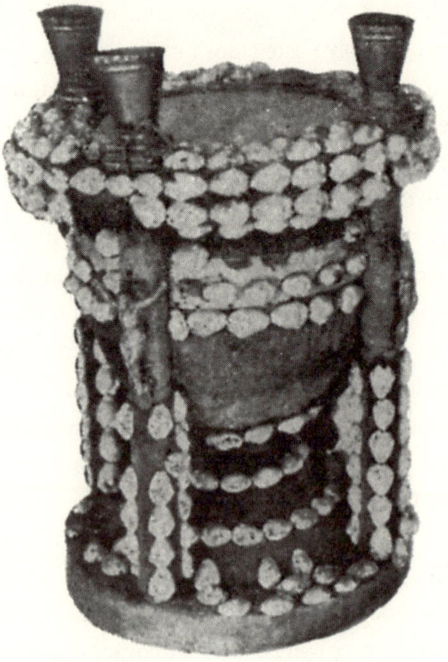

Fig. 294 — Estado actual del *eribó* de la Fig. 293.

Figure 9.11. *"Fig. 294—Present state of the eribó of Fig. 293."* The damaged Efore Muna Tanze Sese in the early 1950s (as illustrated in Ortiz 1954:67). Note that its cowrie shells are turned "mouths" inward, so as to "guard" rather than "reveal" the "secret." Note also the Dead Christ figure attached to each column. Compare with earlier photograph (figure 9.7) and police line drawing made at the time of its 1914 confiscation (figures 5.6 and 9.5). Courtesy of María Fernanda Ortiz Herrera, Representante Sucesores de Fernando Ortiz.

The museum-accessioned *seses* of Efore Muna Tanze and other lodges provided indispensable data on drum-form history. Yet, perhaps the greatest contributions came in Ortiz's unprecedented study of the *seses'* interior construction and contents. During a police confiscation thirty years before the period of Ortiz's writing (ca. 1920), "the drumskin of the *sese copón* had broken," and the ethnologist was able to examine the sealed goblet's sacred contents, which had been prepared, of course, under the strictest secrecy, by the lodge's *brujo,* Nasakó. "It was seen that its interior was divided into four parts, or receptacles, by means of crossed wood tablets. . . . Each one of those four square holes [quadrants] had a de-

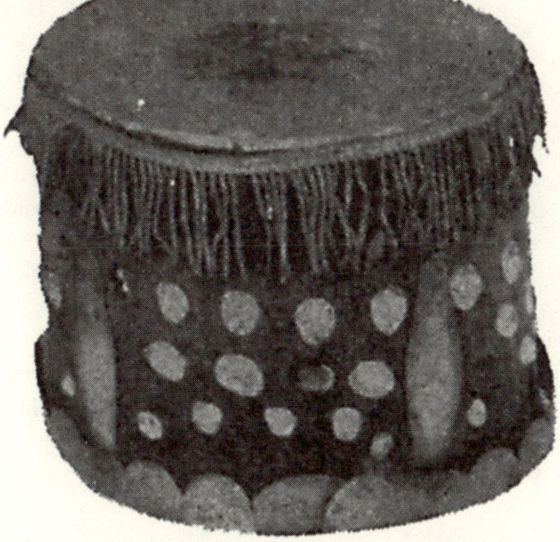

Fig. 291 — *Eribó* adornado con cauris.

Figure 9.12. *"Fig. 291—*Eribó *adorned with cowries."* Ortiz used this "archaic . . . African style" *eribó* in the Montané Anthropological Museum to trace the "transculturation" of this drum type through time, which, he argued, developed in the Efó branch into the goblet *sese* (Ortiz 1954:64). Courtesy of María Fernanda Ortiz Herrera, Representante Sucesores de Fernando Ortiz.

posit of obscure material, shapeless and impossible to identify. Years later we could learn that that was, in effect, the 'charge' of the *sese*" (1954:75).

"Years later" apparently refers to Ortiz's close study of the Efore Muna Tanze *sese de copón* in the Museum of Legal Medicine. Given inadequate storage conditions, the "extraordinarily adorned" *sese* had horribly deteriorated between its photographic documentation when first exhibited and its 1954 publication in Ortiz's *Los instrumentos.* The *plumeros* had "rotted" away, and one of the four flared slots for the plumes around the drumhead had broken off (cf. figures 9.7 and 9.11). Though unfortunate for this great "mother" of Efore Muna Tanze's members—a masterpiece that even the hard-boiled Roche y Monteagudo had characterized as "artistic" and "splendid" (1925:71)—it was still the holy grail for what were, by 1923, called "folklore" studies.

Ortiz's 1954 text uses a series of photographic figures, from different views, of the Efore Muna Tanze *sese,* which "has been opened [and] its cover separated from its body." Ortiz was able to draw conclusions laid out in the culmination of his eighty-five-page chapter, which remain the standard today (1954:66–80; see figures 9.11 and 9.13). Through close laboratory examination that he correlated with his field research, Ortiz identified the *sese*'s contents as four specific *cargas,* each of which empowered and protected one of the four *obones* of the lodge (1954: 75–76). The presence and kinds of *carga* enabled Ortiz to substantiate his observations of the morphological differences between the *brujería*-driven Efó *sese namokimbán* of Andrés Petít and the "empty *sese*" of the Efí branch. As well, he could now conclude that *ñáñigo* ceremonies "are fundamentally of a magical character," permitting him to revise old-style anthropological conjectures that they were part of "sexual and agrarian rites, that is, reproductive and resurrectional mysteries related to the harvest, the hunt, men's initiations or 'rites of passage' and the evocation of the dead" (1954: 67–68).

Under modern ethnological analysis, had Fernández Carrillo's "brilliant light of the sun" finally penetrated the innermost recesses of the "dark" *ñáñigo* secret, the "mysterious" *carga* of the Abakuá "Holy Sacrament"? Not entirely. Fernando Ortiz, as a theoretically self-conscious researcher, remained aware of the epistemological and practical limits of the sci-

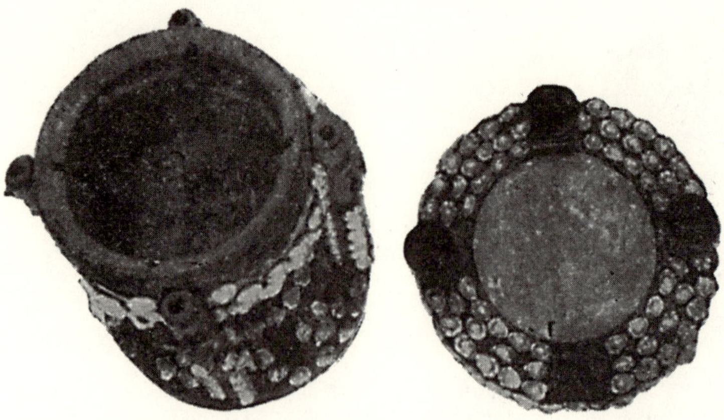

Fig. 295 — La caja abierta y la tapa del *eribó* de la Fig. 293.

Figure 9.13. *"Fig. 295—The open vessel and the top of the* eribó *of Fig. 293."* Illustration of the confiscated Efore Muna Tanze cowrie-encrusted goblet *sese* in the Criminological Museum, as opened by Fernando Ortiz for his 1954 study. By opening the *sese,* Ortiz discovered the contents of its various *cargas,* and, thereby, determined that it contained protective material for each of the four *obones* of the lodge. In turn, he concluded that Abakuá "rites" were of a "fundamentally . . . magical character" (Ortiz 1954:67–68). Courtesy of María Fernanda Ortiz Herrera, Representante Sucesores de Fernando Ortiz.

entific enterprise. Ortiz knew when he had hit a wall. Though a lawyer, professor, and statesman, he was neither an Andrés Petít nor the Abakuá officer who confects the *sese*'s contents. While the opened Efore Muna Tanze goblet permitted him to "observe the interior of the *sese,*" he had not really "discovered a secret," he conceded. For *"what is missing is the real secret . . . the word of Nasakó"* (1954:76, emphasis added). Nasakó, after all, held the spiritual key to the "light inside." As in Fernández Carrillo's assessment of Landaluze's *El Ñáñigo,* the form had been captured, but *El Ñáñigo* remained mysteriously "quiet." Don José Trujillo y Monagas was desperate to hear it "speak," but neither he nor his successors would be so lucky. In the laboratory, *ekue* was silent. This improbable task would be left to the emerging field of Cuban "folklore" studies as developed by Lydia Cabrera, Ortiz's sister-in-law, who published *The Abakuá Secret Society: Narrated by Old Adepts* in 1958.

Conclusion

Without doubt, the contexts and motivations for the raids and confiscations on suspected *brujo* and *ñáñigo* houses are to be found in the tense, and often violent, social and political struggles during the first two or more decades of the nation: black disenfranchisement and the government's backlash against the political organizing of people of color after the Second War of Independence, culminating in the massacres of 1912, propaganda-driven hysteria over the alleged ritual killings of white children by black *brujos* in Havana and Matanzas, the August Revolution against Cuba's first government of Tomás Estrada Palma (1906), which brought the second American occupation, and the visible social and political power of the Abakuá Society in relation to Cuba's increasingly U.S.-dominated economy (see Helg 1995:169–226; Pérez 1988:391; Palmié 2002:218–225). Still, although these contexts help explain the confiscation of, and earliest writings about, *ñáñigo* and *brujo* objects from 1906 to 1916, changing ideas about the objects' significances led to their donation, and use in publications, well after the 1920s. Early on, Fernando Ortiz illustrated the objects of *brujería* in social scientific arguments for wiping out "centers of infection" within the new nation (1906). Roche y Monteagudo simply did his job, with extreme prejudice, of course, illustrating the objects in order to educate cops and trumpet their successes against the mysterious criminal hydra. In 1916, following President Menocal's violent assault on *brujería* and *ñañiguismo,* Castellanos produced his scientific study of black atavism and stigmata—not only offering the diagnostics of what today is called "racial profiling," but also reinforcing the basis for a eugenic program, which began with Ortiz's early works in penology and criminal ethnology.

Clearly, *ñáñigo* and *brujo* objects in the great national university's museums would help train the next generations of doctors in legal medicine, so their talents could be applied where most needed, including in the continued war against the "dark of night," wherever it lifted its ugly head. At the same time, ideas about the significance of the objects began to change with the emergence of more liberal and radical cultural ideas starting in the early 1920s. In the hands of Fernando Ortiz and his colleagues, *ñáñigo* and *brujo* objects would come to perform a different conceptual labor: they became documents to substantiate Ortiz's "transculturation" theory in relation to the Cuban nation's distinctive creole, or *mestizo,* identity—particularly its difference from Europe and the United States. For Castellanos in 1928, albeit in the bristling language of "adulteration," and for Ortiz between 1923 and the end of his life, *El Ñáñigo* and the *sese de copón* could illuminate the alchemy of Cubanidad in the mixing of the "white" and the "negro."

10 From Atavism to Modern Primitivism

By 1920, Landaluze's *El Ñáñigo* had reemerged, this time within Fernando Ortiz's historical analysis of the old "Day of Kings" carnival (1920). Instead of figuring atavism and blight in Cuba's history, Landaluze's 1881 *El Ñañigo* illustrates a vital component of old-style African "nation" carnival performance, a signal event in a national narrative just beginning its revision. *El Ñáñigo* thus graduated, though quite tentatively in 1920, toward the role of folkloric personage. It is true that the early 1920s Ortiz still regarded the *diablitos* as the "demagogic fetish priests" of the old African *cabildos.* And carnival's creole features, such as the sartorial splendor of royal *cabildo* personnel on parade, were little more than an "imitation" of the whites. Still, Ortiz respectfully regarded the nations' internal organization, protocols, fraternal values of mutual aid, and the "drum dances—inoffensive and so appreciated by the Africans" (Ortiz 1960:22, 33; 1921:29–31). Indeed, writing in a companion article of 1921, Ortiz wished that the mutual-aid dimension of the *cabildos* had survived into the Republic, rather than the thinly veiled, "savage animist fetishism" at the rotten core of the Afro-Cuban "houses" or "temples." The colonial government's suppression of the *cabildos* in the era of emancipation merely had driven these African atavisms underground, from whence they reemerged as the scourge of the new nation.[1] This thesis, along with an increasing fascination with the laudable cultural dimension of colonial black life, went a long way toward the recuperation of carefully selected aspects of *lo afrocubano*—singing, drumming, and dancing, in particular—as "inoffensive" folklore suitable even for the consumption of Cuba's middle class and foreign visitors.

By the mid-1920s, Ortiz had penned unprecedented, ethnographically neutral pieces on Afro-Cuban sociocultural institutions (1921), vernacular language (1924a), cuisine (1923), and folkloric figures (1924b). The great Cuban historian Julio de la Riverend notes Ortiz's "rupture with criminal and juristic studies" during this period, which was signaled by a decisive shift away from the analysis of Cuban culture in terms of social pathology (de la Riverend quoted in Moore 1997:38), toward a pluralist consideration of its contribution to Cuban national culture. Though *costumbrista* arts had been dismissed by Ortiz's early scientific colleague as useless for "ethnographic" inquiry, Ortiz resurrected them as significant documents for historical folklore study. Thus, he prominently featured Landaluze's 1881 *El Ñáñigo* in his illustrations for the "Old Festival of the 'Day of Kings,'" first published in 1920 and reprinted as a small book in 1960. In the 1960 edition, the illustration shares a page with a reproduction of an 1838 painting by the French *costumbrista* Pierre Toussaint Frédéric Miahle. Previously isolated within Roche y Monteagudo's police narrative, not to mention against Landaluze's own seamless background itself, *El Ñáñigo* now gains contextualization within Ortiz's analysis of the institutions and meanings of historical carnival. In other words, as paired with Miahle's dramatic horizontal street scene of multifarious *diablitos* and dancers, *El Ñáñigo* leaps off the page as a stellar example of carnival performance, of a vital and valid historical Afro-Cuban *culture.* Moreover, the work locates *El Ñáñigo* within a set of transatlantic and regional performance genres. Finally, Ortiz went far in revealing the pejorative term *diablito* as a function of the dominant peninsular language and attitude, providing, in turn, a host of appropriate, culturally specific Black Atlantic terms for a range of maskers, such as *moko jumbia, culona, mojiganga, bacumbi, vegigante, egungún, John Canoe,* and, most important, a Carabalí-Abakuá term for certain *íreme* masquerades, *amirifimo* [*sic*] (1960:21–33; see *Efimeremé* and *Efimeremo* in Cabrera 1988:150–151). Undoubtedly of African origin, the multifarious maskers of the *cabildo* "nations" had been labeled "little devils" by observers whose frame of reference was the individual "grotesque" masquerade tradition of historical Iberian and colonial Catholic festival. "Surely," Ortiz explains, "upon having to name them, the whites found in the motley disguises, leaps and cabrioles, horns and masks, of the Africans, a certain analogy to the *diablitos,* or masks simulating the devil, which long ago accompanied the Catholic Corpus Christi processions in Cuba, as in Spain and other countries" (Ortiz 1960:29). In short, within Ibero-Cuban hierarchies of civilization, the Abakuá *íreme,* liturgy, and institutions had been discursively assigned to, and imprisoned within, the "savage slot" (Troulliot 1991).

Ortiz's reshaping of *El Ñáñigo*'s identity and status cannot be underestimated. His vast writings on every aspect of Cuban society, his central participation in seminal national organizations, his role in the reform of Cuban law, and his occupations as lawyer, professor, and diplomatic consul placed him among the most venerated figures of his generation and Cuban intellectual history as a whole. Among the larger progressive movement within Cuban society in the 1920s and 1930s, Ortiz and his colleagues formed one important constituency among a multidisciplinary cultural front of writers, artists, poets, scientists, searching for resources that would foster "national renovation and reaffirmation" (see Martínez 1994:37–46; Blanc 1992:54–57).

The national renovation movement (1923–34), known as the "revolutionary acclamation of the patria," represented a direct response to perceived oppressive patterns of the old colonial system, "foreign domination, crass materialism, blatant social inequality, and government malfeasance." The most immediate political targets were the corrupt governments of President Alfredo Zayas (1921–24), whose first three years in office came under the direct control of U.S. special envoy General Enoch H. Crowder, and the dictator Gerardo Machado (1924–33), who was deposed in the triumphant *machadato* of 1933 (see Pérez 1988:392–394).[2] In socioeconomic perspective, the "fantastic sugar prices" during World War I and the "horizontal consolidation" of U.S. control of the Cuban sugar industry by 1922 had created the ostentatious and materialistic "Dance of the Millions" during the early 1920s. Social inequality, the immiseration of the rural proletariat, and black disenfranchisement were outstanding features of the period. The collapse of sugar prices and general economic instability and depression were key economic factors in increasing national discontent and revolutionary stirrings during the 1930s (see Ayala 1999: 23–47, 182, 203–220, 231–247). Given ongoing neocolonial control of Cuba by the United States, politically cemented through the Platt Amendment and corporate ownership, cultural movements associated with national renovation, such as "Afro-Cubanism" and "Black Poetry," were intended to provide "antidotes to Wall Street" through the tropes of blackness and *mestizaje* (Kutzinski 1993:134–162).[3]

Still, though Fernando Ortiz stood at the forefront of many new organizations, such as the Society of Cuban Folklore and the Junta of National Renovation (both founded in 1923),[4] he remained more conservative and pro–North American than other Cuban writers. Culturally, though fascinated with things Afro-Cuban, he continued to valorize primarily Hispanic and European culture from an elite perspective. Indeed, as Robin Moore suggests, though Ortiz employed the term *ajiaco* (stew) as a felicitous metaphor for Cuban cultural mixture *(mestizaje)*, he continued to stress through the early 1950s the need to discard lingering African as well as lower-class Spanish "atavisms," which putrefied rather than lent wholesome flavor to the national stew (Palmié 1998).[5] In my reading, Ortiz's progressive agenda for the nation, in many ways based in neo-evolutionist ideas, hampered his much-lauded theory of "transculturation." The idea of transculturation has the potential to be a nonhierarchical, culturally relativist process of mutual influence rather than the Eurocentric though "progressive" program that it was: that of "raising" *lo afrocubano* through successive levels of wholesome *cubanidad* that other groups had already ostensibly achieved (Palmié 1998:368–371; see Ortiz 1973: 242). Indeed, central ideas undergirding transculturation theory can be found in the seminal nineteenth-century Cuban progressive writings of José Antonio Saco y López (1797–1879) and creole planter Francisco de Arango y Parreño (1765–1837), who stressed the "positive effects of racial intermarriage," envisioning a "plan . . . to whiten our negroes." As Arango y Parreño continued, "Nature herself shows us the simplest and most certain path to this end. She shows us that black yields to white and that it disappears if one continues mixing both races. Let us protect these mixtures instead of preventing them and let us qualify their offspring to enjoy all civil rights to the full. In my opinion this measure is worth more than all others that could be taken for the present and future security of Cuba" (quoted in Martínez-Alier 1974: 35; see also p. 37). Ortiz's "transculturation" of the 1920s onward continued to rely on a hidden "blood based logic" (Apter 1991:238), rearticulating notions of mixture's positive social effects in modern cultural terms. Between the lines, "transculturation" meant cleansing black culture of its atavisms in order to convert it to modern "folklore" in the service of the new nation.[6] The forms of Afro-Cuban culture Ortiz chose to show the public—the old-style "inoffensive" singing, drumming, and dancing—were appropriate for middle-class consumption (Moore 1984:39–47).

Though bold and unprecedented, and demonstrative of his crucial shift from exclusively archival research to interaction with living culture bearers, Ortiz's presentation of "authentic" Lucumí *batá* drum music on the stage in 1937 (see Ortiz 1938; 1954: 235–238) in fact constituted a new, elite audience and readership for this African religious material now valorized as "folkloric." On the whole, staged *afrocubanismo* remained disconnected from the ritual systems still considered by the majority to be malign "witchcraft" *(brujería* and *ñañiguismo)*. True, Ortiz earnestly founded the Society for Afrocuban Studies along with Nicolás Guillén, Emilio Roig de Leuchenring, Emilio Ballagas, José Luciano Franco, Israel Castellanos, Teodoro Ramos Blanco,[7] and other luminaries of arts, letters, and science in 1937 on the principle of "objective criteria" in the research of Afro-Cuban culture. Echoing key humanistic and democratic themes of José Martí as well as Saco and Arango y Parreño, their platform emphasized the "coexistence of diverse races in Cuba" and vowed to "achieve greater egalitarian interaction among the diverse components of the Cuban nation, in order to move toward the felicitous realization of their common historical destinies" (see Rubin 1998:32; Roldán 1940:1059).

Still, some ideas die hard. Five years after the founding of the Society of Cuban Folklore, nineteenth-century racialist, evolutionary, and criminological theories continued to raise their ugly heads as seen in Israel Castellanos's 1928 *diablito* article. Though Ortiz had dropped criminal ethnology by 1930, its theoretical baggage exerted its influence on others through at least 1937, while Israel Castellanos reigned as the director of the country's Bureau of Identification. Indeed, in the same year that Castellanos cofounded the Society for Afrocuban Studies with Ortiz, he republished his bizarre *La brujería y el ñañiguismo* criminology text (1916), now titled *Afro-Cuban Legal Medicine and Criminology.* Castellanos faithfully cites as precedents José Trujillo y Monagas, Cesare Lombroso, Henri Dumont, and, not least, the Ortiz of the *Negros brujos* period. An indication of how backward Castellanos remained is seen in a peculiar internationalist gesture to the Black Atlantic that departs from that of the *afrocubanismo* cultural movements in Cuba. Castellanos dedicates his 1937 work to the famous Brazilian psychologist Dr. Arthur Ramos, "who, in his beautiful volumes on the bio-sociological manifestations of the *negro* in his country, has cited our humble contribution to Afro-Cuban ethnography." Whereas a generation of progressive artists, writers, and intellectuals was celebrating Afro-Cuban and Abakuá cultural themes in its works, such as the first modern Afro-Cuban-style novel by Alejo Carpentier (*Ecue Yamba O!* 1933), Castellanos dwells on bio-sociological atavisms. Unsurprisingly, he chose a familiar figure as the frontispiece to *Afro-Cuban Legal Medicine and Criminology.*

Landaluze's brightly painted *diablito* of ca. 1878 opens Castellanos's tedious publication on the delinquency of Cuban *ñáñigos* and *brujos.* Whereas Ortiz had recontextualized *El Ñáñigo* by pairing it with Mialhe's exuberant 1838 street scene, Castellanos surgically removes Landaluze's *diablito* by cutting it out of the artist's charming Day of Kings street scene and pasting it onto a bleak white background as "Figure 1" like a butterfly specimen (figure 10.1; compare with plate 20). Clearly, in order to reiterate the fetishistic and atavistic background of the island's Afro-Cubans, Castellanos directly followed Landaluze's *diablito* with an old photograph of a bare-chested "African Curandero Type" (figure 10.2). On its own, and in our time, the document could be a handsome and sympathetic representation of an African elder. However, given its location in this criminological context, direct comparison with Havana's contemporary Afro-Cubans would not have been lost on Castellanos's readers. African-style dress—head ties and beads—had been standard fixtures on Havana's streets and

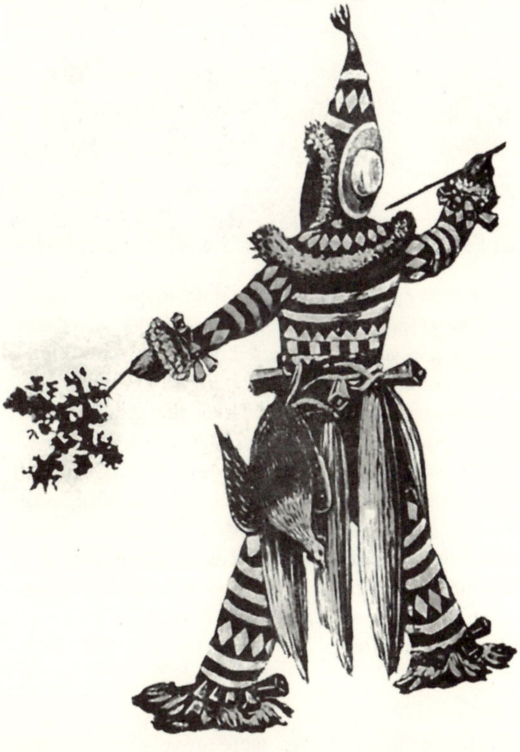

Figure 10.1. ***"Fig. 1—El*** **diablito** ***o*** **írime** ***of the Ñáñigos."*** **Frontispiece to Israel Castellanos's 1937** ***Afro-Cuban Legal Medicine and Criminology.*** **Castellanos cut and pasted a version of the** ***El Ñáñigo*** **figure from a ca. 1878 oil by Victor Patricio de Landaluze (see plate 20). The original painting features this pacific figure standing before a charmed middle-class family during Carnival, while its recontextualization isolates the figure as a specimen and constitutes it as the apotheosis of Abakuá delinquency. Courtesy of María Fernanda Ortiz Herrera, Representante Sucesores de Fernando Ortiz.**

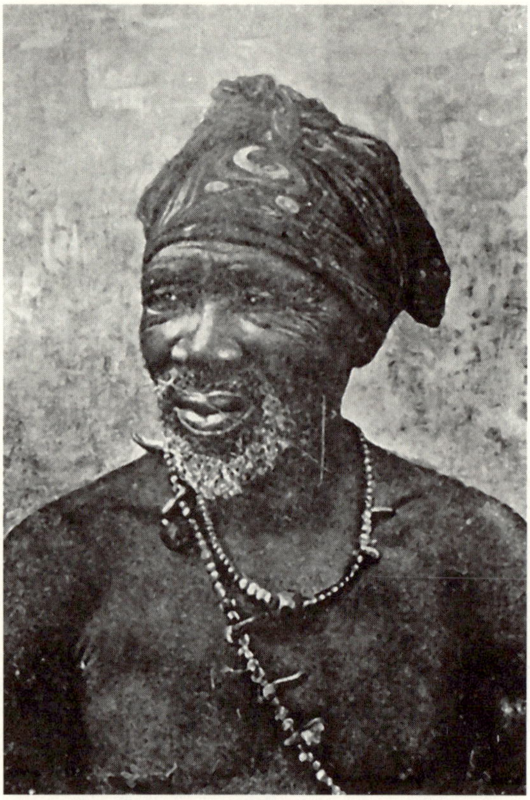

Figure 10.2. *"Fig. 2—Type of African healer, according to Hutchinson."* The second illustration in Castellanos's 1937 *Afro-Cuban Legal Medicine and Criminology.* It directly follows the Landaluze masquerade of figure 10.1, suggesting the twin terms of *ñáñiguismo* and *brujería* in Cuba, and that primitive African magic is behind the Cuban *ñáñigo.* The African features, headtie, and beads would not have been lost on a Cuban audience as references to ordinary black Cubans, as well as sorcerers. Despite the elegance and dignity of the subject, as we see it today, before the mid-nineteenth century it would have been interpreted by general audiences in Cuba as a frightening presence, a sorcerer capable of kidnapping and ritually killing white children.

plantations for centuries, were universally described in *costumbrista* works, and, more insidiously, were stereotypical fixtures of the vernacular blackface theater in the nineteenth and twentieth centuries, the equivalents of chicken, watermelon, and banjos in American minstrelsy (figures 10.3, 10.4).

During the thick of national reform, the twin demons still apparently cast a pall over Havana and peopled the nightmares of middle- and upper-class white Cubans. Elite white Cubans raised during the 1930s through the 1950s remember their parents' near-hysterical prohibition against going anywhere near the window, let alone going outside, on the feast days celebrated by Afro-Cubans. Parents feared their children being shot, knifed, kidnapped, or *embrujado*—that is, ensorcelled. In short, the *brujo* and the *ñáñigo* remained the bogeymen of Cuban cultural fantasy through the 1950s, if not later, lurking just behind the scrim of aestheticized folkloric representation.[8] Still, a number of courageous Cubans began asking what was wrong with this picture. For example, the Afro-Cuban anthropologist Rómulo Lachatañeré sharply critiqued Fernando Ortiz's pejorative usage of *brujo* and published sympathetic ethnographies on Afro-Cuban religious traditions and their contemporary presence (see Ortiz 1939; Lachatañeré 1938, 1942, 1961).

At the cultural forefront of the national renovation movement was Grupo Minorista, founded in 1923. Counted among its core members were Cuba's most renowned minds in arts, letters, and sciences, such as the lawyer, journalist, and Marxist historian Emilio Roig de Leuchenring, the poet, lawyer, and socialist Juan Marinello Vidaurreta, the novelist and ethnomusicologist Alejo Carpentier, the oil painter Jorge Mañach, and numerous other avant-garde artists, all born around the turn of the last century (see Suchlicki 2001). Though not formal members of Grupo Minorista, the elders Fernando Ortiz and Enrique José Varona (1849–1933) acted as the group's mentors and consultants. Grupo Minorista's members were greatly influenced by the progressive, antiauthoritarian ideals of José Martí's "Our America" (1891).[9] The group's writers and artists began to translate into "narrative or symbolic form the sociopolitical preoccupations of its generation" (Martínez 1994:48). In particular, they focused on the injustices Cubans had experienced during years of dominance from abroad (the United States) and corruption and political tyranny at home (the Zayas administration of 1920–24 and that of Machado, 1924–33).

The artists and writers among Grupo Minorista

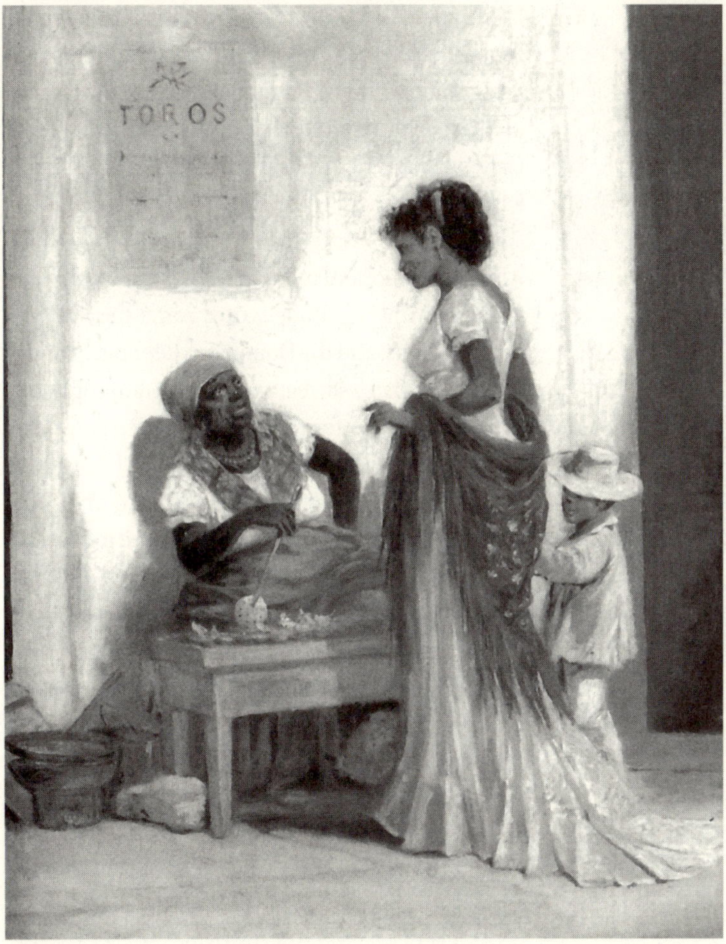

Figure 10.3. Víctor Patricio de Landaluze, *La Bollera,* ca. 1878–80, oil on canvas, 36 × 28 cm. Landaluze depicts the colorful everyday street scene of an African vendor of fritters, dressed in typical headtie, necklaces, full skirts, and colorful *pañuelo* about the shoulders. The customer and her son, in contrast, are of the higher *mulata* class, likely free creoles. Courtesy of the Museo Nacional de Bellas Artes, Havana.

were aware of modernist movements in the United States (including the Harlem Renaissance), Paris (postimpressionism, cubism, fauvism, expressionism, and surrealism), Mexico (themes of vernacular expression and socialist revolution in modern muralism), and the Caribbean (Negritude literature). It has become a commonplace in the contemporary art historical literature that these artists sought to "build Cuban identity upon a heritage that combined representations of the Afro-Cuban, *guajiro* [rural] culture and urban life, with its Cubanized Spanish baroque aesthetic" (Blanc 1992:57; Martínez 1994:37–49). In doing so, they rebelled against the old Academy of San Alejandro, founded in 1818, which "was hopelessly conservative" by the twentieth century and "out of step with the modern art currents that began with postimpressionism" (Martínez 1994:3). Thus, Cuban painting by the first two vanguard generations (1920s–30s and 1940s)[10] attempted to produce the signs of a flavorful national *ajiaco,* conceived as both diverse—inclusive of hitherto neglected elements—and benign, rather than "putrefied." To this end it applied a range of modernist approaches to an inherited body of "vernacular" representations found in the *marquillas cigarreras* and *costumbrista* realism, as well as to traditional artistic subjects that had already been reinterpreted by Parisian modernists (e.g., abstracted still-life paintings and portraits; see Martínez 1994:11–92). Some, but not all, Cuban artists and writers more narrowly confined their agenda to fashioning a "national identity." Though not always explicitly articulated, many engaged in ex-

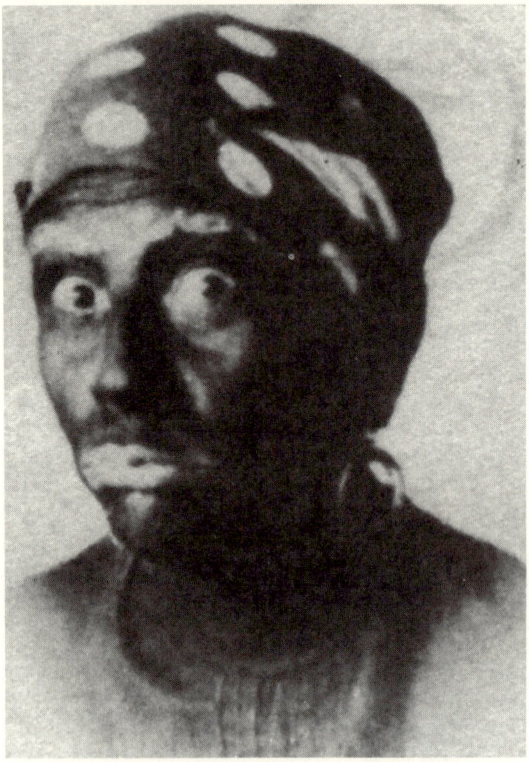

Figure 10.4. Blanca Becerra in blackface costume depicting a *negra conga* in the tradition of nineteenth-century "vernacular theater" (R. Moore 1997:150). The figure resonates with American minstrelsy.

plorations that now are called "transnational," particularly around their immersion in and identification with Africa's contribution to Cuba, as well as direct intellectual exchanges with African, Caribbean, and North American exponents of Negritude and black internationalism (see Powell 1997:19–22, 78–80, 108–114; Herzberg 1992:37; Sims 1992:74; Ellis 1998). One Cuban artist and one Cuban writer, in particular, stand among contemporary critics as central figures of what writers now read as a mid-twentieth-century transnational artistic practice.

Lam and His Contemporaries: *El Ñáñigo* as Modernist Genre Figure

When the Afro-Chinese Cuban painter Wifredo Lam (1902–1982) returned from Paris to his "native land"[11] in 1941, his future collaborator, Lydia Cabrera (1899–1991), had already written and published a book of Afro-Cuban "folktales" and had begun unprecedented local fieldwork with Havana's black religious communities (Cabrera 1940; Intar Gallery 1984:14; Suchlicki 2001:89; Blanc 1992:57). Lam, fleeing Nazi-occupied France with a boatload of surrealists and intellectuals, reached Cuba via a brief African Diaspora island tour: Martinique (where he engaged with Negritude writer Aimé Césaire), the Virgin Islands, and the Dominican Republic. Though Parisian cubism, surrealism, and the appropriation of African-based forms represented fertile ground for Lam's early artistic experiences in his France years (1938–41), he transformed these resources after 1941 into a unique Cuban and Caribbean mode. Lam and several of his Cuban contemporaries, like their literary counterparts, celebrated the figures of Santería, Abakuá, Carnival, and other popular figures and forms as markers of a complex modern *cubanidad,* wrought through the blending of cultures and histories.[12]

Within Cuban modernism, the *diablito,*[13] as the "supreme incarnation" of the Abakuá, as Castellanos had said, thus graduated once again. Cast in a variety of styles, the *íreme* came to occupy a central place in the visual language of modernist easel painting during World War II, particularly in the cubist-surrealist canvases of Wifredo Lam. Still, as deployed within the mid-century Cuban context of cultural meaning and political relevance, the *diablito*'s treatment was uneven. In cases, though employing modernist approaches, the period's artists merely reproduced nineteenth-century stereotypes as much as revised them. For example, a number of painters, including Eduardo Abela, Lorenzo Romero Arciaga, Carlos Enríquez, Antonio Gattorno, and Jaime Valls, all of whom illustrated the flagship journal of the Cuban modernist movement, *Revista de Avance,* tended to portray Afro-Cubans and popular folk as "'noble savages' who lived close to nature, as musicians and dancers seemingly possessed, as menial workers scraping out a living, and as strong mothers caring for their children" (Martínez 1994:80–81). If they drew upon living Afro-Cubans as models, they also drew upon inherited representations of Africans and Cuban folk, particularly as found in the *costumbrista* works of the nineteenth century. Many "re-recreated old picturesque or exotic forms" based on earlier work, such as that of Landaluze and Miahle (see Martínez 1994:82). Paintings such as Eduardo Abela's 1928 *El Gallo Místico,* art historian Juan Martínez argues, were the "modern successor[s] to Miahle's and Landaluze's *Día de los Reyes*" (Martínez 1994:85). Generations of Cuban artists worked in self-conscious relationship to earlier works painted on the island, and art historians therefore begin their narratives of Afro-Cuban visual traditions with Miahle and Landaluze (see Blanc 1992:53–54; Martínez 1994:50–53, 79–92).

For some Cuban artists, critics argue, African-based elements served not merely as formal sources for a variety of modernist primitivisms as they had in Paris (see W. Rubin 1984). For Wifredo Lam, it appears, figures such as the *diablito* and the *orishas* of the Lucumí religion became what art historian Richard Powell calls "historical, cultural, and personal locator[s]" (Powell 1991:25; see Blanc 1992). This argument has much to recommend it. Early educated at the conservative San Alejandro Academy (1918–23), Lam then studied the range of European modernisms in Spain and France between 1923 and 1941, including various surrealisms and Parisian cubism, with its pioneering use of African sculpture. Still, Lam's particular use of things African and Afro-Cuban, critics argue, diverged from his Parisian and Cuban contemporaries. Afro-Cuban imagery reconnected Lam not only to the African-derived cultures of his upbringing, it is widely believed, but also to Diaspora-wide and pan-African currents. Though much writing on the Cuban avant-garde locates the island's modernists within the "search for a nationalist ethos" (e.g., Blanc 1992; Martínez 1994), Lam's African Diaspora identifications can be read to resist wholesale nationalist claims upon his art. Analogously, in terms elaborated by postmodern-oriented critics, Fernando Ortiz's concept of the Cuban *ajiaco,* properly understood, can be employed to revise reductive modern nationalisms and crypto-essentialist multiculturalisms. Lam's work, for example, registers internationalist or transnationalist connections and processes, immersed as it is in Black Atlantic currents and Cuban creolizations (Mosquera 1996a, 1996b; Americas Society 1992; Sims 1992; Benítez-Rojo 1992; Merewether 1992; Fisher 1994). The latter perspective is persuasive. I believe, however, that it became much too tempting in the 1990s for contemporary critics to appropriate Lam either as an essentialized figure whose art gushed forth from his recuperated Afro-Cuban self, or as the poster boy for postmodern, postcolonial, transnational artistic agendas in the art world—particularly in countering the Eurocentric notion that Lam's work was merely an extension of Pablo Picasso's use of African art in his surrealism within flat cubist space (see Sims 1992; Herzberg 1992).

Rather than become mired in the foregoing debates, I prefer to look closely at selected works, in order to elicit how Lam and certain contemporaries utilized the *diablito,* and, hence, how they shifted the ground of its representation and meaning between the early 1940s and the late 1950s. Here I walk something of a middle path. Lam clearly approached the *diablito* figure in unique ways. Still, like his contemporaries, he relied, for example, on older conventions established by Víctor Patricio de Landaluze—the lone *íreme,* the *fambá* (temple) interior, and the street carnival *diablito.* He also relied on his literary and ethnographic colleagues, in some cases, to title his works, so that they appear to carry specific intentionalities they may not have had. Moreover, Lam's extraordinary feel for aspects of the Afro-Cuban religions does not add up to what recent critics see as a thoroughgoing cultural communion, virtually a form of Santería priesthood (Herzberg 1992). I sense that his work on the island emerged as much from collective thinking and study with colleagues—a historical characteristic of Cuban intellectual endeavor, the "group"—who approached *lo afrocubano* from varied disciplinary angles, as from "within," as it were.

Some experiments by Cuban artists merely appropriated the *diablito* in bald primitivisms, rehearsing the stereotyped or romantic treatment of Afro-Cubans in decades past. I believe that Lam used the *diablito* as a formal and cultural source in order to explore the phenomena of spiritual and material transformation, a project that owed as much to African and Afro-Cuban categories of religious experience as to surrealist experiments with other orders of reality. In this sense, Lam did go *monte adentro* ("inside the sacred forest") and did glimpse something of the "light inside," though this journey took place as much in his studio, the museum, collegial discourse, and the texts of Lydia Cabrera as in the *tierra* of *ekue*.

From 1943 through the mid-1950s, employing selected formal resources of surrealism and cubism, Wifredo Lam approached the *ñáñigo* subject with increasing abstraction, moving from more legible representations of the *diablito*, an icon shared among his contemporaries, to ingeniously constructed abstract figures in ambiguous spaces. In doing so, Lam moved from reliance on old and current generic conventions to unique meditations on mysterious principles of force and transformation. In 1943 Lam painted one of his first *ñáñigo* subjects: a full-length, schematically delineated *diablito* playing a drum (plate 21). In subsequent bodies of work, Lam distilled the *diablito* masquerade into a series of geometric figures, often elaborated with biomorphic appendages. His most recognizable geometric figure remains the iconic vertical diamond with one or two eyelike circles (figures 10.5–10.7).

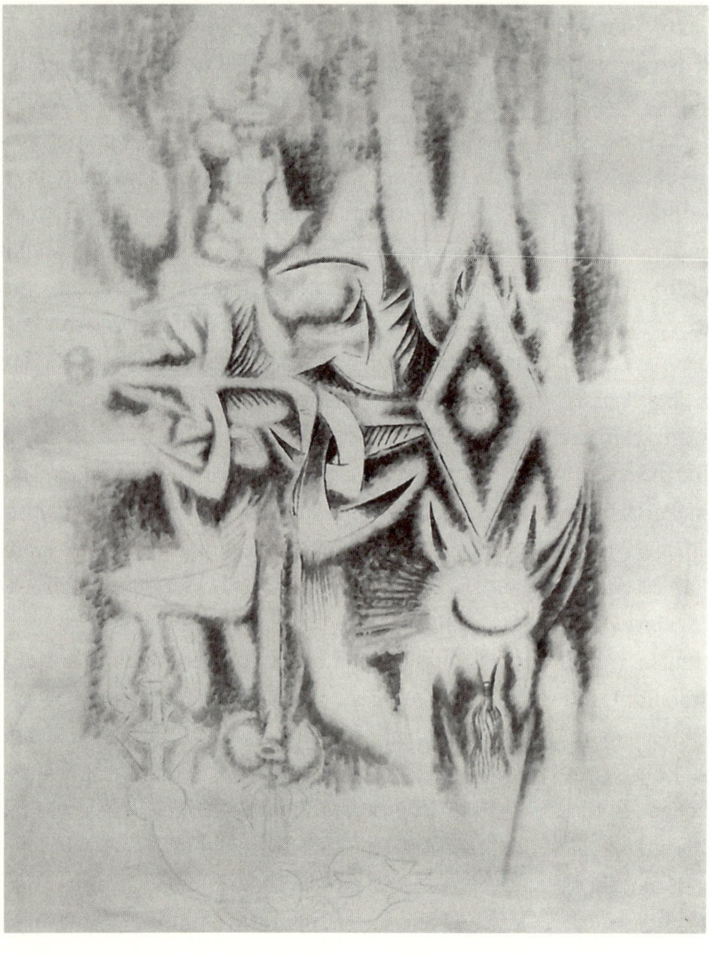

Figure 10.5. Wifredo Lam, *Au Défaut du Jour*, 1945, oil on canvas. Lam abstracts the standing *íreme* figure playing a drum (right) with biomorphism and distills the conical headdress with the two large eyes into a diamond-shaped emblem with two glowing, vertically stacked eyes; this also may reflect diamond-shaped elements in Abakuá writing. Copyright © 2002 Artists Rights Society (ARS), New York/ADAGP, Paris.

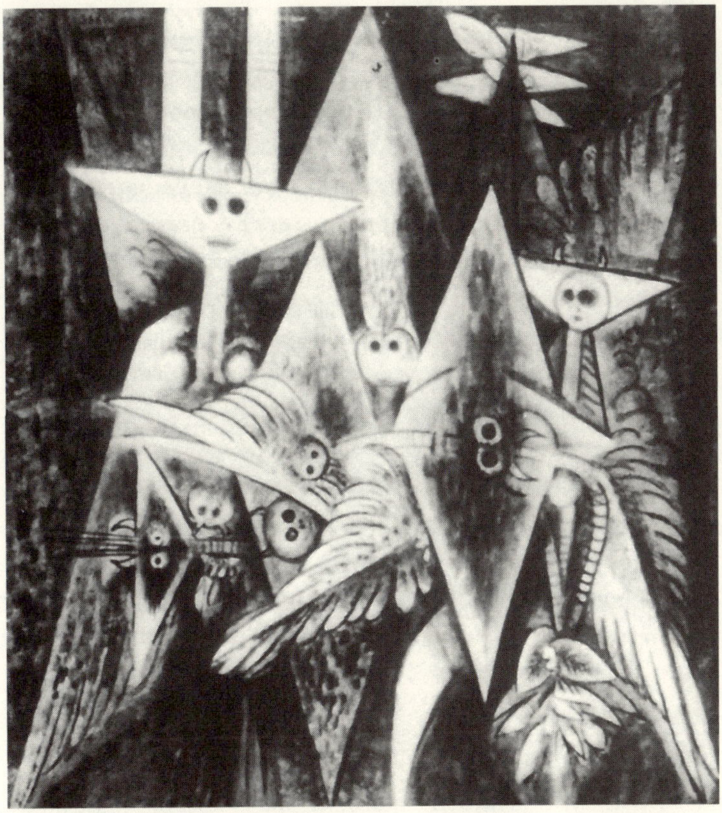

Figure 10.6. Wifredo Lam, *La Parade Antillaise,* 1945, oil on canvas, 50.5 × 42.75 inches. Lam combines and interconnects the diamond icon with birdlike wings, triangular and circular head forms with horns, and foliage. The circular heads probably derive from Eleguá figures (cf. figure 5.5).

The 1943 work combines figural and atmospheric abstraction in flattened space (plate 21). Most readable are the *diablito*'s conical hood with its pronounced almond eyes and rudimentary arms with biomorphic hands, which touch a goblet-shaped drum. Lam references the figure's masked body, stance, and activity with painted black contour lines, producing shapes that are skeletally filled with broad brushstrokes. Shading along certain contour lines, as on the left arm and the circular drumhead, lend a sense of volume, albeit minimal. A rising arm holding an implement and suggestions of other figures flank this central standing figure. These last elements, along with hot atmospheric color, suggest the presence and feeling of Caribbean festive activity, perhaps carnival. In a schematic way, the composition recalls, in fact, Ramón Meza's nineteenth-century description of Day of Kings participants "pressed together" behind the *diablito.* This subject matter would have been legible and meaningful to contemporaneous viewers because the work employs genre conventions utilized by a number of the period's artists: a prominent *diablito* flanked by festive, dancing, or mystically possessed figures, with a drum in the foreground—most often goblet-shaped (plates 21 and 22; figure 10.5; see plate 19, center and right).

That *íreme* masquerades do not play drums, and that Abakuá musical drums are not goblet-shaped or ovoid, suggest Lam's work as a composite stylization of Cuban festive and religious performance using generic elements, much as Landaluze and Miahle had done; for example, Landaluze placed a similar *El Ñáñigo* in a number of compositions. Landaluze himself had juxtaposed a version of *El Ñáñigo* and an ovoid drum with bas-relief bands and surface fluting in a ca. 1880 painting (see plates 8, 19, 20). Moreover, between 1943 and 1944 Lam's contemporary Mario Carreño (b. 1913) painted multiple, fluted, goblet-

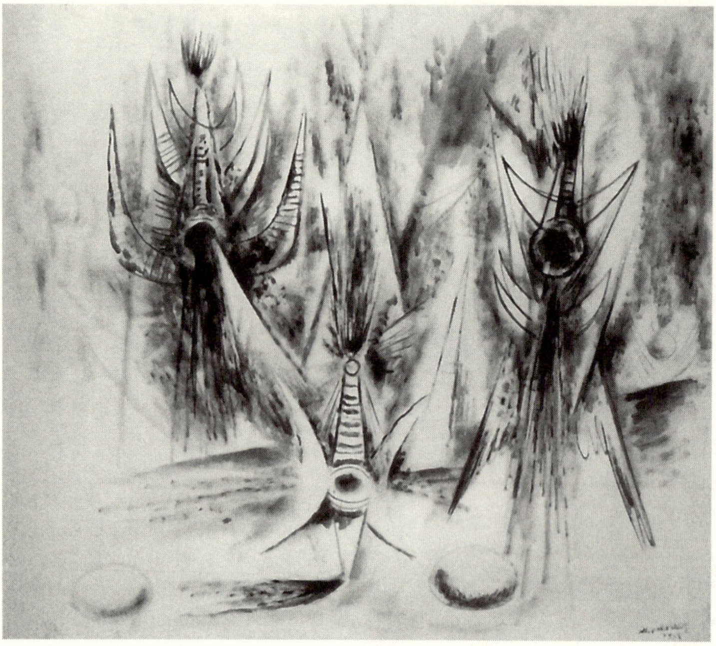

Figure 10.7. Wifredo Lam, *Les Oiseaux Voiles* (The Birds-Sails), 1945, oil on canvas. Lam realizes the hybrid *íreme* and bird figures more ethereally, wherein the *sombrereta* becomes a portal that emits lines of force, as in Boccioni's Futurism. Against and among triangular "sails" and with raised hornlike appendages, the figures float and appear to ascend upward like angels. "Birds" and "sails" deal with movement and natural elements, such as wind, water, force, and light, in addition to dealing with transformations between domains, as in plate 21 and figures 10.5 and 10.6. Courtesy of the Collection of Mr. and. Mrs. Melvin Knyper, Aspen, Colorado. Copyright © 2002 Artists Rights Society (ARS), New York/ADAGP, Paris.

shaped drums in two works. The former features a goblet-shaped, fluted drum with a masklike bas-relief face (figures 10.8 and 10.9). It is unlikely that any observer of Havana carnival or Abakuá ceremony would have seen such a drum, particularly the figurated example, in use anywhere in Havana. Such drums were meant to be played not singly, but in stationary drum batteries, and they remained hidden within the old, secretive Arará *cabildos* of Matanzas, Jovellanos, Agramonte, and Perico one hundred kilometers to the east. Nevertheless, closer to home and more accessible would have been the nation's unique captive model for the artists' painted representations. This grand drum, long considered a "jewel" of Cuba's National Museum, had been confiscated thirty years earlier from one of Matanzas's Arará *cabildos* destroyed during President Menocal's Afro-Cuban persecutions between 1913 and 1914 (see Ortiz 1952: 333–336) (figure 10.10). The modernists' representation of this "African drum" may have resulted from the time-honored practice of countless classically trained artists: copying "Old Master" works in the museum. During this modernist-primitivist moment, the "Old Masters" were Africans and Afro-Cubans, at least insofar as their objects served as raw material—with thanks, of course, to Mario García Menocal, the police, an ethnologist, and at least one museum director.

Lam first rehearses and then revises the foregoing genre conventions through figural abstraction. At the same time, he interrupts figural and spatial representation and fixed semantic references. In the 1943 work, Lam references the devices of realistic representation, for example, figural modeling through contour line and shadow and perspective through overlapping forms. Yet, Lam disrupts the figure's integrity and the figure-ground distinction through aborted contour line, which results in open-ended shapes, and with interpenetrating color application. The resulting permeable, diaphanous figure, thusly, floats within an ambiguous, flattened yellow-orange space made atmospheric with dappled color in red and green. Lam uses these forms of abstraction not for their own sake, but apparently in order to open up other, or deeper, semantic and experiential possibilities. The painterly field "behind" the figure is dabbed with green, which, in view of his prior work, suggests foliage. Moreover, the transparency of the

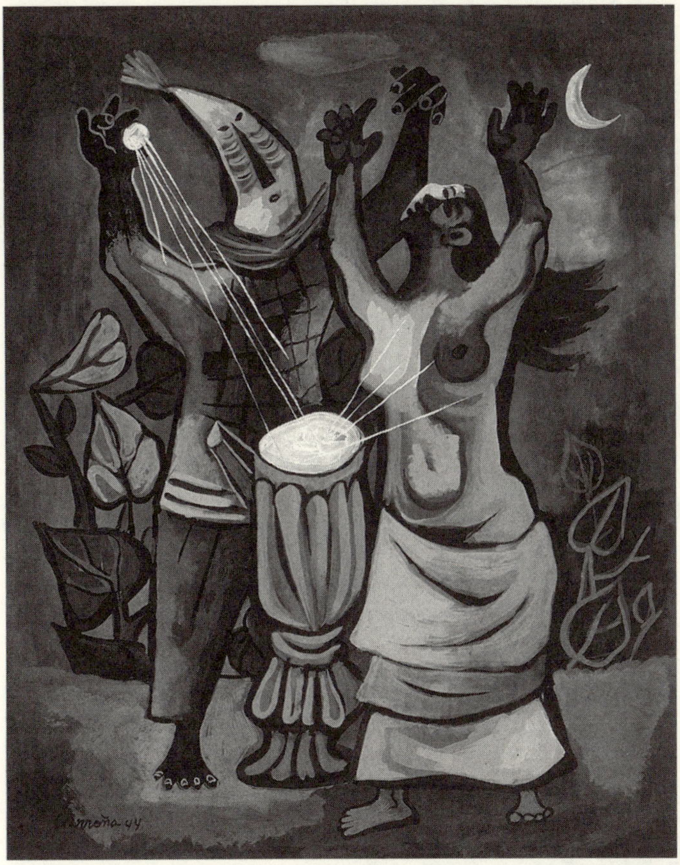

Figure 10.8. Mario Carreño, *Afro-Cuban Dance,* 1944, oil on canvas. Courtesy Art Museum of the Americas, Organization of American States (OAS), Washington, D.C.

figure makes it possible to read the broadly brushed lines within the *diablito*'s thorax both as a ribcage and as a plantlike form that rises vertically up through the conical hood to form the masquerade's *pon-pon.* In other words, the figure references at once bodily integrity, permeation, and alternate structuring by a "skeleton" of the plant kingdom, as well as a mysterious transparency and ephemerality.

The 1943 work upholds and revises contemporaneous *ñáñigo* genre conventions calling for prominent tropical foliage. Lam's colleagues used wild and potted foliage as compositional framing devices and dramatic punctuations, undoubtedly to reference the unique tropical environment of Cuba. When Lam's use of foliage and figure is considered in relation to previous works, particularly his 1942 masterpiece *La Jungla* (The Jungle), one suspects that the 1943 painting also concerns the interpenetration and mediation of at least three different realms: the human, natural, and supernatural. Lam's contemporaries painted *ñáñigo* and Afro-Cuban "themes" through representations of dance, ritual, and musical activity. They employed figural abstractions within plausible, though often flattened, spaces; Lam's works draw on such generic raw material, but he uses it to thematize transformation and the mediation of worldly and otherworldly realms.

Lam had been developing juxtapositions and interconnections between human and animal figures—particular female and equine features—since at least 1941, when he produced the drawings for André Breton's *Fata Morgana* series. *La Jungla,* as indicated not least by its title, combines those two elements with a third, the forest. Julia Herzberg observes that in 1942, Lam had attempted to move beyond the use of the Picasso-like hybrid woman-horse motif. He con-

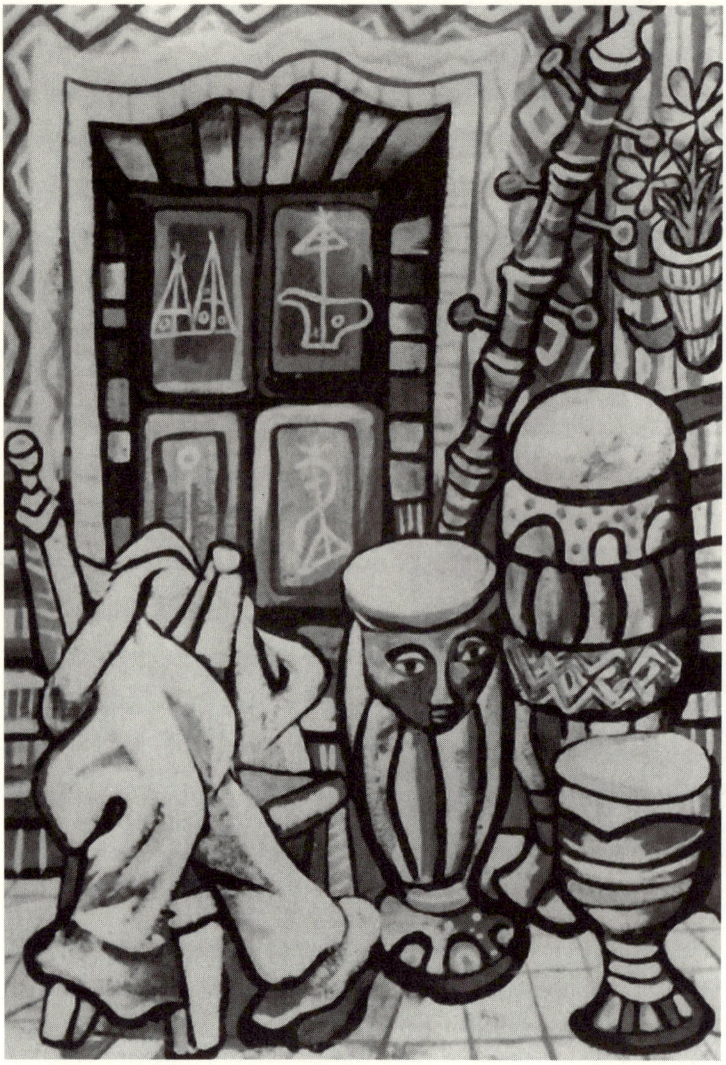

Figure 10.9. Mario Carreño, *Cuarto Fambá,* 1943, oil on canvas (Blanc 1992:65). Carreño creates an *ajiaco* of Cuban interior design, blending indigenizing Cuban themes—the African drum, the *íreme* suit, realistic drawn Abakuá signs, tropical potted flora, and elements of baroque decorative interior architecture, that is, the curvy portal with its stained glass border. In School of Paris modernist style, Carreño renders the drum, plants, coat rack, and, particularly, the crumpled *íreme* suit hung over a chair as geometrically interesting still-life elements. The goblet-shaped figurated and fluted drum, lower right, resembles a plumeless *sese.* It must have been copied from or influenced by the famous Arará example in the National Museum, which was confiscated by the police around 1913–14 (figure 10.10) (illustration from Blanc 1992:65).

sciously embraced a surrealist-based vocabulary, including biomorphism, in flat cubist space, an approach that connected him with the New York surrealists. His move was "consistent with Lam's vision of a world in which the human, animal, and plant kingdoms are united" (Herzberg 1992:32–33). And this vision, Herzberg argues, "also grew out of an Afro-Cuban world view . . . [in which] the horse motif . . . alludes" to possession trance, a transformation that conjoins the worldly and otherworldly (Herzberg 1992:32–33; see also Sims 1992:93–96).[14]

In order to contextualize selected *diablito* examples by Lam created between 1943 and 1947, it is well worth examining similar themes painted by his close Cuban modernist contemporaries. In 1940, Victor Manuel García (1897–1969) employed a neo-naive approach to the *ñáñigo* theme in *Carnival* (plate 22). García centers the yellow *diablito* before other figures in a high-affect environment, using a palette of hot but limited colors. His figures are significantly unmodulated, physiognomically simplified, and outlined in black. Clusters of yellow dots, perhaps references to the lighted *farolas* twirled above in carnival processions, punctuate the night sky.[15] This festive street scene of mixed participants, with its prominent masker in the foreground flanked by com-

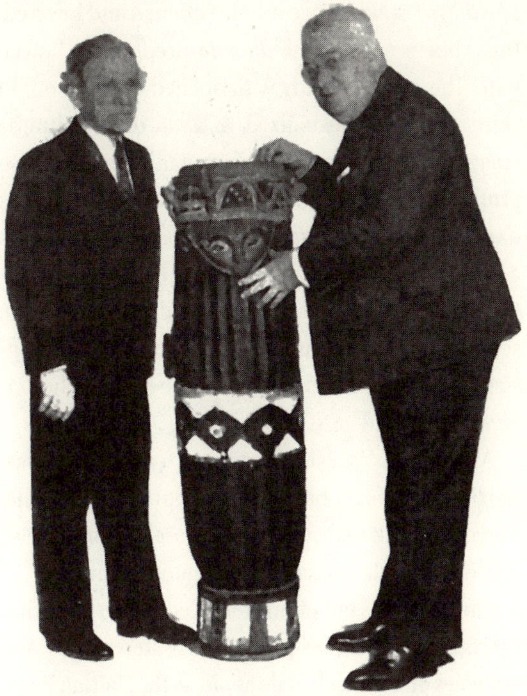

Figure 10.10. *"Fig. 227—J. Rodríguez Morey, director del Museo Nacional de Cuba y el autor de este libro examinando la esculpida cara antropomorfa que adorna un tambor arará* (J. Rodríguez Morey, director of the National Museum of Cuba, and the author examining the sculptured anthropomorphic face that adorns an Arará drum; Ortiz 1952:335, fig. 227). Courtesy of María Fernanda Ortiz Herrera, Representante Sucesores de Fernando Ortiz.

pacted, overlapping figures, bears some generic resemblance to Lam's 1943 *Untitled (Ñáñigo)* and two works from 1945, including *La Parade Antillaise* (figure 10.6). In *Carnival*, for example, an arm rises above the *diablito*'s right shoulder, just as it does in Lam's 1943 work. Still, García's *Carnival* was interested in neither cubist/surrealist abstraction nor the alternative psychological orders of reality some practitioners sought; it is interested in instantiating a popular Afro-Cuban theme, cast in a cartoonlike social realism shaped by modernist approaches. García does so by rehearsing generic content and composition only with the addition of figural simplification and distortion, along with exoticized hot color. These modernist, primitivizing markers within the moderately abstracted figurative mode are not unlike those used by urban African American artists in the 1930s and 1940s, such as Archibald Motley Jr. (see Robinson and Greenhouse 1991). Consonant with the period's culinary leitmotif, the work emerges as one visual equivalent of Fernando Ortiz's Cuban *ajiaco*. The carnival participants' varied skin tones, including white, along with the round faces and almond eyes of the majority, suggest the creole mixture of *lo negro, lo gallego,* and *lo chino*. This effect is visually emphasized by the formal resonance of the African *diablito*'s conical hood with numerous triangular carnival hats, including Asian and harlequin headgear. Still, the *ajiaco*'s biggest ingredient remains the foregrounded Afro-Cuban *diablito*. Though related in its generic role, this is not at all the classicizing *El Ñáñigo* of Landaluze. Though García uses figural simplification and distortion for expressive effect, this *diablito*'s gangly body and outsized black feet and hands ultimately signify *lo africano* through grotesque stereotypes inherited from the nineteenth-century *marquillas cigarreras* and vernacular theater's minstrelsy (see, e.g., figure 8.3).

In contributing his own modernist angle on the creole *ajiaco*, Mario Carreño confronted the *diablito* in *Afro-Cuban Dance* (figure 10.11), painted the same year as Lam's untitled *ñáñigo*. Carreño blends classical motifs from the Western art tradition with Afro-Cuban ones: classical "rape," *ñañiguismo*, and festive "dance," along with tropical male fantasy. In fulfilling the requirements of the theme, Carreño utilizes primitivizing conventions similar to those of García's *Carnival*. *Afro-Cuban Dance* represents a charged encounter between a *diablito* and a woman against a forest background of leaves and vertical *caña brava* (bamboo). Tension is added as the figures are compressed and overlapped in a tightly cropped composition. Stylistically, Carreño combines at least two modernisms: the geometricized and palimpsestic figuration of Picasso's earliest cubism, exemplified in *Les Demoiselles d'Avignon* (1907), which appropriated African mask forms, and the "muscular," distorted figuration of the Mexican muralist David Alfaro Siquieros (see Blanc 1992:63). The *diablito*'s masklike face, split and splayed obliquely into three diamond-like sections, features offset circular eyes and a wide mouth with prominent clenched teeth. As a whole, the *diablito* faithfully copies the principal elements of Landaluze's 1881 *El Ñáñigo* down to the smallest details: zigzag leg cuff and repeated triangular hood designs, a checkerboard back, bells about the waist, an articulated face with conspicuous teeth, a wide stance and arms gesturing forward (compare with figure 4.1). Still, Carreño abbreviates Landaluze's comprehensive costume to reveal the black dancer's massive right arm and radically inflates the hand, both of which combine palimpsestic, geometrized, and muscular figuration. Integral to the composition's swirling center, the ominous curved arm sweeps the eye upward and around the female "dancer," creating a charged circle that unifies the two figures, indicates the *diablito*'s potential grasp, and locks the mask's gaze on the woman's bare breasts. *El Ñáñigo*'s staid stance is here widened and lowered; thus, like a spring, the *diablito* prepares to "vaccinate" the woman, ready with opened legs and raised skirts, with the sexualized *vacunao* of the Rumba Guaguancó. The muscular woman's body is also grotesque. In a jumble of ambivalences, she moves in dance, recoils at the *diablito*'s approach, and displays a dispassionate face; all the while, her taut, preposterous breasts and erect nipples indicate arousal. In semidefensive response, only the woman's own outsized, grotesque hand presents an obstacle to the *diablito*'s grasp and gaze.

Against this forest background, Landaluze's classicizing *El Ñáñigo* becomes an aggressive, sexually frenzied, black male presence before an ambivalent, half-nude creole woman of ambiguous ethnicity. The theme generates out of an eroticized modernist primitivism, which trades on Western stereotypes and fantasies of the black male as old as the Haitian Revo-

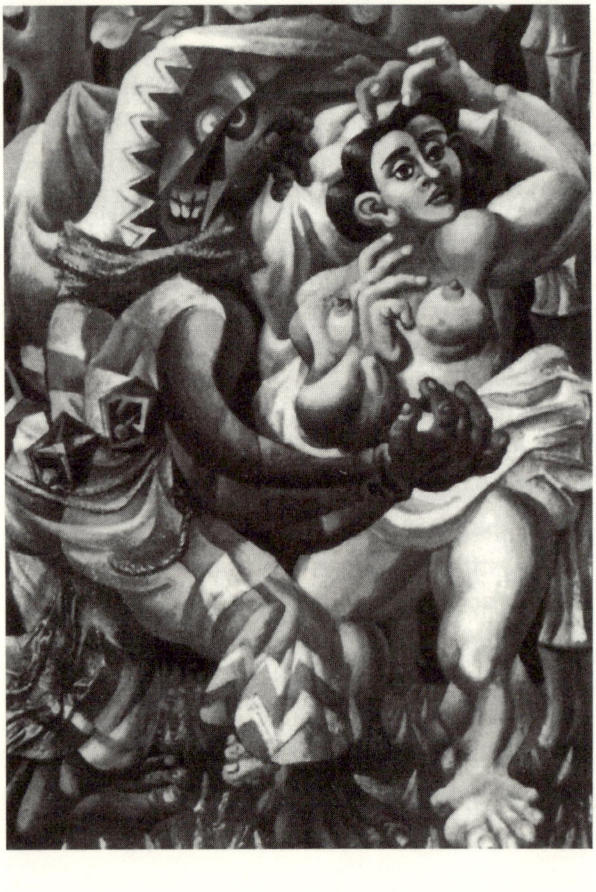

Figure 10.11. Mario Carreño, *Afro-Cuban Dance,* 1943, oil on canvas (Blanc 1992:64). Carreño, offering another version of the eroticized "Afro-Cuban Dance" theme (see his 1943 work, figure 10.8), centers on a frenzied *íreme* and a Cuban *mulata* or *guajira* in an eroticized near-embrace. The *íreme* derives from Landaluze's *El Ñáñigo* and other *diablitos* (1878–81) in its costume design and articulated face. The artist creates a painted *ajiaco* of indigenizing Cuban themes, though marked as "modern" by casting the *diablito* and the woman in the physiognomic styles of Picasso (1906–7; the face from his experimentation with African masks as seen in *Les Demoiselles d'Avignon,* and muscular bodies from just before this period), as well as the muscular physiognomy of the figures from David Alfaro Siquieros's Mexican muralism.

lution. Still, the scene also resuscitates, and recharges through the Afro-Cuban theme, High Renaissance and baroque "rape" motifs based on classical allegories (e.g., Correggio's *Jupiter and Io* [ca. 1532] or Peter Paul Rubens's *Abduction of the Daughters of Leucippus* [1617]; see *Gardner's Art through the Ages* 1997: 762, 850).

Formally and thematically, Africa meets the West in the Caribbean, producing a complicated *ajiaco* indeed. Is Cuba, in part, figured by this ethnically ambiguous *criolla,* whose enlarged nose, lips, ears, and almond eyes combine with her black *pelo lasio* (smooth, "good hair")? She is not quite *mulata* or *morena,* though perhaps of eastern Cuban *mestiza* peasant stock (i.e., a *guajira* of Spanish and Indian descent), a figure often painted during this period. Indeed, Carreño seems to combine two contemporaneous genres, the "*ñáñigo* dance" and the "tropical gypsy" of Victor Manuel García (1929; see Martínez 1994, plate 2). If Victor Manuel's elegant abstracted portrait represented one ingredient of Cuba's identity, Carreño aggressively mixes up the stew, for better or worse. In any event, the scene presents the specter of second-order mixing: African and creole Cubana, made modern through abstraction, in the sexual production of further mixture. Still, any reading of this eroticized easel painting must account for the third term, which completes a triangulation of desire: the beholder. Carreño delivers up the fecund and sexually aroused, though ambivalent, woman to the beholder's (male) gaze via the African's.

This work's lurid primitivism, though cast within a triangulation of desire, is made clearer by another Carreño *Afro-Cuban Dance* (1944; figure 10.8). With raised outstretched arms, as if casting a spell, a *diablito* enchants a woman to a form of ecstasy that conflates the spiritual and the sexual. Holding a glowing charm or mirror, the *diablito* bounces magical light off the skin of the goblet-shaped African drum directly to her breasts. She is presumably aroused by such stimulation, which produces its intended effect. Her uplifted, grotesque arms and Picasso-like palimpsestic face—one facet dark, one facet light—indicate her transformation against a haloed background. The glowing charm, the moon, and the drum skin, in addition to her right breast and half face/mask, form a triangle of pseudomystical force. Amid the painting's myriad details, the drum remains the work's center of gravity. Bisecting the frame and mediating the composition's light and dark zones, the tall wood drum stands erect before the *diablito*'s groin. It is the enchanter's principal machine and conduit of the woman's ecstasy. This gendered member of the African percussion family takes on transcendent significance; an *axis mundi,* its illuminated skin head and godhead reflect its lit counterpart in the sky directly above. The presumed attraction of the "Afro-Cuban Dance" theme was its invocation of license to shed civilization's restraints, via *lo africano.* In this case, the hypersexualized figure of the African enables male fantasies to lay claim to exotic women—*mulatas* and *guajiras*—loosened up, of course, by *afrocubanismo*'s primitive tom-tom. It comes as little surprise that the Cuban term, *bongosero,* for the player of the little double drum held between the knees remains a double entendre, referring to the guy who loves "banging" women, particularly from behind. Ironically, while ostensibly elevating *ñáñigo* material to modernist art, the work trades on precisely the same logic used in Fernández Carrillo's 1881 diatribe against the white *ñáñigos:* be a *ñáñigo* and you can seduce nonwhite women.

Does the racially mixed woman-as-passive-vessel, whose body is nothing less than the *ajiaco*'s gendered cooking pot, produce out of benignly presented "rape" a series of dark offspring or other contrasting complexions? This will of course, depend on the race of the beholder, in all probability, white and upper class. In the potent gustatory metaphors of genetic and cultural exchange developed by a host of New World scholars, the postslavery nation's racially democratic destiny intimately involved the blend of "milk" *(leite)* and "coffee" *(café)* and the "counterpoint" of "sugar and tobacco" earlier proposed by Arango y Parreño (see Browning 1995:17–22; Ortiz 1947; see also Bastide 1978:70–73, Martínez-Alier 1974:33–41). Carreño's painted national *ajiaco*, a "danced" encounter of crossed gazes, complexions, and generative potential, participates in the working out of the island's fraught identity through the "erotics of Cuban nationalism" (see Kutzinski 1993). The flavorful *ajiaco* sought by vanguardist *afrocubanismo* and folklore movements, though tempered by the ethnographic interests of Fernando Ortiz and Lydia Cabrera, turned out bittersweet. Having graduated from criminality and atavism, *El Ñáñigo* now faced new challenges in hypersexuality and primitivism within modernist art. Meanwhile, and perhaps, unsurprisingly, *afrocubanismo* identified Wifredo Lam himself as a walking avatar of the Cuban *ajiaco*, an innate biracial mediator between the primitive and civilized.

Lam's unique approach, apparent personal channel to the mystical, and his Caribbean racial mixture of African and Chinese, enchanted a host of Parisian and American writers, painters, dealers, collectors, and curators, as well as his Cuban avant-garde contemporaries. Not a few admirers characterized Lam as the vehicle and goal of surrealism, that is, a mediator par excellence between the "primitive" and the "civilized," and between the conscious and unconscious.[16] Such sentiments reflect their historical moment but have returned to the thick of contemporary cultural and racial politics. Despite the destabilizations of essentialism proffered by 1990s postmodernism, it has become satisfying, if not obligatory, to ground Lam's embrace of Afro-Cuban icons, aesthetics, and religious principles in a particular "identity," however multiplex. Somehow, in order to explain his interests and their realization in oil paint and canvas, Lam must become not only a cultural "insider," as opposed to Picasso, the "outsider" (Sims 1992:20), but also a "devotee" of Santería (Herzberg 1992:31–32, 51). Lam was "trained in [Santería's] beliefs and rituals by his godmother, Mantonica Wilson, when he was a child in Cuba" (Sims 1992:19). Clearly, Lam did narrate his early experiences of African-based spiritual practices in detail to Max-Pol Fouchet, the principal source of this tantalizing biographical information (Fouchet 1986:14).[17] As the story continues, Lam reconnected with an early-developed consciousness when he returned to his native land in 1941, the point of departure for his Afro-Cuban work. To my mind, the question is less whether these facts are true or untrue than how critics and the artist himself (especially in retrospect) fashioned narratives about his artistic production. Such narratives satisfied the contemporaneous concerns of mid-century modernist primitivism and have met the requirements of certain 1990s identity politics.

Inarguably, Lam's self, artistic personage, and bodies of work were emergent—evolving through lived experience and art *practice*, he didn't necessarily know where he would end up at each step he took. At the same time, the charged critical accounts in question fold Lam's early biography—an already motivated story—into a prophetic narrative of "homecoming" following remote sojourn. It comes to seem inevitable that Lam's Afro-Cuban "identity" would be reawakened or recovered upon the "return to his native land" in 1941 (see Powell 1991). Rather than debate and thereby entangle my own narrative with such accounts, I prefer to look closely at the resources and results of Lam's work during the 1940s and 1950s in Havana in order to pose alternative hypotheses.

Lam, *El Ñáñigo*, and Ethnographic Mediation

If Lam was at all "trained" early on as a "devotee" of Santería, his critical engagement with Afro-Cuban representations came about more substantially through mediated interactions—socially, discursively, and textually. As argued earlier, Lam's 1943 *Untitled (Ñáñigo)* represents, and revises, old and new genre conventions with the modernist stylistic markers of cubism and surrealism. Between 1941 and 1952 in Cuba, Lam recreated himself and was created by others as an epistemologically specific class of "insider" through keen observation, ethnographic reading, passionate mutual reflection with like-minded artists and intellectuals, and endless studio time. To my mind, this art-*work* processed, indeed constituted, whatever personal, ethnic, and spiritual sentiments are credited to any original native insiderism. Received wisdom tells us that Lam's Santería training goes far in explaining paintings in which references to the Lucumí *orishas* and Afro-Cuban phenomenology appear. Of course, because Lam's early memories evidently do not include Abakuá experiences, his intensive post-return communion with the *ñáñigos* in Havana seems to explain the genesis of his *diablito* works.

Clearly, as of the end of 1942, Lam attended some Abakuá *plantes* and other Afro-Cuban rituals with Lydia Cabrera, Alejo Carpentier, and his Parisian dealer, Pierre Loeb. This was a period of intense interchange—personally, professionally, and textually. Carpentier and Cabrera were as enchanted with Lam's insightful artistic expressions as he was with their knowledge of and connections with the practitioner community, which Lam evidently harvested in ways useful to his enterprise. Cabrera and Carpentier, as well as Fernando Ortiz, gushed about Lam in reviews of his work (Carpentier 1989; Cabrera 1942, 1943, 1944, 1946; Ortiz 1950c). At the same time, Lam undoubtedly had at his disposal their works and works-in-progress, stories of their fieldwork through ongoing conversation, and many artifacts in the anthropology, criminology, and national museums, including *costumbrista* painting (see Carpentier 1933, 1946; Ortiz 1920, 1921, 1924b,1950a, 1950b, 1951; Cabrera 1940, 1947, 1994). For Carpentier, Lam's work was eye-opening and confirming of his own discoveries, as the paintings "seemed to reveal everything that is magical, imponderable, and mysterious in the Cuban world" (Herzberg 1992:40; Blanc 1992:93). For Cabrera, Lam's work resonated with her lifelong experiences of Cuba's Africanness and her fascination with syncretism; "two old cultures—Asia and Africa—imprint in [Lam's] work this precious accent of beloved, ancestral truthfulness, and in no way could the artistic language that speaks his exalted and purified forms be called 'exotic'—in the vulgar sense that the word has taken on" (Cabrera 1994:222). Cabrera, an upper-class artist, writer, and folklorist, may have romanticized about the authenticity of her own sources as "pure" (e.g., 1983:27), but her assessment of Lam's avoidance of the "exotic," as seen in Carreño, is well taken. Still, Cabrera's essentialist insight into Lam's "ancestral truthfulness"—a product of "two old cultures"—lurks behind more recent assessments of the artist.

Lam's experiences with Santería and the Abakuá were mediated by collaboration with Cabrera and her ongoing ethnographic tutelage. Indisputably, Lam's contact with the Abakuá Society on several occasions was as close as an uninitiated observer could get. From early 1942 until 1944, Lam and his partner, Helena Holzer, lived in Marianao, the Havana suburb that contained the poor, mostly black *barrio* of Pogolotti. Cabrera had earlier renovated and established a residence in the Quinta San José mansion, also in Marianao and close to this *barrio* (1940). Along with the arduous restoration of the eighteenth-century Santa María del Rosario church (as of 1941), Cabrera resumed her intensive fieldwork in 1942, which she had begun in Pogolotti in as early as 1930 (Intar Gallery 1984:10, 14; Cabrera 1994:205–218). Lam accompanied her to Afro-Cuban rituals and drummings (Herzberg 1992:39). During this same year, 1942, Cabrera, Lam, Carpentier, and the Parisian dealer Pierre Loeb, who had just arrived in Havana with his family, attended Abakuá *plantes* together (Blanc 1992:93). They would have been permitted to sit within the walled courtyard and observe the public festivities: chanted *enkame* prayers by Ekueñón, the chalking of *anaforuana* on the ground, the ritual cleansings of initiates by Eribangandó, the sacrifice of *mbori* with the help of Aberisún and Aberiñán, the *plazas'* procession of attributes, dancing *íremes,* and the preparation of the communal meal by Encandemo. They would not have been allowed to enter the *fambá,* though Lam may have seen photographs of the *fambá* drums, staffs, and drawn signs taken by Cabrera's partner María Teresa de Rojas in the late 1940s, if not the objects themselves (see Cabrera 1958:144–145).

Lam's attitude toward this subject matter, his ethnographic tutelage, and the vagaries of memory are revealed in an homage he wrote to Pierre Loeb almost forty years later (1979): "Pierre in Cuba under the signs of the deities of Africa among the palm-trees I went with you to secret ñáñigo rites. During those rituals Naña-Yreme [*sic*], or the masked [*diablito*],[18] with his baton and sacrificial roosters attached to his belt, accepted new adherents to the . . . sect. During the ceremony the Naña-Yreme [*sic*] drew signs of all different colors on the backs of the new adherents. The masked [*diablito*] then threw food to the four cardinal points and afterward the tom-toms began their mysterious language" (Herzberg 1992:41).

The account, which suffers greatly in translation, nevertheless, reflects both the opportunities and limits within which Lam experienced the Abakuá and later remembered the ceremonies. Overall, the fascinating narrative combines the antiquated descriptors of the first half of the twentieth century *(ñáñigo, diablito),* the romantic sentiments of an enchanted outside observer ("tom-toms," "under the signs of the African deities among the palm trees"), wishful embellishment upon the details, and some neutral ethnographic description.[19] Lam, an artistic savant and conscientious Cuban of part-African descent, was clearly not a scholar of the Abakuá Society and the Afro-Cuban religions, nor did he possess vast "inside" knowledge, though he was a sensitive observer. There are no "African deities" in Abakuá rites, and this fact is decisive in distinguishing the Santería religion and the spiritually empowered Carabalí-derived *sociedad.* There are no "tom-toms"; instead, there is the *biankomeko* of three *enkomos* and one long, tapered *bonkó enchemiyá,* which Cabrera and Ortiz knew well at the time. It is imaginable that the "Yreme" did gesture in four directions, though the gesture's significance, "the four cardinal points," may have been interpreted to Lam in situ, or afterward by one of his colleagues. A masker "with his baton and sacrificial roosters attached to his belt" (Eribangandó), undoubtedly presided over one phase of that initiation ceremony. However, it should not be discounted that Lam's memory was reinforced then or later by the widely published and valorized images of Landaluze's *El Ñáñigo,* with his baton and rooster on the belt, which, by 1979, had guided the conventions for representing this figure for fifty or more years. Finally, Lam's shift between an insider term, *"íreme,"* and an outsider term, "masked *diablito,*" is disciplinarily styled, a reflection of ethnographic discourse. The indigenous term is stated first, and then translated for a nonspecialist readership. At the same time, this helpful gesture constitutes the authority of the narrator to represent the subject from an insider perspective to his reader (Pierre Loeb). Still, to the extent that Lam is to be taken as an insider, and given his colleague Lydia Cabrera's decisive revision of the terms *ñáñigo* and *diablito* (to Abakuá Society and *íreme*) between 1954 and 1958 in widely read works (see Cabrera 1954 and 1958), why the continued pejorative use of *ñáñigo* and *diablito,* the conspicuous absence of the term *Abakuá,* and the switching of descriptors in 1979?

Similar questions have been raised about the descriptive or evocative titles of Lam's works as of 1942. Lam began to incorporate apparent visual references to particular Afro-Cuban *orishas* and other spirits around 1942, icons of which he had undoubtedly seen in practitioners' homes, if not also in field photographs.[20] During this period, Lydia Cabrera "began to give titles to many of Lam's works, a practice that continued for several years. According to Helena Holzer . . . Cabrera suggested titles because the images in the paintings reminded her of specific experiences she was documenting" (Herzberg 1992:40). This does not in the least detract from Lam's penetrating work. Indeed, it suggests just how on the mark his emergent forms were in relation to this powerful subject matter, as well as for members of the same cultural movement who were preoccupied both with *lo afrocubano* and Lam's own painting. Still, it might be said that Lam's research, visual experience, and artistic production during this period were "collaborative" and heteroglossic, to some extent, the product of discursive and textual processes as much as his own essentialized Afro-Cuban genius.

Lam's *ñáñigo* paintings during the middle third of the 1940s seem to become both more personal and universal. Relying less on *afrocubanismo* genre conventions of representation, Lam turns to metaphor and allegory. Relying first on a biomorphism now even more diaphanous and, later, on automatist, surrealist mark-making, he evokes other orders of reality in a fresh way. Beginning in 1945, Lam pared down and transformed the full, more referential figure of the *diablito* into two powerful signs: a long vertical diamond with two burning eyes in the center and a schematic cone that sprouts the fringes of the *íreme*'s *pon-pon* (figures 10.5 and 10.7). *La Parade Antillaise* (figure 10.6), in addition to its diamond icon, contains multiple abstracted, spiritlike figures, which are packed together in an overlapping field of forms. Located centrally, this "parade" evokes again the apparent Carnival group of the 1943 work. In the 1945 *Les Oiseaux Voiles* (Birds–Sails), two tall cones, surmounted by *pon-pons* and fitted with circular *sombretetas,* float among a series of ethereal, staggered triangular forms. One of these two abbreviated *diablitos* sprouts a set of feathered wings that taper downward. Both feature upward aspiring, crescent-like extensions, looking much like rudimentary arms or horns. A third, more diminutive, cone/*pon-pon*/ triangle assemblage spreads its diffused crescent wings outward. Like the other two, with its pointed conical hood freed from any humanoid body of realistic representation, the figure can potentially soar (figure 10.7). Landaluze's *El Ñáñigo,* feet planted firmly upon the ground, is here a bird ready for flight among diaphanous "sails." In order to emphasize trajectory and upward movement, Lam appears to draw upon another modernist resource. The inner circles of the tall *diablitos' sombreretas* become platforms or portals for downward "lines of force," as one sees in the Italian Futurist Umberto Boccioni's (1882–1916) work. Lam thus appears to combine an interest in transforming figures, hybrid species, and atmospheric spaces with movement and unseen natural and supernatural forces. For example, wind is indexed by wings and sails, and conspires with nature's wings to produce the mystery of flight. Lam's "force lines" index not only movement but also unseen vectors of energy. These force lines could not be more different from Carreño's magico-sexual energy lines so prominent in *Afro-Cuban Dance* from the year before.

In short, Lam's shift from the more referential *íreme* of 1943 to the highly reduced and abstracted diamond emblem or hybrid ethereal figure with a conical apex signals a new set of inclinations. His reduction and abstraction produce a concise, potent symbol that far transcends social and cultural referents, aspiring toward the ineffable, imponderable, mystical, and transcendent. At the same time, as surrealism might have it, he transforms and is transformed by his art practice. Lam seems to demonstrate this principle in his stunning revision of another *ñáñigo* genre inherited by his generation from Víctor Patricio de Landaluze: the *fambá* interior (see plate 8).

Employing a compositional layout similar to Mario Carreño's 1943 *Cuarto Fambá* (Famba Room; figure 10.9), Lam paints his own *Cuarto Fambá* four years later, though in horizontal rather than vertical format (figure 10.12). Both rooms are flattened, though perspective and a sense of space are retained through their shared use of a receding floor tile pattern and other strong diagonals and overlapping objects, some of which are shaded. Carreño places proportionally larger objects in the immediate foreground, including two goblet-shaped Arará drums, a *sese,* and a *diablito* masquerade heaped on a chair. The room contains a mix of styles: the middle drum's bas-relief visage is a ringer for Picasso's later cubist faces, with its almond eyes and simplified features heavily outlined in black; in Cézanne fashion, the empty *diablito* suit's form takes on a geometric life of its own. At the same time, Carreño's space is highly decorative and cluttered. Indeed, this *fambá* interior is nothing less than the Cuban colonial era baroque style that fascinated the period's culturati, as seen, for example, in the restorations of Cabrera's Quinta San José. The *fambá*'s prominent shuttered window is framed with the signal stained glass that fills the paintings of Cuban modernist Amelia Peláez de Casal (1895–

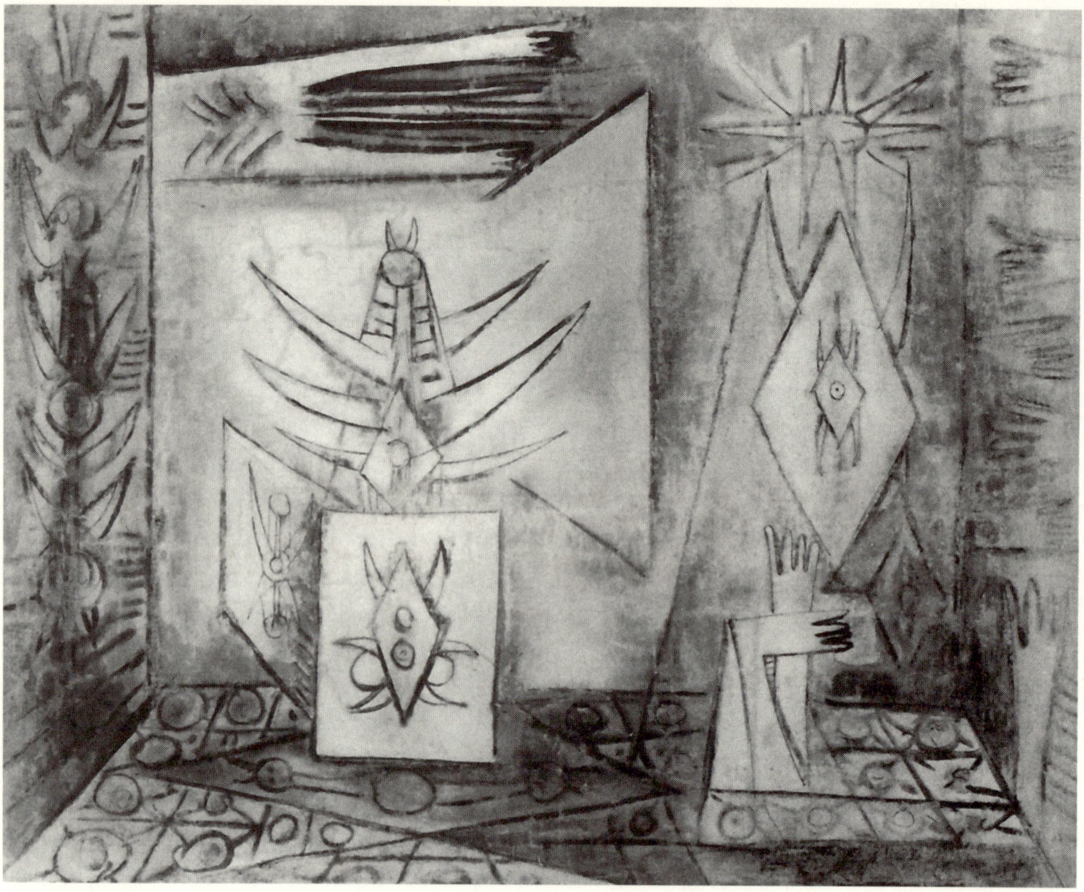

Figure 10.12. Wifredo Lam, *Cuarto Fambá,* 1947, oil on canvas, approx. 25 × 31.5 inches. Unlike Carreño, Lam presents an abstracted space filled with representations of his *diablitos* as well as surrealist symbol grids (see figure 10.11). Copyright © 2002 Artists Rights Society (ARS), New York/ADAGP, Paris.

1968) (figure 10.13). In short, Carreño's contribution deploys modernist formal markers and the genre conventions of *afrocubanismo*—drums, foliage, *ñáñigo* suit and ritual signs—to reenvision Cuban interior design sensibility, producing a unique, creole architectural *ajiaco* that bridges the eighteenth and twentieth centuries (see Blanc 1992:63).

Lam's 1947 *fambá* composition, including the placement of its interior panels, diagonals, and objects, mirrors Carreño's of 1943, if it does not also directly signify upon it. Lam's cubist space remains spare and minimal, at one level; as a horizontal composition, it is open and expansive, though ambiguous. At another level, the interior becomes dense with intricate visual activity. Instead of the decorative clutter of architectural and natural features, such as drums and plants referenced representationally, it is filled with Lam's schematic, hybrid *diablito* figures and horned diamond icons, in addition to surrealist symbols and calligraphic automatism. A vast panel with a looming *diablito*-like figure replaces Carreño's baroque window frame. On the right, a sail-like triangle, a sketched sunburst, two smaller geometric panels, and three rising schematic hands replace Carreño's chair, bamboo coat rack, potted plant, and three drums. More hands and rising *diablitos* replace Carreño's wall patterns, while circular and stick figure symbols comprehensively fill the floor tiles.

Both paintings share a common theme and object: the transformation of the artist's studio into a *fambá.*

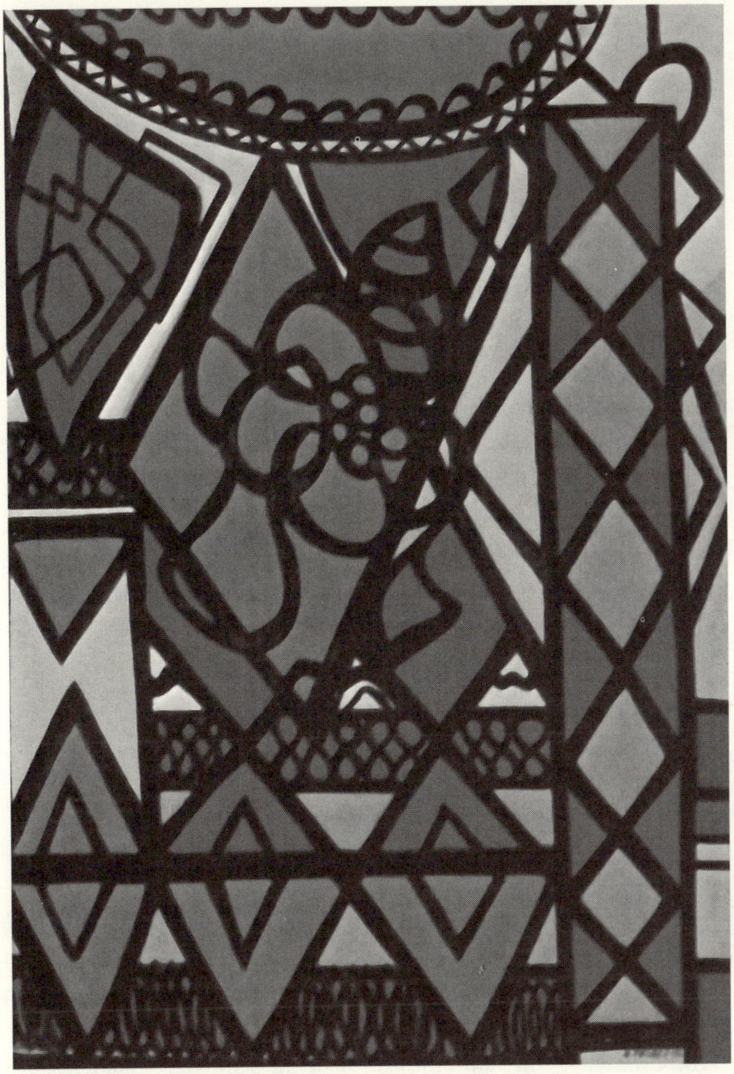

Figure 10.13. Amelia Peláez, *Still Life,* 1955, oil on canvas. Peláez abstractly represents Cuban interiors, including geometric stained-glass windows. Courtesy of the Museum of Arts and Science, Daytona Beach, Florida.

Carreño's space is filled with domestic and Afro-Cubanized still-life models, as well as the drawn products of the vanguard artist's labor: realistic *ñáñigo* signs. In Lam's *Cuarto Fambá,* the large panel, the leaning rectangle, and hanging diamond, all featuring Lam's signature figures, suggest canvases. Within this studio-cum-*fambá,* the artist's agency and graphic resources develop their analogue in the *ñáñigo* "scribe" of the Abakuá lodge, Mpegó, who chalks the sacred *firmas* on all objects, including cloth, drumskin, staffs, bodies, and the floor (see figures 3.13, 4.8, 4.9). Unlike Carreño, Lam chooses not to reproduce Abakuá *firmas* realistically, though he undoubtedly had the live and published resources to do so. As an alternative, Lam draws streamlined personal facsimiles of such signs into the Cuban tile floor. As a result, he recreates and revises both the signs themselves and the New York surrealist symbol grids of the pre-abstract expressionist periods of Jackson Pollock and Adolf Gottlieb, who drew on symbol making and calligraphic automatism in their surrealist phases prior to 1950s Abstract Expressionism (see figure 10.14). Where this branch of the emerging New York school appropriated signs and symbols from African, Native American, and imaginary sources to reference primitive myth and the collective unconscious, Lam drew

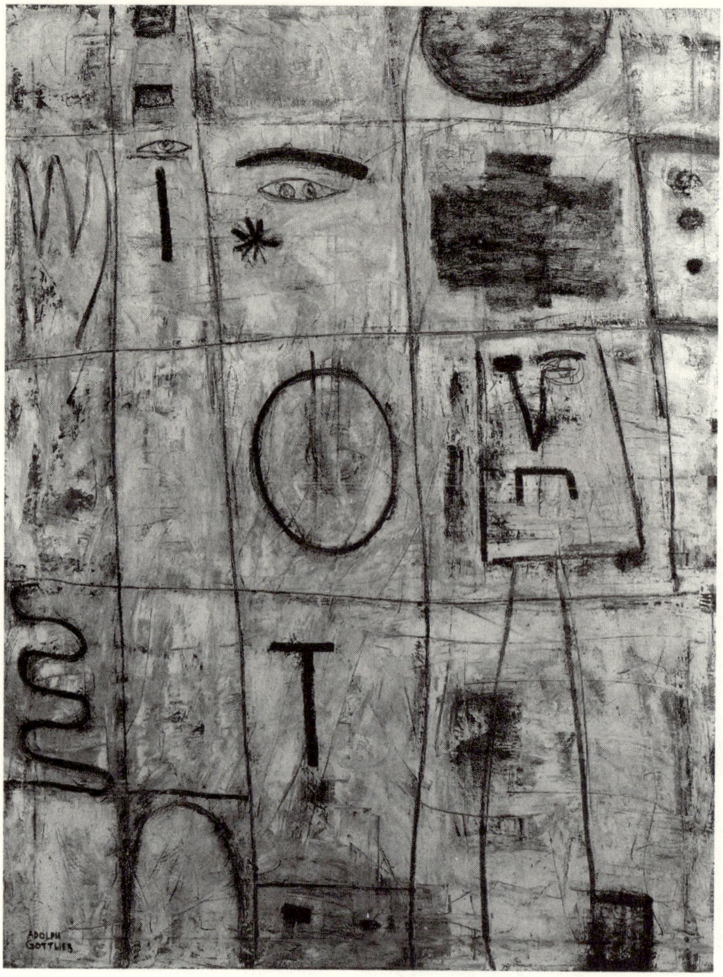

Figure 10.14. Adolf Gottlieb, *T,* 1950, oil on canvas (Blanc 1992:151). Gottlieb places "primitive" symbols and surrealist calligraphic marks in a grid. Courtesy of the Metropolitan Museum of Art.

on the model of Abakuá *anaforuana.* Where the New York School's modernists sought local primitive roots (e.g., Native American) for their own abstractions in order to distinguish their New World from the Old, Lam and his *vanguardia* contemporaries did something of the same. Within the studio-*fambá,* a mystical space of modernist cultural production, the Afro-Cubanist surrealist artist is now the maker of icons and sacred marks, the Carabalí Mpegó.

Within the studios of Cuba's *vanguardia, El Ñáñigo* graduated, for better or worse, into a modernist icon. Through the conventions of mid-century modernist primitivism, and as reshaped by figurative abstraction, *El Ñáñigo* could remain the dark sexual carnivore of Fernández Carrillo's 1881 profile, though now, in paint, the vehicle of the gendered beholder's fantasies. To Lam's credit, he recast the *El Ñáñigo* convention as an open-ended, transformative icon-in-progress of human, natural, and supernatural forces. Lam's *Les Oiseaux Voiles* demonstrates that *El Ñáñigo* could index visible and invisible powers (light and wind, vital forces of culture and nature) and processes (movement, elevation, transformation), rather than refer to fixed social referents. *Cuarto Fambá* thematizes the "work" or performance of transformation-through-writing within the creative subject's practical and psychic space: the studio/*fambá.* These works reflect upon, and revise, modern primitivist and modern ethnological definitions, thus permitting *El Ñáñigo* to unfold as an open ended or "deferred" process of inscription.[21]

11 From Primitivism to Folklore

Within six years of Wifredo Lam's return to Paris in early 1952, Fernando Ortiz and Lydia Cabrera published their most important works—*the* most important works—of Afro-Cuban ethnography (Ortiz 1950a, 1951, 1952–55; Cabrera 1954, 1957, 1970). They remain among the most important works of the African Diaspora literature today.[1] A brief exploration of selected texts reveals how *El Ñáñigo* figured within Ortiz's ethnology and Cabrera's folklore writing during the 1950s. Their efforts, particularly those of Ortiz, because he remained in Cuba after the "triumph of the revolution," as Cubans say, laid the foundations for "folklore" theory and practice from the 1960s forward. Via Ortiz's works, *El Ñáñigo* gains further respect as the legitimate descendant of West African practices, though he remains an anonymous social-scientific illustration in the ongoing "transculturation" narrative of *lo africano* in Cuba. Through Cabrera's textual orchestration, in contrast, *El Ñáñigo* approaches the status of subject and agent via the recorded "narratives" of her "old adept" sources. Still, *El Ñáñigo* remains a folkloric personage, a traditional cultural figure, within a circumscribed expressive world that remains socially and historically decontextualized.

Fernando Ortiz's Organology

Fernando Ortiz's works are heavily analytical ethnologies. They subordinate particular archival and informant sources to social scientific and taxonomic classification. With Ortiz, these data undergo exhaustive etymological scrutiny, particularly in the tracing of African ethnic and linguistic origins in order to substantiate their Cuban "transculturations." Nuggets of anecdote, mentions of colorful living or historical personages, and passages of "oral history" do occasionally emerge (e.g., 1954:314–315), but Ortiz's sources rarely have names and biographies; they do not speak. The voices of his informants, whom he often interviewed in his Vedado office, and formerly "living" *fundamentos,* already museum pieces, become objective data to be absorbed into third-person social-scientific discourse. Thus, the Abakuá Society, its adepts, and its creations exist not in, and for, themselves, but as documentary illustrations of higher-order anthropological, historical, and philological categories.[2]

Ortiz's miraculous five-volume *Instruments of Afro-Cuban Music* (1952–55) is not really ethnography or "ethnomusicology"—an account of indigenous cultural (musical) production. It is an organology, which classifies Afro-Cuban music-making artifacts into categories and meta-categories of instrument types. Instruments or types of them appear in alphabetical organization, and each is painstakingly unpacked from every conceivable angle. Thus, Abakuá instruments and attributes do not appear together, of an ethnographic piece, but are distributed throughout at least three different volumes. The orchestra and "symbolic" drums appear within the "open bottomed, single membrane" category of drum form *(membranófono abierto)* in volume IV, and then within the *Ñ*—for Ñáñigo—chapter, followed by the *Ogudu* and *Pandero* of other Afro-Cuban ethnic groups. Ekue appears under the "friction" drum category *(los fricativos)* in volume V. Other instruments appear in volume II within the categories of "shaken" *(sacuditivo)* and "iron" *(los hierros)* objects, such as the *erikundé* and *maruga,* the *ekón,* and the *enkaniká.*[3] Because the *ekón* is hit percussively with a stick *(palo),* it is technically an *hierro.* Meanwhile, because the *enkaniká* has its own internal clapper, it appears later under the "bells" *(campanas)* subcategory.

Life Imitates Art: *El Ñáñigo* as Artifice

For Fernando Ortiz, the verisimilitude of Landaluze's realistic *diablitos* permitted their use as ethnographic documents. Indeed, Ortiz referred to Landaluze's 1881 *Tipos y costumbres* as "an ethnographic museum." Thus, Ortiz was able, he believed, to prove the existence in Cuba of a colonial-era *diablito* of the Gangá nation through positive comparison of the artist's work with a more recent photograph of a Central African Kuba helmet mask (see Ortiz 1951:449; 1953) of the *Mwaash a mbooy* type. In Ortiz's grand 1951 work, Landaluze's *El Ñáñigo* and other artistic documents illustrate extensive discussions of Abakuá *íreme* dance performance, its African background, and the street theater of *diablitos* during Cuba's Day of Kings carnival (1951:465–472). In the organology, though Ortiz extensively discusses *ñáñigo* history, personnel, and ritual in volume IV, Landaluze's 1881 *El Ñáñigo* is used to illustrate a single, minor instrument type in volume II—quite a demotion, given that *El Ñáñigo* had formerly served as the "supreme incarnation" of *ñañiguismo* and "delinquency" (I. Castellanos 1928). In 1908, Inspector Roche y Monteagudo had captioned Landaluze's figure as "Ñáñigo outfitted with the *saco*" in order to make the attributes of *ñáñigo* personnel legible for purposes of criminal identification. In contrast, Ortiz captions his illustration "Fig. 111—Ñáñigo Diablito with *enkaniká*" in order to identify the precise type, use, and position of a series of squarish Abakuá bells *(enkaniká)* worn about the *íreme*'s waist.

Landaluze's *El Ñáñigo* is exquisitely appropriate for the task. Ironically, its usefulness as a modern scientific illustration in Ortiz's organology is enabled as much by the artifice of classical draftsmanship as by the ostensible transparency of this "ethnographic document." The *costumbrista* consciously chose particular formal means to throw the figure's surfaces and details into relief. Landaluze drew the figure against a neutral background, meticulously modeling its volumes. In its profile perspective, the figure's *enkaniká* sharply stand out and become immediately legible against this background (1952:277). There is neither reason nor evidence to presume a unique "original scene" that the capable artist merely recorded ethnographically, as if taking a photograph. Quite apparently, Landaluze placed a single *ñáñigo diablito* type within different compositions, though it remains unclear whether the artist drew and painted from sketches of multiple fleeting observations on the street or had a single masquerade model for him in the studio. In any event, Landaluze's *El Ñáñigo* was, and remains, a "type," and it singlehandedly created an artistic genre (Abakuá masking) from the popular "customs" of urban Cuba.

Within the contextualization of Ortiz's organology, *El Ñáñigo* becomes a function of higher-order classification. In situ, he might express himself through his *enkaniká* as well as through his "pantomime." But the organology does not intend to lend *El Ñáñigo* the contextualization he might need in order to do so. Thus, in 1952, *El Ñáñigo* still does not "speak," as José Trujillo y Monagas would have wished. The task of getting *El Ñáñigo* to express himself would be left to Fernando Ortiz's sister-in-law, Lydia Cabrera.[4] Ortiz excels in the analytical representation of indigenous concepts, categories, objects, and terminology. These are subordinated to the narrator's firm, omniscient, free indirect discourse, a marked stylistic feature of modern scientific ethnology (see Clifford 1988:47–48). The narrator's voice never varies from its sober, scholarly tone. In contrast, Lydia Cabrera's works come partly in the style of folklore studies, which are then shaped by her idiosyncratic literary bent. These studies include the collection and compilation of oral legends and history, informant glosses of myth and ritual, genealogical recitations, plant lore, and vocabulary. A versatile researcher and writer, Cabrera variously absorbed these materials into compact retold "stories" (1940), juxtaposed them with extensive analytical sections, such as her massive ethnobotanical catalog in *El Monte* (1954), organized them into recognizably ethnographic re-presentations (1958, 1986a, 1986b), cast them as theme-based works (1980b), subordinated them into glossaries or catalogs (1957, 1975, 1988), or presented them in indigenous didactic style (1980a). Thus, for example, her folklore study of the "Abakuá Secret Society" (1958) is prominently subtitled "narrated by old adepts."

Lydia Cabrera and her "Old Informants"

In order to appreciate how *El Ñáñigo* graduates to a valorized folkloric personage with a level of agency within Cabrera's works, it is worth exploring her approach to *lo afrocubano.* Cabrera's ethnographic-style works rightly fall under anthropology's folklore subfield, inasmuch as they concentrate primarily on experience-near representation of expressive culture and oral history through indigenous "voices." Cabrera accomplished this by eliminating heavy redaction of her field notes and emphasizing direct discourse on the published page. Her method, she said, was imposed "by the inextricable explanations and digressions of my informants. . . . I have not omitted repetitions and contradictions. . . . I want their voices to be heard without intermediaries, exactly as they talked to me" (Intar Gallery 1984:6).[5] Such compilation, unrestrained by subordinating analytical frameworks, permitted certain thematic emphases to stand out in their very repetition. Thus, indigenous categories via names, toponyms, natural formations, and ritual objects and principles come to organize her work. For example, *El Monte* thematically revolves around two sacred trees, the royal palm and the *ceiba.* Her scheme narratively choreographs a welter of liturgical and cosmological detail through an indigenous meta-organizing principle, "the sacred forest" *(El Monte).* Still, as if to throw into relief culturally divergent, historically produced principles for organizing any given object of study, the second half of *El Monte* provides a radically reconfigured counterpart to the first. It subordinates loose oral testimony on plants, ritual, and cosmology to scientific classification by common and Latin names, based heavily on the work of Juan Tomás Roig y Mesa (1962) conducted at the famous ethnobotanical station in the Havana microclimate of Santiago de las Vegas. At the same time, because the 550 plants' common and Latin names are followed by their Lucumí and Congo names, as well as the identification of their *orisha* owners, the "initiated" reader can re-sort ostensibly scientific data into Afro-Cuban "nation"- and pantheon-based sacred categories.

Equally important to the open-textured effect of Cabrera's earlier works are her innovative narrative strategies, particularly the ingenious modulations and positional shifts in the narrator's voice, comparable to those encountered in Zora Neale Hurston's folklore studies (1935). In contrast to Ortiz's scientistic narration, dominated by a consistent third-person voice, Cabrera juxtaposes straightforward ethnographic description with romantic asides about her informants in a personal tone and shifts in the narrator's voice from more standard to vernacular expression (see, e.g., 1954:23–28, 86–98). Her narrator's voice strengthens and recedes in authority and tone, and thickens and thins in density of articulation relative to interventions of practitioners' voices. Short bursts of practitioner speech or whole paragraphs pop up unintroduced and left without follow-up. Sentences are often broken up by commas, semicolons, and dashes separating alternate, quoted, or italicized phrasings and rephrasings in several lexicons (Spanish, Bozal, Lucumí, Congo, Abakuá). Though the author stages these alternative voices relative to the narrator's, her works remain significantly open-textured, even "polyphonic" or "heteroglossic," particularly *El Monte* (1954; see Clifford 1988:41–50). This makes the material often difficult to read and understand. The corollary of multiple voices in different languages, language varieties, and idioms is divided, even mystified, address—that is to say, multiple hypothetical readerships with different levels of competence. Hence, often practitioners can read these texts with ease, whereas scholars remain stumped. In Cabrera's case, these textual features apparently resulted as much from her lifelong literary-poetic bent as her thorough lack of training in anthropology. It remains to be discovered whether such textual features, arguably a counterpoint to modern professional ethnographic discourse, emerged along with her avant-garde interests and influences in surrealism. "I'm neither anthropologist nor anthropophagus [cannibal]," she declared: Was this a defense of her intimacy with Afro-Cubans, whom the public still considered bogeymen and parasites set to consume the white race, or a wry critique of the malign colonialist underpinnings of modern anthropological fieldwork?

Though Cabrera is credited with close and enduring relationships with her sources, such as Calixta Morales (Oddedeí) (figure 11.1) and the Abakuá sage Saibeke, caution might be exercised in order not to romanticize her work too much or disconnect her from issues of class, race, and gender in Cuban society from 1900 to 1960—the year she left the island with the wealthy white "first wave" of exiles. A number of the "Old Adepts," such as Teresa Muñoz Omí Tomí, were black employees of her upper-class family (Cabrera 1954:26–27) or were former cane workers at the vast Matanzas sugar mill *(ingenio)* owned by the family of photographer and close friend

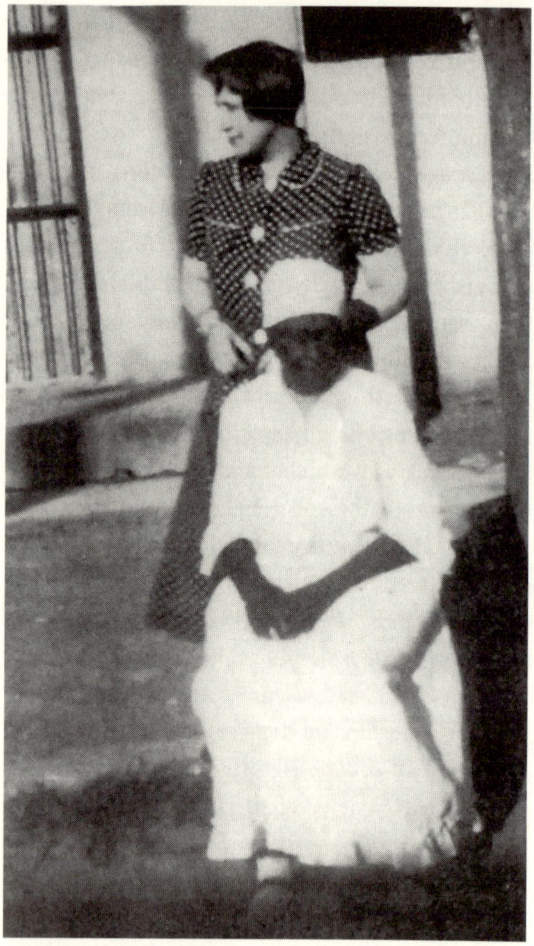

Figure 11.1. Lydia Cabrera with Calixta Morales (Oddedeí) in Pogolotti, 1930 (Intar Gallery 1984). Cabrera met Oddedeí in 1930 and worked with her intensively as an informant as of the early 1940s. Courtesy of the Estate of Lydia Cabrera.

Josefina Tarafa.[6] Cabrera (1899–1991) knew some of her sources from when she was a precocious, liberally educated society girl who became a bohemian intellectual, artist, curator, and businesswoman in Paris in the 1920s and 1930s (Intar Gallery 1984:6–9).[7] It is claimed that Cabrera's first book, *Cuentos negros de Cuba,* part oral tradition and part fiction, was based on the "remember[ed] . . . world of her childhood, a world dominated by the inventions of Black nannies, cooks, and seamstresses" (Intar Gallery 1984:9). Still, the book was written not in Cuba but Paris in 1934, in order "to entertain" her ill partner, the Latin American radical novelist Teresa de la Parra. This work of "folklore" was thus the product of highly mediated transmission, in which, as an emerging literary and artistic type, Cabrera styled herself as a storyteller within a very peculiar performance context. The work may also have provided certain avant-garde cultural credentials in a late-1920s and 1930s Paris enchanted by things "primitive." Following her return to Cuba in 1938, Cabrera moved in with María Teresa de Rojas, owner of the landmark eighteenth-century Quinta San José mansion in Marianao, which the two women restored and filled with arts and crafts. Her close Chilean poet friend visiting from Paris, Gabriela Mistral, was "scandalized by Lydia's wealthy acquaintances. . . . I am pained to have found you rather bourgeois this time, like a French lady from Lyon or Blois. . . . You're wasting yourself like precious land under the Spanish regime of abandon and laziness" (Intar Gallery 1984:10). Appearances aside, as "an emancipated woman who never broke with her family or class," Cabrera led a "highly unorthodox" lifestyle, living in a gay partnership in a colonial mansion next to the impoverished black *barrio* of Pogolotti, where she recommenced her research in 1942 (Intar Gallery 1984:10–11, 14). Cabrera's lifestyle did have its contradictions; however, it would be very surprising to find that her novel fieldwork approach, textual heteroglossia, and divided address were without highly interesting correlates in the social cleavages she experienced.

Cabrera's *Íremes*

In the Cuban literature, the Abakuá receive their first respectful, nonjudgmental treatment in the works of Lydia Cabrera (1954, 1958). It is the first time that information about the Abakuá comes almost entirely from the mouths of its members. And Abakuá masquerade is represented for the first time as a benign, living phenomenon. An Abakuá member dressed in an *íreme* suit poses in various positions before the great *ceiba* tree, for which the 1954 chapter is named (see figure 11.2). The photographs illustrate the dense, twenty-five-page *El Monte* chapter titled "Ukano Bekonsí: The Ceiba Tree and the Secret Society of the Abakuá or Ñáñigos" (1954:195–220). Cabrera's information seems to have been gleaned mostly on Abakuá turf, though her "informants" may have passed time with Cabrera in her office and on the patio of the Quinta San José. That two women, Cabrera and her photographer on occasion, María Teresa de Rojas, were permitted into the Abakuá compound in order to ask questions and photograph sacred objects must also be a first in the group's history on the island. Cabrera's narrative allows her sources to debunk popular prejudices when they define the Abakuá as "a mutual aid society of fraternal support, in which all members are brothers, who guard the secrets of the society, and worship their secret as our elders in Africa did. The ñáñigos are the masons of Africa, and we Cubans, their descendants. Ñañiguismo is not at all what people think it is" (1954:198–199). Abakuá history is left relatively unprocessed, represented, as told to her, in the genres of genealogical recitation and hagiography. This stunning 1954 chapter was the precursor to the first major monograph[8] on the 122-year-old Afro-Cuban tradition, *The Abakuá Secret Society* (1958); it was the first work to foreground the non-pejorative denomination "Abakuá."

Víctor Patricio de Landaluze's *El Ñáñigo* prominently appears among very few illustrations in Cabrera's 1958 work. Cabrera's representation of "old adept narratives" provides the space for *El Ñáñigo* to

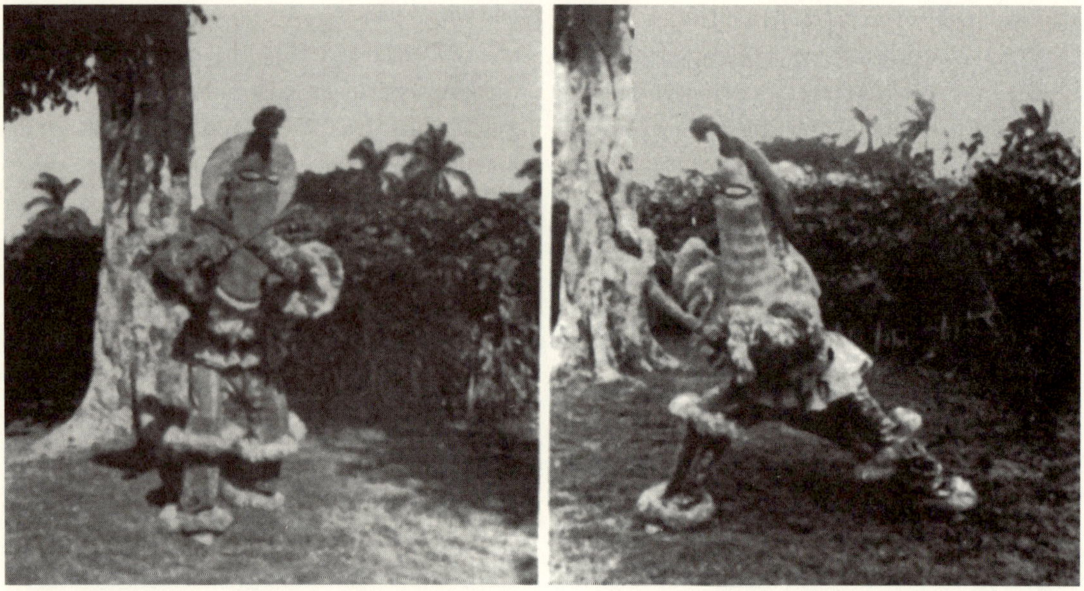

Figure 11.2. An *íreme* photographed by María Teresa de Rojas, 1940s–early 1950s, for Lydia Cabrera's *El Monte.* Courtesy of the Estate of Lydia Cabrera.

gain a kind of identity it had never had in the literature. The work is organized around recitations of genealogy, stories of Sikán and Tanze, the mapping of Abakuá "geography of sacred memory" in West Africa, oral history of Cuba's Abakuá, and descriptions of lodge organization. Lodge offices appear as a series of rich capsule portraits, including the *íremes.* Landaluze's *El Ñáñigo* is one of two illustrations within the section devoted to the *íremes,* and it appears on the verso of a contemporaneous field photograph of an *íreme* photographed in situ by French ethnographer Pierre Verger when he visited Cuba in 1957 (figure 11.3).[9] Captioned *"Diablito,"* Landaluze's 1881 lithograph illustrates the historical role this figure played during the old Day of Kings carnival. Though *diablito* is antiquated, it does represent the popular term applied to Day of Kings maskers. At the same time, *El Ñáñigo* finds sympathetic companionship: Landaluze's subject and Verger's *íreme* are spatialized in a way that bridges 1881 and 1954, leapfrogging the topoi of criminality and delinquency and grounding the two within a living tradition. Cabrera does not attempt to identify the particular *íreme* type that Landaluze drew, but *El Ñáñigo* gains unprecedented substance and significance within a web of *íreme* stories. The following passage precedes the two illustrations:

Ireme Eribangandó

Eribá, lo llama algún obonékue. Era uno de los pescadores que oyó, como Insuá (Isunékue) y otros, bramar a Ekue en las aguas de Fokondó. . . . *Eribangandó mutu chekéndéke.* El que tuvo valor. Pues, cuando Nasakó hizo sacrificar a Sikán y el Espíritu de Tánze chilló en el Secreto unido al de Sikán—la piel de Sikán sobre la piel de Tánze—todos los restos de las ofrendas, las sangres, cuanto se utilizó para la obtención de la Voz, fueron llevadas por Eribangandó a una cueva sagrada, a orillas del río. Cueva profunda, negra como boca de lobo, inspiraba tal terror, que nadie entrada. Allí en lo hondo, vivían unidos el Majá—ñangabión—y el Cocodrillo—mokombé—que salían juntos a comer. (A recibir las ofrendas). . . .

Eribangandó no temía a estos seres misteriosos, que son materializaciones de fuerzas ocultas, de Espíritus fluviales, y no hacen daño a los que están iniciados en los secretos, "saben de las cosas del otro mundo, han hecho alianza con los espíritus." (Cabrera 1970:208)

Eribá, some initiates call him. He was one of the fishermen who heard, as did Insuá (Isunékue) and others, the roar [of] Ekue in the waters of Fokondó. . . . *Eribangandó mutu chekéndéke.* He that had valor. So, when Nasakó sacrificed Sikán, and the Spirit of Tánze shrieked from within the Secret that was united with [her], [i.e.]—the skin of Sikán placed over the skin of Tánze—the remains of the offerings [and] the various kinds of blood . . . were carried by Eribangandó to a sacred cave, at the bank of the river. A deep cave, black as the mouth of a wolf, it used to inspire such terror that no one entered. There, in the deep, the Majá [serpent]—ñáñgabión—and the Crocodile—mokombá—lived together and came out together to eat. (To receive the offerings).

Eribangandó wasn't afraid of these mysterious beings, which were materializations of hidden forces, of river Spirits, and they didn't harm those who were initiated into the secrets, "they know the things of the other world, they have made an alliance with the spirits."

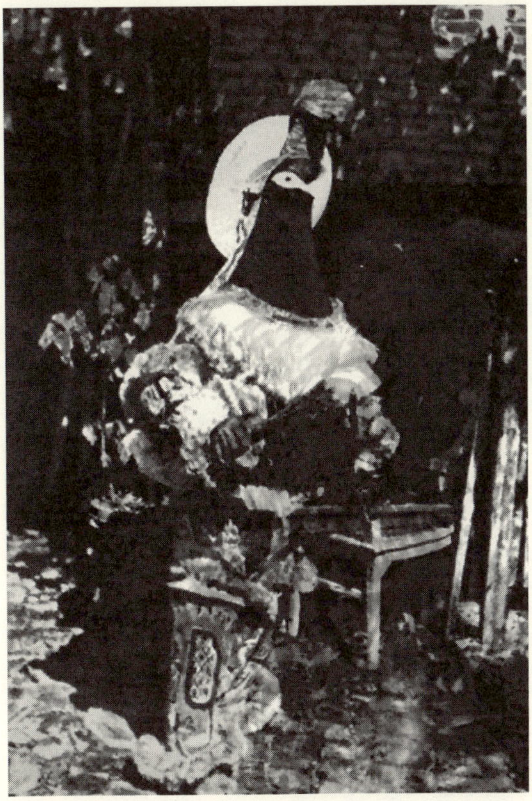

Figure 11.3. Composite image constructed by this author simulating Landaluze's 1881 *El Ñáñigo* as printed on the verso of this 1957 *íreme* photograph in Cabrera's 1958 work *The Abakuá Secret Society.* Courtesy of the Estate of Lydia Cabrera.

As suspended within a web of stories, rather than a web of criminal evidence or ethnological analysis, *El Ñáñigo* graduates from specimen or illustration to virtual personage. The story of Eribangandó, though it does not necessarily identify Landaluze's *El Ñáñigo,* grants him the kinds of markers that constitute subjectivity within the Abakuá idiom: his origin, character traits, and deeds in relation to the mysteries of *ekue.* As an ancestral being, he had a vocation; he had valor and was fearless; he performed essential tasks in the founding of a tradition as the liaison to Ñangabión and Macombá. The *íreme*'s textual portrait is represented in quoted practitioner speech and the narrator's minimal explanatory recapitulation. Nevertheless, this is not transparent ethnography in which everything is explained. Mysterious actions and the "deep" places characters inhabit do not give over easily to the logic of the everyday world of the reader. Cabrera's goal was to "offer the specialists . . . material that has not gone through the dangerous filter of interpretation" (Intar Gallery 1984:6); but, in practice, the work requires not merely a specialized but a kind of initiated or culturally prepared reader. Her writing was, and remains, difficult enough for scholars who need no courses in cultural relativism. Her work was undoubtedly a dare in 1958, when *ñañiguismo* was still illicit.

In the context of Cabrera's narrative, *El Ñáñigo* exemplifies deep knowledge, including knowledge of what cannot be known or understood by ordinary human beings. In a word, he exemplifies defamiliarization. *Eribangandó did not fear those mysterious beings. . . . The spirits don't harm those who are initiated into the secrets. El Ñáñigo,* like his other *íreme* brothers, "knows the things of the other world, they have made an alliance with the spirits." *El Ñáñigo* expresses himself in Cabrera's pages, though not in a manner that would have satisfied José Trujillo y Monagas. Neither might Cabrera's kind of narrative have fully satisfied Fernando Ortiz, who sought to uncover the "secret" mostly in archives and the laboratory, though he had to admit that he never found it. Perhaps the "word of Nasakó" was hidden somewhere in the labyrinth of Cabrera's *El Monte.* Ortiz, an heir of the enlightenment, was, ultimately, professionally wedded to scientific discovery in the service of the nation's progress and positive "transculturation." Cabrera, wedded to her idiosyncratic, open-ended literary and painterly method, left Cuba in the first wave of exiles in 1960. Ortiz stayed, and his influence on the Cuban academy remained dominant and has not ceased. Whatever "light inside" was left to be discovered by observers, it would, of necessity, be wedded to the cultural and political aims of the revolution.

12 We Were Teaching How to Ask the Black Man about Very Private, Personal Things

Afrocubana, *the Triumph of the Revolution, and Socialist Folklore*

In March 1964, the José Martí National Library and the Folklore Department of the National Theater (Teatro Nacional) of Cuba produced an unprecedented evening performance, *El Concierto de Música Abakuá.* It was directed by Argeliers León, an ethnomusicologist and protégé of Fernando Ortiz. The oversized program book,[1] printed on thick, elegant white stock, reproduced an elaborate Abakuá *firma* forming a cryptic geography of sacred memory (figure 12.1). The cover's interconnected radiating signs delineated the "sun illuminating the capital of Efori Isun," from which emanated the "other ancient homelands of the Efó and Efí." Inside, three double-columned bilingual pages explained in rich detail the history, myth, ritual, dramatis personae, and music of the Abakuá. The fourth page of program notes provided background on the show's twenty-three acts in two parts, and the last page transcribed the corresponding twenty-three Abakuá songs in the Brícamo language. These pages were separated by two beautiful poster-size inserts of more *firmas,* with concise explanations of their significance. Like Fernando Ortiz's presentation of Lucumí *batá* music in 1937, León's "concert" was the first time that the feared and misunderstood *ñáñigo*—now, irrevocably, the "Abakuá"—was celebrated on a state-sanctioned stage. Cuba and the world were finally meant to witness the "sun illuminating" the rebirth of the Abakuá Society (see Hagedorn 2001:136–143). In 1959, *El Ñáñigo* could cross over to become a new kind of actor, a hybrid of ethnographic phenomenon and didactic theatrical presence. With the *Concierto Abakuá* he would effortlessly bear on his shoulder the vision of the revolution's "New Man," as Abasonga had carried *ekue* from one side of the Oddán River to the other.

Music and dance theater constituted the March evening's show. Argeliers León provided ethnographic and historical context with apparently neutral program notes. Echoing the sense of Fernando Ortiz's 1937 concert, indeed, the very notion of "transculturation" as applied to Cuban *cosas de negro,* the text concluded: "The musical ex-

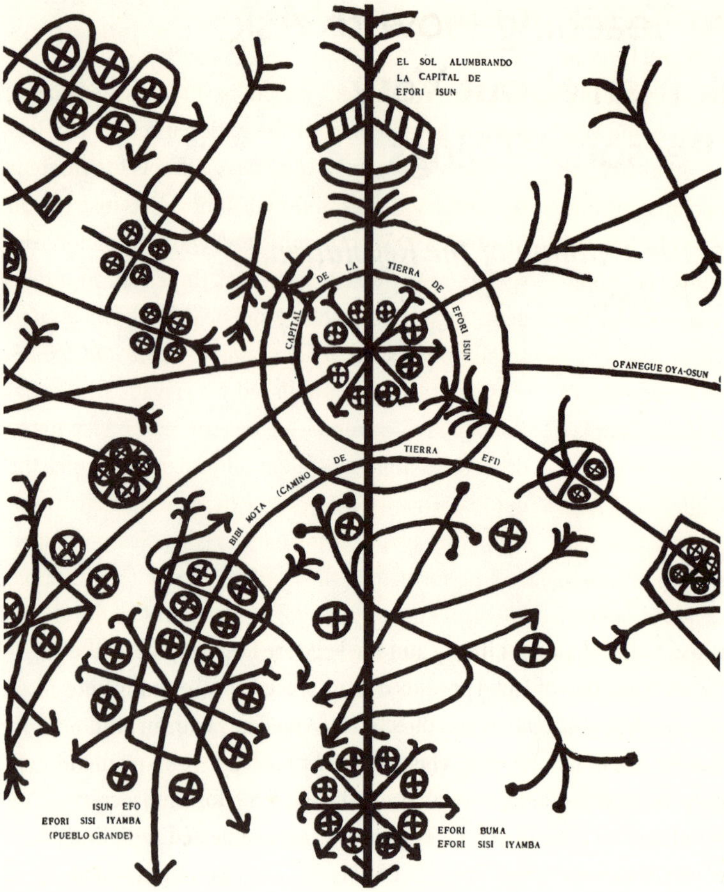

Figure 12.1. Cover of the program for the *Concierto de Música Abakuá,* directed by Argeliers León in the National Theater, March 1964, featuring elaborate *anaforuana* signs delineating the territories of Abakuá origin in Africa.

pression of the Abakuá, *completely isolatable from the hold that ritual has on them,* and their rhythmic and melodic value, are what the Department of Music of the José Martí National Library presents today, as an effort to rescue the cultural expressions of our people" (León 1964, emphasis added). Things Abakuá, at least as theoretically represented in the folkloric concert stage setting, could and would no longer be stigmatized. Yet the intent behind *Concierto Abakuá* was more than aesthetic and theatrical. Significant social change would occur in and through such newly institutionalized kinds of performance. "The revolution was going to make life in Cuba egalitarian in all senses of the word. . . . The Teatro Nacional was going to express these values through its performances" (Hagedorn 1995:225). This socialist vision of "the cultural expressions of our people" as fuel for the transformation of colony into independent socialist nation took on its unique Cuban direction, but resonated with similar projects throughout the Third World. Similar sentiments are found, for example, in the vision of Eric Williams, Trinidad's first prime minister following independence (1962), in dramatist Rex Nettleford's work on Jamaican dance and cultural identity (Nettleford 1978), and in Errol Hill's *Trinidad Carnival: Mandate for a National Theater* (Hill 1972; Franco 2001).

The new National Theater of Cuba was founded soon after the January 1959 triumphal entrance of Fidel Castro into Havana and the American-sponsored flight of dictator Fulgencio Batista into exile. It was housed in the modern National Theater building, which stood adjacent to the great Plaza of the Revolution, with its monument to José Martí and Ernesto "Ché" Guevara. The Plaza would thus inextricably link, in a seamless ideological line, Cuba's second War of Independence from Spain and the 1959 Revolution, as it has become a space reconsecrated around the martyrdom of El Ché. Before the revolution, the National Theater had supported avant-garde, popular, and folkloric performance, particularly under the direction of Ramiro Guerra (Hagedorn 2001:137–138; Roldán 1055–1056). Established by a group of revolutionary intellectuals connected to the People's Socialist Party, the institution was composed of five departments: music, dance, theater, singing, and folklore. The last was headed by Argeliers León, who had attended Ortiz's famous "Afrocubanist" seminars in the 1930s and 1940s. In turn, the Department of Folklore gave birth to the multidisciplinary National Folklore Group of Cuba (Conjunto Folklórico Nacional de Cuba) in 1962. The Conjunto would constitute the principal platform for the theory and practice of applied national folklore, from its teaching and dissemination at all levels of the society to the highly refined performances by its professionals before international audiences. It would, in time, also become a key component of Cuban cultural tourism (see Hagedorn 2001:6–10, 137–138, 221–225).[2]

Folklore was taken so seriously in the revolutionary cultural and educational agenda that a new body, the Institute of Ethnology and Folklore, to be directed by León, was founded in 1961 under the Consejo de Cultura (Council of Culture), a branch of the Ministry of Education. In 1962 the Institute for Ethnology and Folklore gained a more specialized scholarly niche. It came under the Academy of Sciences (Hagedorn 2001:139–140), a great institution of learning that had been inaugurated in 1860 to establish the hard and social science disciplines in Cuba—which would later include anthropology and legal medicine. It claimed a library of more than 110,000 volumes and maintained museums of natural history, zoology, botany, archaeology, and anthropology (Roldán 1940:1047).

El Ñáñigo's School Days

Folklore education, including music and dance, quickly became part of the national school curriculum, and a system of *aficionado* schools for amateur performers was established. Innovative instruction manuals for performance teachers and folklore designers were published. One of these was an intelligent, exceedingly clear, and beautifully illustrated small book called *Study Guide: Costume and Its Importance in Dance,* published by Havana's Editorial Pueblo y Educación (see Lamerán 1982). Like many other contemporary Cuban cultural publications, the guide is organized according to the official genres of the Afro-Cuban performance repertoire developed and performed by the Conjunto Folklórico: Rumba, Guajiro, Lucumí, Congo, Abakuá, and so on. In the kind of concise ethnographic encapsulations developed to present and explain staged folklore, the guide features effective summaries of these genres' origins, history, meanings, style of performance, and costuming *(el vestuario).* Each section is accompanied by a vivid color illustration of folkloric performers engaged in a particular dance style: Guaguancó, Yambú, Colúmbia, Santería, Palo, Abakuá, and the like. The costumes depicted directly follow from the pithy conventions early established by the National Folklore Group of Cuba. Female rumba performers wear the *conguita* dress; the Santería dancer for each deity appears in a highly codified *orisha* costume, along with its appropriate colors and hand-held attribute. In the Abakuá illustration, a barefoot Moruá Yuansá officer wears white, with *pañuelos* (kerchiefs) about the head, shoulders, and waist. He carries his cruciform rattle *(erikundé)* to direct the *íreme.* The outsized *íreme,* who carries the basil branch and rod, as in Landaluze's depictions, dances before the Moruá (plate 23). The *íreme*'s movement reflects not the subtle angularity of the Abakuá *plante* but the exaggerations of thoroughgoing theatricality. Landaluze's *El Ñáñigo* regulated the *íreme*'s movement through classical figuration (see figure 4.1). Roche y Monteagudo turned the *íreme*'s conscientious adherence to the command of Enkríkamo or Moruá on its head, making the *íreme* the evil mastermind of mafia-style street execution (see figure 2.4). Israel Castellanos's Landaluze *ñáñigo* became an isolated cutout, a dead butterfly on a specimen board (see figure 10.1). Here, Lamerán's study guide turns *El Ñáñigo* into an over-the-top stage ham who responds like a performing seal to the command of the Moruá. His left leg and right arm are raised, as he stands planted on one foot. His body careens dramatically backward. In short, the *íreme*'s traditional bodily disposition and movements, already constituted as "folklore" in Ortiz's midcentury writing on Abakuá "pantomime," become a source of spectacular amusement, reflecting a highly mediated and commodified repertoire. The *íreme*'s presentation is consciously directed to audience effect and affect—a secondary transformation Katherine Hagedorn calls "folkloricization" (2001:67–69).

The Construction of Folkloric Authenticity

Argeliers León's "authentic" staged spectacles *(espectáculos)* were extremely popular, and the 1964 concert was the most memorable of these. It was extremely successful not merely in theatricalizing the Abakuá narrative, but also in modeling a form of popular socialist theater in which the audience could participate. Never had *ñañiguismo,* formerly scorned and attacked, been seen live in this way by so many people. As León told Hagedorn before his death, black performers sang the "same songs" as they would have in their "rituals" (Hagedorn 2001:142). The audience was diverse. It included many Abakuá practitioners, who entered into dialogue with the actors "as if it were real." The foreign audience members, including high-profile fellow travelers, were enchanted with this interaction. Ortiz's "tragedy of the Ñáñigos" (see 1950b), built around their central mythical narrative, could be effectively realized on stage with a few key figures, props, and scores. As León remembered, "We had the river, the *diablitos,* the whole thing. Jean-Paul Sartre was there, and he loved it. He said he had seen a type of drama comparable to that of the great Greek dramas, because it established a dialogue between the audience and the performer." Indeed, "fistfights" broke out because some practitioners in the audience felt that the actors "gave away too many secrets" (Hagedorn 2001:142–143). A revolutionary cultural institution could bridge, or so it seemed, an emergent new Cuban society, the Abakuá, and an international audience for the greater good. *El Ñáñigo* had graduated from jail to specimen board, to folklore text, to the national stage. Savage African "rituals" had been elevated and assimilated to modern versions of classical drama in Caribbean socialist space.

Revolutionary Folklore and Racial Authenticity

The enduring axes of race and class formation, though publicly unspoken, have played significant roles in the Conjunto's hierarchy of creative labor, credentialing, and self-promotion, as well as its internal contradictions. The early experiments in the National Theater and the National Folklore group of Cuba sought to achieve what Argeliers León called "authenticity" precisely as they came to terms with these two axes. As Hagedorn paraphrases the recognized accomplishment of León and his colleagues, "the dancers and musicians were not *aficionados,* that is, they had not taken dance classes and such. Rather, they were simply townspeople of these same religious groups" (Hagedorn 2001:140). "Townspeople" operates as a revolutionarily legible euphemism for a distinctive class or subcultural formation that both legitimated the state as a popularly supported institution and that was (to be) uplifted within the new socialist society. The Conjunto, at least on its official face, would teach not religion to these townspeople, Cuban society, and the world, but music and art, "cultural values," which were "isolatable from the hold that ritual has on them."

As a result of León's pioneering work, built on the enduring transculturative vision of Fernando Ortiz, the critical relationship between the "townspeople" and the "intellectuals" was institutionalized in the methodology of Cuban folkloric practice. The former group became the pool of "informants," and the latter were directors, researchers, choreographers, and presenters. The "intellectuals"—the "Director," "Choreographer," and "Designer"—were academically trained white professionals. The performers were virtually all dark-skinned from the poorer *barrios* (see Consejo Nacional de Cultura 1963; Hagedorn 2001:166).[3] The ethnographic go-between and *asesor de folklore* ("folklore consultant") among the intellectuals and the informants was the young *mulato* scholar Rogelio Martínez Furé, a member of Argeliers León's Institute of Ethnology and Folklore under the bureaucratic umbrella of the Academy of Sciences. Intriguingly, the ethnographic consultant's most significant published work, of ostensible Afro-Cuban content, consisted of "dialogues" between himself and the late Don Fernando Ortiz, not folk practitioners (1979). His ethnographic gaze soared upward toward the great theorist of transculturation and black uplift before it swooped downward into the *hampa cubana* (black underworld) in order to rise once again with "folklore" in its sights.

The new institution's organization reflected the historical demographic profile of Cuban government, academy, media, and society in general. Black faces were simply hard to find in the new revolutionary hierarchy, but they were plentiful in the performance stratum of the Conjunto. Ironically, despite post-1959 declarations that racism no longer existed in Cuba, the pattern recalls the historical slots delegated to blacks in other areas of the African Diaspora: entertainment and, soon, sports (Hagedorn 2001:236–238; Abrahams and Szwed 1983:48). Until the 1930s, middle- and upper-class Cuban audiences would not accept Afro-Cubans on the stage, let alone in any sector of the public transcript except the police blotter. In the 1930s, according to Robin Moore, whites, who had been performing stereotyped Afro-Cuban theatrical characters and "cabaret rumba" in blackface for more than half a century, were swept from the stage; foreign tourists, vacationing in increasing numbers, demanded the authenticity of actual black faces playing and dancing rumba (figures 7.4 and 7.5; see Moore 1997:41–61). It is likely that the Conjunto Folklórico's direct prototype, Fernando Ortiz's 1937 public "folkloric conference" of Lucumí music played by Afro-Cuban drummers, could not have taken place in the 1920s or before. It may just be that a public avenue opened for Ortiz's applied ethnology of transculturation in the 1930s, during the very historical conjuncture Robin Moore describes. This trend was welcome, but the concentration of black faces among the "informants" was strategically intended to lend "authenticity" to folklore of African origin, though the practitioners' race and ethnicity had in fact greatly diversified since at least 1900.

The typology of intellectuals and informants was expressed through enduring signifiers of race, class, and institutional positionality. Though the demographics of the Conjunto hierarchy reflected long-held Cuban racial, class, and cultural norms, the institution turned to a very specific rhetorical gloss on the black informants in order to construct their new status within the folkloric display apparatus. They were "authentic" "townspeople" bearing the "cultural values" of "art," "music," and "dance." Their institutional incorporation as modern professionals indexed the shedding of the atavistic, the mystical, and the antisocial as they rose from *bajo nivel cultural* ("low cultural development") to higher levels of culture, in the older senses of "organic cultivation" and "civilization" (see Williams 1976:77–79). This was accomplished partly through the racialized, sartorial, and selective biographical representation of the informants, particularly in contrast to the intellectuals. In a series of photographic portraits (figure 12.2), the Conjunto's visually dazzling first program book presents the latter group, the hierarchy's upper and middle rungs, in crisp modern dress. In contrast, the black female informants wear simple white blouses or, in some cases, more flamboyant costume. Outsized necklaces and earrings abound. These were conventions that had dominated *costumbrista* representations of Afro-Cuban women in Landaluze's time and the modernist primitivism of Victor Manuel García's time: the Conjunto women appear as regal, exotic, or quietly spiritual. Most strikingly, all of the male informants appear as shirtless bust portraits. In three-quarter or frontal pose, often with uplifted visage and illumination upon the forehead, they come across as powerful, dignified, and naturally inspired Afro-Cuban men. Clearly, these are some of the most compelling and dignified portraits ever made of Cuba's black men, particularly as in contrast to the historically stereotyped images of blacks as criminals and buffoons. At the same time, such portraits are directly comparable to some ethnographic portraits of primitive Africans taken at the end of the nineteenth century (figure 10.2).

Still, these stunning male photographic portraits perform a difficult, even magical, conceptual labor: they rhetorically resolve the historical tension in Cuban social thought between *lo africano* and *la cubanidad,* as prior representations tried to do via the image of the *mulata,* the grotesque *negro* of the *marquilla cigarrera* (see Kutzinski 1993), or the "anomalous" *brujo* or *ñáñigo* with his physical "stigmata" (see I. Castellanos 1916). On one hand, these Afro-Cuban men appear as representatives of the "townspeople." Bare chests provide the visual ingredient of the natural, essential, and authentic, throwing into relief, albeit in moderately primitivizing form, the informants' Africanness. But the portraits are not merely Cuban socialist remakes of *National Geographic*'s countless naked indigenes. The bust portrait form effectively shifts upward the myriad traits of historical bodies toward the transhistorical realm of mythical bodies and superorganic "cultural values." The hierarchy of creative labor between intellectuals and informants guaranteed that the head would truly rule the body. Here, black men appear to be bold, but also benign and safe, in contrast to those historical blacks, whose supposed racial, class, and cultural traits had put fear in the hearts of white and official Cuba since the Haitian Revolution of 1791, the 1844 Escalera Conspiracy, the Africanization of Cuba scare, and political organizing before 1912. On the other hand, the informants' identities were framed by modern professional résumés, detailing their substantial careers in theater, television, film, and international recording (Consejo de Cultura 1963; see figure 12.2). No direct mention was made of their specific roots as religious priests, singers, and drummers within the Afro-Cuban *ritual* context. The term *sacred* does slip out, albeit in muted fashion. For example, the handsome and powerful Trinidad Torregrosa appears as a "singer, drummer, and constructor of Cuban *musical instruments,* being one of the few that conserve the *art* of making the batá, sacred drums of Cuba" (Consejo de

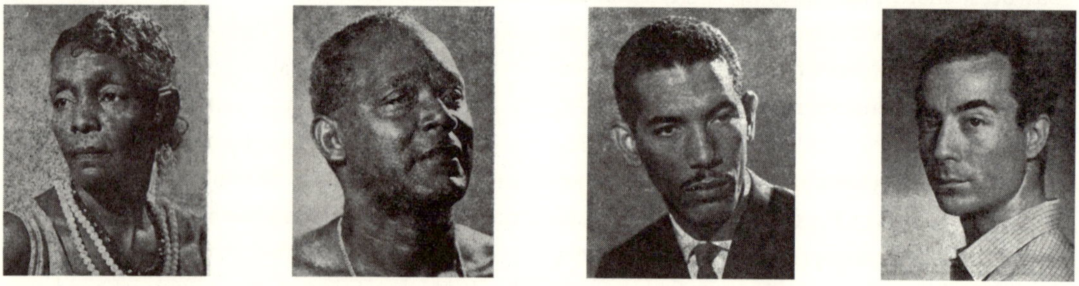

Figure 12.2. Four early portraits from the Conjunto Folklórico Nacional de Cuba. This is a composite of four portraits the author constructed from the Conjunto's first program book from the early 1960s. The black practitioner-"informants," ostensible representatives of the "townspeople," were presented in elegant portraits with modern résumé-"biographies." The first "folklore consultant" was Rogelio Martínez Furé (second from right). The first choreographer was Rodolfo Reyes Cortéz (right). The majority of the "intellectuals" were white and presented in suits; the "informants" were black. The go-between was a mulatto—he was both connected to the Afro-Cuban traditions and a scholarly and ideological descendant of Don Fernando Ortiz. The women informants were presented as humble, exotic, and/or spiritualized, and the men were presented bare-chested, as exuberant, natural, spiritually inspired, but optimally transculturated, Afro-Cuban men. Left, Nieves Fresneda; second from left, Jesús Pérez.

Cultura 1963, emphasis added). The other great elder in the group, Jesús Pérez (see figure 12.2), appears as "the *student* of the famous batá player Pablo Roche (Akilakua)." Pérez's connection to Pablo Roche is valorized by their participation together "in the first conference on Cuban folklore," presented by Fernando Ortiz in 1937 on stage, not by the crucial fact that, musically and spiritually, Jesús Pérez was reared in intimate proximity to great religious sages and the most famous *Añá* (sacred drum set) in Cuban history, handed down from its Yoruba ex-slave creators Atandá and Añabí, through the master Andrés "Sublime" Roche, Pablo Roche's father. This crucial component of Afro-Cuban oral history had been widely known among intellectuals since at least 1954, when Ortiz published the story (1954:316). Lázaro Ros, credited as "one of the best akpwones or singers of Lucumí and Arará music in Cuba," gains an important credential as a professional in his participation in an early world music recording, *Chant du Monde,* produced in Paris in the 1950s. Such positive professional characterizations of Afro-Cubans from poor *barrios* became theoretically possible via Ortiz's theory and practice of "transculturation." Given Ortiz's lifelong interest in flavoring the emergent Cuban *ajiaco* with wholesome "drum dances" while leaving less savory practices behind in the process of transculturation (e.g., "savage fetishism"), it is unsurprising that his students, committed to the ideals of the new regime, would reintroduce the principle that "music," "art," and "dance" were "completely isolatable from the hold that ritual has on them." In short, these authentic Afro-Cuban males were not noble savages, as mid-century avant-garde painters thought, but, in Ortizian terms, the perfect modern transculturates, wherein the program book's elegant photographic portraits, along with professional résumés, provided the seal of approval.

The Conjunto's parent organization, the Consejo de Cultura, sought to "teach" the whole population that Afro-Cuban "folklore" belonged to everyone. Still, if the performances intended to conjoin stage and audience in cultural communion, it sought to do so in a way that assimilated African-based religious liturgy and its priestly agents along with "townspeople" into a secularized and spectacularized form of edification. It is not hard to imagine that such performances, at least in theory, were intended to be cooptive mechanisms for transforming religious institutions, historically independent of the state, into state-regulated "cultural" practices through "folklorization." In large part, Ortiz's "folklore" idea, which aestheticized Afro-Cuban performance in order to enrich and sweeten the Cuban *ajiaco,* was not formally different from the Conjunto Folklórico's charge to create a "national folklore" of the "townspeople's" music and dance. Ortiz remained the eminence grise of Afro-Cuban studies until his death in 1969. Rogelio Martínez Furé, the scholar in charge of rewriting the Afro-Cuban religions as narrative material fit for the Conjunto's mission, in fact, developed a theory of "positive" and "negative" folklore in his "imaginary dialogues" with Fernando Ortiz. Martínez Furé "promoted the transformation and development of folklore, essentially by cleaning up the folk" in an attempt to fashion an appropriate revolutionary national culture (figure 12.2) (Hagedorn 2001:173; Martínez Furé 1979:267):

> The development of a country's folklore can be stimulated in an intelligent and scientific way. So-called *negative* folklore (superstitions, taboos without a scientific basis, idealistic conceptions about supernatural forces that govern the lives of men, curanderistic practices, coprophagy, xenophobia, etc.) can be eliminated, little by little, while enriching and employing *positive* folklore (all that helps in the harmonious development of society, all that contributes to the reinforcement of the solidarity between men, all that exalts the traditions of fighting against oppression, scientific and beneficial pharmacology and the artistic forms that grew up around popular religious conceptions, but that possess cultural values independent of their idealistic content, that can be purified, that can be given a new social revolutionary function. (1979:267; translation by Katherine Hagedorn [2001:174])

Martínez Furé had conserved Ortiz's focus upon social hygiene through folklore and his national high-mindedness; but his application of scientific materialism (read atheism) to Afro-Cuban religion and his vision of government programs to recreate Cubans in the image of socialist man was new to the island, of course (see Padula 1993:22). Undoubtedly, many Conjunto informants agreed with the use of "cultural values" to create solidarity and end oppression, not least because Afro-Cubans had always been central to Cuba's historical struggle against slavery, foreign domination, and discrimination. However, the institutional model that defined their roles within the program of implementation encountered pitfalls in practice.

The intellectuals' folkloric utopia was more precarious that it first seemed, as revealed in an interview Katherine Hagedorn conducted with one of the Conjunto's most revered past directors. Evidently, the Conjunto's hierarchical division of labor and its structure of cultural authority did not sit well with the informants. As Hagedorn shows, the bureaucratic system of artistic development and presentation became a site of contest from almost the outset. To a significant degree, the informants eventually took over the internal organization of the Conjunto Folklórico, reproducing within it the authority relations of the townspeople's "ritual networks" from which the performers came—in other words, their "houses" of Ocha, Palo, and Abakuá. From time to time quarrels, and even violence, erupted between the "informants" and the "intellectuals" in tense settings crosscut by personality, race, and "class"—or institutional position. In one interview, Hagedorn's white interviewee recalls being scandalized by the townspeople's personal behavior on the Conjunto's first European tour, for example, when they cooked their own food in their hotel rooms. In the teariest part of the exchange, interviewer and interviewee weep together when the latter relates that a Conjunto informant burst into her office and shot her with a handgun. Apparently, the Conjunto's official face did not permit its transculturated townspeople the same slack as Cubans grant to their countrymen: *"tanto los defectos como las virtudes"* (defects as well as virtues). In short, at least some of the intellectuals, consciously or unconsciously, believed that you could take the informant out of the *mala vida cubana,* but you could not take the *mala vida cubana* out of the informant. This belief has remained an open secret and potential embarrassment within the Conjunto until today. During the period of her research, Hagedorn's most important source, because of his deep religious conviction and consummate professionalism, attempted without success to shield her from one of the group's most famous singers, who was a shameless drunk given to desecrating his own Santería altar (Hagedorn 2001:151–166).

In their reconfiguration and, in effect, subversion, of the Conjunto Folklórico from the bottom up and inside out, the informants revised the institution's folkloricizing project dedicated to purging "popular religion" and "superstition" from the nation's unifying "cultural values." Still, according to Hagedorn's interviews among early informants, the informants remained clear from the beginning as to the distinction between their state "job" and their "religion" (Hagedorn 2001:85, 98–99). On the job, the informants took their work very seriously as professional performers and teachers of their traditions. Thus, the Conjunto, at least, got to do what it intended on the stage—"authentic folklore." Though undoubtedly shaped by their on stage experiences, many of the informants tried not to take "folklore" home to their "ritual networks." In order to fulfill their religious obligations, they would still have to "clean" people with live roosters and sacrificial goats.

Of course, secularized "folklore" and sacred "ritual networks" should not be taken for granted as a priori distinct zones. It may be that the performers' distinction between "job" and "religion" was a powerful *effect,* a strategic response, to a new set of fraught institutional conditions. Though Afro-Cuban *religiosos* had always maintained their core practices as secret and private, the revolution's folkloricization project may have, in effect, produced new criteria of religious autonomy and purity—rather than the reverse, that folklore diluted and co-opted some nostalgically conceived original sacred purity. There is an often-heard phrase among Afro-Cuban practitioners, *"la religión no tiene nada que ver con la política"* (religion has nothing to do with politics—read the government's political ideology and institutions). In Cuba, the very fact that something is asserted to have "nothing to do" with politics makes it starkly political, even counterrevolutionary; one of Fidel Castro's most memorable admonitions is, "Inside the Revolution, everything; outside the Revolution, nothing."

Ultimately, it may be that the "townspeople's" religion has been transformed, in some ways, by folkloricization. For one thing, the religious vocations of some folklore professionals were affected by stardom—which had much to do with Cuba's development of cultural tourism and a world market for Afro-Cuban folklore recordings and performances. At the same time, the powerful public visibility of *orishas, palos,* and *íremes* on the state stage, as locally decoded by followers, may have lent increasing legitimacy to the religions themselves, mitigating secularizing forces from above in the process. Highly visible performer-priests, Afro-Cuban men and women of knowledge, already could claim cultural and ritual authority within their *barrios.* Now, the revolution had greatly enhanced their visibility, social mobility, and freedom to travel.

Though one of Louis Althusser's premier neo-Marxist concepts was developed for arguments about the capitalist state, the Conjunto Folklórico has, arguably, functioned as an ISA, or "Institutional State Apparatus." ISAs are practical sites of ideological struggle within hegemonic systems. The state, as Stuart Hall has amplified the concept, attempts to establish consensus as to a particular interpretation of reality, most powerfully through communications media. The Catholic Church represents an important historical example of an ISA, for example, as its conversion practices formed a crucial ideological arm of social control during slavery. In Gramscian theory, hegemony is always fraught, never complete, and the respective positions of the constituencies struggling within ISAs are never pure; the ISA must always confront rupture and contest, and the system's social contradictions continue to be reproduced within it (Althusser 1971; see also Hall 1977). For example, during the slavery period, Africans sought to control from within the very ISAs intended to divide and conquer them, the Catholic religious fraternity *(cofradía)* (see Bastide 1978:55, 114; López Valdés 1987: 7). As a result, African-based religions were significantly conserved through forms of "syncretism" as much as through "pure retentions" (see Herskovits 1958). In the case of the Conjunto Folklórico, control, or at least influence, of a state institution from within by Afro-Cuban principles of organization looks intriguingly similar. As theorists of hegemony insist, counterhegemonies always perpetuate as they resist (Comaroff 1985). The Conjunto's music, dance, and costuming remained powerfully representative of their living presence among these "townspeople," albeit aesthetically shaped and ideologically contextualized to fit the economy of the socialist folkloric stage (Hagedorn 2001).

Folkloric Modernity: ISAs and the World Market

Cuba's need for hard currency on the world market increased the stakes around this folkloric ISA, particularly after the collapse of the Soviet Union and the Eastern Bloc. Cuban folkloric performance was already becoming central to commercialized touristic spectacle by the mid-1980s. In the big picture, socialism had begun to make its pact with the universal commodity. In the 1990s, the government established "joint ventures" with Canadian, European, and Latin American hotel and tour corporations, as well as other related businesses. Folklore venues had spread and varied widely, from Havana in the west to Santiago de Cuba in the east. *Folklórico* spectacles *(espectáculos)* could be seen not only in the National Theater and the Conjunto's own compound in El Vedado on "Rumba Saturday" *(Sábado de la Rumba),* but also in tourist hotels, big restaurants, "ethnographic" museums, and selected religious "houses" in

Guanabacoa and Madruga that were slotted into tour-bus itineraries (figure 12.3).[4] In a hotel, for example, an evening's *espectáculo* might consist of a program of Afro-Cuban *folklórico,* comedy skits, and the ever-popular *desfile de moda* (fashion show) chock full of stunning models showcasing clothes that no Cuban could afford. The state-sponsored fashion industry seeks to entertain tourists and demonstrate Cuba's contemporary cachet over lobster and champagne in mansions once owned by the bourgeoisie. Foreign diplomats and business men have the opportunity to use these models to lubricate social events. And Cuba's beautiful young women often seek entry into the profession precisely to meet, and possibly marry, foreign men, who could take them away from the island's deprivations. In this context, *folklórico* is never far from neocolonialist male sexual fantasy and *interés,* which, not a few young Cubans believe, has led to the death of romantic love on the island.

As a result, the processes and outcomes of folkloric performance became varied and complex, indeed, as Katherine Hagedorn shows. The large audience for the Conjunto's Rumba Saturday, for example, includes a constituency of older *santeras* who come to enjoy the spectacle, but also to lend authenticity to it. Tourists are always enchanted. The possession dances are so realistic that even scholars come away with a sense that they have seen the *orishas.*[5] Young Cubans congregate there, too. Some are curious to observe the goings-on, inasmuch as they have little to do in Havana. During the early 1990s, Hagedorn noted, a good percentage of the young attendees were *jineteros* and *jineteras* (male hustlers and female prostitutes), who take advantage of the event to meet

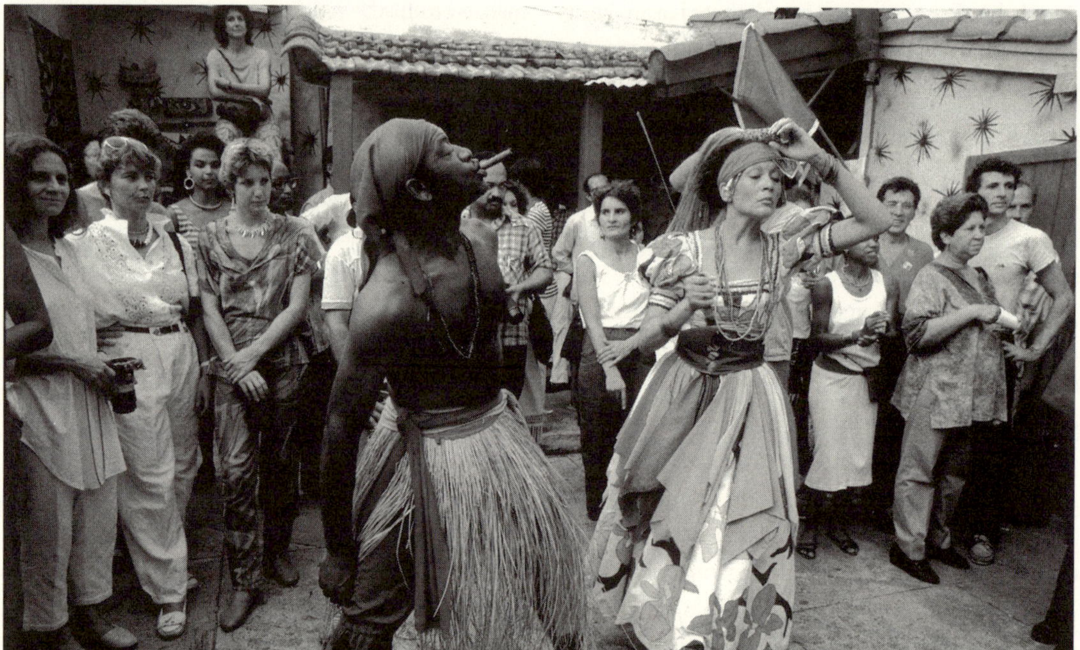

Figure 12.3. Ogún and Oyá do battle in a "folkloric" performance of a Lucumí *batá* drumming before an audience of foreign tourists and the international press, 1986. The drummers and performers were top professionals of the National Folklore Group of Cuba. It was held in the Osha house of the late Rigoberto Rodríguez Duque, which has become a small tourist museum now managed by Fredesvinda Rosell, in Madruga, Havana, Cuba. Photograph by David H. Brown.

cash-toting foreigners. These youth are drawn to the stage, but not to receive a wholesome cultural education; they utilize the state institution to *luchar* in order to *resolver* ("struggle," "hustle," to "resolve" daily needs; see Hagedorn 2001:203). Others, in my experience, did in fact go to seek an education, but one that the excellent urban secondary school system apparently did not provide; like the youth who frequent the oceanside Malecón in Havana, they seek out foreigners, particularly Americans, to find out about news and happenings outside of Cuba: Was there a lot of violence in New York? Are the streets of U.S. cities filled with homeless people? Were all the kids on drugs? Did all Americans have AIDS?

Via the folkloric pipeline, many Afro-Cuban performers would gain international recognition, through recording contracts and becoming the *santería* "godparents" to foreigners who wanted to be initiated into the religions, study drumming, or purchase consecrated drums.[6] The great ritual singer Lázaro Ros is the subject of an earnest, though romanticized, feature film, which confuses the ethical distinction many Conjunto performers made between their "jobs" and their "religion," that is, that Lázaro Ros, an authentic folkloric personage, is who he is and does what he does, on and off stage. In the 1990s, some of the smaller professional troupes that conserve regional Afro-Cuban traditions, such as Los Muñequitos and Grupo AfroCuba of Matanzas, achieved through recording and touring as much world renown as the always popular National Folklore Group of Cuba. Ironically, as the over-the-top beach resort of Varadero has become a tourist blockbuster and cash cow for the government, the nearby city of Matanzas, once called "the Athens of Cuba," has become a depressed backwater.

In a phenomenon that began as early as the 1940s and 1950s, when Fernando Ortiz developed his influential performative taxonomies of *lo afrocubano*, and when drummers such as Chano Pozo and Mongo Santamaría achieved commercial popularity in the United States, the Afro-Cuban repertoire has been highly codified into convenient genre categories. For example, Grupo AfroCuba's first recording, *Rituales afrocubanos* (1993), represented "Música Yoruba," "Música Arará," and "Música Bantú" (Grupo Afro-Cuba de Matanzas 1993). The recordings of Grupo AfroCuba and Los Muñequitos, as well as of lesser groups, have typically included, among the various ritual and rumba song types *(yambú, guaguancó, colúmbia)*, a track simply called "Abakuá" or "Abacuá." One or two festive songs of a huge Abakuá Society repertoire, as well as one or two stylized songs about the Abakuá, have come to stand for "Música Abakuá" in the stage repertoire (see Table 12.1).[7] Grupo AfroCuba performed compact representations of Santería, Iyesá, Palo, Arará, and Abakuá ceremonies on the Mall at the 1989 Smithsonian Institution's Festival of American Folklife, complete with Abakuá attributes, drums, and *íremes.* Though representations of *rumba, orisha,* and *palo* have dominated the public performances of these and other groups, Abakuá representations are catching up. An *íreme* was recently featured on a program of Grupo AfroCuba's recent U.S. tour and regularly accompanies Muñequito performances around the world (figure 12.4).

If such genre categories correctly reflect age-old cultural differences between the African "nations," genre labels also work to distill such differences as musical "styles," which can then be academically

Table 12.1

Track List for *Raíces Africanas* by Grupo AfroCuba de Matanzas

1. Caridad (BataRumba)
2. Ogún (Iyesá)
3. Ogún (Iyesá)
4. Changó (Batá)
5. Ananú (Arará)
6. Eleguá (Bembé)
7. Palo (Bantú)
8. Palo (Bantú)
9. Pá Los Mayores (Yambú Matancero)
10. Enigue Nigue (Guaguancó)
11. Aguado Koloya (Rumba Columbia)
12. Bríkamo
13. Abakuá
14. Baila Mi Guaguancó (BataRumba)

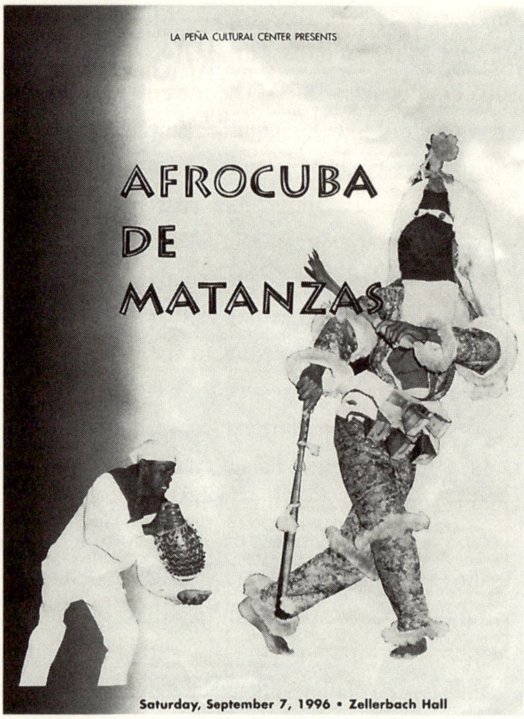

Figure 12.4. Cover from local promotional material for the 1996 Grupo AfroCuba de Matanzas U.S. tour, showing an Abakuá *íreme.* Grupo AfroCuba presented a staged Abakuá ceremony on the National Mall in 1989 at the Festival of American Folklife, including an *íreme* dancer, the symbolic drums, and the orchestra.

taught to competent and not so competent musicians. Internationally available recordings clearly have long facilitated the ability of non-Cuban Santería practitioners to learn the repertoire in order to function in religious communities outside of Cuba. It remains to be discovered what kinds of effects this process of mediated musical pedagogy and production has had on the form and content of religious music. However, one listen to a recent CD set (Cabrera and Tarafa 2001a, 2001b) of urban (Havana) and rural (Matanzas) Santería music, recorded by Lydia Cabrera and Josefina Tarafa on the eve of revolution in 1957, suggests that the religion's musical genres have changed dramatically in style and apparent polish since then. For example, the blended harmonies of the most recent recordings in Cuba and the United States are absent from the 1957 recordings. The drums sound flat and untuned, and the rhythms seem to lack the technical crispness of contemporary ensembles. I leave it to ethnomusicologists to assess fully the significance of such apparent differences, including drumming style and technique.

The revolution's applied folklore program, with its nation- and culture-building goals, has had wide-ranging and varied effects, not all of which were envisioned by the intellectuals and the informants. Clearly, *lo afrocubano* and its practitioners gained a kind of visibility and legitimacy as of the early 1960s, which they had never before experienced. Struggles over authority and meaning within folkloric institutions and the inextricable relationship folklore took on with tourism's dollar both reflected prerevolutionary patterns and upped the ante. Afro-Cubans had gained access to the commercial and folkloric stages in the 1930s and 1940s via the cabaret and university sponsorship, respectively. The former led to new socioeconomic opportunities, but also, Argeliers León argued, to exploitation on the island and a kind of brain drain of Cuban talent in relation to the metropole, New York (León 1984:302). In the scholarly context, Afro-Cuban traditions were redefined in ways that contradicted age-old social stigma and persecution, but also attempted to "transculturate" them of perceived atavisms for the greater good of the national *ajiaco* and the taste of the middle class. As of 1964, *El Ñáñigo* was well on his way to becoming an icon of Cuban national folklore. However, as during the prerevolutionary period that Cubans call the "pseudo-Republic," state and society would remain highly ambivalent about Abakuá practice. Museums would fill with Abakuá attributes and dollar stores with *ñáñigo* tourist souvenirs, while the gates of Abakuá lodges still remained subject to police vigilance.

13 "The Ethnographic Museum" and the Cuban Revolution

The new public visibility and definition of Afro-Cuban folkloric traditions, as represented within national and local museums, historically corresponded to the flowering of staged folklore as of 1963. "Ethnographic" museums gained new support and prominence, and each would showcase marvelous Afro-Cuban attributes, including full-size mannequins dressed in vintage *sacos de íreme.*

The Ethnographic Museum of Guanabacoa, a town that remains one of the bastions of the Afro-Cuban religions, opened with great fanfare in 1964. In contrast to other Cuban ethnographic and historical museums, however, many of the objects in the permanent collection had never been used by practitioners. According to the current museum director, the majority of costumes and beadwork, for example, were "commissioned out" to local priests and artists for the purpose of "ethnographic" display. Indeed, in further contrast to Cuban "collection" methods historically, these and other objects were not the results of police confiscation. They were bought outright. For the 1964 opening, the Museum's vitrines were filled with eye-popping beadwork and grand satin *orisha* costumes with metallic trim and prodigious attributes. Massive altars and dioramas filling entire rooms were constructed.

One exception to the policy of commissioning objects seems to prove the rule, as it were, for it reveals the museum as folkloricizing machine as much as anything else. The museum reconstructed an entire Santería altar of a recently deceased Guanabacoa *santero,* Arcadio Calvo.[1] Calvo (Echú Carirí) was a nationally known priest of Eleguá and the Tata Nkisi patriarch of the Buey Suelto Palo Monte branch. A *palero* from Regla and a *babalawo* raised by elder *paleros* in Guanabacoa related to me that with Calvo's death and the consequent breakup of his *cabildo,* the Sons of Saint Anthony *(los Hijos de San Antonio),* Calvo's nephew sold off the house's decorative and religious pieces. The Museum of Guanabacoa bought the lion's share. Calvo's Santería objects came to occupy one large room, and his sacred Congo cauldron figured into an altar in the Palo Monte display. In this instant "ethnographic" museum, dedicated, as it was, to "the townspeople's" folklore, neither local history nor the acknowledgment of local Afro-Cuban religious practice seem to have played any part in the institution's mission or profile. None of the objects' contemporary makers are identified by wall plaques; the marvelous beadwork is labeled, for example, "necklace of Oshún, deity of the River," and two remarkable Abakuá *sacos de íreme* are simply labeled, "Íreme Suits of Embema and Anamangüí." There are few Guanabacoa religious practitioners who do not know, and few tourists who do, that Calvo's sacred *nganga* cauldron on view, named "Buey Suelto" (Loose Ox), was "born" from Cota Lima, one of the first *ngangas* in Cuba and the root of the now international Briyumba Cota Lima Palo Monte lineage.[2] The museum's display formula, though lamentable, maintains an agenda. That its displays are static, agentless, and transparent to a superorganic "cultural" source is apparently preferable to acknowledging living local religious creators. The objects would be dead relics, save for the fact that their living purpose is, it seems, to burnish the nation's official self-image as a racial democracy with distinctive folkloric "traditions."

The Guanabacoa Museum's displays are more theatrical than ethnographically didactic. Religion and folklore, it seems, have been assimilated to spectacle. A set of distinct spaces corresponds to each of three major Afro-Cuban practices, Abakuá, Lucumí, and Palo Monte. The three spaces, some of which are subdivided themselves, are filled with vitrines abundantly filled with attributes, including a number of Abakuá *íremes* and altar objects. There are no explanations of the meaning or function of any object to be found. Colorful, impressive altars stand in many of the corners. A grand, tiered Santería altar, replete with vases of artificial flowers, is set before curtains and theatrically lit (plate 24). The Lucumí and Palo rooms contain charming diorama-like presentations. The former comes complete with a lifelike black mannequin representing an old, grizzled *babalawo* sitting next to his Ifá divining equipment before an *orisha* cabinet (figure 13.1). The Palo Monte space features a massive black cauldron set before a colorful mythological mural depicting the natural elements. The cauldron is a facsimile, serving purely dramatic purposes, though the smaller pot next to it is believed by some to be Calvo's Buey Suelto (plate 25, center-right rear).

The salons and capacious *solar* (courtyard) of this former bourgeois mansion serve as stages for folkloric performances of Afro-Cuban rituals. Elegant portals divide the courtyard, which is shaded by royal

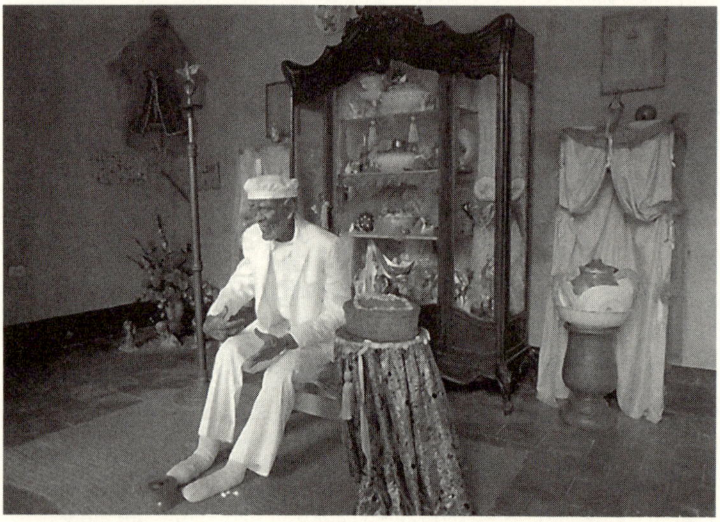

Figure 13.1. Tourist postcard showing facsimile of a Santería priest's *cuarto de santo* (sacred room) with a *babalawo* diviner mannequin; Lukumí salon of the Ethnographic Museum of Guanabacoa.

palm and *ceiba* trees. Fanciful artistic versions of altars adorn the bases of the trees. During public events, the courtyard fills with folklore professionals dancing as the *orishas* or *íremes*. A popular tourist poster provides the visitor a memento of one such performance, a *plante* Abakuá. One half features the drawn *anaforuanas* of Mokongo and the *obonekue;* the other half pictures the courtyard filled with *íreme* masquerades, *plazas* with attributes, and the orchestra. The photograph reveals no touristic audience, thereby suggesting the enactment of a real ceremony. If one were not clear as to just who and what these odd figures in garish costumes represent, the poster copy leaves no doubt: CUBA/FOLKLORE/ABAKUÁ (figure 13.2). Though scholars Fernando Ortiz and Lydia Cabrera succeeded in reinscribing *ñañiguismo* as "Abakuá" and criminality as "folklore" in their academic texts, who else among the pre-1959 social and governing elite would ever have imagined these three terms so intimately and inextricably linked? As of 1964, the linkage was a natural for the revolutionary cultural vanguard. And, as geared mostly to external consumption, the poster preaches to the converted: foreign tourists with expectations that Caribbean countries ought to have colorful national folklore.

The Ethnographic Museum's shop sells postcards of the collections and associated activities by folklore professionals or *aficionados* (plates 24 and 25, figures 13.1 and 13.3). These, among other souvenirs, such as little dolls dressed as the different *orishas* and *íremes* and found all over Cuba, particularly in the airports, were produced in great numbers, apparently starting in the late 1970s. Not surprisingly, several postcards of the *orishas* feature top "informants" of the National Folklore Group of Cuba, such as first soloist dancers Jorge "Chiqui" Dixon as Shangó and Juan Jesús "Petít" Ortiz as Echú-Eleguá. Dixon's Shangó is tall, bold, and imperial. As photographed in the Conjunto's own dance studios in Vedado, Petít's Eleguá gets the deity's attributes correct, but, curiously, embodies not the *orisha* many of us have seen at drummings but a blackface minstrel, complete with grease paint, big white eye sockets, a wide grin, and jazzy hand gestures (compare figure 13.3 with figure 10.4). Toward the goal of touristic spectacle, this convention of representation looks back half a century to the black buffoon in order to figure the mischievousness of Eleguá the trickster. How an accomplished, serious professional was encouraged to adopt this representation remains unclear.

Like the countless dolls, posters, paintings, and other kinds of folkloric display via vitrine or stage, the postcards not only people an imaginary Cuba with exotic figures. They work to codify for consumption Afro-Cuban personages and attributes, just as, for example, Rumba Saturday performances distill

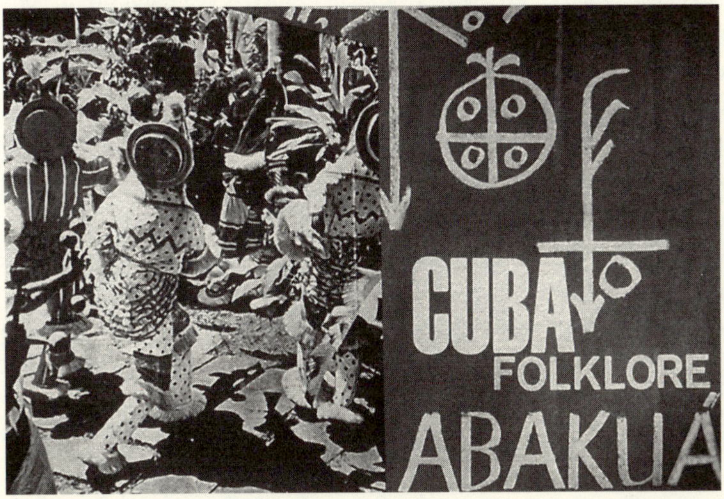

Figure 13.2. ***Cuba/Folklore/Abakuá.*** **Tourism poster of a folkloric Abakuá performance in the courtyard of the Ethnographic Museum of Guanabacoa. The photograph shows several** ***íremes*** **and dignitaries (left rear).**

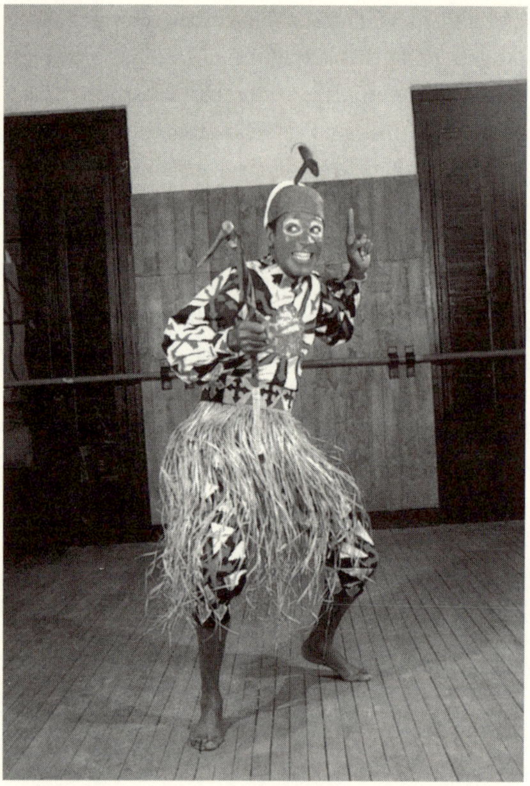

Figure 13.3. Tourist postcard showing Conjunto Folklórico principal dancer Juan Jesús "Petít" Ortiz performing Eleguá in a style that reproduces the Cuban tradition of blackface minstrelsy characteristic of *El Negrito* or "congo" figures.

capsule *orisha* portraits in dance. Printed in Spain and Cuba,[3] the postcards' pithy texts follow directly from folkloric genre categories, as do the liner notes of professional recordings, the teacher's folklore manual, and the museum salons. In a sense, the postcards are the touristic, commercial equivalents of popular religious chromolithographs of the saints (see figures 5.11 and 6.8). One card reminds visitors of *CUBA* via the *Museo de Guanabacoa* and its colorful tiered *orisha* altar, captioned *Altar de Santería.* A photographic cameo of an Afro-Cuban *santera,* swaddled in white and wearing necklaces, completes the picture (plate 24). The cameo is, in effect, a *costumbrista* representation revised for the age of tourism.

Some touristic mementos of Cuban national folklore, particularly mass-produced miniature *íremes,* not only co-opt iconography in order to dominate local cultural ideas and images—that is, theology and liturgy—but, in practice, also work to dislodge independent sources of marketable cultural production. For example, miniature *íremes* have been commonly produced by Havana's Abakuá for a good part of the twentieth century, it seems, as suggested by a stunningly realistic example displayed alongside actual *íreme* costumes in the Casa de Africa Fernando Ortiz Collection (plate 26). For many years, an Abakuá family in Regla has produced beautiful *íreme* scale models with leftover and found materials. The standing dolls, ranging from fifteen to forty inches tall, are painstakingly made from tightly sewn layers of cloth over cotton batting, supported by wire armatures. Very detailed, they feature a hood of *saco de yute,* body suits of colorful cloth adorned with beads and sequins, fringe bordering cut from brooms, painted signatures that identify the *íreme,* appliqué panels bearing the image of Obon Tanze, hand-held batons and brooms, and wood bases appropriately covered with goatskin. They are titled and signed by the artists (plate 27). To their makers, these miniature *íremes* are commemorative art objects; though "cultural" rather than religious, they nevertheless resonate deeply with the family's Abakuá identity, generating deep satisfaction and pride. This tradition has been a public way to valorize a secret and much maligned private practice for a long time. Not least, using knowledge acquired within the Abakuá, their art has helped them to survive economically. In contrast, the airport *diablitos* and related representations, though varied, are mass-produced in state factories and are modeled after other generic images, including *costumbrista* arts (figure 13.4). Colorful souvenir plates printed with images of Cuban carnival, for example, typically derive compositionally from nineteenth-century works by Landaluze and Miahle and center on versions of Landaluze's *El Ñáñigo* itself (plate 28; compare with figure 4.1). Landaluze's checked *El Ñáñigo* holds the same classical pose but reigns over carnival in tropical colors. Here mass culture has produced its own art historical *ajiaco* on a souvenir plate; the dancing *íreme* before a

The present Cuban government has succeeded in rescuing cultural values in the African traditions and customs which played such a great part in forming the

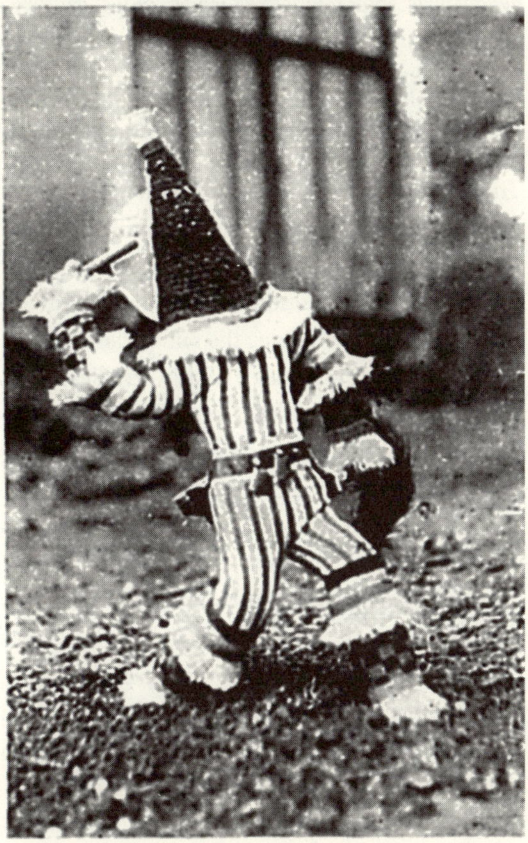

Ireme or little devil

OF THE ABAKUA SOCIETY

national identity, while removing their mystical element.

Figure 13.4. *"Ireme or little devil of the Abakuá Society,"* illustrating Balea's (1984) review of the Ethnographic Museum of Guanabacoa. Such dolls, in this case perhaps five to seven inches tall, are the bread and butter of museum, hotel, and airport shops. This one is mass-produced.

Carnival crowd approximates Victor Manuel García's 1940 *Carnival* (plate 22), as well as *costumbrista* conventions (see plate 19).

Thus, *El Ñáñigo* takes two possible career paths following his graduation to miniature cultural icon for sale to tourists; one is a centrally produced and distributed state product; the other emerges from a tiny, marginalized cottage industry. One is stacked on store shelves in the state-controlled dollar stores, along with the gamut of "cultural" mementos that serve as currency in the burgeoning tourist economy: *orishas, guajiros,* rumba dancers, bongos, miniature *batá* drums, and T-shirts silkscreened with Ché Guevara's iconic face; in contrast, the handmade *íremes* are sold, one by one, for dollars in the street, in local parks, and in front of churches, where others sell popular Catholic ex-votos and *estampitas* of the saints. Not surprisingly, the anemic little dollar store *diablito* brooks no competition. It is illegal to sell anything without state permission. Though the Regla family members have tried to sell their *íremes* on the street, and sometimes succeeded, they have been threatened with arrest and confiscation of their wares. Thus barred from such illicit activity, and swept from public space, the family has had no other choice than to sell their *íremes* to state-sanctioned cultural institutions, which have permission to sell products for dollars. It comes as no surprise that one of the institutions most interested in selling their *íremes* recently has been the Yoruba Cultural Association (AYC). Whereas the family formerly sold their *íremes* on the street for between ten and twenty dollars, with immediate return, they must hand over their dolls to be sold in the AYC store for around seventy-five dollars, I was told, and receive a meager return only when the dolls are sold. In this sense, the diminutive, but aggressive, tourist *diablito* not only co-opted Abakuá ideas but also appropriated the private means of trading on specialized cultural knowledge for purposes of independent survival.

The labor performed by Cuban folkloric display produces results for external as well as internal political consumption. Internally, as argued, it seeks to co-opt the living sources from which "folklore" is mined. For external consumption, as well as for internal pedagogy, "ethnographic" and "folkloric" displays rewrite history in order to substantiate the revolution and its ideological goals. Apparently as part of Cuba's interest in actively promoting cultural tourism in the mid-1980s, the Ethnographic Museum of Guanabacoa was reviewed in the international English edition of *Prisma,* one of the state's premier magazines for foreign consumption. Journalist Mirta Balea wrote approvingly of the Guanabacoa Museum's Afro-Cuban salons in an article called "Black roots: African slaves had a powerful influence on Cuban culture" (figure 13.4). A tourist *íreme* figured among several illustrations. Expanding the review genre well beyond what most visitors would have expected of a glossy tourist magazine, Balea cogently summarizes the relation of African roots to revolutionary ideology. The Ethnographic Museum of Guanabacoa, it seems, was intended to participate in a larger mission to place the oppressive colonial past and the present socialist struggle in proper perspective. Referring to Santería, Palo Monte, and the Abakuá Society, she writes:

> Historians explain the deeply rooted nature of these cults in Cuba by the need of the slaves, and later other underprivileged sectors, to defend themselves against an oppressive society.
>
> The present Cuban government has succeeded in rescuing cultural values in the African traditions and customs which played such a great part in forming the national identity, while removing their mystical element. . . . The authorities have tried to eradicate the anti-social and dangerous practices of the past.
>
> At the same time it has been official policy to incorporate believers in the tasks of building a new society without religious discrimination. The ignorance on which all religions are based can only be countered by adequate social and scientific education. (Balea 1984)

Balea's rundown of cultic religion's defensive function in class struggle, the ignorance of religion in general, the necessary removal of false consciousness, and the role of "cultural values" in revolutionary nation building is standard modern socialist stuff. The review reiterates Argeliers León's 1964 statement on selective cultural "rescue"; but it embraces more militant rhetoric with a familiar ring to it. Early twentieth-century social hygiene and mid-twentieth-century transculturation are here recast for revolutionary use. Those "black roots" amenable to recasting as "cultural values" for national education are "rescued"; those "black roots" adjudged "mystical" and "antisocial" are "eradicated," just as *brujería* and *ñañiguismo* were to be wiped out like the yellow fever epidemic at the turn of the last century.[4]

The Revolution, the Abakuá, and "Retrograde Obscurantism"

Though Balea's 1984 article extols for an international audience the selective conservation of "black roots," it also glimpses a policy that the government might not be willing to admit so baldly: "The authorities have tried to *eradicate* the anti-social and dangerous practices of the past." Clearly, "eradication" is a much stronger term than "folkloricization." In effect, the admission all but confirms what exile historian Carlos Moore charged in print during the same period (C. Moore 1986). Moore argues that the government continues the historical suppression of Afro-Cuban socioreligious institutions. For Moore, it is just the kind of invidious treatment of Afro-Cubans that, official policies of nondiscrimination notwithstanding, were hallmarks of the Spanish colonial and Republican regimes (C. Moore 1986). With respect to the Abakuá, which was far more secretive and hermetic than the other Afro-Cuban practices, Moore argues, they simply held too much independent social power. In 1970, for the first time since Fidel Castro came to power, according to Moore, the Abakuá leveled a "successful twenty-four-hour strike" that paralyzed "the entire port of Havana" (Moore 1988:306). Cuba's actions against religious adherence and adherents, in general, have been regularly reported by the U.S. State Department and independent international human rights organizations[5] (Human Rights Watch 1999; Amnesty International 2000). However, evidence of the systematic targeting of the Afro-Cuban religions by the government remains anecdotal and has yet to be compiled and published. Moore's impressive later writing attempts to link Cuba's 1960s and 1970s foreign policy goals in Africa to the remaking of its national profile vis-à-vis the Afro-Cuban population (1988). Still, hard data on

Afro-Cubans of the kind compiled by Amnesty International and Human Rights Watch would test, and might reinforce, Moore's theses.

Balea's admission of an official policy of "eradication," however qualified by the revolution's egalitarian rhetoric, offers a tantalizing glimpse at ideas that do not get much press in *Prisma* or folklore journals. Rather, official thinking about the Abakuá has been disseminated within obscure, inaccessible political and military journals. Social historian Lauren Derby, who studied Cuban criminology, society, and culture, gained access to several such journals published in the late 1960s and early 1970s, including *Revista Judicial Militar* and *Policía Nacional Revolucionaria (Judicial-Military Journal* and *National Revolutionary Police).*[6] Derby permitted me to quote her research summary of these "exceedingly intelligent and well thought-out" articles. By 1972, the revolutionary police and military had, apparently, been on the case for a number of years:

> The revolution perceived Abakua societies as a negative influence on the public life of the city [Havana] due to their authoritarian structure, violence, anti-trade union ethos, atavistic machismo (perceived as a form of false consciousness) and excessively aggressive masculinity, comportment [that] should be curbed, not fostered, since it encouraged the treatment of women as "instruments of sex" (it seems that during the 1960s in Havana, white youths were flocking to the Abakua, particularly the *díscolos, buscapleitos, guapos* [young toughs] and those seeking *jevas* [easy women]). The Revolution came to see Ñañiguismo as [a] "retrograde obscurantism" that should be overcome as part of efforts [to redress] the lack of culture, backwardness and *subdesarollo* of Cuban society, in favor of the values of discipline, work, ethics, and dignity. (Derby 1995:4)

Revealing of actual government attitudes in the 1960s and 1970s, the articles are, in design and effect, companion pieces to Balea's "cultural" review, just as Roche y Monteagudo's police chronicles complemented Ortiz's early ethnology. In other words, "cultural" programs to promote "positive" folklore on the stage and in the museum vitrines formed just one half of the contemporary story. Ironically, the pseudo-scientific criminological discourse of the "pseudo-Republic" before 1959 continued to shape the official underside of public folkloric display during the first two decades of the revolution. Writing produced by the state apparatus and its cultural critics transparently parroted core notions from early Lombrosian discourse, though warmed over for socialist consumption: *Ñañiguismo* means "backwardness" (primitive atavism), authoritarianism (despotism), and the inculcation of false consciousness in susceptible white youth. Indeed, for a state attempting to instill in its first generations born after the Triumph of the Revolution a host of official ideals, *ñañiguismo,* in its alleged negation of the socialist work ethic, egalitarianism, and gender equality, was clearly an inappropriate model. Some Cubans I queried clearly remember a surge in *guapería* among male youth in the poorer *barrios,* particularly whites, during the 1960s and 1970s. In other words, they remember roughnecking, drinking, fighting, gratuitous violence against bystanders on the street and in packed dance clubs, typically with razors hidden in handkerchiefs, as well as petty crime, all of which they associated, correctly or incorrectly, with "Abakuá" membership. Even some elder Abakuá members I talked with, who consider themselves "humble workers," lament that period and rue the sometimes violent *hombría* (machismo) still found among younger Abakuá members. Still, as former dockworkers and *combatientes* of the revolution, these elders do not identify "the Abakuá" as the cause. The question of what a dispassionate analysis of contemporary Cuban youth behavior over the last forty or so years would reveal remains to be addressed by scholars in a way not possible here.

In brief, the police and military journal articles are not necessarily incorrect in observing certain behaviors among 1970s youth. Still, the analyses and conclusions drawn suggest that the writers first saw what they believed, and then spent some time in the library among antiquated texts for reinforcement. They put pen to paper, uncritically or willfully embracing all the old chestnuts. The articles mystify the systemic causes of certain social behaviors through the invention of a conveniently ill-defined anti-type, or fetish, *ñañiguismo.* Historically, this official fetish emerged, by negative implication, out of late colonial and neocolonial struggles over national definition vis-à-vis modernity (see Palmié 2002:201–259). The dominant, invidious criteria of national definition were class-, race-, and, implicitly, gender-based. As a result, during the consolidation of Cuban nationalism, the War of Independence, the American occupations, and the birth of the nation, Afro-Cubans were terrorized and killed (1902–1910s), and "white" working-class men were jailed and deported. If the opportunities of all *women* were circumscribed by Cuba's patriarchal institutions, and black women, in particular, continued to be funneled into grinding domestic work, the *gender* implications were more subtle.[7] Vestigial gender codes of the former West African "leopard societies" notwithstanding, the hypermasculinized Abakuá code articulated with Cuba's own patriarchal patterns. Perhaps its extremity is an effect of intra- and interclass and racial struggle in Cuba's northern port cities between the mid-nineteenth and mid-twentieth centuries, where the Abakuá Society was the only safety net for working-class men. The building of Abakuá social capital required the feminization of its demographically complex audience for the enactment of its social power. Thus, where U.S. corporate interests and successive Cuban puppet governments required tight social control to make the nation safe for corruption and profit, the secretive, autonomous, labor-organizing institutions of black, *mulato,* and "white" proletarians could not be a good thing. *Ñañiguismo,* a catch-all for social disorder, and prosecuted for illegal assembly early on, might or might not have been Abakuá proper in any given case during the colonial period, though between 1889 and the 1910s the Abakuá Society had become one fixed target among several other "delinquent" practices with "black roots." Ironically, with the "triumph of the revolution" in 1959, this former bastion of workers' self-defense and mutual aid, the Abakuá Society, became an anti–trade union element vis-à-vis the emerging socialist *sindicato* system. Perhaps unsurprisingly, one had to worry about "white youth" once again falling prey to ideological contagion—though its etiology remains publicly unanalyzed and unspoken. That the first young "white" *ñáñigos* in Havana (1860–1870s) and Regla's new "white" branches (1874–1916) raised the greatest government and elite concern should signal to scholars of contemporary urban Cuba the continuing relevance of historically deep racial and class issues. Regla, a town originally abundant with Africans, along with a militantly racist colonial elite of nobles and merchants, apparently became more "white" following the expulsions of Afro-Cubans in the aftermath of the 1912 "race war."[8] Regla's elite is no more, but the town remains a bastion of resistance to the revolutionary government, and its white inhabitants' racial attitudes are somewhat reminiscent of American working-class and southern whites.[9]

Thus, arguments about the systematic persecution of Afro-Cuban institutions in recent treatments, which overly binarize Cuban racial politics (C. Moore 1986, 1988; Helg 1995; R. Moore 1997), might benefit from more nuanced analyses of race as it meets class, ethnicity, gender, and very specific local histories. This does not mean that the specific targeting of Africans and Afro-Cubans should not be addressed. Nineteenth-century nationalists, early Cuban governments, and progressive intellectuals were always more anxious about the societal effects of "atavism" and "promiscuity" vis-à-vis working-class "white" susceptibility than they were about Africans and Afro-Cubans themselves, who most often functioned as scapegoats in a sad history of atrocities.

The Africa House: The Ethnographic Museum as a National Showcase of "Afro-Castroism"

A close look at Havana's Casa de Africa illuminates the meanings of ethnographic display, Afro-Cuban culture, and *El Ñáñigo* in the decades following the founding of Guanabacoa's Ethnographic Museum. By 1986, the *íreme* had come full circle from his early days as carnival curiosity, police evidence, and exhibition specimen in the Museum of Criminology and Legal Medicine; he was now to be exhibited as a prized, wholesome exemplar of Afro-Cuban culture in the "Africa House" in the heart of historic Old Havana. At the same time, he would come full circle in his public reconnection with the name of Don Fernando Ortiz, for whom the newly assembled collection would be named.

The Casa de Africa would build on the Guanabacoa museum's folkloric displays of "black roots," but its official aims embraced a broader cultural and political horizon. Appropriately enough, the Casa de Africa was inaugurated on January 6, 1986, the annual slot for the old Day of Kings, when *íremes* first hit the streets a century and a half earlier. The Casa de Africa's home, a massive three-story ca. 1717 mansion, had belonged to several old Spanish families. For a time it served as a tobacco warehouse. Sited on Calle Obrapía, Number 157, between Mercaderes and San Ignacio, the building and its former inhabitants must have witnessed the pounding drums, shouts for *aguinaldo,* and the awesome *diablitos* of African nation processions for 167 years until the festival was banned in 1884 (Ortiz 1921:20–22).

In its new museum home, the *íreme* easily moved back and forth across the space now called the Black Atlantic. The affirmation of the historical and cultural links between Cuba and Africa was key to the Casa de Africa's mission. Its purpose, wrote its first director, Claudia Mola Fernández, was to "disseminate African history and culture to the world" through the exhibition and ethnographic study of two principal collections: the Don Fernando Ortiz Collection of Afrocubana and the "historical African collection of our Commander in Chief and President of the Council of State and Government . . . Fidel Castro Ruz." Mola Fernández continued: Africa "needed its ancient traditional cultures to be disseminated and valued [particularly] in just recognition of the contribution of the Black Continent, which, since the sixteenth century, via the shameless slave trade, influenced the specific forms of the major currents that make up the Cuban nationality." In turn, these collections would "permit [Cuba] to disseminate to Africa . . . its cultural and historical patrimony . . . and preserve it for posterity." Finally, Africa House, "through the Ministry of Exterior Relations would coordinate along with African diplomatic representatives the commemoration of national festivals: the most important historical and cultural events of the African peoples" (Mola Fernández n.d.).

By 1986, this rhetoric was built on more than twenty years of Cuban political courtship, solidarity, and bridge-building with African nations and leftist movements there, including Cuba's intensive, costly, and divisive military intervention in Angola from 1975 to 1989 (see Padula 1993:26–27; Suchlicki 2001: 28–29, 39). Key to the politics of "Afrocastroism" and the enhancing of Cuba's international "Afrophilic profile," terms employed by outspoken exile critic Carlos Moore, was the concerted use of "ethnicity as a bridge to Africa." The year 1972, Moore notes, "marked the beginning of an officially approved 'African Decade.'" Cuba organized a "steady flow of visiting African, Caribbean, and black American leaders, delegations and cultural groups," including the South African singer Miriam Makeba and African American activist Angela Davis (C. Moore 1988:301–302, 319–322).

Still, this was a period of dilemmas and contradictions. Indeed, even during the 1970s, "while Cuba supported black nationalism in Africa, it was frowned on at home. Afro haircuts and [independent] black organizations were not permitted. The government's attitude toward Afro-Cuban religions wavered from hostility to support" (Padula 1993:27). Social fallout on the home front was becoming apparent from the losses and casualties in the Angola war; responses to the "national unity" call of the 1960s were uneven; the government was observing a generational crisis among the youth, including among Union of Communist Youth (UJC) members, as well as the beginnings of the *friki* and *hipi* movements, and it reasserted the importance of socialist discipline and ideology in all sectors (D. Fernández 1993:193–198). Though Cuba glowed during its "banner year" in 1979, not least because of apparent successes in its support of Latin American revolution, the Mariel Exodus debacle of 1980, the newly visible addiction to material pleasures among Cuba's "big shot" class *(los mayimbes)*, along with a huge black market in dollars and goods on the street, presented stark contradictions. In April 1986, Fidel Castro declared that Cuba had lost the spirit of sacrifice and *conciencia* exemplified by Ernesto "Ché" Guevara. He announced a "rectification of errors" campaign, clamping down on "middlemen," "profiteers," and padded employment rolls. At the same time, apparently to reign in profit making so that it served the national good, the state began to focus on international tourism, including the building of grand hotel resorts in Varadero and the expansion of the "dollar store" economy (Padula 1993:28–29). Therefore, the Africa idea in the 1980s was not that of the 1970s—based heavily as it was on socialist military and diplomatic goals. Mola Fernández's 1986 rhetoric casts the Casa de Africa as an international link in transatlantic culture and education, but this cannot be isolated historically from Cuba's increasing need to resolve sources of hard currency and scarce resources. In some ways, the Casa de Africa represented a perfect venue for the coming together of international economic feelers with First and Third World nations, profitable island tourism, and the increasingly "cultural" and "historic" currency on which Cuba realized that it could trade. The planned restoration of Old Havana would recreate a historical and architectural jewel for the world. The Casa de Africa's new home was restored in the two years prior to 1986 by the Department of Architecture of the Museum of the City, as part of Eusebio Leal's vision to restore Old Havana, which was granted United Nations conservation funds beginning in the 1970s and designated a Heritage of Humanity by UNESCO in 1982 (Suchlicki 2001:286).

A heady, complicated 1987 event demonstrates what potential the Casa de Africa could realize through the manipulation of Black Atlantic culture. The year after the Casa de Africa's inauguration, President Fidel Castro received the Ọ́ọ̀ni of Ifẹ̀, the king of Nigeria's spiritual capital of the traditional Yoruba religion. For the occasion, the Cuban government recruited a group of elder Lucumí *babalawos* to participate in receiving the king; they were given official permission to form an Ifá cultural organization (Ifá Yesterday, Ifá Today, Ifá Tomorrow), the first of its kind under the revolution.[10] The Lucumí religious leaders were at first genuinely enthusiastic about an audience with the king. The state was interested in lubricating the king's visit, primarily economic in nature, with activities of Afro-Cuban cultural interest. Heavily documented meetings, press conferences, cultural performances, and pompous ceremonials were held in the Casa de Africa. Before the cameras, four elder *babalawos* ceremoniously placed a bead necklace of Orunmila, the Yoruba-Lucumí deity of Ifá divination, whose mythological origin is Ifẹ̀, over the king's head. The king had supposedly made a pilgrimage to the still-beating sacred heart of at least one million West African souls lost to Cuba in the slave trade; for the *babalawos* at hand, his visit meant a newfound international recognition and legitimacy. Within their religious practices, many of these *babalawos* were inspired by the Yoruba king's visit to adopt antisyncretic agendas to recover African roots, such as dressing in Yoruba clothes and learning the Yoruba language.

Much did not go as envisioned. Several of the *babalawos* had been promised state visits to Ifẹ̀, among other things, which were never realized, partly because of internal conflicts within the organization and because the state wanted to select any delegate that would represent Cuba. The trip never happened. The priestly organization eventually splintered among much argument. *Babalawos* who originally attended the events with enthusiasm were left with the feeling that they had been badly used in Cuba's negotiations with Nigeria over oil imports. The king was never really interested in them, they felt, not least because he turned out to be a Muslim. Ultimately, the organization was taken over from the inside by a *babalawo* former member of the organization with deep state connections. This laid the groundwork for the new Yoruba Cultural Association (AYC), which effectively co-opts religion into "culture"-as-international-exchange value. The AYC has worked, for example, to co-opt the important annual, countrywide Ifá divination ceremony called the "Reading of the Year," which provides oracular advice to all of Cuba's Lucumí "families." With state support, the AYC conducts its own reading and transmits its watered-down oracular results to the international press; this undoubtedly intends to demonstrate tolerance for religious activity in Cuba. In 2000, the AYC oversaw the $250,000 renovation of a grand mansion in Old Havana to serve as the association's headquarters, a center for research and conferences, and a Museum of the Orishas. In short, the AYC functions to process Cuban religious resources and information for consumption by tourists, journalists, scholars, and foreign religious practitioners, with the goal of marginalizing independent religious organizations and making money, *babalawos* believe. As such, its underlying mission has been similar to the public dissemination of religion as "folklore." Old Havana's renaissance as a jewel of humanity's heritage is inextricably enmeshed with the manipulation of Cuban "culture" as an international currency for the new millennium.

El Ñáñigo Graduates from Curbside to Third Floor Salon

In order to create contemporary cultural and hard currency out of religious and ethnographic material, the revolution's museological arm had to write another chapter in *El Ñáñigo*'s biography. During the historic Day of Kings celebration, the African nation's *diablitos* performed on the street, and then, looking up, petitioned for *aguinaldo* from the elite, who observed the half-amusing, half-repugnant festivities from their balconies above (plate 19). Imaginably, many a *diablito* sought *aguinaldo* while standing on the very paving stones beneath the balconies of Obrapía Number 157 in the heart of Old Havana. In August 1985, a year before the new Casa de Africa's inauguration, perhaps a dozen or more *sacos de íreme* were rescued from virtual abjection, entered the mansion's front door, climbed the three steep flights of worn white marble steps, and settled into a roomy salon in the mansion's third floor. It was a long and complicated upward climb, which is reflected in the passages of *El Ñáñigo*'s biography.

Between August and November 1985, Claudia Mola Fernández worked with members of the Department of Ethnology in the Academy of Sciences, including researcher and curator Raisa Formaguera,[11] to move a large collection of Afro-Cuban objects to the Casa de Africa. This visible and high-level transfer represented the objects' most recent passage in a long history of movement between different kinds and levels of Cuban institutions. Out of necessity and, apparently, out of the significant cultural status that Afro-Cuban objects had taken on by the mid-1980s, this virtually abject trove was given new life. The Department of Ethnology had found itself in the possession of the objects, which were formerly spread among various entities, including the National Museum, the Palacio de Aldama (now the Institute of History), and the Museum of Legal Medicine. Most had been long ago confiscated by the police and suffered terribly from lack of conservation. With the holding institutions unable to conserve the collection, according to Raisa Formaguera, an agreement was reached among several top players in Havana's cultural bureaucracy: Margarita Fonseca, chief of the Department of Ethnology; Eusebio Leal, the historian of the City of Havana; and María Teresa Linares, director of Old Havana's grand Museum of Music. Leal, head of the Old City's renovation, is one of the most important men in Havana, having extraordinary authority and untold resources for directing Havana's renaissance. Linares, a respected ethnomusicologist, a former director of the Conjunto Folklórico Nacional, and the wife of the late Argeliers León, would receive extraordinary sets of drums and other instruments for her museum. The Casa de Africa, which falls under the Museum of the City's authority, would receive the lion's share of the collection's Lucumí,

Palo, and Abakuá objects. Raisa Formaguera worked with Claudia Mola Fernández on three occasions to move the objects from the Academy of Sciences building to their new home in the Casa de Africa. The exhibition of the objects in salons in the great mansion on Obrapía and Mercaderes was the first time many of them had seen the light of day for more than twenty-six years—others, perhaps, for more than three-quarters of a century. Early confiscated by the police, then collected by Steegers, and later studied by Castellanos and Ortiz, a number of the pieces were finally exhibited to the public at the dawn of the revolution by J. Rodríguez Morey, then director of the National Museum (1960). Their biography thus includes moments of heightened legal and social concern, close study under the microscopes of forensic science and ethnology, periods of languishing and rotting in damp storage rooms, small exhibitions accessible to specialists (Legal Medicine and Anthropology), a grand showing on the revolution's early utopian cultural stage, and, finally, specific promotion under the banner of Cuba's African heritage, to be given back to Africa and the world (plates 4, 6, 16, and 18).

The *sacos de íreme,* along with myriad Abakuá altar objects, found themselves in the company of Lucumí and Palo Monte pieces within a collection to be named for Fernando Ortiz. Though it might be inferred that the objects belonged to Ortiz's "private collection," the third floor's rooms in fact bring together objects that Ortiz personally acquired, occasional donations from other individuals and institutions, and the surviving contents of perhaps two and a half decades of police confiscations from the early twentieth century.[12] Meanwhile, the "historical" African collection of President Fidel Castro occupies the second floor of the Casa de Africa. It consists mostly of third-rate ritual sculpture, glossy touristic pieces, and exotic artisanal furniture given to the president as gifts by representatives of twenty-six African countries. Indisputably, the third floor's collection of historical Afrocubana is the largest and best of its kind in the world.

New Curatorship and Professional Informants

Following and revising established conventions for the display of Afrocubana, Claudia Mola Fernández and her staff created three principal Afro-Cuban salons: Lucumí, Palo, and Abakuá, preceded by a didactic foyer display dedicated to the history of the old African *cabildos* and the biography of Fernando Ortiz. The work of organization, conservation, and installation took four to five years. By February 1990, with the inauguration of the Palo Monte salon, the third floor was complete. As opposed to prior exhibitions, which were curated mostly from the top down, Claudia Mola Fernández collaborated with elder Lucumí, Palo Monte, and Abakuá members to install the objects within experience-near display contexts. Indeed, the Palo Monte salon, in what must have been a first in the history of Cuban museums, was inaugurated and sacralized by Efori Eñongo's Perico Abasonga, an elder *palero* who consecrated the installation as if it were within a real *munanso,* a Palo temple (figure 13.5).

As opposed to earlier exhibitions organized by non–Afro-Cubans and nonpractitioners, Mola Fernández could claim genuine insider credentials in her curatorial role. A Cuban of color, she had received initiations within the Lucumí religion, was married to a *babalawo,* and conducted research herself in West Africa among the Yoruba and other groups. Still, the permanently exhibited "Fernando Ortiz Collection" within the Museum of the City's Casa de Africa became legible within a set of frames appropriate to the moment: continuing scholarly legitimation of Afro-Cuban cultural display via the Ortiz model of Cuban ethnology, a high-profile homage to "the third discoverer of Cuba,"[13] Fernando Ortiz, the internationally invested restoration of Eusebio Leal's fiefdom, and Cuba's transition in earnest to a tourist-based economy, in line with the government's shift between the 1970s and 1990s from revolutionary tutor to global economic contender. The last role would, of course, vaporize between 1989 and 1991 with the collapse of the Soviet bloc, the disappearance

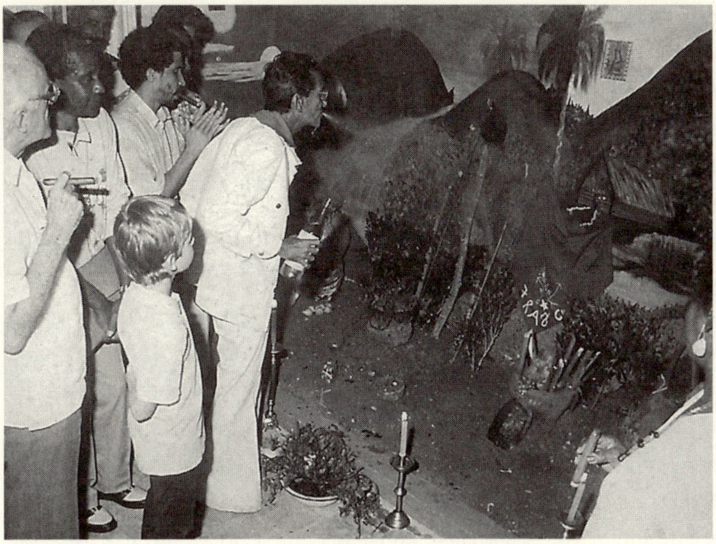

Figure 13.5. Inauguration of the Palo Monte Salon in the Fernando Ortiz Collection of the Casa de Africa, February 1990. A typical Palo altar, set apart by a cement lip, is filled with earth. The "charged" cauldrons are covered with foliage, and a mural, representing mountains, trees and forest, and remote *bohío* dwelling, is painted behind. Perico Abasonga of Regla sprays a libation of *aguardiente* on the shrine. Director Claudia Mola Fernández stands to the far right with a cigar in her hand. Photograph courtesy private collection, Regla.

of trading partners, the end of subsidies, and the onset of the devastating Special Period (1991–97).

Claudia Mola Fernández called upon two old Reglanos in the installation of the Abakuá and Palo Monte objects. Although the Lucumí salon was primarily installed with conventional, though crude, museological methods by the Casa de Africa, Mola Fernández had other things in mind for the Abakuá and Palo Monte salons. Instead of isolated vitrines, random groupings, or cheesy diorama installations, the Casa de Africa would strive for an unprecedented level of ritual authenticity. Mola Fernández called upon Regla's Juan Mokongo to install the Abakuá salon, and, as noted, his close colleague from Efori Eñongo, Perico Abasonga, a venerated *palero,* to install the Palo Monte salon. Juan was already known as an Abakuá sage within museum circles, particularly by the director of the Museum of Regla across the bay from Old Havana, Pedro Cosme Baños. As a result, groups of objects were reintegrated into an altar display context for the first time since their confiscation from many a *fambá* up to three-quarters of a century earlier. As Wifredo Lam had reimagined a conventional space of high art production, his studio, as a *fambá,* so the third-floor upper room in a colonial mansion owned by slaveholders was also converted into a facsimile of the Abakuá temple's interior.

The Fernando Ortiz Collection, as first accessioned by the Casa de Africa, was, in fact, a jumble of objects, which bore incomplete or nonexistent provenances. From their beginnings, no one with the exception of generations of now-deceased dockworkers was ever very interested in the makers' real identities. The pieces had arrived at the Casa de Africa with various museums' accession numbers painted on them, but without corresponding documents. In short, they could be, to most, merely anonymous examples of "the Abakuá Society," formerly *ñañiguismo.* As the direct descendant of such dockworkers and Abakuá object makers, Juan came to this jumble with a bit more preparation. He had to make some sense out of it. Juan meticulously organized the altar around a set of staffs that clearly went together, along with a selection of drums. He added a Catholic crucifix and wine goblet, two divining horns of Nasakó, and a small *pandero* drum to complete the altar top. Behind the altar he hung a brilliant satin dossal bearing the signs of the top Abakuá officers. In front, he placed two candelabra, the clay vessel of Sikán, and the ritual shakers *(maruga* and *erikundé)* used in the orchestra and the choreography of the *íremes* (plate 6). From elements of distinct origins, Juan explained to me, he built an altar that reflected the conventions of a rare branch of Cuba's Abakuá.

The Orú, he said, customarily used seven staffs, rather than the four of the Efó and Efí branches. The other altar objects had come from different sources, such as a beautiful leopardskin-covered *sese* of the Efó. As appropriate to any *fambá* interior, the collection's *sacos de íreme* were hung side by side, as if ready to be taken down and danced during a *plante* (plate 4).

These gorgeous suits, as well as the altar objects, could claim different origins within the Abakuá and histories within Cuban institutions—in short, they could claim rich but complicated biographies. Close visual comparison of the Casa de Africa's *íreme* collection on display and published ethnographic documents indicate that at least two of the *íreme* suits formerly belonged to the Steegers criminological collection in the Museum of Legal Medicine of the University of Havana. These are the elaborate satin appliqué "creole" suits closely studied by Israel Castellanos for his 1928 article (compare figure 9.6 with plate 4, extreme right and left, respectively). Finally, a third suit, one of the most astonishing collected among the Abakuá, is the same Akuaramina masquerade that Pierre Verger photographed during his 1957 visit with Lydia Cabrera (compare plate 18, figure 13.6). According to Raisa Formaguera, it seems to have belonged previously to the National Museum. Apparently photographed in situ in 1957 and then exhibited by Rodríguez Morey in 1960, this *saco de íreme* would seem to have the shortest official institutional biography of the suits now exhibited in the Casa de Africa. Though neither its provenance nor mode of "collection" is known, its biography, as formally written up by scholars, differs from the other suits. Indeed, where some suits had disappeared into Cuban state institutions, some believed that the Akuaramina met a worse fate. Art historian Robert Farris Thompson reproduced Verger's photograph of the same Akuaramina and reported that the suit was "inadvertently destroyed in 1961," leaving the in-situ document as a reflection of "a vanished moment in Afro-Cuban art" (1983:239). Like many other tenacious denizens of the Cuban cultural landscape, the Akuaramina did not, in fact, die—it just lay around in darkness until it was recycled. Thus, while other suits had languished in storerooms for many decades, the Akuaramina seems to have made a relatively swift transition from *fambá* to the National Museum sometime after 1957—when it was still being performed in situ—perhaps via the stewardship and resources of Lydia Cabrera or Fernando Ortiz. Now it was a jewel of the House of Africa.

The last third of the 1980s was a heady moment for new forms and contexts of Afrocubana display. The Casa de Africa, with its practitioner-directed installations and ritually sacralized inaugurations, surpassed the Guanabacoa Museum's theatricalized diorama approach. Perico Abasonga's libations of rum and cigar smoke over the Palo Monte altar resacralized socially dead and long-scorned objects, reconnecting them to spiritual currents past and present. In this sense, the Casa de Africa's collection could claim far more authenticity and legitimacy than that of the Guanabacoa Museum, though the objects' biographies harbored contradictions, given the contexts of their original "collection" and heavy mediation by cultural and political agendas. At minimum, the museum's direction by a curator-priestess and its practitioner-driven installations and "consecrations" created an exhibition form of more explicitly divided address. Like Lydia Cabrera's "old adept"–driven narratives and the Conjunto Folklórico's Rumba Saturday *orisha* dances, it could "mean" different things to different viewing constituencies. Within the exhibition's *fambá* Abakuá, the *íreme* would experience a kind of rebirth among sacred attributes dear and familiar to him. Of course, museum visitors, upon entering the third-floor galleries, would have to pass under the visage and name of Don Fernando Ortiz before anything else. Was the "subject" of the collection the African legacy in Cuba, the persecution of the *ñáñigos,* Don Fernando Ortiz and his legacy to Havana as Cuba's "third discoverer," or the blood, sweat, and tears of "humble" dockworkers such as Quirino Valdés, Juan Mokongo, and Perico Abasonga? Or, once again, was it the revival of Old Havana as a touristic cash cow?

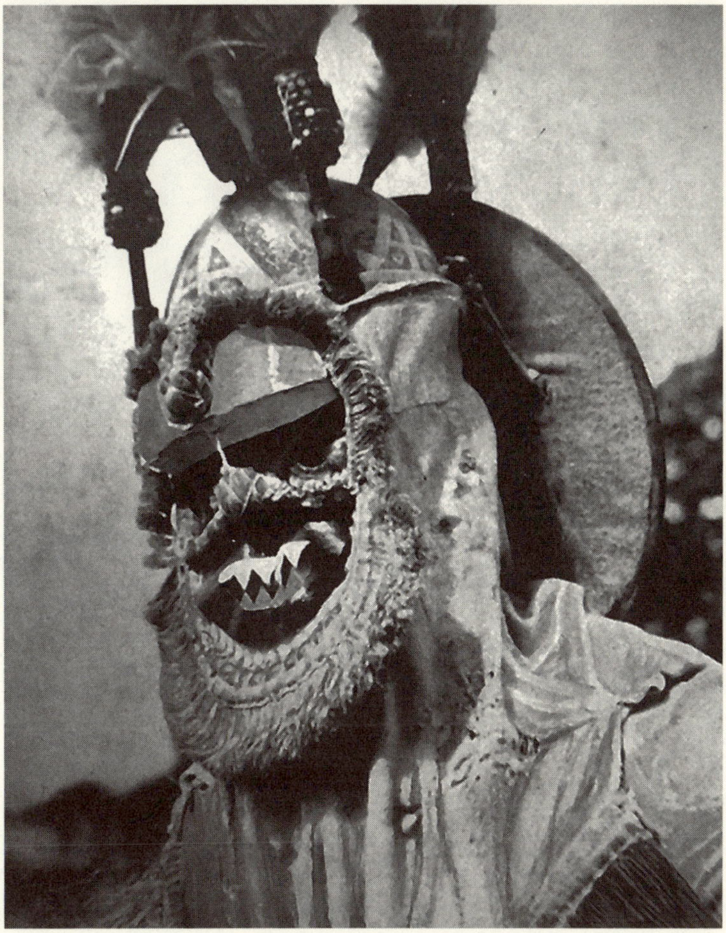

Figure 13.6. *Íreme* Akuaramina, 1957. Pierre Verger photographed the Akuaramina in situ during his Havana visit with Lydia Cabrera in 1957, one year before her 1958 *Sociedad secreta abakuá* title was published (Cabrera 1958, frontispiece). Courtesy of the Estate of Lydia Cabrera.

The Casa de Africa's objects would take on larger meanings not within a young, utopian revolutionary Havana but one struggling to reposition itself within international cultural currents and hard currencies. During the same moment, a small museum just a short ferry hop across the Bay of Havana was beginning to shift its thematic focus and display strategies, though within a variant curatorial direction.

Local History and the "Polyvalent Museum of Regla"

El Museo Polívalente de Regla, an antiquarian, ethnographic, and local history museum, sits on Regla's main artery, the bustling Calle Martí, just up the hill from the church of the town's black Virgin. The museum houses a large collection of possessions belonging to the town's former colonial and republican aristocracy and middle class: furniture, clocks, oil paintings, pianos, domestic Roman Catholic altar pieces, commercial safes, crystal, flatware, porcelains, clothing, and documents. It also owns numerous religious pieces salvaged from local houses of Ocha and Palo Monte, whose elderly owners passed without the support of ritual families to bequeath or dispatch their attributes properly. Director Pedro Cosme Baños explains that the building, a grand single-story mansion with a lovely brick courtyard, belonged to upper-class families until the nineteenth century. A free woman of color of some resources purchased the house, situated on a prominent block in Regla's white First District, a stone's throw from the hilltop mansion of the town's founders, the Recio family. Not long after, she sold it under duress to a white family in order that the racial hierarchies preferred by the town's oligarchy be preserved.[14] By the time of the 1959 revolution, another white upper-class family was living in the house. As things went, the state moved them around the corner to a smaller house facing the bay and the church, and the mansion on Calle Martí was dedicated as the Regla Museum.

In the mid-1980s, under Cosme's direction, the museum moved to recognize hitherto ignored contributions to the town's culture and history. Cosme, an optimistic Afro-Cuban supporter of the revolution, is particularly interested in Regla's African, Chinese, and Spanish/Canary Island working-class heritages. He wrote a book on Regla's Chinese population (Cosme Baños 1998), researched in the Canaries, dedicated salons and vitrines in the museum to objects from the town's principal Yoruba-Lucumí *cabildo,* and recently acquired Abakuá objects for a permanent installation.[15] The museum's cultural and historical "polyvalence" is highlighted in a most poignant juxtaposition. An elegant portrait of the enslaved Yoruba Ño Remigio Herrera Adechina (ca. 1811–1905), a great founder of Ifá who lived and died in Regla, shares the museum's lobby space with other local luminaries, including Regla's fallen combatants of the Wars of Independence and the 1959 revolution (figure 13.7). Adechina's vitrine, directly across the lobby from examples of the Recio family riches, contains iron manacles such as those Adechina may himself have worn in the Middle Passage or on the plantation. Next to them is a Yoruba-Cuban *orisha* object believed to have been made by Adechina's own hands: the conical head of Eshu, the trickster and opener of roads.

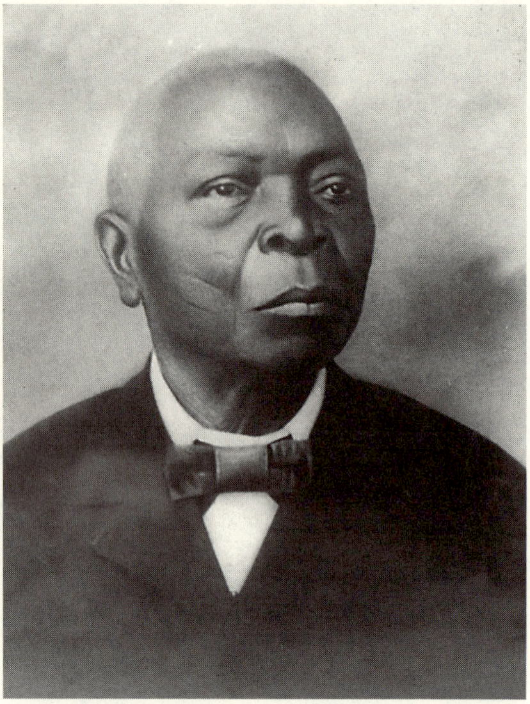

Figure 13.7. Portrait of Ño Remigio Herrera Adechina in the Museum of Regla. A Yoruba, Adechina was a principal founder of Ifá practice in Cuba. Photograph by David H. Brown.

In order to stay in step with recent developments in Havana's cultural infrastructure, Cosme raised funds to expand the museum; he talks about developing a small hotel to house foreign visitors across the street; and he regularly conducts local tours for groups of Europeans and Asian tourists. Under Cosme's direction, the museum has become a respected institution among Regla's folk. Cosme has become a cultural and historical arbiter, and he fancies himself a mayoral figure. The museum's public events are often-touching local tributes, which skirt the institutional pomp of cultural forums across the bay. For example, every Tuesday afternoon, Cosme puts on a Lucumí drumming party *(güiro)* for locals, tourists, and the museum's employees, centered on a performance by a group from Perdomo Street in Regla's traditionally Afro-Cuban Third Barrio. Cosme prepares the hors d'oeuvres himself: sausage and crackers, along with fresh papaya and mango, which most Reglanos never see on their own tables.

The Museum of Regla distinguishes itself from the Casa de Africa and Guanabacoa venues by its particular mission and methods. A local history museum, its collection consists of objects from the town itself, which have been more easily attributable, not anonymous pieces previously cobbled together in the judicial, criminological, and ethnological institutions of Havana. Another distinction worth noting is that most of the Casa de Africa's objects, though now predicated by the benignly represented subject of Fernando Ortiz, were "collected" under conditions of extreme state violence toward specifically targeted groups. In Regla, Afro-Cubans clearly did not escape stigma and violence. Still, the objects in the collection mostly fell to the museum by default or through focused salvage and conservation efforts following the deaths of their elderly owners. The Afro-Cuban objects have been treated to the same historical and museological rigor as other pieces in the collection. Virtually every piece is identified by its former owner, and meticulous accession records are kept. In one case, the entire altar of a deceased Regla priestess was conserved and is on view in the permanent exhibition salon devoted to the Lucumí religion. A special 1999 exhibition, devoted to festive altars, contextualized Lucumí practice in Regla with historical reference to specific persons, including photographs of two of the town's most venerated early twentieth-century priestesses. A photograph of Susana Cantero Omí Toké flanked the installation, rather than, say, a photograph of Fernando Ortiz (figure 13.8, right). This contexualizing device of ancestral photographs rings true to museum visitors and locals precisely because it is modeled after an actual altar installation for the Virgin of Regla/Yemayá in an old Santería house nearby, owned by Norma Cárdenas. In its front room, open for public viewing, photographs of the house's founders, Norma's mother and grandmother, Marcelina and Panchita Cárdenas respectively, frame the altar. The museum's collection can therefore identify, and teach through exhibition, the contributions of specific individuals to Regla's history. In contrast, while the Casa de Africa's collection emphatically marks the African contribution to Cuba's cultural history, it must rely entirely on ethnographic and historical synecdoche. The recreated Abakuá salon, for example, is a part that stands for the whole, though the altar does mark the Orú nation; it represents, in a general way, the "culture" or "folklore" of several hundred lodges (and several thousand anonymous individuals and their families) that comprised the "Abakuá Society" in Cuba. Moreover, the Regla Museum's "polyvalent" collection represents the Municipality of Regla's history, conceived by its current administration as a plurality of cultures, classes, races, ethnicities, and religions. The "Africa House," in effect, spatially segregates Afro-Cuban culture and regrounds it in Cuba's links with Africa in order to fulfill a particular high-profile political purpose. The Guanabacoa Museum's approach is even more generalizing, though its meaning is no less interesting. Apart from the Arcadio Calvo pieces, which have been made anonymous through folkloricized display, the collection represents a vague ethnographic present, not a living local culture. In contrast to the Regla Museum's tranquil locale, which retains its small-town historical feel, the Casa de Africa's immediate environment has increasingly gained the feel of an urban Colonial Williamsburg with a touristic Caribbean twist. The area is filled with period-dressed *mulatas* with colorful turbans and *caleseros* with their fancy horse-driven coaches. New boutiques, restored old bars and grand hotels, a Chinese restaurant, a pizza parlor, and a gay teahouse jostle with blocky Soviet-style administrative buildings nearby. The legions of young prostitutes and male hustlers *(jineteras* and *jineteros)* on the street are matched only by the legions of Havana policemen, there to protect groups of camera-toting tourists from molestation by these supposed delinquents. The *mulatas* and *caleseros* are paid state employees, and neither the *jineteras* nor the policemen are Havana natives, but mostly come from the *campo,* that is, the eastern provinces. More and more locals are being moved out of Old Havana every year to the packed high-rise apartments in Alamar to the east, which Cubans call "Palomar"—that is, it resembles a pigeon *(paloma)* coop.

Recently, the Regla Museum confronted a curatorial challenge around the accession of Abakuá objects, which highlights how the institution conceives its special role. Until 2000, the collection of Afrocubana consisted principally of Lucumí and Palo Monte objects from town itself. In that year, as the result of an arrangement with the old Museum of Legal Medi-

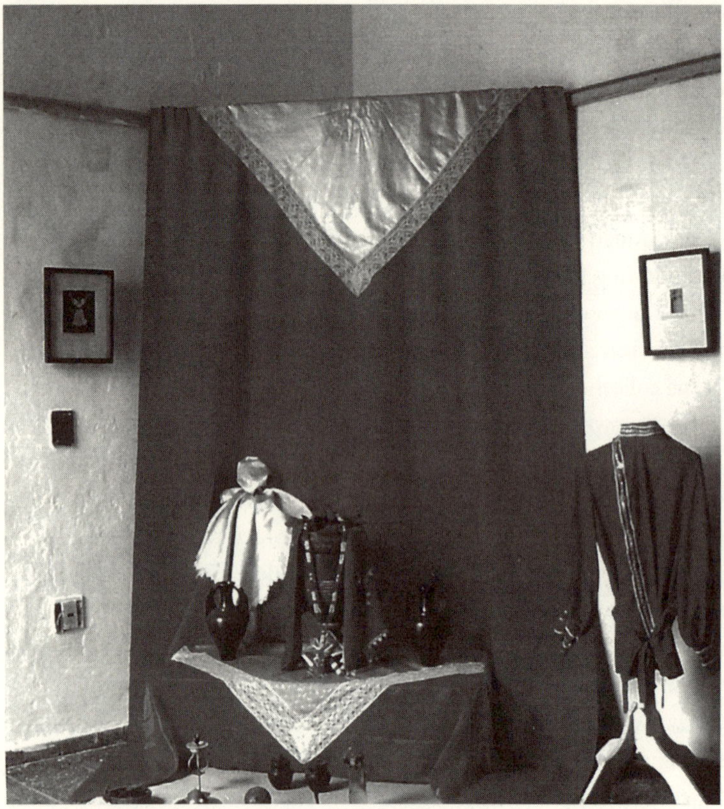

Figure 13.8. Special exhibition of Santería altars and ritual clothes in the Museum of Regla, featuring photographs of two of the town's founding Lucumí priestesses, Susana Cantero Omí Toké and Josefa Herrera Echubí, 1999. The altar ("throne") is dedicated to Shangó. Photograph by David H. Brown, courtesy of the Museum of Regla.

cine in Havana, the Regla Museum acquired a set of Abakuá orchestra drums, an *íreme* masquerade costume, and some minor instruments. In exchange, art historian and museologist Luís Alberto Pedroso reinstalled Legal Medicine's collection. In contrast to the objects in the Regla Museum's collection, the Abakuá pieces, confiscated early in the twentieth century, remain anonymous. Still, though they were most likely not produced by the members of Regla's famous old Abakuá Efó, Enyegueyé, Obon Tanze, or Abarakó Chiquito lodges, their recontextualization in a forthcoming exhibition will endow them with local significance. Though not directly attributable, the Abakuá objects will come to symbolically represent, the director says, *"el pueblo de Regla"* (the people of Regla), the town's colonial and neocolonial history, the contributions of its lodges, and past Abakuá luminaries such as Manuel de Jesús "Chuchú" Capáz, Quirino Valdés, Juan Gutiérrez Montojo, and Juan Mokongo, who were revolutionary fighters, labor leaders, politicians, and workers on Regla's wharves. In this sense, these Abakuá leaders will be reinserted not merely into a general display about "the Abakuá Society," as if Abakuá "traditions" were separate from Regla's history. These figures performed many of the same services and sacrifices as other local heroes now represented in the museum's vitrines. The new Abakuá objects will thus be located, in the museum's rereading, within the town's emerging historical narrative. In a larger framework, such exhibitions will amplify the Abakuá contribution toward Cuban freedom; Regla's Abakuá, such as Quirino Valdés, Chuchú Capáz, Juan Gutiérrez Montojo, and Juan Mokongo, were, it is believed, "humble workers" who organized institutions of self-defense against their colonial and neocolonial capitalist masters (see also López Valdés 1985; Quiñones 1998, n.d.). In this last context, *El Ñáñigo*, figuratively speaking, graduates from criminal delinquent, atavistic specimen, modern-primitivist icon, figure of Cuban national culture to a locally situated, self-conscious, working-class revolutionary subject.

In contrast to the general folkloric relationship the Conjunto Folklórico or the Guanabacoa Museum maintains with the "townspeople" of Cuba, the Museum of Regla bears a more local burden. Afro-Cuban and Abakuá display carries a practical responsibility the museum believes it must maintain toward its own townspeople. Regla is full of functioning Abakuá lodges, and any exhibition will be seen and critiqued by members. The museum is dependent on them for information and the authority to represent the Abakuá Society. Given this proximity and intimacy, the museum feels limits on the kinds of Abakuá objects it can appropriately exhibit. Whereas the Legal Medicine Museum and the Casa de Africa display the otherwise secret and guarded, albeit anonymous, *sese* and Ekue drums, the Regla Museum chose to accession and exhibit only those pieces that are most regularly seen by the public within Abakuá ceremonies themselves: orchestra drums and *íreme* costumes. In its assumption to the status of contemporary museum piece, *El Ñáñigo* was thus reanimated in different ways. In Guanabacoa, *El Ñáñigo* maintains a somewhat reduced vitality as the subject of socialist folklore. In the Casa de Africa, *El Ñáñigo* resides as a subject of Afro-Cuban culture and as a function of Fernando Ortiz's hagiography. In Regla, *El Ñáñigo* lives under the umbrella of local sensitivities, including the Abakuá code.

Conclusion: A Biographical Summary

The Abakuá pieces now in the Casa de Africa and those soon to be exhibited in the Regla Museum carry substantial "biographies." The objects began as *fundamentos* of specific *juegos,* became police evidence, and, then, the dry specimens of two scientific museums and the National Museum. With the revolution, they were reanimated in the Casa de Africa under the banner of an Africanized national identity and the authenticating personage of Fernando Ortiz. With the exception of the Efore Muna Tanze pieces on more or less continuous display in the Museum of Legal Medicine, many objects apparently languished for years, if not decades, in the bowels of various institutions, including the National Museum and the Academy of Sciences. Thus, one chapter of their biography must be their liminal storage and invisibility, if not abjection. They were written, mostly by default, out of the public transcript, just as some were violently written into it between 1874 and Roche y Monteagudo's 1925 police chronicle. Others were more benignly and neutrally written into academic discourse in their use as illustrations within Fernando Ortiz's seminal volumes on Afro-Cuban culture in the 1950s. A selection emerged briefly in Rodríguez Morey's 1960 exhibition at the dawn of the revolution, followed by a rush of interesting Afro-Cuban cultural projects during the early 1960s, such as León's Abakuá Concert, the Guanabacoa Museum, and the Conjunto Folklórico Nacional. Still, it was not until the mid-1980s, in the wake of the "Africa Decade," that they were resurrected within the Casa de Africa.

After their accession to the vitrines of Legal Medicine and Anthropology, and thanks to *afrocubanismo* and modern primitivist painting, the objects were on their way to "national folklore" via the revolutionary cultural agenda, influenced as it was by Ortiz's transculturation theories. Still, the Abakuá objects were reanimated under variant institutional agendas within contemporary Cuba. The meanings of the Abakuá objects in the Casa de Africa, in the still-functioning Museum of Legal Medicine, and in the Museum of Regla overlap but are not identical. Each collection speaks in a different tone to different audiences: tourists, schoolchildren, Cuban and foreign scholars, visiting African dignitaries, university medical students, and religious practitioners. At the Casa de Africa, Juan Mokongo and Perico Abasonga were far more interested in the traditions and history of the Abakuá from the inside than in international politics—though they never disconnected Abakuá from grander proletarian, revolutionary, and humanistic sentiments. Cuban scholars are mostly interested in straightforward ethnographic and historical study in relation to national narratives, as well as locating the Afro-Cuban religions as the defensive necessities of the capitalist past. Visiting foreign scholars have mostly been interested in the Africanness of the objects. Regla schoolchildren learn about their local and national heritage, which is linked to Cuba's heroic liberation struggles. European tourists are charmed by the objects' exotic qualities during their brief vacations on an exotic island.

Juan Mokongo—Abakuá, Reglano, *combatiente,* stevedore, barber, and professional folklore "informant"—represented a special kind of contemporary creator and beholder. He was a living link between a number of the contexts delineated here. He was mentored in the Abakuá tradition of working men who used their sacred and social resources to transform their conditions between 1863 through the 1940s. He was the product of a proud yet much maligned tradition, which he felt to be only belatedly recognized. Juan came to critical awareness of his Abakuá practice long before he became an informant and collaborator with the Casa de Africa and the Museum of Regla. His mentor, Chuchú Capáz, is remembered as having worked closely with Lydia Cabrera and other scholars. Juan closely studied and memorized the private, handwritten notebooks he painstakingly copied from those of Chuchú, and he could translate at will from Spanish to Brícamo and back again. He was welcome in every *fambá* in the country, and could substitute with perfect competence for any missing officer. Like one of his idols, the old *mambí,* Quirino Valdés, Juan had fought as a revolutionary *combatiente.* And he was an Abakuá from Regla, where centralized authority—the Spanish, the Republican governments, and even the Communist state—has always been regarded ambivalently. He was a "white" Abakuá in the tradition of Andrés Facundo Cristo de los Dolores Petít, but always insisted on his connection to his African ancestors, not least because he was a priest of Shangó in the Lucumí religion and Siete Rayos in Palo. One of the ironies of Juan's life became highly marked, and remarked upon, by his friends only after his death. Ultimately, given the slow but marked shift in the regime's stance toward the day-to-day practice of the Afro-Cuban traditions in the mid-1990s, Juan could have a state funeral attended by five thousand people, for which he was dressed in a specially assembled suit: split and sewn down the middle, one half was the lavish red satin consecration garment of Changó, and the other half was the khaki fatigues of the *combatiente.* An Abakuá procession, including six dancing *íremes,* accompanied his coffin to the cemetery of Regla, where he was interred in the pantheon of revolutionary heroes. Quite a graduation ceremony for *El Ñáñigo.*

Despite the grand funeral, his friends remembered his great humility. Juan was a retired stevedore who worked as a barber on a dusty corner by the Via Blanca highway entrance in order to eke out a living. He never asked the state for anything in return for his brave service to the revolution, according to his friends. He lived the last years of his life in a house with a collapsed roof. During the worst part of the Special Period (1991–94), Juan and his wife, María, and the families of their two married sons often had to share a single bar of soap between them. The only fork in the house was reserved for foreign guests invited for dinner. Only after Juan's death did the state give his wife a new two-story house in one of the several famous *barrios* Abakuá, called Pati Larga.

Coda: *El Ñáñigo* in Cuban Contemporary Art: Pedro Álvarez's *Site*

Familiar figures from the Cuban past populate Pedro Álvarez's 1998 near-panoramic canvas *Site (Homage to Wifredo Lam)* (plate 29). Here is the island's long and tangled national narrative as critically seen through the lens of art history. Sad monumental ruins, clawed and defeated by the roots of ancient *ceiba* trees, frame the space, which resembles a stage set. The thick twisted roots and massive stone arch recall the remains of dinosaurs. Thickly layered palms and blocky ramparts contribute to the complex backdrop, while blue pastel sky and Caribbean light selectively illuminate elements of the mysterious blue-green foreground. Within this stretched Claudian composition of the kind borrowed by America's nineteenth-century romantic landscape painters,[16] Álvarez deploys figures appropriated from Víctor Patricio de Landaluze's black colonial "types," sleek 1940s and 1950s American commercial imagery, and socialist sloganeering. Shades of neo-Dada and Pop Art arise in the subtle, all-over collaged repetition of hundred-dollar bills in the background. Two nearly hidden signature reminders of Cuba's great mid-twentieth-century modernist hint at the painting's parenthetical subtitle.

Pedro Álvarez's disjunctive and ironic work, an epic—or better, counter-epic—perfectly encapsulates the nostalgia, suffering, and the near, or false, triumphs that fill Cuba's historical experience. Four iconic Landaluze figures populate the mysterious landscape: the ox-drawn sugar cane cart of Cuba's principal industry; the itinerant seller of pineapples, accompanied by the ubiquitous side bag–toting urchin (see plate 19, far right); the seated urban *bollera,* selling her fritters to a mixed-race, fancily dressed mother with child in tow (figure 10.3); and Landaluze's *Diablito Mongo* (ca. 1878), one of many variants of *El Ñáñigo* (see plate 8).[17]

Álvarez did not choose his references to be charming mementos. Via conventional imagery, Álvarez evokes and rotates 360 degrees for inspection the ecological, social, and economic history of Cuba. Moreover, in his shrewd use of just such conventions, Álvarez reflects upon a specific Cuban history of representation itself. The little ox-cart tableau, with its driver, ominous overseer, and plantation grandmother-granddaughter pair, evokes the emergent capitalist basis of Cuba's Atlantic economy: sugar, with its attendant hierarchies of race and power. The *bollera,* an urban slave or freewoman, references the quasi-autonomy and internal market system of Havana's Afro-Cuban barrios and the daily interactions on Cuba's cobblestone streets among the social hierarchy of people of color. The dark-skinned itinerant fruit seller, wearing a plaid African-style wrap and balancing her wares in classic African head portage style, brings the products of her *conuco* (a personal garden for sustenance and surplus) into the urban setting. The street urchin, with his sombrero and side bag, is an archetype of movement and exchange, as well as the orphaned product of social dislocation. He is a kind of child trickster of roads and urban warrens, like the Lucumí Eshú (see figure 5.5). Drawing thus on Landaluze, Álvarez brings the dynamic of country and city, planter and merchant economy, together in Havana's now-ruined "sugar palace," though from the vantage point of its quotidian black underside, which Fernando Ortiz called *la hampa cubana.* Nothing more starkly embodied the fearsome *hampa cubana* and its *mala vida* than *El Ñáñigo* and *La Brujería,* which are marked by two foreground elements. Landaluze's *Diablito Mongo,* wielding his rod and rooster, and the iron cauldron of the warrior *orisha* Ogún stake their terrain at the trunk of the giant *ceiba* tree—powerful in the Afro-Cuban religious sphere and the national imagination. Havana was officially founded at the foot of a great ceiba in 1524 near the Plaza de Armas in what is now Old Havana. Fruit rises from Ogún's cauldron, and a bunch of purple grapes form the outline of the African continent—signifying a principal vine of ethnic and cultural descent on the island. The two, *diablito* and cauldron, doubly involve Lam, who absorbed the form of the *diablito* into his cubist-surrealist abstractions. And, among the fruit—in many ways, the painting's leitmotif—rises one of Wifredo Lam's signature Afro-Cubanist figures, seen throughout his 1940s and 1950s work: a horned, devilish Eshú. Eshú appears as a flat modernist silhouette (see, e.g., figure 10.6, center right) amid the realist, modeled detail of Landaluze's *costumbrista* genre.

Álvarez signifies upon his art historical forebears, as well as the fallen optimists of Cuban nationhood, by rendering Cuba's urban landscape as a bittersweet *jungla* (jungle), the exuberant and transformative forest of Lam's 1942 monumental work. Álvarez's *Site,* laid out via conventional elements of nineteenth-century academic landscape painting, sets up the tension of denial and revelation. The scene is a stage for disjunction, tragedy, folly, and the return of the repressed. In proximity to Landaluze's quaint "types," lush framing foliage, monumental ruins, and warm, nearly sublime light, the statue of a lion close to the composition's center might suggest this landscape as a romantic national idyll, but for its odd angle and pathos. Massive *ceiba* roots cast the statue askew. The king of the jungle no longer stands out. In green monochrome, this noble and fearsome animal, now dwarfed, recedes into the gloomy immediate environment, as if some pall had descended. Landaluze's charming "types" and "customs," along with Cuba's age-old dreams of independence and hygienic modern nationhood, are rendered radically ambivalent. The azure skies, gentle palms, and brilliant yellow light of a heavily promoted Caribbean paradise encounter darkness and failure where colonialism, slavery, global capital, and race meet on the island's shores. Painting in the 1990s, the young Álvarez does not want to romanticize Cuba's colonial past. There never existed a pristine, antediluvian Cuba, where lions roamed freely and ruled benignly. And those who would make themselves lions through revolution and nationhood are exposed as paper tigers. Even an innocent spirituality remains compromised as a remedy or consolation, as the natural efficacy of spiritually imbued fruit offered to the *orishas* is circumscribed by history.

In *Site,* Álvarez revisits the conjuncture of the Capitalist Atlantic and the Black Atlantic in a complex scene of modernity and its malcontents on the island of Cuba. On this island, everything, including some of its most cherished self-representations, is underpainted, literally, with the grid of U.S. currency and the repeated visage of Benjamin Franklin—putatively known as the "The First American" and archetypal self-made man (Brands 2000). The underpainted dollar grid belies the primacy of national foundation stones, indeed, of nature and the land themselves as essential grounds of the island's identity. Probably not lost on Álvarez, the green dollar, as underpainting, a formal device for manipulating palette, influences everything painted atop it. Moreover, the dollar's dominant color (green) and its repeated form (rectangle grid of collaged reproductions of the bill) become the true building blocks of society and culture. Ultimately, the green dollar, the universal commodity, replaces nature as the artist's ground and inspiration. Hereafter, all representation necessarily arises within the simulacrum (see A. Fernández 1999:44).

Given Álvarez's awareness of prior art history and international avant-gardes, it comes as no surprise that the serially repeated dollar grid evokes the neo-Dada postmodernism of Jasper Johns and the Pop Art of Andy Warhol. Johns's conceptually shrewd targets, American flags, and grids of numbers and alphabets derived from extant, quotidian systems of representation, thereby extracting art making from the post-Renaissance myth of the heroic, inspired artist, whose expression came from on high, from nature, or from within the self. Andy Warhol, with much more humor and irony, in his serial repetition of the already represented (that is, mass and consumer visual culture) questioned the privileged role of the artist; his work both celebrated and critiqued the simulacrum as the starting point for all signifying practice. Similarly, Álvarez's postmodern "Homage to Wifredo Lam" both celebrates and critiques the context in which Lam's *Jungla* and other Cuban modernist works were produced. Lam worked within the international market-driven matrix of modernist art production; as an Afro-Chinese Cuban who had studied in the academy, and among the Parisian avant-garde, his paintings crossed and sundered national, social, phenomenological, and artistic boundaries.

Álvarez's *Site* suggests that the ostensibly natural fruits of the earth and the creative production of the human hand have been enmeshed with the universal commodity since the age of exploration, European enclosure laws of property, and slave ship–driven Atlantic modernity (see Linebaugh and Rediker 2000). In one important local Atlantic "site," contemporary Cuba, the icon of world exchange, the hundred-dollar bill, has special resonance. Cuban youth have called the Franklin-faced note *una risa,* literally, "a smile," when referring to this global object of desire, the "C-note." Whether the smile is turned up or down is a matter of circumstance, prearranged high above and far from the streets of Cuban *barrios.* The Franklin smile, Mona Lisa–like, is a particularly inaccessible denomination of *fula* or *wanikiki* (American dollars), *dólares* that became known as *dolores de cabeza* (headaches) during the Special Period (officially 1991–97) after the collapse of the Soviet bloc and its subsidies of Cuba's economy.

Thus far, it is evident that things "International," as they touch on this national and local site, form one of the work's central themes. A banana-yellow truck, an American-built International, literally slices through the sun-dappled, cool green middle ground. This sleek symbol of modern American commerce, a frivolous pineapple-shaped marble throne of the ages, and a striking red banner remain the only elements in the composition hit fully broadside by the sun. These are setups, of course, allusive props for a tragicomic historical play. What better place to hide the truth than in broad daylight. Juxtaposed and theatrically lit for drama, these three bold elements bespeak the promises and failures of both capitalist expansion—in this case, its banana republics—and socialist revolution. It was, of course, in the shadow of industrializing monocrop agriculture, stolen wars of independence in order to make the island safe for profit, puppet governments, and glossy corporate self-promotion that slaves and workers have toiled in the Cuban countryside and city. In the shadow of Big Fruit's pineapple throne, a black woman ekes out a living toting the very same fruit on her head that such giants as United Fruit wrenched from the land and sold abroad. Ironically, in revolutionary Cuba, Cubans themselves do not normally get to taste pineapples. They are exported abroad, along with sugar, cigars, coffee, and medicine in order to produce the *risa.* Of course, for ordinary Cubans, this smile is a shit-eating grin, complete with all the trappings that the state's egalitarian and tourist facades are capable of providing. Periodically, ordinary Cubans get to taste fruit at the end of Santería drummings, but only after the *orishas* have "eaten" these locally scarce agribusiness products. During the Special Period, a group of hungry Havana kids hijacked crates of fruit intended for the zoo's animals, and then spent an hour throwing banana peels and orange rinds at the monkeys.

If northern Big Fruit once ruled, it now stands in decay, humiliated by the banana peel of post-1959 business nationalization. In *Site,* American International itself is poised to slip on its own cherished product, a sight gag from American movie comedies that brought the mighty low. At the same time, supposed revolutionary triumphs appear in a red banner overhead, such as *Never Work Again* (*Ne Travaillez Jam* [Jamais]), a slogan of the anticapitalist Situationist International, led by such intellectual luminaries as Guy Debord (Anon. 1968; Debord and Sanguinetti 1972). It was probably not lost on Álvarez that this battle cry of the 1968 Paris student revolt and general strike, along with "Down with the Spectacle Commodity Society" and "Abolish Class Society," was heard in France the same year in which Castro made his decisive *intervención* to uproot once and for all bourgeois practice from Cuban society. By 1991, however, the slogans themselves and the cherished principles behind them had become empty spectacles. For some, the socialist state merely became the biggest employer, albeit also the biggest provider of health care and education. With their smarts and sense of entitlement, Cuban youth had already subverted the slogan "Socialism or Death" into "Socialism Is Death" by the early 1990s. If Karl Marx dreamed of hunting and fishing in the morning and writing poetry in the afternoon, many Cuban workers during the Special Period really had the luxury of not having to work at all. First under bloated employment rolls and then with the grave shortages of the Special Period, many workers had nothing to do on the job. No paper, no pens, no will. Just as Afro-Cubans had eked out unofficial livings selling their wares on the streets, doctors and administrators became cab drivers and schoolgirls became prostitutes as Cubans turned to underground economies to survive after 1991. The revolution can gaze back upon the fallen fruit empire, but only from the point of view of a monocrop status quo and continued dependence on the world sugar market. The government, recently coming to its senses, nevertheless has chosen to replace one monocrop with another in the new millennium—namely, tourism. The workers' slogan on the gala banner thus rings hollow in this troubled, small socialist country. Here, pretty much only the government, military, party, new business elites, and street *bizneros* have *dólares,* while everyone else has *dolores de cabeza.*

Álvarez sums up the contradictions of globalizing Cuba with a stroke of brilliance, which amounts to the real homage to Wifredo Lam. We find Eshú, the *orisha* who opens and closes the road, the author of discord, ruptures, and subversion, behind the wheel of American International. Is Eshú to be read as a hero of sorts, coming out for ordinary Cubans? Álvarez, a brainy skeptic does not seem to hold out religion or indigenous spirituality as a force of identity, empowerment, rectification, or equity, as might be read into the works of José Bedia and Juan Francisco Elso Padilla. Elso, for example, was "preoccupied with the dynamics of colonization and, in a parallel way, with Santeria . . . [focusing] on a mythical America" while searching for a "Latin American spirituality" (Camnitzer 1994:41–46, 51–52). Álvarez seems more prepared to seek humanity and dignity in the revelation of the contradictions underpinning social life, historical memory, and representation itself. In Cuba, religion and spirituality push up through the cracks in the pavement but have been given little chance to grow in broad daylight.

Evident to everyone, the revolution banned discrimination, but it persecuted organized religion and discouraged individual spirituality before it had to relent during the worst of the Special Period, 1993. Through applied transculturation theory, the state had raised *lo afrocubano* to the status of national folklore. Afro-Cuban religions lurked in the shadows until recently, yet now they, too, have become as "commercialized," or *metalizado,* in some quarters, just as other globally promoted products.

Álvarez does not directly confront the viewer with social and historical facts. His work is not didactic but allegorical. His modus operandi lies in the pastiche of already mediated figures from popular culture and art history. Social and cultural life is born, grows, dies, and then, decomposes, within the simulacrum (A. Fernández 1999:44). The near-panoramic *Site,* both archaeological excavation and contemporary arena of conflict, constitutes a compressed stage set. Before the beholder, it is an ambiguous zone of desire and identity charged with the traces of oppression and violence, all of which have constituted Cuba's yesterday, today, and tomorrow. Thus, *Site* might be read as a counternarrative of Cuba's epic historical narrative, wherein the unique and indigenous *ajiaco* was perfected with the recipe of transculturation. Modernity, so wished for in the first half of the twentieth century, appears as a sleek American commercial truck. The Situationist, socialist (post)-modernity of the century's second half is reduced to window bunting.

Pedro Álvarez's work and ideas about the possibilities of representation in contemporary Cuba grow out of art developed as of the early 1980s. In many ways, *Site* encapsulates these developments. Historical accounts of recent Cuban art foreground *Volumen I,* an important exhibition held at the Centro de Arte Internacional in Havana on January 14, 1981. It "has come to symbolize the emergence of the new art in Cuba for artists and critics alike" (Camnitzer 1994:1). The "new art" critically reflected upon 1960s and 1970s precedents in form and content. As important, the show and the work that followed helped redefine the possibilities of art in relation to a seemingly implacable rule: "Within the Revolution, everything; outside the Revolution, nothing" (Camnitzer 1994: 129; see Castro 1980). The eleven artists of *Volumen I,* all born between 1948 and 1959—the oldest being Tomás Sánchez and the youngest José Bedia—were children of the revolution, many of whom greatly benefited from the state's systematic emphasis on art education and cultural institutions, not least being the Instituto Superior de Arte (Graduate Institute of Art), created in 1976 (Camnitzer 1994:3, 159). Many highly trained artists had embraced the revolution's opportunities and ideals, became aware of its limitations, and took a proactive stance in order to push the envelope of expression, particularly vis-à-vis the relation of Cuban art to the rest of the world. As Luís Camnitzer shows, though the idea of the self-conscious art "group" preceded them, *Volumen I* represented the "symptom of a new use, in Cuba, of planned strategy as an instrument in art affairs" (Camnitzer 1994:7). That is, these artists embraced and transformed the principle of the collective, which mediates all Cuban revolutionary social life, for the purposes of creative and intellectual action—both within and against institutionalized art practice and historical constraint.

Drawing on previous style and content bases from the 1960s and 1970s, not least realism and revolutionary iconography, the artists of *Volumen I* also revisited with a vengeance key issues dealt with by previous Cuban art movements: modernism, nationalism, internationalism, creolization, the vernacular, *lo afrocubano,* and, not least, the problem of the bourgeoisie. Their educations and opportunities to exhibit outside of Cuba had brought them to critical awareness of world art history and international avant-gardes. They reflected heavily on the tensions between nationalism and internationalism. They confronted Cuba's legacy of colonialism. And, they were forced to confront, daily, the tensions between dogma, social control, and propaganda on one hand and individual creation and freedom of expression on the other (Camnitzer 1994:8–17, 100–129).

The artists of *Volumen I* and at least two succeeding "generations" focused with an ironic eye on themes of the revolutionary, the popular, the international, and the commercial, drawing inspiration from American neo-Dada and Pop art, particularly in the use of serial imagery and the use of ready-mades—including drawing revolutionary icons and slogans from the poster arts (e.g., Leandro Soto) made by the revolution's 1960s artists (e.g., Raúl Martínez and Mayito). The melodramatic use of everyday cast-offs and "kitsch," in particular, permitted artists to defamiliarize colonial imports and prerevolutionary signs of social class, which permeated Cuban cultural history, yet had returned in the form of the island's privileged groups (e.g., the work of Flavio Garciandia and Rubén Torres Llorca). Recycling offered an artistic modus operandi consistent with how ordinary Cubans had to survive—that is, by scrounging. As Cuba's first avant-gardes (1920s–1940s) sought to develop a modern iconography around the themes of *cubanidad, mestizaje,* and *africanidad* in order to approach the question of national identity, the post–*Volumen I* generations used similar themes, but self-reflexively, ironically, and with sustained attention to pain and tragedy. They located Cuban art on a global map, but drew less on European abstractionisms, as the mid-century modernists did, than on the American contemporary modes of conceptualism, photorealism, performance, sited sculpture, and photography. Artist-Santería priests such as Manuel Mendive beautifully, if not unreflectively, had depicted the *orishas* through complex performances of ritually painted bodies. José Bedia, an initiate of Palo Monte, would later meditate upon Amerindian and Cuba's African cultures through complex installations, which forcefully tapped signs of religious power, but also searingly referenced the tragedies of indigenous exterminations, the Middle Passage, and the dangerous crossings of the Straits of Florida to U.S. shores. Marta María Pérez Bravo inserted her own female body into the ritual passages of the Afro-Cuban religions, demonstrating in photographs both its power and vulnerability. María Magdalena Campos Pons used multimedia installations first to approach the relation of feminism and spirituality, and later the theme of her African ancestry, the Middle Passage, and her own migration to the north. The late Belkys Ayón responded to the exclusivist male power of the Abakuá Society. She embraced and monumentalized the female figure of Sikán, inserting her own hand forcefully into the reinscription of Abakuá mythology in large, heavily worked prints.

Clearly seen in Pedro Álvarez's work are aspects of developments in Cuban art during the past thirty years, particularly his fascination with ready-made and conventionalized imagery recontextualized within pastiche in order to expose entrenched myths and create commentary through ironic juxtapositions. In recuperating and resituating the works of Landaluze, Álvarez returns to a foundation stone of Cuban art history. These enduring representations of Afro-Cubans, with their detailed references to ostensibly indigenous "types" and "customs," in a sense were the first to project the terms and conditions of Cuban "folklore," forty-two years before the Society of Cuban Folklore's founding in 1923. Writers and artists continued to draw upon Landaluze's representations, as much in strategies for wiping out atavisms as in elevating Afro-selected Cuban forms as modern icons. Nowadays, Landaluze's iconography lives as much on the touristic stage of the Conjunto Folklórico Nacional de Cuba—in its naturalized and celebratory representations of Afro-Cuban and peasant performance—as it does in the dollar tourist shops, with their dolls, T-shirts, trinkets, *íreme* refrigerator magnets, and miniature drums. Álvarez is clearly aware of this complex iconographic history in his work. He seems less interested in *ñañiguismo*'s ostensible content than in the conflicted contexts of its representation. Like Israel Castellanos (1937), Álvarez cuts and pastes *El Ñáñigo* from Landaluze's late 1870s paintings into his work. Unlike Castellanos, he does not constitute a demon. He deconstructs a Cuban national fetish to reveal the conceptual and practical labor that *El Ñáñigo* and other signs of the folk and *hampa cubana* have played for more or less benign elites, including contemporary art movements. "This is not strange," notes Cuban artist and critic Antonio Elígio Fernández ("Tonel"), "if we consider where this art is coming from: a country announcing its advance toward a socialist future while at the same time slowly yet steadfastly incorporating itself into the globalizing, inexorable network of the market—in other words, reverting to its capitalist past" (Fernández 1999:45).

It comes as no surprise that Álvarez's penchant for irony and the international reach of his vision would lead him, in one recent work, to consider the underside of this "inexorable network of the market" in relation to the history of representation. Invariably, *El Ñáñigo,* though he struggled to maintain his dignity as a "humble worker," early found himself first an object of curiosity, a target of criminal persecution, a specimen of pseudoscientific study, a disempowered source of modernist-primitivist appropriation, and an aestheticized ingredient in the Cuban cultural *ajiaco.* Though *El Ñáñigo* would be celebrated in the utopian early years of the revolution (e.g., León 1964), Cuba's "incorporation . . . into the globalizing, inexorable network of the market" would demand from the "new art" a different kind of recontextualization. In one recent work by Álvarez, as Marilyn Zeitlin notes, "before a background of the Capitolio in Havana, a member of the African secret society Abakuá washes the windshield of a fin-laden car. The degradation of this member of the all-male Afro-Cuban secret society, bedecked in his traditional costume, tells us what Álvarez sees as the current level of progress in eradicating racism" (Zeitlin 1999:134). Though Zeitlin's interpretation deserves nuance, it does underscore the point that, despite various nods to the *íreme*'s cultural value from the 1940s down through the present, Álvarez is telling us that *El Ñáñigo* has graduated to little more than a marginal, homeless squeegeeman. If *El Ñáñigo* and other representations of *lo afrocubano,* the land, and the indigene ever stood for a unique Cuban national identity, this tragicomic squeegeeman must give us pause. For it seems to make little difference whether the "fin-laden car," a mark of a twentieth-century globalizing Cuban landscape, takes us back to the eve of the revolution in the 1950s, or to Old Havana in the contemporary moment of the *dolor de cabeza,* the *jinetero,* and state employees dressed as Landaluze types to enchant tourists: the *mulata* and the *calesero.*

14 Conclusion

The Abakuá Society and the National Narrative

As the story goes, the Abakuá Society, founded in 1836 in Regla, witnessed an exponential expansion through the 1850s, a tumultuous period at the height of Cuba's sugar fortunes, which included numerous slave insurrections. It was founded as an institution of self-defense, mutual support, and empowerment within the slave society. It began among black creole slaves, and its self-conscious Carabalí elders regulated the "pure blood" of its initiated members. It expanded within the Havana *barrios* from 1836 through 1863 on this basis. Local *barrio* identity, masculine identity, trade identity, social status, self-protection through organization, economic interdependence, recreation, and the extension of African-based cultural tradition, as well as some incidents of criminal behavior, were key to its profile. With massive demographic shifts during the mid-nineteenth century, leading to an overwhelming presence of immigrant laboring nonblack males in western Cuba's port cities, the Abakuá institution expanded to include new constituencies of skilled, semiskilled, and unskilled workers, as well as some wealthy whites, around the ports of Havana, Matanzas, and, later, Cárdenas. The shift coincided with the increasing power of American shipping lines and domination over the Cuban economy through the first decades of the republic. The expansion of the Abakuá created as much conflict as solidarity between the original "black" Efí and Efó branches on the one hand and the new Akanarán Efó branch godfathered by Bakokó, whose relatively diverse members were or became "white" *(blanco)* within the Cuban social structure. The Bakokó-descended Efó branch, founded by the *mulato* Andrés Facundo Cristo de los Dolores Petít, took on "syncretic" features, which were both consonant with the Catholic origins of many of the new "whites" and functioned strategically to deflect scrutiny and persecution. The aesthetics of Abakuá attributes among the new Efó line became much more elaborate, given wealthy patronage and competition between the various *juegos.* Such competition undoubtedly articulated with the dynamics of *barrio* and racial identity, as well as the economies of the growing urban port populations.

A peculiar set of narratives constitutes the accounts of Cuba's Abakuá, from the earliest substantial reports of Fernández Carrillo (1881), Alejandro Rodríguez (1881), José Trujillo y Monagas (1882), and Rafael Roche y Monteagudo (1908, 1914, 1925) through the folkloric ethnography of Fernando Ortiz (1950a, 1950b, 1951, 1952–55) and Lydia Cabrera (1958). Ostensibly "objective" ethnographic reporting is always a narrative, with a beginning, middle, and end. All of these accounts, in one way or another, begin with the emergence of Efik Buton from Cabildo Carabalí Brícamo Appapá Efí in 1836; move through the founding of Akanarán Efó Ocobio Mukarará in 1863; address changes within the institution and the conflicts with the black old guard, including the debate over Andrés Petít's "selling of the secret"; detail basic practices, ritual and aesthetic; relate the persecution of the Abakuá Society by the police; and so on. The older accounts are rich in data from confiscated notebooks. The later folkloric accounts depend on the more subjective and variant "narratives of old adepts." My own account essentially follows this pattern.

Ironically, accounts that appear to detail "events" within the context of the historical fulcrum of slavery, independence, and nationhood are, in fact, produced or shaped by the narrative of Cuban nationalism itself. This narrative turns on the struggle against outside oppression, a progressive struggle out of old-world controls, and the invention of tropes of national identity, including the land, the peasant, the Afro-Cuban, the *mulata,* and so on. These are the tropes of *mestizaje.* The flavorful *ajiaco* metaphor best sums up the core figure. Though the "atavistic," "despotic," "personalistic," and pathologically "criminal" Abakuá Society represented a thorn in the side of the emerging body politic, the story of the Abakuá is often a creature of that narrative. The Abakuá Society begins as an "African" form; its "whitening" causes conflict; this conflict is resolved as the Abakuá Society becomes "mixed" or "integrated." All of this is accomplished through the efforts of a mediating, complex *mulato* figure, Andrés Petít (see Kutzinski 1993; Mosquera 1996a:256; and note 29 to chapter 5 of the present volume). The avant-garde takes up Abakuá iconography, among other representations, in the transvaluation of old colonial, European, and corrupted values in order to produce representations of Cuban modernity. Ultimately, the Cuban Revolution, which incorporated the nationalist message of previous revolutions, portrayed the Afro-Latin history of Cuba as one of workers' struggle against foreign oppression and exploitation, notwithstanding the state's early great antipathy and continuing ambivalence toward the Abakuá Society as an independent institution on a state-controlled island. Though his beloved Afro-Cuban religion had been maligned and attacked even by the post-1959 regime, Juan Mokongo's double burial suit brought the two together: he was a *combatiente* and a priest of Changó.

What would an alternative narrative of the Abakuá within slavery and the emerging Cuban nation look like—for example, a narrative written entirely from the perspective of the descendants of Efik Buton and other "black" Efí lodges? Are there grounds, and is there a rationale, for a "black" Cuban Abakuá narrative, one that would not fit as comfortably within the national narrative of *mestizaje* and cleave more closely to Carlos Moore's indictment of state racism? The early literary and painterly *mestizaje* narrative depended on sensual *mulatas* and stereotyped *negritos, negritas, brujos,* and *brujas.* Later, it was taken up by a modernist primitivism, the basis of which continued to be *mestizaje* (Kutzinski 1993; Moore 1997; Blanc 1992; Martínez 1994). The social science *mestizaje* or *ajiaco* depended on the theory of "transculturation," which, in significant part, depended on vestigial notions of evolutionary development, social "hygiene," and progressive uplift through "education." Materially, a majority of the population, particularly Afro-Cubans and peasants, nevertheless remained illiterate and without social supports until the 1959 revolution. Even the most recent multicultural and postmodern accounts of Afro-Cuban culture, which depend on diversity (the former) and pastiche and boundary-crossing (the latter), can diminish the idea of the African "presence" in Cuba (see Mosquera 1996a, 1996b). Paul Gilroy, the dean of Black Atlantic studies and no essentialist, recognizes distinct historical phases of identity formation within the Diaspora, and on that basis he has criticized writers for a kind of "'premature pluralism,' a postmodern evasion" that dismisses certain identity formations based on race and ethnicity that are necessary to cultural resistance (Clifford 1994: 319–320; Gilroy 1993:100–101). In other words, *mestizaje*, multiculturalism, and postmodernism may have the effect of erasing blackness and the African presence.

Carlos Moore (1986, 1988) has been one of the only voices decrying the continuing oppression of Afro-Cubans and the suppression of their institutions, particularly the *cabildos* and the *juegos*, under the revolutionary regime. And, though he might be accused of wearing the ideological lenses of black American nationalism, applying American racial categories to Cuba, John Mason once, perhaps with good reason, critiqued a panel presenter on the Abakuá Society for ignoring the "real" "black" tradition of the Abakuá, which is encountered in Matanzas, but not Havana.[1] Much more research and thinking are necessary to reconcile the received accounts of the Abakuá and the Afro-Cuban religions with alternative perspectives. It is evident, at least, that the notion of a "real" "black" Abakuá tradition in Matanzas carries an ideological load. The term *black* in Cuba has wide berth. The notion of some more "real" tradition in Matanzas, as opposed to an inauthentic or adulterated tradition in Havana, depends upon African Diaspora fallacies about the increasing purity of traditions as one moves further from big urban complexes (Havana to Matanzas). Was not the reported Chinese Abakuá lodge of Matanzas, to which belonged the legendary Yoruba *babalawo* Adechina, just as "real" as any ostensibly "black" lodge? In any case, it is, perhaps, less interesting to ask what is "real," authentic, and original, than to explore the "truth effect" of narratives about authenticity and origin that enchant particular historical constituencies—for example, black nationalists and antisyncretic practitioners. The latter position has been particularly complex, in that it has been advocated by "white" as well as black Cubans. Their antisyncretic, anticreole, and Africanist narratives and practices reinforce, but do not mirror, black nationalist ones. Battle lines in Cuba are not always drawn on the basis of generalized notions of race or ethnicity, but on much more locally marked distinctions: most pertinently, where the Abakuá are concerned, "Efí" versus "Efó," though white Regla Abakuá in the early twentieth century clearly intended to take jobs away from Havana's black dockworkers. Already in the 1960s or early 1970s, Francisco Hurtado de Mendosa ("Yenequita"), the venerated white Isué of Usagaré Munankebé, sought to honor the original island root, Efik Buton, by reinstituting the "empty" *sese de kankomo*, thereby breaking with the *sese de copón* tradition of the mulatto Isué Andrés Petít of Bakokó Efor and his Akanarán Efó line of "white Abakuá." The current premier maker of Abakuá altar objects, another white Abakuá from Regla, self-consciously rejects the *sese de copón* as a mere creole invention, preferring, instead, the Efí *sese*, which, for him, is the authentic, original, true representation of what the Africans brought to Cuba. What led Cuban whites to seek Abakuá initiation in the first place, and what now motivates white Abakuá to venerate their "black roots"?

Another set of questions we might ask has to do with the category of gender. What would the core Abakuá myth and Cuban Abakuá historical practice look like in a narrative written by one of the principal "audiences" of the Abakuá institution, women? This is something the late Belkys Ayón attempted to do, with her close focus on the figure of Sikán. The Abakuá is an exclusively male secret society, which constitutes a particular, hypermacho Cuban social type. This subject remains for future research. In any event, whether or not one believes that the Abakuá institution and liturgy reflect or constitute the "myth" of Sikán, it would be worth focusing attention on the meaning of this myth as it has been invoked in the particular setting of Cuba during different epochs. Even a cursory reading of the myth raises the question of how and why a particular discovery by a woman provokes such interest and leads to her death—execution or "sacrifice"—as well as her immortalization as the "mother of the Abakuá." What has been the meaning and purpose of the myth of the "second mother," the *sese,* in Cuban social history, and why does it continue to be powerful? Two of the questions one must ask are "Whose myth is it" and "Whose interests does it serve?" (Slotkin 1985).

Though "myths" and oral tradition can carry valuable and verifiable historical information (Vansina 1985), they are always deployed—told or otherwise enacted—in particular, situated presents. That is, their telling and enactment have specific contexts. Myths "mean" as much in terms of present concerns and arrangements—including relations of power and authority—as they do in terms of supposed historical origins. The motivated tellers and retellers of such stories have particular interests in recreating and projecting these stories to particular hearers. Moreover, scholars who interpret such stories do so from within particular fields and from particular ideological perspectives. All of these different agents and contexts have their "edges," and it is worth exploring the meanings generated at those edges, as Renato Rosaldo suggests, in our "combing of the past" (see Rosaldo 1980, cited and quoted in Cohen 1994).

The Abakuá Narrative and Regimes of Knowledge Production

An account of the arts, ritual, and organization of the Abakuá Society is undoubtedly enriched when located within historical context: diasporic and local. Still, a "historical" account built around an ostensibly objective historical "context" remains limited unless the sources—the "archive" and the voices of living sources—are subject to scrutiny, particularly to reveal their own historicity. Information, or what we call "data," is constituted by historically specific regimes of knowledge production. Ethnographic sources from Africa and the Americas were produced, for example, within the data collection modes and theoretical agendas of nineteenth-century missionaries and twentieth-century anthropologists. The former were produced within imperial hierarchies of colonization, trade, and missionization. Professional anthropological studies followed on colonialism's coattails. Whereas nineteenth-century texts worked on the assumptions of an evolutionary concept of "civilization," modern anthropological texts began with a "horizontal," relativist concept of "culture." *A* culture was a bounded, territorially situated unit that could be "written" up with reference to its principal constituent parts—for example, social organization, the life cycle, religion, and the like. Between the 1920s and the 1970s, the culture concept shifted from reliance on structural-functional, normative models through Marxist-based material analyses to cognitive and interpretive models. In the 1980s the concepts of "culture" and the "nation," as bounded, territorialized entities, were undercut by emerging postmodern emphases on multiculturalisms, transnationalisms, internationalism, and the concept of "diaspora."

My ethnohistorical and art-historical account of Abakuá objects in the first part of this book rehearsed received patterns and critiqued them. My point of departure for the interpretation of objects assumed, in part, the contemporary perspective that things Abakuá can be considered "art" and meaningful cultural performance rather than, say, delinquency and contagion. My narrative also assumed that the diasporic transmission of "Carabalí" cultural ideas and practices were creolized, or syncretized, in Cuba, particularly as figures such as Andrés Petít innovated the "white" branch of the Abakuá. This narrative is heavily influenced by the lifelong work of Fernando Ortiz, which, unsurprisingly, reflects the Cuban national narrative of indigenization and *mestizaje.* At the same time, I critiqued art-historical interpretive approaches by introducing the complexities of creative intentionality and sociohistorical context in the production of Abakuá objects and performances. I showed how the objects of one lodge's altar might be glossed by general symbolic meanings, but might be better served by close attention to a reflective artist's personal history and the particular historical contexts "cued" by his work (see Bauman and Briggs 1990:69).

The second part of this book sought to historicize the consideration of Abakuá objects and performances as art and as bearers of morally wholesome cultural significance—less to disagree with this assessment than to illuminate the "cultural biography" of things Abakuá between the mid-nineteenth century and the present. That is to say, consideration of things Abakuá as art is quite recent. This is true particularly in Cuba, where they, and even their benign representation in Landaluze's works, suffered mostly as distasteful *cosas de negro* through the 1950s (Ortiz 1953), except in the minds of some members of the intelligentsia. Since the early 1960s on the island, *cosas de negro* labor mostly under the yoke of spectacular "folklore," as transculturated *cosas de Cuba.* Nevertheless, makers of Abakuá objects, probably never considered their work to be less than artful; recent makers do, in fact, consider themselves artists, and their work, art, not folklore, not ethnographic specimen, and not illicit goods—though prior to the 1990s, they remained clear that the state regarded Abakuá practice with suspicion. In the United States, things Abakuá became viable material for ethnographic and folkloric study just before the mid-twentieth century (Courlander 1944). They were valorized as viable material for art historical study by the mid-1970s, following forty years of serious research on southeastern Nigerian arts, reaching their apogee in 1983 as "art and philosophy" (Thompson 1974:173–188, 1978, 1983:227–268; see G. I. Jones 1988).

What I tried to accomplish in the second part of this book is a contextualization of the "archive," as it were. I seek to place the changing "discourses" that appropriated and presented things Abakuá in perspective. Though I am not a social historian, and thus do not write intensively on social and political context, I do reveal the ideological load carried in the rhetorical and organizational forms of accounts treating the Abakuá Society. Knowledge was produced about the Abakuá Society within the discourses of *costumbrista* writing and art, proto- and scientific criminology, ethnology and folklore, and Third World socialist culture-building under the Cuban Revolution. Much of the knowledge produced at each stage drew on, revised, and accommodated itself to what came before it. Thus, for example, Fernando Ortiz, the great lawyer, statesman, and ethnologist, who experienced and participated in a long series of discursive shifts, from *costumbrista* through criminology to Cuban national culture, and who stayed on the island through his death in 1969, was hailed as the "Third Discoverer of Cuba." He remained *Don* Fernando Ortiz, and continues as such in the memories and research of Cuban scholars and the public. Though his work shifted from an emphasis on criminological social hygiene to "folklore," the old evolutionary baggage never disappeared from his notion of transculturation. Ortiz's rigorous scientific and taxonomic analyses of Afro-Cuban culture, as well as his aestheticization of Afro-Cuban "folklore," were modified little by his students and followers after the Triumph of the Revolution. His protégé, Argeliers León, the principal vehicle for "folklore" studies, presentation, pedagogy, and cultural display during the first two decades of the revolution, added a Marxist spin to some of his historical analyses (León 1964, 1984) and a more utopian gloss to the master's progressive ideas (see Hagedorn 2001). The Fernando Ortiz Collection of the Casa de Africa in Old Havana is a feather in the regime's cultural cap, as is the new Fundación Fernando Ortiz under Ortiz's former student Miguel Barnet, which occupies Ortiz's former house on the corner of L Street and 27th in El Vedado.

While on research trips to Cuba, I have lived in an apartment directly across the street from Ortiz's former house and retraced many of the spaces and paths Ortiz followed on his way to the university and to the *barrios* of Havana. As an *extranjero,* I consume the products of Cuba's state institutions of tourism and cultural production. I write articles and books based on my research with practitioners, as well as library research and interaction with Cuban scholars. I publish in the United States, having opportunities that Cuban scholars do not have. Like scholars before me, I "penetrated" the Abakuá Society through "friendships" with three elder Abakuá from Eforí Eñongo. One day, they permitted me to photograph the *íremes* and orchestra at a *plante.* No sooner had the flash started to go off than the younger Abakuá members began to yell and scream, starting a brawl. My hosts gently suggested that I leave. Afterward, the family of Juan Mokongo asked me to write a document stating how much I had benefited from my experience with the members of Eforí Eñongo and that I promised to treat the material respectfully. I was asked to write that in return for the *juego*'s generosity and support, I was making a donation to the group's coffers so that the attributes could be renovated once again. The family then asked me to change the name of the *juego* and erase the real name from the banner. All this was in the interest of protecting the family against criticism and attacks from other members and Abakuá. That is, my work would be seen as benefiting, not exploiting the *juego,* and the family could avoid the accusation that they were commercializing the Abakuá. Indeed, they used the "donation" to renovate Efori Eñongo's *plumeros.*

I had penetrated the Abakuá Society, to a degree, with the generous help and guidance of elder members of Efori Eñongo. Unlike their younger brothers, they were mellow with experience. They knew they were men. They no longer needed to stridently act out *hombría*—manliness—in order to construct their authority. Their mentors had worked with Fernando Ortiz and Lydia Cabrera, so working with anthropologists was not a particularly threatening proposition. Not least, they saw nothing more beneficial than benignly revealing aspects of Abakuá practice in order that people understand what the Abakuá Society is really about, not least, that its men have always been "just humble workers." Still, they already knew what Fernando Ortiz had discovered for himself in 1954. They could discuss the Abakuá Society all day with a researcher. They could permit photography of the altar objects and *sacos.* Their young foreign interlocutor would have documents, recordings, and pictures, but he would never possess the "secret" because, as Ortiz admitted, he did not possess the word of Nasakó.

Notes

1. Introduction: Meanings, Methods, and the Cultural Biography of Things Abakuá

1. Members of the lodge, for purposes of discretion, asked me to alter the name of the lodge, including on the decorative banner that hangs upon the altar.
2. "The light inside" *(la luz interior)* is a phrase used by Jesús Nasakó to characterize the energy that should radiate from his Abakuá artwork as a result of his use of highly contrasting, lustrous, and reflective surface media.
3. By "generalized symbolic meanings" I refer to: (1) transhistorical and archetypal meanings assumed to be fixed and timeless; (2) cognitively based "meanings" or significations within discourse or text; (3) synoptic representations of practices (*practices,* properly understood, are diachronic; they are not exhausted by, and tend to resist, textualization and representation, because they are often highly contingent, ineffable, and on the "hither side of words" or discourse; see Bourdieu 1977; Jackson 1989); (4) significations that bear a narrow 1:1 relationship with a signifier. For example, it was assumed that "primitive symbols" in "tribal art" referred directly to a single concept, for example, symbol *x* = "love" or "fertility." In Renaissance iconology, a burning candle refers to the presence of Christ, a dog to "fidelity," and so on. See Price and Price 1980:188–191; Brown 1996; Bois 1990.

2. The Abakuá Society and the African Diaspora

1. The following is Enrique Sosa Rodríguez's reckoning of ethnicities in Cuba: the Ibo subgroups included the "Isuama," "Olugo," "Isieque," and "Briche." The Ibibio subgroups included the "Orú" and "Efik" ("Efí," also known in Cuba as *appapás chiquitos*); the "Ijaw" included the "Bras" and "Carabalí" (Kalabari proper); the "Ekoi" included the "Kwa"/"Akpá"/"Abakpá" (the Ekoi-Ejagham of Old Calabar), the "Efor"/"Efó"/"Efok" (Efut in Africa), who were also known in Cuba as Brícamos and *appapás grandes* (Sosa Rodríguez 1982:71–72).
2. Forde (1956:72) says that Duke Town is twenty miles from the Calabar River estuary, which does not seem possible according to modern maps (see Lovejoy and Richardson 1999:331).
3. Creek Town is known in Efik as *obio oko* ("that town") and *esik edik* ("net of creek"); it is also known as *ekuritonko,* a word likely of Efut origin (Forde 1956:72).
4. "Old Town" is an anglicization of *Obutong;* Duke Town is an anglicization of *Orok* (town); and Henshaw Town derives from *Nsidun* (Forde 1956:65–68).

5. "The word 'palaver' derives from the Portuguese *palavra* or Spanish *palabra*, 'word,' and signifies any discussion, debate or conference" (Forde 1956:67).
6. As Forde notes, *Egbo* was in common use by Europeans to refer to what was the Efik *ekpe* society: "'egbo' is sanctioned by continual usage among Europeans since the nineteenth century. Egbo . . . [is] more properly *ekpo* since Efik lacks the voiced labial velar *gb*" (1956:66).
7. There, say Nicklin's sources, "Efut mingled with the Efik in the group known as Isangele to the north of Rio del Rey, and some became part of the population of Old Calabar" (Nicklin 1991:12). "The Oron and Amoto [both Efut] elders are certain that in the distant past the secrets . . . were sold to the Efik at Isangele. . . . The head of the delegation was one Effa Effa Effiawat, and asserted that to this day the head of Ekpe in Calabar must be of the Effiawat lineage based in Duke Town. . . . They agree with the people of Bateka [also Efut] that it was the community of Isangele as a whole that sold Ekpe to the Efik," though this group told Nicklin that the secrets of the leopard spirit were sold to one Edem Edem Archibong, who led a delegation from Calabar (Nicklin 1991:12).
8. "Carabalí" resulted from the creolization in Cuba of "Calabar," in which the 'r' and '1'—consonants called "liquids" in creole linguistics—are transposed.
9. Annotating the Efik king Antera Duke's famous diary, Forde writes that the inhabitants of the village of Big Qua Town "are culturally related to the Ejagham Ekoi, and are called abakpa by the Efik" (Forde 1956:66).
10. For most practitioners, "Brícamo" denominates the Abakuá ritual language; undoubtedly it contains terms from the numerous languages spoken by the different "Carabalí" peoples brought to Cuba, including the Ibibio-Efik, the Ejagham, the Efut, and so on. The late Juan Mokongo, a recognized expert among his colleagues, for example, discerned a large quantity of "Isuama" words in Lydia Cabrera's famed Abakuá vocabulary (1988). The Isuama in Cuba were an Ibo people, and an *Isuama cabildo* still exists in the city of Santiago de Cuba.
11. Some practitioners argue that Efik Buton received its secrets from an Appapá Efor *cabildo*, that is, a group of Ekoi origin (Sosa Rodríguez 1982:118). However, the majority opinion of practitioners and scholars seems to be that it emerged from the Carabalí Brícamo Appapá Efí group.
12. This historical account takes the form of a forty-four-page document handwritten in an eight-by-fourteen-inch ledger. Evidently, this 1881 account was published in the newspaper *La Correspondencia de Cuba* shortly after its writing and was then republished in edited form in Don Trujillo y Monagas's *Los criminales de Cuba* (1882:363–373); the data have been made use of by a number of Cuban historians yet are not always cited, for example, in the historical accounts of Roche y Monteagudo (1908:14) and Israel Moliner Castañeda (1988:14).
13. The *intramuros* (inside the walls), now called Old Havana, consisted of the original fortified city of Havana, founded in 1524. The walls were taken down only in the mid-1850s. The *barrios extramuros* consisted in the rapidly growing neighborhoods "outside the walls," populated mostly by free people of color and working-class whites and mulattos. The palace-filled *intramuros* was home to Havana's rich until the late nineteenth century, when they began to move to a ring of developing suburbs such as El Cerro. Many of the buildings of Old Havana were then divided up into numerous small units *(cuarteles)* for poor people, buildings that became known as *solares*—teeming tenements of "delinquency" feared by the middle and upper classes.
14. The *derecho* consisted of a ritual payment of a rooster, if not also money, that had to be delivered to the chief of each *juego* (Rodríguez 1881:5).
15. There were seventy-seven lodges in Havana, four in Regla, and two in Guanabacoa. The greatest number in any location was forty-two in the fifth district of the capital (Rodríguez 1881:19–23; see also Trujillo y Monagas 1882:370–372).
16. He breaks down Akanarán Efó Ekobio Mukarará as: Akanarán Efó (mother of the Efó branch) / Ekobio (brother) / Mukarará (white).
17. According to Cabrera's sources, Akanarán Efó #1 was consecrated in Anche del Norte Street (today Calzada de San Lázaro, between Galiano and San Nicolas) in Central Havana (1986a:1).
18. The personnel were gathered beginning in 1857, although they were not "sworn" until 1863. Akanarán Efó #1 was called Ecobio Efó Macarará by Rafael Roche y Monteagudo (1925:4).
19. Judas was the apostle who betrayed Jesus, "thereby becoming the paradigmatic image of the traitor." Iconographically he was "characterized by the bag of money or thirty pieces of silver" (Apostolos-Cappadona 1994: 194–195). Some say that in 1863 Petít "communicated 'the secret' to the whites"—thereby "betraying" the blacks of the Abakuá Society—for a thousand ounces of gold (17,000 pesos). Others say that it was only thirty ounces and change (2,650 pesos). It is said that the deal was struck given a prior agreement on the part of each rich white slavemaster to emancipate various important

Abakuá, black and mulatto, who were their slaves" (Ortiz 1954:69).

20. The genealogy of Bakokó Efor is unknown. In Cuba, the "Efó" branch was born from the extant Efí branch, according to oral history. The secret writing of each was distinguished by the use of different symbols—Efí uses alternated little circles (o) and crosses (+) within a quartered circle, while Efó uses all (o). However, Bakokó Efor used combinations of these, suggesting its recognition of its Efí roots, though it was a lodge of the Efó "branch." In contrast, Akanarán Efó #1, Bakokó's descendant, used only the little circles within the quartered circle design.
21. Valdés cofounded Abakuá Efó #1 in 1875 and became its Abasonga officer. Abakuá Efó #1 was the second "godchild" of Akanarán Efó, after Ebión Efó, and the first Regla lodge in the line of "white" Abakuá.
22. Some biographical information on Quirino Valdés came from fieldwork with Juan Mokongo and Jesús Nasakó, 1994–1996. His dates and biographical specifics come from Cosme Baños 1998:51.
23. Between the late 1840s and the early 1870s, around 125,000 Chinese contract laborers were imported as indentured workers in Cuba. They worked as sugarcane laborers, in sugar mills, on railroads, and as urban domestic workers (Pérez 1988:115).
24. This is a subject for further reflection and research that is quite complex and more than can be addressed in this work.
25. From my interviews with a number of Havana *babalawos* between 1992 and 2000 for a project on the Yoruba Ifá practice in Cuba.
26. This paragraph and its quotations are drawn from Pérez (1988:117–121).
27. Personal correspondence with A. López of Miami, 30 August 2001. The killing occurred in 1962. The *sese* represents the head of Sikán, the "Mother of the Abakuá"; it is a *fundamento,* a holy sacrament, that "gives birth" to the lodge and all its members.
28. In "guarding the secret," one had to be prepared to "kill for *ekue* if it be necessary" (Sosa Rodríguez 1982: 180–181).
29. For example, the son-in-law of a Cuban man in his fifties recently told me that the latter, affirming his new son-in-law's membership in the family, said, "Now I can kill for you." A member of the Abakuá, as well as *babalawos* and drummers within the Lucumí religion, cannot be homosexual or even mildly effeminate.
30. "Gender matrix" and the "performance" of gender are ideas forming the kernel of recent works by Judith Butler (see 1990 and 1997, respectively).
31. Uriabón Monson Efín is an Efí lodge. The other early Matanzas lodges were Ibiabanga, Ibiabanga Efí, and Embemeré Efó (Moliner Castañeda 1988:14).

3. Abakuá Altar Arts: Ekue, Representation, and the Banner of Regla's Efori Eñongo

1. The full phrase is: "[*Un*] *episodio del proceso defensivo, por mimetismo sincretista, que fueron adoptando los negros afrocubanos para sostener sus ancestrales religiones y ritos*" (Ortiz 1954:79).
2. Carlos Miguel de Céspedes, who ran as second senator for the Liberal Party in 1948 in Matanzas, included calls for voting support in Brícamo in his pamphlets. In a campaign handbill addressed to "Nationalist Abanekues" (Abakuá initiate rank and file), Juan Enseñat Boza, possibly an Abakuá official, endorsed Ricardo Cabanas, who was running for representative: "[Ricardo Cabanas] salutes the *abanekues* and asks them to mark No. 33 Ricardo Cabanas on their ballots, in order to elect him representative" (Sosa Rodríguez 1982, plates).
3. Juan was a priest of Changó in Santería and Siete Rayos in Palo Monte.
4. "Some say that Sikán found Tanze in a calabash, or water vessel, in which the fish hid after she had left it by the river overnight" (León 1964).
5. Hierophany "expresses no more than is implicit in its etymological content, *i.e.,* that *something sacred shows itself to us*. . . . In each case we are confronted by the same mysterious act—the manifestation of something of a wholly different order, a reality that does not belong to our world, in objects that are an integral part of our natural 'profane' world" (Eliade 1959:11).
6. Interview with Jesús Nasakó, 1 July 1994; see Thompson 1983:241 for a similar version. Jesús Nasakó lauded Lydia Cabrera's work (1958) and may have taken parts of his account from her work and mixed it with what he had heard orally. (See Cabrera 1970:88 for a similar explanation.)
7. For example, Cabrera's principal informant, Saibeke, drew a map for her, and Jesús Nasakó drew a similar map for me. Neither document is oriented in terms of compass directions. Moreover, another, more detailed map of "sacred memory" published by Sosa Rodríguez reverses the positions of the Efí and the Efó (1982:452). Whereas Cabrera credits her living informant Saibeke for the map (1970:64), Sosa credits the source of his *geografía del recuerdo sagrado* to a practitioner notebook, presumably in Cuban archives—likely Ortiz's papers—from which he worked (Sosa Rodríguez 1982:452). Though the latter document reverses Saibeke's orientation, Jesús Nasakó

and Juan Mokongo both, like Saibeke, locate the Efó on the left. Sikán is pictured on the left; she was an Efó princess, and her discovery took place in Efó territory. It was later sold "across the water" to the Efí.

8. See Cabrera 1970:70–73 for informants' memories of Cross River cultural geography.
9. The picture's caption reads: "Picture that symbolizes the birth of ñañiguismo in West Africa, next to the river 'Oldan-Ororó,' where the mystery of Ekue was discovered" (Roche y Monteagudo 1925:99).
10. Though not clear when the image was drawn, it was at least seen by Roche just before his 1914 edition but likely after his 1908 edition, inasmuch as it does not appear in this work. Appearing to cite and then gloss the words of this African, Roche relates:

> Thus is explained the foundation of [ñañiguismo] in a navigable river between two hills:
>
> A. *Ekueñón acuá llebengó.*
> B. (Ecueñón . . . kills the tiger). [see upper right]
> A. *Where Sicanecua* [is]. [see center]
> B. (This is the woman who carried the fish within the vessel).
> A./B. Thus, *Eribangando, who is ñáñigo,* goes to the encounter with the woman with his *Moruá,* who commands him and goes behind him [see upper left].
> A. *Enquico.*
> B. (It is the rooster of the consecration that is on the Ororó hill).
> A. *Sicanecua Enquico*
> B. *(Eribangando* and *Morua* are on the Efó Territory, on the . . . [bank] . . . of the river, which is called *Oldán Ororó).*
> A./B. In the middle of the river is the *Embairán,* the canoe that awaits *Sican Ecue,* and the crocodile, *Mocombé,* who lifts his head.
> A./B. On the other bank are encountered *Encoboro ñáñigo, Enkrícamo* and *Mokongo;* later the Palm or *Ucano,* with the water serpent or *Ñangabión* and the goat, or *Emborí.*
> A./B. Nasacó, the sorcerer or doctor, waits at the door of the church or fambá with his *mocuba* or calabash, and smokes a pipe [*cachimba*].
> A./B. At the door is the *encandemo,* the food of the fambá. The moon sees everything . . .
> B. The two hills on the land: the right is Uban and the left hill is that of Ororó Efó.
> The Palm symbolizes the first consecration that was made in Guinea . . .

Roche y Monteagudo 1925:101; presumably the informant is pointing to the image and naming the elements, while Roche is filling in with explication and continuity.

11. Sosa Rodríguez says: "Ubane, it is said in abakuá, is the efik territory, or the territory between efik and efor. All the maps locate the hills and the Oban population in the ekoi territory next to the efik; perhaps Ubane comes from Oban or it was even more to the south, closer to the mouth of the river, next to the ibibio orón" (1982:287). The second river pictured in the banner, to the lower right, is *Odan efin nankulu,* which runs through Efik territory and empties into the sea (interview with Jesús Nasakó, 1 July 1994). Of course, there also exists an "Oban" Hills District deep in the hinterlands northeast of Old Calabar, which was the original Ekoi-Ejagham homeland of the Qua of Old Calabar (Forde 1956:2).
12. The ethnonym Orú may have derived from the Oron group of the Ibibio territory on the western bank of the Cross River. At the same time, it may also refer to the Oron who migrated from there to the Rio del Rey region southeast of Old Calabar. To the extent that the banner's image and various drawn maps can be read in terms of actual geography—that is, the banner's vantage point is from the north, looking south—the Orón/Orú described by Juan and Jesús would be situated in their post-Ibibio home to the southeast of the Cross River's mouth in the Rio del Rey (see map 2.2 and figure 3.7; Nicklin 1991).
13. Cabrera's terms are *Akanúman Kuari* and *Macombe;* Jesús Nasakó's are *Ekokominandubé* and *Macombe.* According to Cabrera's informants, the Oro (Orú) group highly venerated the crocodile. "The old *potencias* founded by the Oros (such as Bibanga, which was the first *potencia* of Matanzas) conserved, in memory of its origins, an embalmed crocodile" (1988:37).
14. Interviews with Juan Mokongo, July 1992; see also Cabrera 1988:424.
15. Interview with Jesús Nasakó, 1 July 1994.
16. Interview with Jesús Nasakó, 1 July 1994. Cabrera's informants related a similar proverb: *"Ñangabión ñene mio okambo nkanima"* (Ñangabión coiled itself around the gourd belonging to the woman who found the fish in the old sacred forest [presumably at the riverbank]) (Cabrera 1988:424). This version of the myth does find itself somewhat at odds with the banner's specific representation, inasmuch as the snake and palm tree are depicted on the Efí bank of the river.
17. For example, various little spirits, the dead, and some *orishas* are believed to live in and around the shadow cast by the spreading, horizontal branches of the great *ceiba* tree in the Lucumí and Palo religions.
18. According to Jesús Nasakó, *Akuriñanga* breaks down as *Akuri* (where is it), and *ñanga* (strange creature, strange reptile); *Akurien yene* (the woman); *Tini awon bibí,* an Ibibio African. *Nandibá fisí* is a plant found at the bank of the river, which is used as a ritual herb by Nasakó (inter-

view of 1 July 1994). Later, when Tanze is cared for by Nasakó in Sikán's water vessel, "the fish lived for some time . . . silent in the gourd [and] always covered by *nandibá fisí* . . . the thistle of the bank" (Cabrera 1970:90).

19. In Taussig's work, Amerindians of Peru discover holy images of the Virgin in the Andean mountains, but they are appropriated by the Church—though the icons also become figures of popular religion that tend to subvert official theologies. In Cuba, the "Three Johns," two mestizos and a black slave, fishermen all, discover the icon of Our Lady of Charity in the middle of the night on the Bay of Nipe in eastern Cuba. The Virgin becomes the patron of the copper-mining town of Cobre, eventually the island of Cuba itself, and the Three Johns and their boat become attributes of the icon, pictured beneath her feet.
20. Nasakó identified the canoe figure as a "Bibi [Ibibio] fisherman" (interview of 1 July 1994). As Forde puts it, for example, the Efik, originally a small branch of the Ibibio-speaking peoples who had moved southeast to waterside settlements on the Cross River estuary where they lived mainly as fishermen, had found their opportunity in the slave trade. Their communities grew and multiplied during the seventeenth and eighteenth centuries with the success of this traffic (Forde 1956:vii).
21. See Janzen 1978:45–47; MacGaffey and Harris 1993:49–51; MacGaffey 1986:171; Cabrera 1986b.
22. Jesús Nasakó and Juan Mokongo identified this figure as Nangobié Nasakó (interviews with Jesús Nasakó, 1 July 1994, and with Juan Mokongo, 1992). Still, Juan Mokongo identified the vessel Nasakó is holding as the pot of *mokuba* (as did the "African" informant of Roche y Monteagudo 1925:101), the herbal concoction of consecration that this ritual doctor prepares. Before Nasakó is the cooking pot of food cooking on a fire, the responsibility of the *plaza* called *Encandemo.* It is the meat from the sacrificial animals for the group to eat.
23. Interview with Jesús Nasakó, interview 1 July 1994.
24. Ekueñón was from the Chenguene Kerombia region of "Congo" (see Sosa Rodríguez 1982:160–161). Jesús Nasakó explains that "Ekueñón was not Bríkamo" (Efór or Efí, etc.). He "was a Congo, not a Carabalí" from this particular region in Congo. Interview with Jesús Nasakó, 1 July 1994.
25. The leopard is commonly represented in Cuba as the *tigre* (tiger). Jesús Nasakó uses the Brícamo term *yevengo* to refer to the *leopardo* and *tigre.*
26. Interview with Jesús Nasakó, 1 July 1994.
27. It is not clear that Mokongo is an Efí in every myth version. In other versions, Sikán is the daughter of Iyamba, the Efó king.
28. Interviews with Jesús Nasakó, 1 July 1994 and 5 January 1996.
29. In a sense, Ekueñón resembles the triumvirate of Lucumí "warriors": a kind of Eleguá (mediator), an Ochosi (itinerant hunter), and Ogún (killer); see Thompson 1983: 18–33, 52–61; J. Mason and Edwards 1985a:8–27; J. Mason 1992:54–116.
30. For an extended discussion on transatlantic friction drum-types, see Ortiz 1955:140–266. I will continue to refer to the "Voice" and spiritual power in general in lowercase as *ekue* and the drum in uppercase as Ekue.
31. The *ekón* was first made out of two pieces of wood, forming a kind of clapper (Cabrera 1970:92; León 1964).
32. The "Seven Tribes of Efor" were Undió, Nandió, Amanandió, Tendió, Nankoboró, Awanerón, and Obonséne Efor (Cabrera 1970:93).
33. Quoted passage translated by Cabrera from the Abakuá idiom *"Mbori Abasí mendó kairán mbori atereremina Ekue"* (1988:339).
34. Cabrera provides a short narrative of how Sikán's body parts were used: "The Fish was given the blood of Sikán in order that it would be tied to his spirit and attract it, just as later [the relics of] Tanze and Sikán were given the blood of the goat in order that together they would come to the [Ekue] drum in the Iriongo [sacred inner sanctum]. . . . And they took her eyes . . . in order to accompany the eyes of Tanze, symbols of the Society. And the skin of her back, in order to cover the new *Fundamento* of Tanze . . . and her intestines . . . in order to make a necklace, in turn, around her decapitated head and to hold the feathers with which it was adorned; and decorate a staff, a scepter, as an immortal memento of Sikán and symbol of command, made for Mokuire [Mokongo]. . . . Of her bones . . . Nasakó would make shims for the Fundamento [drum skin of Ekue]. . . . Her skull . . . was used for his witchcraft. . . . The other bones . . . that were not used by Nasakó were buried at the foot of the Ceiba, Ukano Bekonsí" (Cabrera 1970:107).
35. Through etymological analysis of the Abakuá phrase *"Eshú tu be isán Ekue iyamba enyenisón itiá ororó Usagaré"* ("How did Iyamba make *Ekue* shriek in Africa, [in the] territory of Usagaré"), Fernando Ortiz early speculated that Usagaré could be "Usahaedet" (Ortiz 1955:241–242). Subsequently, presumably following Ortiz and Latham (1973:3), Thompson (1983:241), and Nicklin (1991: 12–13) argue that "Usagaré" is actually "Usaha-Edet" (or Usak-Edet), which Nicklin locates in the Efut/Balondo territory in the Rio del Rey region of southern Cameroon.
36. The *cuica* is a relatively small, single-headed, open-bottomed, friction drum, of wood or metal, in which a

stick is attached with a button to the drum skin *from the inside;* the player reaches into the drum and rubs the stick with wet fingers or a wet cloth, manipulating the pitch by pressuring the drum skin with the fingers of the other hand atop the drumhead. The Abakuá's Iyamba, in contrast, stands the stick, called *yín* or *güín, atop* the drumhead of Ekue, and rubs the stick with fingers moistened with blood or a secret herbal concoction of Nasakó (see Ortiz 1955:166–170; Roberts 1985:13, 225).

37. The *orixás* are the Nagô (Yoruba-Bahian) and Kétu (city of Kétu) deities of the Candomblé of Salvador, Bahia, the cousins of the Lucumí *orishas.*
38. In the oral history, the names of Usagaré and Bekura are often interchangeable.
39. Thompson, citing informant Julito Collazo (1970), Africanizes Eforisún as Efut-nsun (1983:249).

4. Cloth and Signs: West African *Ukara* and the Iconography of Regla's Efori Eñongo

1. Thompson translates *nsibidi* as "cruel letters," the "force" of which is a "mystery" (1983:227); see Thompson's footnotes on African ethnographies that treat this writing system (1983:298). *Nsibidi* became *anaforuana* (Brícamo) and *firma* (Spanish) in Cuba (see Cabrera 1975).
2. Thompson, in a series of important works (1978, 1983), has treated *nsibidi* and *anaforuana* in depth, as did Cabrera (1975). This chapter in no way attempts to be exhaustive, treating a few principal examples that enhance the present set of discussions. See also Talbot (1912), Dayrell (1910, 1911), and MacGregor (1909).
3. The costumes are called *okum-ngbe* in the Ejagham Ngbe society and *idem-ikwo* in the Efik Ekpe society. It is possible that the first two syllables of the Cuban *íreme* derived from *idem,* i.e., *í[d]eme,* wherein, phonologically, the 'd' and 'r' sound similar (see Leib and Romano 1984:54 for Ejagham; Forde 1956:17 for Efik).
4. According to Leib and Romano, "The leopard spirit emerges from the *ekat,* where he has been ritually prepared, passing underneath the starch-resist, blue-and-white dyed *ukara* cloth to the sounds of the Ngbe voice. Numerous *nsibidi* signs on the cloth depict what is to be found in the secret chamber, among them pictographic symbols learned during initiations. The member who can decipher the meaning of the sign also knows the material object it represents. The most common of these signs is the paw print of the leopard, composed of alternating blue and white right triangles. Also found are hieroglyphs of other Ngbe bush animals, most commonly the tortoise, crocodile, bush cow, lizard and snake" (1984:54). According to Forde, "the roar of the leopard is simulated by a secret noise-making apparatus called *mbok.* Whenever the Leopard men produce the noise they always curtain off the room with blue and white Ibo-dyed *ukara* cloth . . . to prevent the entrance of unauthorized persons. Manipulators of the mechanism produce the tones of names, &c., thus enabling the mechanism to 'talk' in a manner analogous to drum signals. [It] is regarded as particularly sacred" (Forde 1956:18).
5. In both cases, individual *plaza* signs and larger unit signs, the authority behind the signs would be collective in time and space. In the first case, the *plaza* sign would include all of the deceased members who had occupied that particular *plaza* back to the original Mokongo or Iyamba, for example; in the second case, the sign, imaginably, might include the collective power of the *potencias* grounding each lodge or determinate group(s) of them.
6. Interview with Jesús Nasakó, 1 July 1994.
7. Interview with Juan Mokongo, 1 July 1993. Because I have changed the name of the lodge, I cannot divulge this information.
8. Each of these represented one of the Seven Tribes of Efor: Undió, Nandió, Amanandió, Tendió, Nankoboró, Awanerón, Obonséne Efor (Cabrera 1970:93).
9. Three, apparently, can also symbolize the three principal "roads" of the Efőr branch, Usagaré, Ibondá (or Bakokó), and Eforisún, as well as three top Abakuá officers: Iyamba, Mokongo, and Isué (see Sosa Rodríguez 1982:176; Cabrera 1988:517).
10. James Clifford writes, "The term *chronotope,* as used by Bakhtin, denotes a configuration of spatial and temporal indicators in a fictional setting (and when) certain activities and stories *take place.* One cannot realistically situate historical detail—putting something 'in its time'—without appealing to explicit or implicit chronotopes" (1988:237).
11. *Jeyeí bariba bacongo!*
Jeyeí bariba bacongo!
Osoiro encaño suabasí (Chorus: *yayó!*)
Osoiro encaño suabasí (Chorus: *yayó!*)
dibo dibo macaro mofe en banbarandibó
asere encomo abasí quiñongo mosongo
abasí yanpan iyá beromo sese eribó erení
asucuaracuantiyén añonomi ecueñon
tanguebo arfia sanga boco enban ñanga
rique asanga maon asanga condo
erigua Efő sese eribo sese condo
eritanse mofe morua un ponpono

Jeyeí bariba bacongo!
Jeyeí bariba bacongo!
Osoiro encaño suabasí (Chorus: *yayó!*)
Osoiro encaño suabasí (Chorus: *yayó!*)

dibo dibo macaro mofe en banbarandibó
asere en eribia econ en eribia econ en dibo
boco eforitanga banbancón butonu ñanga sibonú
asucurucu nandibá emay econ mama
econ mama boco asocaca tie tie in banbaranditó
ecueñon sanga encanima abasí
mayara yara uraña boco betanbre
ecueñon beco beco natan erume eruma
condo abasí acuritan boco asocaca
tie tie acurumina angongo atera
angongo iyá acua anena sisi aborquibié
en conban en bugere mosongo aguara
sese en tarabia amamañan fisi
anandibá fisi mosongo asocaca.

Jeyeí bariba bacongo!
Jeyeí bariba bacongo!
Osoiro encaño suabasí (Chorus: *yayó!*)
Osoiro encaño suabasí (Chorus: *yayó!*)
dibo dibo en banbarandibó macaro mofe banbarandibo
boco bocobia taiboco finbaroco enconban
en bugere acurumina aongobia atongobia
un coro jeguemio eron erume cunanboto
boto que anboto eribo muna guasangando maribá
en teme tararoco iyá condondo acanarán mumié
llanbunbe tindo acanabión bengue iteneñibón
efimereme iyá condondo abacuá anasacó
nantiero erume ñangabión enquiquere acua caitia
caitio eruenbia nairon tanga iforo
efimeremo naguerenba

Jeyeí bariba bacongo!
Jeyeí bariba bacongo!
Osoiro encaño suabasí (Chorus: *yayó!*)
Osoiro encaño suabasí (Chorus: *yayó!*)
Sere buton banban beco anasacó erimacua
ayagara quinquama ucurube ñangabión
mogobión sese buton en calu mapa erie
mosongo moto guana eribó bongó barori
ecun abarori efó añono efí

This is taken from a private Abakuá notebook that Juan Mokongo had hand-copied from the original, which belonged to Manuel de Jesús "Chuchú" Capáz. Juan memorized and performed the prayers from this work; Cabrera (1988:291) records a variant version of Ekueñón's *enkama de rompimiento.*

12. Interview with Jesús Nasakó, 1 July 1994. I attended a number of Abakuá ceremonies from 1992 through 2002 in Regla and Guanabacoa, including a *plante* for the initiation of a new Nasakó officer and a *llanto,* or funerary ceremony.
13. The orchestra, *biankomeko,* consists of three small drums *(enkomos),* the names of which receive different spellings in different sources: *biankomé, obiapá, kuchi-yeremá;* a long tapered tubular drum, *bonkó-enchemillá;* two sticks with which the open end of the *bonkó* is beaten; a bell-gong *(ekón);* and two conical shakers *(maruga* or *erikundé);* see León 1984:88–93; Ortiz 1954:1–41.

5. Altars, Offices, and Multiple Meanings

1. Each *plumero* is stored in a capped PVC tube, and each drum in a five-gallon can.
2. The staffs are, from left to right, Iyamba, Mosongo, Abasonga, and Mokongo.
3. Interview with Jesús Nasakó, 5 January 1996.
4. Interview with Jesús Nasakó, 5 January 1996.
5. The concept of *juramento* is also found within the Yoruba-Lucumí religion, wherein men are "sworn to Añá" as drummers of the sacred *batá* orchestra or "sworn to Osain" as herbalists. In both cases, they become not so much "priests" of Añá or Osain but *facultado*—spiritually authorized and empowered to play sacred drums and work with Osain. In the Congo-Cuban Palo Monte religion, the first *juramento* does not technically make the neophyte a "priest" of Palo Monte, but a kind of spiritual acolyte *(engueyo)* and extension of the *fundamento* or *nganga* of a Palo "house," which is owned by the Tata Nkisi, whose original swearing in was followed by other initiations in which he became the master of the *nganga.*
6. Interview with Jesús Nasakó, 1 July 1996.
7. Interview with Jesús Nasakó, 5 January 1996.
8. *Baroko* refers to the initiation of officers as opposed to that of members.
9. Interview with Jesús Nasakó, 1 July 1996. Jesús Nasakó calls the *baroko "fundamento,"* the complete initiation of thirteen *plazas, "Niñao,"* and the initiation of individual *plazas, "baroko nansao."* Cabrera, in contrast, calls the former *baroko completo* or *"Ninsao"* (1975:134–135).
10. Interview with Jesús Nasakó, 1 July 1996.
11. Interview with Jesús Nasakó, 5 January 1994.
12. See Clarke 1981 and Dixon 1983 and 1986 for brief overviews of the history and demographics of the Cuban exile.
13. During a *baroko* of an Iyamba, only Iyamba officers would be present, and they would use the main room of the temple.
14. See, for example, Nicolás Angarica's discussion of color symbolism within the Lucumí tradition (n.d. [1955]:72).
15. The value of goatskin within the Abakuá resonates with the other Afro-Cuban practices—particularly, as a drumhead—and with Cuban popular culture. The goat is strong and resilient, but the skin remains a symbol of potential eternal payment and suffering for sins commit-

ted in this world: *"chivo que rompe tambor con su pellejo paga"* (The goat that breaks the rhythm [or rules] pays with his skin). A popular song goes: "So said the goat that they were going to kill, 'Don't take my skin to make the drums sound.'" In other words, go ahead and kill me and cook me, but please don't use my skin on a drum so that I would be beaten eternally.

16. The photographic documentation shows at least two ways that the *plumeros* can be inserted into the drums. The metal tangs *(toquillos)* of the *plumeros* of Ekueñón and Mpegó are inserted into metal slots bolted to the sides of the drums. Enkríkamo's *toquillo* is merely inserted into a hole drilled into the top of one of the drum's *cuñas,* or wood tuning shims.
17. Interview with Jesús Nasakó, 5 January 1996.
18. *Nkiko* is alternately spelled *enkiko, enquiko,* and *enquico.* Roosters are the epitome of the macho two-legged sacrificial animal in all the Afro-Cuban ritual systems. They are "fed" to the male warriors in Santería (e.g., Eleguá, Ogún, Oshosi, Shangó) and the powerful male *ngangas* of Palo Monte. They are known for their potentially large size, weight, and their lethal "spur" *(espuela),* which is effective in cockfighting matches. The term *gallo* is also applied to the aggressive male solo singer who competes with his "vassal" *(vasallo)* in competitive Palo song sessions, which include ritualized insults *(mpuyas).* Though the rooster crows loudly, he is also a symbol of discretion.
19. Interview with Jesús Nasakó by telephone, 21 September 2001.
20. Interview with Jesús Nasakó by telephone, 21 September 2001.
21. Iyamba places the stick, about twenty inches long, at the center of Ekue's *parche.* The drum sits directly over the chalked *firma* (a complex quartered circle and four *óvalos*). With fingers moistened in blood, water, or *mokuba*—which apparently contains the blood of a sacrificed rooster—he uses the thumb and forefinger of each hand to rub *(fragayar)* the stick. He can change the sound in different ways. If the stick is put in the center, the sound is very "live"; if on the border, it is much more muted. The pitch can be elevated by pressing the palm into the skin, thereby tightening the drumhead (Ortiz 1955:230–234). A major account reports that Iyamba's staff contains the *yín* (Sosa Rodríguez 1982:157). However, Juan Mokongo and Jesús Nasakó insist that it is Mosongo's.
22. Ortiz gives *saékue, samékue,* and *sambeque* as synonyms for *yín. Yín* and *güín* are used interchangeably, though they apparently have different roots. Ortiz traces *yín* to the Efik term *oyim,* "which means a little hard pointed stick"; *güín* is an "antilleanism," which is applied generally to a stem or stalk of cane that is used in making light utensils. The term *fragayar* is a creolized combination of various Spanish terms such as *fregar, fragollar,* and *fragor* ("to rub," "to crush a grain," and "to make noise") (Ortiz 1955:230).
23. Interview with Jesús Nasakó, 1 July 1994.
24. Sosa Rodríguez understands that the title *Musongo* was the Ekoi [Ejagham] name for the highest grade in the Ngbe society—this may have varied, of course, throughout Ejagham territory—a name that was substituted by the title Iyamba among the Efik of the Atakpa group in Old Calabar, he reports. "It is for this reason," he speculates, that "Musongo could be the ultimate African source for the *ñáñigo* [Abakuá] Mosongo, a personage coming [to have] to be diminished in the evolution of the secret society, first in Africa, and then, in Cuba, despite having conserved some of his major functions reflected in the great relation between Mosongo-Iyamba-ekwe and the coincident character of ekwe-mosongo" (Sosa Rodríguez 1982:163).
25. Interview with Jesús Nasakó, 1 July 1994.
26. Interview with Jesús Nasakó, 1 July 1996.
27. Interview with Jesús Nasakó, 1 July 1994. With respect to another Christ icon Jesús used, he explained: "I put the Christ there with this meaning in mind: the daughter was sacrificed for the tribe just as Christ was sacrificed for the Christians."
28. Within the Lucumí religion, Obatalá, one of the symbolically "white *orishas*" (i.e., spiritually pure and close to God), is the Father of (Lucumí) Heads and is associated with Jesus Christ in the syncretic conception.
29. Commenting on the Afro-Cuban religions as a "collage structure" or "syncretism," in order to make the religions "efficacious in the new milieu" of emergent Cuban society, Mosquera writes: "It is vital that the historic figure of Andrés de los Dolores Petít be retrieved from exclusion so that his *role as a forger of the Cuban nation* may be properly assessed. This 'postmodern' character of the mid-nineteenth century opened the Abakuá Secret Society to whites, converting it into the (first popular integrationist society' in Cuba" (Mosquera 1996a:256 n.3, emphasis added).
30. Cabrera quotes, with regard to Petít's Regla Kimbisa: "It was congo, lucumí, espiritista, catholic. He brought together everything." Another said: "Petít made an *ajiaco,* a scramble, he took everything: he worked with Palo, with Ocha, with Santo; was involved in espiritismo, brujeria, the church, so much was found, in order to conquer/win [*vencer*]" (Cabrera 1986a:3).

    This *ajiaco* stew "of different ingredients [is] cooked

until it makes a broth of synthesis," Gerardo Mosquera comments. "However, the stew is complex, a mosaic as well as a synthesis," he adds, "for the bones remain in the middle of the stew without dissolving although they contribute their marrow to the broth" (Mosquera 1996a:226).

31. Jesús Nasakó was *rayado* (initiated) in Palo on 31 December 1954 at age nine. He was later initiated as a *Padre Nganga* (Father of the Nganga) in 1960 and soon thereafter as a *Tata Nkisi,* the highest level of priesthood. He is a priest of Lucero Mundo. He was "sworn" as an *Olu-Osain* (master of Osain herbalism) on 30 December 1963. He was sworn as an *obonekue* in Efori Eñongo on 24 September 1973. He became the Nasakó of the lodge in 1976. Then he was initiated as a Mason. On 29 June 1988 he was initiated as a priest of Eleguá in the Lucumí religion (Santería), and on 22 April 1993 he was initiated as a *babalawo* of Ifá. In 2002 he became the Iyamba of a new lodge born from Efori Eñongo.
32. The *nkisi* is an assemblage of "spiritual medicines" used by *nganga,* priests, in western Central Africa, and by their descendants in Cuba, who practice the religions of Palo Monte/Mayombe, Briyumba, and Kimbisa. The *nkisi* became *nkiso, nganga, caldero,* or *prenda* in Cuba. See Cabrera 1986a, 1986b; Thompson 1983; Brown 1999; MacGaffey 1986, 1988; MacGaffey and Harris 1993.
33. Quirino Valdés, a heroic personage in the history of Regla, was a boss on Havana's wharves, secretary general of the Regla Warehouse Workers, and the founder of the Workers Federation of the Bay of Havana (Cosme Baños 1998:51).
34. This oral material is confirmed by the genealogical and historical data provided by Sosa Rodríguez 1982:143; see also Roche y Monteagudo 1925:4–5).
35. Interviews with Juan Mokongo, summer 1992.
36. Juan Mokongo and Jesús Nasakó believe this, given what they had been told by their elders. Some of Cabrera's mid-century informants commented negatively on the lavishness of Petít's tradition, implying that what came before it did not reflect personal "enrichment" through adornment.
37. These objects may have belonged to an Orú lodge, and not an Efór or Efí lodge. Orú is the third principal branch of Abakuá in Cuba. Its putative origins lie in the Ibibio-Oron group of the Cross River Delta. Juan Mokongo and Jesús Nasakó hypothesize the Orú provenance by the fact that these lodges' altars displayed seven staffs, as opposed to the three or four of the Efí and Efó.

    Provenance records of the Ortiz, and other, early, collections are sketchy, if not nonexistent. Many of the Abakuá objects confiscated by the Spanish colonial police in the nineteenth century were transported to the Museum of Ultramar in Spain, which Ortiz saw in 1901 (Ortiz 1954:80–81); those confiscated after the birth of the Cuban Republic, 1902, were incorporated into the Museum of the Faculty of Legal Medicine (i.e., criminology), the Museum of Anthropology, and the National Museum. Objects of police confiscation came to form most of the data sample Ortiz studied as well as a portion of the collection later named for him in the Casa de Africa in Havana. For example, the objects confiscated in a major raid on the Efore Muna Tanze lodge of Pogolotti, Marianao, Havana on 20 May 1914 appear in Ortíz's *Los instrumentos de la música afrocubana* section on Abakuá drums (cf. Roche y Monteagudo 1925:73 and Ortiz 1954:66–68). Figure 293 in Ortiz 1954 is a photograph of a display "encountered in the Museum of Legal Medicine of the University of Havana," which I first visited in 1998. The objects remain on display. Rafael Roche y Monteagudo visited the Ultramar museum in 1920 (1925:63).
38. From many personal communications with Juan Mokongo in summer 1992 and Jesús Nasakó in 1994 and 1996.
39. Displays of flamboyant, expensive costume, loud drumming, and vigorous athletically danced performances were seen by spectators from balconies who could, if moved, toss down *aguinaldo* (tips). The great and intricate attention to costume, particularly the kings, queens, and *diablitos,* undoubtedly was intended to impress not only the elevated spectators, but also other carnival groups in a competitive spirit.
40. *La Correspondencia de Cuba,* founded in Havana in 1879, was a daily newspaper with independence-oriented views, focusing on economic-administrative, commercial, and political issues (Roldán 1940:701).
41. Roche added: "*Ecue* is a divine object, all powerful, a Christ, a *santo,* that was baptized by the Efó in the River Oldan [Oddán] that runs through West Africa; and in turn *Ecue* baptized the *Efó,* the same as that which San Juan did to Jesus; and this is what the [Cuban] ñáñigo expresses in his orations when he says: *Nacué uracundó Ecue baracundó efomiremo Ecue Efó,* as *Efí* gave clothes to the *Efó,* and the Efó to the Efí" (1925:33).
42. Robert S. Nelson prefers "appropriation" to Barthes's notion of "myth." Barthes's notion emphasizes an impersonal play of signification within language, while Nelson's emphasizes one driven by "personal agency." For this reason, Nelson dwells on the etymology of "appropriation" itself, which derives from *ad* (effectively, "rendering to") and *proprius* ("own or personal"), adding up to "to make one's own" (Nelson and Shiff 1996:117–119).

43. Interviews with Juan Mokongo, July 1992.

44. Interview with Jesús Nasakó, 5 January 1996.

45. Interviews with Juan Mokongo, summer 1992. Jesús Nasakó, agreeing with Juan Mokongo, explains, for example, that "Mokongo Moküire—Moküire was his [proper name] aside from his office name, Mokongo—is the father of Sikán." Interview with Juan Mokongo, summer 1992, and with Jesús Nasakó, 1 July 1994.

According to Sosa Rodríguez, Mokongo is the "*abanderado* [the flagbearer or standard bearer] of the lodge, because his staff (the staff of command) contains fragments of sacrificial offerings that serve to distinguish the spiritual and historical character lodge"; on the outside, as a kind of flagstaff, it is usually adorned with colorful and varied materials, including crucified Christs signifying the "Abakuá Christianization" (Sosa Rodríguez 1982:156). Sosa appears to be incorrect that Mokongo's staff is "hollow," inasmuch as Mosongo's, as I have been able to discover, is the only one made of *caña brava* or drilled-out cedar, though its cap could be charged with secret materials. Juan Mokongo, by contrast, insists that Abasonga carries the *bandera*, banner, of the lodge.

46. The signature of Mokongo was apparently the first legible Abakuá sign that came to the attention of the authorities, appearing on legal documents signed by Margarito Blanco, arrested by the police in 1839 in Havana for illegal assembly (see Deschamps Chapeaux 1964).

47. More specifically, from a Catholic point of view, as Jesús Nasakó explained to me: "The Santo Cristo de Limpias is Christ alive on the cross asking for the salvation of mankind."

48. Interview with Jesús Nasakó, 1 July 1994.

49. Interview with Jesús Nasakó, 1 July 1994.

50. Apostolos-Cappadona 1994:271.

51. "Unique to the Jesuit Order was the emphasis placed on Jesus. . . . The letters IHS (the abbreviation of the Greek form of the name of Jesus commonly found in paintings)" is central to Jesuit iconography (Howard 1995:509). The Jesuits were important missionaries in Latin America, including Brazil and the Spanish possessions, including Mexico, Peru, and the Caribbean—Cuba. "The Jesuits were expelled from Brazil in 1759 and from all Spanish territories in 1767, but they left a considerable cultural legacy" (see Frazer 1995:513–514). For example, Jesuit schools abounded in Cuba; Fidel Castro was a product of this educational system.

52. "Ford's Edsel, named after the only son of Ford's founder, was designed as a two ton, mid-priced monster, so that Ford's customers would have something to 'trade up' to that wasn't a GM or a Chrysler. It was introduced in 1957, just prior to a recession and just before America decided [it] preferred smaller cars. The Edsel promptly developed a reputation as a lemon because early models were full of bugs. Production halted after 3 years; total production for the Edsel rang in at 110,000 cars" (www.theautochannel.com:8080/conten . . . 19960426/news00601.html).

6. "Symbolic Drums": Innovations and Inventions

1. Ortiz 1954:42.

2. There are three squat *enkomos* and one longer *bonkó enchemillá.* According to Juan Mokongo, the *enkomos* are called, individually, from the top in plate 1 and figure 6.1, *cuchi yeremá, arobapá,* and *biapá.*

3. Interview with Jesús Nasakó, 5 January 1996.

4. Interview with Jesús Nasakó, 5 January 1996.

5. Characterizations described by Juan Mokongo and Jesús Nasakó resonate with Cabrera's informants' descriptions (see citations in text).

6. The fringe is sewn into a tubed length of red cloth through which a hemp cord is passed.

7. Interviews with Juan Mokongo, summer 1992.

8. Interviews with Juan Mokongo, summer 1992.

9. Yellow chalk is used for ceremonies of "life," e.g., initiation; white chalk is predominantly used for funerary ceremonies called *llantos,* though many signs are drawn in yellow and then accented with white.

10. This might occur if a lodge finds itself with its Iyamba grade temporarily vacant.

11. From interviews with Jesús Nasakó, 1 July 1994 and 5 January 1996. Ekueñón stands outside the door to the *fambá,* facing the filled courtyard; he taps his drumskin (*tan, tan, ta-tán*—see Ortiz 1954:48ff.) and sings a long *enkame* to call the attention of the members and prepare the way for the procession of *plazas* to leave the temple by "breaking open" the path.

12. Cabrera 1970:156.

13. Interview with Jesús Nasakó, 5 January 1996.

14. From interview with Jesús Nasakó, 1 July 1994.

15. Interviews with Jesús Nasakó, 1 July 1994 and 5 January 1996.

16. Sosa Rodríguez lists the various ingredients, a "concentration of forces," as "cemetery earth, human bones, a rooster head, the ear of a goat, dry wine, cane rum [*aguardiente*], parts of the *mokuba* [Nasakó's herbal concoction], hair of the heads of the notable obones and abanekues, blood soaked cotton from the left side of their chests, holy oil and holy water taken from the Christian Church" (1982:178).

17. Interview with Jesús Nasakó, 1 July 1994. He reiterated

the ingredients in our 5 January 1996 interview, noting that the *sese namokimbán* can, like an *nganga*, contain the *kiyumba* of a woman—that is, the skull, or part of one.

18. "Fetishism" *(fétichisme)*, coined in a French text in 1757, referred to "the direct worship of particular earthly material objects as themselves endowed with quasi-personal intentionality and divine powers capable of gratifying mundane desires. . . . Driven by anxiety regarding the uncertain outcome of events necessary to meet their vital needs, primitive people fixed on certain material objects associated by chance with their fears and desires, and lacking any true scientific understanding of physical causality, they personified the unknown powers of particular material objects as gods whom they might worship and manipulate to bring about passionately desired events. Such a materialist religion was thoroughly nontranscendental and nonuniversal. It was, as the young Karl Marx put it in 1842, quite simply 'the religion of sensuous desire'" (Peitz 1996:198).
19. Jesús Nasakó also calls it *eribo de kankomo*—"empty drum" (in the *kankomo* style, i.e., the squat, tapered, open-bottomed drum).
20. Interview with Jesús Nasakó, 1 July 1994. See also Ortiz 1954:77.
21. Ewe-Fon drums from the Slave Coast, which turn up in Cuba as drums of the "Arará," in Suriname among the Maroons (a Ghanaian variant), and in Haiti in the "Rada" rites, are also goblet-shaped (see Thompson 1995:91–103).
22. The altar's *ciborium* (not referring to the *baldachin*, or canopy, which was also called the *ciborium*, but the monstrance-like object) could be globe-on-stem shaped. The monstrance emphasizes the goblet with an oversized Host upon a gold plate *(paten)* standing vertically atop it—"showing" it to the congregation.
23. Interview with Jesús Nasakó, 1 July 1994.
24. *"Todos los Efó de Cuba somos hijos de Efí. Es al revés de allá [en Africa]. Allá los Efiques son hijos de Efó."* Interviews with Jesús Nasakó, 1 July 1994 and 5 January 1996.
25. Interviews with Jesús Nasakó, 1 July 1994 and 5 January 1996.
26. Within the Lucumí religion, for example, a *babalawo* such as Victor Betancourt of Old Havana has reinstituted the supposedly African initiation system within his house; his initiates into Santería receive just their tutelary deity and Eleguá the messenger *orisha*, as they believe it was done in Africa, rather than the personal pantheon of multiple *orishas* developed with the "modern" system of initiation in Cuba.
27. Interview with Jesús Nasakó, 1 July 1994.
28. Interview with Jesús Nasakó, 1 July 1994.
29. Interview with Jesús Nasakó, 1 July 1994.
30. Thompson emphasizes Tanze as God's avatar, whereas Jesús Nasakó stresses Obon Tanze as the reincarnated "king of the leopard society."
31. Isué, the *sese*'s custodian, occupies right front; Iyamba, left front; Mokongo, right rear; Isunekue left rear.
32. The old Abakuá Efó #1 crown, which I have seen, is now in the possession of Perico Abasonga of Regla's Efori Eñongo.
33. Fernando Ortiz noted this *sese*'s "regal crown of gilt metal, in the high and pompous style of the Spanish Bourbon dynasty" (Ortiz 1954:59). This "profusion of adornments in the creole taste and its Christian-Lucumí syncretism on the altar with the images of the Virgin de la Caridad (Ochún), of Santa Barbara (Changó), etc., went along with the Crucifix and the Holy Sacrament" (Ortiz 1954:55).
34. The evolution of such crown styles begins with the Roman diadem, which itself was based on the golden laurel wreath tied with ribbons, and which Byzantine emperors revised with chains and pendants—vestiges of wreath ribbons. All subsequent crowns, including open crowns and coronets, derive from this type. The *fleur-de-lis* crown was the most common type of Western regalia during the Middle Ages. The double-arched crown was a modification of the original "Crown of Charlemagne" made for the German King Otto II, to which he added arches. Two arches became standard in England, though some crowns, such as that of Elizabeth I of England in the mid-sixteenth century, had four arches (paraphrased from Goodall 1995:79–80).
35. The female *orishas* Oshún and Oyá, within the Cuban Lucumí tradition, wear small cut-out circular metal crowns on their covered vessels.
36. Interview with Jesús Nasakó, 5 January 1996.
37. Interview with Jesús Nasakó, 5 January 1996.
38. The details of Abakuá ceremonial and initiation have been extensively discussed in a number of sources (Cabrera 1954:205–220; 1975:15–65; Sosa Rodríguez 1982:219–250; Ortiz 1950a; Bustamante 1957; Pedro 1961; Moliner Castañeda 1988:17–18). My intention in the following discussion is to highlight selected ritual uses of the altar objects, framed within a sketch of ritual performances narrated to me by Jesús Nasakó.
39. This account is provided by Jesús Nasakó from two taped interviews, 1 July 1994 and 5 January 1996, and numerous informal sessions over the course of four years in which he corrected and amplified my transcriptions.
40. The placing of a *fundamento* upon the initiate's head recalls the *parada* ceremony in the Lucumí religion, in

which the *soperas* (soup tureens) containing the *orishas* are presented to the head one at a time, culminating in the tutelary *orisha*'s being "crowned"; that is, the tutelary *orisha*'s *sopera* is held upon the head while chanted invocations are made. However, in the Lucumí religion, the initiate comes to own those tureens, with their *fundamento* secrets inside, while, in the Abakuá, a single set of *fundamento* objects remain in the lodge's possession. Abakuá are "sworn to" these objects.

41. Interview with Jesús Nasakó, 5 January 1996.
42. As Jesús explains it, the *wemba* and *mokuba* are the approximate equivalents, respectively, of the *osain* and *omiero* within the Lucumí religion, or the *diámbila* and the *llamboso* of the Kongo religion. When the *osain* liquids from different *orishas* are combined, an *omiero* is produced. The former is for "washing" (cleansing), and the latter is for imbibing, incorporating spiritual substance, as well as washing. "*Wemba* is to clean, *mokuba* is to drink," says Jesús Nasakó. Interview, 5 January 1996.
43. This account derives primarily from interviews and personal communications with Jesús Nasakó and draws on some of my observations of the semipublic phases of the ceremonies.

7. The *Íremes* and Their *Sacos*

1. Interview with Jesús Nasakó, 5 January 1996.
2. Interview with Jesús Nasakó, 5 January 1996.
3. The Akuaramina masquerade was apparently performed as late as 1957, when Pierre Verger photographed it in collaboration with Lydia Cabrera (see Cabrera 1970:5). The rare Embema masquerade costume is believed to remain in its Matanzas lodge and has not been performed since the early 1950s. Perico Abasonga keeps photographs from that era in his home. The Akuaramina masquerade photographed by Pierre Verger hangs, damaged, in the Abakuá salon of the Fernando Ortiz Collection of Havana's Casa de Africa.
4. His findings are difficult to verify historically, since the suits in Havana collections, confiscated by the police, have no accession data. Many colonial-era suits were taken to Spain and placed in the Museum of Ultramar; republican-era suits were jumbled together in police and museum store rooms, and many suits must have rotted.
5. The examples displayed in the Casa de Africa's Fernando Ortiz Collection in Old Havana were mostly confiscated by the police in the republican era (as of 1902).
6. Interview with Jesús Nasakó, 5 January 1996.
7. Still, making no vocal sound and having no verbal language, the *íreme* is like neither beast nor human. With the exception of Akuaramina and Embema, the *íremes* have eyes but no mouths.
8. However, because the costumes are quite hot, the dancers often leave the chest open. And, because the hands and forearms are exposed, attributes of the human dancer's ties to other Cuban religions are often apparent, such as bead necklaces and bracelets.
9. I witnessed this at a *llanto,* a funerary ceremony, at the Orú Papá *tierra* in Guanabacoa in 1993.
10. Interview with Jesús Nasakó, 1 July 1994.
11. See, for example, Thompson 1983:260–266.
12. Imaginably, the suitmaker intended these opposed teethlike triangles to make reference to the leopard's jaw, rather than its paw or perhaps even a conspicuous and widely reported characteristic of Cuban Carabalí themselves: filed teeth *(dientes afilados)* (see Deschamps Chapeaux 1969:67). Or perhaps they are mostly decorative.
13. Interview with Jesús Nasakó, 5 January 1996.
14. Interview with Jesús Nasakó, 5 January 1996.

8. Pictures, Performances, and the Police: Changing Contexts for *Costumbrista* Arts

1. Cuba's republic (1902) had been established under the control of the first American military occupation (1899–1902). The American military returned once again (1906–9) to crush the "August Revolution" by disgruntled Liberals against the second term of Cuba's first president, Tomás Estrada Palma (Pérez 1988:390–91). Cuba's infrastructure was a wreck from the Independence and so-called Spanish-American wars (1895–98 and 1898–99, respectively), and the countryside, the economy, and public health had not yet recovered from its massive battering. The Americans mended significant components of the infrastructure and helped put out the great yellow fever epidemic of July 1900, not least because of the U.S. government's continuing interest in a profitable economic and political presence on the island. The Americans also enthusiastically contributed to the war against the twin demons of *brujería* and *ñañiguismo,* with which the epidemic was compared (Helg 1995:107–116). This first decade of the republic also saw the founding of the Agrupación de Color, a political party founded by Afro-Cubans protesting postwar racism and disenfranchisement; the organization was the vanguard of an emergent liberation movement, which was brutally crushed in the "Race War" of 1912 (Pérez 1988:221–222; Helg 1995:117–227, 229).
2. I borrow the term *graduate* from James Clifford's "On Collecting Art and Culture," which explores how "exotic

objects have been contextualized in the West." Objects move and "graduate" from one category, institution, and semantic zone to another; for example, "primitive" objects may graduate from an "ethnographic" context to a "fine art" context, particularly through types of museum display. See also Vogel 1988.

3. Methodologically, Thompson's work built in part on approaches developed by scholars of West Africa since the late 1950s, which had combined formalism, connoisseurship, and iconology with ethnographic fieldwork (see Brown 1996:81–82 and 133 n.18).
4. The show focused on Western art that appropriated "tribal" arts to produce a modernist primitivism in the early twentieth century.
5. Blassingame 1972; Levine 1977; Abrahams, with Szwed 1983; Vlach 1978.
6. *Ethnological:* the science of "races" or groups considered in relation to anthropological perspectives and questions of the evolution of humankind. It is often taxonomic in nature. *Ethnographic:* essentially, the "writing of culture(s)"—that is, approaches to the written account, produced through more or less extensive fieldwork among ethnically or nationally bounded, territorialized, and usually "remote" groups. Classic modern ethnographies constituted their "cultures" along the lines of a social-scientific template, for example, history, ecology, institutions, economy, life cycle, and religion. *Folkloristic:* based mostly in ethnographic fieldwork in the twentieth century, folklore study is a subfield of anthropology, concentrating on genres of expressive practices in speech, arts, and performance that make meaning and, as recently theorized, embody culture through the dialectic of structure (e.g., patterns of tradition) and agency (creative and reflective subjects).
7. As of 1792, the *cabildos* of the African nations were forced outside the city walls, which were taken down only in 1856.
8. I translate *"madero emplumado, símbolo que enarbolaba cada una de aquellas salvajes agrupaciones"* as "feathered wood emblem, the symbol hoisted by each . . . group," rather than "symbolic figurehead" (Jean Stubbs's translation in Bettelheim 1993). Illustrations of Abakuá processions show that Abakuá groups carried an alternative kind of banner, a stretched goatskin symbolic of Sikán's spirit. However, the "feathered wood emblem" referred to by Meza may have been a version of the Ekpe and Ngbe society emblems for particular grades, which hung from large pillars within their lodges: a large fringed wood frame, over which was stretched a woven fiber mat. To the mat were attached drumheads, arrowlike sticks, animal skulls, gourds, palm-rib staffs, feathers, and so on, symbols of the society (see Nicklin 1991).
9. As Efik Buton (or Acuabutón) likely derives from Efik Obutong ("Old Town"), "Ultán" is possibly a Cuban pronunciation of "Old Town" itself. "Old Town" and "Ultán" are similar in morphology and phonology: ol-t-n and ul-t-n.
10. I paraphrase from Pérez (1988:99–100): Following an 1843 uprising in Matanzas involving three hundred slaves from more than fifteen sugar estates, a rebellion involving two hundred slaves broke out on one estate and spread to others. It was, in fact, a "far-flung conspiracy involving hundreds of slaves and thousands of whites and free people of color." More than four thousand arrests were made, and widespread repression followed, including the torture, floggings, and grisly executions of hundreds if not thousands. The use of ladders *(escaleras)* to which prisoners were tied for floggings accounts for the name La Escalera.
11. The photographs of alleged *ñáñigos*, naked, in Roche y Monteagudo's *ñañiguismo* chapter show white men covered in tattoos. Typically, Abakuá have tattooed their grade signs, as well as *íremes* and other religious imagery, on their bodies. These men's bodies betray no such types (1925:24–33).
12. Ortiz studied criminology under Cesare Lombroso and Enrico Ferri in Italy during 1902–5, and Lombroso wrote the *carta-prólogo* to Ortiz's 1906 work *Los negros brujos* (see Ortiz 1973:xx–1).
13. L. Torriente, from *Pintura y escultura en Cuba*, quoted in Borrás 1996, for whom Landaluze "was . . . the most important folkloric painter of Cuba" (Borrás 1996:357–358).
14. José Nicolás de la Escalera's "most important work is a series of paintings in the church of Santa María del Rosario near Havana. Completed in the 1760s, they depict Saint Dominic Guzmán and other Catholic saints" (Blanc 1992:52). It seems that he was the first Cuban artist to depict an Afro-Cuban in a major painting. In July 1943, Wifredo Lam participated with other Cuban modernists in a fundraising exhibition and sale of painted fans at the Lyceum. The event was dedicated to the restoration of the church (Blanc 1992:94). In 1940, Lydia Cabrera had moved into the Quinta San José with María Teresa de Rojas. The house was an abandoned eighteenth-century colonial mansion, an architectural landmark close to the black *barrio* of Pogolotti in Marianao, where Cabrera had first met Calixta Morales (Oddedeí), one of her most important informants, as early as 1930. In addition to restoring the mansion, she began work with others in the restoration of the church in 1941 (Intar Gallery 1984:10, 14).

15. For example, Fernández Carrillo (1881:143) lists one Abakuá grade as "Macombo" (i.e., Mokongo), which Ortiz reproduces in 1920 (1960:31).
16. The "basic metaphor" of cultural evolutionism—common to both Darwinians and ethnologists of the period—was that of the "tree, with present races, 'taken to represent the budding twigs and foliage. The main stem led up to European man: "civilization" was confined to particular races, whose function it has been, by means of war and conquest, to spread the arts among surrounding nations, or to exterminate those whose low state of mental culture rendered them capable of receiving it'. . . . Contemporary aborigines, surviving in a state of 'arrested development,' could serve as living illustrations of those from which they sprang" (Chapman 1985:31).

    As Raymond Williams has written, by 1775, "civilization . . . [indicated] both the state and the process. . . . In the general spirit of the Enlightenment, with its emphasis on secular and progressive human self-development . . . civilization expressed this sense of historical process, but also celebrated the associated sense of modernity: an achieved condition of refinement and order" (Williams 1983:57–58).
17. Abolition originally was to entail a period of gradual emancipation through the *patronato,* a cushion period or middle stage of indentured servitude for ten years, 1880–90, to acclimate the ex-slaves to their new status.
18. 22 October 1882, Akanarán Efó raided; seventeen arrests of whites, confiscation of attributes, *íreme* costumes, and archive; 1883, Abakuá Efó raided; January 1884, raid on a Havana funeral ceremony in a private house; March 1884, raid on white ñáñigos in Regla in a private house with confiscations of attributes and a "luxurious" *íreme* costume (police engaged in "hand-to-hand combat in order to arrest them"); December 1884, raid on funeral of member of Akanarán Efó; 1885–87, numerous raids, "the persecution having weakened the ñáñigos"; June 1888, another raid on members of Akanarán, with arrests and attributes being confiscated; December 1888, the same personnel were arrested in another raid (Roche y Monteagudo 1925:53–55).
19. Alejandro Rodríguez's account, originally handwritten in a ledger and titled "Reseña histórica de los Ñáñigos de Cuba desde su creación hasta la fecha," covers the founding of Efik Buton and the identity of its members, the early participation of the Carabalí *cabildos* and Ñáñigo lodges in the "Day of Kings" carnival of 6 January, the organization, initiation rites, and altar objects of a lodge, the hierarchy and roster of offices, the 1863 foundation of the first white lodge (Akanarán Efó) and its offspring up through 1881, the distribution of lodges over Havana's districts and municipalities, the secret signs used by each lodge, and a glossary of *ñáñigo* vocabulary.
20. From the Akanarán Efó archive, the police discovered a document on the "eternal suspension" of one D. Miguel Martínez from the group, which the police interpreted as the decree for his murder (Roche y Monteagudo 1908:40).
21. Roche's 1908 work opens with a section, modeled after Rodríguez's account, titled "The Ñáñigos," with chapters on "Their Origin and Development," and "Ñáñigo Official Personnel," with subsections and other chapters on language, proverbs, prayers, tattoos, ceremonies, signs, their crimes, and their fate before the civil governor of the island, Rodríguez Batista.
22. There were two *La Lucha* publications in Havana, one founded in 1882, which was a weekly periodical bearing the views of the *autonomista* movement; the other, founded in 1885, was an afternoon daily with views of the *republicano* movement (Roldán 1940:722). It is not clear in which of these the letter appeared.
23. Following the "dissolution" of Macaró Efó (likely Akanarán Efó), Ecoria Efó #1, #2, and #3, and Ebión Efó as of 3 January 1889, the following *juegos* would give up their "most sacred effects" to the police: Enyegueyé #1, Efí Abaracá #1 and #2, Erón Efí, followed by Pitinacorocó, Enllemillá #1, #2, #3, Ibondá Usagaré, Iquerecuá, Cannamberé, Bacocó, Usagaré, and Batanga Efó. Most were apparently "white" *juegos,* with the exception of Erón Efí.

9. Struggle over Possession of the Secret: The "Museuming" of the *Ñáñigos'* "Most Sacred Effects"

1. *Ultramar* means "overseas." I am grateful to Krista Thompson for her research on Ultramar for a paper she wrote in my fall 1996 graduate seminar at Emory University, "Afro-Caribbean Arts and Cuban Secret Societies: Historiography, Methodology, and Politics." The paper was based on my seminar materials in which I demonstrated the visual and historical connection between confiscated Abakuá objects and criminological study by Roche y Monteagudo (1908/1925); Israel Castellanos (1916/1928); and Fernando Ortiz (1906/1953/1954). Pacheco de Amorim's catalog (1934) of the Ultramar Museum, however, does not include any mention of *ñáñigo* objects.
2. See, for example, how Roland Barthes interprets the "stealing" and "mythologizing" of objects, through "second order" signification, to promote colonial order (1972:114–125).

3. *African Voices,* at the Smithsonian's National Museum of Natural History, replaced dry, isolated, minimally and poorly labeled artifacts with a new installation that foregrounds the cultural agency of the makers. "The central voices of authority that tell about the exhibition's themes and 'stories' are African and African Diasporan" (Arnoldi, Kreamer, and Mason 2001:16-17).

   The notion of anthropological fieldwork as dependent on the notion of "remote areas" comes from Ardener 1987. For a persuasive history of changing museum display, see Vogel 1988.

   The Smithsonian Museum of Natural History's Hall of Cultures, which subsumed the African objects, was changed into an exhibition in line with a modern "anthropological interpretation and style of display" in the 1960s to replace an African display that had stood relatively unchanged since the opening of the National Museum building (now the Museum of Natural History) in 1913. In the 1960s installation, the objects were organized into conventional ethnic classification, still with little distinction between the functional and the aesthetic, and with some prejudicial labels mentioning, for example, cannibalism. (See Arnoldi, Kreamer, and Mason 2001:17.)
4. "Fakelore," in 1960s and 1970s folklore study, was the diluted or debased derivative of "genuine," community-based oral literature.
5. A general of the Liberation forces in the Second War of Independence, Nuñez was named Havana's governor in 1899 (Roldán 1940:971). Roche's opening chapter, "Los Ñáñigos," features only three other pages of illustrations, consisting of drawn signs and attributes (figure 5.4).
6. The men have a great variety of tattoos, except they do not have those one expects to see: Abakuá signatures, *íreme* figures, and the like.
7. Cesare Lombroso (1836–1909), the top Italian criminologist, focused his research on the relation between mental and physical disorders. He was a professor of forensic medicine and psychiatry at Turin, where he eventually became the chair of criminal anthropology. When Ortiz was in Turin (1903), he collaborated on Lombroso's journal, *Archive of Criminal Anthropology, Psychiatry and Legal Medicine* (see Rubin 1998:26).
8. Paul Broca (1824–1880) was a French surgeon and physical anthropologist noted for his research on the brain and skull. He studied the comparative morphology of the brain, the topography of the skull and brain, and prehistoric trepanations, as well as discovering the seats of articulate speech in "the convolution of Broca" or "Broca's area."
9. From the text plaque introducing the Steegers collection in the Museum of the Faculty of Legal Medicine and Toxicology at the University of Havana.
10. From the text plaque introducing the Steegers collection in the Museum of the Faculty of Legal Medicine and Toxicology at the University of Havana.
11. From interviews in August 2001 with Dr. Ponce and two medical students, and from posted course schedules in the Legal Medicine and Toxicology school lobby.
12. Description from my notes and drawings from visits to the museum from 1998 to 2000.
13. In the concrete terms of local geography, this was the busy artery of St. Lázarus Avenue, which runs from the University of Havana in El Vedado to the frontier of Old Havana on the Prado. Many of the Abakuá houses raided by the police and listed in Roche y Monteagudo's 1908 work were located on either side of St. Lazarus in the *barrios* now called Cayo Hueso, Príncipe, and Central Havana, if they were not in Marianao, Guanabacoa, or Regla.
14. The carved "frog" *(sapo)* "fetish" of Domingo Bocourt, which was published by Castellanos in 1916 (plate 12 between pages 62 and 63), is still on view in the Museum of Legal Medicine, within what is now called the Calixto García hospital complex behind the University of Havana.
15. *Embó* is an alternate pronunciation of the Yoruba-Lucumí term *ebó,* a ritual "work" toward a defined end, which may include sacrificial offerings, cleansings, prayer, and drumming.
16. Roche y Monteagudo lists the following: "a gold chalice equal to that the Catholics use in the Mass's sacrifice; six small drums and two large ones; a large wood goblet; a crucifix; two *marugas* [musical shakers]; a set of iron bells; a candlestick; three staffs incrusted with white metal and *ñáñigo* symbols; one of these attributes is surmounted by a rooster, another by a cross, and the third with a kind of wheel; two pots; four plates; suits or *sacos* of the Diablitos—one red and the other green; a jacket; four pieces of cloth in different colors; four *sombreros* [*sombreretas*]; a burlap bag; four large *plumeros* and one small one; a knife with a point and [a] handle of black wood; two roosters; a sack containing the remains of a fish and others of food in a state of putrefaction—the leftovers, undoubtedly, of the offerings or *derechos* that the initiates had contributed to the carabalí-brícamo style banquet in order to join in such reprehensible association. . . . We must mention, before concluding this chapter, that as will be observed in the illustration [figures 5.6, 8.1, and 9.4], the *Sese* [that] had certain artistic form, and

the four *plumeros* that adorned it were splendid" (Roche y Monteagudo 1925:71).

17. Not permitted to photograph in the Legal Medicine Museum, I made drawings and compared the exhibition content and organization to photocopies of the Ortiz and Roche illustrations (figures 8.1, 9.5, 9.7, and 9.8) that I had brought along.
18. Up through the 1960s, as Rafael L. López Valdés explained in a personal communication, fieldwork *within* living communities in Cuba was mostly discouraged under the Revolution. The "informant"/"investigator" relationship was highly controlled within state institutions such as the National Folklore Group of Cuba. The musicians and dancers in this group were mostly practitioners. They became the sources from which the investigators would draw material and compose and choreograph "folkloricized" performances (see Hagedorn 2001).
19. Israel Castellanos distinguished "ethnography" from the comparative ethnological science of groups—and intended to document and analyze one type of object of a specific group (though he conducted little fieldwork). In the world at large, in contrast, the 1920s commenced the age of modern fieldwork among living communities within the professional discipline of social anthropology (see, e.g., Malinowski 1961; Radcliffe-Brown 1948; Clifford 1988:26–31; Stocking 1983:71–74).
20. Among those objects "confiscated in Marianao there were patterns for suits, and these corresponded exactly to the patterns [*moldes*] that were confiscated from the *ñáñigos* in Guanabacoa." Typically, all of the suits were made basically the same, with the same number of cut out pieces, from patterns, in their composition. Usefully also, Castellanos attempted to distinguish between examples of "older" suits from the nineteenth century, which used striped (or cross-striped) cloth, called *cotí,* that was commonly used in cushions and pillows, that is, upholstery fabric. More recent, twentieth-century costumes, he argued, used combinations of satin, wool, flannel, and flour sacks. Older models used little adornment beyond fiber fringe, whereas the recent models used complex appliqués of brilliant color over monochromatic bases (Castellanos 1928:30–33).

10. From Atavism to Modern Primitivism

1. Ortiz wrote: "Through government restriction the *cabildos* disappeared, with all the good they had: mutual support, security against sicknesses, the drum dances—inoffensive and so appreciated by the Africans; what remained in exchange, semi-underground, the savage, animist fetishism. . . . How much better the opposite result would be! How much better it would be if today we had *cabildos* of mutual aid and public drum dances, and not *templos brujos* ["witchcraft temples"], tolerated or clandestine!" (1921:29–31; my translation).

   By an official act, the Bando de Buen Gobierno y Policia of 1792, the *cabildos* "were banished . . . to the banks [*orillas*] of the city outside its walls" (Ortiz 1921: 17). A proclamation of 1884 "prohibited the gathering of the *cabildos* of blacks of Africa and their circulation through the streets on Noche-Buena and the Day of the Kings. The African saturnal passed into history. That of 1884 was the last: the 6th of January of 1885 was the first silent Epiphany that Cuba had" (Ortiz 1921:20–22).

   According to historian Rebecca Jarvis Scott, the suppression of the *cabildos de nación* during the 1880s was meant to prevent the further consolidation of African-based subcultures with the emancipation of thousands of Africans, a scenario that portended counterhegemonic loyalties in the national setting (1985:264–278).
2. The following is summarized from Pérez 1988:394: Gerardo Machado was elected to his first term as president in 1924. By 1927 opposition to his government by disaffected liberals led to the establishment of new political organizations, including student groups. At the end of his term (1928), Machado was elected unopposed by unconstitutional means. General strikes commenced by 1930, and abortive uprisings were staged in 1931 by Mario G. Menocal and Carlos Mendieta. The United States dispatched Ambassador Sumner Welles to mediate between Machado and the opposition. A general strike climaxed with a military coup ousting Machado and installing Carlos Manuel De Céspedes as president, followed by a "Sergeant's Revolt" led by Fulgencio Batista. He aided the establishment of a new provisional government headed by Ramón Grau San Martín, which organized massive reforms. In January 1934, Batista overthrew Grau and installed Mendieta as president. Revolutionary responses by Grau, newly recognized communist and workers organizations, and other advocacies led to the promulgation of the new constitution in 1940, and Batista was elected president for a four-year term. He was then succeeded by Grau in 1944 (see Pérez 1988: 394).
3. The Platt Amendment, instituted in 1901 by the American occupation government in return for Cuba's independence, permitted the United States to intervene in Cuba's affairs at any future moment when deemed necessary. The Platt Amendment was abrogated by Cuba in 1934.
4. La Sociedad de Folklore Cubano, founded on 6 January (the traditional Day of Kings) 1923, was convened by

Enrique José Varona Pera, a poet, orator, philosopher, politician, and revolutionary. With Varona, among others, as honorary presidents, Fernando Ortiz was elected president of the governing body, with other posts being filled by a roster of Cuban luminaries, including Emilio Roig de Leuchenring (historian), Manuel Pérez Beato (antiquarian), and Ramiro Guerra (choreographer). Their principal organ was the *Archives of Cuban Folklore* (founded 1924; see Roldán 1940:1055–1056).

5. I am grateful to Stephan Palmié for pointing me in this direction in interpreting Ortiz's notion of the national "stew." Personal communication, 1997; see also Palmié 1998.
6. As Robin Moore astutely notes, Ortiz's theory of transculturation, spelled out most fully in his *Contrapunteo cubano* (1940), still distinguishes between "pure" and "inauthentic" culture. It lacks theorization of dominance, resistance, and accommodation in Cuba's political arena, as these affect transculturation. Moreover, even though Ortiz's 1946 *El engaño de las razas* (The Deception of Race) rejects the linking of race or biology with inherent cultural, emotional, or mental attributes in humans, Moore argues, he continued to speak, as late as 1965, of black culture as having feminine or childlike aspects, as well as sensualism and diabolic lasciviousness. Finally, he never wholly considered Afro-Cuban culture as "beautiful" or aesthetically valid to the same extent as European-style compositions (he wrote that "African music lacks the technical and instrumental possibilities which European [art] music has today"). His 1950 *La africanía,* on Afro-Cuban music, casts African-derived art as a "rough-hewn gemstone that needs to be refined." Thus, he advocated a hybridized "high" musical composition within the Western tradition and made into a "universal art." For this reason he prized the Cuban composers Roldán, Borbolla, García Caturla, and Hilario González and more commercial artists of the mid-century such as Ernesto Lecuona and Gonzalo Roig as the epitome of Cuban artists. García Caturla and Roldán began careers associated with the middle-class *afrocubanismo* movement that developed around 1930 (this account summarized from Moore 1984:42–46). For example, García Caturla created a piece entitled *Danza lucumí* in 1925 (Blanc 1992:57).
7. Guillén was a great poet and an Afro-Cuban, Roig de Leuchenring a writer and historian, Ballagas a poet and leader of the "Black Poetry" movement, Franco a historian, and Ramos Blanco a sculptor and Afro-Cuban.
8. It is, of course, quite common to hear Cuban whites today say that all the crime in Havana is committed by "the blacks" *(los negros).*
9. Martí conceived of a "Mother America"—which included all of the Americas as a greater homeland—free of singular dependence on North America, the United States. "Our America" explored the sufferings and remedies, virtues and defects of this larger homeland, encouraging knowledge of each community, its character, material and spiritual necessities, how governments should proceed. It was against tyranny and dictatorship.
10. The first vanguard generation, members of the Grupo Minorista movement, included Jorge Arche, Eduardo Abela, Carlos Enríquez, Arístides Fernández, Antonio Gattorno, Victor Manuel García, Amelia Peláez del Casal, Marcelo Pogolotti, Fidelio Ponce de León, Domingo Ravenet, and Wifredo Lam, all born around the turn of the twentieth century. The "second" generation, which came to prominence in the 1940s, included Cundo Bermúdez, Luis Martínez Pedro, Mario Carreño, Mariano Rodríguez, and Rene Portocarrero (see Martínez 1994:19–24).
11. Lydia Cabrera and Wifredo Lam collaborated on the important translation into Spanish and illustration of Aimé Césaire's *Retour au pays natal* (Return to the Native Land) in 1943 (see Blanc 1992:94; Cabrera 1994:227–261).
12. The ideal of *cubanidad* had become key in the Cuban nationalist movements of the 1920s and 1930s. *Cubanidad* "implied bonds based on one's place of birth and identity as a member of a nation. The term . . . incorporated a sense of duty, pride, confidence, and the search for and affirmation of that which was Cuban, be it Spanish, African, Indian, or a combination of all three" (Martínez 1994:38).
13. I will use the term *diablito* in reference to Lam's *íreme* figures because I have seen no contemporaneous evidence that he used the latter term, except in writings thirty or more years later. In fact, most of his works in this mode are untitled or use other evocative names and phrases. He and his artist contemporaries continued to use the term *ñáñigo,* though Lydia Cabrera changed this with her 1954 *El Monte* and later *La sociedad secreta abakuá* (1958), which consistently used the terms *íreme* and Abakuá.
14. In Lucumí possession trance, the *orisha* "mounts" its priest/*caballo* (horse).
15. Victor Manuel García depicts the *íreme* with the quasi-realistic details of fringe, diminutive bells at the waist, and *sombrereta,* though the odd one-piece suit draws, perhaps, from a Carnival version of an Abakuá *íreme,* which is still seen today; indeed, the figure holds what appears to be a scorpion (Sp. *alacrán*), which could refer to the famous El Alacrán carnival group of Havana.

16. Dealer Pierre Loeb wrote in 1946 that "It is the privilege of the negro, with Chinese blood, to have rediscovered the mystery without which there is no art, and thanks to Wifredo Lam, it is in the West Indies the instinct of the primitive and the knowledge of civilized man are going to counterbalance one another" (Loeb quoted in Herzberg 1992:47). André Breton, who had adopted the term *surrealism* from Guillaume Apollinaire, published the first *Surrealist Manifesto* in 1924: "Surrealism. Psychic automatism in its pure state, by which one proposes to express—verbally, by means of the written word, or in any other manner—the actual functioning of thought, in the absence of any control exercised by reason, exempt from any aesthetic or moral concern" (Rubin 1968:64). Lam worked with Breton on the *Fata Morgana* collection of writing and collective surrealist illustrations in 1941, and sailed with Breton to the Caribbean from Marseilles; Breton wrote the catalog foreword to Lam's first solo show in New York (1942); and so on (see Blanc 1992:92–94).
17. Max-Pol Fouchet, the principal source of these biographical data and the point of departure for more recent speculations, relates Lam as telling him that he heard African drums every night as he lay in his mother's bed, that he witnessed ritual cleansings after invoking Shangó, and that (Lam's words) he was "attending ceremonies with rites that had come from Dahomey or the Congo," given his introduction to them by Mantonica Wilson (Fouchet 1986:14). Sims (1992:29 n.12) cites an edition of the same Fouchet work.

    Julia Herzberg's attempt to build on this data seems not to be based on solid evidence and depends on circular argumentation. She contends that Mantonica Wilson was a "*lucumí* priestess commonly known as a *santera*." She was a "priestess of Changó, the Yoruba thundergod, who was her tutelary deity. Anyone who came to her for guidance would indirectly receive the guidance of Changó through her. She brought Lam under the guidance of Changó. Although the young Lam was a devotee, he was not an initiate. . . . In connection with her role as spiritual guide, Mantonica Wilson gave Lam a gift of an amulet consecrated under Changó's patronage. . . . This good luck charm has two ribbons and four leaves. Changó's colors are red and white. The original colors of Lam's amulet have changed over the years from a deep red to a lighter shade and from white to pale green" (Herzberg 1992:31). The footnotes suggest, with good reason, that Wilson was a "healer, adviser, and diviner" but the sources do not define her as a Lucumí priestess. The identification of the "amulet" as a Shangó attribute is made on the basis of color and number. Shangó does take red and white, though it not true, as the writer insists, that the number four definitively identifies Shangó. (Six does.) The writer seems to read backward, with little support, from the "Lucumí" "Changó" "amulet" to the identity of Wilson as a Lucumí priestess of Shangó. Within Lucumí tradition, red could represent vital action, war, fire, and problems, relevant to Shangó, but also to any other "warrior," such as Eleguá or Oyá. Red is heavily used in Palo Monte, the Congo-Cuban religion, and it is also used among Catholics for Saint Barbara. There is simply no evidence to support the specificity of the argument that Wilson was a Shangó priestess and Lam was a "devotee," though he may have received "guidance." In any case, certainly he may, as the sources suggest, have attended "cleansing ceremonies" as a youth, but it is clear that, with respect to his post-1941 Afro-Cuban work, he had much ethnographic help from his friends, including Lydia Cabrera's titling of his paintings.
18. The translation says "masked devil." This is, presumably, Herzberg's translation. I have not come across the original and do not know whether it was in French or Spanish.
19. It is possible that the transcription of Lam's account for *L'aventure du Pierre Loeb: La Galerie Pierre, Paris, 1924–1964* (Paris: Galerie Albert Loeb, 1979), p. 35, or Herzberg's translation into English rendered some of the terms in odd or inappropriate ways, such as "tom-tom" and "devil." Aside from this, some embellishment occurs on Lam's part, for example, as the Abakuá signs are not drawn in "all different colors," only in yellow or white chalk.
20. Cabrera apparently took Lam to ritual events and drummings in the houses of Lucumí *santeros* and, possibly, Palo practitioners beginning in early 1942 in Pogolotti, Marianao, and Regla (Herzberg 1992:39). The conical or rounded figures of Eleguá are clearly seen in many paintings.
21. Arguably, they are "postmodern" works (see Mosquera 1996a:225–258), though caution should apply to any such hard-and-fast typologies.

11. From Primitivism to Folklore

1. During Lam's stay in Cuba (1938–52), Lydia Cabrera published two important reviews of his work in the *Diario de la Marina* (1942 and 1944), collaborated with Lam on the translation of Aimé Césaire's *Return to the Native Land* (1943), and wrote the preface to Lam's 1946 exhibition catalogue for the Lyceum. Based on her research, which was most intensive and ongoing from 1942, she published one major article on Afro-Cuban rit-

ual practices in Ortiz's *Revista Bimestre Cubana* (1947). Fernando Ortiz and Lydia Cabrera remain among the pantheon of the African Diaspora field's researcher-writers, who include Raimundo Nina Rodrigues, Pierre Verger, Edson Carniero, and Roger Bastide for Brazil and Melville J. Herskovits and Alfred Métraux for Haiti, for example.

2. Ortiz's independent Abakuá manuscript, which might represent a different focus or approach, may someday be published.
3. The *erikundé* is the Moruá grade's cruciform rattle; the conical or cylindrical fringed *marugas* are carried by auxiliary members of the orchestra; the *ekón* is the sacred invocatory bell, hit with a stick *(palo)*, which was used to summon Tanze's spirit to Ekue (originally it was a wood clapper); and the *enkaniká* is the belt of cowbells worn around the *íreme*'s waist (see Ortiz 1952:99–113, 229–261, 267–278).
4. In 1908 Fernando Ortiz married Ester Cabrera, Lydia Cabrera's sister (Rubin 1998:26).
5. As the late Juan Mokongo, an intimate of one of Cabrera's supposed Abakuá sources, related, Cabrera "just wrote down whatever they told to her." For this reason, he argued, her more recently published Abakuá vocabulary (1988) confounds at least two distinct and distinctive Carabalí lexicons. Juan Mokongo claimed that *La lengua sagrada de los ñáñigos* (The Sacred Language of the Ñáñigos) combined what he called Brícamo and Isuama. It is true that the Efut were called Brícamo during the colonial period, while the Isuama made up another distinct subgroup of Carabalí.
6. Josefina Tarafa's family owned the Central Cuba in Matanzas, where much of Cabrera's research on rural Lucumí and Palo practice was conducted in 1956 (discussions with Elliot Klein, current translator of *El Monte*, summer 2000; Cabrera 1993:7). It is likely that her father was Colonel José Miguel Tarafa (1869–1932), a railroad and sugar magnate (Suchlicki 2001:584).
7. Teresa Muñoz (Omí Tomí), for example, was the seamstress for Lydia Cabrera's grandmother and mother (Cabrera 1954:27).
8. Before Cabrera's first major works (1954, 1958), the noted journalist Juan Luis Martín wrote a dense monograph in two volumes for the *Papeles Cubanos* series, apparently completed in 1930 but not published until 1945. Much of its data was acquired through police sources. In quasi-scientific language, it seeks to determine the ethnic origin of the *ñáñigos*, establish the origin of their common and esoteric language, and put in context their attitudes and behavior in Cuba. Covering in detail many aspects of history, ritual, and language, the account assumes the criminality of the group, though this characteristic is not essential but "accidental." In other words, "although the original purposes of the secret ñáñigo group were not criminal," within the condition of the "colonial worker's existence, as if it were centrifugal," without "cohesion" or "family values," men joined this society. However, given the ties to the "distant African society" it recreated and the coercive "collective order" of the group, and under "menace of terrible mystical pain . . . the voluntary choice of the member disappeared" (1945:21). This, presumably, was the cause of the "despotism" many police and criminologists attributed to the atavistic *ñáñigos*, their indifference to social and legal codes, and the root of their criminality, inasmuch as members were obliged to defend their honor and their brothers in the group through killing.
9. Ironically, Verger returned to Cuba in 1957 (he had briefly passed through in 1936) in order to photograph Ernest Hemingway, who failed to "enchant" the Frenchman. He met Lydia Cabrera in Havana, and she took him to ceremonies and meetings with her sources (see Pivin and Saint Leon 1996:234).

12. We Were Teaching How to Ask the Black Man about Very Private, Personal Things: *Afrocubana*, the Triumph of the Revolution, and Socialist Folklore

1. María Teresa Linares, the widow of Argeliers León, made a gift of a copy of the limited-edition program to me in 1993.
2. This synthesis comes out of Katherine Hagedorn's dissertation (1995) research, a series of conversations we had about her work in 1999 and 2000, and her 2001 book.
3. By definition, the "intellectuals" were not, and could not be, *religiosos*, because religious adherents could not be in the Communist Party or occupy certain professions. This policy began to change around 1993, as the government began to cope with the social tensions produced by the Special Period of economic austerity and its great deprivations; some further relaxations in restrictions on religion seem to have come in 1998 around the pope's visit to Cuba. As of July 2000, for the first time in the Conjunto Folklórico's history, a black Cuban religious practitioner and scholar, Juan García, a founding veteran, became the group's director, replacing Teresa González.
4. For example, the house of the late Rigoberto Rodríguez Duque of Madruga, a Santería house, and that of Enrique Hernández Armenteros, a *babalawo*, *palero*, and Abakuá, feature rooms filled with lavish altars, dramatic performance spaces for drum dances, and a full calendar

of public events. State tour operators take busloads of tourists to these "ceremonies."

5. One American woman, a partially initiated priestess who visited Cuba in the early 1990s on a cultural tour, exclaimed in my presence, "You can see the *orishas everywhere* in Cuba, even on stages!"
6. This is particularly true with the famous Mario "Papo" Angarica, a *babalawo* and *olubatá* (master of drums). In the Conjunto Folklórico, Lázaro Ros and the late Librada Quesada became the "godparents" of many foreign dance students.
7. Grupo AfroCuba, however, recently added a piece with an equally generic title, "Bríkamo" (see table 12.1). Still, the song does derive from the unique tradition of the country's only Brícamo *cabildo*, in the city of Matanzas, the Cabildo Niño Jesús. That this *cabildo* and song are unique—that is, their tradition is not widespread—throws into relief just how generalizing such genre labels are.

13. "The Ethnographic Museum" and the Cuban Revolution

1. Personal communication with Rafael L. López Valdés, 8 May 1985.
2. Interview with Julían González Pérez Sr. and Antonio Martín de Armas Arredondo, 3 August 2000.
3. The Cuban postcards were put out by Ediciones Artex S.A., with photos by Roberto Salas. The Spanish postcards were put out by Ediciones JF, Madrid.
4. In a similar case of "rescuing" "positive folklore" versus eradicating "negative" folklore, the state, under ICAIC, has sponsored numerous ethnographic documentaries of Afro-Cuban ritual practices over the years. One of the earliest ostensible "documentaries" on Afro-Cuban religion, by the then young Octavio Cortázar, uses Russian montage techniques to juxtapose the painful grimaces and ostensibly unsalutary behavior of St. Lazarus's followers dragging themselves on the pavement in their pilgrimage toward his church with the smiling faces of Cuban children doing physical exercise on the beach (Cortázar 1968). Religion was thus cast as an opiate of the people and a brutal anachronism.
5. The U.S. State Department and a number of international human-rights organizations, such as Amnesty International, regularly report on the state of freedom of expression, assembly, and religion, focusing almost exclusively on Christian religion. See, for example, U.S. Department of State 1998; Amnesty International 2000; Human Rights Watch 1999.
6. Though listed in a well-known bibliography by Cuban researcher Tomás Fernández Robaina (1985:72–73), the journals do not turn up in Cuban stores or in collections outside of Cuba, but are confined to the National Library. Fernández Robaina and Derby cite "La sociedad secreta Abakuá [*ñáñigos*]. 1969. *Revista Jurídica Militar* (1):13–24" and "Los ñáñigos o abakuás. 1972. *Policía Nacional Revolucionaria,* revista 1, no. 3 (January–March): 2–16."
7. "This persistence of patriarchy was paradoxical in a revolution that imagined itself to be quintessentially modern; but in certain ways, the Castro regime was an old-fashioned family regime, with Fidel as father and leader" (Padula 1993:25).
8. Violence against blacks and suspected *brujos* was frequent in Regla during this period (see Palmié 2002: 241–242 and 343 n.35; also drawn from personal communications with Reglanos and Guanabacoenses, 2001).
9. If one wants to hear comments such as, "Blacks are lazy and unintelligent," they "screw up everything" including the practice of the Afro-Cuban religions, and the like, Regla is a good place to start.
10. Manuel Ibañez, Feliberto O'Farrill, Eustaquio Delgado, and Reinaldo Blayó formed the initial leadership of Ifá Ayer, Ifá Hoy, Ifá Mañana (Ifá Yesterday, Ifá Today, Ifá Tomorrow).
11. This account is based upon my interview with Lic. Raisa Formaguera, now a museologist at the Museum of Regla, 3 August 2000.
12. Records are slim or nonexistent. The confiscated pieces were rendered anonymous by the conditions of their "collection," and the former director of the Casa de Africa apparently took whatever research files there were out of the country when she left just before the mid-1990s.
13. Christopher Columbus is considered to be the first discoverer, Alexander von Humboldt the second, and, according to Rafael L. López Valdés, probably following the thoughts of Juan Marinello, Ortiz the third (Hagedorn 2001:138; see Marinello Vidaurreta 1989:563).
14. The Spaniard Antón Recio (sixteenth century; Marrero 1986, 13:39), was, according to the museum's director, the original owner of the lands on which the town of Regla was founded (1687). The museum owns objects that belonged to the descendants of Gonzalo Recio de Oquendo, a creole born in Havana who served as lieutenant governor during the English occupation of Havana (1762). Granted the title Marqués de la Real Proclamación in 1764, Gonzalo Recio was the inheritor of the *mayorazgo* (estate) of Antón Recio.
15. It is the Cabildo of the Virgin of Regla/Yemayá, founded

by Ño Remigio Herrera Adechina (ca. 1811–1905) and run by his daughter Josefa Herrera Echubí after his death until her death in 1947. The museum also set up a satellite space adjacent to the town's church with a permanent exhibition of Santería objects.

Using the museum's collection, Cosme has mounted special exhibitions and celebrations to the *cabildo*'s deceased African founders Ño Remigio Herrera Adechina, who is buried in the town's cemetery, and his daughter Josefa Herrera Echubí.

16. From Claude Lorrain (1600–1682), a French landscape painter who became famous in Rome for his landscape compositions, using foreground trees as framing, and a sensitivity to the power of light, which gave significance to foreground objects and groups and limned diaphanous backgrounds. Lorrain influenced the painters of the Hudson River school in the nineteenth century in the United States (see Read 1995:85–86).
17. See Museo de Bellas Artes de Bilbao 1998 for these four oil paintings, among others, produced in the late 1870s.

14. Conclusion: The Abakuá Society and the National Narrative

1. John Mason critiqued a presenter at the ACASA Triennial in Washington, D.C., in 1990.

References

Abrahams, Roger, and John Szwed. 1983. After the myth: Studying Afro-American cultural patterns in the plantation literature. In *The Man-of-Words in the West Indies: Performance and the Emergence of Creole Culture,* 40–54. Baltimore: Johns Hopkins University Press.

Aimes, H. H. S. 1905. African institutions in America. *Journal of American Folklore* 8:15–32.

Althusser, Louis. 1971. *Lenin and Philosophy and Other Essays.* Trans. Ben Brewster. New York: Monthly Review Press.

Amnesty International. 2000. Annual report, Cuba. www.web.amnesty.org/web/ar2000web.nsf.

Angarica, Nicolás Valentín. n.d. [1955]. *Manual de Orihaté: Religión lucumí.* Havana: N.p.

Anon. 1968. Slogans to be spread now by every means: Occupation committee of the People's Free Sorbonne University, Sorbonne, 16 May. Trans. Ken Knab. members.optusnet.com.au/~rkeehan/si/slogans.html.

Apostolos-Cappadona, D. 1994. *Dictionary of Christian Art.* New York: Continuum.

Appiah, Kwame Anthony. 1992. *In My Father's House: Africa in the Philosophy of Culture.* New York: Oxford University Press.

Apter, Andrew. 1991. Herskovits' heritage: Rethinking syncretism in the African diaspora. *Diaspora: A Journal of Transnational Studies* 1 (winter): 235–260.

———. 1992. *Black Critics and Kings: The Hermeneutics of Power in Yoruba Society.* Chicago: University of Chicago Press.

Ardener, Edwin. 1987. "Remote areas": Some theoretical considerations. In Anthony Jackson, ed., *Anthropology at Home,* 38–54. London: Tavistock.

Arens, W., and Ivan Karp, eds. 1989. *Creativity of Power: Cosmology and Action in African Societies.* Washington, D.C.: Smithsonian Institution Press.

Armstrong, Robert Plant. 1989. The etymology of the word "Ogun." In Sandra Barnes, ed., *Africa's Ogun: Old World and New,* 30–38. Bloomington: Indiana University Press.

Arnoldi, Mary Jo, Christine Mullen Kreamer, and Michael Atwood Mason. 2001. Reflections on "African Voices" at the Smithsonian's National Museum of Natural History. *African Arts* 34, no. 2 (summer): 16–17.

Asad, Talal, ed. 1973. *Anthropology and the Colonial Encounter.* New York: Humanities Press.

Ayala, César J. 1999. *American Sugar Kingdom: The Plantation Economy of the Spanish Caribbean, 1898–1934.* Chapel Hill: University of North Carolina Press.

Bakhtin, Mikhail M. 1981. *The Dialogic Imagination: Four Essays.* Ed. Michael Holquist. Austin: University of Texas Press.
Balandier, George. 1968. *Daily Life in the Kingdom of the Kongo, from the Sixteenth to the Eighteenth Century.* London: George Allen and Unwin.
Balea, Mirta. 1984. Guanabacoa museum, black roots: African slaves had a powerful influence on Cuban culture. *Prisma* 2, no. 16 (July): 24–26.
Barber, Karin. 1981. How man makes god in West Africa. *Africa* 5, no. 3: 724–744.
Baron, Robert. 1994. Africa in the Americas: Melville J. Herskovits' folkloristic and anthropological scholarship, 1923–41. Ph.D. diss., University of Pennsylvania.
Barth, Fredrik, ed. 1969. *Ethnic Groups and Boundaries: The Social Organization of Culture Difference.* Bergen, Oslo, and London: Universitets Forlaget and George Allen.
Barthes, Roland. 1972. *Mythologies.* Trans. Annette Lavers. New York: Farrar, Straus & Giroux.
Bastide, Roger. 1972. *African Civilizations in the New World.* Trans. Peter Green. New York: Harper and Row.
———. 1978. *The African Religions of Brazil: Toward a Sociology of the Interpenetration of Civilizations.* Trans. Helen Sebba. Baltimore: Johns Hopkins University Press.
Bauman, Richard, and Charles L. Briggs. 1990. Poetics and performance as critical perspectives on language and social life. *Annual Review of Anthropology* 19:59–88.
Bell, Catherine. 1992. *Ritual Practice, Ritual Theory.* New York: Oxford University Press.
Benítez-Rojo, Antonio. 1992. *The Repeating Island: The Caribbean in Postmodern Perspective.* Trans. James E. Maraniss. Durham, N.C.: Duke University Press.
Bettelheim, Judith, ed. 1993. *Cuban Festivals with Annotated Glossary: The Afro-Cuban Festival "Day of Kings."* New York: Garland.
Blanc, Giulio V., ed. 1992. *Wifredo Lam and His Contemporaries.* New York: The Studio Museum in Harlem.
Blassingame, John. 1972. *The Slave Community: Plantation Life in the Antebellum South.* New York.
Blier, Suzanne. 1995. *African Vodun: Art, Psychology, and Power.* Chicago: University of Chicago Press.
Borrás, María Luisa. 1996. Breve panorama de la pintura cubana. In *Cuba siglo XX: Modernidad y sincretismo,* 25–42, 357–363. La Palma: Centro Atlántico de Arte Moderno.
Bourdieu, Pierre. 1977. *Outline of a Theory of Practice.* Trans. Richard Nice. Cambridge: Cambridge University Press.
———. 1984. *Distinction: A Social Critique of the Judgment of Taste.* Trans. Richard Nice. Cambridge, Mass.: Harvard University Press.
Brands, H. W. 2000. *The First American: The Life and Times of Benjamin Franklin.* New York: Doubleday.
Brown, David H. 1989. Garden in the machine: Afro-Cuban Sacred art and performance in urban New Jersey and New York. Ph.D. diss., Yale University.
———. 1993a. Annotated glossary for Fernando Ortiz's *The Afro-Cuban Festival "Day of the Kings."* In Judith Bettelheim, ed., *Cuban Festivals with Annotated Glossary: The Afro-Cuban Festival "Day of Kings,"* 49–98. New York: Garland.
———. 1993b. Thrones of the Orichas: Afro-Cuban altars in New Jersey, New York, and Havana. *African Arts* 26, no. 4: 44–59, 85–87.
———. 1996. Toward an ethnoaesthetics of Santería ritual arts: The practice of altar-making and gift-exchange. In Arturo Lindsay, ed., *Santería Aesthetics in Contemporary Latin American Art,* 77–148. Washington, D.C.: Smithsonian Institution Press.
———. 2003. *Santería Enthroned: Art, Ritual, and Innovation in an Afro-Cuban Religion.* Chicago: University of Chicago Press.
Browning, Barbara. 1995. *Samba: Resistance in Motion.* Bloomington: Indiana University Press.
Bustamante, Juan A. 1957. El sacrificio totémico en el baroko ñáñigo. *Revista Bimestre Cubana* 73:29–63.
Butler, Judith, 1990. *Gender Trouble: Feminism and the Subversion of Identity.* New York : Routledge.
———. 1997. *Excitable Speech: A Politics of the Performative.* New York: Routledge.
Cabrera, Lydia. 1940. *Cuentos negros de Cuba.* Havana: La Verónica.
———. 1942. Un gran pintor: Wifredo Lam. *Diario de la Marina,* 17 May.
———. 1943. Wifredo Lam. *Diario de la Marina,* 17 May.
———. 1944. Wifredo Lam. *Diario de la Marina,* 30 January.
———. 1946. Catálogo de la primera exposición de Wifredo Lam en Cuba. *Lyceum,* 11–19 April.
———. 1947. Eggüe o Vichichi Nfinda. *Revista Bimestre Cubana* LX, 2d semester: 47–120.
———. 1954. *El Monte; Igbo, Finda; Ewe Orisha, Vititi Nfinda (Notas sobre las religiones, la magia, las supersticiones y el folklore de los negros criollos y del pueblo de Cuba).* Havana: Ediciones C. R.
———. 1957. *Anagó: Vocabulario lucumí (el yoruba que se habla en Cuba).* Havana: Ediciones C. R.
———. 1958. *La sociedad secreta abakuá: Narrada por viejos adeptos.* Havana: Ediciones C. R.
———. 1970. *La sociedad secreta abakuá: Narrada por viejos adeptos.* Miami: Ediciones C. R.

———. 1973. *La laguna sagrada de San Joaquín.* Miami: Ediciones Universal.
———. 1975. *Anaforuana: Ritual y símbolos de la iniciación en la sociedad secreta abakuá.* Madrid: Ediciones R.
———. 1980a. *Koeko Iyawó, aprende novicia: Pequeño tratado de la regla lucumí.* Miami: Ediciones C. R.
———. 1980b. *Yemayá y Ochún: Kariocha, iyalorichas y olorichas.* Miami: Ediciones C. R.
———. 1983. *El Monte; Igbo, Finda; Ewe Orisha, Vititi Nfinda: Notas sobre las religiones, la magia, las supersticiones y el folklore de los negros criollos y del pueblo de Cuba.* Miami: Colección del Chicherekú.
———. 1986a. *La Regla Kimbisa del Santo Cristo del Buen Viaje.* Miami: Ediciones Universal.
———. 1986b. *Reglas de Congo, Palo Monte, Mayombe.* Miami: Colección del Chicherikú en exilo.
———. 1988. *Lengua sagrada de los ñáñigos.* Miami: Colección del Chicherekú en el exilo.
———. 1993. *La laguna sagrada de San Joaquín.* Miami: Ediciones Universal.
———. 1994. Calixta. In Isabel Castellanos, ed., *Lydia Cabrera: Páginas sueltas,* 207–211. Miami: Ediciones Universal.
Cabrera, Lydia, and Josefina Tarafa. 2001a. *Havana, Cuba, ca. 1957: Rhythms and Songs for the Orishas.* CD. Washington, D.C.: Smithsonian Folkways Recordings.
———. 2001b. *Matanzas, Cuba, ca. 1957: Afro-Cuban Sacred Music from the Countryside.* CD. Washington, D.C.: Smithsonian Folkways Recordings.
Camnitzer, Luis. 1994. *New Art of Cuba.* Austin: University of Texas Press.
Caribbean Quarterly. 1956. Vol. 4, nos. 3 and 4 (March/June): 263–274.
Carpentier, Alejo. 1933. *Ecue Yamba O!* Madrid: Editorial España.
———. 1946. *La música en Cuba.* México: Fondo de Cultura Económica.
———. 1989. Reflexiones acerca de la pintura de Wifredo Lam. *Alcance a la revista de la Biblioteca Nacional José Martí* 3:99.
Castellanos, Isabel M. 1977. The use of language in Afro-Cuban religion. Ph.D. diss., Georgetown University.
Castellanos, Israel. 1916. *La brujería y el ñáñiguismo en Cuba desde el punto de vista médico-legal.* Havana: Lloredo.
———. 1928. El "diablito" Ñáñigo. *Archivos del Folklore Cubano* 3, no. 4: 27–37.
———. 1937. *Medicina legal y criminologia afro-cubanas.* Havana: Molina.
Castro, Fidel. 1980. Palabras a los intelectuales. In Víctor López Lemus, ed., *Revolución, letras, arte,* 7–33. Havana: Editorial Letras Cubanas.
Cerny, Charlene, and Suzanne Seriff, eds. 1996. *Recycled, Re-Seen: Folk Art from the Global Scrap Heap.* New York: Harry N. Abrams.
Chambers, Douglas B. 1997. "My own nation": Igbo exiles in the Diaspora. In David Eltis and David Richardson, eds., *Routes to Slavery: Direction, Ethnicity and Mortality in the Atlantic Slave Trade,* 72–98. London: Frank Cass.
Chapman, William Ryan. 1985. Arranging ethnology: A. H. L. F. Pitt Rivers and the typological tradition. In George Stocking, ed., *Objects and Others: Essays on Museums and Material Culture,* 15–48. Madison: University of Wisconsin Press.
Chávez Álvarez, Ernesto. 1991. *El crimen de la niña Cecilia: La brujería en Cuba como fenómeno social (1902–1925).* Havana: Editorial de Ciéncias Sociales.
Clarke, Juan M. 1981. *The 1980 Mariel Exodus: An Assessment and Prospect—A Special Report.* Washington, D.C.: Council for Interamerican Security.
Clifford, James. 1988. *The Predicament of Culture: Twentieth-Century Ethnography, Literature, and Art.* Cambridge, Mass.: Harvard University Press.
———. 1994. Diasporas. *Cultural Anthropology* 9(3):302–338.
Cohen, David William. 1994. *The Combing of History.* Chicago: University of Chicago Press.
Colpe, Carsten. 1987. Syncretism. In Mircea Eliade, ed., *The Encyclopedia of Religion,* 218–227. New York: Macmillan.
Comaroff, Jean. 1985. *Body of Power, Spirit of Resistance: The Culture and History of a South African People.* Chicago: University of Chicago Press.
Consejo Nacional de Cultura. 1963. *Conjunto folklórico nacional.* La Habana: Gobierno del Estado.
Corporación Nacional del Turismo. 1950. *La pintura colonial en Cuba: Exposición en el capitolio nacional.* La Habana: Corporación Nacional del Turismo.
Cortázar, Octavio. 1968. *Acerca de un personaje que unos llaman San Lázaro y otros llaman Babalú.* Film. Havana: Instituto Cubano del Arte e Industria Cinematográficos (ICAIC).
Cosentino, Donald J. 1995a. Introduction: Imagine heaven. In Donald J. Cosentino, ed., *Sacred Arts of Vodou,* 25–55. Los Angeles: Fowler Museum of Cultural History.
———. 1995b. It's all for you, Sen Jak! In Donald J. Cosentino, ed., *Sacred Arts of Vodou,* 243–263. Los Angeles: Fowler Museum of Cultural History.
Cosme Baños, Pedro. 1998. *Los chinos en Regla.* Santiago de Cuba: Editorial Oriente.
Courlander, Harold. 1944. Abakua meeting in Guanabacoa. *Journal of Negro History* XXIX (October): 461–470.

———. 1976. *A Treasury of Afro-American Folklore.* New York: Crown.
———. 1990. Recollections of Haiti in the 1930s and '40s. *African Arts* XXIII (April): 60–70.
Dallas Museum of Art. 1989. *Black Art, Ancestral Legacy: The African Impulse in African-American Art.* Dallas: Dallas Museum of Art.
Dayrell, Elphinstone. 1910. Some "nsibidi" signs. *Man* 67: 112–114.
———. 1911. Further notes on nsibidi signs with their meanings from the Ikon District, Southern Nigeria. *Journal of the Royal Anthropological Institute* XLI: 521–540.
D'Azevedo, Warren L., ed. 1973. *The Traditional Artist in African Society.* Bloomington: Indiana University Press.
Debord, Guy, and Gianfranco Sanguinetti. 1972. Theses on the Situationist International and its time. Trans. Christopher Winks. http://members.optusnet.com.au/~rkeehan/si/sistime.html.
Derby, Lauren. 1995. Research report (on Afro-Cuban cultures and criminological discourse). Unpublished paper.
Deschamps Chapeaux, Pedro. 1964. Margarito Blanco: Ocongo de Ultán. *Boletín del Instituto de Historia del Archivo Nacional* LXV (July–December): 97.
———. 1968. Cabildos: Solo para esclavos. *Cuba: Revista Mensual* (January): 50–51.
———. 1969. Marcas tribales de los esclavos en Cuba. *Etnología y Folklore* 8 (July–December): 65–78.
Desmangles, Leslie G. 1992. *The Faces of the Gods: Vodou and Roman Catholicism in Haiti.* Chapel Hill: University of North Carolina Press.
Dixon, Heriberto. 1983. An overview of the black Cubans among the Mariel entrants. ERIC Documents (ED 233104).
———. 1986. The Cuban-American counterpoint: Black Cubans in the United States. Paper delivered at the International Symposium on the Cultural Expression of Hispanics in the United States (Paris, 12 March).
Douglas, Mary. 1978. *Purity and Danger: An Analysis of Concepts of Pollution and Taboo.* London: Routledge and Kegan Paul.
Drake Boehm, Barbara. 1995. Altar (portable altar). In J. Turner, ed., *Dictionary of Art,* 697–700. New York: Grove Press.
Drewal, Henry, John I. Pemberton, and Roland Abiodun. 1989. *Yoruba: Nine Centuries of African Art and Thought.* New York: Center for African Art and Harry N. Abrams.
Drewal, Margaret. 1992. *Yoruba Ritual: Performers, Play, Agency.* Bloomington: Indiana University Press.
Dumont, Henri. 1915–16. Antropología y patología comparada de los negros esclavos. *Revista Bimestre Cubana* 10, no. 3 (May–June 1915); 11, no 2 (March–April 1916).
———. 1922. *Antropología y patología comparada de los negros esclavos.* Israel Castellanos, trans. Havana: Colección Cubana de Libros y Documentos Ineditados o Raros.
Dumoulin, John. 1962. The participative art of the Afrocuban religions. *Abhandlungen und Berichte des Staatlichen Museums fur Volkerkund* 21:63–67.
Eliade, Mircea. 1959. *The Sacred and the Profane: The Nature of Religion.* Trans. W. R. Trask. New York: Harcourt Brace.
Ellis, Keith. 1998. Nicolás Guillén and Langston Hughes: Convergences and divergences. In Lisa Brock and Digna Castañeda Fuertes, eds., *Between Race and Empire: African-Americans and Cubans before the Cuban Revolution,* 129–167. Philadelphia: Temple University Press.
Eltis, David, and David Richardson. 1997. West Africa and the transatlantic slave trade: New evidence of long-run trends. In David Eltis and David Richardson, eds., *Routes to Slavery: Direction, Ethnicity and Mortality in the Atlantic Slave Trade,* 16–35. London: Frank Cass.
Fabian, Johannes. 1983. *Time and the Other: How Anthropology Makes Its Object.* New York: Columbia University Press.
Fernández, Antonio Elígio ("Tonel"). 1999. Tree of many beaches: Cuban art in motion (1980s–1990s). In Marilyn A. Zeitlin, ed., *Contemporary Art from Cuba: Irony and Survival on the Utopian Island,* 39–52. Tempe and New York: Arizona State University Art Museum and Delano Greenridge Editions.
Fernández, Damián J. 1993. Youth in Cuba: Resistance and accommodation. In Enrique A. Baloryra and James A. Morris, eds., *Conflict and Change in Cuba,* 189–214. Albuquerque: University of New Mexico Press.
Fernández Carrillo, Enrique. 1881. El Ñáñigo: Carta cerrada y abierta. In Víctor Patricio de Landaluze, *Tipos y costumbres de la isla de Cuba,* 141–145. Havana: Miguel de Villa.
Fernández Robaina, Tomás, ed. 1985. *Bibliografía de temas afrocubanos.* Havana: Ministry of Culture, José Martí National Library.
Fischer, Sibylle. 1997. Sketches of a colony: Cuba in the 1800s. Paper presented to the Black Atlantic Project Seminar at the Rutgers Center for Historical Analysis, October 28.
Forde, Daryll, ed. 1956. *Efik Traders of Old Calabar.* London: International African Institute.
Foucault, Michel. 1979. *Discipline and Punish: The Birth of the Prison.* Trans. A. Sheridan. New York: Random House.
Fouchet, Max-Pol. 1986. *Wifredo Lam.* Trans. Kenneth Lyons. Barcelona: Ediciones Polígrafa.
Franco, Pamela. 2001. Shifting ground: An early history of Afro-creole women's mas' in Trinidad Carnival. Ph.D. diss., Emory University.

Frazer, Valerie. 1995. Jesuit order (Latin America; missions). In J. Turner, ed., *Dictionary of Art,* 17:513–514. New York: Grove Press.
Freyre, Gilberto. 1986. *The Masters and the Slaves: A Study in the Development of Brazilian Civilization.* Trans. Samuel Putnam. Berkeley: University of California Press.
Gardner's Art through the Ages. 1997. Eds. Richard G. Tansey and Fred S. Kleiner. Fort Worth: Harcourt Brace.
Gates, Henry Louis, Jr. 1988. *The Signifying Monkey: A Theory of African American Literary Criticism.* New York: Oxford University Press.
Geertz, Clifford. 1973. *The Interpretation of Cultures.* New York: Basic Books.
———. 1983. *Local Knowledge: Further Essays in Interpretive Anthropology.* New York: Basic Books.
Genovese, Eugene. 1976. *Roll Jordan Roll: The World the Slaves Made.* New York: Vintage Books.
Giddens, Anthony. 1976. *New Rules of Sociological Method: A Positive Critique of Interpretive Sociologies.* New York: Basic Books.
Gilroy, Paul. 1993. *The Black Atlantic: Modernity and Double Consciousness.* Cambridge, Mass.: Harvard University Press.
Ginzburg, Carlo. 1980. *The Cheese and the Worms: The Cosmos of a Sixteenth-Century Miller.* Trans. J. Tedeschi and A. Tedeschi. Baltimore: Johns Hopkins University Press.
Gleason, Judith. 1992. *Oyá: In Praise of the African Goddess.* New York: HarperCollins.
Gómez, Michael. 1998. *Exchanging Our Country Marks: The Transformation of African Identities in the Colonial and Antebellum South.* Chapel Hill: University of North Carolina Press.
———. 1999. African identity and slavery in the Americas. *Radical History Review* 75:111–120.
Goodall, Joan A. 1995. Regalia. In J. Turner, ed., *Dictionary of Art,* 26:77–83. New York: Grove Press.
Grupo AfroCuba de Matanzas. 1993. *Rituales afrocubanos.* CD. Havana: Egrem Studios.
———. 1996. *Raíces africanas/African Roots.* CD. Havana and New York: Egrem Studios/Shanachie.
Grupo Yorubá Andabo. 1998. *Del yoruba al son: La isla de la música,* vol. 6. CD. México: Universal Music/Magic Music.
Hagedorn, Katherine J. 1995. *Anatomía del proceso folklórico:* The "folkloricization" of African based religious traditions in Cuba. Ph.D. diss., Brown University.
———. 2001. *Divine Utterances: The Performance of Afro-Cuban Santería.* Washington, D.C.: Smithsonian Institution Press.
Hall, Stuart. 1977. Culture, the media, and the "ideological effect." In J. Curran, M. Gurevitch, and J. Woolacott, eds., *Mass Communications and Society,* 315–347. Beverly Hills: Sage.
Hardin, Kris L. 1993. *The Aesthetics of Action: Continuity and Change in a West African Town.* Washington, D.C.: Smithsonian Institution Press.
Hebdige, Dick. 1979. *Subculture: The Meaning of Style.* London: Methuen.
Helg, Aline. 1995. *Our Rightful Share: The Afro-Cuban Struggle for Equality, 1886–1912.* Chapel Hill: University of North Carolina Press.
Hemeldonck, G. V. 1995. Ciborium. In J. Turner, ed., *Dictionary of Art,* 7:299–304. New York: Grove Press.
Herskovits, Melville J. 1941. *The Myth of the Negro Past.* New York: Harper and Brothers.
———. 1958. Preface to the Beacon Press edition of *The Myth of the Negro Past.* Boston: Beacon Press.
———. 1966. African gods and Catholic saints in New World Negro belief. In Francis S. Herskovits, ed., *The New World Negro: Selected Papers in Afroamerican Studies,* 321–329. Bloomington: Indiana University Press.
Herzberg, Julia P. 1992. Wifredo Lam: The development of a style and world view—the Havana years, 1941–1952. In Giulio V. Blanc, ed., *Wifredo Lam and His Contemporaries,* 31–52. New York: The Studio Museum in Harlem.
Hill, Errol. 1972. *Trinidad Carnival: Mandate for a National Theater.* Austin: University of Texas Press.
Houlberg, Marilyn H. 1983. The texture of change: Yoruba cultural responses to new media. *Cultural Survival Quarterly* 7 (summer): 14–16.
Howard, Deborah. 1995. Jesuit order (iconography). In J. Turner, ed., *Dictionary of Art,* 509–510. New York: Grove Press.
Human Rights Watch. 1999. *Cuba's Repressive Machinery: Human Rights Forty Years after the Revolution.* New York: HRW Publications.
Hurston, Zora Neale. 1935. *Mules and Men.* Philadelphia: J. B. Lippincott.
Intar Gallery. 1984. *Lydia Cabrera: An Intimate Portrait.* New York: Intar Gallery.
Jackson, Michael. 1989. *Paths toward a Clearing: Radical Empiricism and Ethnographic Inquiry.* Bloomington: Indiana University Press.
Jackson, Walter. 1986. Herskovits and the search for Afro-American culture. In George W. Stocking, Jr., ed., *Malinowski, Rivers, Benedict and Others: Essays on Culture and Personality,* 95–126. Madison: University of Wisconsin Press.
Jacobson, Matthew Frye. 1998. *Whiteness of a Different Color: European Immigrants and the Alchemy of Race.* Cambridge, Mass.: Harvard University Press.

Janzen, John. 1978. *The Quest for Therapy: Medical Pluralism in Lower Zaire.* Berkeley: University of California Press.

Jones, G. I. 1988. The Niger-Cross River hinterlands and their masks. In Sidney Kasfir, ed., *West African Masks and Cultural Systems,* 126:123–150. Tervuren: Koninklijk Museum voor Midden-Africa.

Karp, Ivan, and Steven D. Lavine, eds. 1990. *Exhibiting Cultures: The Poetics and Politics of Museum Display.* Washington, D.C.: Smithsonian Institution Press.

Kasfir, Sidney. 1988. Introduction: Masquerading as a cultural system. In Sidney Kasfir, ed., *West African Masks and Cultural Systems,* 126:1–16. Tervuren: Koninklijk Museum voor Midden-Africa.

Kelly, John D., and Martha Kaplan. 1990. History, structure, and ritual. *Annual Review of Anthropology* 19:119–149.

Kirshenblatt-Gimblett, Barbara. 1983. The future of folklore studies in America: The urban frontier. *Folklore Forum* 16, no. 1 (winter): 185–234.

Kopytoff, Igor. 1986. The cultural biography of things: Commoditization as process. In Arjun Appadurai, ed., *The Social Life of Things: Commodities in Cultural Perspective,* 64–94. Cambridge: Cambridge University Press.

Kutzinski, Vera M. 1993. *Sugar's Secrets: Race and the Erotics of Cuban Nationalism.* Charlottesville: University Press of Virginia.

Kuyk, Betty M. 1983. The African derivation of black fraternal orders in the United States. *Comparative Studies in Society and History* 25, no. 4: 559–592.

Lachatañeré, Rómulo. 1938. *"Oh, Mío Yemayá!"* Havana: n.p.

———. 1942. *Manual de santería (el sistema de cultos lucumís).* La Habana: Editorial Caribe.

———. 1961. Las creencias religiosas de los afrocubanos y la falsa aplicación del término brujería. *Actas del Folklore* 1, no. 5: 11–15.

Laman, Karl. 1962. *The Kongo.* III. Uppsala: Almqvist and Wiksells.

Lamerán, Sara. 1982. *Guía de estudio: El vestuario y su importancia en la danza.* Havana: Ministerio de Cultura, Editorial Pueblo y Educación.

Landaluze, Víctor Patricio. 1881. *Tipos y costumbres de la isla de Cuba.* Havana: Miguel de Villa.

Latham, A. J. H. 1973. *Old Calabar: 1600–1891.* Oxford: Clarendon Press.

Lawal, Babatunde. 1974. Some aspects of Yoruba aesthetics. *British Journal of Aesthetics* 14, no. 3 (summer): 239–249.

———. 1996. From Africa to the Americas: Art in Yoruba religion. In Arturo Lindsay, ed., *Santería Aesthetics in Contemporary Latin American Art,* 3–38. Washington, D.C.: Smithsonian Institution Press.

Leib, Elliot, and Renee Romano. 1984. Reign of the leopard: Ngbe ritual. *African Arts* 18, no. 1: 48–56, 95, 96.

León, Argeliers. 1964. Concierto de música Abakuá. Playbill. Havana: Consejo de la Cultura.

———. 1984. *Del canto y el tiempo.* Havana: Editorial Letras Cubanas.

Levine, Lawrence. 1977. *Black Culture and Black Consciousness: Afro-American Folk Thought from Slavery to Freedom.* Oxford: Oxford University Press.

Lévi-Strauss, Claude. 1966. *The Savage Mind.* Chicago: University of Chicago Press.

Limerick, Patricia Nelson. 2002. The Smithsonian scandal that wasn't. History News Network, 22 February (http://hnn.us/articles/748.html).

Linebaugh, Peter, and Marcus Rediker. 2000. *The Many-Headed Hydra: Sailors, Slaves, Commoners, and the Hidden History of the Revolutionary Atlantic.* Boston: Beacon Press.

Lipsitz, George. 1990. Mardi Gras Indians: Carnival and counternarrative in black New Orleans. In *Time Passages: Collective Memory and American Popular Culture,* 233–256. Minneapolis: University of Minnesota Press.

López Valdés, Rafael L. 1985. La sociedad secreta abakuá en un grupo de trabajadores portuarios. In *Componentes africanos en el étnos cubano,* 151–185. Havana: Editorial de Ciencias Sociales.

———. 1987. Las religiones de origen africano en Cuba: Tiempos y conjugaciones. Unpublished paper.

Los Muñequitos de Matanzas. 1992a. *Congo Yambumba.* CD. New York: QBADISC.

———. 1992b. *Rumba caliente 88/77.* CD. Havana: Egrem Studios.

Lovejoy, Paul, and David Richardson. 1999. Trust, pawnship, and Atlantic history: The institutional foundations of the Old Calabar slave trade. *American History Review* 104, no. 2: 331–355.

———. "Pawns will live when slaves is apt to dye": Credit, risk, and trust at Old Calabar in the era of the slave trade. Unpublished manuscript.

Lumsden, Ian. 1996. *Machos, Maricones, and Gays: Cuba and Homosexuality.* Philadelphia: Temple University Press.

MacGaffey, Wyatt. 1986. *Religion and Society in Central Africa: The Bakongo of Lower Zaire.* Chicago: University of Chicago Press.

———. 1988. Complexity, astonishment and power: The visual vocabulary of Kongo minkisi. *Journal of Southern African Studies* 14, no. 2 (January): 188–203.

———, and Michael Harris. 1993. *Astonishment and Power.* Washington, D.C.: Smithsonian Institution Press.

MacGregor, Rev. J. K. 1909. Some notes on *nsibidi*. *Journal of the Royal Anthropological Institute* XXXIX: 209–219.
Magiciens de la terre. 1989. Paris: Centre Pompidou.
Malinowski, Bronislaw. 1948. *Magic, Science and Religion and Other Essays.* Garden City, N.Y.: Doubleday.
———. 1961. *Argonauts of the Western Pacific: An Account of Native Enterprise and Adventure in the Archipelagos of Melanesian New Guinea.* New York: E. P. Dutton.
Marinello Vidaurreta, Juan. 1989. *Cuba: Cultura.* Havana: Editorial Letras Cubanas.
Martín, Juan L. 1945. *Mutiaroco: Sanga recobebá—Los elementos esotéricos del ñañiguismo.* Havana: Editorial Atalaya.
Martínez, Juan. 1994. *Cuban Art and National Identity: The Vanguardia Painters, 1927–1950.* Gainesville: University Press of Florida.
Martínez-Alier, Vera. 1974. *Marriage, Class and Color in Nineteenth-Century Cuba: A Study of Racial Attitudes and Sexual Values in a Slave Society.* Ann Arbor: University of Michigan Press.
Martínez Furé, R. 1979. *Diálogos imaginarios.* Havana: Editorial Arte y Literatura.
Mason, John. 1992. *Orin Òrìṣà: Songs for Selected Heads.* Brooklyn: Yoruba Theological Archministry.
Mason, John, and Gary Edwards. 1985a. *Black Gods: Orisa Studies in the New World.* Brooklyn: Yoruba Theological Archministry.
———. 1985b. *Four New World Yoruba Rituals.* Brooklyn: Yoruba Theological Archministry.
Mason, Michael A. 1997. Practicing santería, performing the self: The social construction of subjectivity in humans and gods in an Afro-Cuban religion. Ph.D. diss., Indiana University.
———. 2002. *Living Santería: Rituals and Experiences in an Afro-Cuban Religion.* Washington, D.C.: Smithsonian Institution Press.
McEvilley, Thomas. 1984. Doctor lawyer Indian chief: "Primitivism in 20th century art" at the Museum of Modern Art in 1984. *Art Forum* (November): 54–60.
Métraux, Alfred. 1972. *Voodoo in Haiti.* Trans. H. Charteris. New York: Schocken Books.
Meza y Suárez Inclán, Ramón. 1891. El día de reyes. *Habana Elegante* 5, no. 2 (January 11).
Mintz, Sidney W., and Richard Price. 1992. *The Birth of African-American Culture: An Anthropological Perspective.* Boston: Beacon Press.
Mola Fernández, Claudia. La Casa de Africa. Brochure. N.p.
Moliner Castañeda, Israel. 1988. Los ñáñigos. *Del Caribe* 5, no. 12: 13–18.
Moore, Carlos. 1986. Congo or Carabalí: Race relations in socialist Cuba. *Caribbean Review* 15, no. 2 (spring): 12–15, 43.
———. 1988. *Castro, the Blacks, and Africa.* Los Angeles: University of California Center for Afro-American Studies.
Moore, Robin D. 1997. *Nationalizing Blackness: Afrocubanismo and Artistic Revolution in Havana, 1920–1940.* Pittsburgh: University of Pittsburgh Press.
Moreno, Denis. 1988. *Un tambor arará.* Havana: Editorial de Ciencias Sociales.
Morgan, Philip D. 1997. The cultural implications of the Atlantic slave trade: African regional origins, American destinations and New World developments. In David Eltis and David Richardson, eds., *Routes to Slavery: Direction, Ethnicity, and Mortality in the Atlantic Slave Trade,* 122–145. London: Frank Cass.
Mosquera, Gerardo. 1996a. Elegguá at the (post?)modern crossroads: The presence of Africa in the visual arts of Cuba. In Arturo Lindsay, ed., *Santería Aesthetics in Contemporary Latin American Art,* 225–258. Washington, D.C.: Smithsonian Institution Press.
———. 1996b. Towards a different postmodernity: Africa in Cuban art. In *Cuba Siglo XX: Modernidad y sincretismo,* 391–411. Las Palmas: Centro Atlántico de Arte Moderno.
Mullen, Edward J. 1987. *Los negros brujos:* A reexamination of the text. *Cuban Studies* 17:111–132.
Murphy, Joseph. 1988. *Santería: An African Religion in America.* Boston: Beacon Press.
Museo de Bellas Artes de Bilbao. 1998. *Víctor Patricio Landaluze, Colleción Museo Nacional de Bellas Artes de la Habana.* Bilbao: Museo de Bellas Artes.
Nelson, Robert S., and Richard Shiff, eds. 1996. *Critical Terms for Art History.* Chicago: University of Chicago Press.
Nettleford, Rex M. 1978. *Caribbean Cultural Identity: The Case of Jamaica—A Case of Cultural Dynamics.* Kingston: Institute of Jamaica.
Nicklin, Keith. 1991. An Ejagham emblem of the Ekpe society. *Tribal Art* (Musée Barbier-Mueller): 3–18.
Nicklin, Keith, and Jill Salmons. 1988. *Ikem:* The history of a masquerade in southeast Nigeria. In Sidney Kasfir, ed., *West African Masks and Cultural Systems,* 126:123–150. Tervuren: Koninklijk Museum voor Midden-Africa.
Numismatic Guaranty Corporation. 2001. NGC photo proof series—1946 Roosevelt dime. http://www.coinsite.com/CoinSite-PF/PParticles/10croos.htm.
Omari, Mikelle Smith. 1984. *From the Inside to the Outside: The Art and Ritual of the Bahian Candomblé.* Los Angeles: University of California Museum of Cultural History.
Ong, Walter. 1982. *Orality and Literacy: The Technologizing of the Word.* London: Methuen.

Ortiz, Fernando. 1906. *Los negros brujos: Apuntes para un estudio de etnología criminal.* Havana: Librería Santa Fe.

———. 1914. Alfonso Bertillón y su sistema antropométrico. *La Reforma Social* 1, no. 1 (April): 7–25.

———. 1916. *Hampa afro-cubana. Los negros esclavos; estudio sociológico y de derecho público.* Havana: Revista Bimestre Cubana.

———. 1920. La fiesta afrocubana del "Día de Reyes." *Revista Bimestre Cubana* 15, no. 1 (January–June): 5–26.

———. 1921. Los cabildos afrocubanos. *Revista Bimestre Cubana* 16, no. 1: 5–39.

———. 1923. La cocina afrocubana. *Revista Bimestre Cubana* 18, no. 6: 401–423.

———. 1924a. *Glosario de afronegrismos.* Havana: Imprenta "El Siglo XX."

———. 1924b. Personajes del folklore afrocubano. *Archivos del Folklore Cubano* 1, no. 1: 62–75; no. 2: 116–119.

———. 1938. La música sagrada de los negros yorubá en Cuba. *Estudios Afrocubanos* 2, no. 1: 80–104.

———. 1939. Brujos o santeros. *Estudios Afrocubanos* 3, no. 3: 85–90.

———. 1940. *Contrapunteo cubano del tabaco y el azúcar: Advertencia de sus contrastes agrarios, económicos, históricos y sociales, su etnografía y su transculturación.* Havana: Jesús Montero.

———. 1947. *Cuban Counterpoint: Tobacco and Sugar.* New York: Alfred A. Knopf.

———. 1950a. *La africanía de la música folklórica de Cuba.* Havana: Ministerio de Educación, Dirección de Cultura.

———. 1950b. La tragedia de los ñáñigos. *Cuadernos Americanos* IX, no. 4 (July–August): 79–101.

———. 1950c. Wifredo Lam y so obra vista a través de significados críticos. *Cuadernos de Arte* 1. Havana: Ministerio de Educación, Dirección de Cultura.

———. 1951. *Los bailes y el teatro de los negros en el folklore de Cuba.* Havana: Ediciones Cardenas y Cia.

———. 1952–55. *Los instrumentos de la música afrocubana.* Havana: Publicaciones de la Dirección de la Cultura del Ministerio de Educación.

———. 1952. *Los instrumentos de la música afrocubana,* vol. II. Havana: Publicaciones de la Dirección de la Cultura del Ministerio de Educación.

———. 1953. Dos "diablitos" de Landaluze. *Bohemia* 45: 36–38, 99–101.

———. 1954. *Los instrumentos de la música afrocubana,* vol. IV. Havana: Publicaciones de la Dirección de la Cultura del Ministerio de Educación.

———. 1955. *Los instrumentos de la música afrocubana,* vol. V. Havana: Publicaciones de la Dirección de la Cultura del Ministerio de Educación.

———. 1960. *La antigua fiesta afrocubana del "Día de Reyes."* Havana: Ministerio de Relaciones Exteriores, Departamento de Asuntos Culturales, División de Publicaciones.

———. 1973. *Los negros brujos: Apuntes para un estudio de etnología criminal.* Miami: Ediciones Universal.

———. 1987. *Los negros esclavos.* Havana: Editorial de Ciencias Sociales.

Pacheco de Amorim, F. 1934. *Catálogo-inventario del Museu de Etnografia do Ultramar.* Coimbra: Institutu de Antropologia da Universidade de Coimbra.

Padula, Alan. 1993. Cuban socialism: Thirty years of controversy. In Enrique A. Baloryra and James A. Morris, eds., *Conflict and Change in Cuba,* 15–37. Albuquerque: University of New Mexico Press.

Palmié, Stephan. 1993. Ethnogenetic processes and cultural transfer in Afro-American slave populations. In W. Binder, ed., *Slavery in the Americas,* 337–363. Würtzburg: Königshausen u. Neumann.

———. 1994. Some notes on space, time, and units of analysis in the historiography of Ekpe/Abakuá. Paper presented at the Centre for African Studies and Latin American Studies Centre, University of London, 7 October 1994.

———. 1997. Ekpe/Abakuá in the Middle Passage. Unpublished manuscript.

———. 1998. Fernando Ortiz and the cooking of history. *Ibero-Amerikanisches Archiv* 24, nos. 3–4: 353–373.

———. 2002. *Wizards and Scientists: Explorations in Afro-Cuban Modernity and Tradition.* Durham, N.C.: Duke University Press.

Panofsky, Erwin. 1955. *Meaning in the Visual Arts.* Garden City, N.Y.: Doubleday.

Patterson, Orlando. 1982. *Slavery and Social Death: A Comparative Study.* Cambridge, Mass.: Harvard University Press.

Pedro, Alberto. 1961. Para iniciarse en la sociedad abakuá. *Actas del Folklore* 1, no. 4: 17–20.

Peitz, William. 1996. Fetish. In Robert S. Nelson and Richard Shiff, eds., *Critical Terms for Art History,* 197–207. Chicago: University of Chicago Press.

Pérez, Louis A. 1988. *Cuba: Between Reform and Revolution.* New York: Oxford University Press.

Pichardo, D. Esteban T. 1874. *Plano de la Habana.* Havana: Agrimensor y Maestro Obras. Geography and Map Division, Library of Congress, filing location: Cuba, Havana (city), 1874, 1:10,000, D. Esteban T. Pichardo.

Picton, John, and John Mack. 1989. *African Textiles.* New York: Harper and Row.

Pivin, Jean Loup, and Pascal Martin Saint Leon. 1996. *Pierre Verger, Le Messager / The Go-Between: Photography, 1932–67.* Paris: Revue Noire.

Polk, Patrick. 1995. Sacred banners and the divine cavalry charge. In Donald Cosentino, ed., *Sacred Arts of Vodou*, 325–347. Los Angeles: Fowler Museum of Cultural History.

Powell, Richard J. 1991. "In my family of primitiveness and tradition": William H. Johnson's Jesus and the Three Marys. *American Art* 5, no. 4 (fall): 21–34.

———. 1997. *Black Art and Culture in the 20th Century.* London: Thames and Hudson.

Preston, George N. 1985. *Sets, Series, and Ensembles in African Art.* New York: Center for African Art.

Price, Sally, and Richard Price. 1980. *Afro-American Arts of the Suriname Rain Forest.* Los Angeles: University of California Press.

Quiñones, Tato. 1994. *Ecorie abakuá: Cuatro ensayos sobre los ñáñigos cubanos.* Havana: Ediciones Unión.

———. 1998. Historia y tradición oral en los sucesos del 27 de noviembre de 1871. *La gaceta de Cuba* 36, no. 5 (September–October): 24–26.

———. n.d. Historia y tradición oral: Tres ejemplos relacionados con las sociedades abacuá cubanas en el siglo XIX. Paper presented to the Fifth International Workshop of Afro-American Social and Cultural Anthropology, Havana.

Rabinow, Paul. 1977. *Reflections on Fieldwork in Morocco.* Berkeley: University of California Press.

Read, Herbert, ed. 1995. *The Thames and Hudson Dictionary of Art and Artists.* London: Thames and Hudson.

Reisman, Karl. 1970. Cultural and linguistic ambiguity in a West Indian village. In John F. Szwed and Norman Whitten, eds., *Afro-American Anthropology: Contemporary Perspectives*, 129–142. New York: Free Press.

Ringling Museum of Art. 1980. *Two Centuries of Cuban Art, 1759–1959.* Sarasota and Daytona Beach, Fla.: John and Mabel Ringling Museum of Art and Museum of Arts and Sciences.

Rippe, María del Carmen. 2001. Historia del Museo Nacional de Bellas Artes. www.lajiribilla.cubaweb.cu/2001/n12_julio/344_12.htmlAlafi.

Robinson, Jontyle, and Wendy Greenhouse. 1991. *The Art of Archibald Motley, Jr.* Chicago: Chicago Historical Society.

Robreño, Gustavo. 1925. *La acera del Louvre: Novela histórica.* Havana: Imprenta y Papeleria de Rambla, Bouza y Ca.

Roche y Monteagudo, R. 1908. *La policía y sus mistérios en Cuba.* Havana: Imprenta "La Prueba."

———. 1914. *La policía y sus mistérios en Cuba; y adicionada con "La policía judicial," procedimientos, formularios, leyes, reglamentos, ordenanzas y disposiciones que conciernen a los cuerpos de seguridad publica.* 2d ed. Havana: Imprenta y Papeleria de Rambla, Bouza y Cia.

———. 1925. Los ñáñigos: Su origen y progresos. In *La policía y sus mistérios en Cuba,* 1–154. Havana: n.p.

Rodman, Selden. 1988. *Where Art Is Joy: Haitian Art—The First Forty Years.* New York: Ruggles de Latour.

Rodríguez, Alejandro. 1881. Reseña histórica de los ñáñigos de Cuba desde su creación hasta la fecha. Unpublished manuscript. Archivo Nacional de Cuba.

Rodríguez Herrera, Esteban. 1958–59. *Léxico mayor de Cuba,* vols. I and II. La Habana: Editorial Lex.

Roig de Leuchenring, Emilio. 1923. La fiesta del día de reyes o de diablitos. *Social* (January): 45.

———. 1950. *Banderas oficiales y revolucionarias de Cuba.* Havana: Oficina del Historiador de la Ciudad de La Habana.

Roig y Mesa, Juan Tomás. 1962. *Diccionario botánico de nombres vulgares cubanos,* 3d ed. 2 vols. Santiago de las Vegas, Cuba: Estación Experimental Agronómica.

Roldán Oliarte, Esteban. 1940. *Cuba en la mano: Enciclopédia popular ilustrada.* Havana: Ucar, García y Cia.

Rosaldo, Renato. 1980. Doing oral history. *Social Analysis* 4 (September): 89–99.

Royal Museum of Fine Arts, Antwerp. *America, Bride of the Sun: 500 years, Latin America and the Low Countries.* 1992. Brussels: Imschoot.

Rubin, Arnold. 1974. *African Accumulative Sculpture: Power and Display.* New York: Pace Gallery.

Rubin, Jane G. 1998. *Miscellanea II of Studies Dedicated to Fernando Ortiz (1881–1969).* New York: InterAmericas.

Rubin, William S. 1968. *Dada, Surrealism, and Their Heritage.* New York: Museum of Modern Art.

———. 1984. *Primitivism in 20th Century Art.* New York: Museum of Modern Art.

Rush, Dana. 1999. Eternal potential: Chromolithographs in Vodunland. *African Arts* 32, no. 4 (winter): 60–75, 94–96.

Schoemaker, George H. 1994. *Mai '68* and the traditionalization of French shadow theatre. *Journal of American Folklore* 107, no. 425: 364–377.

Scott, David. 1991. That event, this memory: Notes on the anthropology of African diasporas in the New World. *Diaspora* 1, no. 3 (winter): 261–284.

Scott, Rebecca Jarvis. 1985. *Slave Emancipation in Cuba: The Transition to Free Labor, 1860–1899.* Princeton: Princeton University Press.

Shaw, Rosalind, and Charles Stewart. 1994. *Syncretism/Anti-Syncretism: The Politics of Religious Synthesis.* London: Routledge.

Sill, Gertrude Grace. 1975. *A Handbook of Symbols in Christian Art.* New York: Collier Books.

Sims, Lowery Stokes. 1992. "Wifredo Lam and the International Avant-Garde." In Giulio V. Blanc, ed., *Wifredo Lam and His Contemporaries,* 17–29. New York: The Studio Museum in Harlem.

Sosa Rodríguez, Enrique. 1982. *Los ñáñigos.* Havana: Ediciones Casa de las Américas.

Stebich, Ute. 1978. *Haitian Art.* Brooklyn: The Brooklyn Museum.

Stocking, George. 1983. The ethnographer's magic: Fieldwork in British anthropology from Tylor to Malinowski. In George W. Stocking, ed., *Observers Observed: Essays on Ethnographic Fieldwork,* 70–120. Madison: University of Wisconsin Press.

Suchlicki, Jaime. 2001. *Historical Dictionary of Cuba.* 2d ed. Lanham, Md.: Scarecrow Press.

Szwed, John F. 1969. An American anthropological dilemma: The politics of Afro-American culture. In Dell Hymes, ed., *Reinventing Anthropology,* 153–181. New York: Pantheon.

Talbot, P. Amaury. 1912. *In the Shadow of the Bush.* London: William Heinemann.

Taussig, Michael. 1987. *Shamanism, Colonialism, and the Wild Man: A Study in Terror and Healing.* Chicago: University of Chicago Press.

Thompson, Robert F. 1969a. Abatan: A master potter of the Egbado Yoruba. In Daniel Biebuyck, ed., *Tradition and Creativity in Tribal Art,* 120–182. Berkeley: University of California Press.

———. 1969b. African influence on the art of the United States. In Armstead L. Robinson, Craig C. Foster, and Donald H. Ogilvie, eds., *Black Studies in the University: A Symposium,* 122–170. New Haven: Yale University Press.

———. 1974. *African Art in Motion: Icon and Act.* Washington, D.C.: National Gallery of Art.

———. 1978. Black ideographic writing: Calabar to Cuba. *Yale Alumni Magazine* (November): 29–33.

———. 1983. *Flash of the Spirit: African and Afro-American Art and Philosophy.* New York: Random House.

———. 1993. *Face of the Gods: Art and Altars of Africa and the African-Americas.* New York: Museum of African Art.

———. 1995. From the isle beneath the sea: Haiti's Africanizing Vodou art. In D. Cosentino, ed., *Sacred Arts of Vodou,* 91–119. Los Angeles: Fowler Museum of Cultural History.

———. 1999. First word: Communiqué from Afro-Atlantis. *African Arts* 32, no. 4 (winter): 1–8.

Triana, José, ed. 1975. *Teatro bufo siglo XIX: Antología,* vol. 1. Havana: Editorial Arte y Literatura.

Troulliot, Michel-Rolph. 1991. Anthropology and the savage slot: The poetics and politics of otherness. In Richard Fox, ed., *Recapturing Anthropology: Working in the Present,* 17–44. Santa Fe: School of American Research Press.

Truettner, William, ed. 1991. *The West as America: Reinterpreting Images of the Frontier, 1820–1920.* Washington, D.C.: Smithsonian Institution Press.

Trujillo y Monagas, Don José. 1882. *Los criminales de Cuba.* Barcelona: Establecimiento Tipográfico de Fidel Ciro.

Tuan, Yi-fu. 1977. *Space and Place: The Perspective of Experience.* Minneapolis: University of Minnesota Press.

Turner, Victor W. 1986. *The Anthropology of Performance.* New York: PAJ Publications.

Urrutía y Blanco, Carlos. 1882. *Los criminales en Cuba y el Inspector Trujillo: Narración de los servicios, prestados en el cuerpo de policía de La Habana.* Barcelona: F. Giró.

U.S. Department of State. 1998. Respect for Human Rights, Section 2: Respect for Civil Liberties, Including, C. Freedom of Religion. Cuba Country Report on Human Rights Practices for 1997. www.state.gov/www/global/human_rights/1997_hrp_report/cuba.html.

Vansina, Jan. 1985. *Oral Tradition as History.* Madison: University of Wisconsin Press.

Vlach, John Michael. 1978. *The Afro-American Tradition in Decorative Arts.* Cleveland: Cleveland Museum of Art.

———. 1984. *Plain Painters: Making Sense of American Folk Art.* Washington, D.C.: Smithsonian Institution Press.

Vogel, Susan, ed. 1988. *ART/Artifact: African Art in Anthropology Collections.* New York: Center for African Art and Prestel Verlag.

Wahlman, Maude Southwell. 1993. *Signs and Symbols: African Images in African-American Quilts.* New York: Studio Books.

Wescott, Joan. 1962. The sculpture and myths of Eshu-Elegba, the Yoruba trickster. *Africa* (October): 336–354.

Williams, Raymond. 1983. *Keywords: A Vocabulary of Culture and Society.* New York: Oxford University Press.

Wilson, Judith. 1994. Will the "New Internationalism" be the same old story? Some art historical considerations. In Jean Fisher, ed., *Global Visions: Towards a New Internationalism in the Visual Arts,* 87–113. London: Kala Press.

Wright, Irene. 1910. *Cuba.* New York: Macmillan.

Zeitlin, Marilyn A., ed. 1999. *Contemporary Art from Cuba: Irony and Survival on the Utopian Island.* Tempe and New York: Arizona State University Art Museum and Delano Greenridge Editions.

Index

Page numbers in **boldface** indicate illustrations